S. Numme

W9-BCM-316

**EMPIRICAL
DEMOCRATIC
THEORY**

EMPIRICAL DEMOCRATIC THEORY

Edited by

CHARLES F. CNUDDE
University of Wisconsin

And

DEANE E. NEUBAUER
University of California, Irvine

MARKHAM PUBLISHING COMPANY / CHICAGO

MARKHAM POLITICAL SCIENCE SERIES
Aaron Wildavsky, Editor

© MARKHAM PUBLISHING COMPANY 1969

ALL RIGHTS RESERVED

PRINTED IN U.S.A.

LIBRARY OF CONGRESS CATALOG CARD NUMBER: 68-24031

CONTENTS

vi

EMPIRICAL DEMOCRATIC THEORY

INTRODUCTION

Empirical Democratic Theory:
Some Preliminary Questions

To entitle a book of readings *Empirical Democratic Theory* and to include in it selections most of which are less than 20 years old, requires, we suspect, both explanation and justification.

All political theories can be cast in one or more of any three modes: normative, empirical, or analytic.[1] Normative theories are argumentative and prescriptive; they attempt to justify the choice of one value or set of values over another and prescribe that behavior (including institutional practices) presumed most appropriate for achieving that valued outcome. Analytic theories are definitional or conceptual expositions, examinations of the logical implications of concepts and their relationship to other concepts. Empirical theories are descriptive and explanatory, constructed from observations of the real world. These three modes of theory are thus differentiated by their intended goals (argumentation and prescription, exposition and implication, or description and explanation) and the kinds of "evidence" which are deemed appropriate as support for a given theory.

Historically, democratic political theory has been cast primarily in the normative and analytic modes. To the extent that these normative and analytic theories have contained an empirical complement, it has been by contemporary standards a most casual empiricism, primarily an attempt by a particular theorist to justify his behavioral assumptions by citing selected and appropriate instances of such behavior. Some traditional political theory, for example that of a Machiavelli, Montesquieu, Madison or Hume, is far more empirically grounded but its empiricism is still highly selective and unsystematic.

The adoption of the empirical mode as a predominant form in the construction of democratic theory is of quite recent origin, a product of the so-called "behavioral" movement in political science. Contemporary empirical democratic theory is distinguished from traditional political theory in several respects. First, it is explicitly non-normative, though like normative theory it is frequently linked to analytic theory. Although almost any empirical finding which bears upon the functioning or dysfunctioning of a democratic political system has normative implications, empirical democratic theorists explicitly eschew attempts to justify values or pre-scriptive statements. Second, empirical democratic theorists are concerned with the description and explanation of observable phenomena, as opposed to hypothesized or conjectured occurrences. And third, empirical demo-cratic theory shares with the broader tradition of modern political analysis a pretention to scientific status. That is, the primary concern of empirical democratic theory is not simply to be empirical, but to be systematically empirical and theoretical in the scientific sense. By this is meant the formulation of hypotheses which may be aggregated in some interrelated fashion into theory and which are in principle capable of being tested at the empirical level, that is, made into operational hypotheses. "Tested" in this sense means applying the hypotheses to data gathered and analyzed according to the agreed-upon tenets of statistical theory.

This characterization of empirical democratic theory is clearly over-simplified and, consequently, misleading. In most of contemporary social science, the actual empirical output of a discipline rarely meets the rigid standards of its methodological canons. Political science and empirical democratic theory are no exceptions. That body of writings and research that we view as constituting empirical democratic theory is unevenly developed. Some studies give evidence of considerable rigor and commit-ment to the methodological principles of social science; others are far more loosely constructed, the hypotheses which they purport to test only marginally operational (if at all), and the data brought to bear on them somewhat suspect. In part, this unevenness in the development of empirical democratic theory is a consequence of the difficulty of the subject matter, in part a consequence of the imprecise analytic and research tools which are available.

The readings selected for this volume display both faults and thus provide ample evidence of this uneven development. They also display, we believe, some of the "payoffs" which can be gained by pursuing the belief that many important questions relating to democratic political organization can be fruitfully investigated through the techniques of modern political analysis. And as we shall argue in our final chapter, we also believe that something approximating *an* empirical theory of democracy has already emerged from the many individual and piecemeal attempts at its construction. The documentation of this assertion is the primary purpose of this volume.

Before proceeding to this task, however, it may be profitable to raise some preliminary questions about the nature and limitations of empirical democratic theory. To be precise: What kinds of questions does empirical theory attempt to pose? How answerable are these, given limitations on our research skills and techniques? What questions in principle lie outside the scope of empirical democratic theory? In what respects is democratic theory any different from other forms of political theory?

SOME PERTINENT QUESTIONS

In terms of the questions which it poses, empirical democratic theory is inherently causal; that is, because its pretentions are towards explanation, the questions which are posed take the form: "How do we account for this variation (or lack of variation)?" Such questions are equivalent to asking: "What factors cause these observable variations?" These questions can further be classified into two sets. One attempts to isolate and account for differences which exist between democratic and non-democratic political systems; the other attempts to isolate and account for differences among democratic political systems.

It has always been presumed that the institutionalization and mainten- ance of democratic political systems is dependent upon a number of *environmental* conditions. Specifying the exact nature of these conditions has been a task of both traditional and modern scholars of democracy. At one time or another, it has been claimed that the success of democratic political organizations is dependent upon such diverse factors as the absence of extreme conflict, a relative equality of social and economic condition, the predominant distribution throughout the population of so-called "democratic personalities," a favorable position in the structure of international relations, a dispersal and heterogeneity of interests, particular features of national character, an underlying structure of social norms conducive to democratic political behavior, etc., as well as a variety of historical accidents. The difficulty with such assertions is twofold. First, often such assertions are in fact normative statements which may take this form: Assertion = "Democracy is predicated upon the existence of equality of condition"; therefore, prescription = "Structure society so as to enhance equality of condition." In this form, the empirical veracity of the assertion is rarely documented. Second, assertions stipulating those conditions presumably necessary for the existence of democracy often focus upon the importance of one factor or set of conditions, e.g., the dispersal and heterogeneity of interests. It is either not clear how one set of supposedly necessary factors relates to another, or the question of sufficiency is begged. For example, it is quite clear that there is some relationship between the level of social and economic development of a country and its likelihood of being democratic; the probability of very poor countries being democratic is very low. But it is equally clear that relative affluence is not necessarily related to a preference for democratic government. A relatively high level of social and economic development is perhaps a necessary condition for democratic government, but it is hardly a sufficient one.

Empirical democratic theory attempts to (a) determine the empirical veracity of these kinds of causal assertions in their simple form, and (b) specify those factors which appear to be causally preeminent in the determination of democratic government. One can accomplish this goal either by examining the distribution of some independent variable across a sample of all countries (democratic and non-democratic) to determine whether the incidence of correlation is higher for democratic than for non-democratic countries; or one can focus on the dependent variable, incidence of democracy, while searching for characteristics which appear common to it. Questions of necessity can be determined in this fashion, assuming of course that one is able to investigate such factors at an acceptable operational level. For the example given above, findings which indicate that relatively high levels of democracy are maintained in the absence of relatively high levels of social and economic development effectively refute the assertion that such factors are necessary conditions for democracy. Establishing the sufficiency of given factors for the establishment and maintenance of democracy is far more complicated. To establish the criteria of sufficiency would be equivalent to establishing closure on the number of causal factors related to democratic government. Although *inordinately difficult* to accomplish in practice, in principle such is possible. What is required is: the full enumeration of those factors associated with the establishment and maintenance of democratic government; the subsumption of related factors under summary concepts; the operationalization of those concepts at a level acceptable to testing across the inherent variations of national differences; and the demonstration through such a test that no democratic political systems exist which do not satisfy such conditions (or alternatively, that such factors are causally present in all observable democratic political systems). So much would establish the necessary and sufficient conditions for the establishment and maintenance of democratic political systems *given the constraints of the existing evidence*. By the constraints of the existing evidence is meant that one could account for all *observable* variation in the phenomena under investigation. Within certain boundary conditions, for example, such as democratic political systems in the "modern," i.e., post industrial period, one could *explain* why some political systems are democratic and some non-democratic. To repeat, the establishment of sufficiency is possible in principle; its possibility in practice is another matter entirely. Not only are the theoretical demands enormous, and perhaps insuperable, the operational difficulties are so profound as to render most questions of establishing sufficiency irrelevant. If these were not sufficient difficulties, one must also confront the problem of measurement error. Since the actual size of measurement error is always unknown, one can at best only approximate it through estimates, a process which serves most needs but necessarily establishes a limit on one's ability to establish sufficiency. At the empirical level, then, it is but the most remote possibility that one can overcome such difficulties to establish criteria of both necessity and sufficiency.

Methodologically, however, it is important to take note of such a possibility if only to suggest what such an outcome would mean for other research goals. For example, it is most important to be aware that the establishment of the necessary and sufficient conditions for democracy results in explanation not *prediction*. Prediction can be gained from explanation in some probabilistic sense, but prediction in any absolute sense is always the subject of subsequent testing and verification. Thus, the elucidation and verification of the necessary and sufficient conditions for democracy on the basis of examining all observable instances of such would give one greater confidence in predicting which conditions are liable to result in democratic or non-democratic government; but short of being able to account for all subsequent eventualities in the future, such predictions can never be more than probabilistic estimates drawn from existing evidence and limited by the assumptions which one employs concerning the regularity of human behavior.

To summarize so far, empirical democratic theory attempts to explain why some political systems are democratic and others are non-democratic. In searching for such explanations, empirical democratic theory focuses upon causal factors with its eventual (but distant) goal the enumeration of the necessary and sufficient conditions for democracy.

Empirical democratic theory is also concerned with attempts to describe and explain those variations which occur within democratic countries. In what respects are democratic countries similar; in what respects are they different? What is the nature of the democratic political process? To what degree are our assumptions about democratic political behavior correct? Given new evidence about the nature of this behavior, what can one say about the democratic political process? Obviously, as questions like these make clear, accurate description is a necessary first step to any theory construction. If one is to explain what is going on, one must first be fairly confident that he knows what is going on. Thus, in recent years considerable energy has been spent in the more or less systematic description of democratic political processes, focused upon both individual and comparative cases.

The largest amount of attention has been given to elections and voting, the formalized modes of citizen participation in democratic society. A very great proportion of the normative rationale of the democratic system is predicated upon certain assumptions about how citizens should and do participate in the democratic political process. Additionally, many explanatory theories of the democratic political process have been offered which assume (either explicitly or implicitly) that citizen participation in the democratic political process is sustained at relatively high levels. Systematic investigation of voting and elections at all levels of government in numerous countries indicates: that despite some basic circumstantial variation, average levels of participation in the electoral process are lower than traditionally supposed; that by and large individuals participate in elections for reasons quite unrelated to "basic" issue questions; and that their concern with the political process, except at times of crisis, is marginal at best. The accumulation and documentation of such facts has resulted in a number of *empirical* theories which attempt to explain various characteristics of the political process—for example, its stability or instability—given the existence of facts such as these. Other assumptions of traditional democratic theory have been treated in similar fashion.

For example, recent studies have investigated such phenomena as: the level of consensus existing in the United States; the operation of majority rule in highly pluralistic democratic societies; the process of representation as reflected in American legislative institutions; the process of bureaucratic decision-making in United States federal agencies; the structure and behavior of political parties; interest groups and other institutions, such as the courts and independent regulatory commissions. Much of the evidence from these studies contradicts the assumptions of traditional theory, and, like the findings of the voting studies, stands as a basis for the construction of an empirical democratic theory substantially different from traditional theory.

Another set of questions raised by contemporary democratic theory has to do with system outputs. In what respects are democratic systems different from non-democratic systems in terms of what they provide for their citizens? How different are democratic systems from one another in this respect? How can one account for such variations? Political systems are, besides other things, mechanisms for the distribution of rewards and benefits. One ostensible function of democratic political systems is to distribute these rewards and benefits in a manner somewhat commensurate with the preferences of the citizenry or at least some demonstrable majority therein. To what degree do democratic systems accomplish this goal? What are the rewards being distributed? Are they material or symbolic? Only a few of these questions have been examined in any systematic fashion. Those studies cited and reproduced in this volume are indicative of a growing interest in the detailed study of political system outputs.

These three sets of questions can be seen to be consistent with one of the standard paradigms of social science, the S-O-R paradigm of stimulus, organism, and response. Because the paradigm appears to fit so nicely with the kinds of questions which have been raised by the empirical democratic theorists, we have adopted it as the organizing framework for the readings in this volume. By *stimulus*, we mean the environment which impinges upon democratic political systems. In environment we include factors such as the social and economic conditions of the system under discussion, its historical tradition, its position in the stream of world affairs, its geographical configurations, the normative content of its culture, etc. By *organism*, we mean the functioning of the democratic political system—the process of preference generation and accommodation, the structure of elite-mass interaction, the pattern of institutional inter-action, and the pattern of organized decision-making. Finally, by *reaction*, we mean the pattern of system outputs—the distribution of political goods which characterizes the system. We assume that these three factors are systematically interrelated; that variations in stimulus will be reflected in characteristic variations in the functioning of the organism, which will in turn effect the reactions or outcomes characteristic of the organism. As we approach these points substantively in the introductions to the readings, we shall comment on these relationships at greater length.

Before turning to the readings which compose the bulk of this volume, it may be worthwhile to take note of some other questions which have been directed toward the empirical theorists. Those who criticize the application of empirical techniques to the study of democracy—and such criticism has been both hostile and friendly—have frequently questioned the status of the findings produced by the use of such techniques. By the very nature of the research enterprise, it is argued, the empiricists are forced to examine narrow and thus generally uninteresting questions about democracy. The important questions of democracy, because of their generality, are out of the "research grasp" of the empiricists. In addition, the research apparatus of the empiricists is both expensive and elaborate, and it has been wondered aloud whether so many scarce resources, both intellectual and material, might be better applied. The least friendly of critics have argued baldly that the empiricists have told us nothing at all that is relevant to the world in which we live; and, therefore, their efforts have been useless. These are serious charges which deserve to be answered.[2]

There are several possible responses one could make to such charges. One could first argue that the value of the empiricist's intellectual product should be judged comparatively on the basis of the available evidence. As we suggested (not with much originality) above, a major consequence of the recent work of the empiricists has been to bring into question the assumptions of traditional democratic theory and, by extension, some of its conclusions. The fact that the real world does not in some important respects resemble the world described or imagined by Rousseau, Locke, Montesquieu, or even Marx is in itself important. In this respect alone, it would seem, the value of the empiricist's findings is established.

But there is a more interesting element present in this criticism which goes beyond a mere assessment of the findings of the empiricists *qua* findings. One senses in much of this criticism a note of disappointment and despair from those whose concerns with democratic theory are normative. Those whom we have called the empiricists have torn down much of traditional democratic theory, and yet, because of their disinclination to engage in normative theorizing themselves, have failed to offer alternative normative theories for those which they have partially discredited. The critics of the empiricists have reacted by condemning the empiricists because they refuse to engage themselves in normative theory, or alternatively by arguing that the empirical theory which the empiricists have created is in fact a normative theory in itself since its explanation of the *status quo* often appears as its justification.[3]

Although this is really a side issue to the present discussion, it is an important one because it summarizes an attitude which many individuals have toward the findings of the empiricists and suggests how the evaluation of those findings can become confused. Democracy is an inherently difficult concept. It means many things to many people. As a general summary concept, it holds numerous implications and connotations which are frequently complex and often contradictory. In addition, as we suggested in our introductory remarks, one's theoretical motivations for studying democracy can also be very different. The upshot of the intersection of these factors is that the *product* of any student of democracy is often interpreted or evaluated on the basis of inappropriate criteria. It is possible to criticize any scholarly product on at least two dimensions—one arguing that the wrong substance or phenomenon is being studied, and second arguing that the substance or phenomenon is being studied badly or wrongly. Much of the criticism of the empiricists confuses these two significantly different criteria of evaluation. Thus, when the empiricists are criticized for their intellectual failings, it is often not a criticism of the quality of their empiricism so much as it is a criticism of their choice of research interest.[4] If one is to evaluate effectively the intellectual products of the empiricists, it is necessary to separate these two criteria of evaluation; for only in this way, can one answer what appears to be the more important question: What are the intellectual limitations of empirical democratic theory? The reason for the necessity of separation is clear. If one independently evaluates the limitations and quality of the techniques utilized by the empiricists for the questions that they have approached, one can then make some judgments about the probable success of investigating other kinds of questions. If, on the other hand, one insists on evaluating the work of the empiricists on the basis of irrelevant criteria—their failure or reluctance to address other kinds of questions—then it is inevitable that such work will be shown to be wanting and very little will be learned about the potential and actual limitations of empirical democratic theory as an intellectual enterprise.

One can phrase the argument somewhat differently. For a variety of reasons (ideological, methodological, professional) many individuals have grown impatient with the efforts of the empiricists and their alleged inability to address "important" questions of democratic theory. This impatience has led to a form of criticism which focuses upon that which the empiricists have not done rather than that which they have. Though it is legitimate to debate the relative importance of alternative research strategies—presumably focused upon the relative "payoffs" from such strategies —at some levels the argument is beyond solution; for the choice of research strategies represents the taste of the researchers and "in matters of taste there can be no debate." Consequently, we shall direct our attentions primarily to what the empiricists have done and limit our comments to suggesting why these choices have been made.

There are three kinds of constraints on empirical democratic theory, which for the sake of convenience may be termed conceptual, operational, and data constraints. Briefly, these constraints are interrelated in the following manner. Because the phenomena encompassed by the concept "democracy" are extremely varied and complex, prior to any empirical examination of those phenomena it is necessary to impose closure upon that segment of behavior to be investigated. This process of "delineating the subject matter" is most complicated by the fact that our "theories" of democracy frequently fail to specify which variables are critical to a given occurrence and which are not. This imprecise delineation of the subject matter leads often to empirical confusion and reduces the level of rigor which can be brought to any given investigation. Perhaps an example will make this more clear. Consider the concept democracy to represent a set of behavior. This set is composed of many subsets of behavior, which together comprise the set democracy. In principle, it is possible to specify the names of the subsets and particularly to specify their properties with respect to all other subsets. The result of such an exercise might be a display of Ven-type diagrams in which the intersection of properties of every individual subset would be clearly specified. (E.g., two behaviors included in the set democracy are represented by those institutional arrangements established to obtain the goals of majority rule and minority rights, each of which might constitute a subset of observable behaviors. In practice these goals are not independently achieved; and thus an interaction effect is created. The diagrams illustrating this case would show a considerable intersection of the two sets.) The precise specification of these intersections would be tantamount to the precise delineation of phenomena, i.e., stating which variables are relevant for any given empirical investigation. This process of delineation is usually recognized as the ubiquitous "definitional problem" wherein a given author provides a definition for a concept which in fact delimits by attribution the range of phenomena in which he is interested.

This process of delineation operates as a constraint in two ways. First, when the subject to be delineated is the democratic process, one is confronted with what might be called a very noisy communications channel. The common names of the subset behaviors are very common indeed, having themselves very nearly as many attributed or stipulated meanings as the universal set. A very frequent result is the necessity of engaging in complicated analytic exercises merely to establish the types of behavior in which one has an empirical interest. (This delineation problem is closely related to a number of operational problems, about which we will speak below.) Almost any example would suffice to clarify the point. For example, assume that one is interested in how majority rule operates in a democratic political system. What is meant by majority rule? How has the term been used traditionally? How are those meanings related to the one which might be useful for this investigation? In order to make one's findings intelligible to any external audience—and by intelligible is meant making one's findings relatively free of ambiguity—it is first necessary to clarify the preferred usage from other existent usages. Very simply, one is constrained in his investigations by the substance of the intellectual tradition which embraces the subject matter under discussion. And to repeat, when this subject matter is the democratic process, the constraints may be considerable.

The second delineational constraint is that mentioned above—the specification of the phenomenological interrelationships between concepts. If one is to operate with confidence at the empirical level, it is necessary to have some relatively sound notions about how the phenomena in which one is interested are affected by other behaviors. Before one can proceed to the operational level, then, one must engage first in concept delineation, and, second, one must be knowledgeable about the behavioral environment which impinges upon his subject matter.

Conceptual constraints are closely related to operational constraints. Operationalization refers to the formulation of concepts such that they accord with some observable and perhaps measurable empirical reality. Clearly, for any set of concepts which have some empirical referents, the more precisely delineated those concepts, the easier the operational task. Conversely, the more abstract and imprecise the concepts under discussion, the more difficult it will be to isolate and measure the appropriate empirical referents. Let us illustrate the point with some examples. Most everyone has some intuitive notion of what constitutes political equality; some probably feel that they have some quite precise ideas about the concept. How does one measure, i.e., operationalize, political equality? First, as suggested, some rough form of delineation at the empirical level is necessary. In what spheres of activity are we interested in measuring equality? We might decide, for example, to give the concept "political equality" empirical substance by defining it as the "ability of all adult citizens to interject their preferences for decision-making purposes whenever they feel intense about the decision to be made." This definition obviously includes some elements of what most of us would take to be political equality, while excluding others like the equal treatment of preferences after they have been voiced; but it informs us about none of the conditions which must guide our measurement. Since it fails to stipulate the criteria of measurement within the content of the definition, it is not an operational definition. An operational definition of political equality would more easily proceed from a definition which delineated the concept into several possible behaviors, each of which might be measured independently, or one of which might be taken as a representative indicator of the others.

Our example also points to another difficulty of operationalizing very abstract concepts, especially democratic theory concepts. Many of the concepts utilized in democratic theory are, by virtue of the intellectual tradition from which they emerged, normative or maximizational concepts. They refer to goals to be achieved by a given social organization, in this case the democratic polity. Thus, the concept "political equality," while basic to almost any discussion of democracy, has no literal empirical referent for the simple reason that no political organization of any significant size is capable of achieving full political equality (and one could add political liberty, freedom, etc.). To repeat, the concept is stipulative; it postulates a goal to be maximized. Operationally, then, it can be a quite literally "meaningless" concept because it has no empirical referent. However, the concept does, of course, provide the basis for constructing a measurement, the degree to which actual, existing democratic political organizations approximate the condition of political equality. Thus, one can cite elections as instances in which individual citizens are permitted to express their preferences on certain issues. Since elections differ considerably with respect to who is allowed to vote, how equally the votes are treated, and the like, the examination of various features of elections provides one with an empirical indicator of the degree to which political equality is realized in democratic polities. Whether or not one wishes only this indicator, that is to say, whether or not this one test is accepted as a sufficient operational definition of the concept political equality, depends entirely on the uses to which such evidence is to be put. One may wish to construct several tests, to enforce several conditional applications to gain a useful measure. Again, within the context of our example, it might be felt that differences in the implementation of political equality through the electoral system are not sufficient for one's purposes. One might also examine the expression of citizens' preferences in circumstances other than elections, e.g., as aggregated and transmitted through interest groups.

Very quickly, however, one is certain to run afoul of the constraints placed upon one's investigations by the absence of suitable data or the costs of obtaining suitable data. The limitations on empirical research very frequently are neither methodological, theoretical, nor operational, but are the simple product of insufficient data. One very good reason for attempting to measure political equality by focusing on the electoral system is because most of the reliable and comparable data that we have is electoral data. Other measures which might very well focus upon interest groups, upon various governmental institutions, or upon individual citizen behavior require the gathering of new data from a wide variety of disparate sources. The inordinate costs both of time and money of gathering such data are sufficient to deter most researchers from attempting the task.

Almost any example would adequately illustrate these points. Any major problem in democratic theory is subject to these constraints, especially the constraints on data availability. In a very literal sense, the kinds of problems which have been treated by the empiricists have been primarily dictated by the availability of data, which in an overwhelming number of cases has been either electoral or survey data. This, of course, speaks to a major criticism of empirical democratic theory and returns us to the point at which we began. As our remarks make quite clear, we agree with the critics that obtaining appropriate data is very costly and that very great expense is often spent to provide reliable evidence for points of relatively small theoretical interest. We disagree with the critics with respect to the conclusions to be drawn from this premise. The critics have focused upon this limitation of empirical democratic theory as a compelling argument against an enterprise which they would like to see terminated for quite other reasons. We focus upon this limitation to identify it as the major bottleneck preventing a more systematic investigation of interesting and important questions. It is often piously remarked at the conclusion of almost any conference in the social sciences that "we need more theory" to solve whatever problem has been under discussion. We strongly suspect that democratic theory has riches and insights which vastly outstrip the quality and quantity of the data which have been brought to bear on that theory.

We have argued, then, that three sets of constraints—conceptual, operational, and data constraints—limit in one way or another the kinds of democratic theory questions which can be addressed empirically. We have not ourselves addressed the question which is often posed in this context: What kinds of questions cannot be treated by empirical democratic theory? The import of this question is really to differentiate those questions which have traditionally been handled by normative democratic theory and those treated by empirical theory. It is clear that empirical democratic theory cannot deal with value questions in the same manner as normative theory, since empirical theorists refrain from offering prescriptions based upon their investigations. But empirical theory may be a most valuable aid to those who wish to engage in normative theory. Presumably, if one is to make prescriptive kinds of statements it is preferable to make them on the basis of correct rather than false premises; and in this respect empirical democratic theory can be most helpful.

The other side of this issue—What questions in principle lie outside the scope of empirical democratic theory?—is much more difficult to answer. First, and obviously, empirical democratic theory is constrained by any and all of the limitations which impinge upon social science in general. The limitations of social theory of any sort to predict individual occurrences or individual behaviors is well known; consequently, the ability to answer predictive questions in general is similarly limited. But the development of explanatory theory can bear heavily upon the kinds of predictions which one might make, such as, suggesting the probabilities of given occurrences. Thus, as we will argue in our final chapter, we are aware that certain factors are related to the stability of democratic political systems, and from this knowledge we infer that a *significant* change in one of those factors will contribute toward instability. Though we are not so sophisticated as to be able to specify the exact point at which a change in one variable will produce a *critical* change in the other, we at least can specify these relationships in operational terms, e.g., the relationship between level of political participation and system stability. As another example, from his qualitative examination of the budgetary process, Aaron Wildavsky and his associates have constructed a model of that process which when applied to time sequence quantitative budgetary data "explains" a large portion of the variation in that process. Wildavsky's model is not able to "predict" certain budgetary occurrences, such as, sudden increases in defense expenditures brought about by a far greater involvement in the Viet Nam war; but the discernable regularity in the process is such that most events can be predicted and allowance made overall for such un-expected occurrences. (See Chapter 21, below.)

Second, and equally important, whole sets of questions *in their stated form* are outside the scope of empirical theory in general because their abstract formulation places them beyond the operational capability of empirical investigation. The language of much of democratic theory is extremely general and abstract, a result of attempts to provide propositions which apply to the whole of a political system. One could list any number of examples: Madison's propositions on the control of conflict by its pluralistic dispersion; Mill's assumptions and assertions concerning the psychic gratifications which man receives from living in a democratic society; Marx's propositions about the relationship of economic to political power. These propositions are not capable of being tested in their present form; they must first be transformed by some relatively inventive "re-theorizing" into researchable problems. This process of re-theorizing is by no means simple; but on the other hand it is by no means impossible.[5] All that one can say at this point, admittedly a feeble reply to those impatient for empirical answers to difficult questions, is that one cannot know which of these questions are soluble and which are not until they have been raised in the appropriate context and sufficient effort expended upon them to constitute a proper test. As has been the case since the beginning of social science investigation, the questions of today which appear insoluble may quite likely yield solutions tomorrow, only to be replaced by the unveiling of an even more difficult set still to be answered. Consequently, to speak more about what empirical democratic theory cannot do is probably futile. Our real concern, the concern of this volume, is to attempt some assessment of what it has done.

The readings selected for this volume illustrate most of the points made in this introduction. They range from highly rigorous, fairly narrow, very quantitative studies to less rigorous, broadly focused, qualitative analy-ses. They address very many of the major questions which are embraced by democratic theory. Taken as a whole, we believe that they are a repre-sentative sampling of this subfield of political investigation. The reader is encouraged to evaluate their merit with reference to the critical questions raised, but only partially answered in this introduction.

NOTES

[1] For a similar statement, see Giovanni Sartori, *Democratic Theory* (New York: Praeger, 1965), Chap. 8.

[2] Few criticisms are so harsh; but the position represents a natural extension of many of the criticisms leveled against the "behaviorists" in general. To examine this issue in its least restrained form, see: Herbert J. Storing, ed., *Essays on the Scientific Study of Politics* (New York: Holt, Rinehart, and Winston, 1962); the review of this volume by John H. Schaar and Sheldon S. Wolin, "Essays on the Scientific Study of Politics: A Critique," *American Political Science Review*, Vol. 57 (March, 1963), pp. 125–50; and the reply to Schaar and Wolin by Herbert J. Storing, Leo Strauss, *et al.*, in the same volume. A more recent criticism has been leveled by George Kateb, "The Use of the Old Books of Political Theory," a paper prepared for the American Political Science Association (mimeograph) (Chicago, 1967).

[3] For an example of this kind of argument, see Peter Bachrach, *A Theory of Democratic Elitism* (Boston: Little, Brown and Co., 1967).

[4] Again, Bachrach makes this criticism very clear. See *op. cit.*

[5] Cf. Dahl's brilliant reinterpretation of Madisonian theory. Robert A. Dahl, *A Preface to Democratic Theory* (Chicago: University of Chicago Press, 1956), Chap. 1.

PART ONE

Defining Democracy

For a variety of reasons (some of which were enumerated in the Introduction), most empirical studies in the social sciences begin with some form of definitional exercise. The language of social science is sufficiently imprecise that usually it is necessary to clarify the concepts with which one is working in order to provide them with operational precision. The language of democracy is particularly cluttered. Faced with this clutter, one has a number of strategies available which he may employ to impose a temporary order suitable to his purposes. In general, one can define a concept by stipulating a meaning for it ("by x I mean y") or by deriving a meaning from attribution ("when people say x they seem to mean y, z, and so on"). Much of the imprecision and ambiguity of the concept *democracy* and its subsidiary concepts comes from the fact that many generations of students have utilized identical concept names to stipulate new meanings for those concepts, a practice which has in turn led others to derive a wide variety of attributional meanings for these concepts.

The situation is further complicated by the fact that the reality, the empirical substance, to which these concepts refer changes considerably over periods of time. Athenian democracy was substantially different from nineteenth-century English democracy which, in turn, is different from democracy in the United States in the 1960's. Changes in technology, in culture, in size, and in the interaction pattern of the individuals involved have created a quite different set of empirical referents for old and familiar concepts. We rarely attempt to accept the full import of the consequences which flow from this fact, since to do so implies nothing less than a fundamental restructuring of the language to make it completely situationally relevant. Two alternatives to this fundamental restructuring of the language are the coining of new terms (a form of stipulation) and negative differentiation (a form of attribution). The creation of new terms to isolate the pheno-mena of reference can, if done well, result in useful clarification; if done badly, it can result in the creation of useless jargon. The test would seem to be the appropriateness of the renaming with respect to the empirical phenomena being discussed. For example, in some of his earlier work, Robert Dahl wished to focus rather exclusively on the control relational aspects of democracy, the interaction patterns of leaders and non-leaders. To facilitate his purpose, Dahl (and originally Charles E. Lindblom) coined the term *polyarchy* to refer to that particular control relationship in which the behavior of leaders was controlled by non-leaders, *and* he provided a set of specific conditions which identify the existence of this relationship. (Cf. Dahl and Lindblom, *Politics, Economics, and Welfare* [New York: Harper & Row, 1953], and Robert A. Dahl, *A Preface to Democratic Theory* [Chicago: University of Chicago Press, 1956].) Thus, polyarchy is not simply "Dahl's name for democracy" (as it has sometimes been called), but rather is a particular stipulative definition which delineates one form of democratic behavior from another (or others) and has by virtue of its definitional conditions a set of clear empirical referents. This form of stipulation clearly differs from that in which traditional concept names are used without further qualification (e.g., "by democracy I mean political equality, political liberty, and majority rule).

Negative attribution is definition by systematic exclusion. This is the technique utilized by Giovanni Sartori in the selection, "What Democracy Is Not" (Chapter 1). The technique of negative attribution has dramatic effect and in principle is a quite legitimate method of defining any concept. Complications arise when the concept in question has a large number of connotations (as democracy does) or when the phenomenological family to which the concept is kin is very large. In these circumstances, obtaining a clear and precise residual (which is the purpose of negative attribution) is very costly since the amount of exclusionary effort needed is consequently large. This technique, however, fits Sartori's purpose well since a major preliminary effort (not reprinted here) is devoted to the consideration of other definitional entanglements, including the prescriptive and behavioral definitions of democracy. The *ex adverso* definition provided by Sartori helps to complete the limits assigned to the concept by positive definitions.

Ranney and Kendall's attempt to construct a model of democracy based on the interaction of four fundamental principles of political de-mocracy represents a combination of stipulative and attributional defini-tions. In their sweeping analysis of the American party system, Ranney and Kendall found that before they could accurately appraise that system as an agency of democratic government, it was first necessary to have some work-ing definition of democratic government compatible with the political tradition of the United States. In the selection reprinted here, "Basic Principles for a Model of Democracy" (Chapter 2), Ranney and Kendall argue that in order for a government to be considered democratic, it must exhibit three minimum characteristics: "(1) Those who hold office in it must stand ready, *in some sense*, to do whatever the people want them to do, and to refrain from doing anything the people oppose; (2) each member of the 'community' for which it acts should have, *in some sense*, as good a chance as his fellows to participate in the community's decision-making— no better and no worse; and (3) it must operate in terms of an understanding that when the enfranchised members of the community disagree as to what ought to be done, the last word lies, *in some sense*, with the larger number and never the smaller . . . ." From these three minima, Ranney and Kendall derive the four basic principles of democracy which constitute their model—popular sovereignty, political equality, popular consultation and majority rule.

The two selections in Part One represent much more than merely a matter of taste over which definitional form is to be preferred. Ranney and Kendall are arguing, in effect, that democracy is constituted by the simultaneous satisfaction of these four conditions at some satisfactory level of performance. The authors' discussion of the definitional construct (model) raises two important questions: In what way are the performance differences combined, and how does one specify the thresholds which mark the existence of democratic organization?

The authors make no attempt to answer the first question. They do imply, however, that the absence of any one condition is sufficient to cause the governmental form under question to be disqualified as democratic. This means that political systems can be classified only as not democratic or as democratic. Those systems that satisfy none, one, two, or three conditions *are not* democratic, and only those that satisfy all four *are* democratic.

On the other hand, the authors give considerable attention to the question of thresholds. Determining which countries are democratic and which are not is similar, it is argued, to defining in an operational sense when to classify a bald man as bald. Given the fact that baldness is an incremental process in which one slowly loses hair, at which increment does one cease to have a full head of hair and become bald? To satisfy such a question, Ranney and Kendall contend, one needs to employ the example of a spectrum, establishing one end of it as the model (the complete absence of hair) and the incremental loss of hair as the scale of measurement. "What purposes does this spectrum serve? It enables us to measure and compare individual men as to their *degrees* of baldness, and it permits us to make sense of the statement about a man, 'He is getting bald'—i.e., it enables us to determine the direction of change. . . . So it is with our model of democracy. It will serve to fix one end of a spectrum, which, in turn, will enable us to measure the degrees of democracy of existing governments and institutions and to compare them with each other. In terms of such a spectrum—but only in terms of it—it is perfectly legitimate to call some existing governments 'democracies.' . . . [A]lthough the United States can hardly be placed at the democratic extreme of our spectrum, and may even be less near to our model than, say Switzerland or Great Britain, it is nevertheless so much nearer to it than, say, the Soviet Union or Red China that we are justified in saying that *compared to* the Communist nations the United States *is* a democracy." What this argument says is that it is empirically not possible to specify the location of the threshold levels of democratic performance. In principle it is possible to locate such thresholds (this is the underlying rationale of the four continua as measuring devices), but in practice it is not. Consequently, they will in fact compare countries with each other with respect to this model or standard (the four principles). The net result of this empirical concession to their model formulation is to divide any empirical sample of countries into democratic and non-democratic depending on where they might exist with respect to the unlocatable threshold conditions. Thus, because of problems in combining performance differences and in specifying thresholds, what began as an exercise in scalar measurement becomes, in practice, an exercise in classification.

Sartori very clearly recognizes the difficulty of defining democracy in terms of continua which have a clear empirical referent. A major purpose of his *ex adverso* definition is to make clear what set of behaviors would constitute the complete opposite of democracy. His argument rejects numerous logical candidates (tyranny, despotism, absolutism, dictatorship, authoritarianism and totalitarianism, the coercion-consensus continuum, and the monocracy-polyarchy distinction) and concludes with the choice of autocracy as the best opposite of democracy because "the semantic indication conveyed by autocracy is precise, and we are immediately able to elucidate the concepts and to draw the line that clearly separates democracy from what it is not." Justifying his conclusion further, he suggests that "the difference between democracy and its opposite lies in the fact that in a democracy power is scattered, limited, controlled, and exercised in rotation; whereas in an autocracy power is concentrated, uncontrolled, indefinite, unlimited. What democracy *is not* is, in one word, autocracy."

Sartori's dichotomy is very appealing, but it is clear after some consideration that the neatness of the distinction is more apparent than real. Semantically, it is true that if democracy means that power is "scattered, limited, controlled, and exercised in rotation" and autocracy means that power is "concentrated, uncontrolled, indefinite, and unlimited," then autocracy and democracy are opposites. But is this all we wish to know? If our sole goal is the intellectual satisfaction of knowing that these terms can be defined as opposites, then our goal is easily satisfied. If, however, our purpose is to find the real world opposite of democracy in order to, as Sartori suggests, more precisely bound our notion of democracy, then we are immediately confronted with the fact that the terms used to establish the meaning of the dichotomy have no such conveniently precise meanings. In the real world, the exercise of power in both democracies and auto- cracies is a complicated affair. It involves, among other things, the exercise of power by various groups and individuals over a considerable number of specific situations. Over this range of phenomena it is not always possible to know to what degree power is scattered or limited or controlled or exercised in rotation. Empirically, one finds that sometimes, in some situations, it is and at other times it is not, just as in those regimes which we would define as autocratic, power will not always be in application concentrated, uncontrolled, indefinite, or unlimited. On the basis of closer examination then, one can see that Sartori has not yet escaped from the necessity, at least at the operational level, of employing concepts which are really continua along which some form of measurement must, in prin- ciple, be employed.

CHAPTER 1

What Democracy Is Not

Giovanni Sartori

1. THE "EX ADVERSO" DEFINITION

To define means to assign limits, to delimit. A concept is undefined as long as it is unlimited. That is to say that a definition must embrace the whole of what it defines, but no more. Therefore, if we want to complete our definition of democracy, we also have to see what democracy *is not*, that is, what is the opposite of democracy.

Generally, definitions *ex adverso* are the easiest. As it is difficult to say what white is, we usually say that it is the opposite of black. When we try to define politics positively, we are bound to get into trouble, so we solve the problem by saying that it is neither ethics nor economics, and so forth. Likewise, while it is complicated to say what is meant by democracy, it is, or should be, easier to say what is not meant by it. Except that—and this is more than a coincidence—as soon as we have become aware of the importance of locating accurately the boundaries of democracy, and thereby of clearly establishing the difference between it and its counterfeits, our way of indicating the opposite of democracy has become less and less precise.

Formerly, the contrary of democracy was indicated by words like tyranny, despotism, autocracy, absolutism and dictatorship.[1] But we have recently coined two new terms, totalitarianism and authoritarianism. Thus, when the question, "What is the opposite of democracy?" is asked, we tend to reply, nowadays, "Totalitarianism," or "Authoritarianism." Franz Neumann's last book, for instance, has been given the title *The Democratic and the Authoritarian State*, and totalitarianism has been spelled out by Nisbet as the very negation of democracy despite the warning that "we merely delude ourselves if we suppose that there is always necessary conflict between totalitarian governments and the desires and aspirations of the masses."[2]

Reprinted from Giovanni Sartori, *Democratic Theory* (Detroit: Wayne State University Press, 1962), Chap. VII, pp. 135–57, by permission of the Wayne State University Press. Footnotes have been renumbered.

Now, there is no doubt that our political vocabulary was in need of some enrichment. But I question whether these two innovations are happy ones or are being used correctly. In fact, I do not consider "authoritarianism" a felicitous terminological coinage and, while "totalitarianism" is a very useful addition to our vocabulary, I wonder to what extent it is suitable as a proper antithesis to democracy.

Of course, it would be pedantic to ostracize the word authoritarianism or to reproach everybody who opposes totalitarianism to democracy. But since we are living in the age of confused democracy—so confused that it is even difficult to determine what democracy is not—we should be put on guard against the misunderstandings that stem from the use of these concepts. There is nothing wrong in that we enjoy saying "authoritarianism" or "totalitarianism." But it is somewhat strange that the antonyms that are less satisfying are being used so much more than the apposite ones.

When we oppose democracy to autocracy, for instance, we can easily and surely determine the point where democracy ends, notwithstanding all of its possible variants and transformations. Whereas when we speak of democracy and totalitarianism, we place a vast no-man's-land between democracy and its opposite. And it is my contention that authoritarianism is even less satisfactory as an antithesis. Thus, to begin with, the problem of the definition *a contrario* of democracy confronts us with this puzzling fact: that the label which should be used most is actually the label that is used least.

2. AUTHORITARIANISM AND AUTHORITY

In the word authoritarianism, the suffix -*ism* indicates a particularly, not to say excessively, energetic authority—an authority which crushes liberty. "Authoritarianism" is thus a pejorative term. But authoritarianism comes from "authority", and the word authority tends instead to have a favorable connotation.

The original meaning of "authority" is probably related to the Latin verb *augere*, to augment. Therefore, in its earliest meaning it indicated that those in authority add something, supplement, confirm, or sanction a course of action or thought. However, as Hannah Arendt has pertinently pointed out, this original meaning has been completely lost, because *auctoritas* derived its meaning from a strictly traditionalistic mental pattern. For the Romans the authority of the living depended on and stemmed from the authority of the city's founders. Thus, what is "augmented" by those in authority is the foundation. *Auctor* was not *artifex*, i.e., was not the actual maker or inventor. History was not seen as the adventure of man's breaking with the past and introducing change, but, on the contrary, as an augmentation of the past, as the expansion and confirmation of an *Ursprung*. The opposite is true for us. In our view of the world, *auctor* has become associated with *artifex*, with the author, the inventor, the maker. We take a dynamic view of history, and thus we do not think of growth as directed towards the past, but towards the future.[3] However, notwithstanding our different perspective, and therefore notwithstanding the fact that *auctor* has become *author*—thereby suggesting the idea of creation, innovation, and initiative—"authority" has always been and still is an approbative term. And it is hard to see how it could be otherwise.[4]

It is all very well to say that the political process is a "power process." But once we have said this, we must distinguish between one type of power and another: between *potestas* and *auctoritas*, between power as force (or domination) and power as authority, between power to coerce and power to get things done. Thus, "authority" is the term that we need for the purpose of indicating not the power that is suspended from above over those who have to submit to it, but, on the contrary, the power that comes from spontaneous investiture and draws its force and efficacy from the fact that it is acknowledged.[5] Authority is, we could say, a power that is based on persuasion, prestige, deference. And when we speak of authority we refer to a leadership that arouses and receives spontaneous support.[6]

In regard to our problem, the distinction between power and authority is serviceable in that it allows us to specify that democracy is the political system which is built on the mode of exercising power that is called authority, in the sense that the typical feature of democracy is that it tends to transform power into authority, a *vis coactiva* into a *vis directiva*. Far from being repugnant to democracy, authority is its power formula par excellence. The ideal cherished by those who look forward to a genuine democracy is not the conquest of power but, on the contrary, its minimization, and therefore the replacement of "power holders" by what we might call "authority holders."

In the light of this conclusion, it is easy to understand how disturbing the label "authoritarianism" is. There are three reasons for this. In the first place it tends to make our attitude toward the idea of authority ambivalent and vacillating, torn as we are between the consciousness of its desirability and the distressing associations it arouses. As a consequence some people have again started to confuse *auctoritas* with *potestas*, authority with power, with the result that all the typology concerning the different forms of power has been muddled once more[7] and that the very notion of authority has been made meaningless.[8] A second incongruity comes from the fact that "authoritarianism" casts over the problems of the present the shadow of an outworn and gratuitous philosophy of history. The term has in this respect a singularly anti-historical flavor, since authority started to be used in a pejorative sense when the idea of liberty without authority, of a happy state of natural anarchy, had already been long extinct. In the third place, thanks to the interference of the term authoritarianism, we are forced to be real virtuosi of language in order to make a proper use of our terminology. This may seem a frivolous reason for disapproving of its use, but I submit that a democracy cannot permit itself the luxury of defending itself as if its audience were made up of philologists and glottologists.

Since authority and democracy are so closely interwoven that we can hardly speak of democracy without speaking of authority, let us suppose that at a certain point in the discussion we have to use the adjectival form instead of the noun. What are we supposed to say? Shall we call democracy an "authoritarian" system? This is clearly inadvisable. Thus if we wish to convey the idea that democracy typically requires power as authority, our only escape is to resort to the subtle distinction between *authoritarian* (non-democratic) authority, and *authoritative* (democratic) authority, with the result that we find ourselves with the not very appealing expression "authoritative system" to connote a democracy.[9] And in order to avoid misunderstandings, we would have to resort to similar refinements quite frequently. For example, "authoritarianism" has suggested the epithet "authoritarian personality" to indicate the type of personality structure that is not adapted to the democratic way of life.[10] The trouble is, again, that this term leaves the impression that the type of personality which can best serve democracy should be authority-less. Of course, this is not so. But in order to correct this erroneous impression, we shall have to make a distinction between the authoritarian personality and the authoritative personality, with the understanding that the successful functioning of a democratic system depends on the latter type of personality structure.[11]

We can see from all this that we do indeed have to be virtuosi. And I wonder whether it is wise to establish the difference between democracy and its opposite by such fine distinctions. Furthermore, I am also brought to wonder why we should honor modern dictatorships with a distinctive mark that they do not deserve. It is true that when we say "authoritarian State" we mean to express censure; but in the censure a certain amount of praise is also implied.[12] "Authoritarianism" does suggest that an excessive use of authority is involved; yet, this excess remains linked to something that is praiseworthy, it is an excess of authority. And authority is a legitimate need, no society is possible without it. Actually, if the use of "authoritarianism" had not clouded the waters so much, and if we could follow the sensible and usual practice of giving it the meaning of its root (authority) we would assert the very opposite of what is commonly accepted, that is, that it is inappropriate to use a word that evokes the idea of authority in speaking of a tyrannical system, for true authority is destroyed by despotisms, whereas the authoritative personality is necessary to a free society.[13]

If, then, we are seeking the correct antithesis of democracy, authoritarianism will not do, for a word that creates confusion and gives rise to so many unnecessary problems cannot be the proper antithesis. And it should be added that, even setting aside all the foregoing reasons, authoritarianism is not, in any case, a *vis-à-vis* of democracy, for the good reason that the concept of authority is correlative to the concept of freedom.[14]

True freedom, it is said, accepts authority, just as true authority recognizes freedom. Freedom that does not acknowledge authority is arbitrary freedom, *licentia* not *libertas*. Vice versa, authority that does not recognize freedom is authoritarianism. This means that authoritarianism is the opposite of liberty and therefore the opposite of what is historically known as liberalism rather than as democracy. And the difference is not in the least irrelevant. For one thing it still has to be proved that democracy cannot be illiberal, or at any rate a-liberal. And in this hypothesis the use of the term authoritarianism would demand the inclusion of "authoritarian democracy" as a possible category—another confirmation of our assertion that if it is the opposite of democracy that we are seeking, we have not found it.

THE "TOTAL STATE" DEMOCRACY AND ABSOLUTISM

Let us get on to "totalitarianism." Totalitarianism comes from "totality," and simply expresses, as such, the idea of extension, of something that embraces and pervades everything; and, in a derived sense, the idea of all-pervading penetration and intensity. But according to this meaning it could hardly be denied that, in some degree, a tendency towards totality characterizes every modern State. Demographic pressure, the continually increasing interdependence of all aspects of the industrial society, technological progress and the resultant search for more and more rational, functional, and planned societal forms, to mention only the more conspicuous reasons, lead present-day governments, *bon gré mal gré*, to concern themselves increasingly with everybody and everything.

In this respect, then, we could easily argue that the law of inertia of modern States tends to make them more and more totalitarian, in the literal meaning of the term. All modern States are developing in the direction of the "total State." And the democratic State is no exception. As a matter of fact, the hypothesis that a democratic State can become totalitarian, meaning that it can become an all-pervading total State, is perfectly plausible. For, in principle, no political formula can justify a totalitarian expansion of political power as easily as democracy. Democracy is the government *of* all, and as such it is vested with a greater right than any other ethico-political formula to exercise jurisdiction *over* all. The power that originates in everyone is authorized, *ex hypothesi*, to do everything. "The democratic fiction," de Jouvenel remarks, "lends the leaders the authority of the whole. It is the whole that wills, it is the whole that acts."[15]

It will be objected that this is not the sense in which "totalitarianism" was coined and accepted into the political vocabulary, since in this context it has a technical connotation and should thus be considered a synonym of "authoritarianism" or "absolutism." The reason for this is that, in politics, attention is not paid so much to the extent of power—to its amount—as to the way it is *exercised*. This may be true, but once we have decided that totalitarianism does not indicate an extension—a total State—but has to be understood as an equivalent of absolutism, or of authoritarianism, we have not made much progress. On the contrary.

I shall not embark again on a discussion of authoritarianism, because, whatever the worth and appropriateness of the concept itself, any identification of authoritarianism with totalitarianism is patently arbitrary. Even if it is plausible that every totalitarian system is authoritarian, the opposite, i.e. that every authoritarian system is totalitarian, is not plausible. The only necessary consequence of authoritarian exercise of power is that the freedom of the subjects will be trampled on and, more precisely, that coercion will be at a maximum intensity while voluntarization will be feeble and peripheral. That this should take place in a totalitarian manner is a further condition or hypothesis, which certainly cannot be explained if we make totalitarianism synonymous with authoritarianism.

Rather, it is useful to examine the other equation, namely, that totalitarianism is analogous to absolutism. For this purpose it will be worthwhile to investigate the concept of absolutism, and this in two respects—to see if it can help us to clarify the concept of totalitarianism, and to ascertain at the same time whether the term is by any chance satisfactory as an opposite of democracy.

Absolutus is a term used by the Latin commentators of the Aristotelian concept of *pambasileia* (translated as *rex absolutus*) and it did not have, for a long time, a derogatory meaning. *Potestas absoluta*, absolute power, merely indicated a supreme, perfect, complete, and (in this context and reference) intangible power. It is only with Machiavelli, and especially with Guicciardini, that a *potestà assoluta* is linked with virtual tyranny (and this only in a peripheral way), and that the Latin root *absolvere*, which conveys the meaning of "setting free," begins to be associated with the idea of lack and thereby of imperfection.[16] However, it was not until the 18th century that "absolutism" was coined and used in its modern derogatory sense of "released from" something that we praise. In the modern connotation, then, the absolute power of absolutism denotes a power set free from controls, released from restraints: a limitless, discretional exercise of power that allows no opposition. And the concept appears definite because we are reminded, by association of ideas, of the absolute 17th and 18th century monarchies.

But what interests us is not the past. I mean that if we have to use the word "absolutism" for the present, the fact that it recalls an example from the past is confusing, not only because absolute monarchies no longer exist in the West, but especially because this imagery is related to the patrimonial concept of the State, that is, to a political system in which the State is conceived of as the monarch's estate. Therefore it is obvious that a democracy cannot be absolute in the sense that absolute monarchies were; but that does not prove that a democracy cannot become absolute in some other way.

In what we might term its material meaning, a power that is not opposed by adequate *de facto* countervailing powers is an absolute power. In this connotation, absolutism is related to the concentration of power. The more a society loses its pluralistic structure and the more its intermediary forces are levelled and weakened, the more easily the conditions that make absolutism possible are created. Thus, any State that concentrates all the power in itself is potentially a State that can exercise absolute power. And this implies that even an overcentralized democracy[17] that tends to replace the spontaneous interplay of a multi-group society with its own unicentric will is in a position to exercise an absolutist kind of pressure. Let us not forget, in this connection, that "democratic centralization" was Lenin's slogan.

In a second sense, we have absolute power when it is not disciplined and limited by law. In this meaning the absolute State is the non-constitutional State, that is, a State in which the power holders are not restrained by, or have become released from, constitutional checks and restraints. In this connection the query is: Is the democratic State necessarily a liberal-constitutional State, and more precisely a *Rechtsstaat* of the "garantist" type in which the sovereign *demos* (no less than the former *princeps*) is not *legibus solutus?* Genetically, that is historically speaking, this has been the case. But if we say "necessarily," then the answer is: No, democracy and constitutionalism are not inevitably linked. Actually, present-day maximization of democracy seeks, or at any rate entails, a minimization of the "garantist" aspects of liberal constitutionalism. Democratic perfectionism in particular rejects the classic constitutional State in its impatience to obtain more quickly more than the system allows. But then we cannot fail to see that even in the constitutional meaning of the expression a democracy may become absolute. Incidentally, let us be reminded that this has already been the trend with ancient democracies.

There is finally a third, general and generic, sense of "absolutism" that refers to a mental pattern, to a personality type. The so-called constitutional gentleman, with his internalized moral self-restraints, typifies its opposite, the non-absolute kind of leader. But the constitutional gentleman has become a very rare specimen in our time. Therefore, even from this broad angle, I do not see why the assertion that a democratic absolutism is within the range of possibility should be considered disrespectful. If democracy is not absolutist it is not because it cannot, *ex hypothesi*, become so, but rather because we are made aware of this danger and thereby take the necessary precautions.

In effect many authoritative scholars have emphasized that the principle of democracy, in itself, can easily imply absolutism, or that in any case it leaves many openings which may lead to what is meant by saying "absolutism." Democratic legitimacy implies the limitation of power only insofar as it opposes autocratic power, so that once the adversary is defeated, popular sovereignty may well come to resemble its former enemy. A limited power while fighting or resisting another power, popular sovereignty becomes, in its own way, a source of unlimited power when the counter-powers disappear.

E.g., if we contend that democracy is achieved by taking all the power from the despot with one hand to give it to the people with the other, all this operation accomplishes is to present us with an absolutism in reverse. And in this case one is perfectly justified in maintaining that it is precisely democratic legitimacy that gives absolute sanction to power. For there is no appeal when sovereignty is exercised in the name of the people: we are already in the final court of appeal.

As anyone can easily see, the antithesis under discussion is neither clear-cut nor axiomatic. By saying this I do not intend to affirm that democracy and absolutism are compatible. I only wish to make clear that I cannot demonstrate what democracy *is not*—or can never be—if I have to argue the problem on the basis of the concept of absolutism.

The answer to my second question, namely, whether totalitarianism and absolutism should be used as synonyms, and whether the latter concept helps in determining the meaning of the former, is implicit in what I have already said. Absolutism is a loose concept that cannot be pinned down easily. Therefore, it is not very helpful in explaining an already obscure term like totalitarianism. Two one-legged men do not make a two-legged man. I should also like to make, in principle, an objection concerning the economy of language. "Totalitarianism" is a modern word which was invented to give the idea of a phenomenon that seems to us without precedent. What sense does it make then to waste this neologism by dressing it in old clothes? If totalitarianism has to be understood as meaning absolutism, why coin this new term, which has the additional defect of being even more obscure than the previous one, since we have to use "absolutism" to explain it?

4. TOTALITARIANISM

Instead of resorting to synonyms that are not even synonyms, let us return to the direct question: What does "totalitarianism" mean? A perusal of the views put forward by a number of authors in the book *Totalitarianism*[18] shows how ambiguous the word is, and how difficult it is to agree on its meaning. The fundamental question seems to be whether the word should be used to indicate a trait that is common to many different State-societies, or whether it should designate a particular type of political system characterized by its own special syndrome of features.[19] Another question, which is related to the former one, is: Should "totalitarianism" be used for all epochs, including ancient times, or should it be reserved for our time, to indicate an experience whose novelty we wish to emphasize?

It is my opinion that if we take the first path we cannot give a sufficiently definite meaning to the term, nor employ it most fruitfully. Certainly, if we wish, we can say that the ancient *polis* was totalitarian, or, as Franz Neumann remarked, that the government of Sparta and the regime of Diocletian are examples of totalitarianism.[20] Except that the analogy is superficial, and, as Karl Loewenstein rightly points out in this connection, "We are not entitled to qualify certain ancient autocracies as totalitarian because the *telos* of the State society . . . , rarely articulated in secular terms, was accepted without disagreement by the power holders and the power addressees alike, and so deeply ingrained in tradition that it required neither ideological formulation nor enforcement."[21] When we apply "totalitarianism" to a past epoch, we lose sight of the profound qualitative difference that exists between total domination taken as a matter of course because it is based on tradition and religion, and the total domination which emerges in the modern world, superimposing itself on a Christian, liberal, and democratic civilization.[22]

Besides, following this line, we can come to the point of reducing the notion of totalitarianism to a vanishing point, as E. H. Carr has done. He defines totalitarianism as "the belief that some organized group or institution, whether church or government or party, has a special access to truth."[23] Now, the reason that Carr arrives at such a patently arbitrary definition is that he wants to demonstrate that totalitarianism is as old as the world, that it has always existed and always will, except for a brief parenthesis which he calls the "age of individualism."[24] But what he really manages to demonstrate is the futility of employing the term to interpret the entire course of history. The danger of taking this line is that we arrive at wholly arbitrary stipulations that have no basis whatever in the semantic potential of the word, or at any rate that we give "totalitarianism" so broad a meaning that it becomes meaningless.[25]

The second approach, which is the one indicated by Friedrich, is thus more fruitful, even though it presents considerable difficulties. In his contribution to "Totalitarianism" Friedrich lists five requisites for a totalitarian system: (a) an official ideology, (b) a single mass party controlled by an oligarchy, (c) government monopoly of arms, (d) government monopoly of mass media, and (e) a terroristic police system.[26] It is symptomatic that this list is varied even by those contributors who agree with Friedrich that totalitarianism is a specific political system characterized by several traits.[27] Nevertheless the area of disagreement can easily be reduced to a question of detail if an agreement is reached on the following points: (i) the opportunity of using "totalitarianism" to denote only a present-day phenomenon, and (ii) the necessity of adhering to the semantic connotation of the word, which means remaining within the orbit of the idea of totality.

It is my thesis, then, that a new term has a *raison d'être* if it expresses a new idea. Therefore "totalitarianism" can be used fruitfully if by it we mean to indicate the unprecedented intensity, pervasiveness, and penetration— both in breadth and in depth—that political domination can assume. Our world is revealing such a new aspect and dimension of power as not even the prophets of a new age—Marx and Nietzsche, for instance—have glimpsed or suspected. Hobbes's Leviathan is a baby monster when confronted with Orwell's, and the tyrannies of the past seem innocent and innocuous compared to what totalitarian dictatorships are, or can become.[28] A term was needed to indicate this difference, and "totalitarianism" is effective as this term.[29]

What I disapprove of is its use as a noun, for when used as the grammatical and logical subject of discourse, "totalitarianism" does not say enough, since it designates neither a form of government nor a way of governing. Instead, it becomes meaningful when it is in its adjectival form, when used as a predicate. It is correct to say "totalitarian party" because the specification indicates that it is a party that wishes to suppress all other parties. And it is correct, and necessary, to speak of "totalitarian autocracy" because thus we indicate the modern type of despotism and tyranny. Whereas, on the other hand, it is useless as well as misleading to adopt "totalitarianism" as a substantive to replace the pre-existing terminology.

It is a confusing waste because in this case totalitarianism becomes a cosmic notion that is interpreted by everyone as he thinks fit, and thereby distracts our attention from the essential point. The essential point being that totalitarianism denotes the imprisonment of the whole of society *within* the State, an all-pervasive political domination over the extra-political life of man. When in Italy the saying was, "Everything in the State, nothing outside the State, nothing against the State," this was little more than a rhetorical phrase. But if the proposition "everything in the State" is taken seriously and applied to its limit by the instruments of coercion which technological power has at its disposal, we indeed find ourselves confronted with the thing; that is, "the ultimate invasion of human privacy,"[30] the destruction of everything that is spontaneous, independent, diversified, and autonomous in the life of human collectivities; in short, a huge political garrison where a mass society has been incapsulated into the State. And this is precisely what distinguishes totalitarianism from absolutism: "The destruction of the line between State and society and the total politicization of society. . . . This is not merely a question of more or less political power. The difference is one of quality, not quantity."[31]

Yet in these terms we have described only a tendency, an objective, or, as it has been so well expressed, a "nightmare."[32] We have not described a definite type of State, or a definite power structure. And since the possibility of pursuing totalitarian ends strictly depends on the form of the State, we must first determine what the non-democratic form of power structure is— and this will be the opposite of democracy which will permit us to conclude that totalitarianism and democracy are incompatible.

5. DEMOCRACY VERSUS AUTOCRACY

We may now review with sufficient accuracy the range of the possible opposites of democracy, or at any rate the ways of indicating its boundaries with the greatest possible clarity. I shall proceed to examine the following concepts, arranged in five groups: (i) tyranny, despotism, absolutism; (ii) dictatorship; (iii) authoritarianism and totalitarianism; (iv) the coercion-consensus continuum, or the monocracy-polycracy distinction; (v) autocracy.

Tyranny, despotism, and absolutism are the old-fashioned terms. Actually they survive in our vocabulary mostly as scare words. Tyranny, it is true, has a long and elaborate record in the history of political thought. It is sufficient to recall the distinction of Bartolo da Sassoferrato and of Coluccio Salutati between tyranny *quoad exercitium* (relating to the way of exercising power) and tyranny *ex defectu tituli* (relating to the illegitimate or violent acquisition of power) and all the following literature of the Monarchomachs on the right to kill the tyrant. Nevertheless it is hard to see how these distinctions, and for that matter all the Renaissance literature on the subject, apply to modern conditions and to the present-day terms of the problem. Our plebiscitary dictators can hardly be considered tyrants *ex defectu tituli*, and our criteria for spelling out a tyranny *exercitio* are too different from the

Greek and the Renaissance moral and natural law criteria. On the other hand, despotism is a very inarticulate concept in the political literature, and we have seen the difficulties inherent in the use of absolutism. All in all, these terms only render the general idea of a displeasing and oppressive *exercitium* of State power. And if we want to know more about the tyrannical despotic, and absolute way of exercising power—as well as of the form of State which is related to this *exercitium*—we must refer to the more modern concepts.

Dictatorship is actually the term that has come to replace tyranny. However, our use of dictatorship in the meaning formerly given to tyranny is very recent.[33] Indeed so recent that our concept is still very rough and inarticulate.[34] One could almost say that whereas tyranny has been reduced out of its old age to being a scare word, dictatorship still has to emerge from the juvenile stage of being little more than a mere "boo word." For up to the present moment there is no satisfactory theory of dictatorship which establishes a typology and relates the concept to a certain kind of allocation of power, distribution of power, elite recruitment, decision-making, and—in sum—to a definite form and *exercitium* of State power.[35] It is true that if we are making little progress in this direction this is because, or partly because, we have been unable, as yet, to build a frame of reference to replace the obsolete traditional classification of political systems.[36] But it is also true, on the other hand, that present-day scholars are making a generous use of the term but have dedicated little attention to the concept, concentrating, as it were, not on dictatorship but on authoritarianism and totalitarianism. We know comparatively less about our dictatorships than previous authors knew about tyranny, and consequently our queries have to be once again passed over to those new terminological coins.

Totalitarianism and authoritarianism, however, cannot solve our problem either. In opposing authoritarianism to democracy we confuse the issues of liberty and of democracy, we reinforce the obsolete notion of an authority-less democratic ideal, and at the same time we provide a very inadequate image of what awaits us in a technological totalitarian autocracy. As for totalitarianism, its ineffectiveness as an *ex adverso* determination of democracy is revealed by the fact that in the expression "totalitarian democracy," which has been put into circulation by J. B. Talmon,[37] the two alleged opposites have been coupled. We need not discuss whether Talmon's label is pertinent, intrinsically contradictory, or paradoxical. It is sufficient to note that its very adoption points out the weakness of the antithesis democracy-versus-totalitarianism. And it is a real weakness, for in this alternative we are unable to spell out and define clearly one horn of the dilemma, i.e., totalitarianism as a noun. Democracy is in itself an extremely difficult and controversial concept. If we try to define it *per differentiam* with even vaguer and more ambiguous notions, we are just furthering the confusion of ideas.

It might be suggested at this point that we should change approach, and search for what democracy *is not* by having recourse to distinctions of the power-authority, or the coercion-consensus kind (and the like). But in this approach we have a continuum; and this means that conceptual overlaps are not only inevitable but considerable. Who could deny, for instance, that every coercion requires a minimum of consent, and vice versa that hardly any consent is exempt from some degree of coercion? This does not mean in the least that the distinctions are not useful. On the contrary, they are essential. But it does mean that if we use them for the purpose of pinning down the difference between democracy and non-democracy they may well lead us to what I have called a balanced nihilism.

We might switch, however, to Karl Loewenstein's suggestion: "The basic dichotomy of political systems and the patterns of government included therein would be terminologically best expressed by the pair of opposites 'polycracy' and 'monocracy,' the former denoting shared and the latter concentrated exercise of political power."[38] I agree with Loewenstein when he remarks that complex classifications defeat their purpose, and I agree very much with his subsequent treatment of the topic.[39] But regarding this specific suggestion it should be pointed out that also the "polycracy-monocracy" contrast can hardly prevent overlaps, for the argument will always be brought up that even a monocracy is based, somehow or other, on a polycracy.[40] I grant that the objection is not insuperable, but let me again pose the question: Why choose overlapping, or (as in the cases examined previously) misleading and ambiguous concepts when we do have, after all, an unequivocal term which expresses the contrary of democracy?[41]

We are left, thus, with autocracy. It is quite true that even autocracy can be criticized on the grounds that it has not been elaborated any better than dictatorship and the other poorly defined and somewhat inarticulate concepts on our list. Nevertheless, autocracy does have an advantage over the other concepts in that it focuses the attention on the strategic juncture of the argument, namely, on the method of creation of the power holders, and on the source of their legitimacy. So, given the fact that we do not possess an articulate agreed-upon general framework for the classification of political systems, it follows that in the present state of our conceptual tools only autocracy is serviceable for the purpose of defining democracy *a contrario*. Despite other possible drawbacks, if the alternative is "democracy or autocracy," the semantic indication conveyed by autocracy is precise, and we are immediately able to elucidate the concepts and to draw the line that clearly separates democracy from what it is not.

Democracy, viewed as non-autocracy, denotes a political system characterized by the absence of personal power, and more particularly a system that hinges on the principle that no one can proclaim himself ruler, that no one can hold power irrevocably in his own name. Precisely because the autocratic principle is repudiated, the democratic axiom is that man's power over man can only be granted by others. Furthermore, if the designation of leaders does not come from consensus, there is no democracy. Nor is there democracy when consensus is counterfeit and extorted, for there is no consensus if those who are to give it are not free to dissent and if it does not result from choice among a number of alternatives. And no terminological falsification, as well as no amount of subtle display of dialectics, can erase boundary-posts that are as clear and easily identifiable as these.

From this correct *ex adverso* approach we also understand more clearly the meaning and *raison d'être* of liberal-democratic institutions, that is, of the constitutional precautions which, by separating the exercise of power from its investiture and by binding public officials to preordained juridical structures, make it possible to replace leaders, to limit their time in office, to hold them responsible to the people, and to avert abuses of power. The *a contrario* definition of democracy is therefore the following: In democracy no one can choose himself, no one can invest himself with the power to rule, and therefore no one can arrogate to himself unconditional and unlimited power. The difference between democracy and its opposite lies in the fact that in a democracy power is scattered, limited, controlled, and exercised in rotation; whereas in an autocracy power is concentrated, uncontrolled indefinite, and unlimited. What democracy is *not* is, in one word, autocracy

NOTES

[1] The terms are arranged in chronological order. Tyrant and despot are Greek names. Absolutism and autocracy have been used only since the 18th century. One might wonder why I have listed dictatorship, a Latin term, as last. In its Roman meaning, dictatorship was not a political system but an extraordinary magistracy limited in time and functions. We have to wait until we are well into the 20th century before dictatorship denotes a non-democratic regime. Therefore, the meaning of dictatorship which concerns us is really a very recent one. These concepts are examined below in Section V.

[2] Cf. R. A. Nisbet, *The Quest for Community* (New York, 1953), p. 194.

[3] Cf. Hannah Arendt in *Authority*, ed. C. J. Friedrich (Cambridge, 1958), pp. 99–102; cf. also Friedrich's essay, p. 30.

[4] For greater development and depth see in general the volume ed. by Friedrich, *Authority*, which contains excellent contributions. Cf. also the good collection *Freedom and Authority in Our Time*, eds. Bryson, Finkelstein, MacIver and McKeon (New York

and London, 1953); as well as Dolf Sternberger, *Autoritat, Freiheit und Befehlsgewalt* (Tubingen, 1959).

[5] The *Bulletin international des sciences sociales* in the series of terminological studies under the auspices of UNESCO indicates the following common usage of "authority": "Power that is accepted, respected, recognized, legitimate." (IV, 1955, p. 718.) With reference to the distinction which Friedrich makes between corporeal or substantive power (power as a *thing had*) and relational power, or power *over* (cf. *Constitutional Government and Democracy*, pp. 22–24 and 584), authority would be the desirable form of the "relational" mode of power.

[6] In a somewhat poetic but effective manner, Jacques Maritain writes: "We shall call 'authority' the right to lead and command, to be listened to and obeyed by others: and we shall name 'power' the force by means of which others can be obliged to listen and obey. . . . To the extent to which it is power, authority reaches down to the physical level; insofar as it is authority, power is raised to the moral level. . . ." "Democratie et Autorite" in *Le Pouvoir*, eds. R. P. McKeon, C. J. Friedrich, *et al.* (Paris, 1957), II.

[7] Many contemporary writers, in fact, use "power" and others use "authority" for all possible cases, without any precise reason, and without explaining why; thereby revealing that they are blind to the problem which Plato had already seen, that is, whether *auctoritas* is to be explained in terms of *potestas* (Thrasymachus' thesis), or whether *potestas* is to be converted into *auctoritas*. Yet is it on the basis of this distinction that one poses the fundamental alternative between "politics as war" (the *auctoritas* which is might) and "legalitarian politics" (the *auctoritas* which is not *potestas*). . . .

[8] Cf. e.r., Robert Bierstedt's essay, "The Problem of Authority," in *Freedom and Control in Modern Society*, eds. Berger, Abel, and Page (New York, 1954), in which authority is defined as "institutionalized power" (p. 78), legality is confused with legitimacy (following Merriam), and a number of distinctions are either misleading or irrelevant. Lasswell and Kaplan's (and Merriam's) definition, "authority is formal power" (*Power and Society*, p. 133), also seems inadequate.

[9] Perhaps it is for this reason, that is, because he had implicitly in mind authority rather than authoritarianism, that David Easton speaks of "authoritative allocation" and "authoritative decisions." If this is the case, it would seem helpful to contemplate also a strict use of the notion, distinguishing between authoritative and coercive allocations. Cf. *The Political System* (New York, 1953), Chap. V.

[10] Cf. for instance T. W. Adorno *et al.*, *The Authoritarian Personality* (New York, 1950); M. Janowitz and D. Marvick, "Authoritarianism and Political Behavior," in *Public Opinion Quarterly* (1953), pp. 185–201; and *Studies in the Scope and Method of the Authoritarian Personality*, eds. R. Christie and M. Jahoda (Glencoe, 1954).

[11] Aside from the terminological confusion because of which we should on the one hand approve of authority but on the other beware of the authoritarian personality, I am under the impression that many of the extrapolations derived from this questionable ideal-type are either of little significance (because much more important variables should be taken into account) or arbitrary, e.g., is it really true that an authoritarian family structure supports an authoritarian political regime? And if it is true (actually the opposite can be claimed), is this extremely remote antecedent really relevant?

[12] One should bear in mind that "authoritarianism" was coined by authoritarian regimes, and this, obviously, in order to exploit the approbatory connotation of the semantics.

[13] Cf. Friedrich: "In a very real sense, in a totalitarian society true authority is altogether destroyed," in *Totalitarianism* (New Haven, 1954), p. 274. This thesis is developed by Friedrich in *Confluence*, No. 3 (1954), pp. 307–16, and elaborated further in a very stimulating way in *Authority*, p. 28f. Cf. also Hannah Arendt, "Authority in the Twentieth Century," in *Review of Politics*, IV (1956). This was also, despite the different wording and approach, Gugliemo Ferrero's thesis when he distinguished between the power that "comes from above" and the legitimate power that "comes from below," and

related the crisis of our times to the "disappearance of the sense of legitimacy." Cf. *Il potere* (Milano, 1947), *passim*.

[14] Cf. the history of the idea in G. Quadri, *Il Problema dell 'autorita* (Firenze, 1940), two vols.

[15] *Le Pouvoir*, p. 316.

[16] Cf. R. De Mattei "Assolutismo" in *Enciclopedia del diritto* (Milano, 1958), Vol. III, pp. 917f. Cf. also Emilio Bussi, "Reflexions critiques sur la notion d'absolutisme" in *Bulletin de la Societe d'Histoire Moderne*, November–December, 1955.

[17] Lasswell and Kaplan distinguish between centralization and concentration of power, and rightly point out that the latter, not the former, is a characteristic of despotic rule (*Power and Society*, pp. 224–25). Accordingly, I use "over-centralization" for a centralization which acquires the nature of a concentration.

[18] Cf. *Totalitarianism: Proceedings of a Conference Held at the American Academy of Arts and Sciences*, March, 1953, ed. C. J. Friedrich.

[19] Cf. N. S. Timasheff in *Totalitarianism*, p. 39.

[20] Cf. *The Democratic and the Authoritarian State* (Glencoe, 1957), pp. 246–47.

[21] *Political Power and the Governmental Process* (Chicago, 1957), pp. 59–60.

[22] Other examples of totalitarian anticipations are furnished by Barrington Moore, Jr., *Political Power and Social Theory* (Cambridge, 1958), Chap. II, "Totalitarian Elements in Pre-industrial Societies." Still, it seems to me that our terms (such as dictatorship and totalitarianism) cannot, without being arbitrary, be superimposed on preliterate societies and on oriental despotisms.

[23] E. H. Carr, *The Soviet Impact on the Western World* (New York, 1949), p. 110.

[24] *Op. cit.* This is also the underlying central thesis of Carr's history of the Russian Revolution, *The Bolshevik Revolution* (London, 1950–58), 5 vols.

[25] Cf. R. A. Nisbet's remark: "Totalitarianism has unfortunately become one of those omnibus words used to absorb indiscriminately every element of the past and present that we regard as detestable." (*The Quest for Community*, p. 192.)

[26] Cf. pp. 52–53. In a successive volume, *Totalitarian Dictatorship and Autocracy*, written in collaboration with Z. K. Brzezinski (New Haven, 1956), Friedrich adds to the five above-mentioned characteristics a sixth one, "a centrally directed economy" (cf. pp. 9, 177–236). It is understood that these five or six traits are interwoven, with a totalitarian system as their syndrome; for the monopoly of armed force as well as economic planning pertain, or, in the latter case, can pertain also to democratic systems.

[27] Cf. in *Totalitarianism* the communications of Alex Inkeles and Karl W. Deutsch, pp. 87f., 308f. It turns out that if we follow, for example, the criteria suggested by Deutsch, Peter the Great would be a totalitarian despot, while to Friedrich he would not (cf. p. 334).

[28] The unique and modern character of totalitarian dictatorship is rendered very well by Friedrich and Brzezinski, *Totalitarian Dictatorship and Autocracy*, esp. pp. 10–13 *et passim*. The authors opportunely point out, as a confirmation of the "modernity" of the totalitarian systems, that four of the six traits they enumerate are "technologically conditioned," and that the two remaining ones (the official ideology and the single party) link the totalitarian dictatorship to modern democracy, of which they are a perversion. "In summary," the authors conclude , "these regimes could have arisen only within the context of mass democracy and modern technology" (p. 13). This genealogy is generally recognized. Gabriel A. Almond has well synthesized on his part the novelty of this concept as follows: "Totalitarianism is tyranny with a rational bureaucracy, a monopoly of the modern technology of communication, and a monopoly of the modern technology of violence." "Comparative Political Systems" in *Political Behavior—A Reader*, eds. Eulau, Eldersveld, Janowitz (Glencoe, 1956), p. 39.

[29] In this sense, totalitarianism is perhaps the very word that Tocqueville was trying to find when he wrote: "I believe that the kind of oppression which threatens democratic nations will not resemble any other form previously experienced in the world; our contemporaries would not be able to find anything like it in their memories. Try as I may I cannot find an expression that can reproduce the exact idea I have formed of it; the

ancient words despotism and tyranny are entirely inadequate. It is something new; I must therefore attempt to define it, for I cannot name it." *De la democratie en Amerique* (Paris, 1951), Vol. II, Pt. IV, Chap. VI, p. 324.

[30] R. A. Nisbet, *The Quest for Community*, p. 202.

[31] Franz Neumann, *op. cit.*, p. 245.

[32] "When I try to picture totalitarianism to myself as a general phenomenon," writes G. F. Kennan, "what comes into my mind most prominently is neither the Soviet picture nor the Nazi picture as I have known them in the flesh, but rather the fictional and symbolic images created by such people as Orwell or Kafka or Koestler or the early Soviet satirists. The purest expression of the phenomenon, in other words, seems to me to have been rendered not in its physical reality but in its power as a dream, or a nightmare." *Totalitarianism*, pp. 19–20.

[33] It is well to remember in this connection that dictatorship was still used in a very innocent meaning in the age of the Italian *Risorgimento*. Farini in Emilia in 1859 and Garibaldi in Sicily in 1860 proclaimed themselves dictators, and Marx used "dictatorship of the proletariat" in a sense that to him seemed quite compatible with that of democracy. This is because "dictatorship" still denoted either a magistracy (according to the Roman origin of the term), or (as in Marx, who was echoing Blanqui) simply the idea of recourse to the use of force.

[34] What has happened to the concept of dictatorship is to some extent parallel to what has occurred to the idea of absolutism. Absolutism could not be understood in a defective sense—as the release of the ruler from obligations from which he should not be freed—until the idea of *potestas amplissima* was confronted with that of *princeps legibus obligatus*, and in a special way, ultimately, with the concept of a State bound by law (the constitutional State). This is indeed why the negative meaning of absolutism is not fully affirmed until the 18th century (and never without reservations, as is evidenced by the concept of enlightened absolutism). This applies also to dictatorship. It is only after an adequate and successful experience of "government by consent" that we begin to perceive that *dictare* (to dictate) can stand for a distinct type of political system. It is only at this point that dictatorship can take on a negative connotation (as the opposite of government by consent). Outside of this opposition, the need of *dictare* is implicit in any form of government. Cf. my article "Dittatura" in *Enciclopedia del Diritto*, IX (Milano).

[35] Strange as it may seem, the bibliography on the subject is surprisingly poor. The old and very questionable text of Carl Schmitt, *Die Diktatur* (2nd ed., 1928), is still the one most cited, and has not been superseded. The very classification of the concept is still in the embryo stage, as evidenced by the incomplete study left by Franz Neumann, "Notes on the Theory of Dictatorship," in *The Democratic and Authoritarian State*, pp. 233–56. On the other hand, Alfred Coppan's *Dictatorship—Its History and Theory* (London, 1939) remains by far—despite the 1954 volume of G. W. F. Hallgarten *Histoire des dictatures* (French transl., Paris, 1961)—the best historical interpretation.

[36] The attempt made by Lasswell and Kaplan with *Power and Society* to provide this framework (see especially Part III, Chaps. VIII, IX) is perhaps the most convincing example at hand. Despite innumerable valuable precisions and insights, I find it difficult to agree with most of the definitions and classifications adopted. Perhaps their effort would have been more rewarding if a historian of political theories had been part of the team, since a large part of their conceptualization of the key political terms seems to lack historical dimension, that is, the role those terms have played and the purpose for which they were invented and elaborated. . . .

[37] Cf. *The Origins of Totalitarian Democracy* (London, 1952).

[38] *Political Power and the Governmental Process*, p. 13.

[39] Actually, Loewenstein too starts from autocracy, taking as the basic classification the distinction between (i) constitutionlism as shared and (ii) autocracy as concentrated exercise of power. Cf. *op. cit.*, p. 29 *et passim*.

[40] Cf. e.g., how Lasswell and Kaplan use a threefold division, breaking the dichotomic approach into (i) autocracies, (ii) oligarchies, and (iii) republics (cf. *Power and*

Society, p. 218f.). Although this classification is widely opened to question, it points out that Loewenstein's conceptualization inevitably raises the problem of an intermediary or mixed pattern.

[41] In conclusion, if we start from the terminal democracy (and there are good reasons why we should), then "autocracy" has a more precise symmetry, even though "monocracy" can be effectively used to point out that when the investiture of power is autocratic, a concentrated exercise of power is correlative to it.

CHAPTER 2

Basic Principles
for a Model of Democracy

Austin Ranney
Willmoore Kendall

Prominent among the obstacles that confront our effort to appraise the American party system as an agency of *democratic* government is the widespread disagreement among Americans about just what democratic government is—a disagreement stemming largely from the powerful emotional appeal of the word "democracy" to most Americans and their consequent desire to identify "democratic" government with their varying conceptions of *good* government.[1]

In the present chapter, nevertheless, the authors will offer their own conception of the basic principles of democracy. They undertake these tasks because of their conviction that one can appraise the American party system—or any other institution—as an agency of democratic government only in the light of some kind of model.

Let us therefore begin our inquiry by asking what a "model" is, and how it can and cannot be usefully employed in social and political analysis.

THE NATURE OF MODELS

Existing Governments and "Forms" of Government

When we reflect upon the nature of the governments that actually exist in the world today and upon the way in which men customarily think and talk about them, one of the first things we notice is that all existing governments are alike in some respects. For example, they all make rules for the conduct of their peoples, and they all use force to punish persons who disobey the rules. On the other hand, no two governments are exactly alike in *every* respect; each one, in fact, differs considerably from all the others. Yet despite the fact that all governments are somewhat alike but each government differs materially from all others, most men believe (and have long believed) that governments can usefully be classified as to their *form*—that they can legitimately be described, for example, either as "monarchies," "aristocracies," and "democracies," or as "democracies" and "dictatorships."

Now just what do we mean when we talk about the "form" of governments—when, for example, we call the United States and Great Britain "democracies," and the Soviet Union and Red China "dictatorships"? Surely we do not mean thereby that the first two are exactly alike; nor do we mean that they are completely unlike the latter two. We mean rather that *in certain respects* the first two are alike, and that in those particular respects they are unlike the latter two. In other words, in deciding whether an existing government is a democracy, we are not concerned with *all* its characteristics; we look at only *part* of them—the part which, in our opinion, determines whether or not any government is a democracy. But how do we decide which of its many parts to base our judgment on? There is only one possible answer: We decide in terms of a mental picture of the *essential* nature of democracy—in terms of a model of democracy.

Model Governments and Actual Governments

What is a "model of democracy" in this context, and how does it differ from the actual governments men generally call "democratic"? A *model* of democracy, as we shall henceforth use the term, is a mental picture of a *type* or *kind* of government stripped of all its nonessential and irrelevant characteristics—a government reduced to its differentiae, i.e., to the *principles of organization* that make it different from a "monarchy" or an "aristocracy," each of which in turn has its basic principles of organization and its model.

As a means of grasping the difference between a model of a government and an actual government, let us look for a moment at how models are used in economics. In speaking of the model "market economy," Wilhelm Röpke warns that

we must make a sharp distinction between the *principle* of a market economy as such—bound as it is to no historical period but representing rather one of the permanent elements out of which an historical economic order can be put together—and the *actual development* which during the nineteenth and twentieth centuries has led to the historical form of market economy. One is a philosophical category [in our terminology, a "model" economy], the other an historical individuality; one is a simple structural element [i.e., a carefully worked-out principle of organization], the other an historical and therefore unique, a non-recurrent *compound* of economic, social, legal, political, moral and cultural elements, a compound which, in this highly complicated mixture of ingredients, never occurred before and will never recur hereafter.[2]

Our point is that anyone who talks about the "form" or "type" of existing governments—and this includes most of us—is speaking, consciously or unconsciously, in terms of models. Anyone who applies the label "democratic" to an actual government or institution must in doing so appeal to a mental picture of an ideal or model democracy, which is there whether he recognizes its presence or not.

If this is true, the only choice open to the writer on democracy is this: he can leave his model implicit in his comments on existing institutions and have his readers dig it out for themselves; or he can present his model, explicitly and in as clear and straightforward a manner as possible, before he starts talking about existing institutions. The latter procedure is likely to make for better communication between writer and reader; and the purpose of the present chapter is to make clear the model we have in mind when we use the term "democracy."[3]

THE FUNCTION OF MODELS

Throughout this book we shall be examining various American institutions, and particularly those of our party system, with a view to answering two fundamental questions: What kind of government do these institutions add up to? And to what extent is this the kind of government the American people appear to want? In the course of this inquiry we shall doubtless discover that some of these institutions serve the purposes of democracy less well than others, and that the total governing system of the United States does not, therefore, correspond exactly to our model of democracy. Such a procedure may well disturb many of our readers—some of them to the point that they will ask in dismay, "Aren't you really saying that America is not a democracy?"

Stated in such terms, this question involves a misconception as to the sort of inquiry we are attempting, and cannot be answered Yes or No. Certainly we do not propose to compare all existing governments with our model of democracy and then label "democratic" all those governments that measure up to it in every respect, and lump together all those that do not as "undemocratic." If this were our purpose, we should have great difficulty in finding an acceptable candidate for the "democratic" category, and even some difficulty in discovering a completely eligible candidate for the "undemocratic" category.

Our model of democracy will serve rather to fix one end of a spectrum or scale, along which we can place various existing institutions and governments. The notion of the spectrum is, in fact, so basic to our whole project that we must pause to explain in some detail its nature and its relation to our model of democracy. Let us take the common word "bald" as an illustration. We could take any number of men with varying amounts of hair, some of whom we could all agree are "bald," count the number of hairs on each, and range them along a scale in the order of the number of hairs each possesses. At this point we should have a great deal of difficulty deciding just where "baldness" begins. Would we, for example, select a certain number of hairs and say that a man with only one less hair than that is "bald"? Clearly not. Or do we call "bald" only the man who has no hair at all? This certainly is not the way most of us use the word. Yet we still feel justified—and properly so—in calling the men at one end of the scale "bald" even though each one has some hair and even though the variations from man to man as we ascend the scale are minute.

We now have an example of a spectrum. We have set up a "model"— the complete absence of hair—and we have established a scale of increasing distance from the model. Along this scale any particular man can be placed according to the number of hairs he has on his head. But the scale, the measuring, and indeed any use of the term "bald" makes sense only in terms of the model that fixes one end of the spectrum. What purposes does this spectrum serve? It enables us to measure and compare individual men as to their *degrees* of baldness, and it permits us to make sense of the statement about a man, "He is getting bald"—i.e., it enables us to determine the direction of change.

So it is with our model of democracy. It will serve to fix one end of a spectrum, which, in turn, will enable us to measure the degrees of democracy of existing governments and institutions and to compare them with each other. In terms of such a spectrum—but only in terms of it—it is perfectly legitimate to call some existing governments "democracies." Thus, to return to the hypothetical question that touched off the present discussion, although the United States can hardly be placed at the democratic extreme of our spectrum, and may even be less near to our model than, say, Switzerland or Great Britain, it is nevertheless so much nearer to it than, say, the Soviet Union or Red China that we are justified in saying that *compared to* the Communist nations the United States *is* a democracy.[4]

The kind of spectrum we have been talking about, we repeat, can perform its functions only if one end of the scale has been clearly and unequivocally fixed by the construction of a model. And that model, in turn, can perform its functions only if we bear in mind at least two considerations. First, the model is a conception of the *most democratic* government possible, and not necessarily a conception of the *best* government possible. In other words, the fact that a particular person does not "believe in" such a government (that is, does not wish the actual community in which he lives to be governed in exactly that fashion) need not keep him from using the model as a purely *analytical* device in the manner described above. And second, a model of democracy is not identical with the "historic compound" of traits found in any of the existing governments that are generally called "democracies."

CONSTRUCTING A MODEL OF DEMOCRACY

In the remainder of the present chapter the authors of this book will present the basic principles on which, in their opinion, a model of democracy for the modern nation-state should be built. They believe that a fairly strong case can be made out on common-sense grounds for reserving the term "democracy" for these principles and the resulting model. But having presented the broad outlines of that case in the ensuing pages, they will press no quarrel with the reader who refuses to go along with it—provided he remembers that this is what "democracy" means wherever it is used in the rest of *this* book.

The authors urge the reader to accompany them in adopting the following point of view: The most important tasks for any student of forms of government are: (a) to "isolate the alternatives" (i.e., to answer the question, What kinds of government are there, in fact or in theory, from which a people or group may choose in establishing a system for making its political decisions?); (b) to make sure we understand their differentiae (i.e., the essential, bedrock differences between them); (c) to try to bring about a situation in which we can refer first to one alternative and then to another without any danger of misunderstanding each other; and (d) to shed what light we can on what results a people may expect when it chooses one of them and passes up the others.

In other words, what matters to the United States or to any nation is the kind of government it *has*. The important thing is that each of us should have a clear idea of the kind of governing institutions we want—whether they are called "democracy" or "numbersocracy" or whatever—and that he should have an accurate picture of the extent to which the institutions we actually have do or do not provide us with what he wants. And the kind of inquiry we shall make in the present chapter may help the reader to raise and answer these questions for himself.

PRINCIPLES OF DEMOCRACY

Most writers on democracy, whatever else they may insist must be present in order for a government to be called a "democracy," are . . . committed to the view that it must exhibit the following minimum characteristics:

(1) Those who hold office in it must stand ready, *in some sense*, to do whatever the people want them to do, and to refrain from doing anything the people oppose; (2) each member of the "community" for which it acts should have, *in some sense*, as good a chance as his fellows to participate in the community's decision-making—no better and no worse; and (3) it must operate in terms of an understanding that when the enfranchised members of the community disagree as to what ought to be done, the last word lies, *in some sense*, with the larger number and never the smaller—i.e., the majority of the electorate and not the minority should carry the day. So much, we repeat, seems to be pretty well agreed on all sides.

One of the basic contentions of this chapter is that once one has committed himself to that much, he has committed himself to at least the broad outline of a highly meaningful conception of democratic government. Another is that this conception of democratic government, despite the presence of the words "in some sense" in the foregoing statements, leaves less room to move around in, and be "different," than is commonly supposed.

Anyone who carefully analyzes the above three minima will find that the conception as a whole breaks down into four, not three, principles. These are (a) popular sovereignty, (b) political equality, (c) popular consultation, and (d) majority rule. In the ensuing subsections we shall inquire what logically is involved in each of these principles.

Popular Sovereignty

We observe that the word "democracy," through most of its history and to most people, has meant "government ruled by all"—as opposed to "government ruled by a few" ("aristocracy") and "government ruled by one" ("monarchy"). "Popular sovereignty," if we mean by it sovereignty of the entire people, is undoubtedly therefore the *oldest* of the ideas associated with democracy. As Lord Bryce put it:

> The word Democracy has been used ever since the time of Herodotus to denote that form of government in which the ruling power of a State is legally vested, not in any particular class or classes, but *in the members of the community as a whole.*[5]

For a full understanding of what is involved in popular sovereignty (and thus in one major element of democracy), we might now look closely at each of the key phrases in Bryce's statement in order to understand all that it has to say:

(1) "The ruling power of a State." To speak of "popular sovereignty" is to take for granted something called "sovereignty," which can be either "popular" or "non-popular." "Sovereignty," as the term is ordinarily used in traditional political science, denotes *the* definite source of *final* decisions,

the power to make and enforce laws (Bryce's "ruling power of a State") above which there is no law. It is, traditional political science holds, present as a matter of course in every genuine "political community"—and so much as a matter of course that where it is not present the "political community" either has not yet been born or has already died. A decision of the "sovereign," so defined, can be revised only by another act of that same "sovereign"; its power to make decisions, furthermore, is subject to no limitations except those it sees fit to impose on *itself* (and even these it can remove at will). No group whose power is limited by some *other* group can, therefore, be called "sovereign." In the political community, power is embodied and institutionalized in the machinery of "the State"; and it is the possession of such sovereign power that sets the State apart from all other social groupings.

The doctrine of "popular sovereignty," then, is that according to which power vests in *all* the members of the community rather than in any part of them or in any one of them. Just as sovereign power is what makes a State a State, sovereign power vested in all the community's members is what makes the State "democratic." Democracy, in other words, is one among several *ways of organizing the State*, one among several answers a community can make to the question as to where within it sovereign power is to be lodged. It is *not* an answer to the question whether such power ought to exist at all, for where it does not (as, for example, in the United Nations Organization) there is no State to organize. In a word, the doctrine of popular sovereignty means it when it says "sovereignty" every bit as much as when it says "popular."

We must notice at once, however, that the notion that popular sovereignty is fundamental to democracy is highly unpalatable to certain present-day writers.[6] Of special importance in this connection are the writers who proclaim that in a true democracy there can be *no* unlimited power—that a State is democratic only so long as certain individual rights are entirely removed from the power of *any* governmental agency, whether popularly controlled or not. To them "limited government" or "constitutional government" is an essential attribute of democracy. Such a position, of course, is difficult to square with the assertion that popular sovereignty is a basic element of democracy; but the whole question is so inextricably interwoven with the problem of majority rule and minority rights that we will reserve further discussion of it for our exposition below of the doctrine of majority rule.

(2) "Is legally vested." When we say that in a democracy sovereignty is "legally" vested in the people, we do not mean to imply that it may "actually" reside elsewhere. Democracy, that is to say, surely does not mean a government whose formal constitution "legally" vests all power in the people, but where the power is "actually"—behind the legal formalisms—

wielded by a dictator. But neither does democracy mean a government in which the sovereign power is "legally" vested in the dictator, but in which the people start a violent revolution and depose the dictator every time he does something they dislike. The phrase means merely that the legal-formal governing institutions of a democracy are such that the government's actions are always made in response to an orderly and nonviolent expression of the popular will. It means, in short, that both the "legal" and the "actual" ruling power reside in the people.

(3) "In the members of the community." Who are "the people"? Are they *all* the individuals who at any point in time happen to be physically present within the geographical boundaries of the democratic community? The answer, it seems to us, is clear: Membership in any community, democratic or otherwise, means something more than mere physical presence among a haphazard agglomeration of individuals tossed together by chance in a given geographic area. The term "community" suggests something *common* among those individuals, something binding them together, some overlap or commonality of interests and feelings—it surely is something more than just an arithmetical term denoting "the total number of any collection of persons."

We do not suggest that a genuine community exists only where each individual completely ignores his own selfish interest and cares only for the welfare of others. Such a suggestion would indeed be naïve. Almost everything we know about the process of politics indicates that dissension and disagreement and "selfishness" are always present—that politics consists to a considerable degree of the struggle for power and satisfaction of their varying desires among numberless antagonistic interest groups.[7] Yet in most countries this struggle for power does not produce the perpetual civil war that we would expect to be its inevitable result; it operates rather within a number of sharp limitations. The various interest groups do not as a rule maintain private armies and use tanks, machine guns, and atomic bombs against one another; their political game is played according to certain rules, and the rules are for the most part obeyed even when obeying them prevents the full victory of one or another of the groups. Why? Rousseau gave us the answer two hundred years ago:

> What made the establishment of societies necessary was . . . the fact that the interests of individuals clashed. But what made their establishment possible was the fact that these same interests *also* coincided. *In other words*, it is the overlap among different interests that creates the social bond, so that no society can possibly exist save as there is some point at which all the interests *concerned* are in harmony.[8]

In other words, the "popular sovereignty" of a democratic State is possible only if its members' desire to continue to live together as a community is at least as strong as their desire to satisfy their separate and antagonistic interests. Mary Parker Follett put it this way:

> Real authority inheres in a genuine whole. The individual is sovereign over himself as far as he unifies the heterogeneous elements of his nature. Two people are sovereign over themselves as far as they are capable of creating one out of two. A group is sovereign over itself as far as it is capable of creating one out of several or many. A state is sovereign only as it has the power of creating one in which all are. Sovereignty is the power engendered by a complete interdependence becoming conscious of itself.[9]

In the pages to come we shall have frequent occasion to talk further of the nature of community and its importance for democracy. But for present purposes it is clear that *any* community, democratic or otherwise, must decide what qualifications should be required as the condition of admittance to full membership (and, in a democratic society, the right to participate in making the community's political decisions). And the decision upon such qualifications is made in a democracy by the same process by which other political decisions are made, and is revisable by the same process.

(4) "Not in any particular class or classes, but in the members of the community as a whole." Little comment is required upon this dictum—for if the community's ruling power *is* vested in a particular class, then such a government would, by definition, be what men have generally called "aristocracy" or "oligarchy."

Political Equality

The second basic principle of democracy is that of political equality. Each member of the community must have the same chance as his fellows to participate in its total decision-making process. Only thus can there be genuine popular sovereignty; for if any individual or group of individuals has *more* power (through such devices as plural voting or special officeholding requirements) than the other members of the community, that group becomes a politically privileged class or elite, and popular sovereignty, as we have defined it above, cannot exist. It is for these reasons that political equality is generally regarded as an essential element of democracy.

It is necessary to point out, however, that political equality involves far more than the classical slogan of "one man, one vote." If equality in voting rights were synonymous with political equality, then—on this score at least—the Communist nations' claim that they are more democratic than their Western opponents would be hard to dispute. After all, they hold elections frequently, and it is probable that a higher percentage of the population holds the suffrage than in any Western nation; and a larger proportion of the eligible voters actually go to the polls. But does this mean that therefore the Communist nations really *do* have a higher degree of political equality than the West?

The answer, we believe, can be found by analyzing the nature of the decision-making process and the part that voting plays therein. What do we do when we make decisions? "Policy-making," says Professor MacIver, "depends upon the *assessing of alternatives* with a view to translating one of them into action."[10] In other words, the essence of making a decision is the *choice among alternatives*. And in order to make a genuine choice, each of these three conditions must obtain for the policy-maker: (1) the presence of genuine alternatives before him; (2) the opportunity to find out about the nature and probable consequences of each alternative; and (3) full freedom to choose whichever of the alternatives seems to him—for whatever reasons he deems sufficient—the most desirable. In the absence of any one of these conditions he can hardly be said to be making a genuine choice. Where, then, does voting come in? At most it is a kind of machinery whereby each policy-maker registers the choice he has made. In other words, voting is just one part—albeit a necessary one—of the total decision-making process, and its significance depends upon the degree to which the other parts of the process have operated *before* voting takes place. In the Communist countries the voter has only the candidates of the Communist party to choose—there are no opposition candidates. In the same manner, in Hitler's Germany the voter was asked in periodic plebiscites if he approved of what his Führer was doing, but on his ballot there was only a *ja* for him to mark. In such "elections" the voters have no choice; and the fact that such impressive percentages of the population mark ballots is no indication at all that the principle of political equality is being observed.

Thus political equality means not only "one man, one vote," but also an equal chance for each member of the community to participate in the total decision-making process of the community.

Popular Consultation

There is general agreement upon the proposition that a democratic government should do what the people want it to do and should not do anything they don't want it to do. And in this chapter we have said that this must mean something more than a state of affairs in which the people, playing the role Locke claims for them in the *Second Treatise*, violently and successfully rebel against the holders of public office whenever these ignore or flout the popular will. In democratic government, that is to say, the people must be "consulted" about the policy they wish those in power to pursue in a given matter—and the holders of office, having learned the popular desire, should proceed to do whatever the people want them to do. Thus "popular consultation" in this sense requires at least these three attributes: (1) on matters of public policy there must *be* a genuine popular will; (2) the office-holders must be aware of what that will requires; and (3) having ascertained the nature of the popular will, they must then faithfully and invariably translate it into action.

A considerable portion of the discussion of democracy rests upon the assumption that once most members of the community are agreed that these things *should* happen they automatically *do* take place—that when democracy is generally regarded as desirable, it springs into being. This book proceeds upon quite a different assumption: that there is nothing at all "automatic" about popular consultation, that some kind of institutional machinery must be set up to accomplish the job, and that the search for such machinery is at once the most difficult and the most urgent job facing anyone who wants to see democracy more fully realized in any particular nation. The purpose of this book, we again remind our readers, is to examine the institutions—particularly those of our party system—which now purport to carry on the process of popular consultation, in order to see how well or how badly they do the job. That the full and effective operation of popular consultation is vital to democracy, however, is undeniable.

Majority Rule

Up to this point in our analysis we have said little that any contemporary theorist of democracy would dispute, though many of them might say (and we should agree) that as yet we have not by any means told the whole story. Actually, all we are asserting up to this point is that no one thinks of democracy as requiring the location of the ruling power in a special elite or ruling class, or necessitating political *in*equality, or making governmental decisions *contrary* to what the people desire.

Our fourth principle of democracy, however, is considerably more controversial than the other three. For we believe that a model democratic government must always be able to justify its actions on the grounds that they accord with the wishes of a majority of the enfranchised members of the community. Or, to put it another way, we believe that when there are two opinions among the members of a democratic community as to whether the government should perform any given action, the opinion of the larger group, which for most purposes we can usefully think of as one-half of the enfranchised members plus at least one, ought to prevail.

This affirmation, of course, plunges us into the middle of the greatest single theoretical controversy about the nature of democracy: "absolute" majority rule versus "limited" majority rule. An understanding of the issues on which this quarrel turns is essential to the case for our conception of democracy. We will therefore explore them as carefully as we can, attempting to state fully and fairly the position contrary to our own, and then showing why we are convinced that "absolute" majority rule is an inescapable attribute of any model of *perfectly* democratic government—that it is, in short, the only decision-making principle that is consistent with the other three principles of democracy we have previously presented.

The "Absolute" Majority Rule Position. Much of the opposition to absolute majority rule results, we believe, from misunderstandings as to what it involves—or, to put this a little differently, from a tendency to attribute to "majoritarian" democratic theorists certain ideas that are not necessary to the position as we have stated it, and that, so far as the present writers have been able to discover, no majoritarian has ever asserted. Before going further, then, let us deal with some of these misunderstandings.

(1) Some critics charge that "the majority," in whom the majoritarians wish to vest the community's decision-making power, really does not exist and is only a convenient fiction invented by the majoritarians to shore up their case. The majoritarian, however, is *not* called upon to show that "the majority" exists, or that he views with favor the continuous exercise of power in the democratic society by one identifiable *and permanent* group of the enfranchised citizens at the expense of all other such groups. Power in the democratic state belongs to the *whole* people; ideally, power in the democratic state is exercised by the *whole* people; and if the people in such a state could be counted upon to reach unanimous decisions on all governmental problems, the issue on which the controversy over majority rule turns could be ignored. For that issue is this: What happens in the democratic state when the people are *divided*—when, as we put it above, there are *two* opinions as to the course to be followed? The majoritarian is saying, above all, that no doctrine of the democratic state is complete that does not deal with that issue. His way of dealing with it is to say, Let the opinion that has the greater number of supporters prevail. But as a democrat he naturally prefers unanimous decisions to nearly unanimous ones, and nearly unanimous ones to decisions opposed by a considerable minority, and decisions opposed by a considerable minority to decisions opposed by a minority accounting for nearly half the population. And, far from being required by his position to demonstrate that *the* majority exists, he knows that a society in which it is possible to point to such a majority—a society, in other words, permanently divided between *a* permanent majority and *a* permanent minority, so that all issues become issues between those two groups—is a society in which democracy is about to become impossible to operate. In short, the majoritarian wishes to locate the decision-making power in popular majorities, not in "*the* majority" conceived as one never-changing group of persons.

(2) Other critics argue that it is impossible for each and every one of the myriad day-to-day decisions a modern government must make to be based upon a specific majority mandate. When the majoritarian says that the government of a democratic state must be able to point to the "wishes of a majority" as justification for any action it takes, however, he is not saying that it must be able to point to a *specific majority mandate* for that specific action (though, admittedly, majoritarians have sometimes talked as though that were the case). For democracy—like aristocracy and monarchy—is a matter of who exercises the *ultimate* ruling power, and the processes by which day-to-day decisions are made become important only when they immediately affect the location and exercise of that ultimate ruling power. To illustrate the point we are making, let us draw an analogy with another form of government. If an absolute monarch called in one of his courtiers and said to him, "I'm tired of figuring out each of my subjects' tax bills, so you take over the job," surely no one would say, "But he can't do that—he's an absolute monarch and must make *all* the decisions." The monarch's absoluteness consists in his ability to take back the tax-fixing power any time and in any case he wants to even if the courtier wants to keep it. And so it is with popular majorities in a democracy: if a majority wishes to entrust such-and-such a type of decision to, say, a supreme court, and thus give that court a "blanket" mandate for all such decisions, it certainly can do so without violating any of the principles of democracy. So long as any future majority can take the power away from the court (even if the court wants to retain it) by the same process by which it initially awarded the power, the majority, and not the court, exercises ultimate power. And to deny the majority the power to "delegate" part of its power or to cancel the "delegation" when it wishes to is to say that in a democracy the whole people has less power than the monarch in an absolute monarchy.

There is also another reason why majoritarian democracy does not demand specific majority mandates on each and every governmental decision. To demand such mandates is to ask of the people what is obviously impossible, and even if it were not impossible something they would be unlikely to do, namely, to give to public affairs an unlimited amount of time and attention (since if they gave less than that some of the necessary mandates would not get formulated). Absolute monarchy does not require that the monarch actually *make* each and every governmental decision, but only that he have the *power* to make whatever decisions he *wishes* to make. And, by the same token, democracy does not require that popular majorities actually *make* each and every governmental decision, but only that they have the *power* to make whatever decisions they *wish* to make.

In short, majoritarian democracy demands only that popular majorities have the *final* word on whatever matters they wish to have the final word on, whether these have to do with the *procedures* by which decisions are made or the *content* of decisions. If on a given matter they are more desirous of preserving a certain procedure (e.g., the Supreme Court's power of judicial review) than of having a particular course of action followed (e.g., preserving racial segregation in the public schools), they can, without any diminution of their ultimate power, decide to let an unpopular decision made by a popular procedure stand. But if the content of the decision is more important to them than preserving the procedure, they should have full power to alter the procedure or set it aside in order to get the particular course of action they wish. So long as it is a majority, and not a minority, that decides whether preserving the procedure or getting the course of action is more important, the requirements of majority-rule democracy are satisfied.

(3) Some critics charge that the case for majority rule rests upon an alleged connection between the rightness or wisdom of a procedure or a policy and the number of people who support it. The majoritarian replies that the difference between a majority and a minority is, to be sure, a difference in numbers; and the technique by which we discover which procedure or policy represents the wishes of the majority is indeed what is called "holding an election" by those who think it a good technique and "counting noses" by those who think it a bad one. But the difference between a people risen unanimously against a dictator on the one hand, and that dictator on the other hand, is also a difference in numbers—as is also the difference between five Supreme Court justices and four, or the difference between two-thirds of the senators present and voting, and two-thirds-minus-one of the senators present and voting, both of which are differences made much of by the anti-majoritarians. In other words, the special fascination with numbers of which majoritarians are frequently accused is characteristic not of majority-rule democracy in particular but of democracy itself. For all who value freedom, a state of affairs where two human beings are subordinated to the arbitrary will of a third is twice as bad as a state of affairs where only one is so subordinated. And the connection upon which the majoritarian insists is not the connection between numbers and rightness but that between numbers and human freedom. A policy or procedure, obviously, does not gain in rightness by picking up enough support to justify the claim that it represents the wishes of the majority, or lose in rightness by losing support. But that is not the point at issue, since what the majoritarian asserts is not the superior intelligence or wisdom or even morality of popular majorities, but the wrongness, from the democratic point of view, of a state of affairs where the few are in position to have their way over the wishes of the many.

The "Limited" Majority Rule Position. The first thing to note about those who oppose "absolute" majority rule is that they do not argue that democracy requires lodging the ultimate decision-making power in the hands of minorities. These writers are above all concerned to deny that the alternatives to majority-rule-versus-minority-rule are exhaustive—since, they say, there is a third alternative, which is the principle a genuine democracy must adopt. Among the proponents of "limited" majority rule, or, as some call it, "*constitutional* democracy," this third alternative appears in one of two versions. The first of these, which is advanced by relatively few present-day theorists, holds that in a genuine democracy there must be certain things that the government may not do *at all*, even if the whole people wishes it to. The question is not, say these writers, whether majorities *or* minorities should rule; in a true democracy *both* majorities *and* minorities should be subordinate to and controlled by a third force—The Law, which, in an American context, we may take to be equivalent to the Constitution. In Dean Roscoe Pound's formulation of this point of view:

> An idea of a covenant of people not to do certain things and only to do certain other things in a certain way was well known in the formative era of our polity. . . . Shall we say then that the foundations of modern democracy were undemocratic, or shall we say that *Demos, no less than Rex, may . . . rule under God and the Law?*[11]

The more often-encountered version of this "third alternative" position holds, not that there are certain things a democratic government may *never* do, but rather that it may do those things only when a "more substantial" popular majority than just 50 per cent plus one wants them done. Such "extraordinary majorities" as two-thirds or three-fourths of the people should, in this view, be required before such action may properly be taken in a democracy.

Although in some disagreement as to *how* to protect certain things from action by bare popular majorities, the opponents of "absolute" majority rule generally agree that such things as free speech, free press, free worship, and "due process" guarantees to persons accused of crime should be protected. A recent variation upon this third-alternative theme is provided by those who argue that certain limitations on majorities are inherent in the principle of majority rule itself—no majority, they say, may rightfully change the conditions (presumably of political freedom) by which it became a majority, because to do so would be to destroy majority rule itself.[12]

Let us summarize the "limited" majority rule position by representing it diagrammatically in Figure 1. The circle represents everything any government could possibly do, from setting up speed limits for automobiles to forcing everyone to have at least three wives. The shaded portion of the circle represents such actions as the latter, which in a democracy bare popular majorities must not be allowed to do. The remainder of the circle represents all the possible governmental actions remaining, which may be taken whenever a popular majority of *any* size wishes them to be taken. As these writers

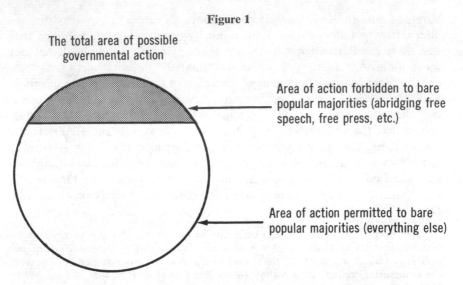

Figure 1

The total area of possible
governmental action

Area of action forbidden to bare
popular majorities (abridging free
speech, free press, etc.)

Area of action permitted to bare
popular majorities (everything else)

view their own position, therefore, they are not asserting that minority rule is more democratic than majority rule. So long as bare popular majorities do not invade the areas which true democracy forbids them to enter, say these writers, such majorities should have full power to rule. So their conclusion is that democracy involves *both* majority rule *and* the protection of individual and minority rights against invasion by bare popular majorities.

A Critique of the "Limited" Majority Rule Position. Before criticizing the "limited" majority rule position, let us recall that in the present chapter we are not drawing up detailed blueprints for the government of any *actual* community; rather we are attempting to reason out a set of principles to guide us in the construction of a *model of democracy*. For the reasons noted in the first section of this chapter, the essential characteristic of such a model must be logical consistency among its various principles. And our basic objection to the "limited" majority rule position is therefore that its "third alternative" to majority rule and minority rule is logically invalid. There is, we believe, no logical alternative to majority rule except minority rule; and of the two, majority rule must be chosen as a principle of democracy, since it is more nearly consistent than minority rule with the other principles of democracy.[13]

The weakness of the position that "limited" majority rule is more democratic than "absolute" majority rule becomes apparent when we ask the question, *How* are popular majorities to be limited without violating the other principles of democracy? In other words, by what institutional mechanisms can such majorities be restrained without introducing the principle of *minority* rule?

The advocates of "limited" majority rule disagree among themselves upon the answer to this question. Their writings appear to contain at least three different answers, each of which is to some degree incompatible with the other two. Briefly summarized, they are as follows.

LIMITATION BY "THE LAW." In 1936, a majority of the United States Supreme Court declared the first Agricultural Adjustment Act unconstitutional. Mr. Justice Owen J. Roberts took the occasion to explain his conception of the role of the court and of the Constitution in determining what the people's elected representatives in Congress may and may not do. As he put it:

> There should be no misunderstanding as to the function of this court in such a case. It is sometimes said that the court assumes a power to overrule or control the action of the people's representatives. This is a misconception. The Constitution is the supreme law of the land ordained and established by the people. All legislation must conform to the principles it lays down. When an act of Congress is appropriately challenged in the courts as not conforming to the constitutional mandate the judicial branch of the government has only one duty,—to lay the article of the Constitution which is invoked beside the statute which is challenged and to decide whether the latter squares with the former.[14]

Relatively few advocates of "limited" majority rule, however, rely upon Mr. Justice Roberts' fiction of "The Constitution" and "The Law" as something that exists entirely apart from what fallible human beings think it is. Most observers recognize that professors of political science, law-school professors, constitutional lawyers, congressmen, and even Supreme Court judges do not agree among themselves about what many crucial parts of the Constitution mean when applied to specific policy-making situations. And this has inclined most of them to conclude that every time a government tries to decide whether or not it should adopt a certain policy, there will be no absolutely "right" answer—that is, there will be available no divine revelation or "scientific" law to indicate *the* proper decision. If there were, government would be a simple matter indeed. But instead there will be only a decision which the members of the community will have to make the best way they can—on the basis of the evidence available and according to their own differing values and differing interpretations of the evidence. If all of them agree about what should be done, then no problem about who should rule arises, for neither a majority nor a minority will exist.

Unanimity on matters of governmental policy is, however, difficult to achieve and rarely present. Consequently, on all yes-or-no issues (which all public issues ultimately become: Shall we or shall we not adopt this specific policy, or elect this candidate instead of that?), all members of the community will fall into either the yes-group or the no-group. Except in cases of a flat tie, one group will be larger than the other. One, in other words, will be the majority and the other the minority.

Seen from this point of view, the issue over the status of majority rule can be put thus: If a majority wishes, for example, to adopt a policy that a minority regards as intolerably destructive of human rights, how can the majority be restrained?

LIMITATION BY FORMAL MINORITY VETO. A second group of writers argue that a true democracy must provide formal institutional devices by which the minority can, in the situation just described, prevent the majority from having its way. Among the devices proposed for this purpose are such familiar American practices as the requirement of extraordinary majorities for such matters as amending the Constitution and ratifying treaties; and, most important of all, the institution of judicial review, which gives a body of judges beyond the control of bare popular majorities the power to nullify any act of such majorities that the judges deem to be an invasion of minority rights.

To limit the power of the majority in this fashion is, we believe, to give the minority an absolute veto over change, and thus to invite the minority, insofar as such a veto makes this possible, to rule whenever it pleases. When, for example, a two-thirds majority is required before some governmental action can be taken, a "no" vote is made to count for just twice as much as a "yes" vote. Not only is this a clear violation of the principle of political equality—which, as we have previously noted; is generally regarded as essential to democracy—but it also means that when 60 per cent of the people want something and 40 per cent don't want it, the smaller and not the larger group gets its way. And the ability to get one's way is nothing other than the power to *rule*. So wherever a two-thirds majority is required for action, it is always possible that a minority, if it is large enough, can carry the day.[15]

"But wait a minute," it might be objected, "the minority doesn't *rule* in such a case—it only keeps the majority from ruling. It, like judicial review, is a *veto* power, not a power to rule." Such an objection, however, ignores the nature of the decision-making process. In any policy-making situation there are always a number of alternatives to choose among, and one of those alternatives is always the retention of the status quo. A veto, to be sure, always chooses the status quo in preference to any of the other alternatives. But to choose the status quo does not mean that no policy at all is chosen; on the contrary, a very definite policy is chosen, for the government is thereby committed to a certain course of action just as much as it would have been committed to another course of action had some alternative other than the status quo been chosen instead. And to give a minority the power to veto any act of a majority is to give it the power to *rule*.

But, it might be further objected to our position on majority rule, suppose a watchdog like the Supreme Court has been given its veto power *by the majority itself?* What if the majority *wants* to give some minority agency the task of keeping the majority on its toes and warning it when it is going too far? Such a situation, it seems to us, is perfectly consonant with democracy so long as everyone knows the watchdog is the agent of and responsible to the majority, and acts accordingly. Those who defend judicial review on the ground that the majority has willed it, however, are simply postponing the day of reckoning with the basic question. For when the watchdog tells the majority that they must give up a certain piece of legislation, and the majority replies that they must have it and let the heavens fall, who wins in such a situation—the majority or their agent-watchdog? This, of course, is another way of asking the familiar question: When the majority wants above all else to do a certain thing and a minority believes that that thing should not be done, which group gets its way? And our answer to the question remains: In any government which can legitimately be called "democratic," the majority and not the minority must carry the day.

LIMITATION BY MAJORITY SELF-RESTRAINT. Some writers who advocate "limited" majority rule do not propose any *formal* limitations upon the power of popular majorities. They hold, instead, that in a true democracy majorities will not *be* restrained but rather will *restrain themselves* from violating human rights. Now if "limited" majority rule means nothing more than this, then the authors of this book have no quarrel with it; for such a "limitation" is no limitation at all upon the *power* of the majority, and therefore cannot become, strictly speaking, minority *rule*. At most it is no more than a way of saying that if the majority chooses to destroy any of the elements of democracy, then democracy will no longer exist—that democracies which have committed suicide are democracies no longer. Since the propositions just stated are undeniable, there are no significant logical differences between this third version of the "limited" majority rule position and the "absolute" majority rule position outlined previously.

Why "Absolute" Majority Rule? For the reasons given in the foregoing pages, any attempt to place *formal* institutional limitations upon the "absolute" power of popular majorities logically results in the establishment of *minority* rule. And from the standpoint of strict logic, "absolute" majority rule must be chosen over minority rule as a principle of ideally *democratic* government, not because there is any magical virtue or omniscience in popular majorities, but because majority rule is more nearly in accord than minority rule with the other principles of democracy that we have previously discussed. It is the only principle of decision-making that men have yet discovered which "grants a perpetual privilege to none and permits an equal share of power to all."[16]

For the prevention of majority "tyranny" and the protection of human rights in our model of democracy, therefore, we must depend upon factors other than formal limitations upon the power of popular majorities. . . .

THE PRINCIPLES CONSIDERED

It is for the reasons given above that we believe that a model of democracy must be constructed according to the principles of popular sovereignty, political equality, popular consultation, and majority rule. Let us conclude our statement of these principles by pointing out two consequences of the position we have taken.

In the first place, it is important to remember that *all four* of these elements must be present, and that each one considered by itself makes democratic sense only as the presence of the other three is assumed. If, for example, we are told that the Supreme Court—or, for that matter, the Politburo—is committed to decisions made by bare majorities of its members and is therefore a "majority-rule institution," we are hardly justified in concluding that the government of which it is a part must be fully democratic. Why not? Because in the total governing system within which each of these institutions operates, the elements of popular sovereignty, political equality, and popular consultation are, in varying degrees, lacking.[17]

Second, we have urged a purely *political* conception of democracy— one according to which democracy is simply and solely a way of making decisions, and the *content* of any particular decision (except insofar as it may affect the nature of the decision-making *process*) is irrelevant to the question of the presence or absence of democracy. We have taken this position partly because the word "democracy" throughout most of its history has denoted a certain form of government only.[18] But, it might be objected, since other words have grown and taken on new meanings, why not "democracy"? The answer is that words acquire new meanings only when those new meanings are generally agreed upon and the words are made more useful thereby—and surely neither of these conditions has resulted from the attempts to add to the original purely political meaning of "democracy."

In any case, even if one does introduce social and economic principles into his conception of democracy, he still must assign priorities. Let us assume, by way of illustrating this point, that we decide that democracy means not only the four principles listed above but also requires a publicly guaranteed minimum standard of living for all. Suppose that in a given community 70 per cent of the people want to end all government aid to the poor, and only 30 per cent want to retain it. What, in such a situation, would be the "democratic" solution? Which is the more fundamental to democracy—that the people get what they want even if it isn't "democratic," or that they be forced to have "democracy" even if they don't want it? To argue the latter position is to give democracy a very peculiar meaning indeed; but the only alternative is to admit that a certain *way* of making decisions is more fundamental to democracy than any particular *kind* of decision—and that is in effect to admit that democracy is basically a political matter. As Sidney Hook puts it:

What do those who contrast economic democracy with political democracy mean by the phrase "economic democracy"? If we examine the social systems which they regard as exemplifications of it, we find that by "economic democracy" they really mean economic security. This is a radically different concept. That it cannot legitimately be regarded as a species of democracy is apparent when we realize that one may be secure without having any control over the conditions of security. . . . Soldiers have economic security, but not democracy.[19]

This, of course, is not to say that it is unimportant to ask what kind of social and economic systems provide the most favorable soil for democracy to flourish in. Clearly this is a highly important question for anyone who wishes to see democracy achieved in his community. We are saying only that the question of what *helps* democracy is entirely different from the question of what *is* democracy. And it is the latter question alone with which we are here concerned.

NOTES

[1] Cf. this judgment by a distinguished pair of logicians: ". . . The emotional associations and overtones of words may often prevent a clear apprehension of the issues at stake. This is particularly true in the social sciences. Words like 'democracy,' 'liberty,' 'duty,' have a powerful emotive function; they are frequently used as battle cries, as appeals to emotions, and as substitutes for thought. Many of the disputes . . . which undoubtedly arise from a conflict of emotional attitudes, would assuredly disappear if the precisely defined equivalents were substituted for these words": Morris R. Cohen and Ernest Nagel, *Introduction to Logic and Scientific Method* (New York: Harcourt, Brace and Company, 1934), p. 232.

[2] Wilhelm Röpke, *Civitas Humana*, translated by C. S. Fox (London: William Hodge and Company, Ltd., 1948), pp. 6–7. Emphasis added. See also Röpke, pp. 7–10. Max Weber offers these illustrations of models or "ideal types": "A panic on the stock exchange can be most conveniently analyzed by attempting to determine first what the course of action would have been if it had not been influenced by irrational effects; it is then possible to introduce the irrational components as accounting for the observed deviations from this hypothetical course. Similarly, in analyzing a political or military campaign it is convenient to determine in the first place what would have been a rational course, given the ends of the participants and adequate knowledge of all circumstances. Only in this way is it possible to assess the causal significance of irrational factors as accounting for deviations of this type. The construction of a purely rational course of action in such cases serves the sociologist as a type ('ideal type') which has the merit of

clear understandability and lack of ambiguity. By comparison with this it is possible to understand the ways in which actual action is influenced by irrational deviation from the line of conduct which would be expected on the hypothesis that the action were purely rational": *The Theory of Social and Economic Organization*, translated by A. R. Henderson and Talcott Parsons, revised and edited by Talcott Parsons (London: William Hodge and Company, Ltd., 1947), pp. 83–84.

[3] On the desirability of frankly and didactically presenting models in social science analysis, see Robert M. MacIver, *The Web of Government* (New York: The Macmillan Company, 1947), pp. 8, 403–04; and M. A. Girshick and Daniel Lerner, "Model Construction in the Social Sciences," *Public Opinion Quarterly*, Vol. XIV (Winter, 1950–51), p. 710–23.

[4] Cf. James Bryce, *Modern Democracies* (New York: The Macmillan Company, 1924), Vol. I, pp. 47–50.

[5] *Op. cit.*, Vol. I, p. 20. Italics added.

[6] The so-called "pluralists" of the 1920's denied the desirability (and some even denied the possibility) of creating a "sovereign State" in this sense; and thus, from the point of view set forth in the text, classified themselves as opponents of the very idea of government, and therefore were neither critics nor supporters of democracy. It is unnecessary for our purposes to go into the rather rarefied academic argument about the idea of sovereignty; but those who would like to pursue the subject further will find a convenient starting place in the summary and evaluation of the pluralist attack on sovereignty in Francis W. Coker, *Recent Political Thought* (New York: D. Appleton-Century Co., Inc., 1934), Chaps. XVIII, XIX. The pluralist point of view, as just defined, appears to have no contemporary exponents, and must be carefully distinguished from contemporary American pluralism, which is a defense of the pluralistic *exercise* of sovereignty—that is, has no quarrel with the idea of sovereignty as such.

[7] The classic statement of this view of the nature of politics is presented in Arthur F. Bentley's *The Process of Government* (Chicago: The University of Chicago Press, 1908). This work has since been reprinted by the Principia Press of Bloomington, Indiana. For an illuminating discussion of Bentley's critics and a restatement of his position, see Richard W. Taylor, "Arthur Bentley's Political Science," *Western Political Quarterly*, V (June, 1952), pp. 214–30. A leading present-day application of Bentley's attitude toward politics is David B. Truman, *The Governmental Process* (New York: Alfred A. Knopf, 1951).

[8] Jean Jacques Rousseau, *The Social Contract*, translated by Willmoore Kendall (Chicago: Henry Regnery Co., 1954), Bk. II, Chap. I, p. 24.

[9] Mary Parker Follett, *The New State* (New York: Longmans, Green and Co., 1918), p. 271. On the nature and necessity of community for democratic government, see also Robert M. MacIver, *Community* (London: Macmillan and Company, Ltd., 1917), pp. 128–29, and *The Web of Government* (New York: The Macmillan Company, 1947), pp. 4ff.; and A. D. Lindsay, *The Essentials of Democracy*, 2nd ed. (London: Oxford University Press, 1935), p. 4.

[10] *The Web of Government*, p. 9. Italics added.

[11] Roscoe Pound, "Law and Federal Government," in *Federalism as a Democratic Process* (New Brunswick, N.J.: Rutgers University Press, 1942), pp. 8–9. Italics added.

[12] Cf. Laurence Stapleton, *The Design of Democracy* (New York: Oxford University Press, 1949), pp. 67–68, 74–76; Herbert McClosky, "The Fallacy of Absolute Majority Rule," *The Journal of Politics*, XI (November, 1949), pp. 637–54; and J. Roland Pennock, "Responsiveness, Responsibility, and Majority Rule," *American Political Science Review*, XLVI (September, 1952), pp. 791–96.

[13] Some readers may agree that the principle of "absolute" majority rule is logically consistent with democracy, but feel that they do not wish to live in an America in which popular majorities exercise their absolute powers in an absolute way. . . .

[14] *United States* v. *Butler* 197 U.S. 1 (1936).

[15] Cf. Hugo Krabbe, *The Modern Idea of the State*, translated by G. H. Sabine and W. J. Shepard, (New York: D. Appleton and Company, 1922), p. 76.

[16] Ladislas Konopczynski, "Majority Rule," *Encyclopedia of the Social Sciences* (New York: The Macmillan Company, 1937), Vol. IX, pp. 55–60.

[17] The easiest way to avoid the obvious error of calling something like the Politburo a "majority-rule" body is to use the term "majority principle" to denote the rule by which *any* decision-making body, however removed from and set over the bulk of the populace, may make its own decisions. The term "majority rule" is most usefully reserved to denote that principle in a total governing system by which all political decisions are ultimately subject to control by at least 50 per cent plus one of the enfranchised citizens: Cf. Willmoore Kendall, *John Locke and the Doctrine of Majority-Rule* (Urbana: University of Illinois Press, 1941), pp. 24–27.

[18] Cf. Carl F. Becker, ". . . as a historian, I am naturally disposed to be satisfied with the meaning which in the history of politics men have commonly attributed to the word—a meaning, needless to say, which derives partly from experience and partly from the aspirations of mankind. So regarded, the term democracy refers primarily to a form of government, and it has always meant government by the many as opposed to government by the one . . .": *Modern Democracy* (New Haven: Yale University Press, 1941), pp. 6–7.

[19] *New York Times Sunday Magazine*, March 16, 1947, pp. 48–49. For another exposition of this position, see Krabbe, *op. cit.*, pp. 6–7.

PART TWO

Some Structures
of Democratic Government

As we suggested in our introduction to the previous section, attempting to specify "irreducible" or "fundamental" principles of the democratic process is a procedure fraught with difficulty. Though one may be able to specify a set of fundamental principles consistent with one's definition at the conceptual level, at the operational level one is likely to be overwhelmed with the variation in application of those principles and the institutional richness of the democratic process in its variety of settings. Thus, to describe accurately the structure of democratic government in a manner consistent with a set of fundamental principles is a task well exceeding the modest limits of this kind of volume. Our strategy in presenting this discussion has been to focus upon some institutional processes which are certainly basic to the democratic process even if they do not represent someone else's set of "most basic" institutional processes. Those which we have chosen to concentrate on are: the voting process, federalism, the structure of political opposition, and the administrative process.

The voting process has received more attention by political analysts than any other feature of the democratic process, in part because of the intrinsic importance of the voting act, in part because the data produced by the voting process are plentiful, relatively easily compared, quantifiable, and inexpensive. In a literal sense, then, we know more about the voting process than about many of the other institutionalized activities of democracy. This is both a blessing and a bother. It is obviously a positive good to have plentiful information and analyses about the voting process; but it is, at the same time, difficult to summarize or represent an accurate sample of such plentiful research. Whatever choice we might make would slight some important segment of research. The article which we have selected to reprint is noteworthy, in part, because it minimizes this fault and also, in part, because it focuses the whole of the voting process in a particularly interesting way. In "Voting and Elections: A Functional Analysis" (Chapter 3), Richard Rose and Harve Mossawir are concerned with the meanings which are given to the voting act and to elections in general. There is a tendency, they argue, to treat elections, wherever they occur and under whatever circumstances, as if they were equal. Thus, it has been common to speak in similar terms of both competitive and non-competitive elections as well as literate and illiterate electorates. One must be aware, Rose and Mossawir state, that radically different conditions can mean that the functions which elections perform both for the individual voter and for the political system may be radically different. Using the voting studies as a source of evidence, they argue that the voting act may perform as many as six different major functions for individual voters and that elections may similarly perform six chief functions for political systems. In order to interpret the meaning of an election, it is, therefore, necessary first to be aware of the conditions under which it is taking place since these, to a significant degree, determine its functional character.

In "Symbols and Political Quiescence" (Chapter 4), Murray Edelman suggests that the meaning of *many* kinds of manifest political activity may deserve to be reassessed in the light of the latent functions which they perform for individuals or groups. Edelman observes that there is a substantial difference between the amount of public activity which surrounds the demand for legislation and that which attends its administration. He also observes that the nature of the groups interested in various kinds of legislation seems to be an important determinant of the kind of activity which surrounds it. From these observations, Edelman concludes that the functions performed by the passage of legislation and its administration are different and that it is the performance of these different functions which accounts for the differences in observed group activity. In short, the passage of legislation or the demand for legislation is, by and large, a symbolic activity, most frequently a response to the demands of some relatively large, poorly organized group (or groups) for a legislative redress to some major social or political ill. Those portions of the legislation which receive most attention are precisely those which are most likely to have the least effect—provisions stating general, non-operational goals, rather than those specifying the administrative machinery of the bill or the actual legal limits of the legislation. The vague, diffuse, but intense group demand that some social or political ill be dealt with legislatively is matched by the only possible response—a symbolic gratification of that demand. The material content of legislation, its administrative reality, is more likely to be the concern of some particularly interested, relatively small, well organized group which is likely to be directly affected by the operation of the legislative provisions rather than by its symbolic content. Whereas the larger, diffuse groups are likely to lapse into quiescence following the enactment of their symbolic gratification (for their group-life lacks the purpose and resources for sustaining the group), those groups interested in the material consequences of legislation are likely to pay close attention to its daily administration and attempt to make use of their continuing influence to insure that their interests are satisfied. As Edelman suggests: "The 'what' of Lasswell's famous definition of politics is a complex universe in itself." It is sufficiently complex, in fact, that the meaning of the outcomes of democratic political systems are very likely to be often misread if symbolic and material gratifications are confused.

If the electoral process and the structure of legislative demand and satisfaction are characteristic features of democratic organization, no less is the pattern of political party interaction, for the eventual focus of all demand and the direct attention of the voter is, in mass democratic political systems, the political party. And to the extent that democratic political systems differ one from another, that difference is probably most reflected in their patterns of political opposition. In a complicated set of causal interactions, the pattern of political opposition is related to the value pattern of the political culture, to the institutional arrangements which impinge upon the process of preference generation and satisfaction, to the legitimacy of regimes, and to many other equally vital factors of the democratic political process. This is because the pattern of political opposition (the limits and extent of political competition) is the empirical result of permissibility in politics and, as such, represents the day to day approximation of those critical values of political freedom and political equality. To suggest so much is to make clear that studying the patterns of political oppositions in democratic countries is likely to be a most profitable focus for comparative analysis; describing various patterns and having some understanding of how and why they differ will have considerable theoretical importance for the study of democracy. In "Patterns of Opposition" (Chapter 5), Robert Dahl provides such a framework for the analysis of political oppositions. Utilizing as data individual country analyses by the contributing authors of his volume, Dahl inductively derives a framework which asserts that oppositions differ in six important respects: the organizational cohesion of concentration of the opponents, the competitiveness of the opposition, the site or setting for the encounter between opposition and those who control the government, the distinctiveness or identifiability of the opposition, the goals of the opposition, and the strategies of the opposition.

Although the ability to describe oppositional differences with respect to these six criteria does not *prima facie* provide explanations for such differences, Dahl's framework is most useful in pointing to some of the institutional bases for oppositional differences in various societies. One of the classical differences between democratic societies in this respect is federalism, for a federal system obviously constitutes a vastly different site for the encounter of opposition with government than does a unitary system of government. This is certainly true in the United States, where it is commonly accepted that the essential decentralized nature of the American party system is a product of its federal organization. In a most provocative essay, *"Baker* v. *Carr* and the Ghost of Federalism" (Chapter 6), Martin Landau argues that the functional rationale of the American federal system, so pressing and immediate at the time of its statement in the *Federalist Papers*, has lost its viability with the economic and social growth of the United States. That system of shared powers, which once loomed as the only possible combination of the diversified interests of the infant states of America, in a time of nationalized social, economic, and political life today serves only to keep alive institutional arrangements which emphasize local and parochial interests. In short, Landau argues that American federalism has outlived its usefulness as a political arrangement. It is, given the contemporary cast of American life, an anachronism which forces the continuation of political practices (like the decentralized party system) which serve the interests of minorities (such as rural areas) at the expense of the interests of the majority (urban areas). *Baker* v. *Carr*, Landau suggests, is primarily an attempt by the Supreme Court to redress the "lag" between this historically determined center of political power and its contemporary source. Landau only hints at the possible future consequences of the demise of American federalism (for example, the creation of a new federal relationship based upon massive urban concentrations), but from his analysis it is clear that as the *de facto* power base of American politics undergoes change, great pressures are generated to ratify that change with *de jure* recognition. If, as Dahl for example has repeatedly argued, the stability of many democratic systems is a function of the dispersion of political power through pluralistic instrumentalities, such as federalism, the death of one federal structure and the emergence of another presages significant change in the character of American democracy. One hypothesis which might be entertained is that as American politics become more and more nationalized, and as these changes are ratified by basic institutional changes, traditionally federalist American democracy will become more nearly alike functionally to traditionally centralized democratic states (but which? Britain? France? Sweden?). Clearly, Landau has raised a question which requires much further attention. Rarely are we, as political analysts, made aware of such basic alterations in the basic structure of our political forms.

CHAPTER 3

Voting and Elections:
A Functional Analysis

Richard Rose
Harve Mossawir

Elections are among the most ubiquitous of contemporary political institutions, and voting is the single act of political participation undertaken by a majority of adults in a majority of the nations in the world today. Although elections are of ancient origin, the practice of voting in nation-wide balloting began to gain importance in Europe only in the 19th century, and become of world-wide significance in the periods after the First and Second World Wars. Voting differs in legal form from nation to nation and from election to election, depending upon the extent to which abstention is permitted or encouraged, alternatives exist within or between parties, each citizen has an equal number of votes and each vote has equal weight in counting. Elections also vary greatly in significance if they concern voting for men or legislation, for legislative or executive officials, for national or local offices, or for office holders or candidates for seats in an electoral college.[1] Yet the same vocabulary is used to describe balloting at all corners of the earth.

The study of voting and elections is now one of the major growth areas within the field of political science. Concern with the practical and theoretical implications of voting and elections was exhibited during 19th-century debates concerning the extension of the franchise and alterations of constitutional procedures. Analysis by more sophisticated statistical and survey techniques began before the Second World War, and in the past two decades has grown so much and spread so widely that at times it seems to some tantamount to the study of political behavior itself. Work in the field is now a recognized sub-discipline within political science. Limited consideration, however, is given to the relevance of voting and elections for the political system as a whole. Many authors discuss these relationships only perfunctorily in the introduction and conclusion of intensive

Reprinted from *Political Studies*, Vol. XV, No. 2 (June, 1967), pp. 173–201. Footnotes have been renumbered.

analyses of voting decisions or of a particular election. The purpose of this paper is to try to redress the resulting imbalance by concentrating detailed attention upon the multiple functions, i.e., observable consequences, of voting for individuals and of elections for political systems in contemporary societies.

I

The literature of politics contains many assertions about the purported functions of elections for individual voters, some but not all of which are dependent upon specific institutional arrangements. The statements may be grouped under six general headings.

First, voting involves individual *choice* of governors or major governmental policies. An approach developed by Joseph Schumpeter and restated by Robert T. McKenzie emphasizes the task of the voter as nothing more and nothing less than that of choosing between teams of competing leaders at general elections.[2] In America, the use of primary elections to choose candidates gives a much greater measure of choice than is present in duopolistic competition, or in simple-plurality general election contests. Referenda and balloting on constitutional amendments afford voters the opportunity to choose or reject specific policies, but this device is now of declining and limited political importance. A number of writers, including V. O. Key in his posthumous *The Responsible Electorate*, have argued that in effect voters do choose between policy alternatives in national elections. Few academic analysts today would go so far as to endorse the assertion that voters can mandate their representatives at an election, although the word "mandate" is still prevalent in the discourse of politicians.[3]

Second, voting permits individuals to participate in a reciprocal and continuing *exchange of influence* with office-holders and candidates. The emphasis here is upon the extent to which the need for election or re-election will lead incumbents and candidates to alter their policies in order to retain or gain office. The attribution of voter influence rather than control of policies avoids many problems arising from representation. Lipset's discussion of elections endorses this doctrine, as does Parsons' very general treatment of American voting behavior.[4] The importance of this approach is that it is dynamic, that is, it considers how alternatives for choice are derived, and what the elected do. Carl Friedrich has described the exchange of influence between elections as arising from "a law of anticipated reactions," in which politicians continuously adjust policy decisions with reference to assumptions about future as well as past voter preferences. This analysis has been endorsed not only by Sir Ivor Jennings, but also by the authors of *The American Voter*, who declare: "The holders of elective or appointive office in democratic government are guided in many of their actions by a calculus of electoral effect."[5] It is sometimes asserted by popular writers that in the exchange of influence at election times the individual voter is, in fact, being manipulated—i.e. unilaterally subjected to influence—through campaign propaganda transmitted by mass media.[6] Voters can also influence the selection of candidates in the absence of primary elections if party leaders are sensitive to popular preferences. Thus, the prospect of a general election can effect the re-nomination of candidates not only in a competitive system (see e.g., the Conservatives' abandonment of Sir Alec Douglas-Home in 1965) but also in one-party states, such as Tanzania, Poland, and even, to a limited degree, in the Soviet Union.[7]

Third, voting contributes to the development or maintenance of an individual's *allegiance* to the existing constitutional regime. In this proposition, the function of voting is seen as that of reinforcing or increasing an individual's predisposition to accept voluntarily the regulations of the regime, regardless of the result of an election or whether the election provides alternative choices. In his seminal discussion of electoral systems, W. J. M. Mackenzie has called attention to this function, and Edward Shils has given extreme expression to this idea.

The granting of universal suffrage without property or literacy qualifications is perhaps the greatest single factor leading to the formation of a political society. . . . The drawing of the whole adult population periodically into contact with the symbols of the center of national political life must, in the course of time, have immeasurable consequences by stirring people up and giving them a sense of their own potential significance, and attaching their sentiments to symbols which comprehend the entire nation.[8]

The importance attached to electoral participation as a means of expressing and reinforcing allegiance can be seen in arguments for compulsory voting by many advocates of universal suffrage. In the late 19th century, these arguments had liberal connotations; in the past three decades, compulsory voting has often been associated with Communist and Fascist regimes. Fear that an individual's allegiance may be increased by voting, whether primarily in response to internalized norms or to external coercion has in consequence produced arguments "In Defence of Apathy."[9]

Fourth, voting contributes to the development or maintenance of a voter's *disaffection* from the existing constitutional regime. Disaffection, the predisposition to refuse voluntary compliance with the regulations of a regime, may be induced by the result of a specific election, or it may have other antecedents, and simply be reinforced by voting or by purposeful abstention. Disaffection as a consequence of a single election result is rare, although the possibility exists wherever extremist parties seek and have a chance to gain office. It would seem more usual for disaffected voters to find their feelings reinforced each time they balloted. The unwillingness of supporters of some extremist parties to report their preferences in sample surveys is a probable indicator that some voters regard their actions as a means of maintaining disaffection. In a few instances, extremist parties have asked disaffected voters to spoil their ballots, or vote for a candidate pledged to reject the legitimacy of the state, e.g., Sinn Fein in British elections. Non-voting is a general phenomenon among a fraction of all electorates, whether large or small. A modicum of non-voting is always to be expected on involuntary grounds. Organized boycotts, such as that of the South Vietnam elections of September, 1966, are infrequent, and interpreting success or failure is difficult insofar as "normal turnout" is often hard to estimate. Major falls in turnout are open to interpretation as evidence of growing voter disaffection, as W. Dean Burnham has argued in an historical analysis of American data.[10]

Fifth, voting has *emotional* significance for individuals. The significance may be in addition to instrumental political values, or it may exclude political functions. The intensity of the emotion may also vary. The act of voting has been compared to participation in a "great eleusinian mystery" by R. B. McCallum, the founder of the Nuffield election studies; more restrainedly, W. J. M. Mackenzie suggests that the ritual function of voting may, at its highest, perhaps be comparable to a Coronation service.[11] In both cases, emotions may have political consequences, in the first instance leading to temporary disorder as in 18th-century England, and in the other to a maintenance of allegiance. The frequent use of metaphorical language from sport or military games suggests that for some persons election contests provide emotional satisfaction akin to watching athletic matches, with the behavior of individual contestants more important than the result. At a much lower level of intensity, one might suggest that the emotional significance of voting may be transitory or superficial, like that derived from "being done good to" by listening to a sermon, or occasionally fulfilling a minor social duty.

Sixth, for some individuals, voting may be *functionless*, i.e., devoid of any emotional or politically significant personal consequences. This extreme form of apathy is not likely to be found among many people who personally record their votes. But turnout figures recorded for many noncompetitive elections are so high as to suggest that a substantial number of voters may have had no personal awareness of voting, or even of an election. One could posit that the act of voting tends to be functionless for individuals in so far as it is devoid of emotional significance, allegiance or disaffection, or any relationship to the choice or influence of men or governmental policies.

The chief functions of an election in a political system are often analogous to functions of voting for an individual, although there need not be an exact correspondence. Six main points can be made.

First, elections are a recognized means of providing *succession* in leadership. The problem of political succession is common to all systems, for even a lifetime dictator will eventually need replacement. At a minimum, an election, even if a plebiscite with only one individual seeking endorsement as dictator, provides a legal means for validating a claim to govern. In the Western world, elections are expected to involve competition between two or more possible claimants to succeed to office, and the presence or absence of competition is a basic characteristic distinguishing "free" elections. Within this framework, however, competition can take place in a variety of forms, for a variety of offices, and under laws which are intended to affect the possibility of one or more groups of candidates achieving success.[12]

Second, elections *control the policy decisions* of government. The development of the devices of initiative, referendum, and repeal institutionalized in large-scale societies, most notably the United States, the possibility for elections to enact or repeal legislation, constitutional amendments or tax levies.[13] While these devices are no longer subjects of agitation, constitutions in many American states enshrine these possibilities, most notably in mandatory provisions for voting on constitutional amendments and tax levies.

Third, elections *influence* the policy decisions of government. Among contemporary students of elections, Stanley Kelley has been exceptional in analysing seriously and at length the use of elections as devices for influencing policy decisions of government. It is sometimes claimed that the development of public opinion polls and party-sponsored market research is now providing an alternative mechanism for voters to influence policy, with sample surveys the immediate means of ascertaining preferences, and the sanction of a general election the incentive for policy-makers to remain continuously interested in voters' policy preferences.[14]

Fourth, elections can help to *secure the legitimation* of a regime, or to maintain legitimacy. Legitimacy, the voluntary compliance by the great majority of the populace with the regulations of a regime, is not yet securely developed in most nations, and achieving it is a major goal of many national leaders. In many countries it is believed voting may lead individuals to become mobilized, i.e., more involved in and receptive to regulations, and elections have been justified on this basis, without regard to competition. Where national integration is the sole goal of leaders, then mobilization through voting may take place without coercive measures, as was the case in early 20th-century Argentina and in some African societies today.[15]

But, as Lipset declares, "The greater the changes in the structure of the society or organization that a governing group is attempting to introduce, the more likely the leadership is to desire and even require a high level of partition by the citizens or members." The abnormally high voting turnouts reported in Communist and other extremist regimes are evidence in support of this hypothesis.[16] In systems where legitimacy antedates universal suffrage, such as Britain, elections may help maintain legitimacy in so far as relatively apathetic and moderate citizens come forward to vote against intense and extremists activists, according to Berelson's ingenious interpretation of the aggregate consequences of differential political involvement. Lipset has also posited that elections may help maintain legitimacy by bringing together in support for a single party individuals who are otherwise remote from or in conflict with each other on grounds such as class, status and religion.[17]

Fifth, in extreme cases, elections may lead to the *repudiation*[18] of a regime because of the intensity of differences of opinion among groups competing for office.[19] Repudiation may take the form of a government refusing to leave office following its apparent defeat, the revolt of losers (e.g., the response of Southern states to the election of Abraham Lincoln in 1860) or the abolition of the existing regime by a newly-elected government. For example, the election of an African government in Northern Rhodesia for the first time made maintenance of the Federation in Central Africa impossible; in the blunt words of Kenneth Kaunda to his opponents, "My friend has lost—and lost forever."[20]

Sixth, to say that an election is *functionless* is to state that it has no observable, verifiable consequences for the political system. It would be possible to hypothesize that in many new nations where elections are unfamiliar, communications poor, and administration primitive, elections *may* tend toward this state, or, in the absence of evidence, this hypothesis is easier to defend than any other. This is not to say that an election which has no observable impact upon control of office is functionless, for an uncontested election in a free society such as Switzerland, can be a slack resource which citizens invoke in case of political controversy.[21]

The substantial body of literature concerning voting and elections is not capable of ready classification in order to ascertain which of the above functions are most important for voters and for political systems. Studies have varied greatly in locale, with the most work done in Western, democratic societies and in primitive African communities. The frameworks of analysis have also varied, with students in the Nuffield tradition concentrating on campaigners, and those in the sociological tradition concentrating upon voters. Even studies within the United States, where rigorous work has most often been done, have left important ambiguities. For example, while the authors of *The American Voter* describe elections as "a device of control" in the preamble and conclusion of their work, the intervening data and analysis strongly suggest much more diffuse and perhaps tenuous political functions. Similarly, V. O. Key has asserted in his final book, "Voters are not fools," but in his penultimate study, *Public Opinion and American Democracy*, he has presented massive evidence and trenchant analysis arguing that voters who think their ballots are influencing or choosing policy are misguided, if not foolish.[22] Robert Dahl has been distinctive in having a model of pluralistic politics which does not rest upon active exchange of influence between voters and governors. In *Who Governs?* he emphasizes, "The first fact, and it overshadows almost everything else, is that *most citizens use their political resources scarcely at all.*" Yet the scope of Dahl's *Political Oppositions* is defined by the existence of opposition parties at elections, and most contributors emphasize electoral competition as of major significance for the political system.[23]

Ideally, in order to sort out existing confusion, one would like to have survey and aggregate data concerning a number of elections in a wide variety of political systems—competitive and non-competitive; developed and underdeveloped; Afro-Asian, Communist and Western. Only a little basic data is available concerning the great majority of electoral systems in the world. The first point arising from this material is that the great majority of nations in the world do have elections. The Yale Data Programme reports that for 100 nations for which information could be obtained, ninety-two had held elections in the preceding six years; the authors of *The Cross-Polity Survey* record ninety countries as currently possessing electoral systems. The quantity of elections is not purely a consequence of the creation of many independent states in the past few years, for the Institute of Electoral Research recorded elections in sixty-eight countries in the period 1954–58.[24] Secondly, elections usually involve the participation of a majority of the population of voting age. The median turnout for the ninety-two national elections reported in the Yale Data Programme fell between Burundi, 68.4 per cent, and Madagascar, 64.8 per cent; in two-thirds of the cases, a majority of the voting-age population was recorded as casting ballots. Thirdly, party competition is absent in half or more of elections. The editors of *The Cross-Polity Survey* classify forty-three countries as possessing competitive electoral systems, compared to thirty with strictly non-competitive systems and seventeen that are ambiguous or virtually one-party. Dahl, employing more stringent criteria to define competition as the presence of full legal opposition by organized parties through a decade, reports that only about 30 of 133 states had competitive elections.[25] Fourthly, the capacity of electors to understand the chief formal and political characteristics of a modern Western political institution is likely to be very imperfect in parts of the world into which it is imported. Of available indicators of voter comprehension, literacy is probably best, since without the ability to read and write in one's native language it is doubtful whether an individual will understand much about the electoral process, or even, the national political system; the fact that an illiterate votes (or is voted) does not mean that his behavior has the same meaning as that of a literate.[26] Literacy figures, as reported by the Yale Data Programme, show that 62 of 118 nations for which data is available have literacy rates of 50 per cent or higher for populations aged 15 and over, and Banks and Textor report that 55 of 105 nations have reached this level.[27]

As the differences in the number of nations classified differs from source to source and from variable to variable, it is clear that the evidence is indicative rather than conclusive. It is sufficient, however, to confirm the proposition that elections can be presumed to have different functions for voters and political systems, for a significant number of cases exist to fit into each cell in the following typology: Competitive elections and majority of voters literate (thirty-four). Competitive elections and majority of voters illiterate (nine). Majority of voters literate but no competition in elections (fifteen). Majority of voters illiterate and no electoral competition (thirty-three).[28] The implication of this finding is that the current practice of reporting electoral data in a form equating ballots in America, Albania and Dahomey is fundamentally mistaken, and the most elaborate concern with statistical comparability of results will be of little avail.[29] Simply because elections have the same institutional characteristics in different countries, it does not follow that their functional significance is comparable.

II

Britain is a good country for intensive analysis of general theoretical questions about elections. Electoral institutions have traditional sources yet have proven adaptable, British procedures have often served as models for other countries, and a substantial mass of descriptive and survey material is readily available as a basis for further research. In order to explore the extent of voters' electorally relevant political demands, attitudes toward the electoral process, and the relationship between electoral attitudes and allegiance to the regime, a survey was undertaken in the Stockport North constituency in February–March 1964.

The constituency was chosen for a number of reasons. On key variables such as social class, housing and population growth, Stockport consistently ranks near the middle among towns in England and Wales.[30]

Politically, the constituency was marginal, and was won by Labour from the Conservatives at the 1964 election. Last and not least, it was relatively convenient to our former University. A total of 889 names were drawn from a fresh electoral register by systematic random sampling methods. Student interviewers conducted all but two dozen interviews, which were undertaken by the senior author. The response rate was 77 per cent of all names drawn; non-respondents included refusals, 6 per cent; moved or absent for a prolonged period, 6 per cent; sick, senile or dead, 6 per cent; not at home after three or more calls by an interviewer, 4 per cent; house demolished, 1 per cent. The research cost of £91 was met by a grant from the Faculty of Economics of Manchester University. Interviewing occurred at a time when an election had to take place within the next eight months. Yet respondents were not interviewed during the election campaign, when an abnormally high interest might have been temporarily generated in the questions. Stockport North was chosen as a marginal constituency with a reasonably representative social ˜structure; moreover, it had been systematically exposed to pre-election propaganda by both parties for more than six months in advance of interviewing. One survey of this type can, of course, only provide illustrative evidence. But in present circumstances, it is highly desirable that general theoretical problems should be considered in relation to data which provides some empirical bearings, and gives suggestions for more special surveys "around" elections.

In order for an election to have the function of voter choice or influence upon policy as well as office-holding, an individual voter must be aware that government influences his life, he must have demands seen as relevant to politics, and he must be willing to consider altering party preferences in response to changes in policies. In addition, a large proportion of voters would be expected to show interest in politics and believe that they possessed political influence.

When Stockport respondents were asked how much effect government had on the lives of people like themselves, 48 per cent attributed a lot of influence, 28 per cent a little influence, and 11 per cent no effect; an additional 13 per cent said they did not know. Among those perceiving some government influence, evaluations of influence were mixed or positive. A total of 44 per cent thought the value of the impact depended upon the situation, and 37 per cent that government usually made things better; 13 per cent replied that government usually made things worse, and 6 per cent said don't know.[31]

When asked to give some examples of the influence of government on their lives, among those perceiving influence, 30 per cent did not offer any example, and only 18 per cent offered more than one example. Reference

Table 1. Main Concern of Respondents

Subject	Per cent
Economic (standard of living, job, pension, housing)	40%
Personal (health, happiness, lead a decent life)	16%
Family (children, relatives)	13%
War	5%
Miscellaneous	5%
None	21%

was most often made to economic policy, welfare measures and taxes.

The relatively low salience of government to the central concerns of the majority of voters is evidenced by answers to the question: "What would you say is the main concern of you and your family today?" (Table 1). Few of the respondents mentioned a problem that was unambiguously personal, such as ill health, or one that was unambiguously political, such as nuclear war. When asked what group outside their family could help them with their chief concerns, the great majority of respondents (71 per cent) saw themselves reliant strictly upon family resources, and could think of no other group to provide assistance. Even though this question was asked immediately after a series about government and 40 per cent had referred to economic concerns, only 15 per cent of persons with a problem referred to obtaining assistance from a government or other political source. To assess the existence of latent demands which could be crystallized by campaigners, individuals were asked whether or not they were satisfied with six things for which governments accept responsibility—their standard of living, job, housing, education today, welfare services generally, and the condition of pensioners. On five of these points, the proportion reporting themselves satisfied ranged from 61 to 75 per cent. Only the condition of pensioners showed a majority of voters dissatisfied, notwithstanding the very intensive criticism of the state of England at the time in the media and among party activists.

When Stockport respondents were asked point-blank what they thought were the most important things the government *ought* to do something about, virtually everyone could give voice to some complaint which they wished government action to remedy. The apparent discrepancy between this response and other evidence of the low salience of politics to the ordinary voter can best be explained by the fact that for the respondent to state a political demand in response to explicit questioning it is only necessary for him to have a minimum cognitive awareness of public affairs, and less than 100 per cent satisfaction with things as they are. It does not necessarily reflect interest or knowledge comparable to that of candidates, political scientists and newspapers that commission public opinion polls.

For example, only 45 per cent of Stockport respondents described themselves as "interested" or "very interested" in politics, 41 per cent knew the name of their M.P. (Sir Norman Hulbert had sat for Stockport since 1935), 10 per cent considered themselves members of a political party, and only 9 per cent described themselves as "very interested" in politics. These figures are consistent with other findings suggesting that no more than one-sixth of the British electorate is in any meaningful sense actively involved in politics.[32]

Voters are also aware that they are not the only members of society seeking to influence government, and that the deference paid them by politicians during election campaigns may not be lasting. In the Stockport survey, 52 per cent said that they thought the pledges made by party leaders during campaigns were sometimes sincere and sometimes not, and 26 per cent thought campaigners usually insincere. Similarly, only 14 per cent claimed that people like themselves had a lot of influence upon the way the country is governed, and 12 per cent some influence; 38 per cent said people like themselves had little influence, and 27 per cent no influence, with the remainder don't know. Attribution of political influence is pluralistic, inasmuch as more than half the respondents credit five groups with substantial, i.e. "a lot" or "too much," impact on government (Table 2). But voters see people like themselves in the lower half among influential groups; only the Queen was thought less likely than voters to have "a lot" of influence and only the Church of England and the Queen were more often said to have no influence. Thus, while recognizing what Dahl calls "dispersed inequalities,"[33] voters seem to think that in the dispersion of inequalities, some people are more unequal than others.

Table 2. Influence of Groups upon Government

	A Lot (%)	Too Much (%)	A Little (%)	None (%)	Don't Know (%)
Prime Minister	62	5	22	5	6
Members of Parliament	54	4	31	8	3
Big business	52	29	11	2	6
The Press	46	11	27	9	7
Trade unions	39	24	24	2	11
Television	36	6	30	18	10
Senior civil servants*	30	6	30	12	22
Church of England	17	2	39	31	11
The Queen	13	2	35	43	7

* Piloting the questionnaire showed that many respondents had no conception of the title or duties of administrative class civil servants; the chief referent for "civil servants" appeared to be a local clerical officer. The term "senior civil servant" was employed as more meaningful to respondents. The Don't Know group was twice as high for civil servants as for any other group.

Given the foregoing attitudes, it is hardly surprising that voters do not see a general election as a time at which a choice of some importance can be made between parties. In fact, the majority of voters do not see it as a time of choice. Only 12 per cent of persons who had voted in the 1959 general election reported altering their party preference in Stockport by March 1964. The reason most often given was the intervention of a Liberal candidate. An additional 19 per cent said they could think of things that the other parties could do that might make them change their vote, e.g. modify welfare policies. But 69 per cent of the voters declared that they could not think of anything that could make them think of voting differently from their established party preference. Moreover, data from the Civic Culture survey shows that only 1 to 7 per cent of respondents in the five nations volunteered references to changing a vote as a means of influencing government.[34] In short, for most individuals the function of voting at a given general election is not that of calculating and registering a fresh choice, but rather re-affirming an allegiance established long ago. To speak of the majority of voters at a given election as "choosing" a party is nearly as misleading as speaking of a worshipper on a Sunday "choosing" to go to an Anglican, rather than a Presbyterian or a Baptist church.

Notwithstanding the relatively low salience of elections as instruments of choice, they do appear to have some meaning to electors, for turnout of voters is consistently high in Britain, with well above three-quarters of persons physically able to do so casting their votes. Particularly in a country where free elections have been a highly valued symbol for generations, one might posit that an individual's participation in elections is primarily motivated by a commitment to the electoral process itself, rather than by expectations of choosing or influencing government. Yet in recent years, the mass media have increasingly discussed the extent to which voters may be manipulated by politicians. Such discussion may influence or reflect considerable cynicism among voters about the electoral process. Alternatively, one might suggest that most voters are as apathetic about the electoral process as they are about other features of politics that command the attention of the opinion elite.

To explore the values and beliefs of voters about the electoral process, Stockport respondents were asked four questions; each of which offered a statement consistent with liberal doctrines of representation and one representing disaffection. The first point to note in the answers is that voters are not apathetic or confused. The maximum expressing no opinion or uncertainty on any question was 8 per cent, and only 4 respondents in 684 had no views on at least three of the four questions (Table 3). Secondly, a clear majority of voters endorsed each of the liberal alternatives, with

Table 3. Attitudes of Voters toward the Electoral Process
(L = Liberal Alternative; D = Disaffected Alternative)

		L (%)	D (%)	No Opinion (%)
1. (L)	Voters have a *big* influence on the way the country is governed, OR			
(D)	Voters *don't* have much influence on government.	60	35	5
2. (L)	Most people *do* think about how they vote, OR			
(D)	Most people *don't* think about how they vote.	57	35	8
3. (L)	There *is* a real difference between the parties, OR			
(D)	There's *no* real difference to choose from between the parties.	73	23	4
4. (L)	Voters should vote for the *party* they think best, OR			
(D)	Voters should vote for the *men* they think best without regard to party.	68	28	4

support ranging from 57 per cent to 73 per cent. Thirdly, the median voter endorsed liberal values and beliefs. A total of 56 per cent of respondents opted for the liberal alternative at least three out of four times, and only 12 per cent opted for a disaffected alternative at least three times.[35] Moreover, cross-analysis by conventional demographic variables showed that endorsement of these values is found in all strata of the electorate.

The voters' support for the electoral process on grounds that appear to be more symbolic and expressive than instrumental[36] suggests the possibility that voting may be an end in itself, providing emotional gratifications for those who participate in elections. The important question then becomes whether elections have a strong or a very limited emotional function, and whether emotional responses are favorable or unfavorable. The Stockport survey found that 54 per cent said that elections had no emotional effect at all upon them, as against 31 per cent who enjoyed elections, and 8 per cent reporting annoyance. Similarly, Almond and Verba found that a majority of their respondents did not report a feeling of satisfaction when voting.[37] Interestingly, on all five comparative measures American respondents showed markedly higher emotional response to elections than respondents in Britain, Germany, Italy or Mexico. One might speculate that the enthusiasm of American social scientists for voting studies reflects, among other things, a general cultural orientation, and that in America elections as well as election studies are more important than in other countries.

The low emotional effect of elections suggests that for most voters the gratification obtained from voting is a result of having done a necessary but not particularly pleasurable duty. The duty of voting is the only act of political participation expected of a majority of persons in Britain, and stressed in pre-adult socialization. When an election is at hand, an individual can hardly avoid awareness of polling, because of intensive and extensive publicity through the mass media; for example in Stockport in March 1964, 89 per cent were already aware an election would be held sometime later in the year. On election day, the social norms internalized by the individual will make him feel impelled to cast a vote. The cost of voting, in terms of time and effort, is usually low in highly urbanized Britain. By voting, an individual may achieve a sense of emotional gratification from doing a duty or he will at least avoid tension and possible guilt feelings which could have arisen through failure to do his duty. The sense of duty may, of course, be reinforced or counteracted by either personal and social pressures, e.g. a sense of party identification making it a duty to vote for a particular party whether it has a chance of victory or not in the constituency, or a sense of social solidarity, making it important to vote if one's family, friends and fellow-workers are voting.

Evidence in support of this line of analysis is found in the Stockport survey. When asked whether you don't have to vote unless you feel like it, or whether voting is a duty, 82 per cent replied that they thought voting a duty. Many surveys of turnout have consistently shown that as the importance of voting varies, so does the propensity to vote, whether variations be caused by differences in individual political involvement, in types of elections (e.g. national and local government) or in differential socialization into prevailing cultural norms.[38] In Britain and other free societies, the duty to vote, through a process of socialization, becomes a response to an internal compulsion. In many countries, however, an individual may vote primarily because he fears external sanctions may be brought to bear upon him if he fails to support the party organizing the election. In both types of situation, voting is not so much behavior freely undertaken by an individual seeking to initiate or advance interests, but rather a more-or-less passive response by an individual to continuing social pressures, whether the demands are manifested overtly by mobilization through a single party or transmitted more subtly through a diffuse process of socialization.

Such analysis points to the importance of voting for the political system generally, as a means of building or maintaining individual allegiance, i.e. voluntary acceptance of the constitutional arrangements and specific regulations of a regime. A presumption of the legitimacy of Cabinet government in Britain is customary. In the Stockport survey, a crude but direct attempt was made to assess support for the regime by asking,

"Broadly speaking, what do you think about the general arrangements for governing the country with a Parliament, a Prime Minister, and a Cabinet?" Of all respondents, 73 per cent positively endorsed the regime, and only 10 per cent gave unfavorable replies; additionally, 5 per cent said ambiguously "could be better," 4 per cent gave miscellaneous answers, and 8 per cent were "don't knows."

A large number of potential sources of legitimacy exist in Britain.[39] What is required is some sense of the relative importance of elections for allegiance by comparison with traditional orientations, fear of coercion, and other factors. The Stockport survey contained a section which attempted to explore this problem empirically. Individuals were asked whether they agreed or disagreed with a list of five reasons given for justifying allegiance to the regime (Table 4). While the responses are illustrative rather than conclusive, it is noteworthy that the reason linked to electoral choice was endorsed by 66 per cent of respondents, thus placing it second in importance. Moreover, popular choice was much more important than two other justifications often given for allegiance—provision of benefits and tradition.

General approval of a regime does not necessarily lead to acceptance of specific constitutional provisions or laws.[40] Hence respondents were also asked about obedience to laws. A total of 46 per cent said that they could think of circumstances in which it would be all right to break a law. Probing showed that the examples most frequently cited—e.g. helping a person in an emergency—were not likely to undermine general allegiance to the regime. When asked specifically whether it would be all right to break traffic laws, fiddle income tax, steal food if in poverty, or break laws against conscience, the proportion giving definite approval to law violations varied from 19 to 27 per cent. In short, individual Englishmen have internalized support for everyday regulations of the regime, as well as for its basic constitutional structure. When asked to evaluate a variety of reasons sometimes given for obeying laws, the consent of the electorate again ranked high

Table 4. Justification of Allegiance

	Agree (%)	Disagree (%)	Don't Know (%)
It's the best form of government we know	77	19	4
It's the kind of government the people want	66	25	9
We've got to accept it whatever we think	65	32	3
It usually provides the right things for people	49	40	10
It's good because it is traditional	44	49	7

in importance, slightly surpassing the importance attributed to the threat of punishment (Table 5). Again, justification on traditional grounds was ranked last in importance.

Additional evidence of the importance of elections in maintaining allegiance can be found by abstracting from the total number of respondents three groups of persons whose orientations toward politics most nearly conform to ideal-type models. Because relatively stringent criteria were employed, only 28 per cent of all respondents could be put in one of three distinctive and very different categories—the activist who fulfills liberal expectations of the voter; the subject aware of governmental output but little concerned with influencing government; and the parochial scarcely aware of governmental activities.[41] Among these three groups, 78 per cent of the activists endorsed the regime because it is the kind of government the people want, compared to 69 per cent of subjects and 37 per cent of parochials. Similarly, when asked about reasons for obeying laws, 94 per cent of activists endorsed the statement that laws are made by people we elect. By comparison, only 67 per cent of subjects and 68 per cent of parochials agreed with this reason.

Because individuals tend to say that elections are important in justifying allegiance, it does not follow that elections are of primary significance in the historical process of legitimation. Particularly in Britain, it would seem that the allegiance of individuals to the regime antedates universal suffrage. Nonetheless, it is noteworthy that elections provide contemporary re-enforcement for traditional orientations of allegiance, and that the importance attributed to various sources of legitimacy seems now to have shifted, with less significance attached to tradition and more to elections. This interpretation is underscored by the fact that voters seem motivated to turn out at the polls by a sense of duty. The equilibrium of the British political system today thus does not arise so much from high voter satisfaction caused by office-holders satisfying many electoral demands;

Table 5. Justification for Obeying Laws

	Agree (%)	Disagree (%)	Don't Know (%)
Laws are generally sensible	90	8	2
Laws are made by people we elect	75	20	5
Laws are fairly enforced	75	18	7
You'll be punished if you break laws	74	22	4
People who make the laws know what you ought to do	64	29	6
Everyone has always done so	45	51	4

instead, it is more likely to arise because voters expect little from government and are satisfied with whatever they receive. This discounting of
expectations can be particularly important in times of social strain; in the
words of one Mass-Observation respondent in 1943:

Beyond saying that I hope for more than I expect, it seems to me that "blessed is
he that expecteth nothing, for he shall not be disappointed." In other words, I
hope for very little because I fear I shall not get it.[42]

In such circumstances, one might agree with W. J. M. Mackenzie's assertion, "Every electoral system is a sort of confidence trick. . . . Elections
only work because we believe they are going to work"[43]—as long as it is
understood that the maintenance of legitimacy through such "tricks" as
elections is a basic concern of all governments.

III

Generalizing about politics on the basis of limited data is always difficult
and rarely done well; we still lack, for example, a good typology of elections.
In the present state of electoral studies it is both necessary and practicable
to generalize. It is necessary because the steady and increasing accumulation
of studies of voters and elections tend to follow a few lines, ones that rarely
converge and still leave gaps in our knowledge. More studies will not
provide more understanding unless more attention is given to the problem
of synthesizing what we already know, and relating this knowledge to basic
problems of political systems. It is practicable because voting is usually
regarded as one political activity that is suitable to comparison on a cross-
national basis. The many studies of voting and campaigning in a variety of
Western, East European and non-Western nations provide ample material
to test the plausibility, if not the conclusiveness, of generalizations. The
emphasis in this paper upon British survey data is perhaps preferable to the
conventional use of American material, given the fact that British experience of elections, unlike American but like most countries, is rooted in an
elitist tradition.[44]

Voting has much greater significance for the political scientist or the
candidate than it has for the voter. For individuals, the chief functions of
voting[45] are emotional or allegiance-maintaining. Only a limited fraction of
the electorate seems able or willing to act so that their votes can consciously
have for them the function of choosing governors or influencing government
policy. Within the field of social science, a model from social psychology
would seem best suited to the data. In democratic and non-democratic
societies alike, voting is a norm. When this norm is internalized by an
individual and/or supported by strong social pressures, a majority of

individuals will vote, even if lacking in partisanship, anticipating a one-sided result, expressing not much interest in the campaign, having no concern about the election outcome, and a low sense of political efficacy.[46] For such individuals, voting may provide a mild gratification, or simply dissipate tension arising from failing to act according to established norms. In such a model, motivations to vote are not to be evaluated as "rational" or "irrational," but rather as "compelling" or "failing to compel."

The non-political significance of a formally political act is better understood if one follows out the full implications of the Michigan dictum: "Our approach is in the main dependent on the point of view of the actor."[47] The language of political science unfortunately leads us to narrow our attention from the multiplicity of an individual's roles when we speak of him in terms of one relatively minor and intermittent role, that of "voter." The word "voter" refers to an abstraction, just as much as does the term "economic man." The chief social roles of an individual are those of spouse, parent, relative, wage-earner, friend, etc. For most individuals, though not for activists, the role of "citizen" or "subject" is likely to be of little significance; the very limited obligation of his role as voter exhausts his commitment to activity within the political sub-system of society. It would thus be much more accurate and only a little cumbersome if, instead of writing about voting behavior, we wrote about the behavior of ordinary individuals in electoral situations.

It is important to emphasize that this argument does not mean that politics is relatively less important for an individual than participation in other more-or-less voluntary social organizations. A key finding of comparative studies of associational life is that only a minority of the adult population participates in formally organized social groups. The Civic Culture study, for example, found the figure varied from 26 per cent in Mexican urban areas to 57 per cent in America. Except in America, the great majority of individuals belonged to only one organization and had never held an office in it. While not exactly comparable between nations, figures for "civic-political" group membership showed that it was neither among the highest nor the lowest of the eleven types of organizations categorized.[48] Intensive studies of religious behavior and of trade union activities confirm that low levels of active participation in social organizations are not specific to politics. In religion and, by analogy in trade unionism, it is clear that the great majority of individuals do have a group identification, as is the case in politics; yet there too, only a small minority go beyond identification and regularly participate in activities of the groups with which they identify.[49] Depending upon criteria employed, the politically important activists are seen to be minorities of a few per cent to about one-sixth of their society.[50] The great bulk of individuals are much more concerned with primary group relationships outside or even inside formal organizations than they are with the larger, society-wide goals of institutions of which they are aware, but with which they are only intermittently and superficially involved.

The failure of the literature on voting behavior to cope properly with this phenomenon is partly methodological. In a situation in which each adult is eligible to vote, studying voters by means of a national cross-section sample is logical, even though economic constraints on sample size mean that insufficient activists are likely to be found for intensive analysis, and the great majority will be answering questions of far more interest to the surveyors rather than the surveyed. Confronted by an interviewer asking questions about politics, a substantial number of individuals may give a long series of "don't know" answers or else give answers of low intensity, consistency or durability. For example, Converse has found that individuals re-interviewed after a two-year time lag showed correlations of only 0.2 to 0.4 in opinions reported on basic political issues.[51]

Methodological considerations also influence the intellectual predispositions of authors of voting studies. The importance of psychological and statistical training in voting research, as well as the importance of serendipity, has meant that the landmark studies of voting could not have been written by persons trained in the political science of the time. Moreover, research projects were often not strictly motivated by a concern with political problems.[52] A common complaint, as expressed by V. O. Key in 1960, is that most voting studies "have been about behavior in political situations, but only infrequently have they contributed much to the explanations of the political import of the behavior observed".[53]

The social scientists concerned could, with justice, reply that their concentration on studying voters was a natural and desirable reaction to the importance attached to the electorate in formal theories of politics a quarter of a century ago and today. Only recently have studies begun to emerge which focus survey techniques and sociological concepts upon campaigners and office-holders rather than voters.[54]

The reception within the academic community of findings emphasizing the relatively apolitical nature of members of the electorate tells us much about the intellectual climate of opinion prevailing in the world of social science in recent decades. The results were widely interpreted as an attack upon conventional empirical and normative theories of democratic government, and welcomed or denounced according to the reader's predisposition toward iconoclasm or liberalism.[55] Some who felt affronted denied the validity of the survey findings, whereas others denied the relevance. Specially worth quoting is the assertion of two philosophers in a recent British review of the literature:

To claim that sociological findings can show these older political theories to be demonstrably invalid is seriously to misunderstand the most basic features of much political theory, which often touches reality only at the edges and is only at that point open to empirical refutation.[56]

It is worth pointing out that there is a tradition of political theory whose main spokesmen—Walter Bagehot, Graham Wallas and the Anglicized A. L. Lowell and Walter Lippmann—would have had little occasion to be surprised by modern findings about voters. Continental writers, such as Ostrogorski and Michels, seem to have swung from an extreme faith in elections and electors to the extreme of wishing to see them abolished.[57] Schumpeter, whose classic study of *Capitalism, Socialism and Democracy* was first published in 1942 remains untypically relevant to contemporary electoral research findings.

Theories which attribute the function of choice or political influence to voting usually include assumptions about the presumed "rationality" of voters. The crux of the problem is that the term "rationality," while familiar and symbolically potent, is one for which there is no standardized meaning. Usage suggests that "rationality" in voting would require individuals to have a high degree of political information and powers of logical reasoning. Yet Downs has shown that logically it is "irrational" for a voter to meet the criteria of rationality outlined above. Moreover, the authors of *The American Voter* have estimated that only about one-seventh of the electorate can give a reasonably detailed and consistent explanation of their party preferences.[58] The question then arises: Is the valued symbol of rationality to be conferred only upon persons with a high degree of verbal facility in discussing party preferences? Failure to discuss politics intelligently may be regarded as "irrational," but it is not proof that an individual votes "unreasonably." As John Plamenatz has argued, "A choice is reasonable, not because the chooser, when challenged, can give a satisfactory explanation of why he made it, but because *if he could give an explanation*, it would be satisfactory."[59] Studies of voting behavior make it clear that the great majority of voters cannot give satisfactory explanations of their own volition. Yet careful reading of illustrations of levels of conceptualization cited in *The American Voter*, or of any set of life-history interviews, makes it clear that intellectually satisfactory justifications of choice can be elucidated for many inarticulate voters, e.g. illiterate Negroes, bitter coal-miners, elderly spinsters, etc., recorded as conceptualizing politics in terms of group benefits or the nature of the times, as well as in ideological terms. If this criterion is accepted, then approximately three-quarters of the American and, presumably, of other Western electorates could be classified as "reasonable" voters.[60]

In terms of the political system, the chief function of elections is constituent, affecting the structure more than the performance of government, through the provision of a recognized means of performing a necessary political function, succession in leadership, either through confirmation or substitution of men in office. The extent to which elections determine who governs is a matter of degree. In Britain, the two-party system has tended to present a duopolistic choice since 1945. Coalitions of parties and minority governments, influenced by but not determined by election results are characteristic of the majority of competitive party systems, however, and up to 1945 were frequently found in Britain.[61] The fusion of the legislature and the executive means that control of government is undivided, by comparison with America; yet 10 of the 17 times a new Prime Minister has take office in Britain in this century have occurred between elections rather than immediately following a poll. The fact that an election in Britain gives an individual a chance to vote for only one office formally facilitates the accountability of office-holders to voters. But the absence of voter influence upon the nomination of candidates and upon the choice of men to hold key administrative posts reduces the significance of elections, by contrast with, say, America, where primary elections greatly increase voters' choice and influence upon one-party areas, and the long ballot in a federal system gives individuals a form of proportional representation little known in Europe, that arising from being an elector in constituencies very differently constituted and voting for large numbers of nominally administrative officials. It is implicit in the proposition that securing succession is a necessary function of a political system that alternative methods exist, in the absence of competitive elections or parallel with them. Alternatives include hereditary kingship on well defined principles, clan chieftainship, co-option, bloodless coups organized by cliques within government, violent coups, and insurrection and civil war. In many instances, changes in control of government also involve changes in the form of the regime, as in the advent of de Gaulle to office in France in 1958. Dankwart Rustow concludes in his review of "Succession in the Twentieth Century":

In empirical fact, it would seem that in all three parts of the world—democratic, Communist and developing—changes of regime have been more frequent than have orderly changes of government within a continuing regime (i.e. changes resulting from elections).[62]

The influence of elections upon policies prevailing within a political system is extremely complicated, for the basic difficulty is conceptual. The word "policy" is often used to refer to pre-election pledges by campaigners or to statements of intentions by elected officials. It does not follow that differences in policy intentions between competing parties will result in different policy outcomes, i.e. tangible differences in allocation of government resources. Campaigners may abandon pre-election pledges once in office, for good reasons or bad, or official statements of intentions may not be implemented for reasons within or outside their control. Moreover, if one is to argue that policy intentions or outcomes in a given situation would be different with party X rather than party Y in office, one is then comparing observable behavior with hypothetical behavior. It would seem most sensible to regard "policy" as referring to party-capabilities to produce different outcomes when in office. This is conventionally held to be important in elections, although of diminished importance in "end-of-ideology" interpretations of contemporary politics.

From a British point of view, there is substantial evidence to suggest that the policy-influencing function of elections is small. The lengthy historical analysis of public expenditure by Peacock and Wiseman concludes that wars have been of greater force than any other factor in altering the quantity and distribution of public resources.[63] The structure of British central government is weighted against innovation, not only because routine, pattern-maintaining activities dominate many of the bureaucracy's activities, but also because a general election traditionally introduces no more than about seventy new political ministers to "control" more than two dozen departments. There are good theoretical reasons for assuming that this number of persons is too small to redirect many policies; there are practical reasons too, arising from the varying skills and outlooks of ministers in Cabinet government. It may be argued that in the long run electoral competition leads to greater distribution of public benefits among more numerous categories of voters in response to voter influence. Studies of politicians indicate, however, that many do not attend to electoral preferences, or perceive them accurately. Moreover, adjusting policies in response to voter influence is only one of a number of possible strategies open to a political party.[64]

Statistical analyses of the relationship between party competition at elections and expenditure on different forms of public welfare suggest that socio-economic factors account for more variation in expenditure than do levels of party competition or non-competition.[65] The most clear-cut cases where policy may be assumed important occur when Communist or Fascist parties have substantial electoral support. While major policy changes would follow an extremist victory, subsequent elections in a one-party regime would likely be devoid of policy influence. Generally, there is sufficient evidence to suggest that even if the policy-making function of an election is not nil, it is sufficiently low so as to be less important than the function of providing for succession. An election might thus be compared in political significance with the work of a supreme court. Every political system has a highest judicial authority for constituent reasons. Some may be able to void particular acts of government, although others may not. Occasionally this body may make a decision of major importance for the political system, but most policy processes do not involve reference to it, and its decisions have very little or narrowly confined impact on policy decisions.[66]

The significance of elections in building legitimacy is also difficult to measure. There is a strong case argued that the way in which political elites responded to past demands for the vote from the unenfranchised has had major consequences for legitimation or repudiation of the regime, depending upon whether new social groups were welcomed into the electorate, or excluded and driven to alternative and sometimes extra-constitutional outlets.[67] At a minimum, political leaders appear to have believed that some form of balloting, even a plebiscite without effective choice, was helpful in building legitimacy. As Louis Napoleon is reported to have said, "Election was like baptism—it was essential but one did not want to spend one's life in the font."[68] Yet, as in Louis Napoleon's case, it did not follow that this ritual was sufficient to confer full legitimacy on a regime in the throes of development.

History shows sufficient cases of regimes with electoral systems failing to achieve legitimacy, so that elections are a contributory rather than a controlling factor in legitimacy. Contemporary data is unsatisfactory because many regimes and states are so new and under such strains that it is impossible to tell whether they have operational electoral systems and/or legitimacy. The *Cross-Polity* study indicates that among forty-four nations classified as now possessing competitive electoral systems, only fifteen have evidenced political stability since before the Second World War, with an additional nine having had political stability since the war.[69] While the coding for "stability" is not precisely suitable, it is nonetheless close enough to legitimacy to justify the assertion that political systems with competitive elections have not necessarily achieved legitimacy. There remains however the possibility that adoption of competitive elections may contribute to building legitimacy.

When the significance of electoral research for general theories of the political system is discussed, implicitly or occasionally explicitly many writers seem to employ or endorse a simple input-output model of the type best outlined by David Easton.[70] This model is set into operation by the assumption that political societies arise from the unsatisfied demands of individuals and groups. This leads to the creation of a regime. The material outputs of the regime then increase or reduce its support, according to their approximation to demands. The prime mover is the individual with demands; the regime and its governments react and individuals then modify preferences according to their evaluation of regime activity.

The foregoing model has the attractiveness and the unreality of contract theories of government. It is historically very misleading, for constitutional development customarily begins with a group holding power over a given territory. The individual is expected to react to the demands of the regime for taxes, military service, change of religion, etc. In contemporary terms, it seems more meaningful to think in terms of a model in which the prime mover is the regime rather than the individual. The government of the day provides inputs in the form of legal regulations or exhortations which are not legally binding. The individual can then respond in a number of ways—e.g. by parochially remaining unaware of demands, by complying with them, by partial compliance, or by intentional or unintentional action contrary to demands.

Unlike voting, such actions provide continuing feedback to the government. In addition, an individual may react to government through non-electoral political channels such as pressure groups; through extra-constititional, overtly illegal activities; or by "market behavior," i.e. unconcerted actions taken without political intent, but having political consequences. The most obvious examples are activities which lead birth-rates to rise contrary to official projections, with substantial implications for public education, health and welfare policies. In economic market behavior, an individual may vote with his feet by changing jobs, reducing efforts or immigrating. Whereas the disequilibrium arising from a shift in voting preference may be slight and is intermittent, that arising from market behavior can be immediate and invoke tangible and often immediate constraints upon governments.

Such a simple but fundamental rearrangement of relationships has three possible advantages. First, it relates the importance of a vote as an influence resource to other influence resources of an individual. Secondly, it relates elections as a device for influencing governments or governmental mobilization of support, to other forms of governmental–individual interaction. Thirdly, it points out ways in which electoral research findings can be related to other well studied areas of political science, as well as to areas which are currently under-researched.

NOTES

* This article has been written while the first-named author held an American Social Science Research Council grant for the study of legitimacy and allegiance; the data reported in Section II were analyzed by the second author while holding a Fulbright Scholarship at the University of Manchester, 1964–65.

[1] For fuller discussion of important but often neglected comparative and conceptual problems arising from historical analysis, see Stein Rokkan, "The Comparative Study of Political Participation," in *Essays on the Behavioral Study of Politics*, ed. Austin Ranney (Urbana: University of Illinois Press, 1962), pp. 70ff.; Reinhard Bendix, *Nation-Building and Citizenship* (New York: Wiley, 1964), pp. 74ff.; and W. J. M. Mackenzie, "Elections: Theory and Functions" (mimeograph article prepared for publication in the *International Encyclopaedia of the Social Sciences*).

[2] See Joseph A. Schumpeter, *Capitalism, Socialism and Democracy* (London: Allen & Unwin, 4th ed., 1952), Chaps. 21–23; and R. T. McKenzie, *British Political Parties* (London: Heinemann, 1964 ed.), Chap. 11.

[3] For a discussion of the rise and decline of belief in the mandate, see A. H. Birch, *Representative and Responsible Government* (London: Allen & Unwin, 1964), especially pp. 116ff.

[4] See S. M. Lipset, *Political Man* (New York: Doubleday, 1960), especially pp. 280–81, 307; and Talcott Parsons, "Voting and the Equilibrium of the American Political System," in *American Voting Behavior*, eds. Eugene Burdick and A. J. Brodbeck (Glencoe, Illinois: Free Press, 1959), pp. 86ff.

[5] Angus Campbell, *et al.*, *The American Voter* (New York: Wiley, 1960), p. 4. See also, Carl J. Friedrich, *Constitutional Government and Democracy* (New York: Harper, 1937), pp. 203ff.; and Sir Ivor Jennings, *The British Constitution* (Cambridge: Cambridge University Press, 4th ed., 1961), pp. 188–89.

[6] See e.g., Vance Packard, *The Hidden Persuaders* (Harmondsworth, England: Penguin, 1960 ed.), pp. 149ff. The claim has little academic currency, and detailed research has consistently shown it to be unfounded. See, e.g., Joseph T. Klapper, *The Effects of Mass Communication* (Glencoe, Illinois: Free Press, 1960).

[7] See William Tordoff, "The General Election in Tanzania," *Journal of Commonwealth Political Studies*, Vol. IV, no. 2 (1966); Jerzy J. Wiatr, "Elections and Voting Behavior in Poland," pp. 239ff., in Austin Ranney, ed., *op. cit.*; and Howard R. Swearer, "The Functions of Soviet Local Elections," *Midwest Journal of Political Science*, Vol. V, no. 2 (1961), pp. 138ff.

[8] *Political Development in the New States* ('s Gravenhage: Mouton, 1962), p. 38. See also W. J. M. Mackenzie, "Representation in Plural Societies," and "The Export of Electoral Systems," *Political Studies*, Vol. II, no. 2 (1954), and Vol. V, no. 3 (1957).

[9] The title of an article by W. H. Morris-Jones, *Political Studies*, Vol. II, no. 1 (1954). On the movement for compulsory voting, see Herbert Tingsten, *Political Behaviour* (London: P. S. King, 1937), Chap. 4; and, for latter-day discussion, S. M. Lipset, *op. cit.*, Chap. 6.

[10] "The Changing Shape of the American Political Universe," *American Political Science Review*, Vol. LIX, no. 1 (1965). See also Rodney Stiefbold, "The Significance of Void Ballots in West German Elections," *ibid.*, Vol. LIX, no. 2; and, for data on refusing to report votes, G. Almond and S. Verba, *The Civic Culture* (Princeton: Princeton University Press, 1963), p. 117.

[11] For the reference to Greece, see R. B. McCallum, "The Study of Psephology," *Parliamentary Affairs*, Vol. VIII, no. 4 (1955), p. 509. Note also W. J. M. Mackenzie's articles referred to in footnote 8. Mackenzie seems to attribute "more" rather than "less" emotional significance to elections.

[12] The point is aptly illustrated for France, a country in which elections are not the only means of providing succession; see Peter Campbell, *French Electoral Systems and Elections since 1789* (London: Faber, 2nd ed., 1966).

[13] See A. L. Lowell, *Public Opinion and Popular Government* (New York: Longmans, 1914), Chap. 11–15.

[14] Stanley Kelley, *Political Campaigning: Problems in Creating an Informed Elector-ate* (Washington: Brookings Institution, 1960); and "Die Professionalisierung des Wahlkampfes," in *Zur Soziologie der Wahl*, eds. Erwin Scheuch and Rudolph Wilden-mann (Cologne and Opladen: Westdeutscher Verlag, 1965), pp. 50–54.

[15] See Dario Canton, "Universal Suffrage as an Agent of Mobilization" (Evian: Sixth World Congress of Sociology, mimeograph, 1966), pp. 8ff.; and Szymon Chodak, "The Societal Functions of Party Systems in Sub-Saharan Africa," in *Cleavages, Ideologies and Party Systems*, ed. E. Allardt and Y. Littunen (Helsinki: Westermarck Society, 1964), pp. 266ff.

[16] See S. M. Lipset, *op. cit.*, p. 180; and for a case study, Howard Swearer, *op. cit.*, pp. 144ff. Recent elections in Poland are said to seek legitimation without coercion, and, from descriptions, suggest there are significant variations within non-competitive Communist elections. See not only Jerzy Wiatr, *op. cit.*, but also Z. Pelczynski, "Poland, 1957," in *Elections Abroad*, ed. D. E. Butler (London: Macmillan, 1959); and Zygmunt Gostkowski, "Popular Interest in the Municipal Election in Lodz, Poland," *Public Opinion Quarterly*, Vol. XXIII, no. 3 (1959).

[17] S. M. Lipset, *op. cit.*, pp. 130–31; and for a case study, Philip Williams, "The French Presidential Election of 1965," *Parliamentary Affairs*, Vol. XIX, no. 1 (1966). Cf. B. Berelson, *et al.*, *Voting* (Chicago: Chicago University Press, 1954), pp. 312ff.; and Gerald Garvey, "The Theory of Party Equilibrium," *American Political Science Review*, Vol. LX, no. 1 (1966).

[18] The terms allegiance and disaffection are used to denote individual orientations towards regimes, and the terms legitimacy and repudiation for properties of political systems. Explicit and operational definitions are offered, and the senior author is doing continuing research in this field. The terms are used, in preference to the much over-worked words "concensus" and "cleavage," because the latter are rarely defined opera-tionally, and now threaten to obscure rigorous analysis.

[19] For an analysis of the problem of voters with preferences of different intensities all having votes of equal value, see Robert A. Dahl, *A Preface to Democratic Theory* (Chicago: Chicago University Press, 1956), pp. 95ff.

[20] Quoted in D. C. Mulford, *The Northern Rhodesia General Election, 1962* (Nairobi: Oxford University Press, 1964), p. 186.

[21] For data on uncontested elections in Switzerland, see Roger Girod, "Geography of the Swiss Party System," pp. 145ff., in E. Allardt and Y. Littunen, eds., *op. cit.*

[22] Cf. *Public Opinion and American Democracy* (New York: Knopf, 1961), Chap. 21, with *The Responsible Electorate*, with the assistance of Milton C. Cummings Jr. (Cam-bridge, Massachusetts: Harvard University Press, 1966). In the latter book, Key is arguing that it is the parallelism of voters' preferences and party policy that is significant; he explicitly makes no claim that there is a causal link between the two. See also Angus Campbell, *et al.*, *op. cit.*, p. 541.

[23] See *Who Governs?* (New Haven: Yale University Press, 1961), pp. 276ff., and pp. 322–25. Italics in the original. Contrast *Political Oppositions in Western Democracies* (New Haven: Yale University Press, 1966), pp. 339 and 395.

[24] See Bruce Russett, *et al.*, *World Handbook of Political and Social Indicators* (New Haven: Yale University Press, 1964), Table 24; Arthur Banks and Robert Textor, *The Cross-Polity Survey* (Cambridge, Massachusetts: MIT Press, 1963), p. 86; and *A Review of Elections, 1954–58* (London: Institute of Electoral Research, 1960).

[25] Arthur Banks and Robert Textor, *op. cit.*, pp. 86 and 97–98, and Robert Dahl, *Political Oppositions*, p. xi.

[26] This point is made explicitly by T. E. Smith, *Elections in Developing Countries* (London: Macmillan, 1960), p. 255, although he rejects the notion earlier, at pp. 1–2 and p. 207ff. W. J. M. Mackenzie reduces the difference between literate and illiterate voters by querying the sophistication of literates, "Representation in Plural Societies," pp. 67–68. Cf. Mohammed Ayub Khan, "Pakistan Perspective," *Foreign Affairs*, Vol. XXXVIII, no. 4 (1960); and Fred Riggs, "Bureaucrats and Political Development: A

Paradoxical View," in *Bureaucracy and Political Development*, ed. J. LaPalombara (Princeton: Princeton University Press, 1963), pp. 131ff.

[27] *Op. Cit.*, p. 66; and Bruce M. Russett, *et al.*, *op. cit.*, Table 64.

[28] Derived from Arthur Banks and Robert Textor, *op. cit.*, Raw Characteristics 12 and 29; and Bruce Russett, *et al.*, *op. cit.*, Table 64.

[29] The author is obviously indebted to the compilers of such data, for it is useful information to have at hand. Nonetheless, given the presence of sophisticated commentary on sources of data error in Russett, *et al.*, *op. cit.*, pp. 82–83, it is all the more noteworthy that a final caveat was not inserted about problems of functional significance.

[30] See C. A. Moser and Wolf Scott, *British Towns* (Edinburgh: Oliver and Boyd, 1961), pp. 112–13.

[31] Similar answers for Britain, America and Germany were obtained in *The Civic Culture* survey, but that survey reported far higher proportions unambiguously seeing government as improving conditions, since the question employed offered a polarized choice: "31b. On the whole, do the activities of the national government tend to improve conditions in this country or would we be better off without them?" *Op. cit.*, pp. 80ff. and p. 529.

[32] See Richard Rose, *Politics in England* (London: Faber, 1965), Chap. 4. See also G. Almond and S. Verba, *op. cit.*, p. 188, showing that only about 15 per cent of all British respondents claim ever to have tried to influence local government. Germany, Italy and Mexico have fewer activists, when those claiming activity are taken as a percentage of all adult respondents.

[33] *Who Governs?*, p. 228. Attributions of influence were similar in a nation-wide Gallup Poll survey on the same theme, reported in *Gallup Political Index* (London), No. 37, January, 1963, pp. 15–16.

[34] *Op. cit.*, pp. 203ff. For detailed discussion of changers defined in this article as individuals switching support from one party to another, see R. S. Milne and H. C. Mackenzie, "The Floating Vote," *Political Studies*, Vol. III, no. 1; and, more generally, H. Daudt, *Floating Voters and the Floating Vote* (Leiden: Stenfert Kroese, 1961). The definitive account of voting shifts in British elections should appear in the forthcoming study of D. E. Butler and Donald Stokes of the 1964 and 1966 British elections.

[35] The position of the liberal and disaffected alternatives were reversed on questions 2 and 4 in order to avoid response-set bias.

[36] Elections are not the only political institution capable of analysis for symbolic meaning. See e.g. Thurman Arnold, *The Symbols of Government* (New York: 1935); and, more recently, Murray Edelman, *The Symbolic Uses of Politics* (Urbana: Illinois University Press, 1964).

[37] *Op. cit.*, p. 146. The published table reports that 71 per cent in America showed satisfaction when going to the polls, but this percentage is calculated only in relation to recent voters, and they are much fewer in America than elsewhere. The proportion of total respondents expressing satisfaction is only about 44 per cent.

[38] See e.g. Angus Campbell, *et al.*, *op. cit.*, Chap. 5; Angus Campbell, "Surge and Decline: A Study of Electoral Change," *Public Opinion Quarterly*, Vol. XXIV, no. 3 (1960), and R. E. Lane, *op. cit.*, especially pp. 350ff.; and, on London local government, L. J. Sharpe, *A Metropolis Votes* (London School of Economics: Greater London Papers No. 8, 1962), pp. 18ff. Cf. Dilys M. Hill, "Democracy in Local Government" (University of Leeds: Ph.D. thesis, 1966), especially Chaps. 3–4.

[39] See Richard Rose, *Politics in England*, Chap. 10.

[40] See especially, James W. Prothro and Charles W. Grigg, "Fundamental Principles of Democracy," *Journal of Politics*, Vol. XXII, no. 11 (1960).

[41] Full details of classification are contained in Harve Mossawir, *The Significance of an Election* (Manchester: M.A.Econ. thesis, 1965), Chaps. 3–4. The difficulties in classification confirm discussion by G. Almond and S. Verba, *op. cit.*, Chap. 15, that the mixture of outlooks in a political culture is likely to involve the mixing of outlooks within individuals, rather than the mixture in society of individuals who conform closely to different ideal-types.

[42] Quoted from "The World of Politics" (London: Mass Observation typescript, c. 1949), p. 5. The continued success of the Conservatives *vis-à-vis* Labour in inter-war Britain is further evidence in this direction.

[43] Representation in Plural Societies," *op. cit.*, p. 69.

[44] Cf. S. Rokkan, *op. cit.*, with Robert E. Lane, *op. cit.*, Chap. 2, especially p. 9.

[45] That is, the decision to vote or to abstain.

[46] The proportions ranking lowest on these indices who nonetheless voted ranged from 52 to 70 per cent in American elections in 1952 and 1956, according to data in A. Campbell. *et al.*, *op. cit.*, pp. 97–105.

[47] *Ibid.*, pp. 27ff.

[48] G. Almond and S. Verba, *op. cit.*, pp. 302ff. For a more general discussion of organized groups in political life, see William Kornhauser, *The Politics of Mass Society* (London: Routledge, 1960).

[49] Cf. data in Michael Argyle, *Religious Behaviour* (London: Routledge, 1958), especially Chaps. 2–4, and Martin Harrison, *Trade Unions and the Labour Party Since 1945* (London: Allen & Unwin, 1960), Chap. 3, with Richard Rose, *Politics in England*, Chap. 4. Roman Catholics are an exception to this generalization, but it is worth noting that the Church, like some political parties determined to secure very high voting turnout, claims influence upon the totality of an individual's social relationships.

[50] For comparative data, see the special issue on political participation of the *International Social Science Journal*, Vol. XII, no. 1 (1960).

[51] Philip E. Converse, "New Dimensions of Meaning for Cross-Section Sample Surveys in Politics," *International Social Science Journal*, Vol. XVI, no. 1 (1964), p. 23. See also, V. O. Key, Jr., *Public Opinion and American Democracy*, Chaps. 7–11, and, for a hyper-critical statement, D. E. G. Plowman, "Public Opinion and the Polls," *British Journal of Sociology*, Vol. XIII, no. 4 (1962).

[52] For important material on the origins of the Erie County, Elmira and University of Michigan surveys, see Peter Rossi, "Four Landmarks in Voting Research," in E. Burdick and A. J. Brodbeck, *op. cit.*, pp. 15ff. Only two of the eight authors of *The People's Choice*, *Voting*, and *The American Voter* took their Ph.D. in political science. On Britain, see Richard Rose, "The Nuffield Election Studies Come of Age," *The Times*, October 27, 1966.

[53] "The Politically Relevant in Surveys," *Public Opinion Quarterly*, Vol. XXIV, no. 2 (1960), p. 54. Key then proceeds to praise *The American Voter* as an exception to this generalization.

[54] The pioneering effort, a 1958 study of Congressional representation by Warren Miller and Donald Stokes, has yet to be published in book form. See their joint article, "Constituency Influence in Congress," *American Political Science Review*, Vol. LVII, no. 1 (1963), and Miller's article "Majority Rule and the Representative System of Government," in E. Allardt and Y. Littunen, *op. cit.* For British studies, see D. E. Butler and A. S. King, *The British General Election of 1964* (London: Macmillan, 1965), Chaps. 3–6; Richard Rose, *Influencing Voters* (London: Faber, 1967), and the results of a postal survey of M.P.s and candidates, given preliminary analysis in Richard Rose and Dennis Kavanagh, "Campaigning for Parliament," *New Society*, July 28, 1966.

[55] See e.g. various contributors to E. Burdick and A. J. Brodbeck, *op. cit.* and more recently, Arthur Maass's foreword to V. O. Key's *The Responsible Electorate*.

[56] Grame Duncan and Steven Lukes, "The New Democracy," *Political Studies*, Vol. XI, no. 2 (1963), p. 163. The authors make the statement in rejecting an argument by Robert Dahl concerning the need to rethink political theories in the light of findings of voting studies. For an interesting survey on the historical relationship between liberal economic theories and liberal theories of the franchise, see T. W. Hutchison, *Markets and the Franchise* (London: Institute of Economic Affairs, 1966).

[57] For a valuable attempt to explain Michels' shift from "pure democracy" to Fascist leanings, see J. D. May, "Democracy, Organization, Michels," in the *American Political Science Review*, Vol. LIX, no. 2 (1965). More generally, see Giovanni Sartori,

"Electoral Studies and Democratic Theory: A Continental View," in *Political Studies,* Vol. VI, no. 1 (1958).

[58] See *An Economic Theory of Democracy* (New York: Harper, 1957), Part III, and Angus Campbell, *et al., op. cit.,* Chap. 10.

[59] "Electoral Studies and Democratic Theory: A British View," in *Political Studies,* Vol. VI, no. 1 (1958), p. 9. Italics supplied.

[60] See Angus Campbell, *et al., op. cit.,* Table 10.1, p. 249.

[61] See Robert Dahl, *Political Oppositions,* pp. 332ff.

[62] *Journal of International Affairs,* Vol. XVIII, no. 1, p. 107.

[63] See Alan Peacock and Jack Wiseman, *The Growth of Public Expenditure in the United Kingdom* (Princeton: Princeton University Press, 1961).

[64] See Warren Miller, *op. cit.,* pp. 375–76; Richard Rose, *Influencing Voters,* especially Chaps. 8–10, and Robert Dahl, *Political Oppositions,* pp. 344ff.

[65] See Richard Dawson and James Robinson, "Inter-Party Competition, Economic Variables and Welfare Policies in American States," *Journal of Politics,* Vol. XXV, no. 2 (1965).

[66] For a discussion of policy processes independent of elections in the British context, see Richard Rose, *Politics in England,* Chap. 9.

[67] See e.g. Stein Rokkan, *op. cit.,* and Reinhard Bendix, *op. cit.* For case studies, compare Guenther Roth, on "negative integration" of *The Social Democrats in Imperial Germany* (Totowa, N.J.: Bedminster Press, 1963), and T. H. Marshall, *Citizenship and Social Class* (Cambridge: Cambridge University Press, 1950).

[68] Quoted in Peter Campbell, *op cit.,* p. 13.

[69] Derived from data classified as Raw Characteristics 27 and 29, *op. cit.,* pp. 84–87.

[70] "An Approach to the Analysis of Political Systems," *World Politics,* Vol. IX, no. 3 (1957).

CHAPTER 4

Symbols and Political Quiescence

Murray Edelman

Few explanations of political phenomena are more common than the assertion that the success of some group was facilitated by the "apathy" of other groups with opposing interests. If apathy is not observable in a political context because it connotes an individual's mental state, quiescence is observable. This chapter specifies some conditions associated with political quiescence in the formation of business regulation policies. Although the same general conditions are apparently applicable to the formation of public policies in any area, the argument and the examples used here focus upon the field of government regulation of business in order to permit more intensive treatment.

Political quiescence toward a policy area can be assumed to be a function either of lack of interest or of the satisfaction of whatever interest the quiescent group may have in the policy in question. Our concern here is with the forms of satisfaction. In analyzing the various means by which it can come to pass, the following discussion distinguishes between interests in resources (whether goods or freedoms to act) and interests in symbols connoting the suppression of threats to the group in question.

Three related hypotheses will be considered:

(1) The interests of organized groups in tangible resources or in substantive power are less easily satiable than are interests in symbolic reassurance.

(2) Conditions associated with the occurrence of an interest in symbolic reassurance are:

  (a) the existence of economic conditions threatening the security of a large group;

  (b) the absence of organization for the purpose of furthering the common interest of that group.

(3) The pattern of political activity represented by lack of organization, interests in symbolic reassurance, and quiescence is a key element in

Reprinted from Murray Edelman, *The Symbolic Uses of Politics* (Urbana: University of Illinois Press, 1964), Chap. 2, pp. 22–43, by permission of the University of Illinois.

the ability of organized groups to use political agencies in order to make good their claims on tangible resources and power, thus continuing the threat to the unorganized.

Evidence bearing on these hypotheses is marshaled as follows. First, some widely accepted propositions regarding group claims, quiescence, and techniques for satisfying group interests in governmental regulation of business are summarized. Next, some pertinent experimental and empirical findings of other disciplines are considered. Finally, we explore the possibility of integrating the various findings and applying them to the propositions listed above.

I

If the regulatory process is examined in terms of a divergence between political and legal promises on the one hand and resource allocations and group reactions on the other hand, the largely symbolic character of the entire process becomes apparent. What do the studies of government regulation of business tell us of the role and functions of that amorphous group who are affected by these policies, but who are not organized to pursue their interests? The following generalizations would probably be accepted by most students, perhaps with occasional changes of emphasis:

(1) Tangible resources and benefits are frequently not distributed to unorganized political group interests as promised in regulatory statutes and the propaganda attending their enactment.

This is true of the values held out to (or demanded by) groups which regard themselves as disadvantaged and which presumably anticipate benefits from a regulatory policy. There is virtually unanimous agreement among students of the antitrust laws, the Clayton and Federal Trade Commission acts, the Interstate Commerce acts, the public utility statutes and the right-to-work laws, for example, that through much of the history of their administration these statutes have been ineffective in the sense that many of the values they promised have not in fact been realized. The story has not been uniform, of course; but the general point hardly needs detailed documentation at this late date. Herring,[1] Leiserson,[2] Truman,[3] and Bernstein[4] all conclude that few regulatory policies have been pursued unless they proved acceptable to the regulated groups or served the interests of these groups. Redford,[5] Bernstein,[6] and others have offered a "life cycle" theory of regulatory history, showing a more or less regular pattern of loss of vigor by regulatory agencies. For purposes of the present argument it need not be assumed that this always happens but only that it frequently happens in important cases.[7]

(2) When it does happen, the deprived groups often display little tendency to protest or to assert their awareness of the deprivation.

The fervent display of public wrath, or enthusiasm, in the course of the initial legislative attack on forces seen as threatening "the little man" is a common American spectacle. It is about as predictable as the subsequent lapse of the same fervor. Again, it does not always occur, but it happens often enough to call for thorough explanation. The leading students of regulatory processes have all remarked upon it; but most of these scholars, who ordinarily display a close regard for rigor and full exploration, dismiss this highly significant political behavior rather casually. Thus, Redford declares that, "In the course of time the administrator finds that the initial public drive and congressional sentiment behind his directive has wilted and that political support for change from the existing pattern is lacking."[8]

Although the presumed beneficiaries of regulatory legislation often show little or no concern with its failure to protect them, they are nevertheless assumed to constitute a potential base of political support for the retention of these statutes in the law books. The professional politician is probably quite correct when he acts on the assumption that his advocacy of this regulatory legislation, in principle, is a widely popular move, even though actual resource allocations inconsistent with the promise of the statutes are met with quiescence. These responses (support of the statute together with apathy toward failure to allocate resources as the statute promises) define the meanings of the law so far as the presumed beneficiaries are concerned.[9] It is the frequent inconsistency between the two types of response that is puzzling.

(3) The most intensive dissemination of symbols commonly attends the enactment of legislation which is most meaningless in its effects upon resource allocation. In the legislative history of particular regulatory statutes the provisions least significant for resource allocation are most widely publicized and the most significant provisions are least widely publicized.

The statutes listed under Proposition 1 as having promised something substantially different from what was delivered are also the ones which have been most intensively publicized as symbolizing protection of widely shared interests. Trust-busting, "Labor's Magna Carta" (the Clayton Act), protection against price discrimination and deceptive trade practices, protection against excessive public utility charges, tight control of union bureaucracies (or, by other groups, the "slave labor law"), federal income taxation according to "ability to pay," are the terms and symbols widely disseminated to the public as descriptive of much of the leading federal and state regulation of the last seven decades, and they are precisely the descriptions shown by careful students to be most misleading. Nor is it any less misleading if one quotes the exact language of the most widely publicized specific provisions of these laws: Section 1 of the Sherman Act,

Sections 6 and 20 of the Clayton Act, or the closed shop, secondary boycott, or emergency strike provisions of Taft–Hartley, for example. In none of these instances would a reading of either the text of the statutory provision or the attendant claims and publicity enable an observer to predict even the direction of future regulatory policy, let alone its precise objectives.

Other features of these statutes also stand as the symbols of threats stalemated, if not checkmated, by the forces of right and justice. Typically, a preamble (which does not pretend to be more than symbolic, even in legal theory) includes strong assurances that the public or the public interest will be protected, and the most widely publicized regulatory provisions always include other non-operational standards connoting fairness, balance, or equity.

If one asks, on the other hand, for examples of changes in resource allocations that have been influenced substantially and directly by public policy, it quickly appears that the outstanding examples have been publicized relatively little. One thinks of such legislation as the silver purchase provisions, the court definitions of the word "lawful" in the Clayton Act's labor sections, the procedural provisions of Taft–Hartley and the Railway Labor Act, the severe postwar cuts in grazing service appropriations, and changes in the parity formula requiring that such items as interest, taxes, freight rates, and wages be included as components of the index of prices paid by farmers.

Illuminating descriptions of the operational meaning of statutory mandates are found in Truman's study and in Earl Latham's *The Group Basis of Politics*.[10] Both emphasize the importance of contending groups and organizations in day-to-day decision-making as the dynamic element in policy formation; and both distinguish this element from statutory language as such.[11]

We are only beginning to get some serious studies of the familiarity of voters with current public issues and of the intensity of their feelings about issues; but successful political professionals have evidently long acted on the assumption that there is in fact relatively little familiarity, that expressions of deep concern are rare, that quiescence is common, and that, in general, the congressman can count upon stereotyped reactions rather than persistent, organized pursuit of material interests on the part of most constituents.[12]

(4) Policies severely denying resources to large numbers of people can be pursued indefinitely without serious controversy.

The silver purchase policy, the farm policy, and a great many other subsidies are obvious examples. The antitrust laws, utility regulations, and other statutes ostensibly intended to protect the small operator or the consumer are less obvious examples, though there is ample evidence, some of it cited below, that these usually support the proposition as well.

The federal income tax law offers a rather neat illustration of the divergence between a widely publicized symbol and actual resource allocation patterns. The historic constitutional struggle leading up to the Sixteenth Amendment, the warm defenses of the principle of ability to pay, and the frequent attacks upon the principle through such widely discussed proposals as that for a 25 per cent limit on rates have made the federal tax law a major symbol of justice. While the fervent rhetoric from both sides turns upon the symbol of a progressive tax and bolsters the assumption that the system is highly progressive, the bite of the law into people's resources depends upon quite other provisions and activities that are little publicized and that often seriously qualify its progressive character. Special tax treatments arise from such devices as family partnerships, gifts *inter vivos*, income-splitting, multiple trusts, percentage depletion, and deferred compensation.

Tax evasion alone goes far toward making the symbol of "ability to pay" hollow semantically though potent symbolically. While 95 per cent of income from wages and salaries is taxed as provided by law, taxes are actually collected on only 67 per cent of taxable income from interest, dividends, and fiduciary investments and on only about 36 per cent of taxable farm income.[13] By and large, the recipients of larger incomes can most easily benefit from exemptions, avoidance, and evasions. This may or may not be desirable public policy, but it certainly marks a disparity between symbol and effect upon resources.

II

These phenomena are significant for the study of the political process for two reasons. First, there is a substantial degree of consistency in the group interest patterns associated with policies on highly diverse subject matters. Second, they suggest that nonrational reaction to symbols among people sharing a common governmental interest is a key element in the process. The disciplines of sociology, social psychology, and semantics have produced some pertinent data on the second point, to which we now turn.

Harold Lasswell wrote three decades ago that "Politics is the process by which the irrational bases of society are brought out into the open." He marshaled some support in case studies for several propositions that have since been confirmed with richer and more direct experimental evidence. "The rational and dialectical phases of politics," he said, "are subsidiary to the process of redefining an emotional consensus." He argued that "widespread and disturbing changes in the life-situation of many members of society" produce adjustment problems which are resolved largely through symbolization, and he suggested that "Political demands probably bear but a limited relevance to social needs."[14]

The frame of reference suggested by these statements is sometimes accepted by political scientists today when they study voting behavior and when they analyze the legislative process. Its bearing on policy formation in the administrative process is not so widely recognized. It is true that cognition and rationality are central to administrative procedures to a degree not true of legislation or voting. But this is not the same thing as saying that administrative policies or administrative politics are necessarily insulated from the "process of redefining an emotional consensus."

Let us consider now some experimental findings and conclusions specifying conditions under which groups or personality types are prone to respond strongly to symbolic appeals and to distort or ignore reality in a fashion that can be politically significant.

(1) People read their own meanings into situations that are unclear or provocative of emotion. As phrased by Fensterheim, "The less well defined the stimulus situation, or the more emotionally laden, the greater will be the contribution of the perceiver."[15] This proposition is no longer doubted by psychologists. It is the justification for so-called projective techniques and is supported by a great deal of experimental evidence.

Now it is precisely in emotionally laden and poorly defined situations that the most widely and loudly publicized public regulatory policies are launched and administered. If, as we have every reason to suppose, there is little cognitive familiarity with issues, the "interest" of most of the public is likely to be a function of other sociopsychological factors. What these other factors are is suggested by certain additional findings.

(2) It is characteristic of large numbers of people in our society that they see and think in terms of stereotypes, personalization, and oversimplifications, that they cannot recognize or tolerate ambiguous and complex situations, and that they accordingly respond chiefly to symbols that oversimplify and distort. This form of behavior (together with other characteristics less relevant to the political process) is especially likely to occur where there is insecurity occasioned by failure to adjust to real or perceived problems.[16] Frenkel-Brunswik has noted that "such objective factors as economic conditions" may contribute to the appearance of the syndrome, and hence to its importance as a widespread group phenomenon attending the formulation of public policy.[17] Such behavior is sufficiently persistent and widespread to be politically significant only when there is social reinforcement of faith in the symbol. When insecurity is individual, without communication and reinforcement from others, there is little correlation with ethnocentricity or its characteristics.[18]

A different kind of study suggests the extent to which reality can become irrelevant for persons very strongly committed to an emotion-satisfying symbol. Festinger and his associates, as participant-observers, studied a group of fifteen persons who were persuaded that the world would come to an end on a particular day in 1956 and that they as believers would be carried away in a flying saucer. With few exceptions the participants refused to give up their belief even after the appointed day had passed. The Festinger study concludes that commitment to a belief is likely to be strengthened and reaffirmed in the face of clear disproof of its validity where there is a strong prior commitment (many of the individuals involved had actually given away their worldly goods) and where there is continuing social support of the commitment by others (two members who lost faith lived where they had no further contact with fellow members of the group; those who retained their faith had continued to see each other). What we know of previous messianic movements of this sort supports this hypothesis.[19]

(3) Emotional commitment to a symbol is associated with contentment and quiescence regarding problems that would otherwise arouse concern.

It is a striking fact that this effect has been noticed and stressed by careful observers in a number of disparate fields, using quite different data and methods. Adorno reports it as an important finding in *The Authoritarian Personality*: "Since political and economic events make themselves felt apparently down to the most private and intimate realms of the individual, there is reliance upon stereotype and similar avoidance of reality to alleviate psychologically the feeling of anxiety and uncertainty and provide the individual with the illusion of some kind of intellectual security."[20]

In addition to the support it gets from psychological experiment, the phenomenon has been remarked by scholars in the fields of semantics, organizational theory, and political science. Albert Salomon points out that "Manipulation of social images makes it possible for members of society to believe that they live not in a jungle, but in a well organized and good society."[21] Harold Lasswell put it as follows:

It should not be hastily assumed that because a particular set of controversies passes out of the public mind that the implied problems were solved in any fundamental sense. Quite often a solution is a magical solution which changes nothing in the conditions affecting the tension level of the community, and which merely permits the community to distract its attention to another set of equally irrelevant symbols. The number of statutes which pass the legislature, or the number of decrees which are handed down by the executive, but which change nothing in the permanent practices of society, is a rough index of the role of magic in politics. . . . Political symbolization has its catharsis function. . . .[22]

Chester Barnard, an uncommonly astute analyst of his own long experience as an executive, concluded that "Neither authority nor co-operative disposition . . . will stand much overt division on formal issues in the present stage of human development. Most laws, executive orders, decisions, etc., are in effect formal notice that all is well—there is agreement, authority is not questioned."[23]

Kenneth Burke makes much the same point. Designating political rhetoric as "secular prayer," he declares that its function is "to sharpen up the pointless and blunt the too sharply pointed."[24] Elsewhere, he points out that laws themselves serve this function, alleging that positive law is *itself* "the test of a judgment's judiciousness."[25]

(4) An active demand for increased economic resources or fewer political restrictions on action is not always operative. It is, rather, a function of comparison and contrast with reference groups, usually those not far removed in socioeconomic status.

This is, of course, one of the most firmly established propositions about social dynamics; one that has been supported by macrosociological analysis,[26] by psychological experiment,[27] and by observation of the political process, particularly through contrast between political quiescence and protest or revolutionary activity.[28]

The proposition helps explain failure to demand additional resources where such behavior is socially sanctioned and supported. It also helps explain the insatiability of the demand by some organized groups for additional resources (i.e., the absence of quiescence) where there is competition for such resources among rival organizations and where it is acquisitiveness that is socially supported.

(5) The phenomena discussed above (the supplying of meaning in vague situations, stereotypes, oversimplification, political quiescence) are in large measure associated with social, economic, or cultural factors affecting large segments of the population. They acquire political meaning as group phenomena.

Even among the psychologists, some of whom have been notably insensitive to socialization and environment as explanations and phases of the individual traits they identify, there are impressive experimental findings to support the proposition. In analyzing the interview material of his *authoritarian personality* study, Adorno concluded that "our general cultural climate" is basic in political ideology and in stereotyped political thinking, and he catalogued some standardizing aspects of that climate.[29] His finding, quoted above, regarding the relation of symbols to quiescence is also phrased to emphasize its social character. Lindesmith and Strauss make a similar point, emphasizing the association between symbols and the reference groups to which people adhere.[30]

Another type of research has demonstrated that because interests are typically bound up with people's social situation, attitudes are not typically changed by ex parte appeals. The function of propaganda is rather to activate socially rooted interests. One empirical study which arrives at this conclusion sums up the thesis as follows: "Political writers have the task of providing 'rational' men with good and acceptable reasons to dress up the choice which is more effectively determined by underlying social affiliations."[31]

George Herbert Mead makes the fundamental point that symbolization itself has no meaning apart from social activity: "Symbolization constitutes objects . . . which would not exist except for the context of social relationships wherein symbolization occurs."[32]

III

These studies offer a basis for understanding more clearly what it is that different types of groups expect from government and under what circumstances they are likely to be satisfied or restive about what is forthcoming. Two broad patterns of group interest activity vis-à-vis public regulatory policy are evidently identifiable on the basis of these various modes of observing the social scene. The two patterns may be summarized in the following shorthand fashion:

(1) Pattern A: a relatively high degree of organization—rational, cognitive procedures—precise information—an effective interest in specifically identified, tangible resources—a favorably perceived strategic position with respect to reference groups—relatively small numbers.

(2) Pattern B: shared interest in improvement of status through protest activity—an unfavorably perceived strategic position with respect to reference groups—distorted, stereotyped, inexact information and perception—response to symbols connoting suppression of threats—relative ineffectiveness in securing tangible resources through political activity—little organization for purposeful action—quiescence—relatively large numbers.

It is very likely misleading to assume that some of these observations can be regarded as causes or consequences of others. That they often occur together is both a more accurate observation and more significant. It is also evident that each of the patterns is realized in different degrees at different times.

While political scientists and students of organizational theory have gone far toward a sophisticated description and analysis of Pattern A there is far less agreement and precision in describing and analyzing Pattern B and in explaining how it intermeshes with Pattern A.

The most common explanation of the relative inability of large numbers of people to realize their economic aspirations in public policy is in terms of invisibility. The explanation is usually implicit rather than explicit, but it evidently assumes that public regulatory policy facilitating the exploitation of resources by knowledgeable organized groups (usually the "regulated") at the expense of taxpayers, consumers, or other unorganized groups is possible only because the latter do not really know it is happening. What is invisible to them does not arouse either interest or political sanctions.

On a superficial level of explanation this assumption is no doubt valid. But it is an example of the danger to the social scientist of failure to inquire transactionally: of assuming, in this instance, (1) that an answer to a questioner, or a questionnaire, about what an individual "knows" of a regulatory policy at any point in time is in any sense equivalent to specification of a group political interest: and (2) that the sum of many individual knowings (or not knowings) as reported to a questioner is a *cause* of effective (or ineffective) organization, rather than a consequence of it, or simply a concomitant phase of the same environment. If one is interested in policy formation, what count are the assumptions of legislators and administrators about the determinants of future political disaffection and political sanctions. Observable political behavior, as well as psychological findings, reveal something of these assumptions.

There is, in fact, persuasive evidence of the reality of a political interest in continuing assurances of protection against economic forces understood as powerful and threatening. The most relevant evidence lies in the continuing utility of old political issues in campaigns. Monopoly and economic concentration, antitrust policy, public utility regulation, banking controls, and curbs on management and labor are themes that party professionals regard as good for votes in one campaign after another, and doubtless with good reason. They know that these are areas in which concern is easily stirred. In evaluating allegations that the public has lost "interest" in these policies the politician has only to ask himself how much apathy would remain if an effort were made formally to repeal the antitrust, public utility, banking, or labor laws. The answers and the point become clear at once.

The laws may be repealed in effect by administrative policy, budgetary starvation, or other little publicized means; but the laws as symbols must stand because they satisfy interests that are very strong indeed: interests that politicians fear will be expressed actively if a large number of voters are led to believe that their shield against a threat has been removed.

More than that, it is largely as symbols of this sort that these statutes have utility to most of the voters. If they function as reassurances that threats in the economic environment are under control, their indirect effect is to permit greater claims upon tangible resources by the organized groups concerned than would be possible if the legal symbols were absent.

To say this is not to assume that everyone objectively affected by a policy is simply quiescent rather than apathetic or even completely unaware of the issue. It is to say that those who are potentially able and willing to apply political sanctions constitute the politically significant group. It is to suggest as well that incumbent or aspiring congressmen are less concerned with individual constituents' familiarity or unfamiliarity with an issue as of any given moment than with the possibility that the interest of a substantial number of them *could* be aroused and organized if he should cast a potentially unpopular vote on a bill or if a change in their economic situation should occur. The shrewder and more effective politicians probably appreciate intuitively the validity of the psychological finding noted earlier: that where public understanding is vague and information rare, interests in reassurance will be all the more potent and all the more susceptible to manipulation by political symbols.

We have already noted that it is one of the demonstrable functions of symbolization that it induces a feeling of well-being: the resolution of tension. Not only is this a major function of widely publicized regulatory statutes, but it is also a major function of their administration. Some of the most widely publicized administrative activities can most confidently be expected to convey a sense of well-being to the onlooker because they suggest vigorous activity while in fact signifying inactivity or protection of the "regulated."

One form this phenomenon takes is noisy attacks on trivia. The Federal Trade Commission, for example, has long been noted for its hit-and-miss attacks on many relatively small firms involved in deceptive advertising or unfair trade practices while it continues to overlook much of the really significant activity it is ostensibly established to regulate: monopoly, interlocking directorates, and so on.[33]

Another form it takes is prolonged, repeated, well-publicized attention to a significant problem which is never solved. A notable example is the approach of the Federal Communications Commission to surveillance of program content in general and to discussion of public issues on the air in particular. In the postwar period we have had the Blue Book, and the Mayflower Policy, the abolition of the Mayflower Policy, and the announcement of a substitute policy; but the radio or television licensee is in practice perfectly free, as he has been all along, to editorialize, with or without opportunity for opposing views to be heard, or to avoid serious discussion of public affairs entirely.

The most obvious kinds of dissemination of symbolic satisfactions are to be found in administrative dicta accompanying decisions and orders, in press releases, and in annual reports. It is not uncommon to give the rhetoric to one side and the decision to the other. Nowhere does the FCC wax so emphatic in emphasizing public service responsibility, for example, as in decisions permitting greater concentration of control in an area, condoning license transfers at inflated prices, refusing to impose sanctions for flagrantly sacrificing program quality to profits, and so on.[34]

The integral connection is apparent between symbolic satisfaction of the disorganized, on the one hand, and the success of the organized, on the other, in using governmental instrumentalities as aids in securing the tangible resources they claim.

Public policy may usefully be understood as the resultant of the interplay among groups.[35] But the political and sociopsychological processes discussed here mean that groups which present claims upon resources may be rendered quiescent by their success in securing non-tangible values. Far from representing an obstacle to organized producers and sellers, they become defenders of the very system of law which permits the organized to pursue their interests effectively.

Thurman Arnold has pointed out how the antitrust laws perform precisely this function:

The actual result of the antitrust laws was to promote the growth of great industrial organizations by deflecting the attack on them into purely moral and ceremonial channels . . . every scheme for direct control broke to pieces on the great protective rock of the antitrust laws. . . .

The antitrust laws remained as a most important symbol. Whenever anyone demanded practical regulation, they formed an effective moral obstacle, since all the liberals would answer with a demand that the antitrust laws be enforced. Men like Senator Borah founded political careers on the continuance of such crusades, which were entirely futile but enormously picturesque, and which paid big dividends in terms of personal prestige.[36]

Arnold's subsequent career as chief of the antitrust division of the Department of Justice did as much to prove his point as his writings. For a five-year period he instilled unprecedented vigor into the division, and his efforts were widely publicized. He thereby unquestionably made the laws a more important symbol of the protection of the public; but despite his impressive intentions and talents, monopoly, concentration of capital, and restraint of trade were not seriously threatened or affected.

This is not to suggest that signs or symbols in themselves have any magical force as narcotics. They are, rather, the only means by which groups not in a position to analyze a complex situation rationally may adjust themselves to it, through stereotypization, oversimplification, and reassurance.

There have, of course, been many instances of effective administration and enforcement of regulatory statutes. In each such instance it will be found that organized groups have had an informed interest in effective administration. Sometimes the existence of these groups is explicable as a holdover from the campaign for legislative enactment of the basic statute; and often the initial administrative appointees are informed, dedicated adherents of these interests. They are thus in a position to secure pertinent data and to act strategically, helping furnish "organization" to the groups they represent. Sometimes the resources involved are such that there is organization on both sides; or the more effective organization may be on the "reform" side. The securities exchange legislation is an illuminating example, for after Richard Whitney's conviction for embezzlement, key officials of the New York Stock Exchange recognized their own interest in supporting controls over less scrupulous elements. This interest configuration doubtless explains the relative popularity of the SEC in the 1930's both with regulated groups and with organized liberal groups.

IV

The evidence considered here suggests that we can make an encouraging start toward defining the conditions in which myth and symbolic reassurance become key elements in the governmental process. The conditions[37] are present in substantial degree in many policy areas other than business regulation. They may well be maximal in the foreign policy area, and a similar approach to the study of foreign policy formation would doubtless be revealing.

Because the requisite conditions are always present in some degree, every instance of policy formulations involves a "mix" of symbolic effect and rational reflection of interests in resources, though one or the other may be dominant in any particular case. One type of mix is exemplified by such governmental programs outside the business regulation field as public education and social security. There can be no doubt that these programs do confer important tangible benefits upon a very wide public, very much as they promise to do. They do so for the reasons suggested earlier. Business organizations, labor organizations, teachers' organizations, and other organized groups benefit from these programs and have historically served to focus public attention upon the resources to be gained or lost. Their task has been all the easier because the techniques for achieving the benefits are fairly readily recognizable.

But the financing of these same programs involves public policies of a different order. Here the symbol of "free" education and other benefits, the complexity of the revenue and administrative structure, and the absence of organization have facilitated the emergence of highly regressive payroll, property, and head taxes as the major sources of revenue. Thus, business organizations, which by and large support the public schools that provide their trained personnel and the social security programs that minimize the costs of industrial pensions, pay relatively little for these services, while the direct beneficiaries of the "free" programs pay a relatively high proportion of the costs. Careful analysis of the "mix" in particular programs should prove illuminating.

If the conditions facilitating symbolic reassurance are correctly specified, there is reason to question some common assumptions about strategic variables in policy formulation and reason also to devise some more imaginative models in designing research in this area. The theory discussed here suggests, for example, a tie between the emergence of conditions promoting interests in symbolic reassurance and widened freedom of policy maneuver for the organized. It implies that the number of adherents of a political interest may have more to do with whether the political benefit offered is tangible or symbolic than with the quantity or quality of tangible resources allocated. It suggests that the factors that explain voting behavior can be quite different from the factors that explain resource allocations through government. The fact that large numbers of people are objectively affected by a governmental program may actually serve in some contexts to weaken their capacity to exert a political claim upon tangible values.

A number of recent writers, to take another example, have suggested that it is the "independence" of the independent regulatory commissions which chiefly accounts for their tendency to become tools of the groups they regulate. The hypotheses suggested here apply to regulatory programs administered in cabinet departments as well; and their operation is discernible in some of these programs when the specified conditions are present. The grazing service and the antitrust division are examples.

In terms of research design, the implications of the analysis probably lie chiefly in the direction of emphasizing an integral tie of political behavior to underlying and extensive social interaction. Analysts of political dynamics must have a theory of relevance; but the directly relevant may run farther afield than has sometimes been assumed. Political activities of all kinds require the most exhaustive scrutiny to ascertain whether their chief function is symbolic or substantive. The "what" of Lasswell's famous definition of politics is a complex universe in itself.

NOTES

[1] E. Pendleton Herring, *Public Administration and the Public Interest* (New York, 1936), p. 213.

[2] Avery Leiserson, *Administrative Regulation: A Study in Representation of Interests* (Chicago, 1942), p. 14.

[3] David Truman, *The Governmental Process* (New York, 1951), Chap. 5.

[4] Marver Bernstein, *Regulating Business by Independent Commissions* (New York, 1955), Chap. 3.

[5] Emmette S. Redford, *Administration of National Economic Control* (New York, 1952), pp. 385–86.

[6] Bernstein, *op. cit.*

[7] In addition to the statements in these analytical treatments of the administrative process, evidence for the proposition that regulatory statutes often fail to have their promised consequences in terms of resource allocation are found in general studies of government regulation of business and in empirical research on particular statutes. As an example of the former see Clair Wilcox, *Public Policies Toward Business* (Chicago, 1955). As examples of the latter, see Frederic Meyers, *"Right to Work" in Practice* (New York, 1959); Walton Hamilton and Irene Till, *Antitrust in Action*, TNEC Monograph 16 (Washington D.C., GPO, 1950).

[8] Redford, *op. cit.*, p. 383. Similar explanations appear in Herring, *op. cit.*, p. 227, and Bernstein, *op. cit.*, pp. 82–83. Some writers have briefly suggested more rigorous explanations, consistent with the hypotheses discussed in this paper, though they do not consider the possible role of interests in symbolic reassurance. Thus Truman calls attention to organizational factors, emphasizing the ineffectiveness of interest groups "whose interactions on the basis of the interest are not sufficiently frequent or stabilized to produce an intervening organization and whose multiple memberships, on the same account, are a constant threat to the strength of the claim." Truman, *op. cit.*, p. 441. Multiple group memberships are, of course, characteristic of individuals in all organizations, stable and unstable; and "infrequent interactions" is a phenomenon that itself calls for explanation if a common interest is recognized. Bernstein, *loc. cit.*, refers to the "undramatic nature" of administration and to the assumption that the administrative agency will protect the public.

[9] Compare the discussion of meaning in George Herbert Mead, *Mind, Self and Society* (Chicago, 1934), pp. 78–79.

[10] Truman, *op. cit.*, pp. 439–46; Earl Latham, *The Group Basis of Politics* (Ithaca, N.Y., 1952), Chap. 1.

[11] I have explored this effect in labor legislation in "Interest Representation and Labor Law Administration," *Labor Law Journal*, Vol. 9 (1958), pp. 218–26.

[12] See Lewis A. Dexter, "Candidates Must Make the Issues and Give Them Meaning," *Public Opinion Quarterly*, Vol. 10 (1955–56), pp. 408–14.

[13] Randolph E. Paul, "Erosion of the Tax Base and Rate Structure," in Joint Committee on the Economic Report, *Federal Tax Policy for Economic Growth and Stability*, 84th Congress, 1st Session, 1955, pp. 123–38.

[14] *Psychopathology and Politics* (New York, 1960), pp. 184, 185.

[15] Herbert Fensterheim, "The Influence of Value Systems on the Perception of People," *Journal of Abnormal and Social Psychology*, Vol. 48 (1953), p. 93. Fensterheim cites the following studies in support of the proposition: D. Krech and R. S. Crutchfield, *Theory and Problems of Social Psychology* (New York, 1948); A. S. Luchins, "An Evaluation of Some Current Criticisms of Gestalt Psychological Work on Perception," *Psychological Review*, Vol. 58 (1951), pp. 69–95; J. S. Bruner, "One Kind of Perception: A Reply to Professor Luchins," *Psychological Review*, Vol. 58 (1951), pp. 306–12; and chapters by Bruner, Frenkel-Brunswik, and Klein in R. R. Blake and G. V. Ramsey, *Perception: An Approach to Personality* (New York, 1951). See also Charles Osgood, Percy Tannenbaum, and George Suci, *The Measurement of Meaning* (Urbana, Ill., 1957).

[16] Among the leading general and experimental studies dealing with the phenomenon are: M. Rokeach, "Generalized Mental Rigidity as a Factor in Ethnocentrism," *Journal of Abnormal and Social Psychology*, Vol. 43 (1948), pp. 259–77; R. R. Canning and J. M. Baker, "Effect of the Group on Authoritarian and Non-authoritarian Persons," *American Journal of Sociology*, Vol. 64 (1959), pp. 579–81; A. H. Maslow, "The Authoritarian Character Structure," *Journal of Social Psychology*, Vol. 18 (1942), p. 403; T. W. Adorno and others, *The Authoritarian Personality* (New York, 1953), pp. 123–38; Erich Fromm, *Escape from Freedom* (New York, 1941); R. K. Merton, *Mass Persuasion* (New York, 1950).

[17] Else Frenkel-Brunswik, "Interaction of Psychological and Sociological Factors in Political Behavior," *The American Political Science Review*, Vol. 46 (1952), pp. 44–65.

[18] Adorno and others, *op. cit.*

[19] Leon Festinger, Henry Riecken, and Stanley Schachter, *When Prophecy Fails* (Minneapolis, 1956).

[20] Adorno and others, *op. cit.*, p. 665.

[21] Albert Salomon, "Symbols and Images in the Constitution of Society," in L. Bryson, L. Finkelstein, H. Hoagland, and R. M. MacIver (eds.), *Symbols and Society* (New York, 1955), p. 110.

[22] Lasswell, *op. cit.*, p. 195.

[23] Chester I. Barnard, *The Functions of the Executive* (Cambridge, Mass., 1938), p. 226.

[24] Kenneth Burke, *A Grammar of Motives* (New York, 1945), p. 393.

[25] *Ibid.*, p. 362.

[26] Mead, *op. cit.*; Ernst Cassirer, *An Essay on Man*.

[27] See James G. March and Herbert A. Simon, *Organizations* (New York, 1958), pp. 65–81.

[28] See, e.g., Murray Edelman, "Causes in Fluctuations of Popular Support for the Italian Communist Party Since 1946," *Journal of Politics*, Vol. 20 (1958), pp. 547–50; Arthur M. Ross, *Trade Union Wage Policy* (Berkeley and Los Angeles, 1948).

[29] Adorno and others, *op. cit.*, p. 655.

[30] Alfred R. Lindesmith and Anselm L. Strauss, *Social Psychology* (New York, 1956), pp. 253–55. For a report of another psychological experiment demonstrating that attitudes are a function of group norms, see I. Sarnoff, D. Katz, and C. McClintock, "Attitude-Change Procedures and Motivating Patterns," in Daniel Katz and others (eds.), *Public Opinion and Propaganda* (New York, 1954), pp. 308–9; also Festinger, Riecken, and Schachter, *op. cit.*

[31] Paul F. Lazarsfeld, Bernard Berelson, and Hazel Gaudet, *The People's Choice* (New York, 1944), p. 83. For an account of an experiment reaching the same conclusion see S. M. Lipset, "Opinion Formation in a Crisis Situation," *Public Opinion Quarterly*, Vol. 17 (1953), pp. 20–46.

[32] Mead, *op. cit.*, p. 78.

[33] Cf. Wilcox, *op. cit.*, pp. 281, 252–55.

[34] Many examples may be found in the writer's study entitled *The Licensing of Radio Services in the United States, 1927 to 1947* (Urbana, Ill., 1950).

[35] For discussion of the utility of this view to social scientists, see Arthur F. Bentley, *The Process of Government* (1908; New York, reprint 1949); Truman, *op. cit.*

[36] *The Folklore of Capitalism* (New Haven, Conn., 1937), pp. 212, 215, 216.

[37] They are listed above under "Pattern B."

CHAPTER 5

Patterns of Opposition

Robert A. Dahl

If one reflects on the differences in the patterns of opposition in the ten countries examined here, the first, the most obvious, and yet the most striking conclusion is likely to be a new awareness of the great variety of different patterns of opposition in democratic systems. The answer to one of the questions posed in the first chapter is clear and unmistakable: there is no single prevailing pattern of opposition in Western democracies.

Can we make order out of the variety we have discovered? The patterns of opposition in the countries discussed in the preceding chapters—not to mention those in the score of democratic countries we have had to ignore—are too complex to repose easily within any classification scheme. Nevertheless, the simplification provided by a typology will prove useful in exploring some of the other questions set out in an earlier chapter. The present chapter will be devoted, therefore, to a search for a helpful way to classify the patterns of opposition revealed in this volume.

Oppositions, it appears, differ in at least six important ways:

1. The organizational cohesion or concentration of the opponents.
2. The competitiveness of the opposition.
3. The site or setting for the encounter between opposition and those who control the government.
4. The distinctiveness or identifiability of the opposition.
5. The goals of the opposition.
6. The strategies of opposition.

Let us examine each of these.

CONCENTRATION

Opponents of a government may display varying degrees of organizational cohesion; they may all be concentrated in a single organization, for example,

Reprinted from *Political Oppositions in Western Democracies*, edited by Robert A. Dahl (New Haven: Yale University Press, 1966), Chap. 11, pp. 332–347, by permission of Yale University Press. Copyright © 1966 by Yale University.

or they may be dispersed in a number of organizations operating independently of one another.

Probably in no country, and certainly in no democratic country, are all the active opponents of government ever concentrated in one organization. If we concern ourselves with political parties, however, the situation is rather different. Because a political party is the most visible manifestation and surely one of the most effective forms of opposition in a democratic country, it is this particular form with which we have been most concerned in this book. However, the extent to which opposition is concentrated depends on the party system of a country. Although genuine one-party systems probably cannot exist and certainly do not now exist except where governments prohibit opposition parties, in a few countries where key civil liberties are by no means wholly impaired, as in Mexico, a single party has enjoyed a near monopoly of votes, or, as in India, of parliamentary seats. In each of these countries, although some opposition is concentrated in small parties, a good deal of opposition operates as factions within the dominant party. The highest degree of concentration of opposition exists in two-party systems, where the out-party has a substantial monopoly of the opposition. In multi-party systems, opposition is likely to be dispersed among several parties.

In the English-speaking world, all thought about opposition has been dominated, at least in this century, by simple two-party models—to which multi-party systems are a kind of unsatisfactory and probably temporary exception. And this view, so confidently held in Britain and the United States, has often been accepted even outside the English-speaking world.

Yet the facts themselves are enough to discredit such a parochial notion. To begin with, the system of two dominant parties has not been much imitated outside the English-speaking world and its zones of influence. Of thirty countries having in 1964 opposition parties, widespread suffrage, and governments based on relatively recent elections, only eight would be considered "two-party systems" in the usual sense.[1] Of these eight countries, all but two (Austria and Uruguay) are either English-speaking democracies or were launched politically under the influence of Britain or the United States.

Moreover, as our essays on Britain, the United States, and Austria make clear, even where there are only two dominant parties the patterns of opposition are often radically different. Indeed, in the English-speaking world, the British two-party system as we now understand it seems to exist only in Britain and in New Zealand. In Australia, one of the two major "parties" is actually a coalition of two parties, while in Canada third parties have been much more significant than in either the United States or Britain.[2] The United States is a paradoxical case. The relative weakness of third parties throughout American history makes the United States an even more clear-cut example of two dominant parties than Britain; yet within this framework of two parties, as we have seen, the American pattern of dispersed opposition has nearly as much in common with some of the European multi-party systems as it does with the "concentrated" British pattern. Finally, as Allen Potter indicates in his essay, the British two-party system as we know it today has not existed for much more than the last four decades. Thanks first to the Irish Nationalists and then to Labor, Britain could scarcely be classified as a genuine two-party system for the forty-year period from about 1880 to 1920; while in the middle decades of the 19th century, the British pattern was rather similar to that of the United States: two heterogeneous parties with an executive drawing support from sympathetic elements in both parties.[3] Hence even in British experience the recent pattern is somewhat abnormal.

In sum, it might be reasonable to consider multi-party systems as the natural way for government and oppositions to manage their conflicts in democracies, while two-party systems, whether resembling the British pattern or the American, are the deviant cases. It is conceivable, of course, that the deviant cases represent superior forms; yet multiparty systems exist in Denmark, Norway, Sweden, the Netherlands, and Switzerland, countries widely thought to have handled their political, social, and economic problems with at least as much skill, justice, and social peace as any other democracies.

In addition to the number of important parties, concentration has yet another dimension. Parties themselves vary enormously in internal unity, as measured, for example, by the way their members vote in parliament; what is formally a single opposition party may in fact disintegrate into a number of factions. Since there are variations in the degree of unity and factionalism among parties even within a particular country, it is difficult to characterize whole systems; in Italy and France the Communists have been highly cohesive in their voting in the parliament, whereas in both countries the other parties are much more divided among themselves.

In order to consider the bearing of concentration on patterns of opposition in the ten countries treated in this volume, it is helpful to combine these two dimensions into four simple categories:[4]

1. Two-party systems with a high degree of internal party unity, as in Britain.
2. Two-party systems with relatively low internal party unity, as in the United States.
3. Multi-party systems with relatively high internal party unity, as in Sweden, Norway, and the Netherlands.
4. Multi-party systems with low internal party unity, as in both Italy and France.

To the extent that an opposition takes the party system of the country into account in selecting the strategy it will pursue, different party systems should be associated with different strategies. Thus an opposition confronted with a party system of the first type is likely to behave somewhat differently from an opposition confronted with one of the other kinds of party systems. I shall return to this point in a moment.

COMPETITIVENESS

How competitive an opposition is depends partly on how concentrated it is. In this case "competitive" does not refer to the psychological orientations of political actors but to the way in which the gains and losses of political opponents in elections and in parliament are related. On the analogy of an equivalent concept in the theory of games, two parties are in a strictly competitive (or zero-sum) relation if they pursue strategies such that, given the election or voting system, the gains of one will exactly equal the losses of another.[5] Because in any given election the number of seats in a legislative body is fixed, whenever only two parties run competing candidates in an election they are necessarily engaged in a strictly competitive contest, since the seats gained by one party will be lost to the other. Applying the notion of strict competition to a legislative body presents some problems; but we can get around most of these by stipulating that two parties are strictly competitive in a legislature if they pursue strategies such that both cannot simultaneously belong to a winning coalition. As an empirical fact, of course, no legislature is strictly competitive all the time; some measures gain overwhelming or unanimous approval, while on others party leaders deliberately permit their followers to vote as they choose. In some legislatures, however, key votes are usually strictly competitive; votes on the formation of a government, votes of confidence, votes on the major legislative and budgeting measures submitted by the government, etc. We can regard parties as strictly competitive in parliament, then, if they are strictly competitive on key votes.

It might be conjectured that in a parliamentary or presidential system monopolized by two highly unified parties, competition would always be strictly competitive. The salient example is, of course, Britain. Yet the parties *could* deliberately decide to collaborate either in parliament or in elections, or in both. During most of two world wars the major parties in Britain agreed to substitute collaboration for competition: coalition cabinets were formed, and elections were delayed until after the end of the war. In Austria from 1947 onward, the People's Party and the Socialist Party formed a coalition government that left virtually no opposition in Parliament; yet at each election the two parties vigorously fought one another for votes. The most extreme displacement of competition by coalition has occurred in Colombia, where the two major parties deliberately entered into a pact to eliminate competition not only in Congress but in national elections; the agreement was intended to last through four elections and four terms of office for a total of sixteen years.

Even in a system with two unified parties, then, strict competition is not inevitable. Yet the temptation to shift from coalition to competition is bound to be very great, particularly for the party that believes it could win a majority of votes.[6] Hence coalition in a two-party system imposes severe strains and probably tends to be an unstable solution. Whether, given these strains, the arrangement in Colombia will run the full sixteen years therefore seems rather dubious.

In the United States, the two major parties are strictly competitive during presidential elections and for the most part during congressional elections; but in Congress party cohesion is weak as compared with Britain, and elements within one party enter into winning coalitions with elements of the other party even on key votes. In multi-party systems strict competition is unlikely; in fact unless one party can form a majority by itself, strict competition is actually impossible; for unless two parties are willing to enter into a coalition, no majority can be formed. Moreover, parties may not be strictly competitive even during elections, for they may enter into electoral alliances that limit competition in various ways, for example by uniting in some districts around a single candidate, as in runoff elections in France.

Thus the competitiveness of opposition (in the sense in which the term is used here) depends in large measure, though not completely, on the number and nature of parties, i.e., on the extent to which opposition is concentrated. The possibilities we have discussed, and for which examples actually exist, extend from a system in which the opposition is concentrated in a party that is strictly competitive both in elections and in parliament, through various systems in which opposition strategies are both cooperative and competitive, to systems in which the minority party that would ordinarily constitute the opposition coalesces with the majority party both in elections and in parliament (see Table 1).

SITE

Because it seeks to bring about a change in the behavior of the government, an opposition will employ some of its political resources to persuade, induce, or compel a government to alter its conduct. The situation or circumstances in which an opposition employs its resources to bring about a change might be called a *site* for encounters between opposition and government.[7]

Table 1. Competition, Cooperation, and Coalescence:
Types of Party Systems

| | Opposition in | | |
Type of System	Elections	Parliament	Examples
I. Strictly competitive	Strictly competitive	Strictly competitive	Britain
II. Cooperative-competitive			
A. Two-party	Strictly competitive	Cooperative and competitive	United States
B. Multi-party	Cooperative and competitive	Cooperative and competitive	France, Italy
III. Coalescent-competitive			
A. Two-party	Strictly competitive	Coalescent	Austria, wartime Britain
B. Multi-party	Cooperative and competitive	Coalescent	
IV. Strictly coalescent	Coalescent	Coalescent	Colombia

All ten of our systems offer oppositions the opportunity to challenge the government by influencing public opinion in order to increase support for themselves, by winning votes and parliamentary seats in elections, by entering into an executive coalition, by gaining support in parliament for legislation, by negotiating with other officials, and by negotiating with unofficial or quasi-official organizations.

The relative importance of these sites varies from one system to another. In some systems one site is relatively decisive: victory in that encounter entails a rather high probability of victory at the rest. But other systems may not offer a decisive site; an opposition may win an encounter at one site and lose at another.

In one sense, to be sure, public opinion is a decisive site in every democracy; for each democracy it would be possible in principle to specify some amount and distribution of opinions that would be decisive. Moreover, aside from the question of "decisiveness," influencing public opinion is highly important because success in that undertaking creates capital that can often be converted into influence at the other sites. Conversely, even if microscopic public backing is by no means always a fatal weakness, it is always a severe handicap, while outright public hostility greatly magnifies the difficulties of gaining influence at any site.

Nonetheless, the amount and distribution of public support required for an opposition to gain victory vary even among different democracies, and specifically among those analyzed in the preceding chapters. Unfortunately, the theoretical and empirical patterns have not, as far as I know, been at all worked out, and I shall not attempt to do so here. However, among the countries described in this volume it is possible to distinguish, in a rough way, four somewhat different patterns of "decisiveness."

First, in Britain, which is unique in this respect, parliamentary elections are relatively decisive. For a political opposition to succeed in changing important government policies, a condition that is ordinarily both necessary and sufficient is for it to win a majority of seats in a parliamentary election. By winning a parliamentary majority, the opposition is able to select the executive; and because of party unity the onetime opposition, now the new government, can count upon its majority in the House of Commons to support its policies. The consequences for opposition strategies are obvious. Ordinarily an opposition will concentrate on winning public opinion to its cause and its candidates so that it can win a future parliamentary majority. Every other use of its resources must be subordinated to this controlling purpose. Parliament itself is not, then, a site for genuine encounters so much as it is a forum from which to influence the next election. Parliamentary debate is not intended to influence Parliament as much as the public—and hence future elections; negotiations to enter into the Cabinet would, on the whole, be futile; and everyone knows it.

Second, in some countries where, unlike Britain, elections are not decisive (even though they are important) the formation of the executive is relatively decisive: an executive coalition is moderately sure of gaining the necessary parliamentary support for the policies the coalition agrees on; a group not in the executive coalition is much less likely to gain support for its policies. This pattern exists in countries with multi-party systems where the parties are cohesive in parliamentary voting, as in Holland and Italy, and also in the unusual Austrian two-party coalition system. In these countries the parties attempt to influence public opinion and win parliamentary seats in elections, but they take it more or less for granted that they cannot govern except as part of a coalition. Hence, unlike the British parties, they shape their strategy to take advantage of opportunities for bargaining their way into the current coalition, replacing it with a different coalition, or forcing new elections that are expected to improve their bargaining position.

Third, some countries that might be placed in the second category because of the working of their parties and the regular governmental institutions have in fact moved closer to a system in which elections and the selection of the executive coalition are decisive only with respect to other *official* sites—parliament, the bureaucracies, local governments, and so on. But on a variety of key issues bargaining has been displaced from these official sites to "bargaining processes between the giant alliances of . . . associations and corporations," as Stein Rokkan says of the "two-tier system" in Norway. So important has this bargaining become in the Scandinavian countries that parliamentary democracy in the conventional sense has been to some extent replaced by a kind of democratic corporatism —or, if one prefers terms less tainted by undemocratic connotations, by a pluralistic democracy with highly organized associations.

The fourth group of countries bears some similarity to the third category because of the dispersed or pluralistic character of key decisions; what distinguishes these countries, however, is the fact that even among official sites none is decisive. For the absence of a decisive site has been produced by a deliberate dispersion of legal authority through constitutional devices such as federalism, separation of powers, and checks and balances. The United States and Switzerland are probably the extreme cases, though West Germany also falls into this category.

DISTINCTIVENESS

The distinctiveness of opposition in a political system is largely a result of the three factors we have just discussed: cohesion, competitiveness, and the relative importance of different sites.

In the classic model, the opposition is clearly identified. The principal sites for encounters between opposition and government are the national parliament, parliamentary elections, and the communications media; hence parliament enjoys a virtual monopoly over official, day-to-day encounters. There are only two major parties, both highly unified; hence the opposition is highly concentrated in a single party. Finally, the two parties are strictly competitive in parliament and in elections. As a result of all these conditions, opposition is so sharply distinguished that it is possible to identify unambiguously *the* opposition. In Britain, which has at various times most closely corresponded to this classic model, the distinctiveness of the opposition is symbolized by its very name, "Her Majesty's Loyal Opposition."

The United States and Switzerland both lie close to the opposite extreme. In the United States the sites at which conflict occurs between supporters and opponents of the conduct of government are scattered among the two houses of Congress, the bureaucracy, the White House itself, the courts, and the fifty states, to mention some of the main official sites. The two parties are decentralized; and in Congress they pursue cooperative–competitive strategies. Hence it is never easy to distinguish "opposition" from "government"; and it is exceedingly difficult, if not impossible, to identify *the* opposition. In Switzerland the opposition is perhaps even less distinctive, for in addition to the features that lessen the distinctiveness of opposition in the United States, the Swiss add a multiparty system, referenda, and a plural executive (the Federal Council), the members of which are drawn from all the major parties (including most recently the Socialists), and by tradition conduct themselves in a nonpartisan fashion.

GOALS

Although it is obvious that oppositions differ in their goals, it is exceedingly difficult to reduce differences in goals to a manageable analytical scheme. Political actors, as we all know, have long-run aims and short-run aims, and their short-run goals are not necessarily deduced from their long-run goals; the short-run goals may so much dominate their choice of strategies that their "long-run" goals are, realistically speaking, nothing more than the outcome of their short-run goals. Everyone knows too that the ostensible goals of a political actor may not be his real goals; his public objectives may differ from his private objectives. There is no simple way to get round these complexities in the notion of aims or goals. The solution I have chosen is a deliberate oversimplification. I simply postulate that certain goals, whether long-run or short-run, public or private, are "dominant" or "controlling"; and I distinguish between (a) aims or goals and (b) strategies.

In the case of an opposition, the *controlling goals* are the objectives that the opposition seeks to arrive at by changing the conduct of the government. The *strategy* of opposition consists of the means it chooses to obtain these goals.

As to goals, an opposition may oppose the conduct of government because it wants to change (or to resist a possible change in): (1) the personnel of government; (2) the specific policies of government; (3) the structure of the political system; or (4) the socioeconomic structure. Although these are by no means sharply distinct categories, for the sake of simplicity we shall speak of them as if they were more clearly distinguishable than in fact they are. The seven most relevant patterns are shown in Table 2.

The fourth type exhibited in Table 2—political reformism that is not policy-oriented but is concerned with changes in the political structure and perhaps in the personnel of government—has been, historically, a somewhat transitory kind of opposition in the Western democracies. The most important distinction is between systems that have relatively little structural opposition and those that have a great deal.

The United States has been something of a deviant case . . . . [O]pposition in the United States has been pretty much limited to the nonstructural varieties because of a rather widespread acceptance of the major political, economic, and social structures. By about 1815, the Federalists had little left to quarrel with even on matters of government policy;

Table 2. Patterns of Opposition: Goals*

Opposition to the Conduct of Government in Order to Change (or Prevent Change) in

Types of Opposition	Personnel of Govt.	Specific Policies of Govt.	Political Structure	Socio-economic Structure	Example
NONSTRUCTURAL OPPOSITION					
1. Pure office-seeking parties	+	−	−	−	U.S. Federalists 1815–30
2. Pressure groups	−	+	−	−	U.S. Farm Bureau Federation
3. Policy-oriented parties	+	+	−	−	U.S. Republican Party
LIMITED STRUCTURAL OPPOSITION					
4. Political reformism (not policy-oriented)	+ or −	−	+	−	Britain: Irish Nationalists; U.S.: Women's suffrage movement
MAJOR STRUCTURAL OPPOSITION					
5. Comprehensive political-structural reformism	+	+	+	−	France: RPF
6. Democratic social-structural reformism	+	+	−	+	Dem.-Socialist parties
7. Revolutionary movements	+	+	+	+	Communist parties

Symbols: + = yes
  − = no

* Note that number 4, limited structural opposition, includes two subpatterns: i.e., either the presence or absence of opposition to the personnel of government. There are sixteen theoretically possible patterns. The remaining eight do not appear in the table because they were felt to be irrelevant or highly unlikely.

their views became more and more indistinguishable from those of the leading Democratic-Republicans. A recent study of Federalism argues that

the single most compelling motive for Federalists to engage in political activity after 1815 was the lure of public office both for its own sake and because it meant that they would once again participate in the day-to-day actions of government. Federalists had always believed themselves peculiarly fitted to rule and their exclusion from office was perhaps more noxious to them than their defeat on public issues.[8]

Although the Democrats and Republicans have not been, most of the time, purely office-seeking (despite their well-known reputation for being as alike as Tweedledum and Tweedledee), in opposition they tend to be policy-oriented and to avoid any challenge to the basic structures of American politics and society. And a great deal of opposition to the conduct of government in the United States manifests itself not in the parties but in the activities of pressure groups, which usually direct their energies to highly specific questions.

Is the United States, then, a gigantic unique case? Or is it the prototype which other stable democracies will tend to emulate? A good case can be made for both points of view. As the preceding chapters have shown, where major structural opposition exists it is for all practical purposes a monopoly of the Communists together with a much smaller element on the extreme Right. Whatever their "ultimate aims," the socialist parties (if we except the small Left-socialist groups) have become essentially policy-oriented—in some cases with strong hankerings after the pleasures of office. This is most clearly evident in Germany, as Kirchheimer has shown in his essay, and in the Scandinavian countries, where the socialists, after more than a generation in office, have either carried out or renounced their major structural reforms and hence, like the Democratic Party in the United States, emphasize policies that would leave the major social, economic, and political structures of the country substantially intact or subject only to evolutionary transformations not directly induced by socialist policies.[9]

Of the countries examined here, only in Italy and France is there today a relatively large structural opposition represented in parliament—or, for that matter, outside it. The decline of structural opposition in the other countries brings them, at least temporarily, closer to the situation that has prevailed in the United States throughout most of its national history.

STRATEGIES

The specific strategies used by opponents in order to change (or to prevent possible change) in the conduct of government are of almost infinite variety. For they are the product of man's enormous capacity for ingenuity, including the special ingenuity of ambitious and unscrupulous men. Even if we confine our attention to democracies, with which we are exclusively concerned here, strategies that have been used at various times defy tidy classification.

Nonetheless, some patterns do emerge from our analysis so far. The strategy an opposition is likely to select depends, in part, on all of the characteristics that have been examined up to this point. Thus strategies obviously depend to some extent on goals: a revolutionary opposition is not likely to follow the same strategy as a pressure group. But as we have seen, given roughly similar goals a strategy that might make a good deal of sense in one system would be inappropriate in another. Putting goals momentarily to one side, then, one might deliberately oversimplify the actual variations in order to formulate the strategic imperatives of our various systems as follows.

Strategy I. Opposition will concentrate above all on strict competition by seeking to gain enough votes in elections to win a majority of seats in parliament and then to form a government (cabinet or executive) consisting only of its own leaders. This strategy is encouraged by a system characterized by two unified parties, where opposition is highly distinctive, and elections are decisive. The only system of this kind among our ten countries is Britain, where the strategy is in fact usually pursued by the opposition party.

Strategy II. An opposition will try to convert additional voters and to gain additional seats in parliamentary elections, but it will assume that it cannot win a parliamentary majority; hence it will concentrate heavily on entering into a governing coalition and gaining as much as it can by intracoalition bargaining. This strategy is encouraged by a system with more than two major parties that have a high degree of party unity, and where the selection of the government (i.e. cabinet or executive) is relatively decisive. This strategy is usually followed by oppositions in Belgium, France, Italy, and Holland.

Strategy III. An opposition will adopt all of Strategy II, but in addition it will assume that many important decisions will be made in quasi-official bargaining among giant associations; hence failure to get into the cabinet need not prevent it from gaining some of its goals by hard bargaining in these quasi-official encounters. This strategy is encouraged by multi-party systems in which Strategy II is appropriate but in which in addition there exists a rather highly developed structure of democratic corporatism. Strategy III is followed most notably in Norway and Sweden, perhaps, but also in the Netherlands and, to some extent, in a good many other countries as well.

Strategy IV. Oppositions will assume that gaining public support and winning votes in elections are both important but neither is always necessary or always sufficient, since any one of a great variety of sites may prove decisive in a specific case and none will prove generally decisive. Hence an opposition will adapt its specific tactics to its resources and to the most vulnerable site or sites. It may concentrate on pressure group activities, intraparty bargaining, legislative maneuvering, gaining favorable judicial decisions, actions at state and local levels, winning elections, or any combination of these. This kind of strategy is encouraged by a system in which constitutional rules and practice prevent any site from being decisive and where opportunities for preventing or inhibiting government action are numerous. The most notable examples of this strategy are provided by the United States; however, among our ten countries, West Germany also seems to approach it.

These, then, are four rather general strategies encouraged by the characteristics of the system in which opposition finds itself, or, more specifically, by what I have described as other elements in the pattern of opposition (concentration, competitiveness, distinctiveness, and sites) without respect, however, to the influence of goals.

Although the goals of an opposition influence its choice of strategies and tactics in ways too various to examine here, two additional strategies (or sets of strategies) may be encouraged in any democratic system where the opposition is motivated by certain kinds of goals.

Strategy V (really a set of strategies) is pursued by an opposition committed to the survival of the political entity when the opposition and the government believe that survival is seriously threatened by severe internal crisis, subversion, war, or the like. A great threat to the political entity encourages overtures by the government to opposition groups to enter into a broader coalition for the duration of the crisis; it encourages all oppositions committed to preserving the political entity (usually, therefore, all the nonrevolutionary oppositions) to adopt coalescent strategies. Coalescent strategies may vary somewhat from one system to another, but in general an opposition tries to enter into a coalition government on the most advantageous terms, seeks to confine conflicts within the cabinet and to prevent them from breaking out in parliament or in public, and keeps open the possibility of reverting to strict competition when the crisis has passed, or at the next election. This is the strategy pursued in Britain in both world wars, by the Swedish parties in the Second World War, and in Italy during the immediate postwar period. Austria is the most interesting example, however, for the coalescent strategy has been pursued by both the major parties long after the dangers that initially encouraged that strategy have declined; what now seems to preserve the strategy is a fear by both parties of the consequences, not so much for the survival of the polity as for the immediate benefits to the parties themselves should the arrangement give way to a competitive pattern.

Strategy VI (also a set of strategies) is often pursued by revolutionary oppositions committed to the destruction of the political entity or the main features of its constitutional system. The essence of this strategy is to use whatever resources the revolutionary opposition has available in order to disrupt the normal operation of political processes, to discredit the system, to impair its legitimacy, and, in general, to increase the vulnerability of the polity to seizure of power by the revolutionary opposition. This was the strategy pursued by the Nazis and the Communists in Weimar Germany. The failure of this strategy for the Communists and its success for the Nazis, the exigencies of Soviet foreign policy created by the threat of Nazi Germany, the wartime Allied coalition and postwar efforts to preserve that coalition all induced the Communist parties at various times to subordinate their revolutionary strategy to cooperative and coalescent strategies. In the intervening years since the end of the Second World War, the failure of revolutionary oppositions to gain or hold power in any European country without outside military assistance, the discrediting of Stalinism since Khrushchev's famous revelations at the Twentieth Party Congress in 1956, the increasing independence of European Communist parties from Soviet control, and the declining importance of the classic proletariat in expanding economies have evidently generated doubts within the two major Communist parties of Western Europe, those of France and Italy, as to the superiority of the revolutionary strategy over Strategy II. Publicly, at least, the French and Italian Communist parties have come to emphasize Strategy II—without, so far, yielding the advantages of a revolutionary strategy when it suits their purposes. Conceivably, the European Communist parties—the only important revolutionary oppositions now remaining in the Western democracies, even in Italy—may be undergoing a fundamental transformation of both goals and strategies, a change that will lead them to abandon revolutionary strategies in Western democracies. Yet it is much too early to leap to that facile conclusion. And even should the present Communist parties do so, it seems likely that a rival "Chinese" variety of Left-Communist would continue in both France and Italy to adhere to a revolutionary strategy, probably as a separate party.

To conclude, therefore, that the strategy of revolution is for all practical purposes dead in the Western democracies is, at the very least, premature.

SOME CONCLUSIONS AND UNSOLVED PROBLEMS

The main conclusions from the discussion in this chapter are, then, these:

First, there exist a great variety of different patterns of opposition in democratic systems.

Second, patterns of opposition differ, among other characteristics, in concentration, competitiveness, relative decisiveness of site, distinctiveness, goals, and strategies.

Third, a choice among strategies is partly determined for an opposition by all the other characteristics of the pattern. The influence of these other characteristics on strategies can be represented schematically as in Figure 1.

Figure 1. A Schematic Representation of the Influence of Various Characteristics of Opposition Patterns on the Choice of Strategies

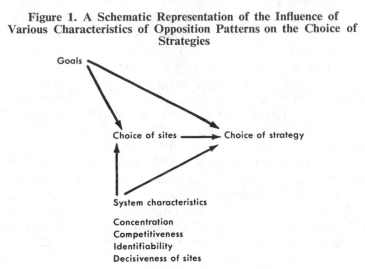

Fourth, although this offers some explanation for the selection of opposition strategies, our analysis so far leaves the other characteristics pretty much unexplained. Evidently, then, a fuller explanation of differences in strategy would require some explanation of the differences that exist with respect to goals, concentration, competitiveness, identifiability, and site. Moreover, ideally one would want to account not only for present differences in these characteristics among our ten countries but also for any significant changes that have occurred, such as a decline in structural opposition.

These are formidable tasks. In the present state of knowledge, explanations will have to remain highly incomplete and conjectural.

NOTES

[1] The eight countries are Australia, Austria, Panama, the Philippines, New Zealand, United Kingdom, the United States, and Uruguay. Even Australia is a highly doubtful case, since it can be included in the two-party class only if the coalition of the Liberal and Country parties is treated as a single party. The tests used to distinguish the two-party systems were somewhat arbitrary, but defensible. Two of the thirty countries, India and Mexico, were excluded because of one-party dominance. The other twenty-one countries were excluded because the proportion of third-party seats in one popularly elected chamber of the national legislature totaled more than 5 per cent. South Africa, which would have qualified as a two-party system by this test, was excluded from the list of thirty democratic countries because of its suffrage restrictions. A more carefully developed classification of party systems could not possibly change the size of the two-party category by much.

[2] "In the thirteen elections to the Canadian Commons between 1921 and 1963, third parties (that is, parties other than the Liberals and Conservatives) secured over 10 per cent of the total popular vote eleven times, and over 25 per cent five times. The low point was 6 per cent in 1930, and the high point 32 per cent in 1945. Although third parties have not been represented in the Commons in the same high proportion as they have in total votes, they have had enough M.P.s to keep either of the major parties from a legislative majority in six (including the two most recent) of the thirteen parliaments elected since 1921. These six parliaments, however, have sat for only 12 of the 43 years from 1921 to 1964, and during several of these 12 years, the Liberals, as at present, have been just short of majority status." Leon D. Epstein, "A Comparative Study of Canadian Parties," *American Political Science Review*, 58 (March, 1964), 49.

[3] *The Economist* observed on April 2, 1864:

The real danger of the present day is that which was pointed out by the great and gifted De Tocqueville. "There are no great topics now to divide parties. There is a concurrence almost unanimous between men of all parties. In consequence, men dispute on small subjects. The old contests of principle become faction fights, mere questions of persons. Governments are turned out perpetually upon questions of no intrinsic importance, just because the Opposition contrive to obtain a temporary and casual majority." Such in substance were the opinions of the great thinker, but they have not been borne out by the recent experience of this country. We have remarked with interest and pleasure that, during the last years of Lord Palmerston's Government, such passions and petty interests as De Tocqueville spoke of have never become predominant, that they have never even obtained substantial influence. The state of things has been most remarkable. The difference between the moderate supporters of the Ministry and its moderate opponents is of the very faintest kind; many men on opposite sides could as a wit has said, "change heads without its being noticed." No great question has arisen to divide or excite them. The Government has been maintained in office by a substantial coalition of the moderate men of both parties. Mr. Bright hates the Government; Mr. Newdegate hates it. But the Liberals who do not go as far as Mr. Bright, the Tories who do not go so far as Mr. Newdegate, by a tacit and informal alliance, have banded together and maintained the Government. Lord Palmerston is in power because sensible persons of average opinions think he ought to be in power. The selection of a Prime Minister by what we may call the common element in the two opposing parties is a new improvement in representative government. It is the only mode in which a strong administration can be upheld in times when parties are equal—when no great opinion divides them. It is the only mode by which the great dangers which De Tocqueville spoke of can be eluded or escaped.

(Quoted in *The Economist*, April 4, 1964, p. 45.)

[4] This scheme would be inadequate for many purposes, but it is sufficient to provide a rough guide to the degree of concentration of opposition in the countries treated in this volume. For a sophisticated treatment of the problem of classifying and analyzing party

systems, see Giovanni Sartori, "The Theory of Parties Revisited," in L. Binder and D. Easton, eds., *Theory and Method in Comparative Politics* (Englewood Cliffs, N.J.: Prentice-Hall, 1965).

[5] This definition puts stress on the strategies of the parties rather than, as in the theory of games, on the objective characteristics of the game or contest itself. For a comparison, see R. D. Luce and H. Raiffa, *Games and Decisions* (New York: Wiley, 1947), Chap. 4; and A. Rapoport, *Fights, Games and Debates* (Ann Arbor: University of Michigan, 1960), Chap. 7.

[6] One of the rare instances in the modern history of British parties when parliamentary party members revolted and displaced their leader occurred in 1922 when Conservatives turned against Austen Chamberlain because of his determination to continue the wartime coalition with the Liberals through the forthcoming election. (R. T. McKenzie, *British Political Parties* [London: Heinemann, 1955], pp. 83ff.) In 1940, however, Neville Chamberlain resigned as Prime Minister because he was *unable* to form a wartime coalition; a few months later he gave up the leadership of the party (*Ibid.*, pp. 47–49).

[7] Or an "arena"; cf. H. D. Lasswell and A. Kaplan, *Power and Society* (New Haven: Yale University Press, 1950), p. 78.

[8] Shaw Livermore, Jr., *The Twilight of Federalism* (Princeton, N.J.: Princeton University Press, 1962), p. 266. A contemporary, Edward Everett, said in 1828 that the lure of office in the United States was much greater than in England. "We have nothing to which the ambitious can aspire, but office. . . . Office here is family, rank, hereditary fortune, in Short Everything, out of the range of private life. This links its possession with innate principles of our Nature; and truly incredible are the efforts Men are willing to Make, the humiliations they are willing to endure, to get it."

[9] See also Kirchheimer's pioneering contribution to this question, "The Waning of Opposition in Parliamentary Regimes," *Social Research* (Summer, 1957), pp. 128–56.

CHAPTER 6

Baker v. *Carr*
and the Ghost of Federalism

Martin Landau

Justice Jackson once remarked on one of the distinctive features of American jurisprudence: That every great movement in our history has produced a leading case in the Supreme Court. By the logic of our system it could not be otherwise—a proposition which I hope will be made clear in the course of these comments.

Baker v. *Carr*[1] appears now as a candidate for admission to that class of events commonly known as "turning points." The issues involved are of formidable proportions: They not only have to do with "the composition of those large contests of policy . . . by which governments and the actions of governments are made and unmade,"[2] but they have a direct bearing on the structural form of the American governmental system. Indeed, I think it quite clear that the effect of the decision to take jurisdiction over the matter of apportionment is, as Justice Harlan put it, to strike deep into the heart of our federal system.[3] The issue in this case is "federalism," and it is this issue which I wish to discuss.

I

There are two major viewpoints reflected in discussions of federalism. On the one hand, federalism is taken as an *end* in and of itself. In this context, the problem which emerges is the maintenance of a specified balance of power and jurisdiction between state and nation. To be sure, jurisdictions are subject to modification and the balances to adjustment but as the Commission on Intergovernmental Relations[4] expressed it, "the enduring values of our federal system fully warrant every effort to preserve and strengthen its essence." On the other hand, federalism is deemed to be an *instrument*[5] of social change, a problem-solving device which possesses

Reprinted from *Reapportionment*, edited by Glendon Schubert (New York: Scribner, 1965), pp. 241–48, with the permission of Charles Scribner's Sons. Copyright © 1965 by Charles Scribner's Sons.

utility only for a specified set of conditions. It furnishes the means to "achieve some union where unity is an impossibility"; the goal involved is the development of that "more perfect union" which "federalists" despair of today. The logic of this view leads one to the position that federalism is "a case of political lag which urgently deserves our attention."[6] The difference in these positions is the difference to be found between the classical concepts of mechanics and evolutionism as they were transferred into the social domain.

II

To suggest that the Constitution of the United States is a monument to the image of the machine is to stress the dominance of the mechanical metaphor in the American Enlightenment. To the 18th century, the Newtonian system represented a cosmological formula so powerful that "Newton became not so much the name of a man as of an infallible world outlook." The true system of the world, D'Alembert had written, has been recognized, developed, and perfected. Geometry was taken as the method of nature, as the prototype of reason; and the paradigm of celestial mechanics—the "perfectly proportioned complete structure"—established the principle of balance as having, in John Adams' phrase, "an unalterable foundation in nature." The set of this time, the prevailing habit of mind, made it axiomatic that government would be stated as a problem in mechanics and its solution a matter of balance.[7]

When, however, scientific models are transferred from their areas of literal meaning, they serve more than heuristic purposes. The transfer itself frequently gives rise to a set of moral principles which precondition the goals to be obtained. What is in science an empirical hypothesis becomes in society a system of norms; what is in the original domain a descriptive proposition becomes in the social context a prescriptive instruction. This, of course, occurs all the more easily when we allow a metaphor to congeal, when we take it literally. To take a metaphor literally is to create a myth, and the more conventional myths become the more difficult they are to dislodge.

To the Founders, society was one great machine. And the perfect workings of any machine depended only on the perfection of adjustment of the pushes and pulls of its constituent elements. Nature's principle was action and reaction, thrust and counterthrust, checks and balances. "Make the system complete in its structure; give a perfect proportion and balance to its parts, and the power you give it will never affect your security," Hamilton assured us. And in the same *Federalist Papers*, Madison instructed that a "natural" government was such that "its several constituent parts may by their proper relations, be the means of keeping each other in their proper places." But it is Jefferson who presents us with the master print of Federalism. "I dare say," he wrote,

that in time all these [states] as well as their central government, like the planets revolving around their common sun, acting and acted upon according to their respective weights and distances, will produce that beautiful equilibrium on which our Constitution is founded, and which I believe it will exhibit to the world in a degree of perfection, unexampled but in the planetary system itself. The enlightened statesman, therefore, will endeavor to preserve the weight and influence of every part, as too much given to any member of it would destroy the general equilibrium.[8]

Formulations of this order were hardly doubted in Philadelphia. Pargellis tells us that "few voices were raised in the convention to offset the clear-cut, beautiful, unreal symbolism of government as an equipoise of equal powers."[9] On the contrary, this was the symbolism that was reified in the constitutional government which was created. The Constitution itself fixed a "legal habit" by which all matters were to be so treated as to preserve the general equilibrium. Accordingly, and however vexatious it has been, as Justice Jackson put it, the historic function of the Supreme Court has been "the maintenance of the constitutional equilibrium between the states and the Federal government."[10] The value of balance is so firmly ingrained in the fabric of American life that one need only reflect on the conventional meanings of the word "unbalanced." Balanced government is a cardinal value in this society; it is one of our cultural myths and a myth subject to all kinds of ritualistic incantation. We endow it with properties it may never have possessed, with virtues that are to be undoubted. It was, therefore, not untoward for the Kestnbaum commission to accept federalism as one of those "enduring values. . . ." But a long time ago Woodrow Wilson cautioned us that "we continue to think . . . according to long accepted constitutional formulas, and it is still politically unorthodox to depart from old-time phraseology . . . but the commonly received opinions concerning federal constitutional balances . . . are many years behind the actual practices of government . . . we are further than most of us realize from the times and policy of the framers of the Constitution."[11]

This statement was formulated when the implications of evolutionism were of such massive proportions that no field of human endeavor remained immune to its influences. Once the image of the biological organism took hold, the Newtonian vision of a closed static structure poised in delicate balance began to yield to an open-ended universe whose only constant appeared to be change (a condition which seemed so perfectly descriptive of the United States in this period). Under the biological metaphor, government began to be seen as "a growing and evolving organism," while the logic of geometry fell before a new pragmatic methodology. The life of the law became experience and the Brandeis brief its expression.

This is the soil which nurtured the instrumental concept of federalism. Here, too, the act of transfer led to the construction of a set of moral principles, the foundation of which was the judgment that "that government is best which combines a stable framework with adequate freedom for the adaptive process to work itself out."[12] This was Wilson's position: We are, he declared, "accountable to Darwin, not to Newton." The Constitution is a living and fecund system: "It is modified by its environment, necessitated by its tasks, shaped to its functions by the sheer pressures of life."[13] The idea that Americans had been seduced by a fictitious analogy (mechanics) led Walter Lippmann to urge that government is not a routine to be followed but a problem to be solved. Vast changes require new instruments: we employ our instruments and we abandon them when they cease to be effective. But if nothing so simply true as this rule prevails in politics, this is one of the problems we shall have to solve. A man, says Lippmann, cannot sleep in his cradle.[14] Nor can a government.

This is the credo of much of American political and legal thought. We are, most of us, Darwinians these days. We represent our governmental systems as "living and fecund" and we doubt not the certainty of this representation. Our government must be "adapted to changing conditions." If it is to be "functional" for a society in change, it must itself change; if it is to survive, it must be fit. We are committed to change, to newness—to new freedoms, new deals, new frontiers. The "new" is our mark of progress, and progress, as we know, is our most important product.

But while we have adopted a new image and, to some extent, a new vocabulary, a paradox becomes readily apparent when one notes, as Wilson put it, "the strange, persistent longevity of power" that the language of mechanics possesses. Really, we have not adopted the biological image as much as we have added it to the older symbolisms. We perhaps think we have abandoned mechanics because we now scoff at slot machine judges, but what we have done is to mix our metaphors. The attendant confusions are especially marked in the case of federalism.

III

The classical concept of American federalism specifies a relatively fixed relationship between two domains of autonomous or sovereign authority in the same territorial unit. Each possesses an exclusive jurisdiction, neither is subordinate to the other, neither can be stripped of its authority by the other. The constitutional formulations of this concept present, in Corwin's phrase, a model of two states locked into a "mutually exclusive, reciprocally limiting" power of relationship.

To remark on the inadequacy of this model today is quite superfluous. We have Wilson's description, in 1885, of the "altered and declining status of the states." A few years later Bryce voiced concern that we are apt to overrate the effects of "mechanical contrivances" in government. The pragmatic Frank Goodnow concludes in 1916 that industrialization has caused the "old distinction" between interstate and intrastate commerce "almost to disappear."[15] And there is Laski's tale of obsolescence[16] and Max Lerner speaking of the ghost of federalism which "haunts a nation in which every force drives toward centralization."[17]

So, we read, the doctrine of dual federalism is dead; if not dead, dying. Our "living Constitution" operates on a new principle, best formulated perhaps by Luther Gulick in 1933: "Nothing effective can be done in the regulation of stabilization of economic affairs unless the area of planning and control has the same boundaries as the economic structure."[18] If the 1930's dramatized this requirement, the decisions of the Roosevelt Court may be taken as the climax—the turning point—of that long, uneven, but inexorable process of transfer—the transfer of authority to the central government.

This is the "crisis of the states." They have had to yield to a "system dominated by the pervasiveness of federal power."[19] They have lost status, prestige, and power. They have lost so much, Leonard White stated, "that competent observers at home and abroad have declared that American federalism is approaching its end." Roscoe Drummond put it more directly: "our federal system no longer exists."[20]

Drummond's conclusion is not sensational. A system so dominated by central power cannot, by definition, be classified as federalist. If, analytically, we stop the system at various times—ranging from 1800 to the present —and if we examine the state of the system at each of these times, i.e., if we compare the operations of government with the classical or constitutional models, we are bound to find less and less correspondence. As a matter of fact this is what our researches have unquestionably demonstrated. Our findings are of such order that it becomes increasingly difficult to represent our governmental system as federalist. It simply does not possess federal characteristics.

Given, however, the "enduring value" of balance and the "legal habit" of our past, this is not a conclusion we are prone to accept. I do not refer only to embattled senators from the South or to a more or less educated public, or to the bar; I refer as well to professional political scientists, to students of constitutional law, to professional commentators of all sorts. Nor does it matter that many of them have accepted the requirements of a nationally integrated society and of a positive and action-oriented central government. The plain fact appears to be that we cannot lay aside the "ghost of federalism." What we have done is to adjust our vocabulary—but not too far. We now use terms that suggest a modified federalism but federalism nevertheless. Thus, there is substituted for "dual federalism" a "cooperative federalism" or a "centralized federalism." There is a "federalism mature" and there is a "national federalism." These are the synonyms of the "new federalism" which may mean upon analysis "no federalism." To mix our metaphors not only leads to a loose and confusing vocabulary; it tortures our logic and results in self-contradictory statements. A rather prominent textbook may be cited in illustration. If, as it states, "it is self-evident" that such social alterations as urbanization and industrialization have a powerful impact on government (p. 105), that "forms" and "patterns" intermesh (p. 889) such that "alterations in procedures . . . have an impact upon . . . structure" (p. 902), and if "the pattern of federalism is being altered" (p. 121) such that "the original system has been adapted to meet the problems of a nation going through vast . . . changes" (p. 32), then it *cannot* follow that "the structure of our federalism is little changed" while "its actual operation has been drastically altered" (p. 101). It is only when we confuse organismic and mechanical models that we can hold to this conclusion while we state that there are "few aspects" of the economy which are not national in scope (pp. 102–7) and that "the national government today . . . has sufficient constitutional power to dispose of virtually any problem of national extent" (pp. 137–38).[21]

IV

I have taken a long way round to *Baker* v. *Carr* only to make clear that the basis for my judgment as to its significance lies within the context of an evolutionary system. That is, I propose to use a biological model for purposes of analysis. To make this statement is to hypothesize that a social community is logically homologous to a biological community; that it displays the properties of mutual interdependence, self-regulation, adaptation to disturbances, and approaches to states of equilibrium; that it develops in constant interaction with an external environment such that its development is determined by external conditions. This is the adaptive process and results in the production of new sets of values, structures, and functions which are to be so integrated as to maintain and sustain the total community organization. Failure to adapt to new sets of external conditions may introduce extreme dysfunction and even threaten survival.[22]

We conceive, then, of government "as if" it were a "living" organism which "grows and evolves" in relation to an external environment which consists of the "total social organization." Government, i.e., is a component of this community and must be "functionally fit" if it is to perform its role for the community. It is, thus, an organization structure which is "intendedly rational" in character operating to satisfy a set of special social needs which themselves arise via the processes of interaction and adaptation. The special purposes which make sense for the external society will influence the structure of government as the structure itself will determine the effectiveness with which the special tasks are fulfilled.[23] In this context "federalism is a function not of constitutions but of societies."[24] And this is the ground upon which I rest analysis of *Baker* v. *Carr*.

Accordingly, it is inconceivable that a government which reflects the properties and needs of an 18th-century environment (society) could be functional, without profound alteration, for a 20th-century society. The collection of thirteen autonomous communities standing in relative isolation to one another, the differences in economy, the rural habit, the diversity of norms and behaviors, the multi-centered system of communication, the existence of sharp local loyalties themselves the product of a "local consciousness," the magnitude of distance—these are some of the characteristics of 18th-century society. Any attempt at unification required the establishment of a structure which would not, in Bryce's words "extinguish their separate administrations, legislatures, and local patriotisms." For the America of 1787, federalism was the only resource. It was a device designed to solve a social problem—a problem of political organization. It was, as Livingston noted in a brilliant essay, "a response to a definite set of stimuli; ... consciously adopted as a means of solving the problems represented by these stimuli."[25] Indeed, it may be viewed as a stroke of social genius; at once it protected the federal qualities of 18th-century society and provided the means for meeting "the desperate need for a modicum of union where unity is impossible."

From a collection of loose, uncentralized or decentralized units, the United States, as we are prone to speak, has evolved into a highly centralized, integrated community which exhibits symbiotic relationships. It no longer possesses federal characteristics. The history (evolution) of the last century is a striking story of vast changes in the structure of society and the needs it generated. That nation concealed under federalism finally emerged. The United States has been for a long time now becoming the United State. To be sure this has not proceeded without significant resistance—some of which has been quite bloody—but the nationalization process is quite visibly revealed in the transfer of authority to the central government. Moreover, the nature of the efforts which are today designed to stem the growth of national power—interstate compacts, uniform state laws, federal-state cooperative agreements, shared tax fields, and tax credits—are themselves testimony to the integrated character of the society. It now appears virtually impossible to identify a state problem—and thus a state domain. On the contrary, those historically local problems as housing, health, education, juvenile delinquency, etc., have already been admitted to the central jurisdiction—some quite a few years ago. The battles which occur today have only to do with substantive programs not with jurisdiction. Nor need I comment upon the extensions of the 14th Amendment or the necessary interest of the central government in metropolitan traffic problems.

On this score, there is an ironic stress in the Kestnbaum reports. This commission to preserve federalism not only urged a grant-in-aid program that would enlarge the functions of the central government but it was forced by experience to find that the metropolitan areas—not the states—were the key units in the intergovernmental complex. Not so long ago, it stated, the primary relations of local communities involved the states; now they "revolve around Federal more than State relations." Thus the need for a Department of Urban Affairs and for a special nationally-oriented Director of Intergovernmental Relations as the Moore Commission proposed for New York City in 1961.[26] Presently, the Mayor of New York City has designated a Deputy Mayor for this function and has authorized the establishment of a lobby in Washington, D.C. Small wonder that New York's governor opposed a national department of urban affairs that wishes to preside over the disintegration of his jurisdiction.

American society is all the time "becoming." But the pace of change— national and international, technological and social, technical and scientific—is so swift that newly generated needs threaten our ability to design new coping instruments. Even more important, however, old instruments, once functional but now quite obstructive, possess a capacity for resistance that challenge a necessary freedom to adapt. Nowhere is this more clearly in evidence than in the election process itself. The logic of our system requires that politics center itself nationally, but the lack of a national party system is the most conspicuous anachronism of our time.

This "lag" which political scientists, almost as a group, attribute to federalism was especially noted by the Committee on Political Parties of the American Political Science Association. "The American political party," it stated, "has its roots in the states. Its regulation and control is conducted almost wholly, although not entirely, by the states acting separately." The consequence of this is clear: "The party system is weighted much more heavily toward the state-local side than is true today of the federal system of government in the United States. *The gap produces serious disabilities in government. It needs to be closed.*"[27]

This, in my judgment, is the historic function of *Baker* v. *Carr*: to close this gap. Tendencies in this direction—in the direction of national parties— have long been observed. It would be a curiosity indeed if the party system remained immune to the press of society. For these tendencies to become characteristic features of our political life, however, requires that the constitutional authorizations of another day be laid aside. It is precisely because the Constitution has traditionally secured such powers as apportionment to the states that a fractionized and decentralized party system has been maintained. The historic justification of this has been the value of local representation but the systems of apportionment in practice have sustained only a spurious and, at best, a technical local interest. The rural areas came first, assumed control and yielded, if at all, only very slowly to the urban shift which, most significantly lies at the base of a national politics.

Justice Harlan's dissent sets the sole issue of *Baker* v. *Carr* as "the right of a state to fix the basis of representation in its own legislature."[28] The Court's decision, he adds, means "to turn our backs on the regard which . . . has always been shown for the judgment of state legislatures and courts *on matters of basically local concern.*"[29]

And this is the point. The decision in *Baker* v. *Carr* is quite to the contrary: The basis of representation for a state legislature is no longer a matter of basic local concern. The Court decision may be interpreted as a move to sustain the urban-national requirements of our time. Justice Frankfurter remarks on the battle between forces whose influence is disparate among the various organs of government. "No shift of power but works a corresponding shift in political influence among the groups composing a society."[30] By the nature of the issue involved, the effect of this decision will be to decrease the power and influence of rural interests and increase the power of metropolitan-urban areas. This will lessen the distance between urban centers and state governments. It will minimize certain types of conflict, allow for more effective planning, and enable a more coordinate attack on pressing urban problems.

The urbanization of state legislatures will be a relatively slow process. It will involve much litigation and conflict. It will involve the courts directly; it will lead to efforts to revamp state constitutions; it will be fought out in the polls as the prime political issue it promises to become. And it will be accompanied by the urbanization of state politics.

The ultimate effect of this shift will be to weigh the party system toward the urban-national side as against the state-local side and this is a necessary condition for the emergence of a national party system. To augment an already developing bypass of the state via direct national-metropolitan relationships with a national party system that is built upon an urban basis must mean a fundamental restructuring of our formal system of government. *Baker* v. *Carr* is a decision on the functional merits of federalism; it does strike deep into its heart.

Is this such a "massive repudiation of our past"? Or is it a development on our past? Once upon a time this country embarked on a voyage to nationhood. The journey was started by the institution of federalism. Its success in enabling a nation to evolve must by the nature of the instrument signal its own demise. The more we become an integrated nation, the less the need for federalism. It is one of those instruments so designed as to outmode itself by its achievements. Sixty years ago New York City was formed as a federal union. The object was to build a unified and coordinate city. This achievement rendered the boroughs quite impractical sixty years later. The life of this city is also marked by a steady transfer of authority to the central government to the point that borough governments exist now in name only. The recent charter proposals remove the last area of governmental activity from these "states." Within the context of evolution "whatever is useful must in the nature of life become useless." Federalism in this country has been a dramatic success.

NOTES

[1] 369 U.S. 186.

[2] J. Frankfurter's dissent. *Ibid.*, p. 287.

[3] J. Harlan's dissent. *Ibid.*, p. 332.

[4] (1955).

[5] See James Bryce, *The American Commonwealth* (1891), Vol. I, p. 342. See also Harvey Manfield, "The States in the American System," in *The Forty-Eight States* (The American Assembly, 1955), p. 13, and see William S. Livingston, "A Note on the Nature of Federalism," *Political Science Quarterly* (March, 1952), pp. 83–84.

[6] Sen. Joseph S. Clark, *Toward National Federalism*, speech of March 28, 1960. Quoted by Robert M. Hutchins, *Two Faces of Federalism* (Center for the Study of Democratic Institutions, 1961), p. 9.

[7] For an analysis of the methodological implications of both mechanics and evolutionism, see Martin Landau, "On the Use of Metaphor in Political Science," *Social Research* (Autumn, 1961).

[8] Quoted in H. W. Schneider, *A History of American Philosophy* (1946), pp. 46–47.

[9] Stanley Pargellis, "The Theory of Balanced Government," in Conyers Read, editor, *The Constitution Reconsidered* (1938), pp. 38–39.

[10] Robert H. Jackson, *The Supreme Court* (1955), p. 65.

[11] *Congressional Government* (1885), Meridian edition, pp. 28–29.

[12] Ellen Rosen, *The United Nations: An Essay in Organization Theory* (1962). Unpublished M.A. thesis, Brooklyn College, p. 4.

[13] *Constitutional Government* (1908), p. 56.

[14] *A Preface to Politics* (1913).

[15] *Principles of Constitutional Government* (1916), pp. 46–47.

[16] "The Obsolescence of Federalism," *The New Republic* (May 3, 1939).

[17] "Minority Rule and Constitutional Tradition," in Read, *op. cit.*, pp. 196–97.

[18] Quoted in E. S. Corwin, *The Twilight of the Supreme Court* (1934), pp. 45–46.

[19] B. Schwartz, "Recent Developments in American Constitutional Law," in A. Junz, editor, *Present Trends in American National Government* (1961), p. 157.

[20] L. White, *The Crisis of the States* (1954), p. 5. White quotes Drummond. See also White, *The Nation and the States* (1953).

[21] J. M. Burns and J. W. Peltason, *Government by the People* (1957).

[22] See L. von Bertalanffy, *Problems of Life* (1952).

[23] See Robert Merton, "Manifest and Latent Functions," in *Social Theory and Social Structure* (1957).

[24] Livingston, *op. cit.*, p. 88.

[25] *Ibid.*, p. 84.

[26] *A New Charter for the City of New York*, New York State Commission on Governmental Operations of the City of New York (1961).

[27] "Toward a More Responsible Two-Party System," *Report of the Committee on Political Parties*, American Political Science Association (1950), p. 26. Emphasis added. See also David Truman, "Federalism and the Party System," in Arthur Macmahon, *Federalism Mature and Emergent* (1955).

[28] 369 U.S. 331.

[29] *Ibid.*, p. 332. Emphasis added.

[30] *Ibid.*, p. 299.

PART THREE

The Prerequisites of Democracy

What are the prerequisites of democracy? It is by answering this question that an empirical theory of democracy will be created, for to answer the question fully requires knowledge of those conditions which must be satisfied for the creation and maintenance of democratic government. Knowing this much, in turn, permits one to explain the failure of democratic government when this is observed. Providing explanations of this form meets the basic requirements of an empirical theory.

As students of democracy, we have obviously only begun to tread this trail, and the studies included in Part Three can hardly be looked upon as constituting such a theory; but they are, we think, noteworthy attempts in that direction. There are numerous ways in which one can conceptualize questions concerning the prerequisites of democracy. Any one method emphasizes some factors at the expense of others. From our survey of recent literature on democracy, we have chosen to emphasize four studies concerned with this question, not necessarily because they are even the most important studies available, but rather because they "fit together" and emphasize the cumulative and integrative possibilities of empirical theorizing in this area.

One set of readings is concerned with the social and economic requisites of democratic development. It is clear that all governmental forms are in important ways products of their environments. It is also clear that governmental forms interact with the environment changing it in various ways. It is of particular theoretical interest whether specific governmental forms are related to specific sets of environmental conditions.

In "Some Social Requisites of Democracy: Economic Development and Political Legitimacy" (Chapter 7), Seymour Martin Lipset empirically examines the familiar proposition that sustaining a democratic regime requires the existence of relatively high levels of economic development. Utilizing selected measures of wealth, industrialization, urbanization, and education as indices of economic development, Lipset finds that "in each case the average wealth, degree of industrialization and urbanization, and level of education is much higher for the more democratic countries." The effects of economic development on the level of democracy are linked to questions of political legitimacy, another prerequisite of any stable political regime.

Lipset's study is of particular interest not simply because of the intrinsic importance of its findings, but also because it has stimulated other scholars to follow the research path which he has opened. Or, with somewhat greater accuracy, Lipset's study is important because it was one of the first to attempt the testing of hypotheses relating to democratic political development with aggregate statistical analysis over a large sample of countries. Economists have long possessed empirical theories of economic development which make use of aggregate statistical analysis. Their efforts to develop such theories have been successful, primarily because there exists among economists some considerable agreement as to what constitutes an adequate measure of an economically-developed country. (The measure is expressed in terms of GNP per capita.) Political analysts concerned with questions of political development have hardly been able to agree with what constitutes political development as a generic process, let alone reach agreement on an adequate statistical measure of democratic political development. Lipset's study is significant because it attempts to bridge this gap, and, it must be added, by employing a most interesting device. He tests his developmental hypothesis by mixing the measurement levels of his independent and dependent variables. Because it is difficult to get agreement on what constitutes democratic political development, and because it is also quite difficult, once one has any such agreement, to devise an empirical measure for which one can obtain reliable data, Lipset simply qualitatively categorizes his sample into four groups: European and English-speaking stable democracies; European and English-speaking unstable democracies and dictatorships; Latin-American democracies and unstable dictatorships; and Latin-American stable dictatorships. This clever solution permits him to test his hypothesis empirically without having to have any precise "measure" of democratic political development, and, as we mentioned above, Lipset's analysis largely confirms the hypothesis that democratic political development is related to the existence of relatively high levels of economic development.

In a somewhat later work, Phillips Cutright, obviously stimulated by Lipset's study, took up the challenge of testing the developmental hypothesis with a higher level of statistical rigor (Chapter 8). To accomplish this task, Cutright devised a scale which he suggests measures the national political development of countries. Whereas Lipset had been explicitly interested in the question of democratic political development, Cutright was proposing to extend the developmental hypothesis suggested by Lipset to include other aspects of political development which he defined as ". . . the degree of complexity and specialization of its national political institutions." Though his intent was to extend the scope of the developmental concept, a close examination of Cutright's index of national political development reveals that it, in fact, measures the degree to which the traditional institutions of liberal democracy are maintained in a country over extended periods of time. What distinguishes Cutright's analysis from Lipset's is the quality of the data and the sophistication of the analysis (multiple regression analysis). Despite his pretentions for extending the developmental concept, Cutright in fact has produced a study which gives excellent replication to Lipset's and strengthens the verification of the original developmental hypothesis. The great service done Lipset by Cutright was to prove that his hypothesis would withstand the test of more rigorous analysis with more sophisticated data.

These two studies, have in turn been directly responsible for the two other articles included in this section: Donald J. McCrone and Charles F. Cnudde's "Toward a Communications Theory of Democratic Political Development: A Causal Model" (Chapter 9), and Deane E. Neubauer's "Some Conditions of Democracy" (Chapter 10). Lipset and Cutright were in some senses proposing a theory of political development—one which has as its focus the specific phenomena of democratic political development. One requirement of an empirical theory is that it state clearly the conditions under which a given phenomena will occur; another is that it provide an explanation of the phenomena when it does occur, i.e., specify the manner in which the conditions interact. Judged by these standards, the studies of Lipset and Cutright are not theories of the political process, but are "studies of the correlates of democratic political development." McCrone and Cnudde have utilized Cutright's political development data to propose a theory of democratic political development which is constructed around a model of communications development. The model they propose is then tested by utilizing Simon–Blalock causal model analysis. Causal model analysis permits one to test a number of possible alternative models and reject those which make predictions inconsistent with the data. The re-analysis of Cutright's data utilizing these tools allows McCrone and Cnudde to make inferences about the causal relationships of such factors as urbanization, education and communications to democratic political development.

The Lipset–Cutright developmental hypothesis and its extension by McCrone and Cnudde suggest that there is a strong linear association beween social and economic development and democratic political development, or as Lipset has put it: "Concretely, this means that the more well-to-do a nation, the greater the chances that it will sustain democracy." The implications of this statement, once one possesses a measure of democracy that is more discriminating than Lipset's simple dichotomies, are not clear. Does the assertion mean also that the *more* "well-to-do," i.e., socially and economically well developed, the *more* democratic a nation is likely to be? This implication persists in Cutright's study which is, of course, based upon a type of interval scale measurement of "national political development." It is this assertion that Neubauer examines. Assuming that the basic developmental hypothesis is correct, he examines a subset of only democratic countries to determine whether increments of social and economic development are correlated with increments of democratic political development— defined in this instance not with Cutright's index of national political development, but with another index which focuses explicitly upon performance features of democratic regimes. Neubauer finds that for this sub-sample of democratic countries the Lipset–Cutright hypothesis is not substantiated; democratic political development so measured is not highly correlated with social and economic development. This leads him to posit that the overall relationship constitutes a threshold phenomenon and that once over the economic development threshold other factors are more important in determining democratic performance.

To repeat, these four studies are rather unique in the literature of democratic theory because they build upon each other and are consequently an explicit attempt to make knowledge in this area cumulative. It is for this reason that we have chosen to represent such a large topic as "the prerequisites of democracy" by this rather narrow definition of prerequisites.

There are obviously many other prerequisites for democracy. Clearly, there must exist some kind of agreement over the "rules of the game," which in turn implies that the predominant values of any given democratic society must evoke agreement above some minimal level. Agreement over critical values also implies that respect for these values probably comes from some common institutional base. Presumably, differences in democratic societies can in part be accounted for by differences in the level of agreement over basic values and by differences in the process of socialization. Extending that presumption, one might also infer that differences among groups in a society with respect to their "democraticness" can in part be explained by differences in these variables. In terms of research problems, there are two things to be determined. First, what is the distribution of values and agreement on those values across a democratic population, and, second, what effect do various distributional patterns have on those systems being investigated?

In "Fundamental Principles of Democracy" (Chapter 11), now a well-known study, James Prothro and Charles Grigg have tested the proposition that "successful" democracy "requires" the existence of high levels of consensus on the norms of democracy. Working with samples of voters from a midwestern (Ann Arbor) and a southern city (Tallahassee), Prothro and Grigg found that although there existed widespread agreement over the norms of democracy stated as abstract principles, when those principles were restated as specific propositions (applications of the principles), agreement over what constitutes desirable behavior quickly disappeared. Analysis of their data indicates that the level of education is the most important variable for determining consistency or inconsistency between agreement with the abstract principle and its application. Prothro and Grigg's findings point directly to a fact often observed but seldom documented: the consistency and substance of beliefs and behavior are likely to vary across groups in the population. Their findings make it clear that the functional requisites of a political system frequently differ from those posited in political theory. Despite the fact that "consensus" does not apparently exist on the application of fundamental principles of democracy, democracy does function to some appreciable degree in both Ann Arbor and Tallahassee. Clearly, other factors are involved. One factor is the cost of action compared with the cost of belief. To express an anti-democratic belief in an ostensibly democratic society is far less costly than to engage in explicitly undemocratic behavior. Apathy, the failure to act on one's beliefs —whatever the precise motivation—thus performs an important function for the democratic system: it keeps undemocratic behavior out of the political arena.

This theme is also treated by Robert Dahl in "Stability, Change, and the Democratic Creed" (Chapter 12). Aware of recent findings (such as those of Prothro and Grigg) which raise questions about the actual level of consensus necessary for the existence of a stable democratic system, Dahl provides some alternative explanations for the existence of a stable democracy in New Haven. In what has been called by others the basis of a theory of "democratic elitism" (cf. Peter Bachrach, The Theory of Democratic Elitism [Boston: Little, Brown and Co., 1966]), Dahl suggests that "consensus,"—an individual's beliefs about the democratic process—can only be understood as a process in which the political professionals, i.e., the political strata, regularly interact with the great bulk of the population. The bulk of the citizenry, characterized by a general agreement with the democratic, is ordinarily unconcerned with the political process and is likely to become engaged only at those times when their interests are perceived to be directly affected. Since it is in precisely this context that citizens are most likely to disagree over the specific application of general democratic principles, their entry into the political arena (the demands made to the professionals), is likely to have the flavor of non-democratic behavior (a challenge to "legitimate" norms). The professionals—who are more familiar with the norms of the creed and more committed to it, especially at the operational level, and who have far greater political resources than the activated citizenry, including experience in dealing with precisely these kinds of situations—are likely to move quickly to dispose of this "challenge" to those norms which traditionally define the pattern of interaction. What results is a process of dynamic socialization in which the elites are forced to respond to some demands for action and are thus informed about an intense preference set and in which the citizenry is informed about which kinds of behaviors are likely to be regarded as legitimate and effective. Over time this process of interaction is likely to result in a relatively stable set of rights and privileges which is appropriate for the resolution of specific grievances, but which may not at any given moment enjoy widespread public support.

Additional support for the two studies described above is provided by Herbert McClosky in "Consensus and Ideology in American Politics" (Chapter 13). Prothro and Grigg found that level of education was most important in determining the likelihood of an individual sustaining consistency between an abstract commitment to a democratic regime and its application in specific situations. Dahl in turn asserts that the professionals are those most committed to the democratic creed, those most able to sustain it in difficult operational circumstances. In this study, McClosky has examined the range of differences which exist between the electorate and the "active minority" on such questions as belief in democratic norms, ability to sustain those norms in specific applications, and the like. His evidence strongly indicates that to the extent that there exists within the population a group characterized by a consensus over a democratic ideology, that group is not the electorate but is the political strata, and it is they who "serve as the major repositories of the public conscience and as the carriers of the Creed." McClosky, like Prothro and Grigg, concludes that in our theorizing about the requisites of democracy, we have given too much emphasis to the role which we assume is played by democratic beliefs or ideas in general. Political behavior in a democracy results from a complex of motives and circumstances, one fortunate coincidence of which is that those who choose to participate most are those who are most characterized by a commitment to democratic beliefs. The implication of McClosky's argument is that widespread participation in the political arena by those whom our evidence suggests are least committed to democratic beliefs is liable to result in undemocratic kinds of behavior, i.e., undemocratic with respect to beliefs about the rights of others in society—not substantive beliefs. Recent experiences in the United States (and in other democracies such as France) would suggest that this hypothesis is quite correct. The civil rights movement and the Viet-Nam war have drawn many individuals into active participation in political affairs for the first time. Whatever one might say about the substantive content of their values, it is clear that these groups, e.g., Black Nationalists and militant peace groups, have less respect for and lower tolerance of those activities normally associated with the democratic creed than do those groups more accustomed to regularized participation in democratic politics. The absence of widespread consensus on democratic norms—or its "concentration" in the influential strata—may in some ways work to the overall advantage of the democratic system; the absence of consensus may have quite disastrous effects on that system when participation of those who do not support the traditional norms becomes intense. These empirical findings have made clear yet another paradox between the traditional view of democracy and the real world of mass democracy. The concept of democracy is obviously predicated upon the assumption that the citizen will participate rather generally in the affairs of his polity. The reality is that when he does decide to participate, he has very little of the "equipment" to do so as a democrat.

The implication of the above is that the citizenries of modern democratic states are not being fully socialized into the norms of democratic behavior. Or, to phrase the observation somewhat less dogmatically, one can observe that the less educated, the less well-off, and those of lower occupational status exhibit a greater tendency to hold anti-democratic beliefs and engage in anti-democratic behavior. Since these behaviors are presumably the result of some learning process, one might gain some insight into the "cause" of differences in the holding of democratic attitudes and beliefs by examining the process of socialization. In their study "The Child's Acquisition of Regime Norms: Political Efficacy" (Chapter 14), David Easton and Jack Dennis report on an investigation of the beliefs of a sample of 12,000 elementary school children between the ages of 7 and 13 with respect to the efficacy of political action in a democracy. The inculcation of this belief is obviously essential in a governmental form which is ostensibly predicated upon the virtue of citizen participation. Easton and Dennis find that notions of efficacy are to be found very early in the life space of children (by grade 3) and that refinement of the attitudes proceeds at a fairly rapid pace throughout the elementary grades. Their findings also indicate that a sense of political efficacy is positively correlated with higher I.Q. and with higher socioeconomic status (but not with sex). The pattern of childhood norm learning, probability of participation in adult life, and commitment to the norms of the democratic creed is an interrelated one. Children who are more intelligent (measured only by I.Q.) and more favorably placed in terms of socioeconomic status criteria are those who learn the norms of the democratic creed at the earliest age and with the greatest degree of sophistication. (Easton and Dennis comment on some of the reasons why this is likely to be the case.) Knowing this much, it then can come as little surprise to find the high participants in the political arena drawn from this repository or to find them more committed to the norms of the political system. With respect to our previous remarks, it should also come as little surprise to find that in times of crisis, when many are drawn into the political arena for the first time, they act undemocratically. Their propensity to do so has, if we are to credit the socialization studies, been long in the making.

CHAPTER 7

Some Social Requisites of Democracy: Economic Development and Political Legitimacy[1]

Seymour Martin Lipset

The conditions associated with the existence and stability of democratic society have been a leading concern of political philosophy. In this paper the problem is attacked from a sociological and behavioral standpoint, by presenting a number of hypotheses concerning some social requisites for democracy, and by discussing some of the data available to test these hypotheses. In its concern with conditions—values, social institutions, historical events—external to the political system itself which sustain different general types of political systems, the paper moves outside the generally recognized province of political sociology. This growing field has dealt largely with the internal analysis of organizations with political goals, or with the determinants of action *within* various political institutions, such as parties, government agencies, or the electoral process.[2] It has in the main left to the political philosopher the larger concern with the relations of the total political system to society as a whole.

I. INTRODUCTION

A sociological analysis of any pattern of behavior, whether referring to a small or a large social system, must result in specific hypotheses, empirically testable statements. Thus, in dealing with democracy, one must be able to point to a set of conditions that have actually existed in a number of countries, and say: democracy has emerged out of these conditions, and has become stabilized because of certain supporting institutions and values, as well as because of its own internal self-maintaining processes. The conditions listed must be ones which differentiate most democratic states from most others.

Reprinted from *American Political Science Review*, Vol. 53, No. 1 (March, 1959), pp. 69–105, by permission of the American Political Science Association.

A recent discussion by a group of political theorists on the "cultural prerequisites to a successfully functioning democracy" points up the difference between the approach of the political sociologist and the political philosopher to a comparable problem.[3] A considerable portion of this symposium is devoted to a debate concerning the contribution of religion, particularly Christian ethics, toward democratic attitudes. The principal author, Ernest Griffith, sees a necessary connection between the Judeo-Christian heritage and attitudes which sustain democratic institutions; the other participants stress the political and economic conditions which may provide the basis for a consensus on basic values which does not depend on religion; and they point to the depression, poverty, and social disorganization which resulted in fascism in Italy and Germany, in spite of strongly religious populations and traditions. What is most striking about this discussion is its lack of a perspective which assumes that theoretical propositions must be subject to test by a systematic comparison of *all* available cases, and which treats a deviant case properly as one case out of many. In this symposium, on the contrary, deviant cases which do not fit a given proposition are cited to demonstrate that there are *no* social conditions which are regularly associated with a given complex political system. So the conflicts among political philosophers about the necessary conditions underlying given political systems often lead to a triumphant demonstration that a given situation clearly violates the thesis of one's opponent, much as if the existence of some wealthy socialists, or poor conservatives, demonstrated that economic factors were not an important determinant of political preference.

The advantage of an attempt such as is presented here, which seeks to dissect the conditions of democracy into several interrelated variables, is that deviant cases fall into proper perspective. The statistical preponderance of evidence supporting the relationship of a variable such as education to democracy indicates that the existence of deviant cases (such as Germany, which succumbed to dictatorship in spite of an advanced educational system) cannot be the sole basis for rejecting the hypothesis. A deviant case, considered within a context which marshals the evidence on all relevant cases, often may actually strengthen the basic hypothesis if an intensive study of it reveals the special conditions which prevented the usual relationship from appearing.[4] Thus, electoral research indicates that a large proportion of the more economically well-to-do Leftists are under-privileged along other dimensions of social status, such as ethnic or religious position.

Controversy in this area stems not only from variations in methodology, but also from use of different definitions. Clearly in order to discuss democracy, or any other phenomenon, it is first necessary to define it.

For the purposes of this paper, democracy (in a complex society) is defined as a political system which supplies regular constitutional opportunities for changing the governing officials. It is a social mechanism for the resolution of the problem of societal decision-making among conflicting interest groups which permits the largest to choose among alternative contenders for political office. In large measure abstracted from the work of Joseph Schumpeter and Max Weber,[5] this definition implies a number of specific conditions: (a) "political formula," a system of beliefs, legitimizing the democratic system and specifying the institutions—parties, a free press, and so forth—which are legitimized, i.e., accepted as proper by all; (b) one set of political leaders in office; and (c) one or more sets of leaders, out of office, who act as a legitimate opposition attempting to gain office.

The need for these conditions is clear. *First*, if a political system is not characterized by a value system allowing the peaceful "play" of power— the adherence by the "outs" to decisions made by "ins" and the recognition by "ins" of the rights of the "outs"—there can be no stable democracy. This has been the problem faced by many Latin-American states. *Second*, if the outcome of the political game is not the periodic awarding of effective authority to one group, a party or stable coalition, then unstable and irresponsible government rather than democracy will result. This state of affairs existed in pre-Fascist Italy, and for much, though not all of the history of the Third and Fourth French Republics, which were character- ized by weak coalition governments, often formed among parties which had major interest and value conflicts with each other. *Third*, if the conditions facilitating the perpetuation of an effective opposition do not exist, then the authority of officials will be maximized, and popular influence on policy will be at a minimum. This is the situation in all one-party states; and by general agreement, at least in the West, these are dictatorships.

Two principal complex characteristics of social systems will be considered here as they bear on the problem of stable democracy: economic development and legitimacy. These will be presented as structural character- istics of a society which sustain a democratic political system. After a discussion of the economic development complex (comprising industriali- zation, wealth, urbanization, and education) and its consequences for democracy, we shall move to two aspects of the problem of legitimacy, or the degree to which institutions are valued for themselves, and considered right and proper. The relations between legitimacy and the effectiveness of the system (the latter primarily a function of economic development) will be followed by a discussion of the sources of cleavage in a society and the ways in which various resolutions of historically crucial issues result either in disruptive forms of cleavage or in cross-cutting affiliations which reduce conflict to a manageable level. Finally, the bearing of these various factors upon the future of democracy will be assessed.

No detailed examination of the political history of individual countries will be undertaken in accordance with the generic definition, since the relative degree or social content of democracy in different countries is not the real problem of this paper. Certain problems of method in the handling of relationships between complex characteristics of total societies do merit brief discussion, however.

An extremely high correlation between aspects of social structure, such as income, education, religion, on the one hand, and democracy, on the other, is not to be anticipated even on the theoretical grounds, because to the extent that the political sub-system of the society operates autonomously, a particular political form may persist under conditions normally adverse to the *emergence* of that form. Or, a political form may develop because of a syndrome of fairly unique historical factors, even though major social characteristics favor another form. Germany is an example of a nation in which the structural changes—growing industrialization, urbanization, wealth, and education—all favored the establishment of a democratic system, but in which a series of adverse historical events prevented democracy from securing legitimacy in the eyes of many important segments of society, and thus weakened German democracy's ability to withstand crisis.

The high correlations which appear in the data to be presented between democracy and other institutional characteristics of societies must not be overly stressed, since unique events may account for *either* the persistence *or* the failure of democracy in any particular society. Max Weber argued strongly that differences in national patterns often reflect key historical events which set one process in motion in one country, and a second process in another. To illustrate his point, he used the analogy of a dice game in which each time the dice came up with a certain number they were increasingly loaded in the direction of coming up with that number again.[6] To Weber, an event predisposing a country toward democracy sets a process in motion which increases the likelihood that in the next critical point in the country's history democracy will win out again. This process can only have meaning if we assume that once established, a democratic political system gathers some momentum and creates some social supports (institutions) to ensure its continued existence. Thus a "premature" democracy which survives will do so by (among other things) facilitating the growth of other conditions conducive to democracy, such as universal literacy, or autonomous private associations. This paper is primarily concerned with explicating the social conditions which serve to *support* a democratic political system, such as education or legitimacy; it will not deal in detail with the kinds of internal mechanisms which serve to *maintain* democratic systems such as the specific rules of the political game.[7]

Comparative generalizations dealing with complex social systems must necessarily deal rather summarily with particular historical features of any one society within the scope of the investigation. In order to test these generalizations bearing on the differences between countries which rank high or low in possession of the attributes associated with democracy, it is necessary to establish some empirical measures of the type of political system. Individual deviations from a particular aspect of democracy are not too important, as long as the definitions unambiguously cover the great majority of nations which are located as democratic or undemocratic. The precise dividing line between "more democratic" and "less democratic" is also not a basic problem, since presumably democracy is *not* a quality of a social system which either does or does not exist, but is rather a complex of characteristics which may be ranked in many different ways. For this reason it was decided to divide the countries under consideration into two groups, rather than to attempt to rank them from highest to lowest. Ranking *individual* countries from the most to the least democratic is much more difficult than splitting the countries into two classes, "more" or "less" democratic, although even here borderline cases such as Mexico pose problems.

Efforts to classify all countries raise a number of problems. Most countries which lack an enduring tradition of political democracy lie in the traditionally underdeveloped sections of the world. It is possible that Max Weber was right when he suggested that modern democracy in its clearest forms can only occur under the unique conditions of capitalist industrialization.[8] Some of the complications introduced by the sharp variations in political practices in different parts of the earth can be reduced by dealing with differences among countries within political culture areas. The two best areas for such internal comparison are Latin America as one, and Europe and the English-speaking countries as the other. More limited comparisons may be made among the Asian states and among the Arab countries.

The main criteria used in this paper to locate European democracies are the uninterrupted continuation of political democracy since World War I, *and* the absence over the past twenty-five years of a major political movement opposed to the democratic "rules of the game."[9] The somewhat less stringent criterion employed for Latin America is whether a given country has had a history of more or less free elections for most of the post-World War I period. Where in Europe we look for stable democracies, in South America we look for countries which have not had fairly constant dictatorial rule (see Table 1). No detailed analysis of the political history

Table 1. Classification of European, English-speaking and Latin-American Nations by Degree of Stable Democracy

European and English-speaking Nations		Latin-American Nations	
Stable Democracies	*Unstable Democracies and Dictatorships*	*Democracies and Unstable Dictatorships*	*Stable Dictatorships*
Australia	Austria	Argentina	Bolivia
Belgium	Bulgaria	Brazil	Cuba
Canada	Czechoslovakia	Chile	Dominican
Denmark	Finland	Colombia	Republic
Ireland	France	Costa Rica	Ecuador
Luxemburg	Germany (West)	Mexico	El Salvador
Netherlands	Greece	Uruguay	Guatemala
New Zealand	Hungary		Haiti
Norway	Iceland		Honduras
Sweden	Italy		Nicaragua
Switzerland	Poland		Panama
United Kingdom	Portugal		Paraguay
United States	Rumania		Peru
	Spain		Venezuela
	Yugoslavia		

of either Europe or Latin America has been made with an eye toward more specific criteria of differentiation; at this point in the examination of the requisites of democracy, election results are sufficient to locate the European countries, and the judgments of experts and impressionistic assessments based on fairly well-known facts of political history will suffice for Latin America.[10]

II. ECONOMIC DEVELOPMENT AND DEMOCRACY

Perhaps the most widespread generalization linking political systems to other aspects of society has been that democracy is related to the state of economic development. Concretely, this means that the more well-to-do a nation, the greater the chances that it will sustain democracy. From Aristotle down to the present, men have argued that only in a wealthy society in which relatively few citizens lived in real poverty could a situation exist in which the mass of the population could intelligently participate in politics and could develop the self-restraint necessary to avoid succumbing to the appeals of irresponsible demagogues. A society divided between a large impoverished mass and a small favored elite would result either in oligarchy (dictatorial rule of the small upper stratum) or in tyranny (popularly based dictatorship). And these two political forms can be given modern labels: tyranny's modern face is Communism or Peronism;

oligarchy appears today in the form of traditionalist dictatorships such as we find in parts of Latin America, Thailand, Spain, or Portugal.

As a means of concretely testing this hypothesis, various indices of economic development—wealth, industrialization, urbanization, and education—have been defined and averages (means) have been computed for the countries which have been classified as more or less democratic in the Anglo-Saxon world and Europe and Latin America.

In each case, the average wealth, degree of industrialization and urbanization, and level of education is much higher for the more democratic countries, as the data presented in Table 2 indicate. If we had combined Latin America and Europe in one table, the differences would have been greater.[11]

The main indices of *wealth* used here are per capita income, number of persons per motor vehicle and per physician, and the number of radios, telephones, and newspapers per thousand persons. The differences are striking on every score, as Table 2 indicates in detail. In the more demo-

Table 2. A Comparison of European, English-speaking and Latin-American Countries, Divided into Two Groups, "More Democratic" and "Less Democratic," by Indices of Wealth, Industrialization, Education, and Urbanization[1]

	A. *Indices of Wealth*					
Means	*Per Capita Income*[2] *in $*	*Thousands of Persons Per Doctor*[3]	*Persons Per Motor Vehicle*[4]	*Telephones Per 1,000 Persons*[5]	*Radios Per 1,000 Persons*[6]	*Newspaper Copies Per 1,000 Persons*[7]
European and English-speaking Stable Democracies	695	.86	17	205	350	341
European and English-speaking Unstable Democracies and Dictatorships	308	1.4	143	58	160	167
Latin-American Democracies and Unstable Dictatorships	171	2.1	99	25	85	102
Latin-American Stable Dictatorships	119	4.4	274	10	43	43
Ranges						
European Stable Democracies	420–1,453	.7– 1.2	3– 62	43–400	160–995	242–570

Table 2—continued

A.   Indices of Wealth—continued

Means	Per Capita Income[2] in $	Thousands of Persons Per Doctor[3]	Persons Per Motor Vehicle[4]	Telephones Per 1,000 Persons[5]	Radios Per 1,000 Persons[6]	Newspaper Copies Per 1,000 Persons[7]
European Dictatorships	128– 482	.6– 4	10–538	7–196	42–307	46–390
Latin-American Democracies	112– 346	.8– 3.3	31–174	12– 58	38–148	51–233
Latin-American Stable Dictatorships	40– 331	1.0–10.8	38–428	1– 24	4–154	4–111

B. Indices of Industrialization

Means	Percentage of Males in Agriculture[8]	Per Capita Energy Consumed[9]
European Stable Democracies	21	3.6
European Dictatorships	41	1.4
Latin-American Democracies	52	.6
Latin-American Stable Dictatorships	67	.25
Ranges		
European Stable Democracies	6–46	1.4 –7.8
European Dictatorships	16–60	.27–3.2
Latin-American Democracies	30–63	.30–0.9
Latin-American Stable Dictatorships	46–87	.02–1.27

C. Indices of Education

Means	Percentage Literate[10]	Primary Education Enrollment Per 1,000 Persons[11]	Post-Primary Enrollment Per 1,000 Persons[12]	Higher Education Enrollment Per 1,000 Persons[13]
European Stable Democracies	96	134	44	4.2
European Dictatorships	85	121	22	3.5
Latin-American Democracies	74	101	13	2.0
Latin-American Dictatorships	46	72	8	1.3
Ranges				
European Stable Democracies	95–100	96–179	19–83	1.7–17.83
European Dictatorships	55–98	61–165	8–37	1.6– 6.1
Latin-American Democracies	48–87	75–137	7–27	.7– 4.6
Latin-American Stable Dictatorships	11–76	11–149	3–24	.2– 3.1

Table 2—continued

D. Indices of Urbanization

Means	Per Cent in Cities over 20,000[14]	Per Cent in Cities over 100,000[15]	Per Cent in Metropolitan Areas[16]
European Stable Democracies	43	28	38
European Dictatorships	24	16	15
Latin-American Democracies	28	22	26
Latin-American Stable Dictatorships	17	12	15
Ranges			
European Stable Democracies	28–54	17–51	22–56
European Dictatorships	12–44	6–33	7–49
Latin-American Democracies	11–48	13–37	17–44
Latin-American Stable Dictatorships	5–36	4–22	7–26

[1] A large part of this table has been compiled from data furnished by International Urban Research, University of California, Berkeley, California.

[2] United Nations, Statistical Office, *National and Per Capita Income in Seventy Countries*, 1949, Statistical Papers, Series E, No. 1, New York, 1950, pp. 14–16.

[3] United Nations, *A Preliminary Report on the World Social Situation, 1952*, Table 11, pp. 46–48.

[4] United Nations, *Statistical Yearbook*, 1956, Table 139, pp. 333–38.

[5] *Ibid.*, Table 149, p. 387.

[6] *Ibid.*, Table 189, p. 641. The population bases for these figures are for different years than those used in reporting the numbers of telephones and radios, but for purposes of group comparisons, the differences are not important.

[7] United Nations, *A Preliminary Report . . .*, *op. cit.*, Appendix B, pp. 86–89.

[8] United Nations, *Demographic Yearbook*, 1956, Table 12, pp. 350–70.

[9] United Nations, *Statistical Yearbook, 1956, op. cit.*, Table 127, pp. 308–10. Figures refer to commercially produced energy, in equivalent numbers of metric tons of coal.

[10] United Nations, *A Preliminary Report . . .*, *op. cit.*, Appendix A, pp. 79–86. A number of countries are listed as more than 95 per cent literate.

[11] *Ibid.*, pp. 86–100. Figures refer to persons enrolled at the earlier year of the primary range, per 1,000 total population, for years ranging from 1946 to 1950. The first primary year varies from five to eight in various countries. The less developed countries have more persons in that age range per 1,000 population than the more developed countries, but this biases the figures presented in the direction of increasing the percentage of the total population in school for the less developed countries, although fewer of the children in that age group attend school. The bias from this source thus reinforces the positive relationship between education and democracy.

[12] *Ibid.*, pp. 86–100.

[13] UNESCO, *World Survey of Education*, Paris, 1955. Figures are the enrollment in higher education per 1,000 population. The years to which the figures apply vary between 1949 and 1952, and the definition of higher education varies for different countries.

[14] Obtained from International Urban Research, University of California, Berkeley, California.

[15] *Ibid.*

[16] *Ibid.*

cratic European countries, there are 17 persons per motor vehicle compared to 143 for the less democratic countries. In the less dictatorial Latin-American countries there are 99 persons per motor vehicle, as against 274 for the more dictatorial ones.[12] Income differences for the groups are also sharp, dropping from an average per capita income of $695 for the more democratic countries of Europe to $308 for the less democratic ones; the corresponding difference for Latin America is from $171 to $119. The ranges are equally consistent, with the lowest per capita income in each group falling in the "less democratic" category, and the highest in the "more democratic" one.

Industrialization—indices of wealth are clearly related to this, of course—is measured by the percentage of employed males in agriculture, and the per capita commercially produced "energy" being used in the country, measured in terms of tons of coal per person per year. Both of these indices show equally consistent results. The average percentage of employed males working in agriculture and related occupations was 21 in the "more democratic" European countries, and 41 in the "less democratic," 52 in the "less dictatorial" Latin-American countries, and 67 in the "more dictatorial." The differences in per capita energy employed in the country are equally large.

The degree of urbanization is also related to the existence of democracy.[13] Three different indices of urbanization are available from data compiled by International Urban Research (Berkeley, California), the percentage of the population in places of 20,000 and over, the percentage in communities of 100,000 and over, and also the percentage residing in standard metropolitan areas. On all three of these indices of urbanization, the more democratic countries score higher than the less democratic, for both of the political culture areas under investigation.

Many have suggested that the better educated the population of a country, the better the chances for democracy, and the comparative data available support this proposition. The "more democratic" countries of Europe are almost entirely literate: the lowest has a rate of 96 per cent, while the "less democratic" nations have an average literacy rate of 85 per cent. In Latin America, the difference is between an average rate of 74 per cent for the "less dictatorial" countries and 46 per cent for the "more dictatorial."[14] The educational enrollment per thousand total population at three different levels, primary, post-primary, and higher educational, is equally consistently related to the degree of democracy. The tremendous disparity is shown by the extreme cases of Haiti and the United States. Haiti has fewer children (11 per thousand) attending school in the primary grades than the United States has attending colleges (almost 18 per thousand).

The relationship between education and democracy is worth more extensive treatment since an entire philosophy of democratic government has seen in increased education the spread of the basic requirement of democracy.[15] As Bryce wrote with special reference to Latin America, "education, if it does not make men good citizens, makes it at least easier for them to become so."[16] Education presumably broadens men's outlooks, enables them to understand the need for norms of tolerance, restrains them from adhering to extremist and monistic doctrines, and increases their capacity to make rational electoral choices.

The evidence bearing on the contribution of education to democracy is even more direct and strong in connection with individual behavior *within* countries, than it is in cross-national correlations. Data gathered by public opinion research agencies which have questioned people in different countries with regard to their belief in various democratic norms of tolerance for opposition, to their attitudes toward ethnic or racial minorities, and with regard to their belief in multi-party as against one-party systems have found that *the most important single factor differentiating those giving democratic responses from others has been education*. The higher one's education, the more likely one is to believe in democratic values and support democratic practices.[17] All the relevant studies indicate that education is far more significant than income or occupation.

These findings should lead us to anticipate a far higher correlation between national levels of education and political practice than in fact we do find. Germany and France have been among the best educated nations of Europe, but this by itself clearly did not stabilize their democracies. It may be, however, that education has served to inhibit other anti-democratic forces. Post-Nazi data from Germany indicate clearly that higher education is linked to rejection of strong-man and one-party government.[18]

If we cannot say that a "high" level of education is a sufficient condition for democracy, the available evidence does suggest that it comes close to being a necessary condition in the modern world. Thus if we turn to Latin America, where widespread illiteracy still exists in many countries, we find that of all the nations in which more than half the population is illiterate, only one, Brazil, can be included in the "more democratic" group.

There is some evidence from other economically impoverished culture areas that literacy is related to democracy. The one member of the Arab League which has maintained democratic institutions since World War II, Lebanon, is by far the best educated (over 80 per cent literacy) of the Arab countries. In the rest of Asia east of the Arab world, only two states, the Philippines and Japan, have maintained democratic regimes without the presence of large anti-democratic parties since 1945. And these two countries, although lower than any European state in per capita income, are among the world's leaders in educational attainment. The Philippines actually ranks second to the United States in its proportion of people attending high school and university, while Japan has a higher level of educational attainment than any European state.[19]

Although the various indices have been presented separately, it seems clear that the factors of industrialization, urbanization, wealth, and education, are so closely interrelated as to form one common factor.[20]

And the factors subsumed under economic development carry with it the political correlate of democracy.[21]

Before moving to a discussion of the inter connections between the development complex and democracy, mention may be made of the study of the Middle East, which, in its essential conclusions, substantiates these empirical relationships for another culture area. A survey of six Middle Eastern countries (Turkey, Lebanon, Egypt, Syria, Jordan, and Iran), conducted by the Columbia University Bureau of Applied Social Research in 1950–51, found high associations betwen urbanization, literacy, voting rates, media consumption and production, and education.[22] Simple and multiple correlations between the four basic variables were computed for all countries for which United Nations statistics were available, in this case, fifty-four. The multiple correlations, regarding each as the dependent variable in turn, are as follows.[23]

Dependent Variable	Multiple Correlation Coefficient
Urbanization	.61
Literacy	.91
Media Participation	.84
Political Participation	.82

In the Middle East, Turkey and Lebanon score higher on most of these indices than do the other four countries analyzed, and Lerner points out that the "great post-war events in Egypt, Syria, Jordan, and Iran have been the violent struggles for the control of power—struggles notably absent in Turkey and Lebanon, where the control of power has been decided by elections."[24]

One of Lerner's contributions is to point to the consequences, for overall stability, of disproportionate development in one direction or another, and the need for coordinated changes in all of these variables. Thus, he compares urbanization and literacy in Egypt and Turkey, and concludes that although Egypt is far more urbanized than Turkey, it is not really "modernized," and does not even have an adequate base for modernization, because literacy has not kept abreast. In Turkey, all of the several indices of modernization have kept pace with each other, with rising voting participation (36 per cent in 1950), rising literacy, urbanization, etc. In Egypt, by contrast, the cities are full of "homeless illiterates," who provide a ready audience for political mobilization in support of extremist ideologies. On Lerner's scale, following the assumption of the functional interdependence of "modernization" factors, Egypt should be twice as literate as Turkey, since it is twice as urbanized. The fact that it is only half as literate explains, for Lerner, the "imbalances" which "tend to become circular and to accelerate social disorganization," political as well as economic.[25]

Lerner introduces one important theoretical addition, the suggestion that these key variables in the modernization process may be viewed as historical phases, with democracy a part of later developments, the "crowning institution of the participant society," one of his terms for a modern industrial society. His view on the relations between these variables, seen as stages, is worth quoting at some length:

The secular evolution of a participant society appears to involve a regular sequence of three phases. Urbanization comes first, for cities alone have developed the complex of skills and resources which characterize the modern industrial economy. Within this urban matrix develop both of the attributes which distinguish the next two phases—literacy and media growth. There is a close reciprocal relationship between these, for the literate develop the media which in turn spread literacy. But, literacy performs the key function in the second phase. The capacity to read, at first acquired by relatively few people, equips them to perform the varied tasks required in the modernizing society. Not until the third phase, when the elaborate technology of industrial development is fairly well advanced, does a society begin to produce newspapers, radio networks, and motion pictures on a massive scale. This in turn accelerates the spread of literacy. Out of this interaction develop those institutions of participation (e.g., voting) which we find in all advanced modern societies.[26]

Lerner's thesis concerning the functional interdependence of these elements of modernization is by no means established by his data, but the material presented in this paper offers an opportunity for research along these lines. Deviant cases, such as Egypt, where "lagging" literacy is associated with serious strains and potential upheaval, may also be found in Europe and in Latin America, and their analysis, a task not attempted here, will clarify further the basic dynamics of modernization, and the problem of social stability in the midst of institutional change.

A number of processes underlie these correlations, observed in many areas of the world, in addition to the effect, already discussed, of a high level of education and literacy in creating or sustaining belief in democratic norms. Perhaps most important is the relationship between modernization and the form of the "class struggle." For the lower strata, economic development, which means increased income, greater economic security, and higher education, permit those in this status to develop longer time perspectives and more complex and gradualist views of politics. A belief in secular reformist gradualism can only be the ideology of a relatively well-to-do lower class.[27] Increased wealth and education also serve democracy by increasing the extent to which the lower strata are exposed to cross pressures which will reduce the intensity of their commitment to given ideologies and make them less receptive to supporting extremist ones. The operation of this process will be discussed in more detail in the second part of the paper, but essentially it functions through enlarging their involvement in an integrated national culture as distinct from an isolated lower-class one, and hence increasing their exposure to middle-class values. Marx argued that the protetariat were a revolutionary force because they have nothing to lose but their chains and can win the whole world. But Tocqueville in analyzing the reasons why the lower strata in America supported the system paraphrased and transposed Marx before Marx ever made this analysis, by pointing out that "only those who have nothing to lose ever revolt."[28]

Increased wealth is not only related causally to the development of democracy by changing the social conditions of the workers, but it also affects the political role of the middle class through changing the shape of the stratification structure so that it shifts from an elongated pyramid, with a large lower-class base, to a diamond with a growing middle class. A large middle class plays a mitigating role in moderating conflict since it is able to reward moderate and democratic parties and penalize extremist groups.

National income is also related to the political values and style of the upper class. The poorer a country, and the lower the absolute standard of living of the lower classes, the greater the pressure on the upper strata to treat the lower classes as beyond the pale of human society, as vulgar, as innately inferior, as a lower caste. The sharp difference in the style of living between those at the top and those at the bottom makes this psychologically necessary. Consequently, the upper strata also tend to regard political rights for the lower strata, particularly the right to share in power, as essentially absurd and immoral. The upper strata not only resist democracy themselves, but their often arrogant political behavior serves to intensify extremist reactions on the part of the lower classes.

The general income level of a nation will also affect its receptivity to democratic political tolerance norms. The values which imply that it does not matter greatly which side rules, that error can be tolerated even in the governing party can best develop where (a) the government has little power to affect the crucial life chances of most powerful groups, or (b) there is enough wealth in the country so that it actually does not make too much difference if some redistribution does take place. If loss of office is seen as meaning serious loss for major power groups, then they will be readier to resort to more drastic measures in seeking to retain or secure office. The wealth level will also affect the extent to which given countries can develop "universalistic" norms among its civil servants and politicians (selection based on competence; performance without favoritism). The poorer the country, the greater the emphasis which is placed on nepotism, i.e., support of kin and friends. The weakness of the universalistic norms reduces the opportunity to develop efficient bureaucracy, a condition for a modern democratic state.[29]

Less directly linked but seemingly still associated with greater wealth is the presence of intermediary organizations and institutions which can act as sources of countervailing power, and recruiters of participants in the political process in the manner discussed by Tocqueville and other exponents of what has come to be known as the theory of the "mass society."[30] They have argued that a society without a multitude of organizations relatively independent of the central state power has a high dictatorial as well as a revolutionary potential. Such organizations serve a number of functions necessary to democracy: they are a source of countervailing power, inhibiting the state or any single major source of private power from dominating all political resources; they are a source of new opinions; they can be the means of communicating ideas, particularly opposition ideas, to a large section of the citizenry; they serve to train men in the skills of politics; and they help increase the level of interest and participation in politics. Although there are no reliable data which bear on the relationship between national patterns of voluntary organizations and national political systems, evidence from studies of individual behavior within a number of different countries demonstrates that, independently of other factors, men who belong to associations are more likely to hold democratic opinions on questions concerning tolerance and party systems, and are more likely to participate in the political process—to be active or to vote. Since we also know that, within countries, the more well-to-do and the better educated one is, the more likely he is to belong to voluntary organizations, it seems likely that the propensity to form such groups is a function of level of income and opportunities for leisure within given nations.[31]

It is obvious that democracy and the conditions related to stable democracy discussed here are essentially located in the countries of northwest Europe and their English-speaking offspring in America and Australasia. It has been argued by Max Weber among others that the factors making for democracy in this area are a historically unique concatenation of elements, part of the complex which also produced capitalism in this area. The basic argument runs that capitalistic economic development (facilitated and most developed in Protestant areas) created the burgher class whose existence was both a catalyst and a necessary condition for democracy. The emphasis within Protestantism on individual responsibility furthered the emergence of democratic values. The greater initial strength of the middle classes in these countries resulted in an alignment between burghers and throne, an alignment which preserved the monarchy, and thus facilitated the legitimation of democracy among the conservative strata. Thus we have an interrelated cluster of economic development, Protestantism, monarchy, gradual political change, legitimacy, and democracy.[32] Men may argue as to whether any aspect of this cluster is primary, but the cluster of factors and forces hangs together.

III. LEGITIMACY AND DEMOCRACY

In this section I turn to an examination of some of the requisites of democracy which are derived from specifically historical elements in this complex, particularly those which relate to the need of a democratic political system for legitimacy, and for mechanisms which reduce the intensity of political cleavage. These requisites are correlated with economic development, but are also distinct from it since they are elements in the political system itself.

Legitimacy and Effectiveness. In the modern world, as the previous section has attempted to document, economic development involving industrialization, urbanization, high educational standards, and a steady increase in the overall wealth of the society, is a basic condition sustaining democracy; it is a mark of the efficiency of the total system.

But the stability of a given democratic system depends not only on the system's efficiency in modernization, but also upon the *effectiveness* and *legitimacy* of the political system. By effectiveness is meant the actual performance of a political system, the extent to which it satisfies the basic functions of government as defined by the expectations of most members of a society, and the expectations of powerful groups within it which might threaten the system, such as the armed forces. The effectiveness of a democratic political system, marked by an efficient bureaucracy and decision-making system, which is able to resolve political problems, can be distinguished from the efficiency of the total system, although breakdown in the functioning of the society as a whole will, of course, affect the political sub-system. Legitimacy involves the capacity of a political system to engender and maintain the belief that existing political institutions are the most appropriate or proper ones for the society. The extent to which contemporary democratic political systems are legitimate depends in large measure upon the ways in which the key issues which have historically divided the society have been resolved. It is the task of these sections of the paper to show *first*, how the degree of legitimacy of a democratic system may affect its capacity to survive the crises of effectiveness, such as depressions or lost wars and *second*, to indicate the ways in which the different resolutions of basic historical cleavages—which determine the legitimacy of various systems—also strengthen or weaken democracy through their effect on contemporary party struggles.

While effectiveness is primarily an instrumental dimension, legitimacy is more affective and evaluative. Groups will regard a political system as legitimate or illegitimate according to the way in which its values fit in with their primary values. Important segments of the German army, civil service, and aristocratic classes rejected the Weimar Republic not because it was ineffective, but because its symbolism and basic values negated their own. Legitimacy, in and of itself, may be associated with many forms of political organization, including oppressive ones. Feudal societies, before the advent of industrialism, undoubtedly enjoyed the basic loyalty of most of their members. Crises of legitimacy are primarily a recent historical phenomenon, following the rise of sharp cleavages among groups which have been able, because of mass communication resources, to organize around different values than those previously considered to be the only legitimate ones for the total society.

A crisis of legitimacy is a crisis of change, and therefore its roots, as a factor affecting the stability of democratic systems, must be sought in the character of change in modern society. It may be hypothesized that crises of legitimacy occur during a transition to a new social structure, if (a) all major groups do not secure access to the political system early in the transitional period, or at least as soon as they develop political demands; or, if (b) the *status* of major conservative institutions is threatened during the period of structural change. After a new social structure is established, if the new system is unable to sustain the expectations of major groups (on the grounds of "effectiveness") for a long enough period to develop legitimacy upon the new basis, a new crisis may develop.

Tocqueville gave a graphic description of the first general type of loss of legitimacy, referring mainly to countries which had moved from aristocratic monarchies to democratic republics: ". . . epochs sometimes occur in the life of a nation when the old customs of a people are changed, public morality is destroyed, religious belief shaken, and the spell of tradition broken. . . . The citizens then have "neither the instinctive patriotism of a monarchy nor the reflecting patriotism of a republic; . . . they have stopped between the two in the midst of confusion and distress."[33]

If, however, the status of major conservative groups and symbols is not threatened during this transitional period even though they lose most of their power, democracy seems to be much more secure. Striking evidence of the link between the preserved legitimacy of conservative institutions and democracy is the relationship between monarchy and democracy. Given the role of the American and French republican revolutions as the initiators of modern democratic political movements, the fact that ten out of twelve of the stable European and English-speaking democracies are monarchies seems a rather ludicrous correlation. Great Britain, Sweden, Norway, Denmark, the Netherlands, Belgium, Luxemburg, Australia, Canada, and New Zealand are kingdoms; while the only republics which meet the twin conditions—of stable democratic procedures since democracy was instituted, and the absence of a major totalitarian movement in the past twenty-five years—are the United States, Switzerland, and Uruguay.

Nations which have moved from absolutism and oligarchy (linked to a state church) to a democratic welfare state, while retaining the forms of monarchy, more frequently seem able to make changes while sustaining a continuous thread of legitimacy for their political institutions.[34]

The preservation of the monarchy has apparently retained for the system the loyalty of the aristocratic, traditionalist, and clerical sectors of the population which resented increased democratization and equalitarianism. And, by more graciously accepting the lower strata, by not resisting to the point that revolution might be necessary, the conservative orders won or retained the loyalty of the new "citizens." Where monarchy was overthrown by revolution, and orderly succession was broken, those forces aligned with monarchy have sometimes continued to refuse legitimacy to republican successors down to the fifth generation or more.

The one constitutional monarchy which became a Fascist dictatorship, Italy, was, like the French Republic, relatively new and still illegitimate for major groups in the society. The House of Savoy alienated the Catholics by destroying the temporal power of the Popes, and was also not a legitimate successor in the old Kingdom of the Two Sicilies. Catholics, in fact, were forbidden by the church to participate in Italian politics until close to World War I, and the church rescinded its original ban only because of its fear of the Socialists. A similar attitude was taken by French Catholics to the Third Republic during the same period. Both Italian and French democracy have had to operate for much of their histories without loyal support from important groups in their society, both on the Left and on the Right. Thus, one main source of legitimacy lies in the continuity of primary conservative and integrative institutions during a transitional period in which new social institutions are emerging.

The second general type of loss of legitimacy is, as indicated above, related to the way in which societies handle the "entry into politics" problem. The determination of when new social groups shall obtain access to the political process affects the legitimacy of the political system, either for conservative or for emerging groups. In the 19th century these new groups were primarily industrial workers; the "entry into politics" crisis of the 20th century typically involves colonial elites, and peasant peoples. Whenever new groups become politically active (e.g., when the workers first seek access to economic and political power through economic organization and the suffrage, when the bourgeoisie demanded access to and participation in government, when colonial elites demand control over their own system), comparatively easy access to the *legitimate* political institutions tends to win the loyalty of the new groups to the system, and they in turn can permit the old dominating strata to maintain their own status integrity. In nations such as Germany, where access was denied for prolonged periods, first to the bourgeoisie and later to the workers, and where force was used to restrict access, the lower strata were alienated from the system, and were led to adopt extremist ideologies which, in turn, alienated the more established groups from an acceptance of the workers' political movement as a legitimate alternative.

Political systems which denied new strata access to power except through revolutionary means also inhibited the growth of legitimacy by introducing millenial hopes into the political arena. Groups which feel obliged to push their way into the body politic through forceful means tend to overexaggerate the possibilities which political participation afford. Their hopes are for far more than the inherent limitations of political stability permit. Consequently, democratic regimes born under such stress will not only face the difficulty of being regarded as illegitimate by those groups loyal to the *ancien régime*, but may be also rejected by those whose millenial hopes were not fulfilled by the change. France seems to offer an example of such a phenomenon. Right-wing clericalists have viewed the Republic as illegitimate, while sections of the lower strata still impatiently await millenial fulfillment. Many of the newly independent nations of Asia and Africa face the problem of winning the loyalties of the masses to democratic states which can do little to fulfill the utopian objectives set by nationalist movements during the period of colonialism, and the transitional struggle to independence.

We have discussed several conditions bearing upon the maintenance, or the initial securing of legitimacy by a political system. Assuming reasonable effectiveness, if the status of major conservative groups is threatened, or if access to the political system is denied at crucial periods, the legitimacy of the system will remain in question. Even in legitimate systems, a breakdown of effectiveness, repeatedly or for a long period, will endanger its stability.

A major test of legitimacy is the extent to which given nations have developed a common "secular political culture," national rituals and holidays which serve to maintain the legitimacy of various democratic practices.[35] The United States has developed a common homogeneous secular political culture as reflected in the veneration and consensus surrounding the Founding Fathers, Jefferson, Lincoln, Theodore Roosevelt and their principles. These common elements to which all American politicians appeal are not present in all democratic societies. In some European countries, the Left and the Right have a different set of symbols, and different historical political heroes. France offers the clearest example of a nation which has not developed such a common heritage. Thus many of the battles involving use of different symbols between the Left and the Right from 1789 down through much of the 19th century are "still in progress, and the issue is still open; every one of these dates (of major political controversy) still divides Left and Right, clerical and anti-clerical, progressive and reactionary, in all their historically determined constellations."[36]

As we have seen, nations may vary in the extent to which their political institutions are viewed as legitimate by different strata. And knowledge concerning the relative degree of legitimacy of a nation's political institutions is of key importance in any effort to analyze the stability of these institutions when faced with a crisis of effectiveness. The relationship between different degrees of legitimacy and effectiveness in specific political systems may be more graphically presented in the form of a four-fold table, with examples of countries characterized by the various possible combinations.

	+ Effectiveness	
	A	B
	C	D

Legitimacy + / −

Societies which fall in box A, those which are high on the scales of both legitimacy and effectiveness, will clearly have stable political systems. Nations like the United States, Sweden, and Britain satisfy the basic political needs of their citizens, have efficient bureaucracies and political decision-making systems, possess traditional legitimacy through long-term continuity of the key symbols of sovereignty, the monarchy or constitution, and do not contain any important minorities whose basic values run counter to those of the system.[37] Ineffective and illegitimate regimes, those which would be found in box D, must, of course, by definition be unstable and break down, unless they are dictatorships maintaining themselves by force such as the governments of Hungary and eastern Germany today. The political experiences of different countries in the early 1930's illustrate the effect of varying combinations of legitimacy and effectiveness. In the late 1920's, neither the German nor the Austrian republics were held legitimate by large and powerful segments of their populations, but nevertheless remained reasonably effective.[38] In the four-fold table, they fell in box C.

When the effectiveness of the governments of the various countries broke down in the 1930's, those societies which were high on the scale of legitimacy remained democratic, while countries which were low, such as Germany, Austria, and Spain, lost their freedom, and France narrowly escaped a similar fate. Or to put the changes in terms of location in the four-fold table, countries which shifted from A to B remained democratic, while the political systems of those which shifted from C to D broke down. It remained for the military defeat in 1940 to prove conclusively the low position of French democracy on the scale of legitimacy. It was the sole defeated democracy which furnished large-scale support for a Quisling regime.[39]

Situations such as those discussed above in which either legitimacy or effectiveness is high while the other is low to demonstrate the utility of this type of analysis. From a short range point of view, a highly effective but illegitimate system, such as a well-governed colony, is more unstable than regimes which are relatively low in effectiveness and high in legitimacy. The social stability of a nation such as Thailand—even with its occasional *coup d'états*—stands out in sharp contrast to the situation in the neighboring former colonial nations of Southeast Asia. The link between the analysis of legitimacy and the earlier discussion of the contribution of economic development to democracy is evident in the processes through which regimes low in legitimacy may gain it, and conversely in those which are related to the collapse of a legitimate system. Prolonged effectiveness which lasts over a number of generations may give legitimacy to a political system; in the modern world, such effectiveness mainly means constant economic development. Thus those nations which adapted most successfully to the requirements of an industrial system had the fewest internal political strains, and either preserved their traditional legitimacy, the monarchy, or developed new strong symbols of legitimacy.

The social and economic structure which Latin America inherited from the Iberian peninsula prevented it from following the lead of the former English colonies, and its republics never developed the symbols and aura of legitimacy. In a large measure, the survival of the new political democracies of Asia and Africa is related to their ability to sustain a prolonged period of effectiveness, of being able to meet the defined instrumental needs of their populations.

Legitimacy and Cleavage Prolonged effectiveness of the system as a whole may, as in the cases of the United States and Switzerland, eventually legitimate the democratic political system. Inherent, however, in all democratic systems is the constant threat that the conflicts among different groups which are the life-blood of the system may crystallize to the point where societal disintegration is threatened. Hence, conditions which serve to moderate the intensity of partisan battle, in addition to effectiveness, are among the key requisites for a democratic political system.

Since the existence of a moderate state of conflict is an inherent aspect of a legitimate democratic system, and is in fact another way of defining it, we should not be surprised that the principal factors determining such an optimum state are closely linked to those which produce legitimacy viewed in terms of continuities of symbols and status. Essentially the character and content of the major cleavages affecting the political stability of a society are largely determined by historical factors which have affected the way in which major issues dividing society have been solved or left unresolved over time.

In modern times, three major issues have emerged in western states. The first was the religious issue: the place of the church and/or various religions within the nation. The second has been the problem of the admission of the lower strata, particularly the workers, to "citizenship," and the establishment of access to power through universal suffrage, and the legitimate right to bargain collectively in the economic sphere. The third has been the continual struggle over the distribution of the national income.

The significant general question here is this: were these major issues dealt with one by one, and each one more or less solved before the next one arose, or did the problems accumulate, so that historical issues and sources of cleavage mixed with newer ones? Resolving tensions one at a time contributes toward a stable political system; carrying over issues from one historical period to another makes for a political atmosphere characterized by bitterness and frustration rather than by tolerance and compromise. Men and parties come to differ with each other, not simply on ways of settling current problems, but rather by fundamental and opposed *Weltanschauungen*. They come to see the political victory of their opponents as a major moral threat; and the total system, as a result, lacks effective value-integration.

The religious issue, the place of the church in the society, was fought through and solved in most of the Protestant nations in the 18th and 19th centuries, and ceased to be a matter of serious political controversy. In some states, such as the United States, the church was disestablished, and it accepted this result. In others, such as Britain, Scandinavia, and Switzerland, religion remains state-supported, but the state churches, like constitutional monarchs, have only nominal sway and have ceased to be major sources of controversy. It remains for the Catholic countries of Europe to provide us with examples of situations in which the historic controversy between clerical and anti-clerical forces, sparked by the French Revolution, has continued to divide men politically down to the present day. Thus in countries such as France, Italy, Spain, and Austria, being Catholic has meant being allied with rightist or conservative groups in politics; while being anti-clerical (or a member of a minority religion) has most often meant alliance with the left. In a number of these countries, newer issues, when they emerged, became superimposed on the religious question: and for the conservative Catholics, the fight against Socialists was not simply an economic struggle, or a controversy over social institutions, but a deep-rooted conflict, between God and Satan, between good and evil.[40] For many secular intellectuals in contemporary Italy, opposition to the church legitimates alliance with the Communists. As long as religious ties reinforce secular political alignments, the chances for democratic give-and-take, and compromise, are weak.

The "citizenship" or "political equality" issue has also been resolved in various ways. Thus the United States and Britain gave citizenship to the workers in the early or mid-19th century. Sweden and a number of European nations resisted through the beginning of the 20th century, and the struggle for citizenship became combined in these countries with socialism as a *political* movement, thereby producing a revolutionary socialism. Or to put this in other terms, where the workers were denied economic and political citizenship rights, their struggle for redistribution of income and status was superimposed on a revolutionary ideology. Where the economic and status struggle developed outside this context, the ideology with which it was linked tended to be that of gradualist reformism. In Hohenzollern Germany, for example, the workers were denied a free and equal suffrage in Prussia until the revolution of 1918. This denial of "citizenship" facilitated the retention of revolutionary Marxism in those parts of Germany where equal suffrage did not exist. In Southern Germany, where full citizenship rights were granted in the late 19th century, reformist, democratic, and non-revolutionary socialism was dominant. The perpetuation of revolutionary dogmas in much of the Social Democratic Party served to give ultra-leftists a voice in party leadership, enabled the Communists to win strength after the military defeat, and perhaps even more important historically, served to frighten large sections of the German middle classes. The latter feared that a socialist victory would really mean an end to all their privileges and status.

In France, the workers won the suffrage but were refused basic economic rights until after World War II. Major groups of French employers denied legitimacy to the French trade unions, and sought to weaken or destroy them following every trade-union victory. The instability of the French unions, their constant need to preserve worker militancy to survive, gave access to the workers to the more revolutionary and extremist political groups. Communist domination of the French labor movement can in large part be traced to the tactics of the French business classes.

The examples presented above do not explain why different countries varied in the way they handled basic national cleavages. They should suffice, however, to illustrate the worth of a hypothesis relating the conditions for stable democratic government to the basis of diversity. Where a number of historic cleavages intermix and create the basis for *Weltanschauung* politics, the democracy will be unstable and weak, for by definition such political views do not include the concept of tolerance.

Weltanschauung politics have also weakened the possibilities for a stable democracy, since parties characterized by such total ideologies have often attempted to create what Sigmund Neumann has called an "integrated" environment, one in which as much as possible of the lives of their members is encapsulated within ideologically linked activities. These actions are based on the assumption that it is important to isolate their followers from contact with "falsehood" expressed by non-believers. Neumann has suggested the need for a basic analytic distinction between parties of representation, which strengthen democracy, and parties of integration which weaken it.[41] The former are typified by most parties in the English-speaking democracies and in Scandinavia, and by most centrist and conservative parties other than the religious ones. They view the party function as primarily one of securing votes around election time. The parties of integration, on the other hand, are concerned with making the world conform to their basic philosophy or *Weltanschauung*. They do not see themselves as contestants in a give-and-take game of pressure politics, in which all parties accept the rules of the game. Rather they view the political or religious struggle as a contest between divine or historic truth on one side and fundamental error on the other. Given this conception of the world, it becomes necessary to prevent their followers from being exposed to the cross-pressures flowing from contact with falsehood, which will reduce their faith.

The two major non-totalitarian groupings which have followed such procedures have been the Catholics and the Socialists. In general, in much of Europe before 1939, the Catholics and Socialists attempted to increase intra-religious or intra-class communications by creating a network of church- and party-linked social and economic organizations within which their followers could live their entire lives. Austria offers perhaps the best example of a situation in which two groups, the Social Catholics and the Social Democrats, divided over all three historic issues and separated the country into two hostile camps, which carried out much of their social activities in party or church-linked organizations.[42]

The totalitarian organizations, Fascist and Communist, expanded the integrationist character of political life to the furthest limit possible. They outdo all other groups in defining the world in struggle terms, and in seeing the corrupting influences either of Judaism or capitalism as requiring the insulation of the believers.

Efforts by democratic parties of integration to isolate their social base from cross-pressures are clearly disruptive of the requirements for a stable democracy in which there is shifting from one election to another, and in which issues between parties are allowed to be resolved over time. Isolation may intensify loyalty to the party or church, but it may also serve to prevent a party from reaching new strata. The Austrian situation also illustrates the frustration of the electoral process which results when most of the electorate is encapsulated within parties of integration. The necessary rules of democratic politics assume that conversion both ways, into and out of a party, is possible and accepted as proper. Parties which hope to gain a majority by democratic methods must ultimately give up their integrationist tendencies. The only justification for isolation from the rest of the culture is a strong commitment to the idea that the party possesses the only truth, that there are certain basic issues which must be resolved by the triumph of historic truth. As the working-class has gained complete citizenship in the political and economic spheres in different countries, the Socialist parties of Europe have dropped their integrationist emphasis. The only non-totalitarian parties which can and do maintain such policies are religious parties such as the Catholic parties, or the Calvinist Anti-Revolutionary party of Holland. Clearly, the Catholic and Dutch Calvinist churches are not "democratic" in the sphere of religion. They insist there is but one truth, as the Communists and Fascists do in politics. Catholics may accept the assumptions of political democracy, but never those of religious tolerance. And where the conflict between religion and irreligion is viewed as salient by Catholics or other believers in a one true church, then a real dilemma exists for the democratic process. Many political issues which in other countries may be easily compromised become aggravated by the religious issue, and cannot be settled.

The intense forms of cleavage developed by that cumulation of unresolved issues which creates *Weltanschauung* politics is sustained by the systematic segregation of different strata of the population in organized political or religious enclaves. Conversely, however, it should be noted that wherever the social structure operates so as naturally to "isolate" individuals or groups with the same political disposition characteristics from contact with differing views, those so isolated tend to back political extremists.

It has been repeatedly remarked, for example, that workers in so-called "isolated" industries, miners, sailors, fishermen, lumbermen, sheep-tenders, and longshoremen, tend to give overwhelming support to the more left-wing tendencies. Such districts tend to vote Communist or Socialist by large majorities, sometimes to the point of having what is essentially a "one-party" system in the areas concerned. Isolation is created by the fact that the requirements of the job make workers in these industries live in communities which are predominately inhabited by others in the same occupation. And this very isolation seems to reduce the pressures on such workers to be tolerant of other points of view, to contain among themselves diverse strains of thought; and makes them receptive to extremist versions of the doctrine generally held by other less isolated members of their class. One should expect that the least "cosmopolitan" (the most isolated) of every political predisposition, or stratum, will be the ones most likely to accept extremism. The political intolerance of farm-based groups in times of crisis may be another illustration of this pattern, since farmers, like workers in isolated industries, tend to have a more homogeneous political environment than do those employed in most urban occupations.[43]

These conclusions are further confirmed by studies of individual voting behavior which indicate that individuals under cross-pressures—those individuals who belong to groups predisposing in different directions, who have friends supporting different parties, who are regularly exposed to the propaganda of different tendencies—are less likely to be strongly committed politically.[44]

Multiple and politically inconsistent affiliations and loyalties are stimuli that serve to reduce the emotion and aggressiveness involved in political choice. For example, in contemporary Germany, a working-class Catholic, pulled in two directions, will most probably vote Christian-Democratic, but is much more tolerant of the Social Democrats than the average middle-class Catholic.[45] Where a man belongs to a variety of groups such that all predispose toward the same political choice, he is in the situation of the isolated worker, and is much less likely to exhibit tolerance of opposition opinions, or view the possibility of their coming to power with equanimity.

The evidence available suggests that the chances for stable democracy are enhanced to the extent that social strata, groups and individuals have a number of cross-cutting politically relevant affiliations. To the degree that a significant proportion of the population is pulled among conflicting forces, such groups and individuals have an interest in reducing the intensity of political conflict.[46] As Robert Dahl and Talcott Parsons have pointed out, such groups and individuals also have an interest in protecting the rights of political minorities.[47]

A stable democracy requires relatively moderate tension among the contending political forces. And political moderation is facilitated by the capacity of a system to resolve key dividing issues before new ones arise. To the extent that the cleavages of religion, citizenship, and "collective bargaining" have been allowed to cumulate and reinforce each other as stimulants of partisan hostility, the system is weakened. The more reinforced and correlated the sources of cleavage, the less the likelihood for political tolerance. Similarly, on the level of group and individual behavior, the greater the isolation from heterogeneous political stimuli, the more that background factors "pile up" in one direction, the greater the chances that the group or individual will have an extremist perspective. These two relationships, one on the level of partisan issues, the other on the nature of party support, are linked together by the fact that parties reflecting accumulated unresolved issues will seek to isolate their followers from conflicting stimuli, to prevent exposure to "error," while isolated individuals and groups will strengthen the intolerant tendencies in the political party system. The conditions maximizing political cosmopolitanism among the electorate are the growth of urbanization, education, communications media, and increased wealth. Most of the obvious isolated occupations, mining, lumbering, agriculture, belong to the category of "primary" occupations, occupations whose relative share of the labor force declines sharply with economic development.[48]

Thus, we see again how the factors involved in modernization or economic development are linked closely to those involved in the historic institutionalization of the values of legitimacy and tolerance. But it should always be noted that correlations are only statements concerning relative degrees of congruence, and that another condition for political action is that the correlation never be so clear-cut that men cannot feel that they can change the direction of affairs by their actions. And this fact of low correlation means also that it is important for analytic purposes to keep variables distinct even if they intercorrelate. For example, the analysis of cleavage presented here suggests specific propositions concerning the ways in which different electoral and constitutional arrangements may affect the chances for democracy. These generalizations are presented in the following section.

IV. SYSTEMS OF GOVERNMENT AND DEMOCRACY

From the hypothesis that cross-cutting bases of cleavage are better for the vitality of democracy, it follows that two-party systems are better than multi-party systems, that electoral systems involving the election of officials on a territorial basis are preferable to systems of proportional representation, and that federalism is superior to a unitary state. In evaluating these propositions, it is important to note again that they are made with the assumption of all other factors being held constant. Clearly, stable democracies are compatible with multi-party systems, with proportional representation, and with a unitary state. And in fact, I would argue that such variations in systems of government, while significant, are much less important than those derived from basic differences in social structure of the sort discussed in the previous sections.

The argument for the two-party system rests on the assumptions that in a complex society, such parties must necessarily be broad coalitions; that they cannot seek to serve only the interests of one major group; that they cannot be parties of integration; and that in building electoral coalitions, they necessarily antagonize support among those most committed to them, and conversely must seek to win support among groups which are preponderantly allied to the opposition party. Thus, the British Conservative or American Republican parties must not so act as to antagonize basically the manual workers, since a large part of the vote must come from them. The Democratic and Labor parties are faced with a similar problem vis-à-vis the middle strata. Parties which are never oriented toward gaining a majority seek to maximize their electoral support from a limited base. Thus a peasant-oriented party will accentuate peasant group interest consciousness, and a party appealing primarily to small businessmen will do the same for its group. Elections, instead of being occasions on which parties seek to find the broadest possible base of support, and so to bring divergent groups to see their common interests, become events in which parties stress the cleavages separating their principal supporters from other groupings.

The proposition that proportional representation weakens rather than strengthens democracy rests on the analysis of the differences between multi-party and majority-party situations. If it is true, as is suggested above, that "multi-partyness" serves to sharpen differences and reduce consensus, then any electoral system which increases the chance for more rather than fewer parties serves democracy badly.

Further, as Georg Simmel pointed out, the system of electing members of parliament to represent territorial constituencies, as contrasted with systems which encourage direct group representation (such as proportional representation), is preferable, since territorial representation helps to stabilize the political systems by forcing interest groups to secure their ends only within an electoral framework that involves some concern with many interests and the need for compromise.[49]

Federalism serves to strengthen democracy by increasing the opportunity for multiple sources of cleavage. It adds regional interests and values to the others such as class, religion and ethnicity which cross cut the social structure.

A major exception to this generalization occurs when federalism divides the country according to lines of basic cleavage, e.g., between the different ethnic, religious, or linguistic areas. In such cases, as in India or in Canada, federalism may then serve to accentuate and reinforce cleavages. Cleavage is desirable within linguistic or religious groups, not between them. But where such divisions do not exist, then federalism seems to serve democracy well. Besides creating a further source of cross-cutting cleavage, it also serves various functions which Tocqueville noted it shared with strong voluntary associations. Among these, it is the source of resistance to centralization of power and a source of training of new political leaders; and it gives the "out" party a stake in the system as a whole, since national "out" parties usually continue to control some units of the system.

Let me repeat that I do not suggest that these aspects of the political structure as such are key conditions for democratic systems. If the underlying social conditions are such as to facilitate democracy, as seems true for Sweden, then the combination of multi-partyness, proportional representation, and a unitary state, do not seriously weaken it. At the most they serve to permit irresponsible minorities to gain a foothold in parliament. On the other hand, where a low level of effectiveness and of legitimacy has operated to weaken the foundations of democracy as occurred in Weimar Germany, or in France, then constitutional factors encouraging multi-partyness serve to reduce the chances that the system will survive.

V. PROBLEMS OF CONTEMPORARY DEMOCRACY

The characteristic pattern of the stable western democracies in the mid-20th century is that of a "post-politics" phase—there is relatively little difference between the democratic Left and Right, the socialists are moderates, and the conservatives accept the welfare state. In large measure this reflects the fact that in these countries the workers have won their fight for citizenship and for political access, i.e., the right to take part in all decisions of the body politic on an equal level with others.[50]

The struggle for citizenship had two aspects, political (access to power through the suffrage) and economic (institutionalization of trade unions' rights to share in the decisions affecting work rewards and conditions). The representatives of the lower strata are now part of the governing classes, members of the club. Political controversy has declined in the wealthier stable democracies because the basic political issue of the industrial revolution, the incorporation of the workers into the legitimate body politic, has been settled. The only key domestic issue today is collective bargaining over differences in the division of the total product within the framework of a Keynesian welfare state; and such issues do not require or precipitate extremism on either side.

In most of the Latin and Eastern European countries, the struggle for working-class integration into the body politic was not settled before the Communists appeared on the scene to take over leadership of the workers. This fact drastically changed the political game, since inherently the Communists could not be absorbed within the system in the way that the Socialists have been. Communist workers, their parties and trade unions, cannot possibly be accorded the right of access by a democratic society. The Communists' self-image and more particularly their ties to the Soviet Union lead them to accept a self-confirming hypothesis. Their self-definition prevents them from being allowed access and this in turn reinforces the sense of alienation from the system (of not being accepted by the other strata) which workers in nations with large Communist parties have. And the more conservative strata are reinforced in their belief that giving increased rights to the workers or their representatives threatens all that is good in life. Thus, the presence of Communists precludes an easy prediction that economic development will stabilize democracy in these European countries.

In the newly independent nations of Asia, the situation is somewhat different. In Europe at the beginning of modern politics, the workers were faced with the problem of winning citizenship, the right to take part in the political game, from the dominant aristocratic and business strata who controlled politics. In Asia the long-term presence of colonial rulers has identified conservatism as an ideology and the more well-to-do classes with subservience to colonialism; while Leftist ideologies, usually of a Marxist variety, have been dominant, being identified with nationalism. The trade unions and the workers' parties of Asia have been part of the political process from the beginning of the democratic system. Conceivably such a situation could mean a stable democracy, except for the fact that these lower-strata rights pre-date the development of a stable economy with a large middle class and an industrial society.

The whole system stands on its head. The Left in the European stable democracies grew gradually in a fight for more democracy, and gave expression to the discontent involved in early industrialization, while the Right retained the support of traditionalist elements in the society, until eventually the system came into an easy balance between a modified Left and Right. In Asia, the Left is in power during the period of population explosion and early industrialization, and must accept responsibility for all the consequent miseries. As in the poorer areas of Europe, the Communists exist to capitalize on all these discontents in completely irresponsible fashion, and currently are a major party, usually the second largest in most Asian states.

Given the existence of poverty-stricken masses, low levels of education, an elongated pyramid class structure, and the "premature" triumph of the democratic Left, the prognosis for the perpetuation of political democracy in Asia and Africa is bleak. The nations which have the best prospects, Israel, Japan, Lebanon, the Philippines and Turkey, tend to resemble Europe in one or more major factors, high educational level (all except Turkey), substantial and growing middle class, and the retention of political legitimacy by non-Leftist groups. The other emerging national states in Asia and Africa are committed more deeply to a certain tempo and pattern of economic development and to national independence, under whatever political form, than they are to the pattern of party politics and free elections which exemplify our model of democracy. It seems likely that in countries which avoid Communist or military dictatorship political developments will follow the pattern developing in countries such as Ghana, Tunisia or Mexico, where an educated minority uses a mass movement expressing Leftist slogans to exercise effective control, and holds elections as a gesture toward ultimate democratic objectives, and as a means of estimating public opinion, not as effective instruments for legitimate turnover in office of governing parties.[51] Given the pressure for rapid industrialization and for the immediate solution of chronic problems of poverty and famine through political agencies, it is unlikely that many of the new governments of Asia and Africa will be characterized by an open party system representing basically different class positions and values.[52]

Latin America, underdeveloped economically like Asia, is, however, politically more like Europe in the early 19th century than like Asia today. Most Latin American countries became independent states before the rise of industrialism and Marxist ideologies, and contain strongholds of traditional conservatism. The countryside is often apolitical or traditional, and the Leftist movements secure support primarily from the industrial proletariat. Latin American Communists, for example, have chosen the European Marxist path of organizing urban workers, rather than the "Yenan way" of Mao, seeking a peasant base.[53] If Latin America is allowed to develop on its own, and is able to increase its productivity and middle classes, there is a good chance that many Latin American countries will follow in the European direction. Recent developments, including the overthrow of a number of dictatorships, in large measure reflect the effects of an increased middle class, growth in wealth, and increased education. There is, however, also the possibility that these countries may yet follow to the French and Italian direction rather than that of northern Europe, that the Communists will seize the leadership of the workers, and that the middle class will be alienated for democracy.

The analysis of the social requisites for democracy contained in this paper has sought to identify some, though obviously far from all, of the structural conditions which are linked to this political system. It has been possible in a very limited fashion to attempt some tests of the hypothesis suggested. These preliminary efforts to apply a method of science to comparative political systems can still be considered only as illustrative since we can say so little about actual variations in national social structures. Considerably more research must be done specifying the boundaries of various societies along many dimensions before reliable comparative analysis of the sort attempted here can be carried out. Although the task obviously presents tremendous difficulties, it is only through such method that we can move beyond the conventional semi-literary methods of giving illustrative examples to support plausible interpretations.

The data available are, however, of a sufficiently consistent character to support strongly the conclusion that a more systematic and up-to-date version of Aristotle's hypothesis concerning the relationship of political forms to social structure is valid. Unfortunately, as has been indicated above, this conclusion does not justify the optimistic liberal's hope that an increase in wealth, in the size of the middle class, in education, and other related factors will necessarily mean the spread of democracy or the stabilization of democracy. As Max Weber, in discussing the chances for democracy in Russia in the early 20th century pointed out: "The spread of Western cultural and capitalistic economy did not, *ipso facto*, guarantee that Russia would also acquire the liberties which had accompanied their emergence in European history. . . . European liberty had been born in unique, perhaps unrepeatable, circumstances at a time when the intellectual and material conditions for it were exceptionally propitious."[54]

These suggestions that the peculiar concatenation of factors which gave rise to western democracy in the 19th century may be unique are not meant to be unduly pessimistic. Political democracy exists and has existed in a variety of circumstances, even if it is most commonly sustained by a limited cluster of conditions. To understand more fully the various conditions under which it has existed may make possible the development of democracy elsewhere. Democracy is not achieved by acts of will alone; but men's wills, through action, can shape institutions and events in directions that reduce or increase the chance for the development and survival of democracy. To aid men's actions in furthering democracy was in some measure Tocqueville's purpose in studying the operation of American democracy, and it remains perhaps the most important substantive intellectual task which students of politics can still set before themselves.

METHODOLOGICAL APPENDIX

The approach to this paper (as has already been indicated) is implicitly different from others which have attempted to handle social phenomena on a total societal level, and it may be useful to make explicit some of the methodological postulates underlying this presentation.

Complex characteristics of a social system, such as democracy, the degree of bureaucratization, the type of stratification system, have usually been handled either by a reductionist approach or by an "ideal-type" approach. The former approach dismisses the possibility of considering those characteristics as system-attributes as such, and maintains that qualities of individual actions are the sum and substance of sociological categories. For this school of thought, the extent of democratic attitudes, or of bureaucratic behavior, or the numbers and types of prestige or power rankings, constitute the essence of the meaning of the attributes of democracy, bureaucracy, or class.

The "ideal-type" approach starts from a similar assumption, but reaches an opposite conclusion. The similar assumption is that societies are a complex order of phenomena, exhibiting such a degree of internal contradiction, that generalizations about them as a whole must necessarily constitute a constructed representation of selected elements, stemming from the particular concerns and perspectives of the scientist. The opposite conclusion is that abstractions of the order of "democracy" or "bureaucracy" have no necessary connection with states or qualities of complex social systems which actually exist, but comprise collections of attributes which are logically interrelated, but characteristic in their entirety of no existing society.[55] An example of this type of abstraction is Weber's concept of "bureaucracy," comprising a set of offices, which are not "owned" by the officeholder, continuously maintained files of records, functionally specified duties, etc. Another is the common definition of democracy in political science, which postulates individual political decisions based on rational knowledge of one's own ends and of the factual political situation.

Criticism of categories, or ideal-types such as this, solely on the basis that they do not correspond to reality is irrelevant, because they are not intended to describe reality, but to provide a basis for comparing different aspects of reality with their deviations from the consistently logical case. Often this approach is quite fruitful, and there is no intention here of substituting another methodological approach in its place, but merely of presenting another possible way of conceptualizing complex characteristics of social systems, stemming from the multivariate analysis pioneered by Paul Lazarsfeld and his colleagues on a quite different level of analysis.[56]

The point at which this approach differs is on the issue of whether generalized theoretical categories can be considered to have a valid relationship to characteristics of total social systems. The implication of the statistical data presented in this paper concerning democracy, and the relations between democracy, economic development, and political legitimacy, is that there are aspects of total social systems which exist, can be stated in theoretical terms, can be compared with similar aspects of other systems, and, at the same time, are derivable from empirical data which can be checked (or questioned) by other researchers. This does not mean at all that situations contradicting the general relationship may not exist, or that at lower levels of social organization, quite different characteristics may not be evident. For example, a country like the United States may be characterized as "democratic" on the national level, even though most secondary organizations within the country may not be democratic. On another level, a church may be characterized as a "non-bureaucratic" organization, when compared with a corporation, even though important segments of the church organization may be as bureaucratized as the most bureaucratic parts of the corporation. On yet another level, it may be quite legitimate, for purposes of psychological evaluation of the total personality, to consider a certain individual as "schizophrenic," even though under certain conditions, he may not act schizophrenically. The point is that when comparisons are being made on a certain level of generalization, referring to the functioning of a total system (whether on a personality, group, organization, or society level), generalizations applicable to a total society have the same kind and degree of validity that those applicable to other systems have, and are subject to the same empirical tests. The lack of systematic and comparative studies of several societies has obscured this point.

This approach also stresses the view that complex characteristics of a total system have multivariate causation, and also multivariate consequences, insofar as the characteristic has some degree of autonomy within the system. Bureaucracy and urbanization, as well as democracy, have many causes and consequences, in this sense.[57]

On this view, it would be difficult to identify any *one* factor crucially associated with, or "causing" any complex social characteristic. Rather, all such characteristics (and this is a methodological assumption to guide research, and not a substantive point) are considered to have multivariate causation, and multivariate consequences. The point may be clarified by a diagram (see Figure 1) of some of the possible connections between democracy, the initial conditions associated with its emergence, and the consequences of an existent democratic system.

Figure 1

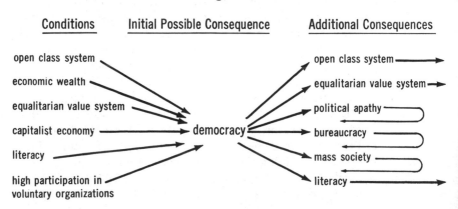

Conditions	Initial Possible Consequence	Additional Consequences
open class system		open class system
economic wealth		equalitarian value system
equalitarian value system		political apathy
capitalist economy	democracy	bureaucracy
literacy		mass society
high participation in voluntary organizations		literacy

The appearance of a factor on both sides of "democracy" implies that it is both an initial condition of democracy, and that democracy, once established, sustains that characteristic of the society, an open class system, for example. On the other hand, some of the initial consequences of democracy, such as bureaucracy, may have the effect of *undermining* democracy, in turn, as the reversing arrows indicate. Appearance of a factor to the right of democracy does not mean that democracy "causes" its appearance, but merely that democracy is an initial condition which favors its development. Similarly, the hypothesis that bureaucracy is one of the consequences of democracy does not imply that democracy is the sole cause, but rather that a democratic system has the effect of encouraging the development of a certain type of bureaucracy, under other additional conditions, which have to be stated if bureaucracy is the focus of the research problem. This diagram is not intended as a complete model of the general social conditions associated with the emergence of democracy, but as a way of clarifying the methodological point concerning the multivariate character of relationships in a total social system.

Thus, in a multivariate system, the focus may be upon any element, and its conditions and consequences may be stated without the implication that we have arrived at a complete theory of the necessary and sufficient conditions of its emergence. This paper does not attempt a *new* theory of democracy, but only the formalizing, and the empirical testing, of certain sets of relationships implied by traditional theories on the level of total social systems.

NOTES

[1] This paper was written as one aspect of a comparative analysis of political behavior in western democracies which is supported by grants from the Behavioral Sciences Division of the Ford Foundation and the Committee on Comparative Politics of the Social Science Research Council. Assistance from Robert Alford and Amitai Etzioni is gratefully acknowledged. It was originally presented at the September, 1958 meetings of the American Political Science Association in St. Louis, Missouri.

[2] See my "Political Sociology, 1945–55," in Hans L. Zetterberg, ed., *Sociology in the USA* (Paris: UNESCO, 1956), pp. 45–55, for a summary of the various areas covered by political sociology. For a discussion of intellectual trends in political sociology and the rationale underlying a focus on the problem of democracy, see my "Political Sociology," in R. K. Merton, *et al.*, eds., *Sociology Today* (New York: Basic Books, 1959), Chap. 3.

[3] Ernest S. Griffith, John Plamenatz, and J. Roland Pennock, "Cultural Prerequisites to a Successfully Functioning Democracy: A Symposium," *American Political Science Review*, Vol. 50 (1956), pp. 101–37.

[4] A detailed example of how a deviant case and analysis advances theory may be found in S. M. Lipset, M. Trow, and J. Coleman, *Union Democracy* (Glencoe: The Free Press, 1956). This book is a study of the political process inside the International Typographical Union, which has a long-term two-party system with free elections and frequent turnover in office, and is thus the clearest exception to Robert Michels' "iron law of oligarchy." The research, however, was not intended as a report on this union, but rather as the best means available to test and amplify Michels' "law." The study could only have been made through a systematic effort to establish a basic theory and derive hypotheses. The best way to add to knowledge about the internal government of voluntary associations seemed to be to study the most deviant case. In the process of examining the particular historical and structural conditions sustaining the two-party system in the ITU, the general theory was clarified.

[5] Joseph Schumpeter, *Capitalism, Socialism, and Democracy*, (New York: Harper and Bros., 1947), pp. 232–302, esp. 269; Max Weber, *Essays in Sociology*, (New York: Oxford University Press, 1946), p. 226.

[6] Max Weber, *The Methodology of the Social Sciences* (Glencoe: The Free Press, 1949), pp. 182–85; see also S. M. Lipset, "A Sociologist Looks at History," *Pacific Sociological Review*, Vol. 1 (Spring, 1958), pp. 13–17.

[7] See Morris Janowitz and Dwaine Marvick, *Competitive Pressure and Democratic Consent*, Michigan Governmental Studies, no. 32 (Bureau of Government, Institute of Public Administration, University of Michigan, 1956), and Robert A. Dahl, *A Preface to Democratic Theory* (Chicago: University of Chicago Press, 1956), esp. pp. 90–123, for recent systematic efforts to specify some of the internal mechanisms of democracy. See David Easton, "An Approach to the Analysis of Political Systems," *World Politics*, Vol. 9 (1957), pp. 383–400, for discussion of problems of internal analysis of political systems.

[8] See Max Weber, "Zur Lage der bürgerlichen Demokratie in Russland," *Archiv fur Sozialwissenschaft und Sozialpolitik*, Vol. 22 (1906), pp. 346 ff.

[9] The latter requirement means that no totalitarian movement, either Fascist or Communist, received 20 per cent of the vote during this time. Actually all the European nations falling on the democratic side of the continuum had totalitarian movements which secured less than 7 per cent of the vote.

[10] The historian Arthur P. Whitaker, for example, has summarized the judgments of experts on Latin America to be that "the countries which have approximated most closely to the democratic ideal have been ... Argentina, Brazil, Chile, Colombia, Costa Rica, and Uruguay." See "The Pathology of Democracy in Latin America: A Historian's Point of View," *American Political Science Review*, Vol. 44 (1950), pp. 101–18. To this group I have added Mexico. Mexico has allowed freedom of the press, of assembly and of organization, to opposition parties, although there is good evidence that it does not allow them the opportunity to win election, since ballots are counted by the incumbents. The existence of opposition groups, contested elections, and adjustments among the various factions of the governing *Partido Revolucionario Institucional* does introduce a considerable element of popular influence in the system.

The interesting effort of Russell Fitzgibbon to secure a "statistical evaluation of Latin American democracy" based on the opinion of various experts is not useful for the purposes of this paper. The judges were asked not only to rank countries as democratic on the basis of purely political criteria, but also to consider the "standard of living" and "educational level." These latter factors may be conditions for democracy, but they are not an aspect of democracy as such. See Russel H. Fitzgibbon, "A Statistical Evaluation of Latin American Democracy," *Western Political Quarterly*, Vol. 9 (1956), pp. 607–19.

[11] Lyle W. Shannon has correlated indices of economic development with whether a country is self-governing or not, and his conclusions are substantially the same. Since Shannon does not give details on the countries categorized as self-governing and non-self-governing, there is no direct measure of the relation between "democratic" and "self-governing" countries. All the countries examined in this paper, however, were

chosen on the assumption that a characterization as "democratic" is meaningless for a non-self-governing country, and therefore, presumably, all of them, whether democratic or dictatorial, would fall within Shannon's "self-governing" category. Shannon shows that underdevelopment is related to lack of self-government; my data indicate that once self-government is attained, development is still related to the character of the political system. See Shannon, ed., *Underdeveloped Areas* (New York: Harper, 1957), and also his article, "Is Level of Government Related to Capacity for Self-Government?" *American Journal of Economics and Sociology*, Vol. 17 (1958), pp. 367–82. In the latter paper, Shannon constructs a composite index of development, using some of the same United Nations sources, as appear in the tables to follow. Shannon's work did not come to my attention until after this paper was prepared, so that the two papers can be considered as separate tests of comparable hypotheses.

¹² It must be remembered that these figures are means, compiled from census figures for the various countries. The data vary widely in accuracy, and there is no way of measuring the validity of compound calculated figures such as those presented here. The consistent direction of all these differences, and their large magnitude, is the main indication of validity.

¹³ Urbanization has often been linked to democracy by political theorists. Harold J. Laski asserted that "organized democracy is the product of urban life," and that it was natural therefore that it should have "made its first effective appearance" in the Greek city states, limited as was their definition of "citizen." See his article "Democracy" in the *Encyclopedia of the Social Sciences* (New York: Macmillan, 1937), Vol. V, pp. 76–85. Max Weber held that the city, as a certain type of political community, is a peculiarly Western, phenomenon, and traced the emergence of the notion of "citizenship" from social developments closely related to urbanization. For a partial statement of his point of view, see the chapter on "Citizenship," in *General Economic History* (Glencoe: The Free Press, 1950), pp. 315–38. It is significant to note that before 1933 the Nazi electoral strength was greatest in small communities and rural areas. Berlin, the only German city of over two million, never gave the Nazis over 25 per cent of the vote in a free election. The modal Nazi, like the modal French Poujadist or Italian neo-Fascist today, was a self employed resident of a small town or rural district. Though the Communists, as a workers' party, are the strongest in the working-class neighborhoods of large cities within countries, they have great electoral strength only in the less urbanized European nations, e.g., Greece, Finland, France, Italy.

¹⁴ The pattern indicated by a comparison of the averages for each group of countries is sustained by the ranges (the high and low extremes) for each index. Most of the ranges overlap, that is, some countries which are in the low category with regard to politics are higher on any given index than some which are high on the scale of democracy. It is noteworthy that in both Europe and Latin America, the nations which are lowest on any of the indices presented in the table are also in the "less democratic" category. Conversely, almost all countries which rank at the top of any of the indices are in the "more democratic" class.

¹⁵ See John Dewey, *Democracy and Education* (New York, 1916).

¹⁶ Quoted in Arthur P. Whitaker, *op. cit.*, p. 112; see also Karl Mannheim, *Freedom, Power and Democratic Planning* (New York, 1950).

¹⁷ See C. H. Smith, "Liberalism and Level of Information," *Journal of Educational Psychology*, Vol. 39 (1948), pp. 65–82; Martin A. Trow, *Right Wing Radicalism and Political Intolerance*, Ph.D. dissertation, Columbia University, 1957, p. 17; Samuel Stouffer, *Communism, Conformity and Civil Liberties* (New York, 1955), pp. 138–39; K. Kido and M. Suyi, "Report of Social Stratification and Mobility in Tokyo, . . . Mobility in Tokyo, III: The Structure of Social Consciousness," *Japanese Sociological Review* (January, 1954), pp. 74–100.

¹⁸ Dewey has suggested that the character of the educational system will influence its effect on democracy, and this may shed some light on the sources of instability in Germany. The purpose of German education, according to Dewey, writing in 1916, was "disciplinary training rather than . . . personal development." The main aim was to

produce "absorption of the aims and meanings of existing institutions," and "thorough-going subordination" to them. This point raises issues which cannot be entered into here, but indicates the complex character of the relationship between democracy and closely related factors, such as education. See Dewey, *Democracy and Education, op. cit.*, pp. 108–10. It suggests caution, too, in drawing optimistic inferences about the prospects of democratic developments in Russia, based on the great expansion of education now taking place there.

[19] Ceylon, which shares with the Philippines and Japan the distinction of being the only democratic countries in South and Far Asia in which the Communists are unimportant electorally, also shares with them the distinction of being the only countries in this area in which a *majority* of the population is literate. It should be noted, however, that Ceylon does have a fairly large Trotskyist party, now the official opposition; and while its educational level is high for Asia, it is much lower than either Japan or the Philippines.

[20] A factor analysis carried out by Leo Schnore, based on data from seventy-five countries, demonstrates this. (To be published.)

[21] This statement is a "statistical" statement, which necessarily means that there will be many exceptions to the correlation. Thus we know that poorer people are more likely to vote for the Democratic or Labor parties in the U.S. and England. The fact that a large minority of the lower strata vote for the more conservative party in these countries does not challenge the proposition that stratification position is the main determinant of party choice, given the multivariate causal process involved in the behavior of people or nations. Clearly social science will never be able to account for (predict) all behavior.

[22] The study is reported in Daniel Lerner, *The Passing of Traditional Society* (Glencoe: The Free Press, 1958). These correlations are derived from census data; the main sections of the survey dealt with reactions to and opinions about the mass media, with inferences as to the personality types appropriate to modern and to traditional society.

[23] *Ibid.*, p. 63. The index of political participation was the per cent voting in the last five elections. These results cannot be considered as independent verification of the relationships presented in this paper, since the data and variables are basically the same (as they are also in the work by Lyle Shannon, *op. cit.*), but the identical results using three entirely different methods, the phi coefficient, multiple correlations, and means and ranges, show decisively that the relationships cannot be attributed to artifacts of the computations. It should also be noted that the three analyses were made without knowledge of each other.

[24] *Ibid.*, pp. 84–85.

[25] *Ibid.*, pp. 87–89. Other theories of underdeveloped areas have also stressed the circular character of the forces sustaining a given level of economic and social development; and in a sense this paper may be regarded as an effort to extend the analysis of the complex of institutions constituting a "modernized" society to the political sphere. Leo Schnore's unpublished monograph, *Economic Development and Urbanization, An Ecological Approach*, relates technological, demographic and organizational (including literacy and per capita income) variables as an interdependent complex. Harvey Leibenstein's recent volume, *Economic Backwardness and Economic Growth* (New York, 1957), views "underdevelopment" within the framework of a "quasi-equilibrium" economic theory, as a complex of associated and mutually supportive aspects of a society, and includes cultural and political characteristics—illiteracy, the lack of a middle class, a crude communications system—as part of the complex. (See pp. 39–41.)

[26] *Ibid.*, p. 60. Lerner also focuses upon certain personality requirements of a "modern" society which may also be related to the personality requirements of democracy. According to him, the physical and social mobility of modern society requires a mobile personality, capable of adaptation to rapid change. Development of a "mobile sensibility so adaptive to change that rearrangement of the self-system is its distinctive mode" has been the work of the 20th century. Its main feature is *empathy*, denoting the " general capacity to see oneself in the other fellow's situation, whether favorably

or unfavorably" (pp. 49 ff.). Whether this psychological characteristic results in a predisposition toward democracy (implying a willingness to accept the viewpoint of others) or is rather associated with the anti-democratic tendencies of a "mass society" type of personality (implying the lack of any solid personal values rooted in rewarding participation) is an open question. Possibly empathy, a more or less "cosmopolitan" outlook, is a general personality characteristic of modern societies, with other special conditions determining whether or not it has the social consequence of tolerance and democratic attitudes, or rootlessness and anomie.

[27] See S. M. Lipset, "Socialism—East and West—Left and Right," *Confluence*, Vol. 7 (Summer, 1958), pp. 173–92.

[28] Alexis de Tocqueville, *Democracy in America*, Vol. I (New York: Alfred A. Knopf, Vintage edition, 1945), p. 258.

[29] For discussion of this problem in a new state, see David Apter, *The Gold Coast in Transition* (Princeton University Press, 1955), esp. Chaps. 9 and 13. Apter shows the importance of efficient bureaucracy, and the acceptance of bureaucratic values and behavior patterns, for the existence of a democratic political order.

[30] See Emil Lederer, *The State of the Masses* (New York, 1940); Hannah Arendt, *Origins of Totalitarianism* (New York, 1950); Max Horkheimer, *Eclipse of Reason* (New York, 1947); Karl Mannheim, *Man and Society in an Age of Reconstruction* (New York, 1940); Philip Selznick, *The Organizational Weapon* (New York, 1952); José Ortega y Gasset, *The Revolt of the Masses* (New York, 1932).

[31] See Edward Banfield, *The Moral Basis of a Backward Society* (Glencoe: The Free Press, 1958), for an excellent description of the way in which abysmal poverty serves to reduce community organization in southern Italy. The data which do exist from polling surveys conducted in the United States, Germany, France, Great Britain, and Sweden show that somewhere between 40 and 50 per cent of the adults in these countries belong to voluntary associations, without lower rates of membership for the less stable democracies, France and Germany, than among the more stable ones, the United States, Great Britain, and Sweden. These results seemingly challenge the general proposition, although no definite conclusion can be made, since most of the studies employed non-comparable categories. This point bears further research in many countries. For the data on these countries see the following studies: for France, Arnold Rose, *Theory and Method in the Social Sciences* (Minneapolis: University of Minnesota Press, 1954), p. 74; and O. R. Gallagher, "Voluntary Associations in France," *Social Forces*, Vol. 36 (December, 1957), pp. 154–56; for Germany, Erich Reigrotski, *Soziale Verflechtungen in der Bundesrepublik* (Tübingen: J. C. B. Mohr, 1956), p. 164; for the U.S., Charles R. Wright and Herbert H. Hyman, "Voluntary Association Memberships of American Adults: Evidence from National Sample Surveys," *American Sociological Review*, Vol. 23 (June, 1958), p. 287, and J. C. Scott, Jr., "Membership and Participation in Voluntary Associations," *ibid.*, Vol. 22 (1957), pp. 315–26; Herbert Maccoby, "The Differential Political Activity of Participants in a Voluntary Association," *ibid.*, Vol. 23 (1958), pp. 524–33; for Great Britain see Mass Observation, *Puzzled People* (London: Victor Gollancz, 1947), p. 119; and Thomas Bottomore, "Social Stratification in Voluntary Organizations," in David Glass, ed., *Social Mobility in Britain* (Glencoe: The Free Press, 1954), p. 354; for Sweden see Gunnar Heckscher, "Pluralist Democracy: The Swedish Experience," *Social Research*, Vol. 15 (December, 1948), pp. 417–61.

[32] In introducing historical events as part of the analysis of factors *external* to the political system, which are part of the causal nexus in which democracy is involved, I am following in good sociological and even functionalist tradition. As Radcliffe-Brown has well put it, ". . . one 'explanation' of a social system will be its history, where we know it—the detailed account of how it came to be, what it is and where it is. Another 'explanation' of the same system is obtained by showing . . . that it is a special exemplification of laws of social psychology or social functioning. The two kinds of explanation do not conflict but supplement one another." A. R. Radcliffe-Brown, "On the Concept of Function in Social Science," *American Anthropologist*, New Series, Vol. 37 (1935), p. 401; see also Max Weber, *The Methodology of the Social Sciences* (Glencoe: The

Free Press, 1949), pp. 164–88, for a detailed discussion of the role of historical analysis in sociological research.

[33] *Op. cit.*, pp. 251–52.

[34] Walter Lippmann, referring to the seemingly greater capacity of the constitutional monarchies than the republics of Europe to "preserve order with freedom," suggests that this may be because "in a republic the governing power, being wholly secularized, loses much of its prestige; it is stripped, if one prefers, of all the illusions of intrinsic majesty." See his *The Public Philosophy* (New York: Mentor Books, 1956), p. 50.

[35] See Gabriel Almond, "Comparative Political Systems," *Journal of Politics*, Vol. 18 (1956), pp. 391–409.

[36] Herbert Luethy, *The State of France* (London: Secker and Warburg, 1955), p. 29.

[37] The race problem in the American South does constitute one basic challenge to the legitimacy of the system, and at one time did cause a breakdown of the national order. The conflict reduces the commitment of many white Southerners to the democratic rules down to the present. Great Britain had a comparable problem as long as Catholic Ireland remained part of the United Kingdom. Effective government could not satisfy Ireland. Political practices by both sides in Northern Ireland, Ulster, also illustrate the problem of a regime which is not legitimate to a large segment of its population.

[38] For an excellent analysis of the permanent crisis of the Austrian republic which flowed from the fact that it was viewed as an illegitimate regime by the Catholics and conservatives, see Charles Gulick, *Austria From Hapsburg to Hitler* (Berkeley: University of California Press, 1948).

[39] The French legitimacy problem is well described by Katherine Munro: "The Right wing parties never quite forgot the possibility of a counter revolution while the Left wing parties revived the Revolution militant in their Marxism or Communism; each side suspected the other of using the Republic to achieve its own ends and of being loyal only so far as it suited it. This suspicion threatened time and time again to make the Republic unworkable, since it led to obstruction in both the political and the economic sphere, and difficulties of government in turn undermined confidence in the regime and its rulers." Quoted in Charles A. Micaud, "French Political Parties: Ideological Myths and Social Realities," in Sigmund Neumann, ed., *Modern Political Parties* (Chicago: University of Chicago Press, 1956), p. 108.

[40] The linkage between democratic instability and Catholicism may also be accounted for by elements inherent in Catholicism as a religious system. Democracy requires a universalistic political belief system in the sense that it legitimates different ideologies. And it might be assumed that religious value systems which are more universalistic in the sense of placing less stress on being the only true church will be more compatible with democracy than those which assume that they have the only truth. The latter belief, held much more strongly by the Catholic than by most other Christian churches, makes it difficult for the religious value system to help legitimate a political system which requires, as part of its basic value system, the belief that "good" is served best through conflict among opposing beliefs.

Kingsley Davis has argued that a Catholic state church tends to be irreconcilable with democracy since "Catholicism attempts to control so many aspects of life, to encourage so much fixity of status and submission to authority, and to remain so independent of secular authority that it invariably clashes with the liberalism, individualism, freedom, mobility and sovereignty of the democratic nation." See his "Political Ambivalence in Latin America," *Journal of Legal and Political Sociology*, Vol. 1 (1943), reprinted in Christensen, *The Evolution of Latin American Government* (New York, 1951), p. 240.

[41] See Sigmund Neumann, *Die Deutschen Parteien: Wesen und Wandel nach dem Kriege* (2nd ed., Berlin, 1932), for exposition of the distinction between parties of integration and parties of representation. Neumann has further distinguished between parties of "democratic integration" (the Catholic, and Social Democratic parties) and those of "total integration" (Fascists and Communist parties) in his more recent chapter,

"Toward a Comparative Study of Political Parties," in the volume which he edited: *Modern Political Parties* (Chicago: University of Chicago Press, 1956), pp. 403–5.

[42] See Charles Gulick, *op. cit.* For their post-World War II formula for compromising this antagonism, see Herbert P. Secher, "Coalition Government: The Case of the Second Austrian Republic," *American Political Science Review*, Vol. 52 (September, 1958), p. 791.

[43] This tendency obviously varies with relation to urban communities, type of rural stratification, and so forth. For a discussion of the role of vocational homogeneity and political communication among farmers, see S. M. Lipset, *Agrarian Socialism* (Berkeley: University of California Press, 1950), Chap. 10, "Social Structure and Political Activity." For evidence on the undemocratic propensities of rural populations see Samuel A. Stouffer, *op. cit.*, pp. 138–39. National Public Opinion Institute of Japan, Report No. 26, *A Survey Concerning the Protection of Civil Liberties* (Tokyo, 1951) reports that the farmers were by far the occupational group least concerned with civil liberties. Carl Friedrich in accounting for the strength of nationalism and Nazism among German farmers suggests similar factors: that "the rural population is more homogeneous, that it contains a smaller number of outsiders and foreigners, that it has much less contact with foreign countries and peoples, and finally that its mobility is much more limited." "The Agricultural Basis of Emotional Nationalism," *Public Opinion Quarterly*, Vol. 1 (1937), pp. 50–51.

[44] Perhaps the first general statement of the consequences of "cross-pressures" on individual and group behavior may be found in Georg Simmel, *Conflict and the Web of Group Affiliations* (Glencoe: The Free Press, 1956), pp. 126–95. It is an interesting example of discontinuity in social research that the concept of cross-pressures was used by Simmel, but had to be independently rediscovered in voting research. For a detailed application of the effect of multiple-group affiliations on the political process in general, see David Truman, *The Governmental Process* (New York, 1951).

[45] See Juan Linz, *The Social Basis of German Politics*, Ph.D. thesis, Columbia University, 1958.

[46] See B. Berelson, P. F. Lazarsfeld, and W. McPhee, *Voting* (Chicago: University of Chicago Press, 1954), for an exposition of the usefulness of cross-pressure as an explanatory concept. Also, see S. M. Lipset, J. Linz, P. F. Lazarsfeld, and A. Barton, "Psychology of Voting," in *Handbook of Social Psychology*, Vol. 2 (Cambridge: Addison-Wesley, 1954), for an attempt to specify the consequences of different group memberships for voting behavior, and a review of the literature.

[47] As Dahl puts it, "if most individuals in the society identify with more than one group, then there is some positive probability that any majority contains individuals who identify for certain purposes with the threatened minority. Members of the threatened minority who strongly prefer their alternative will make their feelings known to those members of the tentative majority who also, at some psychological level, identify with the minority. Some of these sympathizers will shift their support away from the majority alternative and the majority will crumble." See Robert A. Dahl, *A Preface to Democratic Theory* (Chicago: University of Chicago Press, 1956), pp. 104–5. Parsons suggests that "pushing the implications of political difference too far activates the solidarities between adherents of the two parties which exist on other, nonpolitical bases so that majorities come to defend minorities of their own kind who differ from them politically." See Parsons' essay "Voting and the Equilibrium of the American Political System," in the volume edited by E. Burdick and A. Brodbeck, *American Voting Behavior* (Glencoe: The Free Press, 1959).

[48] Colin Clark, *The Conditions of Economic Progress* (New York, 1940).

[49] Georg Simmel, *op. cit.*, pp. 191–94. Talcott Parsons has recently made a similar point, indicating that one of the mechanisms for preventing a "progressively deepening rift in the electorate" is the "involvement of voting with the ramified solidarity structure of the society in such a way, that, though there is a correlation, there is no *exact* correspondence between political polarization and other bases of differentiation." Parsons, *op. cit.*

[50] T. H. Marshall has analyzed the gradual process of incorporation of the working class into the body politic in the 19th century, and has seen that process as the achievement of a "basic human equality, associated with full community membership, which is not inconsistent with a superstructure of economic inequality." See his brief but brilliant book, *Citizenship and Social Class* (Cambridge University Press, 1950), p. 77. Even though universal citizenship opens the way for the challenging of remaining social inequalities, it also provides a basis for believing that the process of social change toward equality will remain within the boundaries of allowable conflict in a democratic system.

[51] See David Apter, *op. cit.*, for a discussion of the evolving political patterns of Ghana. For an interesting brief analysis of the Mexican "one party" system, see L. V. Padgett, "Mexico's One-Party System, a Re-evaluation," *American Political Science Review*, Vol. 51 (1957), pp. 995–1008.

[52] As this paper was being edited for publication, political crises in several poor and illiterate countries occurred, which underline again the instability of democratic government in underdeveloped areas. The government of Pakistan was overthrown peacefully on October 7, 1958, and the new self-appointed president announced that "Western-type democracy cannot function here under present conditions. We have only 16 per cent literacy. In America you have 98 per cent." (*Associated Press* release, October 9, 1958.) The new government proceeded to abolish parliament and all political parties. Similar crises have occurred, almost simultaneously, in Tunisia, Ghana, and even in Burma, which since World War II has been considered one of the more stable governments in Southeast Asia, under Premier U Nu. Guinea has begun life as an independent state with a one-party system.

It is possible that the open emergence of semi-dictatorships without much democratic "front" may reflect the weakening of democratic symbols in these areas under the impact of Soviet ideology, which equates "democracy" with rapid, efficient accomplishment of the "will of the people" by an educated elite, not with particular political forms and methods.

[53] Robert J. Alexander, *Communism in Latin America* (New Brunswick: Rutgers University Press, 1957).

[54] Richard Pipes, "Max Weber and Russia," *World Politics*, Vol. 7 (1955), p. 383.

[55] Max Weber's essay on " 'Objectivity' in Social Science and Social Policy," in his *Methodology of the Social Sciences, op. cit.*, pp. 72–93.

[56] The methodology presuppositions of this approach on the level of the multivariate correlations and interactions of individual behavior with various social characteristics have been presented in Paul F. Lazarsfeld, "Interpretation of Statistical Relations as a Research Operation," in P. F. Lazarsfeld and M. Rosenberg, eds., *The Language of Social Research* (Glencoe: The Free Press, 1955), pp. 115–25; and in H. Hyman *Survey Design and Analysis* (Glencoe: The Free Press, 1955), Chaps. 6 and 7. See also the methodological appendices to Lipset, *et al., Union Democracy, op. cit.*, pp. 419–32; and S. M. Lipset, "The Political Process in Trade Unions: A Theoretical Statement," in M. Berger, *et al.*, eds., *Freedom and Control in Modern Society* (New York: Van Nostrand, 1954), pp. 122–24.

[57] This approach differs from Weber's attempt to trace the origins of modern capitalism. Weber was concerned to establish that *one* antecedent factor, a certain religious ethic, was crucially significant in the syndrome of economic, political, and cultural conditions leading up to the development of Western capitalism. My concern is not to establish the causal necessity of any one factor, but rather the syndrome of conditions which most frequently distinguish nations which may be empirically categorized as "more democratic" or "less democratic," without implying any absolute qualities to the definition.

CHAPTER 8

National Political Development: Measurement and Analysis[*]

Phillips Cutright

Large-scale comparative studies of national political systems offer the social scientist a methodology of great analytic power if only proper use can be made of the material at hand. In this article we examine in some detail a single sociological effort to apply the comparative method to national political systems.

Perhaps the best known and most articulate effort by a sociologist to deal empirically with a large number of contemporary national political systems is that of Seymour M. Lipset.[1] Lipset establishes two groupings of national political systems, stable and unstable democracies, and popular and elite based dictatorships. He then poses the question: What differences in national economic development might explain why a nation would be in one group and not in the other?[2] To answer this question he offers a number of indicators of wealth, industrialization, education, and urbanization. (He does not combine indicators to form a scale of wealth or industrialization, or economic development, although development forms one-half of the central theme of the paper. The other half, "democracy," is not scaled either.)

Lipset presents the statistical means for the nations in each of the two political groups (stable democratic as opposed to all other forms of government) in two areas of the world, the English-speaking and European areas and the Latin-American area. A sample of his analysis of these means is instructive: Among the English-speaking and European stable democracies the average number of telephones per 1,000 persons (a "wealth" indicator) is 205 compared to only 58 per 1,000 in "European and English-speaking unstable democracies and dictatorships." Similar differences favoring democratic nations is revealed for all of the indicators of wealth, industrialization, urbanization and education among the English-speaking and

Reprinted from *American Sociological Review*, Vol. 28 (April, 1963), pp. 253–64, by permission of the American Sociological Association.

European groups and, also, among Latin-American democracies and non-democracies.

Lipset seeks to show the effect of economic development on national political systems. This statistical effect is given as proof that a strong relationship exists. However, comparison of means between two groups may show a difference without telling us the strength of the association between the independent variables that are presumably responsible for the observed difference between the two groups. Thus Lipset notes that stable democracies have 205 telephones per 1,000 persons compared to only 58 per 1,000 in non-democratic nations and infers that there is a "strong" relationship or association between this indicator of national wealth and the type of political system observed.

To give a little more depth to his claims, Lipset presents the ranges for each indicator. Here some curious findings appear. The first and most obvious is that the means between the two types of national governments differ, yet the spread in the values on almost every indicator is so extreme that it appears that it would be very difficult to place a single nation in either the democratic or non-democratic category knowing, for example, only its score on the number of telephones. In the European and English-speaking stable democracies a nation may have from 43 to 400 telephones per 1,000 population while a European dictatorship may have as few as 7 or as many as 196 per 1,000. One wonders about the stable European democracies that have only 43, 60, 90, 130, 150 or even 195 telephones. How do they manage while dictatorial European nations can at the same time have as many as 196 per 1,000? More striking is the case of Latin-American *democracies* in which the average number of telephones is 25 and the range is from 12 to 58. The number of telephones in Latin-American democracies seems paltry when compared to the number of telephones in European dictatorships. European dictatorships have, on the average, double the number of telephones (and "wealth" and "economic development") of Latin-American democracies.

Such a peculiarity can exist for a number of reasons. The first may be a failure to develop a scale of "democracy" that could approximate the scale on which all the independent variables are defined. A nation is either democratic or it is not, according to the Lipset scoring system. It makes little difference that in the verbal discussion of national political systems one talks about shades of democracy if, in the statistical assessment, one cannot distinguish among nations. However, one cannot distinguish among national political systems without a scoring system that assigns values to different nations according to some stated criteria. Although Lipset states his criteria he does not differentiate between France and Albania, Brazil or Chile. We would be better able to assess his descriptive statistics if the dependent variables—the national political system—had been indexed or scaled.

A second reason is a lack of adequate conceptualization of national political systems. A value-laden curiosity about democracies and dictatorships is no substitute for theoretical focus. A theoretical focus means one has a hypothesis to test using a set of predicting variables that are "given" by the theoretical scheme. Lipset seeks to test the hypothesis that democracy will flourish in nations where wealth is distributed rather equally and in which large masses of starving or near starving farmers and workers are not dominated by an elite of wealth and aristocracy. Do populations with a relatively high standard of living possess the "self restraint" necessary to sustain "democratic institutions?" Do impoverished masses languish under an elite dictatorship which further represses them or do they support tyrants (in which they give popular support to a dictatorship) who repress them? Lipset makes no distinction between the varieties of "democratic" or non-democratic political systems. His working hypothesis asks only whether or not a significant difference on each economic indicator exists between nations with two types of political characteristics. When the hypothesis is confirmed he explains the finding through discussion of what people want or what the effects of education might be on self-restraint.

The concept of social change does not appear in Lipset's analysis of his data but he refers to studies by Schnore and Lerner in which statistical assessment of the interdependence of many of the same indicators used by Lipset is demonstrated and, in the case of Lerner, some links between education, communication, urbanization, economic development and individual political participation are tentatively established.[3] Lerner's analysis is, however, restricted to the Middle East.

RESEARCH OBJECTIVES AND HYPOTHESIS

In the first part of this paper we develop an index of political development. The index of political development is operationally defined. The concept that guided construction of the index can be stated simply—a politically developed nation has more complex and specialized national political institutions than a less politically developed nation. Degree of political development can be measured and each nation can be placed on a continuum of development, which will allow it to be compared with any other nation in the world. Operationally we bank heavily on the role played by political parties in national political life in measuring political development.[4]

The principal hypothesis tested is that political institutions are interdependent with educational systems, economic development, communications systems, urbanization, and labor force distribution. A nation's economic system can develop only if its educational system keeps pace, if people concentrate in urban areas, if communication and transportation systems emerge and if changes occur in family and social life that induce people to fit into the demands of the unfolding system. Schnore has measured the interdependence among certain of these factors.[5] But to test the hypothesis that political institutions are not set apart from the rest of a society's social institutions we must construct an index of political development and then test the hypothesis by assessing the association between political development and other measures of national systems.

CONSTRUCTING AN INDEX OF POLITICAL DEVELOPMENT

The following items were selected and given the weights indicated. The time period covered by the data is 1940 through 1960. The score each nation received for the first year was added to the score it received the following year to get a cumulative total score.

A scheme for scoring the nations (in which high scores mean high development) should penalize each nation for political instability which represents "backsliding" and reward it for achieving or retaining more complex political forms of organization. Points for any one year were awarded in the following manner.

1. Legislative Branch of Government.
   Two points for each year in which a parliament existed in which the lower or the only chamber contained representatives of two or more political parties and the minority party or parties had at least 30 per cent of all seats. One point for each year in which a parliament existed whose members were the representatives of one or more political parties, but where the "30 per cent rule" was violated. No points for each year no parliament existed or for years when either of the above types of parliaments was abolished or discarded by executive power. Parliaments whose members are not members of political parties are given a zero. Parliaments that are not self-governing bodies (e.g., the mock parliaments of colonial governments) are given a zero.

2. Executive Branch of Government.
   One point for each year the nation was ruled by a chief executive who was in office by virtue of direct vote in an open election where he faced competition or was selected by a political party in a multi-party system, as defined by the conditions necessary to get 2 points on the legislative branch indicator above. If the parliament ceased being a multi-party parliament because of executive action, the

chief executive stopped getting points. One-half point each year the chief executive was not selected by virtue of his hereditary status but was selected by criteria other than those necessary to attain one point as given above. Colonial governments receive one-half point per year. No points if the nation was governed by a hereditary ruler.

It is possible for a nation to acquire no points, one-half or 1 point depending on the selection of the chief executive. The combined index has a range of zero to 3 points per year. Over the 21-year period of our study it would be possible for a nation to have a total raw score between zero and 63 points.

RELATIONSHIP OF POLITICAL TO OTHER MEASURES OF NATIONAL DEVELOPMENT

This study began with the aim of measuring the degree of association between political development and other types of socioeconomic development. The objective was a statistical assessment of the degree of association between educational development, urbanization, communication development, economic growth and labor force characteristics and the measure of political development.[6] A statistical statement of the proportion of the variation around the mean of the political development index that could be accounted for by covariation with selected independent variables was also sought. Finally, if the association was reasonably close one might build a prediction equation which would describe for each nation whether its level of political development was commensurate with the values it had on the independent variables in a prediction equation.

Of the several independent variables considered, the communications development index[7] had a Pearson zero order association with political development of .81.[8] The communications development index is tightly related to an index of economic development (.95) but is a better predictor of political development than is economic development.[9] The communications index reflects the ability and the need of national systems to maintain differing types of communication systems depending on the varying degrees of literacy of their population and varying levels of integration of the economic social order.

The relationship between national communications development and political development may be seen in graphic form in Figure 1.

This scattergram makes the correlation coefficient more meaningful. The communication development scores on the horizontal axis increase from left to right. The political development scores are on the vertical axis and increase vertically.

The most striking thing about Figure 1 is the steady increase in the level of political development as the level of communication development

Figure 1. Relationship of Communications Development to Political Development*

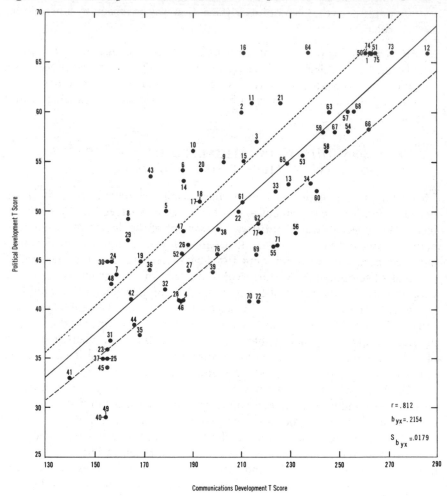

Communications Development T Score

* See Table 2 for the identification of each nation by its number shown here.

increases. The main diagonal is the *regression line.* If every nation's scores were such as to put it exactly on that line, the correlation coefficient would be 1.00. We see, however, that some nations are above the line and some are below. What is the difference? A nation below the line is politically under-developed relative to its given level of communication development.[10] The difference between the communication index scores that the politically overdeveloped nations (above the line) really have and what they would have if they were on the regression line may represent the extent of possible imbalance in the social system of the nation.

Nations below the line face alternative routes to the line. They can increase their level of political development and rise vertically to the line or they can decrease their communications and move to the left until they meet the line—maintaining or perhaps decreasing their level of political development. Such movements as this may seem unlikely to people living in a society in which communication systems are believed to increase steadily, but alternative (even "impossible") movements can occur during revolutions, civil wars and territorial occupation by a foreign power, or through economic disasters. Internal social change may be violent or not, but in any case should result in movement of predictable direction.

Mathematical models have been considered[11] which might be applied to data like these to test the notion that there will be movement toward the line. Empirical testing would be the only way to state whether nations do in fact increase or decrease either variable in order to come into equilibrium. However, if measurements are made each year for a period of years, the movement of nations can be precisely plotted. If empirical tests do not show nations moving toward their equilibrium point, then it is also possible that the same test will reveal different equilibrium points for nations in different socioeconomic conditions. We have conveniently assumed a common set of equilibrium points rather than several (one could have had several equilibrium points simply if different clusters of nations had different regression lines, a possibility to be explored in later research).

The inability of our index to actually distinguish for every nation the refinements of political development, the missing data and substitution of estimates for five communication scores, the mis-reporting of political information—all of these types of error exist and should be considered before refined explanations of minor deviations from the line are attempted.[12] For the benefit of students who may wish to consider these possibilities, the nations that lie between the two broken lines in Figure 1 may be considered as being off the regression line because of measurement and other errors; hence attention may be devoted to nations that are outside the bands for deviant case analysis or comparison of extreme cases on either side of the line.

ACCOUNTING FOR NATIONAL POLITICAL DEVELOPMENT

Inspection of the matrix of correlations in Table 1 reveals a high degree of association between each predicting variable and political development.[13]

Table 1. Matrix of Correlations of National Measures of Political Development, and Levels of Communication, Urbanization, Education and Employment in Agriculture:
N = 77

	2	3	4	5	Means	S.D.
1. Communication	74	88	−86	81	204.5	36.4
2. Urbanization	—	77	−75	69	49.9	8.2
3. Education		—	−78	74	105.8	16.7
4. Agriculture			—	72	53.1	10.5
5. Political Development				—	49.9	9.7

$\hat{Y} = 3.7 + .172X_1 + .232X_2 + .003X_3 + −.014X_4$
$R_y .1234 = .82$
Modified prediction equation used:
$\hat{Y} = 1.97 + .1789X_1 + .2274X_2$
$R_y .12 = .82$

The communications index summed the T scores of newspaper readers per capita, newsprint consumption per capita, the volume of domestic mail per capita and the number of telephones per capita.

The urbanization index is the T score of the proportion of the population of the nation living in cities over 100,000. The education index was formed by combining T scores of literacy with T scores of the number of students per 100,000 enrolled in institutions of higher education, and the proportion of the economically active labor force employed in agriculture was also T scored.

Political development scores were T scored.

Correlations in this matrix use estimated values when no data was available. Although political development values were available for each nation, urban data was missing in 2 of the 77 cases, communication scores in 5, education lacked 4 national scores and agriculture was missing in 18 cases. Estimates were based on the regression of a known value for a nation on the unknown, using regression weights for all of the nations on which data was available. These estimates were then used in the prediction equation.

But the variable most closely associated is the communications development index. If taken alone it accounts for 65 per cent of the variation of the political development scores around the mean.

Computation of a multiple correlation coefficient using all four independent variables simultaneously reveals a multiple R of .82. Thus a total of 67 per cent of the observed variation around the mean of the dependent variable is associated with covariation in the independent variables. This compares with the 65 per cent of variation that could be associated using communications as a single predictor.

The fact that the communication index is highly correlated with the education index, and its .95 correlation with economic development, reveals the highly interdependent nature of national social organization. Thus, the score a nation receives on communications development is itself highly dependent on the national level of educational development, urbanization, labor force movement out of agricultural employment, and economic development. That communications and not economic development, urbanization or education best accounts for the political development of a nation is significant. It should not obscure, however, the essential inter-dependence of this matrix of characteristics which collectively give a distinctive profile to any given nation and collectively interact to yield political outcomes which in turn interact to yield further changes in the independent variables themselves.

USING THE PREDICTION EQUATION TO FULL ADVANTAGE

Political development scores can be used in several ways. We can make a simple statement about the relative position of any nation regarding its political development by comparing the index score of one country with scores of other nations. We can extend the power of such comparison considerably, however, if we use a "prediction equation" to predict what the score of any nation on political development "should be" on the basis of its "complete" profile of national development.[14]

When this calculation is done the predicted value of political development can be compared to the actual value of any nation. If we subtract the predicted value from the actual value we get a number that represents the error of prediction. If the error is positive, the nation has a higher than expected political development score.

For example, the actual political development T score for Canada is 66 and its predicted value is 61.5. The difference is +4.5. Canada has a larger than predicted political development score. On the other hand, Argentina has an actual political development value of 53, but a predicted value 57.4, with a negative residual of −4.5. Argentina's actual political development is less than expected on the basis of its communications and urbanization scores.

These errors may tell us much about some of the factors that influence political development. One such factor is revealed in Table 2 which groups nations according to their geographic location. The size of the average net residual error for the 12 nations in North America, was a positive 5.2. The table also shows that of the 12 nations in North America, 10 had positive residuals. The situation is similar for South America. There, average net residuals reveal greater than predicted political development—an average error of more than three T score values. Looking over the table as a whole, it is clear that nations located in the Western Hemisphere enjoy a considerable advantage in their political development over nations located in Asia or Europe.[15]

We might speculate that the absence of international conflict over the long history of North and South America has resulted in far greater benefits

Table 2. Residual Error of Prediction of Political Development: by Continent and Nation*

North America	Y-Ŷ			Y-Ŷ
1. Canada	4.5	39. Mongolia		−5.0
2. Costa Rica	8.1	40. Muscat		−8.5
3. Cuba	3.9	41. Nepal		−1.5
4. Dom. Republic	−4.8	42. Pakistan		0.6
5. El Salvador	6.7	43. Philippines		10.8
6. Guatemala	8.2	44. Thailand		−2.6
7. Haiti	5.4	45. S. Arabia		−9.8
8. Honduras	8.5	46. Syria		−6.2
9. Mexico	4.6	47. Turkey		2.0
10. Nicaragua	9.4	48. Viet Nam		1.0
11. Panama	8.4	49. Yemen		−8.5
12. United States	−0.1	50. Australia		·1.7
		51. N. Zealand		3.0
South America	Y-Ŷ	*Europe*		Y-Ŷ
13. Argentina	−4.5	52. Albania		1.6
14. Bolivia	7.2	53. Austria		−1.4
15. Brazil	3.7	54. Belgium		0.0
16. Chile	12.7	55. Bulgaria		−5.4
17. Colombia	1.5	56. Czechoslovakia		−6.2
18. Equador	2.9	57. Denmark		−0.5
19. Paraguay	2.2	58. Finland		−1.1
20. Peru	6.6	59. France		1.3
21. Uruguay	5.2	60. W. Germany		−6.7
22. Venezuela	−2.8	61. Greece		0.7
Asia	Y-Ŷ	62. Hungary		−4.1
23. Afghanistan	−3.2	63. Iceland		1.2
24. Burma	5.7	64. Ireland		9.8
25. Cambodia	−4.2	65. Italy		−0.1
26. Ceylon	2.1	66. Luxembourg		−3.2
27. China	−0.9	67. Netherlands		−1.8
28. Fed. of Malaya	−4.4	68. Norway		1.0
29. India	6.4	69. Poland		−6.9
30. Indonesia	5.8	70. Portugal		−9.8
31. Iran	−4.6	71. Romania		−5.7
32. Iraq	−2.5	72. Spain		−12.7
33. Israel	−3.5	73. Sweden		3.2
34. Japan	−6.3	74. Switzerland		4.8
35. Jordan	−4.1	75. United Kingdom		1.0
36. Rep. of Korea	−1.0	76. Yugoslavia		−1.2
37. Laos	−3.8	77. U.S.S.R.		−5.3
38. Lebanon	−3.0			

* Numbers in front of each nation identify it in Figure 1.
† Standard error of estimate of residuals: $s_{y \cdot x} = \pm 5.60$.
Adopted from Edwards, *op. cit.*, p. 162.

for their political development than we anticipated. Our common stereotype of Latin political instability is subject to some re-evaluation when seen from the world perspective. Far from being unstable, the prediction equation suggests that they are not only relatively stable but relatively more developed than *comparable nations* around the world. The absence of international conflict may well be one of the crucial variables to consider as a background to understanding the political development of nations. Of course, in the absence of international conflict within the Western Hemisphere it is impossible to differentiate among nations within the hemisphere. Little can be said about the relation of war to political development because such conflicts do not exist. (*Anything* that does not exist in the Western Hemisphere but does exist in other areas of the world can be invoked as an "explanation" of the direction of the residual values!)[16] In fact a number of Asian nations received their independence largely through the indirect effects of World War II. The Asian nations that have more complex political organization than predicted are India, Indonesia, Burma and the Philippines. These achieved independence *after* the war was over. Most *long run independent* Asian nations have *lower* than predicted political development. There are, in short, no single factor explanations of political development. The presence or absence of international conflict on the territory of a nation, and other violent conflict may, if protracted, influence the development of nations; and complex social systems are especially vulnerable to such changes. Changes that disrupt socioeconomic life may be expected to disrupt other aspects of the national system. We might hypothesize the amount of disruption would be related to the degree of complexity of organization and interdependency within a given nation.[17]

When we compare the predicted with the actual score and find that a nation has departed from its predicted values, we can view it as being under some pressure to move toward the predicted score on political development (or social development). The student interested in mass movements, political change or revolution may have seen in the preceding discussions a means of locating nations that may be experiencing deep strains in the sociopolitical system.

For example, theories of political change which view mass movements as the carriers of political change usually portray such action as taking place when the political institutions are not "adequate" in form or function and are sufficiently out of phase with other areas of national development to set up the conditions that allow traditional bonds of allegiance of the masses to the elites and to existing political institutions to be broken in a mass upheaval. The meaning of the deviation from the "multiple" regression line formed by a set of predicted political scores may be translated in terms of its possible measurement of pressures on certain social classes, economic, or power-elite groups. Kornhauser regards the historic development of national social systems in terms of its rate of development (i.e., rate of urbanization, industrialization, transformation of the educational institutions, and the complexity of the economy and communications systems) in relation to political behavior of certain segments of the population that are affected by rapid change.[18] Other theorists focus on the importance of changes in national character before the economic transformations which lead to political disequilibrium can occur.[19]

The method presented in this paper makes a *prediction* about which nations should experience political movements of a specific type (either toward increasing complexity or decreasing complexity). Theories of change can then be tested against what actually happens. This frees us from the primary and very legitimate criticism leveled against most political change theorists: that they are talking about something that is past and done with. The explanations suffer from *ex post facto* explanation.

Taking Asia as an example, we have already noted the political character of India (6.4), the Philippines (10.8), Burma (5.7); and Indonesia (5.8). These are the only Asian nations whose positive errors of prediction are larger than one standard deviation ($s_{y.x} = +5.60$) of the residuals. Changes *have* been occurring in these nations, and the more dramatic of these changes are political. Burma and Indonesia have turned away from complex political organization and have abandoned multi-party politics. They may move toward the regression line not only by increasing their socioeconomic development scores (a problematic event) but by decreasing their level of political development (a certainty). When they reach the line, the strain to reestablish more complex political forms may return, providing socioeconomic development continues.

The pressures in India and the Philippines toward similar political "backsliding" may also be strong and whether they will follow the same path taken by Burma and Indonesia is problematic. If rapid economic-social development can occur they may achieve political stability.[20]

For the case-study oriented student of social change, this technique supplies a basis on which to pick cases on more than "expert" testimony. Here is a tool for locating deviant cases if one wishes to compare different types of nations in detail to see the institutional mechanisms or other national characteristics that allow a nation to wander far from the regression line for many years. He might wish to contrast, for example, Ireland (9.8) with Spain (-12.7), or Chile (12.7) with Argentina (-4.5).

In tracing out of the social correlates of the political development of nations, one need not wait for the future. The design used here could be taken back to 1930. One might calculate the residual values at five-year intervals and recalculate the deviations, observing the differences among different types of nations. Continued up to 1960, the last sample of points and deviations would look approximately like our own.[21] Such an analysis might reveal cut-off points in social-economic development beyond which change in the political system is apparently unavoidable. It could reveal a cut-off point further down the scale where complex political institutions cannot stand for long. Such a longitudinal study could get at the interaction between political and other institutions in the society. It could measure some of the non-economic aspects of economic growth that trouble students of underdeveloped nations. Does the existence of complex (given their level of socioeconomic development) political organization in Latin American States give them an advantage over their politically backward counterparts in Europe and Asia? What are the effects of sustained political development on other systems within the nation that may allow it to "take off" to new heights of social growth or plunge it into revolution and political traditionalism? What differences in national character sustain political change, economic change or traditionalism, and how is national character affected by increasing levels of organizational complexity in nations?[22]

SUMMARY

This report developed some of the possible applications of an index of political development for 77 independent nations in all continents except Africa. (Africa was omitted for statistical considerations.) Knowledge of the level of the development of the communications system of a nation accounts for 65 per cent of the variation in scores around the mean of the political development index. A multiple regression equation which added educational development, agriculture labor force and degree of urbanization to the communication index as predictors of political development raised the level of explained variation to 67 per cent (Ry. .1234 = .82).

The matrix of high intercorrelations among a variety of indicators of the specialization and level of development of different aspects of national social-economic and political life supported the idea that social systems are indeed systems—that is, their parts are interdependent. The concept of interdependence and the statistical method of this study led us to consider the existence of hypothetical equilibrium points toward which each nation is moving. It is possible for a nation to be politically overdeveloped or underdeveloped, and we suggest that either political or non-political changes will occur to put the nation into equilibrium.

The extent to which a nation diverges from its predicted level of political development was considered and possible ways to utilize these errors of prediction were discussed. Finally, the ability of social scientists to test theories concerning revolution, mass movements and political change was considered.

NOTES

* It is a pleasure to acknowledge the support of the Faculty Research Committee of Dartmouth College. A Ford Foundation Public Affairs grant to Dartmouth College also aided the execution of this research. I was greatly stimulated by and am indebted to Robert A. Dentler for his advice, encouragement and helpful criticism during the initial and final stages of the study. Robert Sokol gave the manuscript a careful reading. My thanks to Robert Van Dam, Lawrence Stifler, Kimberly Holtorff and the other students who helped in the collection of some of the materials. The views expressed here in no way reflect the opinion of the Social Security Administration.

[1] Seymour M. Lipset, "Some Social Requisites of Democracy: Economic Development and Political Legitimacy," *American Political Science Review*, 53 (March, 1959), pp. 69–105. See also Lyle W. Shannon, "Is Level of Development Related to Capacity for Self-Government?" *American Journal of Economics and Sociology*, 17 (July, 1958), pp. 367–82, and a follow-up study also by Shannon, "Socioeconomic Development and Demographic Variables as Predictors of Political Change," *Sociological Quarterly*, III (January, 1962), pp. 27–43. Leo F. Schnore's "The Statistical Measurement of Urbanization and Economic Development," *Land Economics*, XXXVII (August, 1961), pp. 229–245, contains an assessment of the relationship among a number of different non-political indicators of national development we will use in this paper.

[2] Ratings by a single expert or by panels of experts, averaging the opinions of judges concerning their opinions on the condition of the press, political freedoms, etc., are of less value than a more objective indicator of political development. Careful examination of Russell H. Fitzgibbons, "A Statistical Evaluation of Latin-American Democracy," *Western Political Quarterly*, 9 (1956), pp. 607–19, as well as Lipset's attempt to place nations in "democratic" or what amounts to "undemocratic" clusters, reveal the problems of this method of subjective evaluation. The shift in the rank order (by experts) of the Latin-American nations across time periods allows the person using the index to take his pick of the democratic and undemocratic nations. A more crucial point is the lack of agreement among raters concerning the rank order and, with larger numbers of nations, the necessity to abandon subjective evaluations and turn to objective indicators —what expert can be in intimate contact with the political histories of all the nations of the world and also be willing or able to order them on simple scales, let alone multiple dimensions? We can devise statistical and objective methods of measuring political development, just as the economist does when he asks about energy consumption per capita and not what an expert believes the whole economy of a nation has been doing over the past year. This implies that we can also remove ourselves from the world of ethnocentric judgments about the goodness or evil of political systems and turn to other aspects of political systems in order to understand them.

[3] See Daniel Lerner, *The Passing of Traditional Society* (Glencoe: The Free Press, 1958).

[4] The index is, of course, heavily dependent upon available data. The selection among alternative items for the index was guided by the coherent interpretation of Max Weber's political sociology as given by Reinhard Bendix, *Max Weber: An Intellectual Portrait* (Garden City: Doubleday, 1960).

The primary source for the materials used in this study was the *Political Handbook of the World: Parliaments, Parties and Press*, published annually for the Council on Foreign Relations (New York: Harper and Brothers, from 1940 through 1961). Needed supplementary checks were secured by reference to the *Encyclopedia Britannica* and other reference works. Nations included for study are listed in Table 2. With the exception of nations located in Africa, nations recognized by the United Nations as being "independent" nations in the 1960 *Statistical Yearbook* were included in this study. A few very small nations (Monaco, Liechtenstein, Andorra) were omitted. Nearly 100 per cent of the populations of all continents except Africa are thus included. The decision to omit Africa was based on the well known statistical effect of artificially inflated relationships when a large number of the cases cluster at one or both ends of the regression line. Including

African nations would have inflated our correlations because they would have clustered in one corner of the scattergram. Until we develop a more sensitive measure of political development and also accumulate accurate information on the social and economic conditions in most African nations it seemed reasonable to exclude them from this initial study. A total of seventy-seven independent nations are included.

[5] For a matrix of rank order correlations of a number of indicators of these variables see Schnore, *op. cit.*, p. 236. Schnore's correlations tend to be slightly higher than product moment correlations using the T scoring method, but slight differences in the case base included may account for such differences.

See also Alex Inkeles, "National Character and Modern Political Systems," Francis L. K. Hsu, editor, in *Psychological Anthropology* (Homewood, Illinois: The Dorsey Press, 1961), pp. 172–208. He reviews various approaches to this topic and cites studies which suggest connections between national character and modern political systems. However, no conclusions can be drawn from this body of work in part because it lacks a standard measure of political systems against which different national characters might be associated. For a definite point of view on the subject of the importance of personality to social change generally and economic and political change in particular, see Everett E. Hagen, *On the Theory of Social Change* (Homewood, Illinois: The Dorsey Press, 1962). Hagen's theory has the virtue of being testable, but he presents little supporting evidence himself—again, in part, because the evidence simply does not exist. In rejecting economic theories of social change Hagen swings to psychological explanations, but does not completely bypass sociological perspectives.

[6] Social-economic statistics used in this report were drawn from the last reporting year from the following United Nations sourcebooks: *Demographic Yearbook, 1960, Statistical Yearbook, 1960,* and *Report on the World Social Situation, 1957. The Yearbook of Labor Statistics, 1960,* was the source for labor force statistics.

Statistical assessment followed T scoring of all data. A simple technique for computing the T score is given in Allen E. Edwards, *Statistical Methods for the Behavioral Sciences* (New York: Holt, Rinehart and Winston, 1954). For a single item, T scoring of the raw data will yield a mean of fifty and a standard deviation of ten. If we add items together to form an index, four items with a sum of 200 represents a subject (or nation) with an average index score. All single item indicators and combined indices in this paper have been T scored. The original T scoring was done for all independent and territorial political divisions in the world (excluding most Pacific Island dependent territories) for which data was available. Thus the T score for newsprint consumption is based on a case base of ninety-three and not the seventy-seven nations reported here. This fact accounts for the small departures in Table 1 of means and standard deviations one would expect from T scoring.

[7] The communications development index is formed by summing the T scores a given nation received on newspaper consumption, newsprint consumption, telephones and the number of pieces of domestic mail per capita. If one or two indicators of the four were missing we took the average of the two or three available indicators and added their scores to estimate the total index score. Five of the seventy-seven nations had less than two communications indicators and their scores were estimated and used in the prediction equation developed later in the paper.

[8] Variables considered but not included in the matrix because of high intercorrelations with variables in the matrix were an economic development index and the industrial labor force index. Economic development was measured by combining the T scores for a given nation of per capita measures of: energy consumption, steel consumption, income in U.S. dollars and the number of motor vehicles. These items are all highly intercorrelated: See Schnore, *op. cit.*, p. 236.

[9] Product moment correlation of communication development against political development was .81 compared to .68 for economic development against political development.

[10] Our use of the terms politically over- or under-developed should not be understood as a judgment of what the nation should have from a moral or ethical point of view.

A politically underdeveloped nation lacks sufficient points which it could obtain only if it met the criteria set by our political development index. In severe cases it may lack any political party or even a parliament. Our statements of whether or not a nation is underdeveloped or overdeveloped are not made with sole reference to its score of the political development index—a nation is either high, low or in between on the index. This judgment is made with reference to the political development score the nation should have *relative* to its level of communications development. Thus a nation with a one party system may actually be overdeveloped politically relative to its communications system or its level of urbanization and other measures of national growth.

[11] See James S. Coleman, "The Mathematical Study of Small Groups," in Herbert Solomon (ed.), *Mathematical Thinking in the Measurement of Behavior* (Glencoe: The Free Press, 1960), pp. 26–30.

[12] In Figure 1 we have drawn broken lines on either side of the regression line we actually observed for the seventy-seven nations. For these data the sample estimate of the standard error of the regression coefficients can be applied to describe what is a "small" and what is a "large" departure from the regression line. The broken lines on each side of the regression line represent the range of alternative regression lines that would be likely to occur if we were drawing a sample of seventy-seven from a larger population. Although these statistical conditions are not met in this case, the use of a high and a low estimate of alternative regression coefficient establishes a hypothetical band which may help us sort out errors of measurement and other types of error that may result in moving a nation several points away from the line when actually it should be closer to it. Measurement errors may also place a nation on the line when it ought not to be there, but this is less likely than the former movement which decreases correlations.

[13] When intercorrelations are high it becomes impossible to give exact meaning to the size or sign of the beta weights in the prediction equation. This is a favorite pastime of some sociologists but inspection of the correlations and beta weights in Table 1 should make them hesitate to partial out variation to any specific independent variable in a multiple regression analysis. Since I have indulged in this statistical fantasy myself, I feel obliged to bring it to the attention of my colleagues. The use of partial correlations to produce meaningful correlations when intercorrelations are high is also doubtful. Removing the effect of "communication" and then seeing what the partial is between education and political development would reveal a partial of near zero, but this certainly would not mean that education was not a vital factor. Partial correlation is way of finding out what added gain one may expect by including certain variables in a multiple regression equation, but it tends to over-simplify our conception of the world under some conditions. It is what might be called an "anti-systems" statistic, albeit an occasionally useful one.

[14] The new beta weights in the prediction equation show, however, that no gain in prediction would come from using education or agricultural labor force scores and for that reason we use a modified prediction equation which is shown in Table 1. It yields a multiple R identical with that given by all four predictors. Only communication development and urbanization scores are used to calculate the expected political development values for the seventy-seven nations.

[15] The U.S.S.R. is considered to be in Europe and New Zealand and Australia in Asia for the convenience of presentation as well as their geographic location.

[16] See Hagen, *op. cit.*, pp. 185–99 for a statement of social mechanisms that intervene to produce conditions favorable to political development as a consequence of conquest in war or other factors that led to a "withdrawal of status respect" from elite and non-elite groups in the afflicted society. His comments would seem to apply particularly well to certain Asian nations and the consequences of World War II for their political development.

[17] Greater depth of analysis of the variation among nations within continents can be achieved by subtracting out the "bias" effect (the mean of the net residual errors of prediction) that being located on a particular continent gives to a nation, and each nation can then start out on equal terms for further analysis. For example, we could subtract 5.2 from each *actual* score of the North American nations and 3.5 from each South

American nation. In similar vein, we could add 1.5 to each Asian nation and 1.8 to each European nation.

[18] William Kornhauser, *The Politics of Mass Society* (Glencoe: The Free Press, 1959). See also the discussion by Joseph R. Gusfield, "Mass Society and Extremist Politics," *American Sociological Review*, 27 (February, 1962), pp. 19–30.

[19] Hagen, *op. cit.*, and Inkeles, *op cit.*

[20] Philippine deviation may be partially explained by this observation. "While Washington officials and Ambassador Spruance took great pains to maintain neutrality between the candidates, they made it clear to the Philippine government that the conduct of the election was of vital concern to the United States. Had the Liberal Administration been returned to power by means of fraud and violence, it would have been in no position to bargain successfully for badly needed economic assistance and for the much desired revision of the Bell Act!" *Internal pressures* for an honest election, however, are also cited. Willard H. Elsbree, "The 1953 Philippine Presidential Elections," *Pacific Affairs*, XXVII (March, 1954), p. 13. It is, however, interesting to note that representation in the Philippine lower House conformed to our definition of multi-party representation only during the first decade of independence, and has violated the "30 per cent rule" of minority party representation since 1957. In India the Congress party's majorities also override the 30 per cent rule.

[21] Space restrictions prohibit more than mention of the statistical problems of treating change over time: for example, one would need measures of both political and non-political values. It is possible to study development without reference to a nation's relative position in the world. This is the approach usually followed by the case study worker. For a fascinating treatment of the single nation case study which is relevant to many of the concerns of this paper see James C. Davies, "Toward a Theory of Revolution," *American Sociological Review*, 27 (February, 1962), pp. 5–19.

[22] For one example of changes induced by industrialization, see Alex Inkeles and Peter H. Rossi, "National Comparisons of Occupational Prestige," *American Journal of Sociology*, LXI (January, 1956), pp. 329–39, a study of ranking of occupations by inhabitants of six nations. Rankings are highly correlated. The authors interpret this as an outcome of the industrial occupational system and the centralized national state.

CHAPTER 9

Toward a Communications Theory
of Democratic Political Development:
A Causal Model*

Donald J. McCrone
Charles F. Cnudde

The construction of an empirical theory of democratic political development is dependent on the formulation of causal propositions which are
generalizations of the developmental process. To date, several essential
steps in the process of constructing such a theory have been taken. First,
concept formation and clarification by students of political development has
led to an emphasis upon political democracy as one of the dependent variables for the field.[1] Second, the gathering and publication of quantitative
indicators of social, economic, cultural, and political phenomena provide a
firm basis for subsequent empirical inquiry.[2] Finally, correlational analysis
has identified numerous variables which are closely associated with the
development of democratic political institutions.[3]

The next major task is the formulation and testing of empirical models
of democratic political development which provide a basis for inferring
causal relationships by distinguishing between spurious correlations and
indirect and direct effects.[4] The accomplishment of this task would enable
us to derive explanatory propositions concerning the process of democratic
political development.

The purpose of this essay is to suggest the combined utility of two
similar theory-building techniques in the accomplishment of this task and
to take a modest step in the direction of constructing an empirical model of
democratic political development.

I. CONCEPTS OF POLITICAL DEVELOPMENT

Seymour Martin Lipset explicitly adopts democratic political development
as his dependent variable. He defines political democracy as:

Reprinted from *American Political Science Review*, Vol. 61, No. 1 (March, 1967),
pp. 72–79, by permission of the American Political Science Association.

a political system which supplies regular constitutional opportunities for changing the governing officials. It is a social mechanism for the resolution of the problems of societal decision-making among conflicting interest groups which permits the largest to choose among alternative contenders for political office.[5]

For Lipset, this definition of democracy implies three key specific conditions: first, one set of political leaders who occupy official governing positions; second, one or more sets of competing leaders who do not occupy governing positions, but who act as a loyal opposition; third, widespread acceptance of a "political formula" which specifies the legitimate political institutions for the society (political parties, free press, etc.) and legitimizes democratic political competition.[6] European and English-speaking nations are classified as stable democracies or unstable democracies and dictatorships on the basis of whether they fulfilled these specific conditions in the period since World War I. Lipset also adds the condition that there be an absence of Communist or Fascist parties (i.e., political movements opposed to the democratic "political formula") garnering more than 20 per cent of the vote in the last twenty-five years.[7]

Lipset's measurement of political democracy unfortunately has severe limitations. His "all-or-nothing" requirement transforms political democracy from a continuous variable into an attribute. Theoretically, democracy may be most usefully conceived of as a continuum. A political system is not democratic or non-democratic—democracy is not present or absent—rather a political system is more or less democratic. Moreover, even if democracy were best conceived to be an attribute, the problem of selecting nonarbitrary cut-points would still present severe problems.[8] Finally, a dichotomous dependent variable places strains on the power of the statistical techniques that may be applied.

Phillips Cutright, on the other hand, attempts to define political development in terms which do not rely explicitly on liberal democratic standards:

The degree of political development of a nation can be defined by the degree of complexity and specialization of its national political institutions.[9]

Nevertheless, a careful examination of Cutright's political development scoring procedure indicates a reliance on the same standards utilized by Lipset. In fact, Cutright's measurement procedure is an excellent operationalization of Lipset's concept of political democracy. Points are assigned to a political system on the basis of one set of officials in office, one or more sets of political leaders out of office, and reliance on political parties and free elections as the legitimate political institutions for the society.[10] The virtue of the Cutright measure is that it transforms Lipset's democratic attribute into a continuous variable, thereby avoiding the problems cited above. Pending further refinements in this field, democratic political development may best be conceptualized in Lipset's terms and measured by Cutright's procedures.[11]

Both Lipset and Cutright have established correlations between socio-economic factors and democratic political development. Lipset finds that indices of *wealth* (per capita income, thousands of persons per doctor, and persons per motor vehicle), *communication* (telephones, radios, and newspaper copies per thousand persons), *industrialization* (percentages of males in agriculture and per capita energy consumed), *education* (percentage literate, and primary, post-primary, and higher education enrollment per thousand persons), and *urbanization* (per cent in cities over 20,000, 100,000, and in metropolitan areas) are all strongly related to political democracy.[12]

Cutright, using product-moment correlation analysis, identifies indices of *communication* (summed T scores of newspaper readers, newsprint consumption, volume of domestic mail, and number of telephones per capita), *urbanization* (T score of the proportion of the population in cities over 100,000), *education* (combined T scores of literacy and number of students per 100,000 in institutions of higher education), and *agriculture* (T score of the proportion of the economically active labor force employed in agriculture) as being closely associated with political development.[13]

Regardless of the imaginativeness and utility of these studies, they do not constitute theoretical formulations of the process of democratic political development. They remain studies of the correlates of democratic political development.

II. A COMMUNICATIONS DEVELOPMENT MODEL

Communications development suggests itself as a variable around which a theory of the process of democratic political development might be constructed for several reasons.[14] First, both normative and empirical theory point to communications as a prerequisite to a successfully operating political democracy. Normative thinking gives communications networks the role of providing an informed citizenry, while more empirical scholarship sees communications as integrative, producing the social cohesion necessary to prevent disintegration in the face of democratic policy conflict.[15] Second, Cutright finds that communications development is by far the strongest socioeconomic correlate of political development.[16] Third, the most ambitious attempt at a theoretical formulation of the process of democratic political development views communications development as the final prerequisite for a successfully functioning democratic political system.[17]

Daniel Lerner theorizes that the process of democratic political development (which he defines as the "crowning institution of the participant society") is the consequence of a developmental sequence beginning with urbanization:

The secular evolution of a participant society appears to involve a regular sequence of three phases. Urbanization comes first, for cities alone have developed the complex of skills and resources which characterize the modern industrial economy. Within this urban matrix develop both of the attributes which distinguish the next two phases—literacy and media growth. There is a close reciprocal relationship between these, for the literate develop the media which in turn spread literacy. But, literacy performs the key function in the second phase. The capacity to read, at first acquired by relatively few people, equips them to perform the varied tasks required in the modernizing society. Not until the third phase, when the elaborate technology of industrial development is fairly well advanced, does a society begin to produce newspapers, radio networks, and motion pictures on a massive scale. This, in turn, accelerates the spread of literacy. Out of this interaction develop those institutions of participation (e.g. voting) which we find in all advanced modern societies.[18]

Lerner's thesis is not satisfactorily confirmed by his data, but his conceptualization of political development as a developmental sequence provides a basis for a causal formulation of the process of democratic political development.

Figure 1 represents our initial causal model based on the conception of democratic political development as a developmental sequence.

Figure 1. Initial Conception of Democratic Political Development as a Developmental Sequence (U—Urbanization, E—Education, C—Communications, D—Democratic political development)

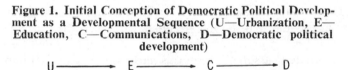

This four-variable causal model is, of course, only one of a whole family of logically alternative models utilizing the same four variables. A means for testing the adequacy of this particular causal model and for eliminating alternative models is clearly needed.

III. TESTING THE MODEL

Two interrelated theory-building techniques are applied in this study in an effort to eliminate logical alternative models and to provide a basis for inferring the adequacy of the postulated model of democratic political development. First, Simon–Blalock causal model analysis is utilized because it enables us

to make causal *inferences* concerning the adequacy of causal models, at least in the sense that we can proceed by eliminating inadequate models that make predictions that are not consistent with the data.[19]

Prediction equations based on the correlation coefficients between variables are computed for each alternative model. Models that make prediction equations inconsistent with the actual relationships between the variables in the system are rejected.[20]

Second, path coefficients are computed for the causal model that is inferred by use of the Simon–Blalock technique. In causal analysis, we are primarily concerned with changes in the dependent variable(s) which are produced by changes in the independent variable(s). The correlation coefficients used in the Simon–Blalock prediction equations only measure the goodness of fit around the regression line. Path coefficients which may be viewed as being analogous to beta weight(s), are used because they measure changes in the dependent variable produced by standardized changes in the independent variable.[21]

The data to be utilized in this study consist of Cutright's previously published intercorrelations computed from four aggregate indicators for seventy-six nations. The four variables are urbanization, education, communication, and political development.[22]

Prior to the analysis of alternative causal models, several fundamental assumptions on which this analysis is based must be explicitly set forth. First, political development is assumed to be the dependent variable and urbanization is conceived not to be dependent on any other variable in the system. Second, relationships between the variables in the system are assumed to be additive and linear. Third, other causes of each of the four variables are assumed to be uncorrelated with the other variables in the system. And fourth, it is necessary to assume uni-directional causation.

Unfortunately, assumptions of this nature are usually left implicit. Yet whenever correlational analysis is attempted with the assumption of which are independent and dependent variables these other assumptions logically follow. The techniques to be applied in this paper merely make the assumptions more explicit. However, this state of affairs should not obscure the basic similarity between making causal inferences from a variety of techniques, whether they be correlation coefficients, regression coefficients, path coefficients, or the Simon–Blalock technique.[23]

Perhaps the least satisfying of these assumptions is that of uni-directional causation. While several respectable hypotheses involving reciprocal effects could be constructed, they would considerably complicate the analysis. We will therefore tentatively exclude such possibilities here. In a subsequent analysis we will try to evaluate these possible reciprocal relationships with a technique devised by one of the authors.[24]

Figure 2 shows the seven logically possible causal relationships between the four variables in the model under the assumptions as set forth above.

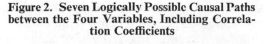

Figure 2. Seven Logically Possible Causal Paths between the Four Variables, Including Correlation Coefficients

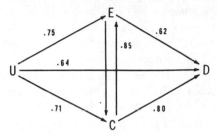

IV. ALTERNATIVE CAUSAL MODELS

Restricting our attention to the first half of the democratic political development model (the relationships between U, E, and C), Figure 3 notes three

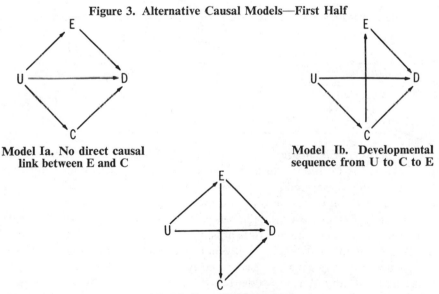

Figure 3. Alternative Causal Models—First Half

Model Ia. No direct causal
link between E and C

Model Ib. Developmental
sequence from U to C to E

Model Ic. Developmental
sequence from U to E to C

logically alternative causal relationships. Model Ia predicts that the relationship between E and C is spurious due to the causal effects of U on both variables. If Model Ia were to fit the data, both educational and communications development would be inferred to be the common consequence of the rise of urbanization with no causal link between education and communication. Model Ib, on the other hand, predicts that the developmental sequence from U to C to E interprets the relationship between U and E. If the prediction equations for Model Ib were correct, urbanization would be seen as producing the spread of communications which would, in turn, produce widespread growth in literacy and education levels. The spread of mass media would be inferred to be a prerequisite to the spread of mass education, rather than the reverse. Model Ic, based on our original model, predicts that the causal links proceed from U to E to C and account for the original relationship between U and C. The success of Model Ic in predicting the actual relationships between these three variables would confirm the notion that urbanization is the prerequisite to the widespread growth of literacy and education. The consequent educational development would then provide the mass public necessary for the growth of the mass media of communication.

The prediction equations for Ia, Ib, and Ic in Table I show the Simon–Blalock test for each of these alternative models. Clearly, the excellence of

Table 1. Prediction Equations and Degree of Fit for Models of Democratic Political Development—First Half

Models	Predictions Predicted	Degree of Fit Actual	Degree of Fit Difference
Ia. $rUErUC = rEC$	$(.75)(.71) = .53$	.85	.32
Ib. $rUCrCE = rUE$	$(.71)(.85) = .60$	.75	.15
Ic. $rUErEC = rUC$	$(.75)(.85) = .64$	.71	.07

the fit between the predicted and actual correlations for Model Ic, as opposed to the results for Ia and Ib, provides a basis for eliminating the latter two alternatives and inferring that the direction of causation is indeed from urbanization to education to communication.

Turning our attention to the second half of the democratic political development model (the relationships between E, C, and D), Figure 4 indicates that only two logically alternative causal models can be posited. This is due to the fact that we have already inferred the direction of causation between E and C from Model Ic. Model IIa predicts that the relationship between C and D is spurious due to common causation by E. If this model were to fit the data, education, not communication, would be confirmed as the final prerequisite to a successfully functioning political democracy. Model IIb posits a developmental sequence from E to C to D as interpreting the original correlation between E and D. If this model is

Figure 4. Alternative Causal Models—Second Half

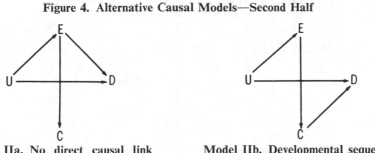

Model IIa. No direct causal link
between C and D

Model IIb. Developmental sequence
from E to C to D

confirmed, communications development will be seen to be the final link in the chain of causation. The spread of mass education creates an informed public that supports the growth of a system of mass communication which penetrates and integrates the society thereby laying the basis for democratic political competition.

Table 2 shows the prediction equations for Models IIa and IIb. These prediction equations confirm the inference that the relationship between

Table 2. Prediction Equations and Degree of Fit for Models of Democratic
Political Development—Second Half

	Predictions		*Degree of Fit*	
Models	*Predicted*	*Actual*	*Difference*	
IIa. $rECrED = rCD$	$(.85)(.62) = .53$	.80	.27	
IIb. $rECrCD = rED$	$(.85)(.80) = .68$	.62	.06	

education and democratic political development is an indirect one through communications.

One final link, the direct original relationship between U and D, remains to be tested. A final logically possible model would postulate that the developmental sequence from U to E to C to D accounts for the entire relationship between U and D. If Model III were to be confirmed, the inference would be that there is no direct relationship between U and D. Figure 5 and Table 3 illustrate and test this possible alternative respectively.

Table 3. Prediction Equation and Degree of Fit for a Model of Democratic
Political Development—Final Link

	Predictions		*Degree of Fit*	
Model	*Predicted*	*Actual*	*Difference*	
III. $rUErECrCD = rUD$	$(.75)(.85)(.80) = .51$	.64	.13	

**Figure 5. Model III—Developmental Sequence
from U to E to C to D**

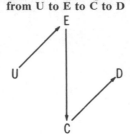

The relatively poor fit (over .10 difference) indicates that Model III can be rejected and the direct link between U and D should be maintained.

Before settling on the final system of causal relationships indicated by use of the Simon–Blalock technique, let us briefly evaluate the direct effects of each of the remaining paths through the computation of path coefficients. The correlation coefficients utilized in the Simon–Blalock analysis, it should be recalled, only measure the degree of association between variables. We found above, for example, that the association between U and D is maintained even when the effect of the path from U to E to C to D was taken into account. Correlation coefficients, however, do not measure the amount of change in the dependent variable which is associated with changes in the independent variable. Our primary concern at this stage is with the measurement of changes in the dependent variable produced by changes in the independent variable path coefficients, therefore, are utilized because they measure the amount of *change* in the dependent variable produced by *standardized changes* in the independent variable.

Figure 6 shows two paths from U to D remain in associational terms. First, there is the developmental sequence from U to D with three links—U

**Figure 6. A Causal Model of Democratic
Political Development Including Path
Coefficients**

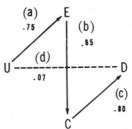

to E, E to C, and C to D. Second, there is the direct link between U and D. Path coefficients for each of these links in the causal model of democratic political development are computed in Table 4.

Table 4. Simultaneous Equations and Path Coefficients for the Causal Model in
Figure 6

Path	Equation	Path Coefficient
a	$bUE + rUE = 0$	.75
b	$bEC + rEC = 0$	.85
c	$bCD + rCD = 0$	.80
d	$bUD + (bCD \times rUC) + rUD = 0$	.07

An examination of the path coefficients placed on each link in Figure 6 indicates that the overwhelmingly important causal links in the process of democratic political development are contained in the developmental sequence from U to E to C to D). The direct effect of urbanization on democratic political development (as indicated by the use of a broken line) is negligible.

The remarkable correspondence between this empirically derived causal model of democratic political development and the original causal model postulated in Figure 1 is clear.

V. CONCLUSION

This causal model, because it represents the beginnings of a parsimonious theory of, rather than mere correlates of, the process of democratic political development enables us to derive a series of empirical propositions concerning this crucial process.

1. Democratic political development occurs when mass communications permeates society.
   Education affects democratic political development by contributing to the growth of mass communications, therefore:
2. Mass communications occurs when literacy and educational levels rise in society.
   Urbanization affects democratic political development primarily by increasing educational levels, which then increase mass communications, therefore:
3. Education and literacy development occur in urbanizing societies.

This causal model, then, is a series of interrelated causal propositions which link urbanization through a developmental sequence to democratic political development.

Since the causal relationships specified in the model are not perfect, the model and the propositions derived therefrom are probabilistic in nature. The r^2 between U and E (.56), E and C (.72), and C and D (.64) leave a significant proportion of the variance unexplained. For this reason, deviant cases (in terms of the model) can be found. Basically, there are two kinds of deviant cases. First, there are those cases where the nation is "over-developed" in one of the variables included in the model. For example, Cutright discusses nations with a relatively low level of communications development which are defined as being relatively highly developed politically.[25] In this case, the democratic political system does not have sufficient communications development to maintain the regime. In terms of our model, this nation is likely to experience severe difficulty in maintaining democratic political competition and may even collapse. The dangers of attempting to impose a democratic regime on socioeconomically under-developed nations in the post-World War II world are indicated by this type of analysis.

Stepping further back in the chain of causation, we may also find nations which are experiencing communications revolutions, but without prior developments in urbanization and education. In this case, disruption of the regime may occur because the citizenry has not been prepared for the sudden exposure and communications development may bring social disintegration, rather than social cohesion. The examination of such deviant cases may give us insight into other factors that produce changes in these four variables and bring such disruptions. Moreover, we may also ascertain the explanatory power of the model by examining the reliability of predictions about disruption based on these discontinuities.

The second type of deviant case is the nation that has fulfilled the requirements for development, in terms of the model, yet fails to maintain a democratic regime. Germany, for example, would seem to have fulfilled the prerequisites for a democratic regime long before the present Federal Republic. Nevertheless, Germany has experienced severe difficulty in establishing and maintaining a democratic regime in the twentieth century. Apparently, the developmental sequence can be disrupted by influences outside the model. Cutright, for example, examines the impact of foreign invasion and war on political development. He finds that such events seem to intervene to upset the normal sequence of events.[26] The examination of this type of deviant case and of time series data may subject our propositions to further tests. For example, the effect of urban growth over time may be quite different from that of variations in urbanization at one point in time. In general, additional research should shed light on other variables that might be included in a more complete model of the process of political development.[27]

A major virtue of this form of causal model analysis is its capacity to elaborate and extend the model by the inclusion of new variables. This type of elaboration may take two forms. First, when variables outside the system are identified and hypothesized to be causal variables in the process of democratic political development, they can be explicitly introduced into the model. The introduction and testing of such variables provides a test of both the causal nature of the specified variable and the adequacy of the existing model. As additional causal variables are identified and included, the model of democratic political development will begin to match the complexity of the phenomenon it seeks to explain.

A second form of elaboration is the introduction and testing of new dependent variables. In this manner, we can gauge the effects of democratic political development. By the introduction of measures of welfare, education, and military expenditures into the model, we can measure the effects of both democratic political systems and the causal factors in development on public policy. More specifically, answers might be obtained to these questions: What is the independent effect of democratic politics on welfare expenditures? What are the effects of education on welfare expenditures? Are the effects of education interpreted through political development? Answers to questions such as these require the testing of several alternative models including welfare expenditures as a new variable.

In a previous study, on an unrelated substantive matter, the authors have expressed the belief that

in regard to the subject of theory building in political science, the cumulative nature of empirical model building needs to be stressed. By explicit articulation of the model of constituency influence and emphasis on establishing empirical relationships, the Miller–Stokes study provides a basis for further development. The application of new techniques and the possible inclusion of new variables is thereby facilitated.[28]

We can only hope that this particular causal model of the process of democratic political development may also facilitate the elaboration and testing of models of development by the application of new techniques and the inclusion of new variables. In this manner, a cumulative body of development theory may arise.

NOTES

* This article is the second of a series on which we are alternating the order of authors' names to indicate that the studies are in every way joint enterprises.

[1] For an interesting discussion of this material as well as important findings on factors which relate to democracy, see Seymour Martin Lipset, "Some Social Requisites of Democracy: Economic Development and Political Legitimacy," *American Political Science Review*, 53 (1959), pp. 69–105.

[2] Bruce M. Russett, *et al.*, *World Handbook of Political and Social Indicators* (New Haven: Yale University Press, 1964).

[3] Phillips Cutright, "National Political Development," in Nelson Polsby, *et al.* (eds.), *Politics and Social Life* (Boston: Houghton Mifflin, 1963), pp. 569–82.

[4] For an example of this type of model testing in political science, see Charles F. Cnudde and Donald J. McCrone, "The Linkage Between Constituency Attitudes and Congressional Voting Behavior: A Causal Model," *American Political Science Review* (1966), pp. 66–72.

[5] Lipset, *op. cit.*, p. 71.

[6] *Loc. cit.*

[7] *Ibid.*, pp. 73–74. Latin-American political systems are classified somewhat differently, but still dichotomously.

[8] For the pitfalls involved in choosing cut-points, see Hubert M. Blalock, Jr., *Causal Inferences in Nonexperimental Research* (Chapel Hill: University of North Carolina Press, 1964).

[9] Cutright, *op. cit.*, p. 571.

[10] *Ibid.*, p. 574. Scores may vary from 0 to 66 based on a total of three for each of twenty-two years (1940–1961).

[11] Of course political scientists' interest in democracy includes more than the existence and maintenance of democratic institutions. Two lines of further refinements have relied upon system-level democratic "behaviors" to make additional distinctions among political systems with democratic institutions. One of these developments deals with Dahl's concept of polyarchy, the other with political equality. While extremely meaningful, these concepts require much ingenuity to operationalize, especially on a cross-national level. For the concept of polyarchy see Robert A. Dahl, *A Preface to Democratic Theory* (Chicago: The University of Chicago Press, 1956), p. 84. For operational measures of the concept see Deane E. Neubauer, "Some Conditions of Democracy," Chapter 10 of this volume, and Haywood R. Alker, Jr., "Causal Inference and Political Analysis" (forthcoming). For an operational measure of political equality within the United States, see Charles F. Cnudde, "Consensus, 'Rules of the Game' and Democratic Politics: The Case of Race Politics in the South" (unpublished Ph.D. dissertation, Department of Political Science, University of North Carolina, 1966).

[12] Lipset, *op. cit.*, pp. 76–77. He relies on means and ranges to establish the relationships.

[13] Cutright, *op. cit.*, p. 577.

[14] For theoretical contributions which indicate the central role of communications systems in more general types of political development, see Lucian W. Pye (ed.), *Communications and Political Development* (Princeton, N.J.: Princeton University Press, 1963).

[15] Karl W. Deutsch, *The Nerves of Government* (New York: The Free Press of Glencoe, 1963); Karl W. Deutsch, "Communication Theory and Political Integration," in Phillip E. Jacob and James V. Toscano (eds.), *The Integration of Political Communities* (Philadelphia and New York: J. B. Lippincott Co., 1964), pp. 46–74. For the relationship between communication and civic cooperation at the individual level in nations which vary in the degree to which democracy is successfully institutionalized, see Gabriel A. Almond and Sidney Verba, *The Civic Culture: Political Attitudes and Democracy in Five Nations* (Princeton: Princeton University Press, 1963), pp. 378–81.

[16] Cutright, *op. cit.*, p. 577.

[17] Daniel Lerner, *The Passing of Traditional Society* (Glencoe: The Free Press, 1958).

[18] *Ibid.*, p. 60.

[19] Blalock, *op. cit.*, p. 62. Also see Herbert A. Simon, "Spurious Correlations: A Causal Interpretation," *Journal of the American Statistical Association*, 49 (1954), pp. 467–79.

[20] Blalock, *op. cit.*, pp. 60–94.

[21] Sewall Wright, "Correlation and Causation," *Journal of Agricultural Research*, 20 (1921), pp. 557–85.

[22] Cutright, *op. cit.*, p. 577.

[23] Social scientists are becoming increasingly aware of the similarities in the logic of these techniques. Boudon, for example, subsumes them all under a more general formulation which he calls "dependence analysis." Raymond Boudon, "A Method of Linear Causal Analysis: Dependence Analysis," *American Sociological Review*, 30 (1965), pp. 365–74.

[24] See Charles F. Cnudde, "Legislative Behavior and Citizen Characteristics: Problems in Theory and Method," (a paper delivered at the Midwest Conference of Political Scientists, Chicago, April 29, 1966).

[25] Cutright, *op. cit.*, pp. 577–81.

[26] *Ibid.*, p. 580.

[27] Clearly, there is no incompatibility between Cutright's technique of using the prediction equation based on the regression line and this type of causal analysis. In fact, Cutright's technique applied at each stage of the developmental process would effectively isolate the deviant cases at each stage. His present research on historical trends in political development should also shed light on the adequacy of this causal model. See *ibid.*, pp. 577–81 for a discussion of Cutright's techniques and research.

[28] Cnudde and McCrone, *op. cit.*, p. 72.

CHAPTER 10

Some Conditions of Democracy*

Deane E. Neubauer

It has been argued that political democracy in nation-states is dependent upon certain levels of social and economic development. Some authors (Lipset and Cutright) argue that a particular complex of social and economic requisites appears necessary for the institutionalization and maintenance of democracy. Others (Lerner and Pye) suggest that national political development of any form is predicated upon the development of a system of communications sufficiently sophisticated to overcome the parochialism of traditional society. Still others (Almond and Verba) find social factors such as education crucial for the development of those attitudes deemed adequate for active citizens of democratic politics.[1]

By definition, political democracy in nation-states requires some minimal level of citizen participation in decision making. Historically the most effective method of institutionalizing such participation is through some form of representative government. This mechanism permits groups of citizens with common preferences to support representatives who will, in turn, attempt to schedule those preferences for decision by the government. Groups of representatives will form coalitions in an attempt to insure that their common preferences will be enacted into public policy. Because preferences in society are likely to vary in direction and intensity, the successful implementation of political democracy imposes two requirements. One, communication of preferences among competing groups, must be widespread. If they are not, it will be difficult for groups with shared preferences to combine their resources such that "majority" preferences can be successfully implemented. Indeed at a more basic level, communication is necessary for the identification and articulation of common preferences. Second, groups within the citizenry holding competing preferences must be socialized into the procedural norms of the system. Most important is the acceptance of the norms of compliance so that

Reprinted from *American Political Science Review*, Vol. 61, No. 4 (December, 1967), pp. 1002–1009, by permission of the American Political Science Association.

groups which "lose" on any given issue (enactment of a preference set) do not withdraw from the decision system or opt to overthrow it. In short, two primary conditions for the maintenance of any system of political democracy are, (1) communication among members of the political system and, (2) socialization into the "rules of the game."

The arguments cited above assert that these conditions are most easily maintained when certain levels of "social and economic development" have been achieved. The reason is clear; in states that are at all large, the most effective method of statewide communication is mass communication, a product of societies with relatively advanced technologies. The existence of such communication systems greatly enhances the development of nationally held values, one of which might be agreement on the norms of governmental decision-making.

The argument encapsulated above represents one major thrust of recent work on "political development." If one intends the argument as a partial explanation for the existence of democratic political organization in one set of countries which are relatively "advanced," as opposed to its absence in another set of countries typified by essentially agricultural economies and traditional cultures, it appears to be sufficiently persuasive not to warrant argument. As the argument is developed in the literature, however, it seems to imply more. Although its proponents are careful to specify that they are speaking of necessary conditions for the achievement of political development (not sufficient conditions), confusions have arisen in the manner in which this particular developmental hypothesis has been presented. For example, Phillips Cutright has posited a linear relationship between socio-economic development and political development. One implication of the linearity assumption is that, as countries become more "advanced" economically and socially, they tend also to become more "advanced" politically. An increment of one is associated with a commensurate increment of the other.[2]

The purpose of this paper is to demonstrate that to a significant degree this assumption is incorrect. The argument proceeds in two parts: (1) the findings which are utilized by Cutright to document his assertions are misleading. The index of national political development does not measure political development as defined by Cutright, but is rather a measure of democratic political development. (2) Democratic political development cannot be adequately measured by Cutright's index of national political development. When one utilizes a more appropriate index, he finds that above the "developmental threshold" there is no significant relationship between democratic political development and socio-economic development.

I. A RE-EXAMINATION OF NATIONAL POLITICAL DEVELOPMENT

Because the studies by Lipset and Cutright state most clearly the relationship of social and economic requisites to democratic political development, a closer examination of them will facilitate the argument to follow.

Lipset's studies indicate that the existence of stable democratic political systems is positively associated with selected indicators of wealth, industrialization, education and urbanization.[3] His correlations suggest that on the basis of these indicators one can distinguish between these regimes and those which are either unstable democracies, popular dictatorships, or elite-based dictatorships. While Lipset's study was the first to give some empirical substance to this previously untested hypothesis, it suffered from methodological shortcomings. (See Cutright for an analysis of Lipset's data). Phillips Cutright attempted to refine Lipset's methods while at the same time broadening the theoretical scope of his findings. Lipset had sought simply to demonstrate that certain gross differences existed between the social and economic composition of different forms of regimes. Cutright, on the other hand, has attempted to demonstrate that "political development" in and of itself is a function of the social and economic characteristics of society. Defining political development as "the degree of complexity and specialization of its (a country's) national political institutions," he attempted to test the hypothesis that "political institutions are interdependent with educational systems, economic institutions, communications systems, degree of urbanization and the distribution of the labor force."[4] To test his hypothesis, Cutright constructed an index of political development by assigning points to nations on the basis of their legislative and executive composition.[5]

The most interesting feature of Cutright's index is that, while it purports to measure "political development," it utilizes indicators which give the highest scores to nations which have established and maintained a set of explicitly democratic political institutions. This index does not measure "political development" in Cutright's definition of the term. It measures "degree of democraticness" by which is meant the extent to which nations institute and maintain overtime multiple party political systems and "open elections." The use of Cutright's index is directly equivalent to asserting that those nations which are characterized by the institutions of liberal democracy, are those which are most highly developed politically. Given another set of normative assumptions one might wish to agree that "most highly developed" means "most democratic," but one cannot, utilizing Cutright's definition of the term "political development," easily equate development with democracy. To cite the most obvious example, many modern states are characterized by political institutions of considerable complexity, but this fact is not related to the existence of a set of democratic political institutions. The Communist countries most clearly fit this category. Impressionistically, it *is* probably the case that the complexity of political institutions is related to the social and economic factors suggested above; this seems to be an inevitable consequence of conducting the affairs of government in large nation-states which maintain or attempt to maintain distributional patterns commensurate with a highly productive and diversified economy. To repeat the important point: Cutright's index does not measure this feature of political development. An appropriate measure of political development defined as institutional complexity should probably focus on the proliferation and specialization of governmental bureaucracies. One might, if one wished, then attempt to associate this measure of political development with the existence of certain types of legislatures and bureaucracies, but this in turn would require an independent theory of governmental organization as related to the phenomenon of organizational complexity.

On balance, then, one can derive from Cutright's analysis the hypothesis that the more socially and economically developed a nation is, the more democratic it is likely to be. There is no question that in gross terms this is correct. The most casual inspection of Cutright's socio-economic data indicates a clustering at one end of the scale of the "underdeveloped" countries (predominately nondemocratic) and at the other end of the scale of the "developed" nations (predominantly European or Anglo-American democracies). What Cutright's data do not make clear is the degree to which this relationship persists beyond the measuring capability of his index. The maximum amount of points that a nation can receive on Cutright's scale is sixty-six, a total achieved by very many of the democratic countries in his sample. Not much can, therefore, be inferred concerning the effect, if any, that differential social and economic development has upon democratic development in these countries. To what extent do *these* countries develop more politically (i.e., democratically) as they attain higher levels of socio-economic development?

In order to suggest the effect which continued socio-economic development has upon democratic development, it is necessary to have an index which goes beyond Cutright's, one which is capable of measuring variation within the sub-sample of "most democratic" countries which are largely undifferentiated on Cutright's index.

We have devised an index of democratic development expressly for this purpose. This index, derived from definitional and empirical constructs of Dahl and Downs, concentrates mainly on electoral features of democratic regimes.[6] Explicitly, the index is composed of four indicators which measure the relative amount of *electoral equality* and *competition* present in a given political system. The rationale behind the index construction is rather simple. The most characteristic feature of democratic regimes is the election of key governmental personnel. As suggested in the introduction, this is the mechanism whereby citizens give some indication of which preferences they wish scheduled for governmental decision. The form of elections alone, however, does not guarantee their democratic substance. Democratic elections are those in which opposition groups are given some opportunity to contest office with ruling groups. Two key indicators of a country's tolerance of electoral opposition groups are the existence of actual electoral competition and the existence of multiple sources of public information. The indicators chosen for the index reflect these considerations. They are:

(a) Per cent of the adult population eligible to vote. This indicator is basic to the concept of "democraticness." The variation between nations on this measure indicates the percentage of the population which is excluded from the suffrage for whatever reasons (sex, race, residence, literacy, etc.). Those nations which score the highest are those which most closely approximate the norm of permitting all adults to participate in the choice of a preferred set of leaders.

(b) Equality of representation. The notion of one man, one vote is basic to modern concepts of democracy. The implication of this norm goes beyond the exclusion of plural voting. It demands that votes be given equal weight in the choice of candidates. We will make use of a measure which calculates the "mean range of distortion" in equating votes with seats in legislatures. The computation is arrived at by determining which parties are most over-represented in the assignment of seats and which are most under-represented. The two are combined to obtain a range of distortion and the mean for all elections studied is then computed.

(c) Information equality. An important condition in Dahl's model, but one which is absent from Downs is: "All individuals possess identical information about the alternatives." Clearly the task of measuring this directly is overwhelming. As an indicator of this condition, we have made use of a measure of the degree to which multiple sources of information are available to citizens of a given country. The measure focuses upon newspapers under the assumption that, if there is considerable "pluralism" in this sphere of mass communications, there is a positive probability that it will exist in other areas of communication. The indicator also attempts to measure the degree to which pluralistic ownership of the press exists. Since adequate data of this form exist only for large cities, the indicator is explicitly concerned with the pattern of newspaper ownership in capital cities. In order to provide for greater comparability among the sample countries, one must also build into the measure some control for the size of the capital city. The formula:

$$\text{number of separately owned papers} \times \frac{\text{average circulation}}{\text{size of capital}}$$

is utilized to derive a coefficient that suggests the relative number and circulation of newspapers in capital cities.[7]

(d) Competition. Electoral competition by political parties is meaningful only if the nature of that competition is such that the alternation in office of competing sets of leaders is probable as well as possible. The measure should reward those countries which come most close to providing the electorate with this alternative. Two measures are utilized.

1. Per cent of the time period in which the dominant party held office. Competition may be close, but if no alternation occurs over a long period of time, the nature of the alternative perceived by the electorate is substantially different than that in which alternation actually takes place.

2. Mean percentage of the vote received by the winning party (parties). This indicator actually measures the closeness of the competition. It distinguishes particularly among those situations in which alternation does not occur. Non-alternation with a margin of 51–49 is thus distinguished from non-alternation with a margin of, say, 90–10.

These two measures eliminate the need of a third, obvious measure— the number of parties competing in the election. Single party states are distinguished from multiple party states by showing no alternation in office, and by the percentage of the vote gained by the winning party.

A sample of twenty-three democratic countries was selected and scored on the above indicators. The scores were then combined into an index of democratic performance.[8]

A multiple regression analysis was undertaken correlating the socio-economic variables with the index of democratic performance. The correlation coefficients are reported in Table 1. If one compares these results with those obtained by Cutright reported in Table 2, it is clear that the two sets of findings are distinctly different. These results could occur for two reasons.

The considerable difference between the two sets of findings could result from either the fact that different samples are employed in the two studies, or because the indexes measure quite different things, or both. The factors are interrelated. It is necessary to use a smaller sample than Cutright for the simple reason that the kind of data necessary for the

**Table 1. Matrix of Correlations of National Measures of
Democratic Performance with Levels of Education, Communication,
Urbanization and Employment in Agriculture**

	1	2	3	4	5
1. Communication		.314	.732	−.698	.424
2. Urbanization	(21)		.578	−.612	−.008
3. Education	(21)	(23)		−.712	.055
4. Agriculture	(21)	(23)	(23)		.016
5. Democratic Performance	(21)	(23)	(23)	(23)	

(Numbers in parentheses represent the sample "N".)

**Table 2. Matrix of Correlations of National Measures of
Political Development with Levels of Education, Communication,
Urbanization and Employment in Agriculture**

	1	2	3	4	5
1. Communication		71	85	−79	80
2. Urbanization	(69)		75	−72	64
3. Education	(69)	(70)		−72	62
4. Agriculture	(57)	(56)	(58)		−56
5. Political Development	(71)	(74)	(72)	(58)	

(Cutright's correlations are multiplied by 100 to produce whole numbers.)

democratic performance indicator come only from democratic countries. But, if the Cutright hypothesis were correct, neither the use of the smaller sample nor the use of the democratic performance index should account for the diminution of the correlation between socio-economic development and democratic "development" assuming Cutright's "political development" index and my democratic performance index measure the same thing. As suggested above, what Cutright terms an index of "political development" is actually an index which measures the existence over time of liberal-democratic regimes. The index of democratic performance, at the conceptual level, attempts to measure the same thing. If socio-economic development were linearly related to democratic development operationalized as institutional maintenance, one would predict that it should also be related to the minimal performance measured by the index of democratic performance. The results indicated above suggest that this is not the case. The correlation between the index of democratic performance and Cutright's index of political development is only .182. This suggests that the two indexes are not measuring the same phenomena. In particular, the low correlation points again to the undifferentiated manner in which relatively well-developed democratic countries are treated in Cutright's index. Close inspection of Cutright's index suggests that its success as a measure of democratic performance is only sustained by the use of countries in the sample which feature wide variation.

II. PATTERNS OF DEMOCRATIC POLITICAL DEVELOPMENT

What then is the status of this particular developmental hypothesis? "Can it be saved?" Assuming that my index of democratic performance differentiates among levels of performance in democratic countries, the answer is no, at least not without serious modification. The data presented in Table 1 suggests that, for this set of democratic countries, there is simply no relationship between level of democratic performance and measures of socio-economic development. (Urbanization, $-.008$, education, $.055$, agriculture, $.016$. The correlation between democratic performance and communication, $.424$, is partially due to the intercorrelation between this measure and the informational equality measures in the performance index.) This in turn suggests that political development, to the extent that it represents democratic political development, is a threshold phenomenon. Certain levels of "basic" socio-economic development appear to be necessary to elevate countries to a level at which they can begin to support complex, nation-wide patterns of political interaction, one of which may be democracy. Once above this threshold, however, the degree to which a country will "maximize" certain forms of democratic practice is no longer a function of continued socio-economic development. In fact, as Table 3 suggests, in a variety of instances one observes some democratic countries that are highly developed socio-economically have high levels of democratic performance, whereas others rank quite low.

Why should this be so? How does one account for this considerable variation in the performance of democratic countries? In answer to these questions, one is tempted to reply that countries perform differently in this respect because democracy is a very complicated form of political organization. The unique feature of democratic political organization is that it permits the variety of interests which characterize society to be translated into controlled social conflict. Although some kinds of political problems are common to all democratic countries, each differs somewhat in its social composition, its pattern of social organization, its political culture and its tradition of resolving political conflict. Thus, if one wishes to explain such variation in performance, it is necessary to examine the effect which these kinds of factors have on the democratic development of a country. In a recent study of ten democratic countries, the author found that, to a considerable degree, such variations in performance could be explained by variations in the patterns of pluralism and cleavages. This study suggests that, when cleavages are intense and disruptive, the level

**Table 3. Ordering of Sample Countries
on Index of Democratic Performance**

1.	Great Britain	236.3
2.	France	231.4
3.	Finland	229.2
4.	Sweden	225.8
5.	Netherlands	220.9
6.	Belgium	214.9
7.	Japan	212.7
8.	Luxembourg	210.1
9.	Norway	209.7
10.	New Zealand	209.4
11.	Denmark	205.7
12.	Israel	203.2
13.	West Germany	199.4
14.	Italy	198.6
15.	Canada	196.8
16.	United States	190.9
17.	Venezuela	188.3
18.	Austria	186.9
19.	Chile	184.6
20.	Ireland	181.4
21.	India	172.7
22.	Switzerland	169.3
23.	Mexico	121.9

of democratic performance is not commensurate with that expected given existing levels of social and economic development. It also suggests the obverse. When some countries are characterized by an ameliorative pattern of pluralism and cleavages, democracy can function relatively well despite a somewhat lower level of social and economic development.[9] Similarly, Robert Dahl has examined the political development of the United States in terms of its pattern of pluralism and cleavages and found this to be a satisfactory explanatory device.[10] In a comparative study of Britain and Germany, Harry Eckstein has suggested that the congruence (or lack of it) between social norms and the authority patterns of regimes may account for the stability or instability of some democratic regimes.[11] In short, variations in the performance of democratic countries appears to be a function of factors such as pluralism and cleavage which, though obviously related to the gross level of socio-economic development, have an effect on performance which extends far beyond this development.

It is also prudent to acknowledge the degree to which choice influences the relationship of socio-economic development to democratic development. The real world is not a deterministic one, and within quite appreciable limits, countries and their leaders are free to choose from a variety of alternatives concerning their form of political organization.

The case of Communist countries is the most clear. Many of these have made remarkable progress toward obtaining higher levels of socio-economic development of the type referred to by Cutright and Lipset. This socio-economic development is not reflected in higher levels of "political development" or democratic development of the form discussed in this study.[12] By choice these regimes prefer a quite different type of institutional structure than that of traditional liberal democracy. Less obvious examples also exist such as India where the governing elite makes considerable efforts on the one hand to extend the suffrage, but limits the effect of citizen participation by supporting a system of representation which heavily over-represents the Congress Party. The examples could be easily multiplied. The point is that the nature and extent of democratic practices in many countries appear to be less a function of their state of social and economic development than of certain values embedded in their political culture; values which, in turn, are related to particular patterns of conflict resolution which need not result in the growth of democratic institutions.

In conclusion, one must be most careful when drawing inferences about the effect which social and economic conditions have on the institutions and practices of nations. It is quite clear, one might say obvious, that extremely poor, traditional societies characterized by illiterate, rural populations in which inter-group communication is barely developed and national identifications and institutions barely extant, will have considerable difficulty in establishing and maintaining political democracy. It is not at all clear that the more well developed these societies are, the more likely they are to become democratic, at least if one wishes to respect differences in the degree to which basic democratic practices are implemented. If we are to have theories of democracy which take into consideration the full range of factors which impede or enhance democratic development, we must go beyond consideration of those factors which are at best threshold conditions.

NOTES

* I would like to thank Lewis A. Froman, Jr., Charles Cnudde and Lyman Drake for their comments on an earlier draft of this paper. The efforts of George Sherinian and Timothy Gilmore in assisting with data gathering are most appreciated.

[1] S. M. Lipset, "Some Social Requisites of Democracy," *American Political Science Review*, 53 (March, 1959), pp. 69–105. See also his *Political Man* (New York: Doubleday, 1960), Chaps. 2 and 3. Phillips Cutright, "National Political Development: Its Measurement and Social Correlates," in Nelson W. Polsby, Robert A. Dentler and Paul A.

Smith (eds.), *Politics and Social Life* (Boston: Houghton Mifflin Co., 1963), pp. 569–82. Daniel Lerner, *The Passing of Traditional Society* (New York: The Free Press, 1958). See also his "Communication Systems and Social Systems: A Statistical Exploration in History and Policy," *Behavioral Science*, 2 (1957), pp. 266–75. Lucian Pye, *Aspects of Political Development* (Boston: Little, Brown & Co., Inc., 1966). Gabriel A. Almond and Sidney Verba, *The Civic Culture* (Princeton: Princeton University Press, 1963).

[2] Cutright, "National Political Development," see especially pp. 577–78.

[3] Lipset, "Some Social Requisites of Democracy," *op. cit.*

[4] Cutright, "National Political Development," *op. cit.*, p. 571.

[5] Nations receive two points for each year that a parliament exists in which the lower or only house contains representatives of two or more political parties and the minority party or parties have at least 30 per cent of the vote. They receive one point if the multiple party rule is operative but the 30 per cent rule violated and no points when neither of these conditions exist. Points are given to the executive branch on the following basis: one point for every year that the nation has a chief executive in office by virtue of a direct vote in an open election in which he faced political competition, or was chosen by a political party in a two- or more-party system as defined by the conditions necessary to gain two points on the legislative point assignment scheme. No points are given for years in which the nation was ruled by a chief executive selected in some manner other than the above. The study covers a twenty-two-year period (1940–1961). It is thus possible for a nation to receive anywhere from 0 to 66 points.

Cutright has used a similar index as a "political representativeness" scale in an examination of the relationship of economic and political development to the growth of social security programs in a number of countries. Many of the criticisms of the index developed in this paper apply to its use as a political representativeness scale. In particular, it is interesting to note that, while in this later study the index is said to measure this political dimension, no attempt was made to build into the index any participation data. Cf. Phillips Cutright, "Political Structure, Economic Development and National Security Programs," *American Journal of Sociology*, 70 (1965), pp. 537–48.

[6] Downs' conditions for a democratic political system are:

1. A single party (or coalition of parties) is chosen by popular election to run the governing apparatus.
2. Such elections are held within periodic intervals, the duration of which cannot be altered by the party in power acting alone.
3. All adults who are permanent residents of the society, are sane and abide by the laws of the land are eligible to vote in each such election.
4. Each voter may cast one and only one vote in each election.
5. Any party (or coalition) receiving the support of a majority of those voting is entitled to take over the powers of government until the next election.
6. The losing parties in an election never try by force or any illegal means to prevent the winning party (or parties) from taking office.
7. The party in power never attempts to restrict the political activities of any citizens or other parties as long as they make no attempt to overthrow the government by force.
8. There are two or more parties competing for control of the governing apparatus in every election.

Anthony Downs, *An Economic Theory of Democracy* (New York: Harper and Row, 1957), pp. 23–24.

Dahl's definitional characteristics of polyarchy are:

During the voting period:

1. Every member of the organization performs the acts we assume to constitute an expression of preference among the scheduled alternatives, e.g., voting.
2. In tabulating these expressions (votes), the weight assigned to the choice of each individual is identical.
3. The alternative with the greatest number of votes is declared the winning choice.

During the prevoting period:

4. Any member who perceives a set of alternatives, at least one of which he regards as preferable to any of the alternatives presently scheduled, can insert his preferred alternative(s) among those scheduled for voting.
5. All individuals possess identical information about the alternatives.

During the postvoting period:

6. Alternatives (leaders or policies) with the greatest number of votes displace any alternatives (leaders or policies) with fewer votes.
7. The orders of elected officials are executed.

During the interelection stage:

8.1 Either all interelection decisions are subordinate or executory to those arrived at during the election stage, i.e., elections are in a sense controlling.
8.2 Or new decisions during the interelection period are governed by the preceding seven conditions, operating, however, under rather different institutional circumstances.
8.3 Or both.

Robert A. Dahl, *A Preface to Democratic Theory* (Chicago: University of Chicago Press, 1956), p. 84. For a modification of Dahl's polyarchy model, see Deane E. Neubauer, *On the Theory of Polyarchy: An Empirical Study of Democracy in Ten Countries* (unpublished Ph.D. dissertation, Yale University, 1965).

[7] For a more comprehensive discussion of this indicator see Neubauer, *op. cit.*

[8] In order to avoid unnecessary complications in comparing these results with those obtained by Cutright, the democratic performance index was constructed in a manner analogous to that used by Cutright to construct the political development index. In fact, to enhance overall comparability between the two studies, his scoring procedure was utilized on all the data. The data for the independent variables (the indexes of communication, urbanization, education and agricultural employment) were obtained by consulting the sources cited by Cutright. The individual scores for each indicator were T-scored, combined (by adding T-scores) into the appropriate indexes and those T-scored. The twenty-three countries comprising the sample were: Austria, Denmark, Belgium, Ireland, the Netherlands, Switzerland, Finland, Luxembourg, Norway, New Zealand, Canada, Israel, Venezuela, United States, Great Britain, France, Sweden, Italy, The Federal Republic, Mexico, Chile, Japan and India. The "N" for the communications index is 21, Luxembourg and Venezuela are not included.

[9] Neubauer, *op. cit.*

[10] Robert A. Dahl, *Pluralist Democracy in the United States: Conflict and Consent* (Chicago: Rand McNally, 1967).

[11] Harry Eckstein, *A Theory of Stable Democracy* (Princeton: Princeton University Press, 1959). For additional uses of this form of explanation see: Giovanni Sartori, "European Political Parties: The Case of Polarized Pluralism," in Joseph LaPalombara and Myron Weiner (eds.), *Political Parties and Political Development* (Princeton: Princeton University Press, 1966), pp. 137–76; Robert A. Dahl (ed.), *Political Oppositions in Western Democracies* (New Haven: Yale University Press, 1966).

[12] With one exception. One of Cutright's indicators gives points to nations which for each year had in existence a parliament "whose members were the representatives of one or more political parties, but where the 30 per cent rule was violated" (p. 547). This is one of the most unfortunate features of his index, for it permits parliaments such as the Soviet parliament to be considered as a functional decision-making organ. Communist states consequently receive scores on the index which are unjustified from any practical point of view.

CHAPTER 11

Fundamental Principles of Democracy: Bases of Agreement and Disagreement

James W. Prothro
Charles M. Grigg

The idea that consensus on fundamental principles is essential to democracy is a recurrent proposition in political theory. Perhaps, because of its general acceptance, the proposition has never been formulated in very precise terms. When authoritative sources state, for example, that "a successful democracy requires the existence of a large measure of consensus in society," exactly what is meant? We assume that the term "successful democracy," although far from precise, carries a widely shared meaning among political scientists. But we are not told in this typical assertion on what *issues* or *problems* consensus must exist. Presumably they are the basic issues about how political power should be won. Nor are we told what degree of agreement democracy requires. Since the word "consensus" is used to refer to "general agreement or concord," however, a "large measure of consensus" presumably falls somewhere close to 100 per cent.[1] For the purpose of examining the proposition as it is generally formulated, then, we interpret it as asserting: a necessary condition for the existence of a democratic government is widespread agreement (approaching 100 per cent) among the adult members of society on at least the basic questions about how political power is won. Specifically, we propose to submit this proposition to empirical examination in an effort to give it more precise meaning and to discover bases of agreement and/or disagreement on fundamental principles.

A recent symposium by three leading political theorists illustrates both the widespread assumption that consensus is necessary and the lack of precision with which the concept of consensus is discussed. In considering the cultural prerequisites of democracy, they all assume the necessity of agreement on basic values, differing only as to the underlying sources of "the attitudes we regard as cultural prerequisites."[2] Ernest S.

Reprinted from *Journal of Politics*, Vol. 22, No. 2 (May, 1960), pp. 276–94, by permission of the Southern Political Science Association.

Griffith supplies an initial list of "the necessary attitudes to sustain demo-cratic institutions," but he is not clear on whether an actual consensus is necessary: ". . . I believe that they must be sufficiently widespread to be accepted as *norms* of desirable conduct, so that deviations therefrom are subject to questioning and usually social disapproval."[3]

John Plamenatz emphasizes individualism as "the sentiment which must be widespread and strong if democracy is to endure," and adds that individualism "has a less general, a less abstract side to it" than the vague "right of every man to order his life as he pleases provided he admits the same right in others." Here the requisite attitudes must be *strong* as well as *widespread*, but when Plamenatz shifts to the specific side he refers to "the faith of the *true* democrat," a somewhat less inclusive reference.[4]

J. Roland Pennock says, "We are in agreement that certain attitudes are essential to democracy," and his initial quantitative requirements are similar to the "widespread" and "strong" criteria: "Unless *the bulk of the society* is committed to a high valuation of these ideals [liberty and equality] it can hardly be expected that institutions predicated upon them will work successfully or long endure."[5] But when he turns to the idea of consensus as such, he withdraws all precision from the phrase "the bulk of the society": "Of course democracy, like other forms of government but to a greater extent, must rest upon a measure of consensus. . . . But can we say with any precision what must be the nature or extent of this consensus, what matters are so fundamental that they must be the subject of general agreement? I doubt it."[6] Here consensus appears necessary as a matter "of course," but we cannot say on what matters it must exist (Pennock cites two opposing views—the necessity of agreement on the substance of policy versus the necessity of agreement on procedures for determining policy); nor need consensus have a great "extent," which presumably means that it can vary from the "great bulk" to even greater portions of society.[7]

Other theorists take similar positions. William Ebenstein, for example, submits that "the *common agreement on fundamentals* is a . . . condition indispensable to . . . political democracy."[8] Bernard R. Berelson asserts, "For political democracy to survive . . . a basic consensus must bind together the contending parties."[9] The same assumption is implicit in Harry V. Jaffa's more specific formulation of the content of consensus: "To be dedicated to this proposition [that 'all men are created equal'], whether by the preservation of equal rights already achieved, or by the preservation of the hope of an equality yet to be achieved, was the 'value' which was the *absolutely necessary condition* of the democratic process."[10]

All of these theorists thus assume the necessity of consensus on some principles but without giving the term any precise meaning.[11] In specifying the principles on which agreement must exist, some differences appear. Although, as Pennock notes, some have gone so far as to argue the need for agreement on the substance of policy, the general position is that consensus is required only on the procedures for winning political power. At the broadest level Ebenstein says that "the most important agreement . . . is the common desire to operate a democratic system,"[12] and Pennock begins his list with "a widespread desire to be self-governing."[13] In addition to this highly general commitment, most theorists speak of consensus on the general values of liberty, equality, individualism, compromise, and acceptance of procedures necessary to majority rule and minority rights. For most of these general principles, the existence (and therefore perhaps the necessity) of consensus is supported by "common sense" observation, by logic, and by opinion survey results. Consensus certainly seems to exist among the American people on the desirability of operating "a democratic system" and on such abstract principles as the idea that "all men are created equal."[14]

But for some of the principles on which agreement is said (without empirical support) to be necessary, the certainty of consensus cannot so easily be taken for granted. Ernest S. Griffith, in maintaining that the essential attitudes of democracy stem from the Christian and Hebrew religions, submits: "Moreover, it would appear that it is these faiths, and especially the Christian faith, that perhaps alone can *cloak such attitudes with the character of 'absolutes'*—a character which is not only *desirable*, but perhaps even *necessary* to democratic survival."[15] Rather than taking absolutist attitudes as desirable or necessary for democracy, Ebenstein asserts that an opposite consensus is necessary: "The dogmatic, totalitarian viewpoint holds that there is only one Truth. The democratic viewpoint holds that different men perceive different aspects of truth . . . and that there will be at least two sides to any major question."[16] At least one of these positions must be incorrect. Does democracy in fact require rejection or acceptance of the "one Truth" idea? In the survey reported in this paper, neither position appears correct: both Midwestern and Southern Americans were found to be closer to a complete absence of consensus than to common agreement in either accepting or rejecting the "one Truth" idea.[17]

Not only do political theorists speak of consensus on abstract principles where none exists, but they also suggest the need for consensus on more specific principles without empirical support. Griffith, for example, insists that the individualistic "view of the nature of individual personality leads straight to true equality of opportunity and treatment as well as to liberty."[18] And this "true equality" must include dedication not only to the old inalienable rights such as freedom of speech, but also to "the right of each one to be treated with dignity as befits a free person—without regard to sex or creed or race or class."[19] As we shall see, the findings below do not support the assumption of general agreement on "true equality" even in such spheres as freedom of speech. And the same is true of the specific proposition that Pennock uses to illustrate the values on which "the bulk of the society" must be agreed—"The proposition that each vote should count for one and none for more than one is doubtless sufficiently implied by the word 'equality'."[20] "True believers" in democracy may be able to make an unimpeachable case for this proposition, but it is not accepted by the bulk of the society.

The discovery that consensus on democratic principles is restricted to a few general and vague formulations might come as a surprise to a person whose only acquaintance with democracy was through the literature of political theory; it will hardly surprise those who have lived in a democracy. Every village cynic knows that the local churchgoer who sings the Creed with greatest fervor often abandons the same ideas when they are put in less lyrical form. Political scientists are certainly not so naive as to expect much greater consistency in a secular sphere. The theorists who argue the necessity of consensus on such matters as the existence or absence of multi-faceted truth, true equality in the right of free speech, and dedication to an equal vote for every citizen are no doubt as aware of these human frailties as the village cynic.[21] But we tend to regard that which seems a *logically necessary* belief in the light of democratic processes as being *empirically necessary* to the existence of those processes. We assume, in a two-step translation, that what people *should* (logically) believe is what they *must* believe (this being a democracy), and that what they *must* believe is what they *do* believe.

In undertaking to discover what kind of consensus actually exists, we assumed that we would find the anticipated agreement on the basic principles of democracy when they were put in a highly abstract form, but that consensus would not be found on more concrete questions involving the application of these principles. We further assumed that regional and class-related variations would be found on the specific formulation of democratic principles. In pinning down these assumptions, we are no doubt demonstrating the obvious—but such a demonstration appears necessary if the obvious is to be incorporated into the logic of political theory. With empirical support for these two assumptions, we can put the proposition about consensus in more precise form and test the following hypothesis: *consensus in a meaningful sense (at both the abstract and specific levels) exists among some segment(s) of the population (which can be called the "carriers of the Creed").* Should our findings support this hypothesis, we could reformulate the proposition about democratic consensus with reference to a smaller group than the total population, whereupon it could be tested more fully, both in the United States and in other democracies, for further refinement.

PROCEDURE

Our research design was based upon the major assumption that the United States is a democracy. Taking this point for granted, we prepared an interviewing schedule around the presumably basic principles of democracy and interviewed samples of voters in two American cities to elicit their attitudes toward these principles.

While the general research design was thus quite simple, the preparation of a questionnaire including the basic points on which agreement is thought to be necessary was a difficult and critical step. From the literature on consensus cited above and from general literature on democracy, however, we conclude that the principles regarded as most essential to democracy are majority rule and minority rights (or freedom to dissent). At the abstract level, then, our interviewers asked for expressions of agreement or disagreement on the following statements:

Principle of Democracy Itself
   Democracy is the best form of government.
Principle of Majority Rule
   Public officials should be chosen by majority vote.
   Every citizen should have an equal chance to influence government policy.
Principle of Minority Rights
   The minority should be free to criticize majority decisions.
   People in the minority should be free to try to win majority support for their opinions.

From these general statements, specific embodiments of the principles of democracy were derived.

Principle of Majority Rule in Specific Terms
   1. In a city referendum, only people who are well-informed about the problem being voted on should be allowed to vote.
   2. In a city referendum deciding on tax-supported undertakings, only taxpayers should be allowed to vote.
   3. If a Negro were legally elected mayor of this city, the white people should not allow him to take office.
   4. If a Communist were legally elected mayor of this city, the people should not allow him to take office.

5. A professional organization like the AMA (the American Medical Association) has a right to try to increase the influence of doctors by getting them to vote as a bloc in elections.

Principle of Minority Rights in Specific Terms

6. If a person wanted to make a speech in this city against churches and religion, he should be allowed to speak.
7. If a person wanted to make a speech in this city favoring government ownership of all the railroads and big industries, he should be allowed to speak.
8. If an admitted Communist wanted to make a speech in this city favoring Communism, he should be allowed to speak.
9. A Negro should not be allowed to run for mayor of this city.
10. A Communist should not be allowed to run for mayor of this city.

These specific propositions are designed to embody the principles of majority rule and minority rights in such a clear fashion that a "correct" or "democratic" response can be deduced from endorsement of the general principles. The democratic responses to statements 1 and 2 are negative, for example, since a restriction of the franchise to the well-informed or to taxpayers would violate the principle that "Every citizen should have an equal chance to influence government policy."[22] The same general principle requires an affirmative answer to the fifth statement, which applies the right of people to "influence government policy" to the election efforts of a specific professional group. The correct responses to statements 3 and 4 are negative because denial of an office to any person "legally elected" would violate the principle that "public officials should be chosen by majority vote."

Of the five statements derived from the broad principle of minority rights, 6, 7, and 8 put the right of "the minority . . . to criticize majority decisions" and "to try to win majority support for their opinions" in terms of specific minority spokesmen; agreement is therefore the correct or democratic answer. Disagreement is the correct response to statements 9 and 10, since denial of the right to seek office to members of minority ethnic or ideological groups directly violates their right "to try to win majority support for their opinions."

Since the proposition being tested asserts the existence of consensus, the interviewing sample could logically have been drawn from any group of Americans. Because we assume regional and class differences, however, we could not rely on the most available respondents, our own college students. The registered voters of two academic communities, Ann Arbor, Michigan, and Tallahassee, Florida, were selected as the sampling population, primarily because they fitted the needs of the hypothesis, and partly because of their accessibility. Although a nationwide survey was ruled out simply on the ground of costs, these atypical communities offer certain advantages for our problem. First, they do permit at least a limited regional comparison of attitudes on democratic fundamentals. Second, they skew the sample by over-representing the more highly educated, thus permitting detailed comparison of the highly educated with the poorly educated, a comparison that could hardly be made with samples from more typical communities.

The over-representation of the highly educated also served to "stack the cards" in favor of the proposition on consensus. Since our hypothesis holds that consensus is limited, we further stacked the cards against the hypothesis by choosing the sample from registered voters rather than from all the residents of the two communities. Although the necessity of consensus is stated in terms of the society as a whole, a line of regression is available in the argument that it need exist only among those who take part in politics. Hence our restriction of the sample to a population of registered voters.

In each city the sample was drawn by the system of random numbers from the official lists of registered voters. The sample represents one per cent of the registered voters from the current registration list in each of the two communities. In a few cases the addresses given were incorrect, but if the person selected could be located in the community, he was included in the sample. A few questions on a limited number of individuals were not recorded in usable form, which accounts for a slight variation in the totals in the tables presented in the paper.

FINDINGS: THE CONSENSUS PROBLEM

In the two communities from which our samples were drawn, consensus can be said to exist among the voters on the basic principles of democracy when they are put in abstract terms. The degree of agreement on these principles ranges from 94.7 to 98.0 per cent, which appears to represent consensus in a truly meaningful sense and to support the first of our preliminary assumptions. On the generalized principles, then, we need not look for "bases of disagreement"—the agreement transcends community, educational, economic, age, sex, party, and other common bases of differences in opinion.[23] We may stop with the conclusion that opinions on these abstract principles have a cultural base.

When these broad principles are translated into more specific propositions, however, consensus breaks down completely. As Table 1 indicates, agreement does not reach 90 per cent on any of the ten propositions, either from the two samples combined or from the communities considered

Table 1. Percentage of "Democratic" Responses to Basic Principles of Democracy Among Selected Population Groups

	Total N = 244	Education†		Ann Arbor N = 144	Talla-hassee N = 100	Income‡	
		High N = 137	Low N = 106			High N = 136	Low N = 99
Majority Rule							
1. Only informed vote*	49.0	61.7	34.7	56.3	38.4	56.6	40.8
2. Only taxpayers vote*	21.0	22.7	18.6	20.8	21.2	20.7	21.0
3. Bar Negro from office*	80.6	89.7	68.6	88.5	66.7	83.2	77.8
4. Bar Communist from office*	46.3	56.1	34.0	46.9	45.5	48.9	43.0
5. AMA right to bloc voting**	45.0	49.6	39.2	44.8	45.5	45.5	44.4
Minority Rights							
6. Allow anti-religious speech**	63.0	77.4	46.5	67.4	56.6	72.8	52.1
7. Allow socialist speech**	79.4	90.2	65.7	81.3	76.8	83.8	73.7
8. Allow Communist speech**	44.0	62.9	23.5	51.4	33.3	52.2	36.7
9. Bar Negro from candidacy*	75.5	86.5	60.2	85.6	58.0	78.6	71.1
10. Bar Communist from candidacy*	41.7	48.1	30.3	44.1	38.2	44.8	34.4

* For these statements, disagreement is recorded as the "democratic" response.
** For these statements, agreement is recorded as the "democratic" response.
† "High education" means more than 12 years of schooling; "low education," 12 years or less.
‡ "High income" means an annual family income of $6,000 or more; "low income," less than $6,000.

separately. Indeed, respondents in both communities are closer to perfect discord than to perfect consensus on over half the statements. If we keep in mind that a 50–50 division represents a total absence of consensus, then degrees of agreement ranging from 25 to 75 per cent can be understood as closer to the total absence of consensus (50 per cent agreement) than to its perfect realization (100 per cent agreement). Responses from voters in both communities fall in this "discord" range on six of the statements (1, 4, 5, 6, 8, and 10); voters in the Southern community approach maximum discord on two additional statements (3 and 9), both of which put democratic principles in terms of Negro participation in public office. These findings strongly support the second of our preliminary assumptions, that consensus does not exist on more concrete questions involving the application of democratic principles.

Three of the statements that evoke more discord than consensus deal with the extension of democratic principles to Communists, a highly unpopular group in the United States. But it should be noted that these statements are put in terms of generally approved behaviors (speaking and seeking public office), not conspiratorial or other reprehensible activities. And the other statements on which discord exceeds consensus refer to groups (as well as activities) that are not in opposition to the American form of government: the right of all citizens to vote, the right of a professional group to maximize its voting strength, and the right to criticize churches and religion.

The extent to which consensus breaks down on the specific formulation of democratic principles is even greater than suggested by our discussion of the range of discord. To this point we have ignored the content of the opinions on these principles, which would permit an overwhelming *rejection* of a democratic principle to be accepted as consensus. Specifically, responses to statement 2 were not counted as falling in the "discord" category, but the approach to consensus in this case lies in rejection of the democratic principle of the "majority vote" with an "equal chance" for "every citizen." But the proposition about consensus holds, of course, that the consensus is in favor of democratic principles. On four statements (2, 4, 5, and 10) a majority of the voters in Ann Arbor express "undemocratic" opinions; and on six statements (1, 2, 4, 5, 8, and 10) a majority of the voters in Tallahassee express "undemocratic" opinions.

However the reactions to our specific statements are approached, they run counter to the idea of extended consensus. On none of them is there the real consensus that we found on the abstract form of the principles; responses to over half of the statements are closer to perfect discord than perfect consensus; and the responses to about half of the statements express the "wrong" answers. Unlike the general statements, then, the specific propositions call for an appraisal of bases of agreement and disagreement.

FINDINGS: BASES OF AGREEMENT AND DISAGREEMENT

The report on findings on the consensus problem has already suggested that regional subcultures are one basis of differences in opinions on democratic principles. Table 1 also shows differences along educational and income lines. Not included are other possible bases of disagreement that were found to have only a negligible effect, for example, age, sex and party.

Community, education and income all have an effect on opinions about democratic principles. More "correct" responses came from the Midwestern than from the Southern community, from those with high education than from those with less education, and from those with high income than from those with low income. The systematic nature of these differences supports the assumption that regional and class-related factors affect attitudes toward democratic principles when they are put in specific terms.

Which of these variables has the greatest effect on attitudes toward basic principles of democracy? Table 1 suggests that education is most important on two counts: (1) for every statement, the greatest difference in opinions is found in the high education–low education dichotomy; (2) for every statement, the grouping with the most "correct" or "democratic" responses is the high education category. Before education can be accepted as the independent variable in relation to democratic attitudes, however, the relationship must be examined for true independence. Since more Ann Arbor than Tallahassee respondents fall in the high education category, and since more high income than low income respondents have high education, the education variable might prove to be spurious—with the concealed community and income factors accounting for its apparent effect. Tables 2 and 3 show that when we control for community and income, differences between the high and low education respondents remain. When we control for education, on the other hand, the smaller differences reported in Table 1 by community and income tend to disappear.[24]

Since educational differences hold up consistently when other factors are "partialled out," education may be accepted as the most consequential basis of opinions on basic democratic principles.[25] Regardless of their other group identifications, people with high education accept democratic principles more than any other grouping. While the highly educated thus come closest to qualifying as the carriers of the democratic creed, the data

Table 2. Percentage of "Democratic" Responses to Basic Principles of Democracy by Education, with Income Controlled

Statement	High-Low Education Differences N = 134 N = 101	Low Income			High Income		
		High Education N = 42	Low Education N = 58	Difference	High Education N = 92	Low Education N = 43	Difference
1	27.0	67.5	22.4	45.1	59.1	51.2	7.9
2	4.1	20.0	22.0	-2.0	23.9	14.0	9.9
3	21.1	94.4	64.4	30.0	87.8	73.2	14.6
4	22.1	55.0	35.0	20.0	56.5	32.6	23.9
5	10.4	52.5	39.0	13.5	48.4	39.5	8.9
6	30.9	67.5	41.1	26.4	81.7	53.5	28.2
7	24.5	87.5	64.4	23.1	91.4	67.4	24.0
8	39.4	59.0	22.0	37.0	64.5	25.6	38.9
9	26.3	86.1	59.6	26.5	86.7	61.0	25.7
10	17.8	41.0	39.8	1.2	51.1	31.0	20.1

Table 3. Percentage of "Democratic" Responses to Basic Principles of Democracy by Education, with Community Controlled

Statement	High–Low Education Differences N = 137 N = 106	Ann Arbor			Tallahassee		
		High Education N = 92	Low Education N = 52	Difference	High Education N = 45	Low Education N = 54	Difference
1	27.0	63.7	42.3	21.4	57.1	26.5	30.6
2	4.1	24.2	15.4	8.8	19.5	22.0	−2.5
3	21.1	94.4	77.6	16.8	78.4	56.8	21.6
4	22.1	56.7	23.8	27.9	54.8	39.2	15.6
5	10.4	48.4	33.5	9.9	53.3	38.9	14.4
6	30.9	80.2	47.1	33.1	71.4	45.8	25.6
7	24.5	92.3	61.5	30.8	85.7	70.0	15.7
8	39.4	67.0	23.1	43.9	53.7	24.5	29.2
9	26.3	96.6	65.3	31.3	62.2	53.8	8.4
10	17.8	48.9	34.6	14.3	46.4	25.5	20.9

do not support our hypothesis; consensus in a meaningful sense (on both the abstract and the specific principles) is not found even among those with high education. On only three of the ten specific statements (3, 7, and 9) does agreement among those with high education reach 90 per cent in Ann Arbor, and in Tallahassee it fails to reach 90 per cent on any of the statements. On the proposition that the vote should be restricted to tax-payers in referenda deciding on tax-supported undertakings, 75.8 per cent of the highly educated in Ann Arbor and 81.5 per cent in Tallahassee reject the democratic principle of an equal vote for every citizen. And on five statements (1, 4, 5, 8, and 10) the highly educated in both communities are closer to perfect discord than to perfect harmony. Even when the necessity of consensus is reformulated in terms of the group most in accord with democratic principles, then, consensus cannot be said to exist.

SUMMARY AND CONCLUSIONS

The attitudes of voters in selected Midwestern and Southern communities offer no support for the hypothesis that democracy requires a large measure of consensus among the carriers of the Creed, i.e., those most consistently in accord with democratic principles. As expected, general consensus was found on the idea of democracy itself and on the broad principles of majority rule and minority rights, but it disappeared when these principles were put in more specific form. Indeed, the voters in both communities were closer to complete discord than to complete consensus; they did not reach consensus on any of the ten specific statements incorporating the principles of majority rule and minority rights; and majorities expressed the "undemocratic" attitude on about half of the statements.

In trying to identify the carriers of the Creed, the expected regional and class-related variations were found in attitudes toward democratic principles in specific form, with education having the most marked effect. While attitudes on democratic fundamentals were not found to vary appreciably according to age, sex or party affiliation, they did vary according to education, community, and income. The greatest difference on every statement was between the high-education group and the low-education group, and the high-education group gave the most democratic response to every question, whether compared with other educational, community or income groupings. Education, but not community or income, held up consistently as a basis of disagreement when other factors were controlled. We accordingly conclude that endorsement of democratic principles is not a function of class as such (of which income is also a criterion), but of greater acquaintance with the logical implications of the broad democratic principles. Note, for example, that the highly educated renounce in much greater degree than any other group the restriction of the vote to the well-informed, a restriction that would presumably affect them least of all.

Although high education was the primary basis of agreement on democratic principles, actual consensus was not found even among this segment of the voting population. The approach to consensus is closer among the highly educated in Ann Arbor, where greater agreement exists on the extension of democratic rights to Negroes, but in both communities the highly educated are closer to discord than consensus on half of the statements. On the basis of these findings, our hypothesis appears to be invalid.

Our failure to find a more extended consensus may, of course, be attributed to the possibility that the statements we formulated do not incorporate the particular "fundamentals" that are actually necessary to democracy.[26] When the approach to consensus is in the "undemocratic" direction—as in the question about restricting the vote to taxpayers—two possible objections to our interviewing schedule are suggested. First, perhaps the question is not a logical derivation from the basic principles with which we began. Second, perhaps the respondents are not interpreting the questions in any uniform way.

On the first point, the logical connection of the specific proposition with the general proposition is virtually self-evident. In syllogistic terms, we have: major premise—every citizen should have an equal chance to influence governmental policy; minor premise—non-taxpayers are citizens; conclusion—non-taxpayers should be allowed to vote in a city referendum deciding on tax-supported undertakings. Since decisions on tax-supported undertakings are clearly matters of governmental policy, rejection of the conclusion is inconsistent with acceptance of the major premise. As a matter of policy, perhaps the vote should be restricted—as it often is—under the circumstances indicated. We simply note that such a position is inconsistent with the unqualified major premise.

As to the second apparent difficulty, varying interpretations of the questions undoubtedly influenced the results. As our pre-test of the questionnaire indicated, the wordings finally chosen conveyed common meanings but tapped different attitudes embedded in different frames of reference. In surveys, as in real political situations, citizens are confronted with the need for making decisions about questions to which they attribute varying implications. We can infer, for example, that the respondents who repudiate free speech for Communists are responding in terms of anti-Communist rather than anti-free speech sentiments, especially since they endorse the idea of free speech in general. Conversely, those who endorse free speech for Communists are presumably reflecting a more consistent dedication to free speech rather than pro-Communist sentiments. But our concern in this study is with the opinions themselves rather than with the varying functions that a given opinion may perform for different individuals.[27] The significant fact is that the opinions (and presumably the frames of reference that produce them) vary systematically from group to group, not randomly or on a meaninglessly idiosyncratic basis.

Assuming that the United States is a democracy, we cannot say without qualification that consensus on fundamental principles is a necessary condition for the existence of democracy. Nor does it appear valid to say that, although consensus need not pervade the entire voting population, it must exist at least among the highly educated, who are the carriers of the Creed. Our data are not inconsistent, of course, with the qualified proposition that consensus on fundamental principles in a highly abstract form is a necessary condition for the existence of democracy. But the implication of political theory that consensus includes more specific principles is empirically invalid. Our findings accordingly suggest that the intuitive insights and logical inferences of political theorists need to be subjected more consistently to empirical validation.

Discussions of consensus tend to overlook the functional nature of apathy for the democratic system. No one is surprised to hear that what people *say* they *believe* and what they *actually do* are not necessarily the same. We usually assume that verbal positions represent a higher level— a more "democratic" stance—than non-verbal behavior. But something close to the opposite may also be true: many people express undemocratic principles in response to questioning but are too apathetic to act on their undemocratic opinions in concrete situations. And in most cases, fortunately for the democratic system, those with the most undemocratic principles are also those who are least likely to act. A sizable number (42.0 per cent) of our Southern respondents said, for example, that "a Negro should not be allowed to run for mayor of this city," but a few months before the survey a Negro actually did conduct an active campaign for that office without any efforts being made by the "white" people to obstruct his candidacy.

In this case, the behavior was more democratic than the verbal expressions. If the leadership elements—the carriers of the Creed—had encouraged undemocratic action, it might have materialized (as it did in Little Rock in the school desegregation crisis). But, in fact, people with basically undemocratic opinions either abstained from acting or acted in a perfectly democratic fashion. "The successful working of the system is not deliberately aimed at by those who work it," John Plamenatz says, "but is the result of their behaving as they do."[28] As J. Roland Pennock puts it, democracy can tolerate less conscious agreement on principles if people are willing to compromise and to follow set rules and procedures.[29] Loose talk of consensus as a self-evident requirement of democracy should have no place beside such insightful observations as these. Carl J. Friedrich appears to have been correct in asserting, eighteen years ago, that democracy depends on habitual patterns of behavior rather than on conscious agreement on democratic "principles."[30] His argument has been largely ignored because, like the position from which he dissented, it was advanced without the support of directly relevant research findings. Our results are offered as a step toward settling the question on empirical grounds.

NOTES

[1] The consensus of Quaker meetings seems to mean unanimity; although no formal vote is recorded, discussion continues until a position emerges on which no dissent is expressed. Similarly, the literature on the family refers to "family consensus" in a way that suggests unanimity; in a family of three or four people, even one dissenter would make it impossible to speak of consensus. At a different extreme, some students of collective behavior employ a functional definition of consensus, taking it to mean that amount of agreement in a group which is necessary for the group to act. Political scientists clearly do not have such limited agreement in mind when they speak of consensus as necessary to democracy. Majorities as large as three-fourths are required by the Constitution (in ratifying amendments), but such a large majority is no more thought of as consensus than a majority of 50 per cent plus one. Our purpose here is not to develop a general definition of consensus. We interpret the vague usage of the term to suggest agreement approaching unanimity. And, since our study actually found agreement as great as 98 per cent on some questions, we regard any degree of agreement that falls significantly below this figure to be less than consensus.

[2] Ernest S. Griffith, John Plamenatz and J. Roland Pennock, "Cultural Prerequisites to a Successfully Functioning Democracy: A Symposium," *The American Political Science Review*, 50 (March, 1956), 101.

[3] *Ibid.*, pp. 103–4. Italics are his.

[4] *Ibid.*, p. 118. Italics are added.

[5] *Ibid.*, pp. 129–31. Italics are added.

[6] *Ibid.*, p. 132.

[7] If the term consensus has any meaning, it is in a great extent of agreement; Pennock's reference to the varying "extent" of consensus must accordingly mean variations from large to even larger majorities.

[8] *Today's Isms* (Englewood Cliffs, 1954), p. 99. Italics are his.

[9] Bernard R. Berelson, Paul F. Lazarsfeld, and William N. McPhee, *Voting: A Study of Opinion Formation in a Presidential Election* (Chicago, 1954), p. 313. Although not a political theorist, Berelson was speaking here on the "theoretical" aspects of "Democratic Practice and Democratic Theory."

[10] " 'Value Consensus' in Democracy: The Issue in the Lincoln-Douglas Debates," *The American Political Science Review*, 52 (September, 1958), p. 753. Italics are added. Among the other theorists who have offered similar conclusions is Norman L. Stamps: "Democracy is a delicate form of government which rests upon conditions which are rather precarious. . . . It is impossible to overestimate the extent to which the success of

parliamentary government is dependent upon a considerable measure of agreement on fundamentals." *Why Democracies Fail: A Critical Evaluation of the Causes of Modern Dictatorship* (Notre Dame, Indiana, 1957), pp. 41–42. Walter Lippmann, in explaining "the decline of the West," cites "the disappearance of the public philosophy—and of a consensus on the first and last things. . . ." *Essays in the Public Philosophy* (Boston, 1955), p. 100. Joseph A. Schumpeter submits: ". . . democratic government will work to full advantage only if all the interests that matter are practically unanimous not only in their allegiance to the country but also in their allegiance to the structural principles of the existing society." *Capitalism, Socialism, and Democracy* (3rd ed., New York, 1950), p. 296.

[11] In Pennock's case, the lack of precision is deliberate, reflecting a well-defined position that the necessary amount of consensus on fundamentals varies according to the strength of two other prerequisites of democracy—"willingness to compromise" and "respect for rules and set procedures." *Op. cit.*, p. 132.

[12] *Op. cit.*, p. 99.

[13] *Op. cit.*, p. 129.

[14] For findings of overwhelming endorsement of the general idea of democracy, see Herbert H. Hyman and Paul B. Sheatsley, "The Current Status of American Public Opinion," in Daniel Katz *et al.* (eds.), *Public Opinion and Propaganda* (New York, 1954), pp. 33–48, reprinted from the *National Council for Social Studies Yearbook*, 1950, Vol. 21, pp. 11–34.

[15] *Op. cit.*, p. 103. Italics are added.

[16] *Op. cit.*, p. 101.

[17] This item is not included in the results below because we report only on those propositions that relate directly to the question of how political power is gained. The recognition of "different aspects of truth" logically underlies the ideas of majority rule and minority rights, but it is not as directly connected with them as the propositions on which we report.

[18] *Op. cit.*, p. 105.

[19] *Ibid.*

[20] *Op. cit.*, p. 131.

[21] That the awareness is so consistently forgotten attests to the need of uniting research in political theory with research in public opinion.

[22] We are not arguing, of course, that these propositions are incorrect in any absolute sense. Good arguments can no doubt be advanced in support of each of the positions we label as "incorrect." Our point is simply that they are incorrect *in the sense* of being undemocratic, i.e., inconsistent with general principles of democracy.

[23] See Angus Campbell and Homer C. Cooper, *Group Differences in Attitudes and Votes* (Ann Arbor, 1956).

[24] Those statements with particular salience for one of the regional subcultures (Southern anti-Negro sentiment) constitute an exception.

[25] For a discussion of this approach to controlling qualitative data, see Herbert Hyman, *Survey Design and Analysis* (Glencoe, 1955), Chap. 7.

[26] The lack of extended consensus cannot, however, be attributed to the possibility that the responses classified as "correct" are actually "incorrect," for we found consensus neither in acceptance nor in rejection of the statements.

[27] The latter approach is, of course, a fruitful type of investigation, but it is not called for by our problem. For a functional analysis of opinions, see M. Brewster Smith, Jerome S. Bruner and Robert W. White, *Opinions and Personality* (New York, 1956).

[28] *Op. cit.*, p. 123.

[29] *Op. cit.*, p. 132.

[30] *The New Belief in the Common Man* (Boston, 1942).

CHAPTER 12

*argues that "Consensus" on
Democratic Belief functions as
a constraint on non-democratic
behaviour by Elite
(Professional).
& i.e. politics*

Stability, Change
and the Democratic Creed

Robert A. Dahl

Leaving to one side as a doubtful case the elected oligarchy that governed
New Haven during its first century and a half, public officials in New
Haven have been selected for the last century and a half through democratic
institutions of a rather advanced sort. For more than a century, indeed, New
Haven's political system has been characterized by well-nigh universal
suffrage, a moderately high participation in elections, a highly competitive
two-party system, opportunity to criticize the conduct and policies of
officials, freedom to seek support for one's views, among officials and
citizens, and surprisingly frequent alternations in office from one party to
the other as electoral majorities have shifted. (Hereafter, when I speak of
the political system of New Haven, I will assume what I have just enumerated to be the defining characteristics of that system: "stability" will mean
the persistence of these characteristics.)

During this period New Haven has not, so far as I can discover, fallen
at any time into the kind of semi-dictatorship occasionally found in other
American communities. Violence is not and seems never to have been a
weapon of importance to New Haven's rulers. Party bosses have existed
and exist today; the parties tend to be highly disciplined, and nominations
are centrally controlled. But despite occasional loose talk to the contrary,
today the parties are too competitive and the community too fragmented
for a party boss to be a community boss as well.

Like every other political system, of course, the political system of New
Haven falls far short of the usual conceptions of an ideal democracy; by
almost any standard, it is obviously full of defects. But to the extent that the
term is ever fairly applied to existing realities, the political system of New
Haven is an example of a democratic system, warts and all. For the past
century it seems to have been a highly stable system.

Theorists have usually assumed that so much stability would be unlikely

Reprinted from Robert A. Dahl, *Who Governs?* (New Haven: Yale University
Press, 1961), pp. 311–25, by permission of Yale University Press. Copyright © 1961 by
Yale University.

and even impossible without widespread agreement among citizens on the key ideas of democracy, including the basic rights, duties, and procedures that serve to distinguish democratic from nondemocratic systems. Tocqueville, you will recall, concluded that among the three causes that maintained democracy among the people of the United States—their physical, social, and economic conditions, their laws, and their customs—it was the customs that constituted "the peculiar cause which renders that people the only one of the American nations that is able to support a democratic government." By "customs," he explained, he meant "the whole moral and intellectual condition of a people." Considering his remarkable eye for relevant detail, Tocqueville was uncharacteristically vague as to the specific nature of these customs. But the general import of his argument is perfectly clear. "Republican notions insinuate themselves," as he says at one place, "into all the ideas, opinions, and habits of the Americans and are formally recognized by the laws; and before the laws could be altered, the whole community must be revolutionized."[1]

Before the days of the sample survey it was difficult to say with confidence how widely shared various ideas of democracy actually were in the United States, or even in New Haven. The data are still inadequate. However, some recent findings[2] cast doubt on the validity of the hypothesis that the stability of the American democratic system depends, as Tocqueville and others seem to argue, on an almost universal belief in the basic rules of the democratic game. These studies offer support for some alternative hypotheses. First, although Americans almost unanimously agree on a number of general propositions about democracy, they disagree about specific applications to crucial cases. Second, a majority of voters frequently hold views contrary to rules of the game actually followed in the political system. Third, a much higher degree of agreement on democratic norms exists among the political stratum than among voters in general. Fourth, even among the political stratum the amount of agreement is hardly high enough to account by itself for the stability of the system.

I propose, therefore, to examine some alternative explanations. Because my data on New Haven are not wholly adequate for the task at hand, the theory I shall sketch out might properly be regarded more as reflections on the process of creating consensus than as a testing of theory by a hard examination of the facts in New Haven. But New Haven will provide a convenient reference point.

SOME ALTERNATIVE EXPLANATIONS

There are at least five alternative ways (aside from denying the validity or generality of recent findings) to account for the stability of the political system in New Haven.

First, one may deny that New Haven is "democratic" and argue that it is in fact run by a covert oligarchy of some sort. Thus the problem, it might be said, is illusory. Yet even in the absence of comparable studies our findings argue strongly that New Haven is not markedly *less* democratic than other supposedly democratic political systems. Some of these, we know, have proved to be unstable; hence the problem does not vanish after all.

Second, one might argue that things were different in the good old days. Yet it is hardly plausible to suppose that in 1910, when slightly less than half the population of New Haven consisted of first- and second-generation immigrants (many of them from countries with few democratic traditions), democratic beliefs were more widespread than they are now. In any case, the main characteristics of the political system—majority rule, the legitimacy of opposition, and so on—do not show any signs of disappearing.

Third, it might be said that the political system of New Haven is scarcely autonomous enough to furnish us with adequate explanations of its own stability, for stability may depend much less on the beliefs of citizens locally than on state and national institutions. There is much truth in this objection, but it does not altogether explain why some American towns, cities, and counties have at various times moved a good deal farther from democratic norms than New Haven has.

Fourth, one might argue that the system has not been entirely stable, that in fact most seemingly stable democratic systems are constantly in transition. Surely this is a valid point, but it is one that cuts both ways. In New Haven, as elsewhere, the rules of the game have altered in quite important, one is tempted to say fundamental, ways over the past century and a half. For example, organized, overt political competition, which was anathema to the patrician oligarchy, seems to have been fully legitimate since about 1840. Consider the electorate—the active voters. Partly as a result of the abolition of property qualifications in 1845, but probably more as a result of party organization and competition, the proportion of voting adults shot up and then stabilized at a moderate level. In most elections from 1800–33 the voters comprised less than a quarter of the adult males and sometimes less than 10 per cent; since 1834, however, they have made up from a half to three-quarters of the adult male (and since 1920, female) population. A final example: throughout the nineteenth century, an implicit norm excluded persons of foreign birth or non-Yankee origins from nomination or election to the mayoralty; since the mayoralty election of 1899, the norm has very nearly come to operate in reverse.

Because of, or in spite of, these changes, however, the essential characteristics of the political system as I described them have remained substantially intact for the past century. With appropriate techniques, probably one could detect and describe significant fluctuations in the "intensity," "degree," or "magnitude" of the various characteristics, but this line of inquiry would not help much in the present problem.

Fifth, one might argue that the stability of New Haven's political system does not depend on a widespread belief that certain democratic norms, rules, or procedures are highly desirable or intrinsically preferable to other rules; in some circumstances a democratic system could be highly stable if a substantial part of the electorate merely *accepted* them. A majority of voters who do not really believe in extending freedom of speech to individuals and groups beyond the pale of popular morality—and who would readily say so during an interview—might nonetheless acquiesce in such extensions on a variety of pragmatic grounds.

There is, I think, a good deal more truth in this view than many enthusiastic democrats care to admit. Let me suggest some circumstances in which this explanation might be valid.

Whenever the costs of disagreement are believed to be very high, there are innumerable conditions under which a collection of people might knowingly agree on a choice that no one preferred, simply because this was the only choice on which they could agree. Stable systems of international politics, such as the balance of power system in the 19th century, surely have been of this kind. Or suppose that 80 per cent of the voters are in favor of a more restricted suffrage than actually exists. Suppose that 40 per cent would like to restrict the suffrage to taxpayers, another 40 per cent would like to restrict it to college graduates, and only 20 per cent would like to retain the present suffrage. Suppose further that their other choices were as follows:

	40% prefer:	40% prefer:	20% prefer:
First choice:	Taxpayers	College graduates	Present requirements
Second choice:	Present requirements	Present requirements	College graduates
Third choice:	College graduates	Taxpayers	Taxpayers

One does not need to assume a great amount of rationality to conclude that they would retain the existing broad suffrage requirements, even though this would be the preferred choice of only a minority.

Moreover, this example hints at the fact that the stability of a political system, even a democratic one, is not merely a matter of the *numbers* of persons who adhere to it but also of the *amount of political resources* they use—or are expected to use—in acting on their beliefs. The amount of political resources an individual is likely to use is a function, among other things, of the amount of resources he has access to, the strength or intensity of his belief, and the relevance he sees in political action as a way of acting on his beliefs. Other things being equal, rules supported only by a wealthy, educated minority (money and knowledge being important political resources) and opposed by the rest of the voters are surely likely to endure longer than rules supported only by a poor, uneducated minority and opposed by the rest of the voters. Likewise, rules that are *strongly* believed in by a minority and weakly opposed by the rest are more likely to endure than rules *weakly* believed in by a majority and strongly opposed by a minority.

In addition to numbers and resources, however, skill is obviously a critical factor. Rules supported by a politically skillful minority may withstand the opposition of a less skilled majority, and in any case are likely to endure longer than if they are supported only by an unskilled minority.

Let us now imagine a society with a political system approximately like that in New Haven. Suppose the rules, procedures, and essential characteristics of this system are strongly supported by a minority which, in comparison with the rest of the population, possesses a high degree of political skill. Suppose further that a majority of voters would prefer rules different from those prevailing, though they might not all prefer the same alternatives. Suppose finally that the majority of voters have access to fewer resources of influence; that their preferences for other rules are not salient or strong; that because of their relative indifference they do not employ what potential influence they have; and that they are not very skillful in using their political resources anyway. Such a political system, it seems to me, might be highly stable.

On the other hand, if any of the characteristics of this hypothetical minority were to shift to the majority, then the system would surely become less stable. Instability would increase, then, if the minority favoring the system no longer had superior resources, or if it became less skillful, or if the question of rules became salient and urgent to a majority of voters.

I should like to advance the hypothesis that the political system we have just been supposing corresponds closely to the facts of New Haven, and in all probability to the United States. If it errs, it is in supposing that *even among the political stratum* the level of agreement on the rules of the game is, at any given moment, high enough to explain the persistence of the rules.

CONSENSUS AS A PROCESS

Most of us, I suppose, are ready to recognize long-run changes in the beliefs expressed by the more articulate segments of the political stratum and the intelligentsia, and we can infer from various kinds of evidence—all of it, alas, highly debatable—that changes of some sort take place over long periods of time in the attitudes about democracy held in the general population. We tend to assume, however, that except for these long-run shifts beliefs about democracy are more or less static. I want to propose an alternative explanation, namely that democratic beliefs, like other political beliefs, are influenced by a recurring *process* of interchange among political professionals, the political stratum, and the great bulk of the population. The process generates enough agreement on rules and norms so as to permit the system to operate, but agreement tends to be incomplete, and typically it decays. So the process is frequently repeated. "Consensus," then, is not at all a static and unchanging attribute of citizens. It is a variable element in a complex and more or less continuous process.

This process seems to me to have the following characteristics:

1. Over long periods of time the great bulk of the citizens possess a fairly stable set of democratic beliefs at a high level of abstraction. Let me call these beliefs the democratic creed. In Ann Arbor and Tallahassee, Prothro and Grigg found that very nearly everyone they interviewed agreed with five abstract democratic propositions.[3] We can, I think, confidently conclude that most Americans believe in democracy as the best form of government, in the desirability of rights and procedures insuring a goodly measure of majority rule and minority freedom, and in a wide but not necessarily comprehensive electorate. At a somewhat lower level of agreement, probably the great majority of citizens also believe in the essential legitimacy of certain specific American political institutions: the presidency, Congress, the Supreme Court, the states, the local governments, etc.

2. Most citizens assume that the American political system is consistent with the democratic creed. Indeed, the common view seems to be that our system is not only democratic but is perhaps the most perfect expression of democracy that exists anywhere; if deficiencies exist, either they can, and ultimately will, be remedied, or else they reflect the usual gap between ideal and reality that men of common sense take for granted. Moreover, because leading officials with key roles in the legitimate political institutions automatically acquire authority for their views on the proper functioning of the political institutions, as long as these various officials seem to agree, the ordinary citizen is inclined to assume that existing ways of carrying on the public business do not violate, at least in an important way, the democratic creed to which he is committed.

3. Widespread adherence to the democratic creed is produced and maintained by a variety of powerful social processes. Of these, probably formal schooling is the most important. The more formal education an American has, the more democratic formulas he knows, expresses, and presumably believes. But almost the entire adult population has been

subjected to *some* degree of indoctrination through the schools. Beliefs acquired in school are reinforced in adult life through normal exposure to the democratic creed, particularly as the creed is articulated by leading political figures and transmitted through the mass media.

These social processes have an enormous impact on the citizen, partly because they begin early in life and partly because the very unanimity with which the creed is espoused makes rejection of it almost impossible. To reject the creed is infinitely more than a simple matter of disagreement. To reject the creed is to reject one's society and one's chances of full acceptance in it—in short, to be an outcast. (As a mental experiment, try to imagine the pyschic and social burdens an American child in an American school would incur if he steadfastly denied to himself and others that democracy is the best form of government.)

To reject the democratic creed is in effect to refuse to be an American. As a nation we have taken great pains to insure that few citizens will ever want to do anything so rash, so preposterous—in fact, so wholly un-American. In New Haven, as in many other parts of the United States, vast social energies have been poured into the process of "Americanization," teaching citizens what is expected in the way of words, beliefs, and behavior if they are to earn acceptance as Americans, for it was obvious to the political stratum that unless the immigrants and their children quickly accepted American political norms, the flood of aliens, particularly from countries with few traditions of self government, would disrupt the political system. In a characteristic response, the Board of Education of the city of New Haven created a supervisor for Americanization (a post, incidentally, that still exists). Something of the feeling of urgency and accomplishment that must have prevailed in many segments of the political stratum shines through these enthusiastic words in the annual report of the New Haven superintendent of schools in 1919:

The public school is the greatest and most effective of all Americanization agencies. This is the one place where all children in a community or district, regardless of nationality, religion, politics, or social status, meet and work together in a cooperative and harmonious spirit. . . . The children work and play together, they catch the school spirit, they live the democratic life, American heroes become their own, American history wins their loyalty, the Stars and Stripes, always before their eyes in the school room, receives their daily salute. Not only are these immigrant children Americanized through the public school, but they, in turn, Americanize their parents carrying into the home many lessons of democracy learned at school.[4]

For their part, the immigrants and their children were highly motivated to learn how to be Americans, for they were desperately, sometimes pathetically, eager to win acceptance as true Americans.

In one form or another the process of Americanization has absorbed enormous social energies all over the United States. As a factor in shaping American behavior and attitudes, the process of Americanization must surely have been as important as the frontier, or industrialization, or urbanization. That regional, ethnic, racial, religious, or economic differences might disrupt the American political system has been a recurring fear among the political stratum of the United States from the very beginning of the republic. Doubtless this anxiety was painfully stimulated by the Civil War. It was aroused again by the influx of immigrants. Throughout the country then the political stratum has seen to it that new citizens, young and old, have been properly trained in "American" principles and beliefs. Everywhere, too, the pupils have been highly motivated to talk, look and believe as Americans should. The result was as astonishing an act of voluntary political and cultural assimilation and speedy elimination of regional, ethnic, and cultural dissimilarities as history can provide. The extent to which Americans agree today on the key propositions about democracy is a measure of the almost unbelievable success of this deliberate attempt to create a seemingly uncoerced nation-wide consensus.

4. Despite wide agreement on a general democratic creed, however, citizens frequently disagree on specific applications. Many citizens oppose what some political philosophers would regard as necessary implications of the creed. Many citizens also disagree with the way the creed is actually applied—or perhaps it would be more accurate to say, with the existing rules of the game, the prevailing political norms. Again and again, for example, surveys indicate that a large number of Americans, sometimes even a majority, do not approve of the extension of important rights, liberties, and privileges to individuals and groups that do in fact enjoy them.

A citizen is able to adhere to these seemingly inconsistent beliefs for a great variety of reasons. For one thing, he himself need not see any inconsistency in his beliefs. The creed is so vague (and incomplete) that strict deductions are difficult or impossible even for sophisticated logicians. Moreover, propositions stated in universal terms are rarely assumed by men of common sense to imply universality in practice; to the frequent dismay of logicians, a common tendency of mankind—and not least of Americans —is to qualify universals in application while leaving them intact in rhetoric. Then, too, the capacity for (or interest in) working out a set of consistent political attitudes is rather limited. As the authors of *The American Voter* have recently shown, most voters seem to operate at a low level of ideological sophistication; even among intelligent (though not necessarily highly educated) citizens, conceptions of politics are often of a simplicity that the political philosopher might find it hard to comprehend.[5] In addition, most citizens operate with a very small fund of political information; often they lack the elementary information required even to be aware of inconsistencies between their views and what is actually happening in the political system, particularly if the subject is (as most questions of rights and procedures are) arcane and complex. Again, questions that bother theorists are often not interesting or salient to most voters; their attention and energies are diverted elsewhere, usually to activities that lie entirely outside the political arena. As long as a citizen believes that democracy is the best political system, that the United States is a democracy, and that the people in office can be trusted, by and large, to apply the abstract creed to specific cases, issues of democratic theory and practice hotly discussed by political philosophers, or even by publicists and columnists, are likely never to penetrate through the manifold barriers to abstract political thinking that are erected by the essentially apolitical culture in which he lives. Finally, even if the issues do manage to get through, many citizens feel themselves incompetent to decide them; this, after all, is what Supreme Court judges, presidents, and members of Congress are supposed to do. Worse yet, many citizens feel that no one in public office will care much about their opinions anyway.

5. Members of the political stratum (who live in a much more politicized culture) are more familiar with the "democratic" norms, more consistent, more ideological, more detailed and explicit in their political attitudes, and more completely in agreement on the norms. They are more in agreement not only on what norms are implied by the abstract democratic creed but also in supporting the norms currently operating. This relatively higher degree of support for the prevailing norms in the existing political system is generated and maintained by a variety of processes. Because members of the political stratum have on the average considerably more formal education than the population as a whole, they have been more thoroughly exposed to the creed and its implications. Because they are more involved in, concerned with, and articulate about politics, they invest more time and effort in elaborating a consistent ideology. Because they participate more extensively in politics, they more frequently express and defend their views, encounter criticism, and face the charge of inconsistency. They know more about politics, read more, experience more, see more.

Within the political stratum, the professionals tend to agree even more on what the norms should be, what they are, and the desirability of maintaining them substantially as they are. Agreement among the professionals is generated by all the factors that account for it among the rest of the political stratum and even among the apolitical strata. Mastery over the existing norms of the political system represents the particular stockpile of skills peculiar to the professional's vocation. Norms also tend to legitimate his power and position in the political system, furnish an agreed-on method of getting on with the immediate tasks at hand, carry the authority of tradition, and help to reduce the baffling uncertainty that surrounds the professional's every choice. Finally, the professional is likely to support the existing norms because his own endorsement of existing norms was initially a criterion in his own recruitment and advancement; complex processes of political selection and rejection tend to exclude the deviant who challenges the prevailing norms of the existing political system. Most of the professionals might properly be called democratic "legitimists."

6. The professionals, of course, have access to extensive political resources which they employ at a high rate with superior efficiency. Consequently, a challenge to the existing norms is bound to be costly to the challenger, for legitimist professionals can quickly shift their skills and resources into the urgent task of doing in the dissenter. As long as the professionals remain substantially legitimist in outlook, therefore, the critic is likely to make little headway. Indeed, the chances are that anyone who advocates extensive changes in the prevailing democratic norms is likely to be treated by the professionals, and even by a fair share of the political stratum, as an outsider, possibly even as a crackpot whose views need not be seriously debated. No worse fate can befall the dissenter, for unless he can gain the attention of the political stratum, it is difficult for him to gain space in the mass media; if he cannot win space in the mass media, it is difficult for him to win a large following; if he cannot win a large following, it is difficult for him to gain the attention of the political stratum.

7. Sometimes, of course, disagreements over the prevailing norms occur within the political stratum and among the professionals themselves. But these disagreements need not, and perhaps ordinarily do not, produce much effort to involve the general public in the dispute. The disagreements are not, to be sure, secret; the electorate is not *legally* barred from finding out about the conflict and becoming involved. It does not need to be. Given the low salience of politics in the life of the average citizen, most conflicts over the prevailing norms might attract more attention if they were held behind locked doors. Unless a professional is willing to invest very great resources in whipping up public interest, he is not likely to get much effective support. In any case, public involvement may seem undesirable to the legitimist, for alterations in the prevailing norms are often subtle matters, better obtained by negotiation than by the crudities and oversimplifications of public debate.

8. Among the rules and procedures supported strongly by the legitimists in the political stratum, and particularly by the professionals, are some that prescribe ways of settling disagreements as to rules and procedures. These involve appeals to authorities who give decisions widely accepted as binding, authoritative, and legitimate—though not necessarily

as "good" or "correct." Typically these include appeals to courts or quasi-judicial institutions that ostensibly arrive at their decisions by appeals to norms, codes, formulas, and beliefs that appear to transcend partisan and policy differences in the political stratum.

9. Ordinarily, then, it is not difficult for a stable system of rights and privileges to exist that, at least in important details, does not have wide-spread public support and occasionally even lacks majority approval. As long as the matter is not a salient public issue—and whether it is or not depends partly on how the political stratum handles it—the question is substantially determined within the political stratum itself. When disagreements arise, these are adjudicated by officials who share the beliefs of the political stratum rather than those of the populace; and even when these officials adopt positions that do not command the undivided support of the political stratum, members of the political stratum, and particularly the professionals, tend to accept a decision as binding until and unless it can be changed through the accepted procedures. This is the essence of their code of democratic legitimism.

10. Occasionally, however, a sizable segment of the political stratum develops doubts that it can ever achieve the changes it seeks through accepted procedures that are, in a sense, internal to the political stratum and the professionals. One or more of these dissenters may push his way into the professional group, or the dissenters may be numerous and vocal enough to acquire a spokesman or two among the professionals. The strategy of the dissenters may now begin to shift. Instead of adjudicating the matter according to the accepted procedures, the dissenters attempt to arouse public support for their proposals, hoping that when a sufficient number of voters are won over to their cause, other professionals—legitimist or not—will have to come around.

The professionals, as I have said, live in a world of uncertainty. They search for omens and portents. If the auguries indicate that the appeal to the populace has failed, then the legitimists may confidently close ranks against the dissenter. But if the auguries are uncertain or unfavorable, then the legitimists, too, are forced to make a counter-appeal to the populace. Since public opinion is often as difficult to interpret as the flights of birds or the entrails of a sheep, political professionals may and frequently do misread the auspices. In October, 1954, the Survey Research Center discovered that only 12 per cent of their sample said they would be more likely to vote for a candidate who had the support of Senator McCarthy; 37 per cent said they would be less likely, and 43 per cent said it would make no difference.[6] In retrospect, these proportions do not look wildly off, but in 1954 belief in McCarthy's mass following was widespread throughout the whole political stratum and not least among the professionals. The legitimists could probably have ignored the late Senator with impunity—as they later did—but he followed a classic strategy—(required, I am suggesting, by the tendency of the legitimists to monopolize the internal devices for adjudicating disputes over norms)—by taking the issue out of the hands of the professionals, where the rules of the game were bound to run against him, and appealing instead to the populace.

If the dissenters succeed in forcing the issue out beyond the political stratum, and dissenters and legitimists begin making appeals to the populace, then the nature of the debate begins to change. Technical questions, subtle distinctions, fine matters of degree are shed. The appeal is now shaped to the simple democratic creed which nearly every citizen believes in. Because the creed does not constitute a tightly logical system, it is possible for the legitimists to demonstrate that existing norms are necessary consequences of the creed, and for the dissenters to show that existing norms run counter to the creed. Because the creed is deeply laden with tradition and sentiment, emotion rises and reasoned discussion declines.

11. Ordinary citizens who normally remain outside these debates now find their attention—and their votes—solicited by both sides. They become aware that the very officials who ordinarily decide these matters, to whom the citizen himself turns for his cues as to what is legitimate and consistent with the creed, are locked in deadly, heated battle. These citizens must now find ways of applying the creed to the issue. One way is to withdraw even more deeply into the political shadows; a citizen can simply refuse to choose. Many do. In March, 1937, at the height of the debate over President Roosevelt's proposal to enlarge the Supreme Court, 50 per cent of the people interviewed in a Gallup poll had listened to neither of the President's two recent radio speeches defending his plan. A month later, one out of seven persons who were asked whether Congress should pass the President's bill expressed no opinion.[7] In New Haven, after several years of public discussion and debate over charter reform, when a sample of registered voters was asked in 1959 whether they personally would do anything if a revision of the charter was proposed that would make the mayor stronger, over 40 per cent of those who disapproved of such an idea said they would do nothing to oppose it, and nearly three-quarters of those who approved said they would do nothing to support it. These seemed to be tolerably honest responses; in the preceding election, after wide discussion among the political stratum and hot debate among the professionals over a new charter, less than half the voters who went to the polls even bothered to vote on the charter.) Thus when dissenters and legitimists appeal to the populace to settle questions they ordinarily decide among themselves, they cannot be at all sure that they will actually produce much of a response no matter how much they try to stir up the public.

However, citizens who *do* make up their minds must find some ways for arriving at a choice. For many citizens the decision is eased by their existing loyalties to parties or political leaders. In April, 1937, 68 per cent of the Democrats in a Gallup poll said that Congress should pass Roosevelt's court plan; 93 per cent of the Republicans said Congress should not. Those who had no strong party identifications were, as one might expect, split—42 per cent in favor and 58 per cent against.[8] In 1954, attitudes toward McCarthy were closely related to party identifications. Among strong Democrats, those who said that McCarthy's support would make them *less* likely to vote for a candidate were six times as great as those who said his support would make them *more* likely; strong Republicans, by contrast, split about evenly. Among Catholics who were strong Democrats, the ratio was two to one against McCarthy; among Catholics who were strong Republicans it was nearly two to one in his favor.[9]

If the parties give no clear guidance, citizens may look to particular leaders or institutions. They may turn to spokesmen in their churches, for example, or trade unions, or regions. They often turn, of course, to attitudes prevalent in their own circle of intimates, friends, associates, acquaintances. If their search yields no consistent cues, they may give up. In the struggle over charter reform in New Haven in 1958, when Democratic leaders were split from the top down, judging from a sample of registered voters interviewed shortly after the election the proportion of people who went to the polls and voted on the general election but did not vote either for or against the charter was higher among Democrats than among either Republicans or independents.

12. An appeal to the populace may terminate in several ways. The appeal may simply fail to create a stir. Interest in political matters wanes rather quickly; since complex issues of democratic norms nearly always lack a direct relation to the on-going life of an individual, they have even less capacity for holding attention than many other issues. However passionately the dissenters feel about their case, life does move on, old questions become tiresome, and the newspapers begin to shove the conflict to the inside pages. Perhaps the legitimists, buoyed by their reading of the electorate, defeat the dissenters in a clear-cut trial of strength and, having done so, close ranks and go on to the next business. Perhaps the dissenters win, or a compromise is worked out; if so the dissenters, like as not, turn into the next generation of legitimists.

THE ROLE OF DEMOCRATIC BELIEFS

The specific beliefs of the average citizen thus have a rather limited though important function. Ordinarily, conflicts over democratic norms are resolved among the professionals, with perhaps some involvement by parts of the political stratum but little or no involvement by most citizens. Thus the fact that a large number of citizens do not believe in the political norms actually applied, particularly extending political liberties to unpopular individuals and groups, has slight effect on the outcome.

The beliefs of the ordinary citizen become relevant only when professionals engage in an intensive appeal to the populace. Even then, the actual outcome of the appeal does not necessarily reflect majority attitudes at all accurately. These are not always known; they are guessed at in a variety of inaccurate ways, and they have to be filtered through the tighter mesh of the political stratum and the professionals before they can become public policy.

Nonetheless, wide consensus on the democratic creed does have two important kinds of consequences. On the one hand, this very consensus makes occasional appeal all but inevitable, for the creed itself gives legitimacy to an appeal to the populace. On the other hand, widespread adherence to the creed limits the character and the course of an appeal. It insures that no appeal is likely to succeed unless it is framed in terms consistent with the creed—which is perhaps not so small a constraint. Some solutions pretty evidently are *not* consistent. Because an appeal must take place in the face of criticism from legitimists and extensive appraisal by members of the political stratum, blatant inconsistencies are likely to be exposed. Moreover, because the appeal is legitimized by the creed, it provides an orderly way to conduct a dispute that exceeds the capacities of the professionals to resolve among themselves.

No one, I imagine, has ever supposed that the existence of the creed entails no risks. People can be deceived by appeals intended to destroy democracy in the name of democracy. Dissenters who believe in the democratic creed may unwittingly advocate or legitimists may insist on preserving rules of the game destined to have unforeseen and unintended consequences disastrous to the stability and perhaps the survival of the democracy.

Nonetheless, we can be reasonably sure of this: even if universal belief in a democratic creed does not guarantee the stability of a democratic system, a substantial decline in the popular consensus would greatly increase the chance of serious instability. How the professionals act, what they advocate, what they are likely to believe, are all constrained by the wide adherence to the creed that exists throughout the community. If a substantial segment of the electorate begins to doubt the creed, professionals will quickly come forth to fan that doubt. The nature and course of an appeal to the populace will change. What today is a question of applying the fundamental norms of democracy will become tomorrow an inquiry into the validity of these norms. If a substantial number of citizens begin to deny not merely to *some* minorities but to minorities *as such* the rights and powers prescribed in the creed, an appeal to the populace is likely to end sooner or later in a call to arms.

Thus consensus on political beliefs and practices has much in common with other aspects of a democratic system. Here, too, leaders lead—and often are led. Citizens are very far indeed from exerting equal influence over the content, application, and development of the political consensus. Yet widely held beliefs by Americans in a creed of democracy and political equality serve as a critical limit on the ways in which leaders can shape the consensus.

Neither the prevailing consensus, the creed, nor even the political system itself are immutable products of democratic ideas, beliefs, and institutions inherited from the past. For better or worse, they are always open, in some measure, to alteration through those complex processes of symbiosis and change that constitute the relations of leaders and citizens in a pluralistic democracy.

NOTES

[1] Tocqueville, *Democracy in America*, pp. 310, 334, 436.

[2] Especially Samuel Stouffer, *Communism, Conformity, and Civil Liberties* (New York: Doubleday, 1955) and James W. Prothro and Charles M. Grigg, "Fundamental Principles of Democracy: Bases of Agreement and Disagreement," *Journal of Politics*, 22 (1960), pp. 276–94.

[3] "Democracy is the best form of government." "Public officials should be chosen by majority vote." "Every citizen should have an equal chance to influence government policy." "The minority should be free to criticize majority decisions." "People in the minority should be free to try to win majority support for their opinions." Prothro and Grigg, "Fundamental Principles of Democracy," pp. 282, 284.

[4] "Report of the Superintendent of Schools," *Annual Report of Education of the New Haven City School District*, 1919.

[5] A. Campbell, P. E. Converse, W. E. Miller, and D. D. Stokes, *The American Voter* (New York: Wiley, 1960), Chaps 9 and 10.

[6] Angus Campbell and Homer C. Cooper, *Group Differences in Attitudes and Votes, A Study of the 1954 Congressional Election* (Ann Arbor, Mich.: University of Michigan Survey Research Center, 1954), p. 145.

[7] Hadley Cantril, ed., *Public Opinion, 1935–1946* (Princeton: Princeton University Press, 1951), p. 150.

[8] *Ibid.*

[9] Campbell and Cooper, *Group Differences in Attitudes*, Tables VI–VIII (p. 92) and B-81 (p. 149). See also Nelson W. Polsby, "Towards an Explanation of McCarthyism," *Political Studies*, 8, No. 3 (1960), p. 250–71.

CHAPTER 13

Consensus and Ideology
in American Politics*

Herbert McClosky

The belief that consensus is a prerequisite of democracy has, since deTocqueville, so often been taken for granted that it is refreshing to find the notion now being challenged. Prothro and Grigg,[1] for example, have questioned whether agreement on "fundamentals" actually exists among the electorate, and have furnished data which indicate that it may not. Dahl,[2] reviewing his study of community decision-makers, has inferred that political stability does not depend upon widespread belief in the superiority of democratic norms and procedures, but only upon their *acceptance*. From the findings turned up by Stouffer,[3] and by Prothro and Grigg, he further conjectures that agreement on democratic norms is greater among the politically active and aware—the "political stratum" as he calls them—than among the voters in general. V. O. Key,[4] going a step further, suggests that the viability of a democracy may depend less upon popular opinion than upon the activities and values of an "aristocratic" strain whose members are set off from the mass by their political influence, their attention to public affairs, and their active role as society's policy makers. "If so, any assessment of the vitality of a democratic system should rest on an examination of the outlook, the sense of purpose, and the beliefs of this sector of society."

Writers who hold consensus to be necessary to a free society have commonly failed to define it precisely or to specify what it must include. Even Tocqueville[5] does not go deeply enough into the matter to satisfy these needs. He tells us that a society can exist and, *a fortiori*, prosper only when "the minds of all the citizens [are] rallied and held together by certain predominant ideas; . . . when a great number of men consider a great number of things from the same aspect, when they hold the same opinions upon many subjects, and when the same occurrences suggest the same thoughts and impressions to their minds"—and he follows this

Reprinted from *American Political Science Review*, Vol. 58, No. 2 (June, 1964) pp. 361–82, by permission of the American Political Science Association.

pronouncement with a list of general principles he believes Americans hold in common. Elsewhere, he speaks of the "customs" of the American nation (its "habits, opinions, usages, and beliefs") as "the peculiar cause which renders that people able to support a democratic government." But nowhere does he set forth explicitly the nature of the agreement upon which a democratic society presumably depends.

Later commentators have not clarified matters much. Some, like A. Lawrence Lowell,[6] have avoided Tocqueville's emphasis upon shared ideas, customs, and opinions in favor of the less demanding view that popular government requires agreement mainly "in regard to the legitimate character of the ruling authority and its right to decide the questions that arise." Consensus, in this view, becomes merely a synonym for legitimacy. Others speak of consensus as a sense of solidarity or social cohesion arising from a common ethos or heritage, which unites men into a community.[7] Political scientists have most frequently employed the term to designate a state of agreement about the "fundamental values" or "rules of the game" considered essential for constitutional government. Rarely, however, have writers on consensus attempted to state what the fundamentals must include, how extensive the agreement must be, and *who* must agree. Is agreement required among all men or only among certain of them? Among the entire electorate or only those who actively participate in public affairs? Is the same type of consensus essential for all democracies at all times, or is a firmer and more sweeping consensus needed for periods of crisis than for periods of calm, for newer, developing democracies than for older stable ones?

While certain of these questions are beyond the scope of this paper (no one, in any event, has done the systematic historical and comparative research needed to answer them satisfactorily), something might be learned about the relation of ideological consensus to democracy by investigating the subject in at least one major democracy, the United States. In the present paper I wish to explore further some of the questions raised by the writers I have cited and to present research findings on several hypotheses relating to those questions.

I. HYPOTHESES AND DEFINITIONS

We expected the data to furnish support for the following hypotheses, among others:

That the American electorate is often divided on "fundamental" democratic values and procedural "rules of the game" and that its understanding of politics and of political ideas is in any event too rudimentary at present to speak of ideological "consensus" among its members.

That, as Prothro and Grigg report for their samples, the electorate exhibits greater support for general, abstract statements of democratic belief than for their specific applications.

That the constituent ideas of American democratic ideology are principally held by the more "articulate" segments of the population, including the political influentials; and that people in these ranks will exhibit a more meaningful and far reaching consensus on democratic and constitutional values than will the general population.

That consensus is far from perfect even among the articulate classes, and will be evidenced on political questions more than on economic ones, on procedural rights more than on public policies, and on freedom more than equality.

That whatever increases the level of political articulateness—education, S.E.S., urban residence, intellectuality, political activity, etc.—strengthens consensus and support for American political ideology and institutions.

Whether a word like ideology can properly be employed in the American context depends, in part, on which of its many connotations one chooses to emphasize. Agreement on the meaning of the term is far from universal, but a tendency can be discerned among contemporary writers to regard ideologies as *systems* of belief that are elaborate, integrated, and coherent, that justify the exercise of power, explain and judge historical events, identify political right and wrong, set forth the interconnections (causal and moral) between politics and other spheres of activity, and furnish guides for action.[8] While liberal democracy does not fulfill perfectly the terms of this definition, it comes close enough, in my opinion, to be considered an ideology.[9] The elements of liberal democratic thought are not nearly so vague as they are sometimes made out to be, and their coalescence into a single body of belief is by no means fortuitous. American democratic "ideology" possesses an elaborately defined theory, a body of interrelated assumptions, axioms, and principles, and a set of ideals that serve as guides for action. Its tenets, postulates, sentiments, and values inspired the great revolutions of the 17th and 18th centuries, and have been repeatedly and explicitly set forth in fundamental documents, such as the Constitution, the Declaration, and the Federalist Papers. They have been restated with remarkable unanimity in the messages of Presidents, in political speeches, in the pronouncements of judges and constitutional commentators, and in the writings of political theorists, historians, and publicists. They are so familiar that we are likely to see them not as a coherent union of ideas and principles embodying a well-defined political tendency, but as a miscellany of slogans and noble sentiments to be trotted out on ceremonial occasions.

Although scholars or Supreme Court justices might argue over fine points of interpretation, they would uniformly recognize as elements of American democratic ideology such concepts as consent, accountability, limited or constitutional government, representation, majority rule, minority rights, the principle of political opposition, freedom of thought, speech, press, and assembly, equality of opportunity, religious toleration, equality before the law, the rights of juridical defense, and individual self-determination over a broad range of personal affairs. How widely such elements of American liberal democracy are approved, by whom and with what measure of understanding, is another question—indeed, it is the central question to be addressed in this paper. But that they form an integrated body of ideas which has become part of the American inheritance seems scarcely open to debate.[10]

The term consensus will be employed in this paper to designate a state of agreement concerning the aforementioned values. It has principally to do with shared beliefs and not with feelings of solidarity, the willingness to live together, to obey the laws, or to accept the existing government as legitimate. Nor does it refer to an abstract or universal state of mind, but to a measurable state of concurrence around values that can be specified. Consensus exists in degree and can be expressed in quantitative form. No one, of course, can say how close one must come to unanimity before consensus is achieved, for the cutting point, as with any continuous variable, is arbitrary. Still, the term in ordinary usage has been reserved for fairly substantial measures of correspondence, and we shall take as a minimal requirement for consensus a level of agreement reaching 75 per cent. This figure, while also arbitrary, recommends itself by being realistically modest (falling as it does midway between a bare majority and unanimity), and by having been designated in this country and elsewhere as the extraordinary majority required for certain constitutional purposes.

Since I shall in subsequent pages frequently (and interchangeably) employ such terms as the "articulate minority," the "political class," the "political elite," the "political influentials," and the "political stratum," I should also clarify what they are intended to signify. I mean them to refer to those people who occupy themselves with public affairs to an unusual degree, such as government officials, elected office holders, active party members, publicists, officers of voluntary associations, and opinion leaders. The terms do not apply to any definable social class in the usual sense, nor to a particular status group or profession. Although the people they designate can be distinguished from other citizens by their activity and concerns, they are in no sense a community, they do not act as a body, and they do not necessarily possess identical or even harmonious interests. "Articulates" or "influentials" can be found scattered throughout the society, at all income levels, in all classes, occupations, ethnic groups, and communities, although some segments of the population will doubtless yield a higher proportion of them than others. I scarcely need to add that the line between the "articulates" and the rest of the population cannot always be sharply drawn, for the qualities that distinguish them vary in form and degree and no single criterion of classification will satisfy every contingency.

The data for the present inquiry have been taken from a national study of political actives and supporters carried out in 1957–58. I have in a previous paper described the procedures of that study in some detail,[11] and will not trouble to repeat that description here. Perhaps it will suffice for present purposes merely to note the following: national surveys were carried out on two separate samples, the first a sample of over 3,000 political "actives" or "leaders" drawn from the delegates and alternates who had attended the Democratic and Republican conventions of 1956; the second a representative national sample of approximately 1,500 adults in the general population drawn by the American Institute of Public Opinion (Gallup Poll). Gallup interviewers also delivered and introduced the questionnaire to all respondents, discussed its contents with them, and furnished both oral and written instructions for its self-administration and completion. (For example characteristics, see Appendix B.)

The party actives may be considered an especially pure sample of the "political stratum," for every person in the sample has marked himself off from the average citizen by his greater political involvement. Although the general population sample may be regarded as a sample of "inarticulates," to be compared with the sample of leaders, there are within it, of course, many persons who by virtue of education, profession, organizational activities, etc. can be classified as "articulates." We shall for certain purposes consider them in this light in order to provide further tests for our hypotheses.

Both samples received the same questionnaire—a lengthy instrument containing questions on personal background, political experience, values, attitudes, opinions, political and economic orientation, party outlooks, and personality characteristics. Many of the questions were direct inquiries in the standard form, but most were single sentence "items" with which the respondent was compelled to express his agreement or disagreement. While each of these items can stand alone and be regarded in its own right as an indicator of a person's opinions or attitudes, each of them is simultaneously an integral element of one of the forty-seven "scales" that was expressly fashioned to afford a more refined and reliable assessment of the attitude and personality predispositions of every respondent. Each of the scales (averaging approximately nine items) has been independently validated either by empirical validation procedures employing appropriate criterion groups, or by a modified Guttman reproducibility procedure (supplemented, in some instances, by a "face validity" procedure utilizing item ratings by experts).

Data on the *scale* scores are presented in Table 4 and are to be distinguished from the "percentage agree" scores for *individual items* presented in the remaining tables.

II. FINDINGS

"Rules of the Game" and Democratic Values

Although the so-called "rules of the game" are often separated from other democratic values, the distinction is to some extent arbitrary. One might, for example, reasonably regard as "rules of the game" many of the norms governing free speech, press, social and political equality, political toleration, and the enforcement of justice. For convenience, nevertheless, we shall treat separately those responses that stand out from the general body of democratic attitudes by their particular emphasis upon fair play, respect for legal procedures, and consideration for the rights of others. A sample of items expressing these values is presented in Table 1.

The responses to these items show plainly that while a majority of the electorate support the "rules of the game," approval of such values is significantly greater and more uniform among the influentials. The latter have achieved consensus (as we have defined it) on eight of the twelve items and near consensus on three of the remaining four items. The electorate, by contrast, does not meet the criterion for consensus on a single item.

Although the *scales* (as distinguished from individual *items*) cannot appropriately be used to measure *consensus*, comparison of the scores on those scales which most nearly embody the "rules of the game" furnishes additional evidence that the political class responds to such norms more favorably than does the electorate. The proportion scoring high[12] on a scale of "faith in direct action" (a scale measuring the inclination to take the law into one's own hands) is 26.1 per cent for the active political minority and 42.5 per cent for the general population. On a scale assessing the willingness to flout the rules of political integrity, the proportions scoring high are 12.2 per cent and 30.6 per cent respectively. On "totalitarianism," a scale measuring the readiness to subordinate the rights of others to the pursuit of some collective political purpose, only 9.7 per cent

Table 1. Political Influentials vs. the Electorate: Response to Items Expressing "Rules of the Game"*

Items	Political Influentials (N = 3,020)	General Electorate (N = 1,484)
	% Agree	
There are times when it almost seems better for the people to take the law into their own hands rather than wait for the machinery of government to act.	13.3	26.9
The majority has the right to abolish minorities if it wants to.	6.8	28.4
We might as well make up our minds that in order to make the world better a lot of innocent people will have to suffer.	27.2	41.6
If congressional committees stuck strictly to the rules and gave every witness his rights, they would never succeed in exposing the many dangerous subversives they have turned up.	24.7	47.4
I don't mind a politician's methods if he manages to get the right things done.	25.6	42.4
Almost any unfairness or brutality may have to be justified when some great purpose is being carried out.	13.3	32.8
Politicians have to cut a few corners if they are going to get anywhere.	29.4	43.2
People ought to be allowed to vote even if they can't do so intelligently.	65.6	47.6
To bring about great changes for the benefit of mankind often requires cruelty and even ruthlessness.	19.4	31.3
Very few politicians have clean records, so why get excited about the mudslinging that sometimes goes on?	14.8	38.1
It is all right to get around the law if you don't actually break it.	21.2	30.2
The true American way of life is disappearing so fast that we may have to use force to save it.	12.8	34.6

* Since respondents were forced to make a choice on each item, the number of omitted or "don't know" responses was, on the average, fewer than 1 per cent, and thus has little influence on the direction or magnitude of the results reported in this and subsequent tables.

of the political actives score high compared with 33.8 per cent of the general population.

These and other results which could be cited support the claim advanced by earlier investigators like Prothro and Grigg, and Hyman and

Sheatsley,[13] that a large proportion of the electorate has failed to grasp certain of the underlying ideas and principles on which the American political system rests. Endorsement of these ideas is not unanimous among the political elite either, but is in every instance greater than that exhibited by the masses.

The picture changes somewhat when we turn from "rules of the game" to items which in a broad, general way express belief in freedom of speech and opinion. As can be seen from Table 2, support for these values is remarkably high for both samples. Both groups, in fact, respond so

Table 2. Political Influentials vs. the Electorate: Responses to Items Expressing Support for General Statements of Free Speech and Opinion

Items	Political Influentials (N = 3,020)	General Electorate (N = 1,484)
	% Agree	
People who hate our way of life should still have a chance to talk and be heard.	86.9	81.8
No matter what a person's political beliefs are, he is entitled to the same legal rights and protections as anyone else.	96.4	94.3
I believe in free speech for all no matter what their views might be.	89.4	88.9
Nobody has a right to tell another person what he should and should not read.	81.4	80.7
You can't really be sure whether an opinion is true or not unless people are free to argue against it.	94.9	90.8
Unless there is freedom for many points of view to be presented, there is little chance that the truth can ever be known.	90.6	85.2
I would not trust any person or group to decide what opinions can be freely expressed and what must be silenced.	79.1	64.6
Freedom of conscience should mean freedom to be an atheist as well as freedom to worship in the church of one's choice.	87.8	77.0

overwhelmingly to abstract statements about freedom that one is tempted to conclude that for these values, at least, a far-reaching consensus has been achieved.[14] These results become even more striking when we consider that the items in the tables are not mere clichés but statements which in some instances closely paraphrase the arguments developed in Mill's essay, *On Liberty*. We cannot, therefore, dismiss them as mere responses to familiar, abstract sentiments which commit the respondent to nothing in particular.

Still, as can readily be discerned from the items in Table 3, previous investigators have been partially correct, at least, in observing that the

Table 3. Political Influentials vs. the Electorate: Response to Items Expressing Support for Specific Applications of Free Speech and Procedural Rights

Items	Political Influentials (N = 3,020) % Agree	General Electorate (N = 1,484) % Agree
Freedom does not give anyone the right to teach foreign ideas in our schools.	45.5	56.7
A man oughtn't to be allowed to speak if he doesn't know what he's talking about.	17.3	36.7
A book that contains wrong political views cannot be a good book and does not deserve to be published.	17.9	50.3
When the country is in great danger we may have to force people to testify against themselves even if it violates their rights.	28.5	36.3
No matter what crime a person is accused of, he should never be convicted unless he has been given the right to face and question his accusers.	90.1	88.1
If a person is convicted of a crime by illegal evidence, he should be set free and the evidence thrown out of court.	79.6	66.1
If someone is suspected of treason or other serious crimes, he shouldn't be entitled to be let out on bail.	33.3	68.9
Any person who hides behind the laws when he is questioned about his activities doesn't deserve much consideration.	55.9	75.7
In dealing with dangerous enemies like the Communists, we can't afford to depend on the courts, the laws and their slow and unreliable methods.	7.4	25.5

principles of freedom and democracy are less widely and enthusiastically favored when they are confronted in their specific, or applied, forms.[15] As Dahl remarks, it is a "common tendency of mankind . . . to qualify universals in application while leaving them intact in rhetoric."[16] This observation, of course, also holds for the political articulates, but to a lesser degree. Not only do they exhibit stronger support for democratic values than does the electorate, but they are also more consistent in applying the general principle to the specific instance.[17] The average citizen has greater difficulty appreciating the importance of certain procedural or juridical rights, especially when he believes the country's internal security is at stake.

Findings which underscore and amplify these conclusions are yielded by a comparison of the scale scores. The data presented in Table 4 confirm that the influentials not only register higher scores on all the pro-democratic scales (faith in freedom, faith in democracy, procedural rights, tolerance),

Table 4. Political Influentials vs. the Electorate: Percentages Scoring High and Low on Democratic and Anti-Democratic Attitude Scales*

Scale	Political Influentials (N = 3,020)	General Electorate (N = 1,484)
	(%s down)	
Faith in Democracy		
% High*	40.1	18.5
% Low	14.4	29.7
Procedural Rights		
% High	58.1	24.1
% Low	12.3	31.3
Tolerance		
% High	61.3	43.1
% Low	16.4	33.2
Faith in Freedom		
% High	63.0	48.4
% Low	17.1	28.4
Ethnocentrism		
% High	27.5	36.5
% Low	46.9	36.3
Elitism		
% High	22.8	38.7
% Low	41.0	22.4
Totalitarianism		
% High	9.7	33.8
% Low	60.1	28.4
Right Wing		
% High	17.5	33.1
% Low	45.3	28.9
Left Wing		
% High	6.7	27.8
% Low	68.7	39.3
California F-Scale		
% High	14.7	33.5
% Low	48.0	23.5

* For explanation of % High and Low see footnote 12. The middle group has been omitted from this table. Differences between the influentials and the electorate on all the scales in this table are, by Kolmogorov–Smirnov and chi-square tests, statistically significant at or beyond the .01 per cent level of significance.

but are more likely to reject anti-democratic sentiments as well. Although they are themselves an elite of a sort, they display greater faith in the capacity of the mass of men to govern themselves, they believe more firmly in political equality, and they more often disdain the "extreme" beliefs embodied in the Right Wing, Left Wing, totalitarian, elitist, and authoritarian scales. Their repudiation of anti-democratic attitudes is by no means unanimous either, but their responses are more uniformly democratic than are those expressed by the electorate.

Equalitarian Values

If Americans concur most strongly about liberty in the abstract, they disagree most strongly about equality. Examples of equalitarian values are presented in Table 5. Both the political stratum and the public divide sharply on these values, a finding which holds for political as well as for social and economic equality. Both are torn not only on the empirical question of whether men are *in fact* equal but also on the normative issue of whether they should be *regarded* as equal. Neither comes close to achieving consensus on such questions as the ability of the people to rule themselves, to know their best interests in the long run, to understand the issues, or to pick their own leaders wisely. Support for these equalitarian features of "popular" democracy, however, is greater among the elite than among the masses.

The reverse is true for the values of economic equality. Among the political stratum, indeed, the weight of opinion is against equality—a result strongly though not exclusively influenced by the pronounced economic conservatism of the Republican leaders in the sample. Support for economic equality is only slightly greater among the electorate. The pattern, furthermore, is extremely spotty, with some policies strongly favored and others as strongly rejected. Thus approval is widespread for public policies (such as social security) that are designed to overcome gross inequalities, but is equally strong for certain features of economic life that promote inequality, such as private enterprise, economic competition, and unlimited pursuit of profit.[18] On social and ethnic equality, both samples are deeply split.

In short, both the public and its leaders are uncertain and ambivalent about equality. The reason, I suspect, lies partly in the fact that the egalitarian aspects of democratic theory have been less adequately thought through than other aspects, and partly in the complications connected with the concept itself. One such complication arises from the historical association of democracy with capitalism, a commingling of egalitarian and inegalitarian elements that has never been (and perhaps never can be)

Table 5. Political Influentials vs. the Electorate: Responses to Items Expressing Belief in Equality

Items	Political Influentials (N = 3,020) % Agree	General Electorate (N = 1,484) % Agree
Political Equality		
The main trouble with democracy is that most people don't really know what's best for them.	40.8	58.0
Few people really know what is in their own best interest in the long run.	42.6	61.1
"Issues" and "arguments" are beyond the understanding of most voters.	37.5	62.3
Most people don't have enough sense to pick their own leaders wisely.	28.0	47.8
It will always be necessary to have a few strong, able people actually running everything.	42.5	56.2
Social and Ethnic Equality		
We have to teach children that all men are created equal but almost everyone knows that some are better than others.	54.7	58.3
Just as is true of fine race horses, some breeds of people are just naturally better than others.	46.0	46.3
Regardless of what some people say, there are certain races in the world that just won't mix with Americans.	37.2	50.4
When it comes to the things that count most, all races are certainly not equal.	45.3	49.0
The trouble with letting certain minority groups into a nice neighborhood is that they gradually give it their own atmosphere.	49.8	57.7
Economic Equality		
Labor does not get its fair share of what it produces.	20.8	44.8
Every person should have a good house, even if the government has to build it for him.	14.9	28.2
I think the government should give a person work if he can't find another job.	23.5	47.3
The government ought to make sure that everyone has a good standard of living.	34.4	55.9
There will always be poverty, so people might as well get used to the idea.	40.4	59.4

perfectly reconciled. Another complication lies in the diffuse and variegated nature of the concept, a result of its application to at least four separate domains: political (e.g., universal suffrage), legal (e.g., equality before the law), economic (e.g., equal distribution of property or opportunity), and moral (e.g., every man's right to be treated as an end and not as a means). Accompanying these are the confusions which result from the common failure to distinguish equality as a *fact* from equality as a *norm*. ("All men are created equal," for example, is taken by some as an empirical statement, by others as a normative one.) Still other complications arise from the differential rewards and opportunities inevitable in any complex society, from the differences in the initial endowment individuals bring into the world, and from the symbolism and fears that so often attend the division of men into ethnic compartments. All these confound the effort to develop a satisfactory theory of democratic equality, and further serve to frustrate the realization of consensus around egalitarian values.

Faith in the Political System

Another perspective on the state of ideology and consensus in America may be obtained by observing how people respond to the political system. How do Americans feel about the political and social institutions by which they are ruled? Do they perceive the system as one they can reach and influence? Are they satisfied that it will govern justly and for the common good?

Sample items relating to these questions are contained in Tables 6 and 7. An assessment of the responses, however, is confounded by an ambivalence in our tradition. Few will question that Americans are patriotic and loyal, that they accept the political system as legitimate, and that they are inclined to shy away from radical or extreme movements which aim to alter or to overthrow the constitutional foundations of the system. Yet Americans are also presumed to have a longstanding suspicion of government—a state of mind which some historians trace back to the depredations of George III and to the habits of self-reliance forced upon our ancestors by frontier life.[19]

It is impossible in the present context to determine the extent to which the scores contained in these tables signify genuine frustration and political disillusionment and the extent to which they represent familiar and largely ritualistic responses. It is plain, however, that Americans are, verbally at least, both confused and divided in their reactions to the political system. Many feel themselves hopelessly ineffectual politically. Approximately half perceive government and politicians as remote, inaccessible, and largely unresponsive to the electorate's needs or opinions.[20] About the same proportion regard politics as squalid and seamy, as an activity in which the participants habitually practice deception, expediency, and self-aggrandizement. Yet by a curious inconsistency which so frequently

Table 6. Political Influentials vs. the Electorate: Responses to Items
Expressing Cynicism toward Government and Politics

Items	Political Influentials (N = 3,020)	General Electorate (N = 1,484)
	% Agree	
Most politicans are looking out for themselves above all else.	36.3	54.3
Both major parties in this country are controlled by the wealthy and are run for their benefit.	7.9	32.1
Many politicians are bought off by some private interest.	43.0	65.3
I avoid dealing with public officials as much as I can.	7.8	39.3
Most politicians can be trusted to do what they think is best for the country.	77.1	58.9
I usually have confidence that the government will do what is right.	81.6	89.6
The people who really "run" the country do not even get known to the voters.	40.2	60.5
The laws of this country are supposed to benefit all of us equally, but the fact is that they're almost all "rich-man's laws."	8.4	33.3
No matter what the people think, a few people will always run things anyway.	30.0	53.8
Most politicans don't seem to me to really mean what they say.	24.7	55.1
There is practically no connection between what a politican says and what he will do once he gets elected.	21.4	54.0
A poor man doesn't have the chance he deserves in the law courts.	20.3	42.9
Most political parties care only about winning elections and nothing more.	28.3	46.2
All politics is controlled by political bosses.	15.6	45.9

frustrates the investigator searching the data for regularities, 89.6 per cent express confidence that the government will do what is right. However strongly they mistrust the men and the procedures through which public policies are fashioned, most voters seem not to be greatly dissatisfied with the outcome. They may be cynical about the operation of the political system, but they do not question its legitimacy.[21]

Although the influentials do not unanimously endorse American political practices either, they are substantially less suspicious and cynical than is the electorate. Indeed, they have achieved consensus or come close

Table 7. Political Influentials vs. the Electorate: Responses to
Items Expressing a Sense of Political Futility

Items	Political Influentials (N = 3,020)	General Electorate (N = 1,484)
	% Agree	
It's no use worrying my head about public affairs; I can't do anything about them anyhow.	2.3	20.5
The people who really "run" the country do not even get known to the voters.	40.2	60.5
I feel that my political leaders hardly care what people like myself think or want.	10.9	39.0
Nothing I ever do seems to have any effect upon what happens in politics.	8.4	61.5
Political parties are so big that the average member hasn't got much to say about what goes on.	37.8	67.5
There doesn't seem to be much connection between what I want and what my representative does.	24.0	43.7
It seems to me that whoever you vote for, things go pretty much the same.	21.1	51.3

to achieving it on most of the items in the two tables. These results are further borne out by the *scale* scores: only 10.1 per cent of the articulates score "high" on the political cynicism scale, as contrasted with 31.3 per cent of the general population; on political suspiciousness the scores are 9 per cent high versus 26.7 per cent; on pessimism they are 12.6 per cent versus 26.7 per cent; and on sense of political futility the influentials score (understandably enough) only 3.1 per cent high compared with 30.2 per cent high for the electorate. The active minority also exhibits a stronger sense of social responsibility than the people do (their respective percentage high scores are 40.7 per cent versus 25.8 per cent) and, as previously noted, they are less tolerant of infractions against ethical political procedures.

Should we not, however, have expected these results as a matter of course, considering that the influentials were selected for study precisely because of their political experience and involvement? Possibly, except that similar (though less pronounced) differences emerge when we distinguish articulates from inarticulates by criteria other than actual political activity. Voters, for example, who have been to college, attained high status occupations or professions, or developed strong intellectual interests are, by a significant margin, also likely to possess more affirmative attitudes toward government, politics, and politicians.[22] They display a greater sense of social and political responsibility, are more optimistic, and are less indulgent of shoddy political methods. The political actives who are highly educated exhibit these attitudes even more strongly. Familiarity, it seems, far from breeding contempt, greatly increases respect, hope and support for the nation's political institutions and practices. Inferential support for this generalization is available from the findings turned up by Almond and Verba in all five countries they investigated in their comparative study of citizenship.[23]

Coherence and Consistency of Attitudes

So far we have explored the question of ideology and consensus mainly from the point of view of agreement on particular values. This, however, is a minimum criterion. Before one can say that a class or group or nation has achieved consensus around an ideology, one should be satisfied that they understand its values in a coherent and correct way. It is a poor consensus in which generalities and slogans are merely echoed with little appreciation of their significance. It seemed appropriate, therefore, to compare the influentials and voters concerning their information and understanding, the relation of their opinions to their party preferences, and the consistency of their views on public affairs.

To begin with, the influentials are more likely than the electorate to have opinions on public questions. For example, 28 per cent of the public are unable (though a few may only be *unwilling*) to classify themselves as liberal, middle of the road, or conservative; while only 1.1 per cent of the articulates fail to make this classification. Forty-eight per cent of the voters, compared to 15 per cent of the actives, do not know in which direction they would turn if the parties were reorganized to reflect ideological differences more clearly. Forty-five per cent of the electorate but only 10.2 per cent of the influentials cannot name any issue that divides the parties. By ratios of approximately three or four to one the electorate is less likely to know which level of government they are mainly interested in, whether they prefer their party to control Congress or the presidency, whether they believe in party discipline and of what type, whether control of the parties should rest at the national or local levels, and so on.

As these and other of our findings suggest, active political involvement heightens one's sense of intellectual order and commitment. This inference is further supported by the data on partisanship. One example may suffice to illustrate the point: when the articulates and the electorate are ranged on a scale assessing their orientation toward fourteen current liberal-conservative issues, the political actives tend to bunch up at the extreme ends of the distribution (the Democratic actives at the "liberal" end, the Republican actives at the "conservative" end), while the rank and file supporters of both parties fall more frequently into the middle or conflicted category. The political influentials, in short, display issue orientations that are more partisan and more consistent with their party preferences.

Essentially the same effect is achieved among the general population by increases in education, economic status, or other factors that raise the level of articulateness. College-educated Democrats and Republicans, for example, disagree more sharply on issues than grade school Democrats and Republicans do. Partisan differences are greater between the informed than between the uninformed, between the upper-class supporters of the two parties than between the lower-class supporters, between the "intellectuals" in both parties than between those who rank low on "intellectuality."

Increases in political knowledge or involvement, hence, cause men not so much to waver as to choose sides and to identify more unswervingly with one political tendency or its opposite. Inarticulateness and distance from the sources of political decision increase intellectual uncertainty and evoke political responses that are random rather than systematic. We are thus led by the findings to a pair of conclusions that may at first appear contradictory but that in reality are not: the political class is more united than the electorate on fundamental political values but divides more sharply by party affiliation on the issues which separate the two parties.[24] Both facts—the greater consensus in the one instance and the sharper cleavage in the other—testify to its superior ideological sophistication.

Not only are the articulates more partisan, but they are also more consistent in their views. Their responses to a wide range of political stimuli are to a greater extent intellectually patterned and informed. They are, for example, better able to name reference groups that correspond with their party affiliation and doctrinal orientation: approximately twice as many active Democrats as ordinary Democratic voters name liberal, Democratically oriented organizations as groups they would seek advice from (e.g., trade unions, Farmers Union, etc.); and by equally large or larger ratios they *reject* as sources of advice such conservative or Republican oriented organizations as the NAM, the Farm Bureau, and the Chamber of Commerce. With some variations, similar findings emerge when Republican leaders are compared with Republican voters. If we also take into account the liberal or conservative issue-orientation of the respondents, the differential ability of party leaders and followers to recognize reference groups becomes even more pronounced. Clearly, the political stratum has a better idea than the public has of who its ideological friends and enemies are. The capacity to recognize sympathetic or hostile reference groups is not highly developed among the public at large.

Compared with the influentials, ordinary voters also show up poorly in their ability to classify themselves politically. For example, among

Democratic actives who score as "liberals" in their views on issues, 82.2 per cent correctly describe themselves as "liberals," while 16.7 per cent call themselves "middle of the roaders" and only 1.1 per cent misclassify themselves as "conservatives." Among Democratic *voters* who actually hold liberal views, only 37 per cent are able to label themselves correctly. The disparity is less striking between Republican leaders and followers but bears out no less conclusively that most voters lack the sophistication to recognize and label accurately the tendency of their own political views. Even their choice of party is frequently discrepant with their actual ideological views: as we reported in a previous paper,[25] not only do Democratic and Republican voters hold fairly similar opinions on issues, but the latter's opinions are closer to the opinions of Democratic leaders than to those of their own leaders.

Data we have gathered on patterns of support for individual political leaders yield similar conclusions: the articulates are far better able than the electorate to select leaders whose political philosophy they share. Often, in fact, voters simultaneously approve of two or more leaders who represent widely different outlooks—for example, Joseph McCarthy and Dwight D. Eisenhower. In a similar vein, a surprisingly large number of voters simultaneously score high on a Right Wing scale and a liberal issues scale, or hold other "discrepant" outlooks. Such inconsistencies are not unknown among the political actives either, but they are much less frequent. Not only does the public have less information than the political class but it does not succeed as well in sorting out and relating the information it does possess.[26]

Most of the relationships reported in the foregoing have been tested with education, occupation, and sometimes with other demographic variables controlled, but the introduction of these factors does not change the direction of the findings, although it sometimes affects the magnitude of the scores.

Comparisons of scores for the two samples have also been made with "acquiescent" response-set controlled. Acquiescence affects the results, but does not eliminate the differences reported or alter the direction or significance of the findings. (See Appendix A.)

III. SUMMARY AND DISCUSSION

Several observations can be offered by way of summarizing and commenting upon the data just reported:

1. American politics is widely thought to be innocent of ideology, but this opinion more appropriately describes the electorate than the active political minority. If American ideology is defined as that cluster of

axioms, values and beliefs which have given form and substance to American democracy and the Constitution, the political influentials manifest by comparison with ordinary voters a more developed sense of ideology and a firmer grasp of its essentials. This is evidenced in their stronger approval of democratic ideas, their greater tolerance and regard for proper procedures and citizen rights, their superior understanding and acceptance of the "rules of the game," and their more affirmative attitudes toward the political system in general. The electorate displays a substantial measure of unity chiefly in its support of freedom in the abstract; on most other features of democratic belief and practice it is sharply divided.

The political views of the influentials are relatively ordered and coherent. As liberals and conservatives, Democrats and Republicans, they take stands on issues, choose reference groups, and express preferences for leaders that are far more consistent than the attitudes and preferences exhibited by the electorate. The latter's opinions do not entirely lack order but are insufficiently integrated to meet the requirements of an ideology.[27] In contrast to the political elite, which tends to be united on basic values but divided on issues by party affiliation (both of which testify to a measure of ideological sophistication), the voters divide on many basic political values and adopt stands on issues with little reference to their party affiliation.

The evidence suggests that it is the articulate classes rather than the public who serve as the major repositories of the public conscience and as the carriers of the Creed. Responsibility for keeping the system going, hence, falls most heavily upon them.[28]

2. Why should consensus and support for democratic ideology be stronger among the political stratum than among the electorate? The answer plainly has to do with the differences in their political activity, involvement and articulateness.

Some observers complain that Americans have little interest in political ideas because they are exclusively concerned with their own personal affairs. Evidence is becoming available, however, that political apathy and ignorance are also widespread among the populations of other countries and may well be endemic in all societies larger than a city-state. It is difficult to imagine any circumstance, short of war or revolutionary crisis, in which the mass of men will evince more interest in the community's affairs than in their own concerns. This is not because they are selfish, thoughtless, or morally deficient, but because the stimuli they receive from public affairs are relatively remote and intangible. One can scarcely expect ordinary men to respond to them as intensely as they respond to the more palpable stimuli in their own everyday lives, which impinge upon them directly and in ways they can understand and do something about. The aphorism which holds man to be a political animal may be supportable on normative grounds but is scarcely defensible as a description of reality. Political apathy seems for most men the more "natural" state. Although political matters are in a sense "everyone's concern," it is just as unreasonable to hope that all men will sustain a lively interest in politics as it would be to expect everyone to become addicted to chamber music, electronics, poetry, or baseball. Since many voters lack education, opportunity, or even tangible and compelling reasons for busying themselves with political ideas, they respond to political stimuli (if they respond at all) without much reflection or consistency. Their life-styles, furthermore, tend to perpetuate this state of affairs, for they are likely to associate with people like themselves whose political opinions are no more informed or consistent than their own. As inarticulates, they are also inclined to avoid the very activities by which they might overcome their indifference and develop a more coherent point of view.

Many voters, in addition, feel remote from the centers of political decision and experience an acute sense of political futility. They know the political world only as a bewildering labyrinth of procedures and unceasing turmoil in which it is difficult to distinguish the just from the wicked, the deserving from the undeserving. The political questions about which they are asked to have opinions are complex and thorny; every solution is imperfect and exacts its price; measures that benefit some groups invariably aggrieve others. The principles which govern the political process seem vague, recondite and impossible to relate to actual events. All this obviously deters voters from developing ideologically, from acquiring insights into the subtleties of the democratic process, and from achieving consensus even on fundamental values.

Although the influentials face some of the same obstacles, they are better able to overcome them. As a group they are distinguished from the mass of the electorate by their above-average education and economic status, their greater political interest and awareness, and their more immediate access to the command posts of community decision. Many of them participate not only in politics but in other public activities as well. This affords them, among other benefits, a more sophisticated understanding of how the society is run and a more intimate association with other men and women who are alert to political ideas and values. Political concepts and abstractions, alien to the vocabulary of many voters, are for the elite familiar items of everyday discourse.

Consider also that the political stratum is, by almost every social criterion we have examined, more homogeneous than the electorate. This promotes communication among them and increases their chances of converging around a common body of attitudes.[29] As Newcomb[30] has remarked, "The actual consequences of communication, as well as the intended ones, are consensus-increasing." Among many segments of the general population, however, communication on matters of political belief either occurs not at all or is so random and cacophonous as to have little utility for the reinforcement of political values. If Louis Wirth is correct in observing that "the limits of consensus are marked by the range of effective communication,"[31] it becomes easier to understand why the active minority achieves consensus more often than the voters do.

Compared with the electorate, whose ordinary members are submerged in an ideological babble of poorly informed and discordant opinions, the members of the political minority inhabit a world in which political ideas are vastly more salient, intellectual consistency is more frequently demanded, attitudes are related to principles, actions are connected to beliefs, "correct" opinions are rewarded and "incorrect" opinions are punished. In addition, as participants in political roles, the actives are compelled (contrary to stereotype) to adopt opinions, to take stands on issues, and to evaluate ideas and events. As *articulates* they are unavoidably exposed to the liberal democratic values which form the main current of our political heritage. The net effect of these influences is to heighten their sensitivity to political ideas and to unite them more firmly behind the values of the American tradition. They may, as a result, be better equipped for the role they are called upon to play in a democracy than the citizens are for *their* role.

The findings furnish little comfort for those who wish to believe that a passion for freedom, tolerance, justice and other democratic values springs spontaneously from the lower depths of the society, and that the plain, homespun, uninitiated yeoman, worker and farmer are the natural hosts of democratic ideology. The mystique of the simple, unworldly, "natural" democrat has been with us since at least the rise of Christianity, and has been assiduously cultivated by Rousseau, Tolstoy, Marx, and numerous lesser writers and social reformers. Usually, the simpler the man, the lower his station in life, and the greater his objective need for equality, the more we have endowed him with a capacity for understanding democracy. We are thus inclined to give the nod to the farmer over the city man, the unlearned over the educated, the poor man over the man of wealth, the "people" over their leaders, the unsophisticated over the sophisticated. Yet every one of these intuitive expectations turns out, upon investigation, to be questionable or false. Democratic beliefs and habits are obviously not "natural" but must be learned; and they are learned more slowly by men and women whose lives are circumscribed by apathy, ignorance, provincialism and social or physical distance from the centers of intellectual activity. In the absence of knowledge and experience—as we can readily

observe from the fidgety course of growth in the newly emerging nations —
the presuppositions and complex obligations of democracy, the rights it
grants and the self-restraints it imposes, cannot be quickly comprehended.
Even in a highly developed democratic nation like the United States,
millions of people continue to possess only the most rudimentary understanding of democratic ideology.

3. While the active political minority affirms the underlying values of
democracy more enthusiastically than the people do, consensus among them
is far from perfect, and we might well inquire why this is so.

Despite the many forces impelling influentials toward agreement on
basic ideological values, counteracting forces are also at work to divide
them. Not all influentials are able to comprehend democratic ideas, to
apply them to concrete contexts, or to thread their way through the
complexities of modern political life. Nor is communication perfect among
them either, despite their greater homogeneity. Many things divide them,
not least of which are differences in education, conflicting economic and
group interests, party competition, factional cleavages and personal political
ambitions.

In demonstrating that the influentials are better prepared than the
masses to receive and reflect upon political ideas, we run the risk of over-
stating the case and of exaggerating their capacity for ideological reasoning. Some members of the political class obviously have no more intellectual concern with politics than the masses do; they are in it for "the
game," for personal reasons, or for almost any reason except ideology.

Then, too, while most democratic ideas are in their most general form
simple enough for almost all members of the elite to understand, they
become considerably more puzzling when one sets out to explicate them,
to relate them to each other, or to apply them to concrete cases. Only a few
of the complications need to be cited to illustrate the point: several of the
ideas, such as equality, are either inherently vague or mean different
things in different contexts. Some democratic (or constitutional) values
turn out in certain situations to be incompatible with other democratic
values (e.g., the majority's right to make and enforce the laws at times
clashes with individual rights, such as the right to stand on one's religious
conscience). As this suggests, democratic ideas and rules of the game are
ordinarily encountered not in pure form or in isolation but in substantive
contexts that are bound to influence the ways in which we react to them.[32]
Many businessmen who consider the regulation of business as an unconstitutional invasion of freedom look upon the regulation of trade
unions as a justifiable curb on lawlessness; trade unionists, needless to
say, lean to the opposite view.

Consider, too, what a heavy burden we place upon a man's normal impulses by asking him to submit unconditionally to democratic values and procedures. Compliance with democratic rules of the game often demands an extraordinary measure of forbearance and self-discipline, a willingness to place constraints upon the use of our collective power and to suffer opinions, actions, and groups we regard as repugnant. The need for such self-restraint is for many people intrinsically difficult to comprehend and still more difficult to honor. Small wonder, then, that consensus around democratic values is imperfect, even among the political influentials who are well situated to appreciate their importance.

4. We turn now to the most crucial question suggested by the research findings, namely, what significance must be assigned to the fact that democratic ideology and consensus are poorly developed among the electorate and only imperfectly realized among the political influentials?

Our first and most obvious conclusion is that, contrary to the familiar claim, a democratic society can survive despite widespread popular misunderstanding and disagreement about basic democratic and constitutional values. The American political system survives and even flourishes under precisely these conditions, and so, we have reason to think, do other viable democracies. What makes this possible is a more conjectural question, though several observations can be offered by way of answering it.

Democratic viability is, to begin with, saved by the fact that those who are most confused about democratic ideas are also likely to be politically apathetic and without significant influence. Their role in the nation's decision process is so small that their "misguided" opinions or nonopinions have little practical consequence for stability. If they contribute little to the vitality of the system, neither are they likely to do much harm. Lipset[33] has pointed out that "apathy undermines consensus," but to this one may add the corollary observation that apathy also furnishes its own partial corrective by keeping the doubters from acting upon their differences. In the United States, at least, their disagreements are *passive* rather than *active*; more the result of political ignorance and indifference than of intellectual conviction or conscious identification with an "alien" political tendency. Most seem not even to be aware of their deviations from the established values. This suggests that there may, after all, be some utility in achieving agreement on large, abstract political sentiments, for it may satisfy men that they share common values when in fact they do not. Not only can this keep conflicts from erupting, but it also permits men who disagree to continue to communicate and thus perhaps to convert their pseudo-consensus on democratic values into a genuine consensus.

I do not mean to suggest, of course, that a nation runs no risk when a large number of its citizens fail to grasp the essential principles on which its constitution is founded. Among Americans, however, the principal danger is not that they will reject democratic ideals in favor of some hostile ideology, but that they will fail to understand the very institutions they believe themselves to be defending and may end up undermining rather than safeguarding them. Our research on "McCarthyism," for example, strongly suggests that popular support for the Senator represented less a conscious rejection of American democratic ideals than a misguided effort to defend them. We found few McCarthy supporters who genuinely shared the attitudes and values associated with his name.[34]

Whether consensus among the influentials is either a necessary or sufficient condition for democratic stability is not really known. Since the influentials act, make public decisions, are more organized, and take political ideas more seriously, agreement among them on constitutional values is widely thought to be essential for viability. At present, however, we do not have enough information (or at least we do not have it in appropriately organized form) to state with satisfactory precision what the actual relation is between elite consensus and democratic stability. Some democratic governments, e.g., Weimar Germany, crumbled when faced with ideological conflicts among their political classes; others, e.g., postwar Italy and France, have until now managed to weather pronounced ideological cleavages. The opinion has long prevailed that consensus is needed to achieve stability, but the converse may be the more correct formulation, i.e., that so long as conditions remain stable, consensus is not required; it becomes essential only when social conditions are disorganized. Consensus may strengthen democratic viability, but its absence in an otherwise stable society need not be fatal or even particularly damaging.

It should also be kept in mind that the existence of intellectual disagreements—even among the influentials—does not necessarily mean that they will be expressed or acted upon. In the United States (and doubtless elsewhere as well), numerous influences are at work to prevent ideological cleavages from assuming an important role in the nation's political life. This is certainly the tendency of such political institutions as federalism, checks and balances, separation of powers, bicameralism, the congressional committee system, the judiciary's practice of accommodating one discrepant law to another, and a system of elections more often fought around local issues and personalities than around urgent national questions. Our two-party system also functions to disguise or soften the genuine disagreements that distinguish active Democrats from active Republicans. The American social system contributes to the same end, for it is a model of the pluralistic society, a profuse collection of diverse groups, interests and organizations spread over a vast and variegated territory. Consensus in such a society becomes difficult to achieve, but by the same token its absence can also more easily be survived. The complexities of a highly pluralistic social and political order tend to diminish the impact of intellectual differences, to compel compromise, and to discourage the holders of divergent views from crystalizing into intransigent doctrinal camps. Thus it seems, paradoxically enough, that the need for consensus on democratic rules of the game increases as the conflict among competing political tendencies becomes sharper, and declines as their differences become more diffused. Italy, by this reasoning, has greater need of consensus than the United States, but has less chance of achieving it. A democratic nation may wisely prefer the American model to the Italian, though what is ideally desired, as Lipset observes,[35] is a balance between cleavage and consensus—the one to give reality and force to the principle of opposition, the other to furnish the secure framework within which that principle might be made continuously effective. Countervailing power within a structure of shared political values would, by this logic be the optimal condition for the maintenance of a democratic society.

5. But even giving this much weight to consensus may exaggerate the role which intellectual factors play in the attainment of democratic stability. The temptation to assign a controlling influence to the place of ideas in the operation of democracy is very great. Partly this results from our tendency to confuse the textbook model of democracy with the reality and to assume the high order of rationality in the system that the model presupposes (e.g., an alert citizenry aware of its rights and duties, cognizant of the basic rules, exercising consent, enjoying perfect information and choosing governors after carefully weighing their qualifications, deliberating over the issues, etc.). It is not my purpose to ridicule this model but to underscore the observation that it can easily mislead us into placing more weight than the facts warrant upon cognitive elements—upon ideas, values, rational choice, consensus, etc.—as the cementing forces of a democratic society. An *ad hominem* consideration may also be relevant here: as intellectuals and students of politics, we are disposed both by training and sensibility to take political ideas seriously and to assign central importance to them in the operation of the state. We are therefore prone to forget that most people take them less seriously than we do, that they pay little attention to issues, rarely worry about the consistency of their opinions, and spend little or no time thinking about the values, presuppositions, and implications which distinguish one political orientation from another. If the viability of a democracy were to depend upon the satisfaction of these intellectual activities, the prognosis would be very grim indeed.

Research from many different lines of inquiry confirms unequivocally that the role heretofore assigned to ideas and to intellectual processes in general has been greatly exaggerated and cannot adequately explain many political phenomena which, on *a priori* grounds, we have expected it to explain. Witness, for example, the research on the non-rational factors which govern the voting decision, on the effects—or rather the non-effects—of ideology on the loyalty and fighting effectiveness of German and American soldiers, on the differences between the views of party leaders and followers, on the influence of personality on political belief, and on group determinants of perception.[36] We now have evidence that patriotism and the strength of one's attachment to a political community need not depend upon one's approval of its intellectual, cultural, or political values. Indeed, our present research clearly confirms that the men and women who express "patriotism" in extreme or chauvinistic form usually have the least knowledge and understanding of American democratic ideals, institutions, and practices.

Abundant anecdotal data from the observation of dictatorial and other nations further corroborate the conclusion that men may become attached to a party, a community, or a nation by forces that have nothing to do with ideology or consensus. Many of these forces are so commonplace that we often neglect them, for they include family, friends, home, employment, property, religion, ethnic attachments, a common language, and familiar surroundings and customs. These may lack the uplifting power of some political doctrines, but their ability to bind men to a society and its govern-ment may nevertheless be great. This observation, of course, is less likely to hold for the intelligentsia than for the inarticulates, but even the political behavior of intellectuals is never governed exclusively by appeals to the mind.

The effect of ideas on democratic viability may also be diminished by the obvious reluctance of most men to press their intellectual differences to the margin and to debate questions that may tear the community apart. So long as no urgent reason arises for bringing such differences to the surface, most men will be satisfied to have them remain dormant. Although there are men and women who are exceptions to this generalization, and who cannot bear to leave basic questions unresolved they are likely to be few, for both the principles and practices of an "open society" strongly reinforce tolerance for variety, contingency and ambiguity in matters of belief and conscience. As our data on freedom of opinion suggest, few Americans expect everyone to value the same things or to hold identical views on public questions. The tendency to ignore, tolerate, or play down differences helps to create an illusion of consensus which for many purposes can be as serviceable as the reality.[37]

6. To conclude, as we have in effect, that ideological awareness and consensus are overvalued as determinants of democratic viability is not to imply that they are of no importance. While disagreements among

Americans on fundamental values have tended to be passive and, owing to apathy and the relative placidity of our politics, easily tolerated; while they do not follow party lines and are rarely insinuated into the party struggle; and while no extremist movement has yet grown large enough to challenge effectively the governing principles of the American Constitution, this happy state of affairs is not permanently guaranteed. Fundamental differences could *become* activated by political and economic crises; party differences could *develop* around fundamental constitutional questions, as they have in France and other democracies; and powerful extremist movements are too familiar a phenomenon of modern political life to take for granted their eternal absence from the American scene.

Obviously a democratic nation also pays a price for an electorate that is weakly developed ideologically. Lacking the intellectual equipment to assess complex political events accurately, the unsophisticated may give support to causes that are contrary to their own or to the national interest. In the name of freedom, democracy, and the Constitution, they may favor a McCarthy, join the John Birch Society, or agitate for the impeachment of a Supreme Court Justice who has worked unstintingly to uphold their constitutional liberties. They may also have difficulty discriminating political integrity from demagoguery, maturity and balanced judgment from fanaticism, honest causes from counterfeits. Our findings on the attitudes shown by ordinary Americans toward "extreme" political beliefs (Left Wing beliefs, Right Wing beliefs, totalitarianism, isolationism, etc.) verify that the possibilities just cited are not merely hypothetical. Those who have the least understanding of American politics subscribe least enthusiastically to its principles, and are most frequently "misled" into attacking constitutional values while acting (as they see it) to defend them.

There is, however, reason to believe that ideological sophistication and the general acceptance of liberal democratic values are increasing rather than declining in the United States. Extreme ideological politics of the type associated with Marxism, fascism and other doctrinaire networks of opinion may be waning, as many sociologists believe,[38] but the same observation does not hold for the influence of democratic ideas. On the contrary, democratic ideology in the United States, linked as it is with the articulate classes, gives promise of growing as the articulate class grows. Many developments in recent American life point to an increase in "articulateness": the extraordinary spread of education, rapid social mobility, urbanization, the proliferation of mass media that disseminate public information, the expansion of the middle class, the decline in the size and number of isolated rural groups, the reduction in the proportion of people with sub-marginal living standards, the incorporation of foreign and minority groups into the culture and their increasing entrance into the professions, and so on. While these developments may on the one side have the effect of reducing the tensions and conflicts on which extreme ideologies feed, they are likely on the other side to beget a more articulate population and a more numerous class of political influentials, committed to liberal democracy and aware of the rights and obligations which attend that commitment.

APPENDIX A. THE EFFECT OF ACQUIESCENCE OR "RESPONSE-SET"

Because responses to scale items are subject to a response-set known as acquiescence, i.e., a tendency to agree (or disagree) with items regardless of what the items say, all procedures in the present study have routinely been run with acquiescence controlled. For this purpose we employed a specially constructed acquiescence scale, consisting of nineteen pairs of contradictory or near-contradictory items. Each respondent received an acquiescence score of 0 to 38, depending upon the number of "agree" and "disagree" responses he registered on the scale. For convenience we have divided our sample into those who scored high, middle, or low on acquiescence, and have compared the influentials and electorate within each acquiescence level.

As the accompanying table shows (Table 8), variations in acquiescence have a powerful effect on the scale scores (and implicitly the item scores) of both the political elite and the public. It is equally plain, nevertheless, that the differences between the two samples on democratic and related ideological values remain large and statistically significant even when acquiescence is held constant; they cannot, therefore, be explained as mere artifacts of response-set. Then, too, although one cannot discern it from these tables, acquiescence functions in the case of some items to reduce rather than to enlarge the "actual" differences between the influentials and the electorate.

The question might also be raised whether we are doing the inquiry a disservice by conceiving acquiescence *entirely* as a response-set which artificially inflates or deflates the scores registered by respondents on certain items or scales. Our research has yielded a vast amount of data on acquiescence which suggests that the tendency to agree or disagree with items indiscriminately reflects personality and cognitive capacities that are strongly associated with the ability to sort out, understand, relate, and internalize norms. Conceivably, therefore, the electorate demonstrates a weaker grasp of democratic and constitutional principles not only because its members are more prone than the influentials to response-set (which means that they say yes to items that happen *in this case* to express

Table 8. Influentials vs. the Electorate: Percentages Scoring High–Low on Selected Scales with Acquiescent Response-Set Controlled

| | %s Down | | | | | |
| | Low Acq. | | Mid. Acq. | | High Acq. | |
	Infl. N = 1,369	*Elect.* 453	*Infl.* 1,159	*Elect.* 520	*Infl.* 492	*Elect.* 471
Faith in Procedural Rights						
High	70	35	56	28	32	10
Low	6	21	13	27	28	45
Faith in Democracy						
High	50	29	36	21	22	6
Low	8	19	16	28	28	42
Tolerance						
High	66	57	62	48	45	27
Low	13	21	15	29	29	48
Faith in Freedom						
High	64	45	63	50	59	50
Low	17	32	15	27	20	26
Totalitarianism						
High	2	11	9	26	35	63
Low	80	52	54	30	21	5
F-Authoritarianism						
High	4	9	14	24	46	67
Low	70	48	38	22	10	2
Political Cynicism						
High	2	9	10	24	31	60
Low	74	51	47	25	20	6
Elitism						
High	12	21	27	35	45	60
Low	53	37	36	23	20	8

undemocratic and "unconstitutional" sentiments), but also because they characteristically lack the habits, skills, or capacities for thinking about these matters in a coherent and sophisticated way. It appears, in short, that the correlation between acquiescence and the expression of certain poorly valued sentiments results not entirely from the influence of the former upon the latter, but also from the influence upon *both* of a common, underlying, mental state.[39]

APPENDIX B. CHARACTERISTICS OF THE PAB GENERAL POPULATION SAMPLE

Because the self-administration and return of questionnaires left with respondents by interviewers represents a somewhat unorthodox sampling procedure, the accompanying table presents a description of the PAB general population sample utilized in this paper. For purposes of compari-

Table 9. Characteristics of McClosky National General Population Sample and Selected Other Samples

	AIPO Samples[a] (January, 1958)	Michigan SRC Sample[b] (1956 Presidential Election)	McClosky-PAB General Population Sample (January, 1958)	Others
	(N = 3,024)	(N = 1,762)	(N = 1,484	
	%	%	%	% (1960 Census)
Sex				
Men	48	44.7	51	48.4
Women	52	55.3	49	51.6
Age (1)				
21–29	16.5		17.3	
30–49	45.5		44.5	
50 +	37.0		37.9	
Undesignated	1.0		.3	
Age (2)				
Under 35		30.2	28	
35–44		25.6	23.6	
45–54		19.1	20.6	
55 +		25.0	27.7	
Race				
White		91.3	93.1	
Negro		8.3	6.5	
Rural–Urban				
Urban (over 2,500)		68	72.2	71.5
Rural (farm–non-farm under 2,500)		32	27.8	28.5
				PAB (Adjusted)
Region				
East	28	25.7	27.7	24.8[c]
Midwest	32	34.4	35.7	35.7
South	25	26.7	19.7	22.8
West	15	13.3	16.9	16.9
Education				
College	15.5	18.7	27.2	
High School	51.5	50.6	51.2	
Grade School	33.0	30.7	21.6	

Table 9—continued

	AIPO Samples[a] (January, 1958)	Michigan SRC Sample[b] (1956 Presidential Election)	McClosky-PAB General Population Sample (January, 1958)	Others
	(N = 3,024)	(N = 1,762)	(N = 1,484)	
	%	%	%	%
Religion				
Catholic		21.1	21.9	
Jew		3.2	2.5	
Prot., Other & NA		75.7	75.6	
Income				
Under 3,000		24.3	20.4	
3,000–5,000		28.8	34.0	
5,000–7,500		25.6	26.6	
7,500–10,000		10.8	9.4	
10,000 +		7.6	5.7	
Refuse, NA, DK		3.6	3.8	
				(Actual Congressional Vote, November, 1958[d])
Party Preference				
Democrat	56[d]	57.1	56.9[e]	56.6
Republican	44	42.9	43.1	43.4

[a] The figures for the AIPO sample are averages computed from two national surveys conducted by the Gallup Poll in January, 1958. The information on the characteristics of these samples was supplied by the AIPO in a letter to the author.

[b] In most cases, the figures from the Michigan SRC sample are computed from the information supplied in the codebook for Deck 6 of Study 417, September 1956. Urban–rural figures are computed from a table in *The American Voter*, p. 454. Criteria for urban–rural are set out on p. 406.

[c] Michigan SRC included Md. and W. Va. in the South, while we had classified these states as Eastern. This column shows the PAB figures with Md. and W. Va. classified as Southern. S.R.C. regional figures combine data from 1952 and 1956 (see *The American Voter*, p. 158).

[d] Data on party preference for the AIPO and the national congressional elections of 1958 are taken from a Gallup news release, May 24, 1959.

[e] Two-party vote only. PAB sample contained 821 Democrats, 623 Republicans, and 40 Independents, Other, and DK's.

son, Table 9 also includes the characteristics of two AIPO (Gallup) samples, interviewed in January–February, 1958; the September–November sample employed by the Survey Research Center, University of Michigan, in its study of the 1956 presidential election; and, where comparable, census and voting data.

As the figures make plain the PAB sample closely resembles in its social characteristics both the AIPO and Michigan SRC samples. Although some of the differences among the samples doubtless arise from the differences in response rate, other differences may be due to the differences in the time of polling as well as differences in the coding criteria employed.

In only one characteristic does the PAB sample deviate substantially from the other samples, namely, in the overrepresentation of the college-educated strata and the corresponding underrepresentation of the grade school educated. This, of course, was to be expected, in light of the length and complexity of the PAB questionnaire and the difficulty associated with its self-administration. It should, however, be kept in mind that oversampling the upper educated has tended to flatten rather than to accentuate the differences between the influentials and the electorate reported in this paper. Since the highly educated tend to embrace democratic values and the "rules of the game" more frequently than the less educated do, the item and scale scores we have reported for the general population of voters are doubtless slightly inflated. In other words, the differences in ideological outlook between the political stratum and the electorate are probably even a bit larger than we have reported. Hence, correcting for the educational bias in the sample would strengthen rather than weaken the conclusions of this paper.

NOTES

* This is a revised version of a paper initially prepared for delivery at the Annual Meeting of the American Political Science Association, Washington, D.C., September, 1962. The research on which it is based has been proposed and analyzed through the Survey Research Center, University of California, Berkeley. Major support for the research was made available by the Social Science Research Council; supplementary support was given by the Rockefeller Foundation and the Institute of Social Sciences, University of California. I am indebted to my research assistant, Beryl L. Crowe, for assistance in the preparation of the research materials. This article may be referred to as number A22 in the Survey Research Center's publication series.

[1] James W. Prothro and C. M. Grigg, "Fundamental Principles of Democracy: Bases of Agreement and Disagreement," *Journal of Politics*, Vol. 22 (Spring, 1960), pp. 276–94.

[2] Robert A. Dahl, *Who Governs?* (New Haven, 1961), Chap. 28.

[3] Samuel A. Stouffer, *Communism, Conformity, and Civil Liberties* (New York, 1955).

[4] V. O. Key, "Public Opinion and the Decay of Democracy," *Virginia Q. Rev.*, Vol. 37 (Autumn, 1961), pp. 481–94. See also David B. Truman, "The American System in Crisis," *Political Science Quarterly*, Vol. 74 (Dec., 1959), pp. 481–97. John Plamenatz, "Cultural Prerequisites to a Successfully Functioning Democracy: A Symposium," *American Political Science Review*, Vol. 50 (March, 1956), p. 123.

[5] Alexis deTocqueville, *Democracy in America* (ed. Phillips Bradley, New York, 1945), II, p. 8; I, pp. 392, 322. The difficulty of specifying the values which underly democracy, and on which consensus is presumed to be required, is illustrated in the exchange between Ernest S. Griffith, John Plamenatz, and J. Roland Pennock, cited above, pp. 101–37. The problem of certifying the "fundamentals" of democratic consensus is directly discussed by Pennock, pp. 132–33. See also Peter Bachrach, "Elite Consensus and Democracy," *Journal of Politics*, Vol. 24 (August, 1962), pp. 449–52.

[6] A. L. Lowell, *Public Opinion and Popular Government* (New York, 1926), p. 9.

[7] Cf., for example, Louis Wirth, *Community Life and Social Policy* (Chicago, 1956), pp. 201–3, 381–82. For a critique of "consensus theory" and the several definitions of consensus see Irving L. Horowitz, "Consensus, Conflict, and Cooperation: a Sociological Inventory," *Social Forces*, Vol. 41 (December, 1962), pp. 177–88.

[8] Cf., Daniel Bell, *The End of Ideology* (Glencoe, 1960), pp. 369–75; Edward Shils, "Ideology and Civility: on the Politics of the Intellectual," *Sewanee Review*, Vol. 66 (Summer, 1958), pp. 450–51; Louis Wirth, *op. cit.*, pp. 202–3.

[9] A persuasive case for considering liberal democracy as an ideology is made by Bernard Williams, "Democracy and Ideology," *Political Science Quarterly*, Vol. 32 (October–December, 1961), pp. 374–84. The nature of ideology in America and some of the other questions addressed in the present paper are discussed by Robert G. McCloskey, "The American Ideology," in Marian D. Irish (ed.), *Continuing Crisis in American Politics* (Englewood Cliffs, N.J., 1963), pp. 10–25.

[10] See Gunnar Myrdal, *An American Dilemma: The Negro Problem and American Democracy* (New York, 1944), Chap. 1. For a comprehensive review of the American value system and evidence concerning its stability over time, see Clyde Kluckhohn, "Have There Been Discernible Shifts in American Values during the Past Generation?" in E. E. Morison (ed.), *The American Style: Essays in Value and Performance* (New York, 1958), pp. 145–217. Kluckhohn concludes (p. 152) that despite some changes, the American value system has been "remarkably stable" since the 18th century and remains "highly influential in the life of the United States."

[11] Herbert McClosky, Paul J. Hoffmann, and Rosemary O'Hara, "Issue Conflict and Consensus Among Party Leaders and Followers," *American Political Science Review*, Vol. 44 (June, 1960), pp. 406–27.

[12] "High" refers to a score made by the upper third of the popular distribution on the scale in question. For example, in the case of the "political indulgence" scale approximately one-third (actually 30.6 per cent) received scores of five or above. Hence, anyone making a score of five or above on this scale is considered to have scored high on "political indulgence." "Low" refers to scores made by the lower third of the distribution.

[13] Prothro and Grigg, *loc. cit.*; Herbert Hyman and Paul B. Sheatsley, "The Current Status of American Public Opinion," in Daniel Katz *et al.* (eds.), *Public Opinion and Propaganda* (New York, 1954), pp. 33–48.

[14] Cf. Robert Lane's report on his "Eastport" sample, in *Political Ideology* (New York, 1962), pp. 461–62.

[15] See Hyman and Sheatsley, *op. cit.*, pp. 40–42; Prothro and Grigg, *op. cit.*

[16] Robert A. Dahl, *loc. cit.* For data on the failure of some people to perceive the relevance of democratic principles for concrete situations see G. D. Wiebe, "The Army-McCarthy Hearings and the Public Conscience," *Public Opinion Quarterly*, Vol. 22 (Winter, 1958–59), pp. 490–502.

[17] See also Stouffer, *op. cit.*, Chap. 2.

[18] These inferences are drawn not only from the few items presented in Table 5, but from data previously reported by H. McClosky, P. J. Hoffmann, and R. O'Hara, *op. cit.*, p. 413; and from the responses to dozens of items in the present study that express attitudes and opinions toward the private enterprise system, taxes, private property, profits, socialism, etc. On the whole, little enthusiasm is registered among either the elite or the masses for a drastic revision of the economy or a major redistribution of the wealth.

[19] Evidence is accumulating that the distrust of politics, often thought to be peculiar to the United States, is also found in many other countries. In fact, Gabriel Almond and Sidney Verba report in their cross-cultural study of citizenship that political interest is higher in the United States than it is in the four other countries they studied (United Kingdom, West Germany, Italy, and Mexico); and that Americans, if anything, are less negative toward politics than are the citizens of the other countries. See *The Civic Culture* (1963), Chaps. III–IV.

[20] See also the Michigan data on voters' sense of "political efficacy" in Angus Campbell, Gerald Gurin, and Warren E. Miller, *The Voter Decides* (Evanston, 1954), pp. 187–94.

[21] For other data on ambivalent attitudes toward government, see Hyman and Sheatsley, *op. cit.*

[22] Similar findings are reported by Robert E. Agger, Marshall N. Goldstein, and Stanley A. Pearl, "Political Cynicism: Measurement and Meaning," *Journal of Politics*, Vol. 23 (1961), pp. 477–506.

[23] Almond and Verba, *op. cit.*, Chap. IV. One can, of course, imagine circumstances, such as political disorganization or revolutionary crises, in which the generalization would not hold—in which, indeed, the political elite might lead the struggle *against* the existing governing institutions. I am speaking, in the present context, of politics under "normal" conditions in established democracies.

[24] See also V. O. Key, *Public Opinion and Democracy* (New York, 1961), pp. 51–52.

[25] McClosky, Hoffmann, and O'Hara, *op. cit.*

[26] For other findings on the state of ideological development among the electorate, see Angus Campbell, Philip E. Converse, Warren E. Miller, and Donald E. Stokes, *The American Voter* (New York, 1960), Chaps. 8–10.

[27] For a similar conclusion on this point, see V. O. Key, *Public Opinion and American Democracy* (New York, 1961), pp. 41, 49. The second chapter of this volume contains an excellent discussion of opinion consensus among the electorate, and touches on a number of the points dealt with in this paper. Evidence on the infrequency of "ideological" thinking among the voters is presented in Campbell, Converse, Miller and Stokes, *op. cit.*, p. 249. By the criteria used the authors were able to classify only 3.5 per cent of the voters as "ideologues" and 12 per cent as "near-ideologues."

[28] V. O. Key, "Public Opinion and the Decay of Democracy," *loc. cit.*

[29] For additional data on the homogeneity of social characteristics and values among American elite groups, see James N. Rosenau, "Consensus-Building in the American National Community: Hypotheses and Supporting Data," *Journal of Politics*, Vol. 24 (November, 1962), pp. 639–61.

[30] Theodore M. Newcomb, "The Study of Consensus," in R. K. Merton *et al.* (eds.), *Sociology Today* (New York, 1959), pp. 277–92.

[31] *Op. cit.*, p. 201.

[32] For a discussion of this point, see Peter Bachrach, "Elite Consensus and Democracy," *Journal of Politics*, Vol. 24 (August, 1962), pp. 439–52.

[33] Seymour Martin Lipset, *Political Man* (New York, 1960), p. 27. Chapter I of this volume provides a stimulating and valuable discussion of the relation of conflict and consensus to the operation of democracy.

[34] Herbert McClosky, "McCarthyism: The Myth and the Reality," unpublished paper delivered at the American Psychological Association, New York, September, 1957. See also Wiebe, *loc. cit.*

[35] Lipset, *op. cit.*, pp. 21–22.

[36] Cf., for example, Campbell *et al.*, *op. cit.*; Bernard R. Berelson, Paul F. Lazarsfeld, and William N. McPhee, *Voting* (Chicago, 1954), especially Chap. 14; Edward A. Shils and Morris Janowitz, "Cohesion and Disintegration in the German Wehrmacht in World War II," *Public Opinion Quarterly*, Vol. 12 (1948), pp. 280–315; Herbert McClosky, "Conservatism and Personality," *American Political Science Review*, Vol. 52 (March, 1958), pp. 27–45; T. W. Adorno *et al.*, *The Authoritarian Personality* (New York,

1950), Chap. XVII; Richard Crutchfield, "Conformity and Character," *American Psychologist*, Vol. 10 (1955), pp. 191–98.

[37] Robert G. McCloskey, *loc. cit.*, suggests that the American political tradition is marked by "ambivalence" toward certain of our fundamental values and that this may discourage the achievement of "consensus" in the usual sense. He believes, however, that Americans have learned to live with, and even to ignore, inconsistencies in the value system, in keeping with our "pragmatic spirit." Whether this ability is uniquely American or whether it is characteristic of all "open," democratic societies is a question well worth investigating. It could, conceivably, be a natural outgrowth of democratic ideology itself, no element of which can be conceived and enforced absolutely without infringing other elements. On this last point, see Sidney Hook, *The Paradoxes of Freedom* (Berkeley, 1962), pp. 14–62.

[38] Cf. Daniel Bell, *The End of Ideology* (Glencoe, 1960), pp. 369–75; S. M. Lipset, *op. cit.*, pp. 403–17; Edward Shils, *loc. cit.*

[39] The full presentation and explication of our findings on acquiescence cannot be accommodated within the limitations of the present paper, and I have put the matter aside for presentation in a separate paper.

CHAPTER 14

The Child's Acquisition
of Regime Norms: Political Efficacy*

David Easton
Jack Dennis

In its broadest conception, a political system is a means through which the wants of the members of a society are converted into binding decisions. To sustain a conversion process of this sort a society must provide a relatively stable context for political interaction, a set of ground rules for participating in all parts of the political process. We may describe this context variously as a constitutional order, a set of fundamental rules, or customary procedures for settling differences. But however this context is defined, it usually includes three elements: some minimal constraints on the general goals of its members, rules or norms governing behavior, and structures of authority through which the members of the system act in making and implementing political outputs. To these goals, norms and structures we may give the traditional name "political regime" or constitutional order in the broadest, non-legal sense of the phrase.

We may hypothesize that if a political system is to persist, one of its major tasks is to provide for the input of at least a minimal level of support for a regime of some kind. A political system that proved unable to sustain a regime, that is, some relatively ordered and stable way of converting inputs into outputs, could not avoid collapsing.[1] Each time a dispute arose it would have to seek to agree on means for settling differences at the same time as it sought to bring about a settlement of the substance of the issue, a virtually impossible combination of tasks for a society to engage in continuously.

A major response mechanism through which political systems typically seek to avert any serious decline in the level of support for an existing regime is to be found in the processes of political socialization. Every society introduces its members to the political system very early in the life cycle. To the extent that the maturing members absorb and become

Reprinted from *American Political Science Review*, Vol. 61, No. 1 (March 1967), pp. 25–38, by permission of the American Political Science Association.

attached to the overarching goals of the system and its basic norms and come to approve its structure of authority as legitimate, we can say that they are learning to contribute support to the regime.

This paper explores an early source of support for a fundamental norm of the American democratic regime. "Norms" we take to be expectations about the way people do or will behave. They may be embodied in laws or constitutional codes; they may be simply customary expectations founded in experience with the system. Through data on over 12,000 elementary-school children we are able to turn to an early stage of the life cycle—childhood between the ages of 7 and 13, a period almost totally neglected in the study of the political regime[2]—in order to discover the origins of attachment to one political norm, called political efficacy.

POLITICAL EFFICACY AS NORM, DISPOSITION AND BEHAVIOR

As a concept, political efficacy appears in three separate although by no means independent guises: as a norm, as a psychological disposition or feeling, and as a form of behavior. Failure to distinguish these three implications of the term has left considerable ambiguity about its theoretical status and utility. For purposes of understanding the contribution of socialization processes to the input of support for this regime norm, it is vital to clarify the relationship among these three elements.

As a norm it refers to the timeless theme of democratic theory that members of a democratic regime ought to regard those who occupy positions of political authority as responsive agents and that the members themselves ought to be disposed to participate in the honors and offices of the system. The *norm* of political efficacy therefore embodies the expectation in democracies that members will feel able to act effectively in politics.

In recent years it has been the burden of considerable research to demonstrate that this democratic norm must entail a corresponding *set of dispositions*. If persons are to be able to live up to the norm and to bring their weight to bear effectively on the political process, we would hypothesize that they are more likely to be able to do so if they have become imbued with a sense of political efficacy.[3] Here efficacy identifies a disposition toward politics, a feeling of effectiveness and capacity in the political sphere.

As compared with the simple statement of the norm, political efficacy as a feeling has turned out to be a surprisingly complex phenomenon. It suggests a number of interwoven sentiments. To be efficacious it would appear that a person must sense his competency at the level of his political self-identity. He must construct a psychic map of the political world with strong lines of force running from himself to the places of officialdom. He must come to believe that when he speaks other political actors will listen. He must also so internalize the expectation of competence that his political self-confidence is not easily eroded by what he will take to be the mistaken indifference which the political process frequently exhibits to his desires. The psychological counterpart to the basic regime rule, involving as it will the mutual expectations of the participating member and the responsive authorities, is therefore a firm conviction by the individual that he is in fact politically effective.

The final element embraced by the term applies to the actual *conduct of a person*. He may or may not act efficaciously. Insofar as he is in fact able to influence the course of events and take a hand in shaping his political destiny, he has demonstrated an observable capacity to behave effectively, regardless of whether he is aware of a principle of political efficacy or has a sense of being efficacious. Because we are dealing with children it is appropriate to set aside this third implication of the term and confine our analysis to the first two.

In distinguishing between political efficacy as a norm and as a disposition or state of feeling, we open up the possibility of using two alternative ways for assessing the input of support for the norm itself. On the one hand, through the standard techniques of attitude testing, we might explore the extent to which members of the American political system are willing to express verbal approval of the norm, explicitly stated. If this procedure were adopted we might expect to discover a high level of consensus if only because the norm accords with stereotyped patriotic rhetoric about the expected role of the ordinary person in a democratic regime.

We were precluded from adopting this procedure by the fact that our respondents were children, not adults. Typically, if we ask children whether they should be able to behave in a certain way, they will respond in the affirmative if in fact that is the way they do behave. Expectations and practice are often undifferentiated. Thus a young child is not likely to respond differently whether he is asked: *Should* ordinary people have a say in what the government does, or *do* ordinary people have such a say. This is particularly likely to be true in areas remote from the concerns and awareness of the child, as in the political sphere. We could not expect to find many children, therefore, who could make the intellectual distinction between the expectation that people should be able to master their political environment and a judgment as to whether people do in fact feel they are politically potent. The responses to items tapping both these opinions would be so highly correlated as to be useless.

However, the fact that, in children, norms and sentiments are so closely interwoven that we could not hope to distinguish them empirically can be put to good use. Insofar as children can be brought to provide us with some clue about the state of their feelings in the matter of efficacy, it will provide us with a reliable if indirect measure of their attitudes toward the norm itself. To the extent that we are able to discover the level of their sense of efficacy we will have an important indication of whether they feel that members of the system should expect to be able to influence the course of political life as it affects them.

We can assume, therefore, that, for children, acquisition of sentiments corresponding to the norm will usually represent psychic incorporation and approval of that ground rule of the regime. This enables us to interpret the presence of a feeling of political efficacy as an attitudinal indicator of confidence in and support for efficacy as a norm in the American democratic regime. In this sense we shall accept the degree to which a child expresses a feeling of efficacy as an index of the extent to which he adheres to the norm.[4]

DEVELOPMENT OF A SENSE OF POLITICAL EFFICACY AND ITS MEASUREMENT

Young children, until quite recently, have been excluded from the sphere of serious political research. They play no manifest or active part in political processes in the American system, adults consider politics to be an arena of interest peculiarly appropriate to themselves, and they have felt that political conflict may indeed be too sordid a tale to bring wittingly before the tender minds of the young. In addition, the child's normal interest in politics in competition with other activities is extremely low.

But in spite of barriers such as these that prevent the child from reaching over into the political sphere, our research reveals that children gradually do acquire an unexpectedly wide range of attitudes and feelings about various aspects of political life. Indeed, it is transparent that if this were not so, sufficient support could hardly be mobilized for major aspects of the political system. By the time that members of the system have reached the degree of social maturity necessary for full participation in the political life of a democratic regime it would be far too late to begin to expose them to the orientations essential for any kind of meaningful involvement. From this perspective it is not really surprising to find that even as subtle and complex a sentiment as that of political efficacy has a tap root that reaches down into the very early part of the life cycle.

Meaning of Political Efficacy

Before we can say when and in what degree feelings of political efficacy are acquired, if at all, we need to clarify the kinds of sentiments included in the idea. Beyond that we will also have to show that in spite of the complexity of the attitudes involved, children do in fact know enough about these matters to be able to express an opinion on them, even during what has wrongly been presumed to be the political void of childhood.

To maintain the continuity and cumulative nature of research, we have followed the description of this sentiment first ventured by the Survey Research Center and reported in *The Voter Decides*, with some necessary modifications. As suggested in this volume,

Sense of political efficacy may be defined as the feeling that individual political action does have, or can have, an impact upon the political process, i.e., that it is worthwhile to perform one's civic duties. It is the feeling that political and social change is possible, and that the individual citizen can play a part in bringing about this change.[5]

To measure political efficacy, the authors employed five items calling for a simple "agree" or "disagree."

1. I don't think public officials care much what people like me think.
2. The way people vote is the main thing that decides how things are run in this country.
3. Voting is the only way that people like me can have any say about how the government runs things.
4. People like me don't have any say about what the government does.
5. Sometimes politics and government seem so complicated that a person like me can't really understand what's going on.[6]

To investigate the child's development of political efficacy, we adapted the S.R.C. questions and added a number of our own in an attempt to form an index. We were not quite ready to accept a priori the view that this attitude complex is unidimensional. Thus we analyzed it initially to unravel its conceptual elements. We have found at least five closely related but separable ideas to be implied.

The first involves a feeling that the government or authorities are responsive to the desires of individuals like the respondent. Here the S.R.C.'s first item ("I don't think public officials care much what people like me think") is the clearest example. This reports the perception by ego that alter (the authorities) is *responsive* to him. Alter is, if not necessarily benign, at least aware of ego's existence and responsively so.

Second, there is the reverse side of the relationship, a feeling that ego is positively and *autonomously* able to affect the course of government, as expressed in items 2 and 4 above. The individual has the capacity to act with an impact upon the political process; therefore civil action is worthwhile and social change is possible. In this element of the feeling, the member of the system does not depend upon the responsiveness of the authorities but rather upon his own inherent powers. It is not simply a case of alter being responsive to ego (for whatever reason), but a case of ego being able to affect alter.

The third closely associated idea is that of the *comprehensibility* of alter to ego, some knowledge about "ruling and being ruled." To be able to comprehend political processes is a highly important part and condition of the sentiment of being an effective participant. In item 5 above we have an expression of this feature of political efficacy. Ego is or is not able to understand what alter is like, to put himself in alter's shoes, and to know what alter does. In part, this is an expression of the psychic distance of ego from alter; in part it reflects a degree of general competence and possession of the means or requisite knowledge to affect alter. Comprehensibility constitutes therefore a third element analytically distinct from the two connected ideas that the individual is an autonomous political actor and that officials are responsive to his demands. All three are contained in the S.R.C. questions.

Two further ideas can plausibly be considered to constitute empirical elements of this attitude complex. One is suggested by the remaining question, "Voting is the only way that people like me can have any say about how the government runs things." Here the basic theme is that the means available to the individual either are or are not limited. We can, of course, conceive of a person who is highly efficacious (on the other items) agreeing to this statement, so that some ambiguity is present. The respondent who agrees but is nevertheless efficacious may do so because he sees the real but singular power of the people in the vote. He believes that voting constitutes the only effective monopoly of legitimate force by ordinary people in the political system; but he may conceive that the effects of this power are quite extensive.

A fifth possible element, and one we would add to the S.R.C. assumptions, is the idea of general inevitability or intractability of government. It could be that both the individual member and the officials are perceived to be caught up in a predestined, unalterable pattern of events from which no escape is possible.[7]

What we have said, then, is that we can analytically distinguish a number of elements which might serve as part of the meaning of political efficacy: a sense of the direct political potency of the individual; a belief in the responsiveness of the government to the desires of individuals; the idea of the comprehensibility of government; the availability of adequate means of influence; and a general resistance to fatalism about the tractability of government to anyone, ruler or ruled.

Crystallization of Political Efficacy

The very complexity and multiplicity of sub-dimensions included in the feeling of political efficacy would seem to militate against any expectation that we could find it in young children, especially as early as 7 and 8 years of age. Before it was possible to probe the nature of the distribution of this feeling among our group of children, we had to assure ourselves that they are likely to have and experience these sentiments, a type hitherto associated only with adults. Furthermore, if they do, we had to discover the age at which we could reasonably anticipate this attitude would take shape and the degree to which it was continuous through childhood. At what age could we say that political efficacy crystallizes as a stable sentiment?

In line with our analysis of the meanings congealed in the idea of political efficacy, we tested eight questionnaire items over our total group of 12,052 children to see whether we would elicit the five major elements distinguished above. These items also represented, in slightly modified form, the S.R.C. questions:[8]

1. Voting is the only way that people like my mother and father can have any say about how the government runs things.
2. Sometimes I can't understand what goes on in the government.
3. What happens in the government will happen no matter what people do. It is like the weather, there is nothing people can do about it.
4. There are some big powerful men in the government who are running the whole thing and they do not care about us ordinary people.
5. My family doesn't have any say about what the government does.
6. I don't think people in the government care much what people like my family think.
7. Citizens don't have a chance to say what they think about running the government.
8. How much do these people *help decide which laws are made for our country:* Very much, Some, Very Little, or Not at all? Put an X for each person or group of people listed below.

For the first seven items, respondents checked one of the options presented in Figure 1 in A. B was used for the eighth item.

Included with these items in the questionnaire were many others concerned with the domain of participant orientations and political commitment. Among them were items having to do with partisan commitment, political interest, activity, political issue sensitivity and national community identification. We intercorrelated all these items, using tetrachoric correlation, after we had dichotomized each item. We then performed at each grade level (3–8), taken separately, a principal axes factor analysis of the r_t matrices and a varimax orthogonal rotation of the resulting principal

Figure 1

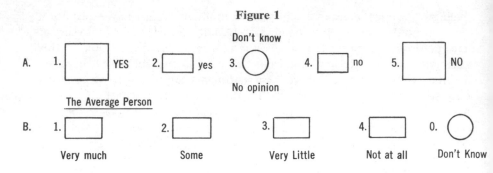

components using as a minimum criterion for rotation an eigenvalue of 1.0.[9] This analysis allowed us to probe related political participant and commitment attitudinal dimensions in children. These dimensions in general were highly consistent and distinct across the grades for our respondents. Inasmuch as this analysis is quite voluminous, we present here only the one portion (and a summary of that) having to do with the dimension we have labelled "sense of political efficacy." In Table 1 appear the rotated factor weights of items correlated with this component at each grade, at the .30 level or above.[10]

The content of the four items which load highest at all grade levels pertains to the responsiveness of officials (items 2 and 4) and to the autonomous power of ordinary people (items 3 and 5). These are the elements evidently at the heart of the early learning of the sense of political efficacy and they are from the beginning closely inter-connected orientations. By the middle of this age span they also become bound up with an associated element, the (lack of) inevitability of government (item 1).

Of the eight items originally devised as measures of political efficacy, seven at some point do load on the component as defined at every grade by the five best items. The item "Voting is the only way . . ." loads, if low, at grades 6 and 7 at least. "The average person helps make the laws of our country" item loads low at grade 8. The item which is not weighted at the .30 level or above on this component has to do with *comprehensibility* (item 2, p. 29 above), and this may be an artifact of our measure. But it may also simply relate to the fact that the government *is* incomprehensible sometimes to every child, even to those who may otherwise have absorbed into their consciousness the regime norm and who correspondingly feel politically efficacious.

One might be tempted to argue that the five high-loading items are associated simply because of response set. Although we cannot discount this possibility entirely, we have tried to guard against it in a number of ways. We stated these questions negatively for the most part thus making it

Table 1. The Political Efficacy Component in Grades 3–8*

	Grade					
	3	4	5	6	7	8
1. "What happens in the government will happen no matter what people do. It is like the weather, there is nothing people can do about it."	.37	.44	.66	.69	.69	.59
2. "There are some big, powerful men in the government who are running the whole thing and they do not care about us ordinary people."	.74	.73	.69	.70	.76	.73
3. "My family doesn't have any say about what the government does."	.71	.67	.72	.73	.72	.70
4. "I don't think people in the government care much about what people like my family think."	.73	.74	.79	.76	.75	.76
5. "Citizens don't have a chance to say what they think about running the government."	.65	.69	.78	.80	.70	.71
Other Items with Factor Weights above .30						
6. "If the Democrats and Republicans disagreed on important things, it would be bad (or good) for the country."	—	−.31	—	—	—	—
7. "How much does the average person help decide which laws are made for our country?"	—	—	—	—	—	.33
8. "Voting is the only way that people like my mother and father can have any say about how the government runs things."	—	—	—	.32	.34	—
Percent of communality over all components	6.1	8.4	12.2	12.6	11.5	13.0
Percent of cummunality over rotated components	9.5	14.1	20.1	20.9	18.9	21.0

* Rotated factor weights $\geq .30$.

harder for children who will agree to almost anything that "sounds" right. We also varied the format of the intervening items and spread the efficacy items throughout the questionnaire, as a further measure to guard against response set. More compelling, however, is the fact that an item with the same format which has a priori to do with a sense of political efficacy (the incomprehensibility item) in effect does not load on the "political efficacy" component. This suggests that children *are* differentiating the meanings of the items and not simply responding in a set fashion. In addition, other items running the same way do not correlate with this factor nor do items running the other way (except the one partisanship item) load negatively. Of course, as better measures of these attitudes are developed, we expect that a better understanding of response-set factors will result.

Summary

The most important conclusion emerging from our principal component analysis is that by grade 3 children have already begun to form an attitude, as revealed in the five high-loading items, which we could call a sense of political efficacy. This basic orientation is likely to become crystallized early in the life of the individual and to be maintained at least through these grades. This does not say, of course, that the third-grade child has developed a *high* sense of political efficacy, nor does it assert that any particular proportion of them experience this sentiment at any level of intensity. It only says that an attitude structure has begun to take shape among the children in their early years.

This development apparently does not depend upon the child's ability to understand the government and to interpret the citizen's role within it. This understanding in any full sense comes later. Nor does this general political attitude depend upon the state of the child's information—scarce and confused as it is—even though cognitive awareness may have important effects upon the later course of efficacy. It would appear that this development is an outgrowth of a general understanding which pervades the child's early environment. For whatever reason, young children in our society begin to develop this attitude by third grade.

IMPLICATIONS OF THE MEASURE OF
POLITICAL EFFICACY

It would be going too far to suggest that in measuring political efficacy in the child with items that resemble those used for adults, this orientation has exactly the same meaning for children. The situation is considerably more complex than that and it testifies to the extreme caution necessary in speaking about any kind of political attitudes and activities among children. At most we have here a projective measure; from the way we discover the child to think about adults, we infer something about the probable state of his own emergent feelings.

On scrutinizing the five index items—those that load highest—we see that we would not be justified in construing them to refer directly either to the child respondent or, projectively, to other children. Rather, they ask the child to make judgments about adults. Thus items 1 and 2 speak vaguely about "ordinary people." Interviews with children of this age group indicated that they are likely to think of these people as adults, particularly when discussion occurs in a political context. Items 3, 4, and 5 inquire about the relationship between government and the child's family or citizens and, in both cases again, unless the child is directed to think otherwise, adults are evoked by the statements.

The reason for pointing the child's attention to efficacy among adults was simple but compelling. Interviews gave us few grounds for believing that we could sensibly expect children to see themselves as having power over such awesome figures as the President, Congress, or the Supreme Court—some of the first concrete political objects to appear on their cognitive screens.[11] It was realistic only to try to get the child to project whatever nascent attitudes he might have onto adults. We are confronted, therefore, with interpreting the meaning of this projective device for eliciting information about the child's own attitudes toward political efficacy, as a sentiment and as a norm.

Although it would be easy to suggest that his opinions on the extent to which adults seem to him to feel efficacious, as measured by our index items, are accurate projections of his own sense of efficacy, this would be putting the matter too bluntly and too sanguinely. It is preferable to begin by taking the child's responses at their face value and to attempt to arrive at a more modest assessment of their significance.

We do not need to interpret the child's perceptions as an indication that even though he is projecting his own feelings onto adults, the items must therefore indirectly measure a developed sense of political efficacy in himself. It would not seem reasonable to expect a child, by age 13 or 14, to develop the fully formed feelings in this area that we find in adults. His political experiences would appear to be too limited. It is more reasonable to interpret the child's responses as an indication that he is learning to think about adults and politics in a certain way. If the child is to become socialized to political norms, it is vital that he learn how to think of adults with respect to their potency in the political sphere. It is this factor that is initially suggested by our index.

But the fact that the child can think of adults in these terms is only half the story. What is even more revealing for our purposes is that it opens up the possibility that, as he learns from adults and patterns himself after them, the child will even begin to think of himself in similar terms as he learns about the political sphere. In this sense only does the index become a projective device to obtain some hint of how the child himself may be learning to feel about his relationship to control over the political sphere.

We can therefore interpret the attitudinal component represented in the index items only as a first but critical step in the child's acquisition of an orientation to political efficacy *as it relates to himself*. He is building up an emotional frame of reference or loose attitudinal structure through which he has come to think about and view expected relationships between adult members of the system and the authorities. Although in the process of norm and attitude crystallization he has not reached a point where he himself necessarily has fully acquired either a norm or sense of efficacy, his capacity to think of adults in these terms repesents a vital preparatory stage in his general political socialization. At some point, perhaps toward late adolescence, he may well begin to think of himself as possessing feelings about his capacity to exercise effective control over government.[12]

The Level of the Child's Sense of Political Efficacy

Now that we have identified this dimension as having empirical reality in these early years, a score can be assigned to each respondent in order to estimate the distribution of feelings, high or low, on political efficacy at various grade levels and for various subgroups.[13] On computing the proportions of children scoring high, medium or low in sense of political efficacy, we find a substantial shift over grades 3–8, as shown in Table 2.

A marked change occurs in these years in the degree of the child's sense of political efficacy. In fact, we see a change consisting of two parts: (1) An increasing number of children at each succeeding grade level is willing to venture an answer other than "I don't know" to the items which compose the index. Thus we can infer that the child is likely to have more and more of an attitudinal basis for responding to these questions the older he becomes. It is noteworthy that only around 5 per cent were not scorable by grade 8 whereas about 26 per cent had been unscorable at grade 3. (2) The shift for those expressing opinions on these questions is distinctly in the direction of a development of a higher sense of political efficacy in these years. Only about 16 per cent of the grade-3 children are high in political efficacy on our index, but about 54 per cent of grade-8 children could be so classified. Correspondingly, those classified as having a low sense of political efficacy show a drop from 56 per cent to 17 per cent over the grades.

The child comes, therefore, both to an awareness of the role of the ordinary individual in the political process and possibly even to some

Table 2. The Development of a Sense of Political Efficacy in Grades 3–8

Grade	Low Efficacy	Medium Efficacy	High Efficacy	Total %	Mean	N Scored*	N Not Scored	% Not Scored†
3	56%	28%	16%	100	8.0	1244	433	26
4	55	27	18	100	8.4	1427	321	18
5	35	29	36	100	10.0	1622	180	10
6	29	27	44	100	10.6	1602	146	8
7	23	29	48	100	11.1	1624	98	6
8	17	29	54	100	11.6	1615	79	5

* Used as a base for percentages.
† Percent not scored is of the total N at each grade level.

emergent sense of his own mastery of the political world as well. This is not to say that he sees himself as synonymous with the Leviathan of the state. Yet he begins to carve out a small piece of political authority for himself—at his own level of consciousness. He is still far away from any actual role that he normally would have in the political process. Even so he begins to feel his political power when it still involves a high degree of projection to those around him and to his future role as an adult member of the system.[14]

GROUP VARIATIONS IN DEVELOPMENT OF POLITICAL EFFICACY

What is there in the processes through which the child becomes socialized in relation to a regime that helps him to acquire these emergent feelings about political efficacy? We may find that among adults the sense of control over political processes is related to such matters as whether their party has consistently won or lost, or whether they have themselves been successful in any attempt to influence public officials or politicians.[15] But children have no such direct experiences. The influences contributing to their reflected feelings about political efficacy must come from other sources.

Due to the limitations of large-scale survey research and the exploratory nature of our inquiry, we did not find it possible to follow up many conceivable lines of explanation. But it is clear that there are three major directions from which influences might impinge on the general political socialization of the child. First, as he matures he will undoubtedly develop certain personality characteristics relating to his general sense of effectiveness in mastering and manipulating his social environment. We might expect that this would have a substantial impact on whether he would attribute like qualities to relevant adults and the rate at which he would absorb political efficacy norms. Our data do not bear frontally on this dimension of the problem. Adequate measures of personality in children, applicable to survey research, do not exist. But one significant variable influencing individual exposure to politics, and possibly related to some aspects of personality could be readily obtained, namely, I.Q.; and it proved to be a significant predictor of attitudes.

Second, as in other areas of socialization, undoubtedly the major sources from which a child draws his political attitudes and convictions are those persons and institutions in his environment that are capable of transmitting to him explicit or subtly implicit messages about the political sphere. Parents, family, schools, mass media, peers and the like are agents of socialization. For reasons related to the index and the pioneer nature of our research we had to forego a detailed inquiry into the operations of these determinants, important as they undoubtedly are.

But third, it is possible to obtain some gross and aggregate measure of the direction in which these agencies carry the socialization of children by examining differences of socialization associated with the particular social class and sex roles which the child performs. Family, schools, and peers operate in a class environment and although cross pressures of many sorts may arise when agents cut across categoric groups—as when middle-class teachers instruct working-class children—we can expect that the broad consequences of class location will not be lost or even effectively masked. In addition to I.Q., our data shed some light on the possible effect of social class and sex on the socialization of the political norm under consideration.

Exposure Potential: I.Q.

One of the general reasons why we might expect a child to acquire any norm of democracy which involves a fairly complicated and in large part abstract set of relationships—as does efficacy—is the child's relative receptivity. We could, of course, in theory apply this to the whole content of political socialization, except for the fact that some "messages" are more difficult to receive and assimilate than others. We would argue that the resources in political communication that the child has are especially likely to affect such acquisition as political efficacy. And our data support this contention when we relate our index of political efficacy to I.Q., as in Table 3.

The relationship between political efficacy and I.Q. is fairly constant over the grades, particularly from grade 5 on. The child who has greater intellectual abilities—as measured by I.Q. tests—is more likely to acquire the norm early and maintain thereafter a greater positive feeling towards it. Probably two things are at work in this relationship, beyond the simple capacity to deal with the abstractions that our questions involve. One is the greater exposure potential of the child with higher intelligence. Although we can only guess as to where cues from his environment originate, the greater the mental capacity of the child the more easily will these cues filter through to him. He is likely to have other supporting informational resources as well. He will have greater facility in recognizing the positive role of the individual in the world of politics if society is teaching that the individual has a role to play.

Secondly, the brighter child will probably enjoy a greater sense of general confidence and effectiveness, other things being equal. He is more likely to maintain the feeling that he can cope with various aspects of his environment successfully and thus with politics. From this perspective his feeling that the ordinary member of the political system has influence is a natural accompaniment of his own greater ego strength and trust in his capacity to deal with the world. This fits with the adult-level findings.[16]

Table 3. The Relationship of I.Q. to Sense of Political Efficacy in Grades 3–8

Grade	I.Q.	Low Efficacy	Medium Efficacy	High Efficacy	Total %*	N†	N Not Scored	Pearson r‡
3	Low	61%	26%	13%	100	361	110	.14
	Medium	53	29	18	100	427	126	
	High	48	32	20	100	203	67	
4	Low	69	22	9	100	467	105	.28
	Medium	50	30	20	100	490	124	
	High	38	32	29	99	302	59	
5	Low	50	29	21	100	475	74	.33
	Medium	34	31	35	100	538	63	
	High	20	26	54	100	420	24	
6	Low	42	26	32	100	522	66	.35
	Medium	28	31	41	100	527	52	
	High	14	21	65	100	414	14	
7	Low	36	34	30	100	543	41	.35
	Medium	19	27	53	99	588	33	
	High	9	24	67	100	362	12	
8	Low	25	35	40	100	559	41	.33
	Medium	15	30	55	100	511	23	
	High	5	23	72	100	392	8	

* Percentages fail to add to 100% in some cases due to rounding error.
† Used as base for percentages.
‡ Computed over the uncollapsed distributions.

Social Location

A related independent variable, socio-economic status,[17] shows a similar if weaker relationship to the sense of political efficacy. This is presented in Table 4.

The child higher on the social ladder is at every grade level likely to be a step or two higher in relative sense of political efficacy. Probably a somewhat similar set of background variables are at work in this relationship as is the case for I.Q.[18] The child whose share of social resources is larger is thereby in a more favorable position to receive relevant information, communications, and reinforcement for adherence to this standard. His position and that of his family in the social structure expose him more frequently to events and interests congruent with this sense. His parents are more likely themselves to be interested and participate in politics and to have a higher sense of political efficacy.[19] The consonance of such a milieu of efficacy and involvement, for the child's own acquisition, is therefore apparent.

Both intellectual ability and social status therefore affect the rate and level of the child's incorporation of a belief that the individual has some force in government. These are quite constant relationships over the grades. They are built into the differential response of children to this norm from the beginning of this form of political awareness. The adult-level findings on social class thus probably reflect a difference which was present in the first learning of this kind. Of course, later experiences related to social class must also have an effect; but we suspect that the effect of social class is a continuing one and something that has roots as deep as the attitude itself. This also leaves the hint that unless I.Q. differences wash themselves out at a later age, it may be that some adult differences in political efficacy are also a product of socialization during childhood. Childhood I.Q. scores of adults may well turn out to be associated with their sense of political efficacy.

Sex

Sex stands as one of the major social categories that distinguishes efficacy among adults. In *The Voter Decides*, for example, it was found that 35 per cent of men but only 20 per cent of women were high in political efficacy.[20] In our data we fail to observe this difference in any marked and consistent way over the grades. Table 5 shows that the sexes come close to being equal. There is a very slight advantage for boys in grades 3–7 but this is reversed in grade 8.

At the very least these data indicate that the sense of political efficacy in females does not begin to drop below that of males before grade 8. Girls show little less confidence than boys that adults are able to handle the

Table 4. The Relationship of Socio-economic Status to Sense of Political Efficacy in Grades 3–8

Grade	SES	Low Efficacy	Medium Efficacy	High Efficacy	Total %*	N†	N Not Scored	Pearson r‡
3	Low	62%	26%	12%	100	302	96	.16
	Medium	56	27	16	99	673	241	
	High	47	34	19	100	269	96	
4	Low	70	20	10	100	325	71	.21
	Medium	54	28	18	100	678	159	
	High	43	31	25	99	424	91	
5	Low	50	25	24	99	383	48	.22
	Medium	33	32	36	101	745	89	
	High	25	30	45	100	494	43	
6	Low	40	26	34	100	355	49	.20
	Medium	32	28	40	100	738	64	
	High	17	26	57	100	509	33	
7	Low	33	28	39	100	388	37	.20
	Medium	24	31	45	100	728	43	
	High	14	26	60	100	508	18	
8	Low	25	34	41	100	364	37	.22
	Medium	18	31	51	100	753	27	
	High	10	24	66	100	498	15	

* Percentages fail to add to 100% in some cases due to rounding error.
† Used as base for percentages.
‡ Computed over the uncollapsed distributions.

Table 5. The Relationship of Sex to Sense of Political Efficacy in Grades 3–8

Grade	Sex	Low Efficacy	Medium Efficacy	High Efficacy	Total %*	N†	N Not Scored
3	Boys	55%	28%	17%	100	669	164
	Girls	57	29	14	100	576	269
4	Boys	52	27	20	99	764	131
	Girls	57	27	16	100	663	191
5	Boys	35	28	37	100	825	86
	Girls	34	31	35	100	798	94
6	Boys	31	24	45	100	819	64
	Girls	28	30	43	101	784	82
7	Boys	23	28	49	100	805	48
	Girls	23	30	47	100	820	50
8	Boys	18	30	52	100	762	37
	Girls	16	29	55	100	854	42

* Percentages fail to add to 100% in some cases due to rounding error.
† Used as base for percentages.

complexities of political life and that their involvement in the political process has some significance; this reflects for young girls a kind of sentiment almost universally less associated with grown women than with men. Yet the strange thing about the finding that girls rate just about as high as boys across the grades is that in other areas of political involvement, in which we test for such attitudes as political participation and interest, we find girls to be markedly lower. In these areas they definitely foreshadow their roles as less politically oriented adults.

These data lend themselves to an interesting interpretation, at least until additional information about adults becomes available. Something must happen between childhood and later phases of the life cycle that leads females into becoming disenchanted with their earlier expected role in political life that they once shared with boys. It may be that when, in succeeding years, it is gradually revealed to maturing girls that male judgments do in fact command dominant attention and respect in the political sphere, a slow, creeping disillusionment results. The shift during adolescence may be imperceptible but in its outcome the disparity between learned expectations and later opportunity for the expression of political concerns will plausibly lead to some sense of helplessness. This is at least a possible pattern of political evolution from girlhood to womanhood that helps to explain the similarity between boys and girls in our data and the later differences between men and women in the realm of political efficacy. Boys, on the other hand, find their expectations fulfilled and with this reinforcement of the norm, feelings of political effectiveness have a better chance of taking root and growing.

But even though women may rank somewhat lower on a political-efficacy scale than men, this does not justify a conclusion that they are any the less supportive of the efficacy norm than are men. If we accept the preceding interpretation as possessing some plausibility, it suggests that the higher feelings of political impotence in women may arise in part because of the expectations girls had been led to apply to *all* adults and subsequent disappointment with their fulfillment. In childhood, females may have learned their political lessons only too well, that is to say, as well as boys. By adulthood, the evidence reveals only that women have developed a lower sense of efficacy than men. But they may still retain their expectation that in a democratic system all adults should have the opportunity to exercise some influence in political life. In fact, long ago the suffragette movement, and its continuation in many indirect ways today, demonstrated that at least some women took the regime norms of democracy literally. Thus, even though women may feel less efficacious than men, it is consistent with this finding that women may continue to be supportive of efficacy as a regime norm, an attitude that a majority of women may learn in childhood.

Unfortunately, research on adults deals only with their feelings of efficacy, not with the degree of their attachment to political efficacy as a norm.

CONCLUSIONS

The fact that from a tender age children are able even to mirror adult feelings of mastery over their political environment and that this feeling gradually takes on a high positive value for increasing proportions of children has vital implications for the input of support for a democratic regime. This is especially so if we are willing to assume that, like imprinting, what is learned early in the life cycle is more difficult to displace than what is learned later[21]—a not unchallengeable proposition, however—and that for children, acquisition of efficacy as a sentiment implies its acceptance as a norm.

The process of interiorization of this norm is of course a complicated matter. As McClosky and Schaar have observed in connection with the learning of social norms, "what is learned is a function of many things: what is actually 'out there' to be learned; the nature and quality of the teaching process; the learner's own ability and motivation; the strength and frequency of reinforcement; the amounts and kinds of impediments to learning, and so forth."[22] In an exploratory study like ours, we cannot hope to comprehend these several facets of the learning process regarding the efficacy norm. As a beginning, however, we can suggest that early attachment to this particular regime norm does not occur in a uniform fashion for all children. The learner's own ability level bears a definite relationship to the process, particularly for the rate of norm acquisition. The child's I.Q., that is, fosters or inhibits his growth of a sense of political effectiveness and the related norm. Similarly his social status, or that of his parents, produces this effect. The acuity of his mental antennae, together with his general social resources, affect how quickly he responds to efficacy cues.

On the other hand, placement in one or the other of the sex roles only marginally influences his orientations to the norm in childhood. The culturally defined, differential political capacities of the sexes which are apparent in adulthood have still to make their appearances. But our findings leave as a moot point whether the high level of childhood attachment of efficacy as a norm may not continue unabated into womanhood. The data on adults refer only to the low sense of efficacy in women and bear little obvious relationship to our understanding of their continued attachment to the regime norm.

The fact that there are differences for groups defined by I.Q. and socio-economic status has important implications for where we may expect to find the strongest initial ties to the regime. But the further fact that by grade

8, 83 per cent (Table 2) of our children felt moderately or highly efficacious does suggest some important possible consequences for the functioning of the American political system. This early acquisition of the norm may operate as a potent and critical force in offsetting later adult experiences which, in a modern, rationally organized mass society, undermine the political importance of the ordinary member. But for the inculcation of this norm at an early and impressionable age, later adult political frustrations in modern mass societies might be less easily contained; disillusionment with this norm of democracy might well find more favorable conditions for growth.

In leading to an early attachment to political efficacy as a legitimate expectation, childhood socialization may thus have central significance for the persistence of a democratic regime. It provides a reservoir of diffuse support upon which the system can automatically draw both in normal times, when members may feel that their capacity to manipulate the political environment is not living up to their expectations, and in special periods of stress, when popular participation may appear to be pure illusion or when political outputs fail to measure up to insistent demands.

The implications of our findings may extend far beyond the particular regime we have been examining. Our study suggests that we need not look only to conflicts and cleavages among interests in the political sphere for the basic sources of persistence and change in that aspect of the political system we have designated as the regime. Rather, a concurrent element contributing to the growth or erosion of support may be found in the orientations to norms acquired very early in the life cycle. We recognize that the early development of support for regime norms such as political efficacy may be unique to the American system, or at least to industrialized systems underpinned by popular education and mass communication. But the probability is otherwise. Our research strongly argues for the need for comparative research as a way of revealing the part played by primary political socialization in the growth and decline of support for political systems in their various aspects.

NOTES

* Research from which this paper was drawn has been supported by a grant from the Office of Education under Cooperative Research Project 1078, Contract SAE 9004. The research design and collection of data were executed jointly by the principal co-investigators, David Easton and Robert D. Hess. The analysis of the political aspects of the data is the primary responsibility of David Easton and Jack Dennis. Jack Dennis is grateful for financial support during the analysis phase of this project from the Research and Development Center for Learning and Re-education at the University of Wisconsin.

¹ For a full extension of these remarks and for discussion of the difference between persistence of a regime, compared to a system as a whole, see D. Easton, *A Systems Analysis of Political Life* (New York: Wiley, 1965), esp. Chaps. 12 and 17ff.

² Although in this paper we concentrate on a single norm, the research from which the analysis proceeds covers other critical norms of the American regime. For further details on the characteristics of our test population see footnote 8.

³ A. Campbell, G. Gurin, and W. E. Miller, *The Voter Decides* (Evanston: Row, Peterson, 1954), p. 190.

⁴ Our interest in the sense of efficacy is clearly and substantially different from concerns that have prevailed in the vast and still growing literature on the subject. For the most part this feeling about politics has been connected with the nature and extent of varying kinds of political participation and involvement, feelings of alienation, anomie and the like. This has reflected the dominant and restrictive interest of political research with allocative problems, the way in which policy is made or put into effect. It has tended to ignore systems persistence concerns, a subject of central theoretical significance. For this see D. Easton, *A Framework for Political Analysis* (New York: Prentice-Hall, 1965); *A Systems Analysis of Political Life*. The literature on political efficacy and its correlates is vast. See for example: G. A. Almond and S. Verba, *The Civic Culture* (Princeton: Princeton University Press, 1963); R. E. Agger, M. N. Goldstein, and S. A. Pearl, "Political Cynicism: Measurement and Meaning," *Journal of Politics*, XIII (1961), 477–506; B. Berelson, P. F. Lazarsfeld, and W. N. McPhee, *Voting* (Chicago: University of Chicago Press, 1954); A. Campbell, G. Gurin, and W. E. Miller, *op. cit.;* A. Campbell, P. E. Converse, W. E. Miller, and D. E. Stokes, *The American Voter* (New York: Wiley, 1960); A. Campbell, "The Passive Citizen," *Acta Sociologica*, VI (fasc. 1–2), 9–21; R. A. Dahl, *Who Governs?* (New Haven: Yale University Press, 1961); E. Douvan and A. M. Walker, "The Sense of Effectiveness in Public Affairs," *Psychological Monographs*, 70 (1956) #32; E. Douvan, "The Sense of Effectiveness and Response to Public Issues," *Journal of Psychology*, 47 (1958), 111–26; S. J. Eldersveld, "Experimental Propaganda Techniques and Voting Behavior," *The American Political Science Review*, L (1956), 154–65; H. Eulau, *Class and Party in the Eisenhower Years* (New York: Free Press of Glencoe, 1962); C. D. Farris, "Authoritarianism as a Political Variable," *Journal of Politics*, XVIII (1956), 61–82; C. D. Farris, "Selected Attitudes on Foreign Affairs as Correlates of Authoritarianism and Political Anomie," *Journal of Politics*, 22 (1960), 50–67; J. E. Horton and W. Thompson, "Powerlessness and Political Negativism," *American Journal of Sociology*, LXVII (1962), 485–93; M. Janowitz and D. Marvick, *Competitive Pressure and Democratic Consent* (Ann Arbor, Michigan: Bureau of Government, 1956); V. O. Key, Jr., *Public Opinion and American Democracy* (New York: Knopf, 1961); A. Kornhauser, H. L. Sheppard, and A. J. Mayer, *When Labor Votes: A Study of Auto Workers* (New York: University Books, 1956); R. E. Lane, "Political Personality and Electoral Choice," *The American Political Science Review*, XLIX (1955), 173–90; *Political Life* (Glencoe: Free Press of Glencoe, 1959); *Political Ideology* (New York: Free Press of Glencoe, 1962); M. R. Levin, *The Alienated Voter: Politics in Boston* (New York: Holt, Rinehart and Winston, 1960); E. Litt, "Political Cynicism and Political Futility," *Journal of Politics*, XXV (1963), 312–23; H. McClosky, "Consensus and Ideology in American Politics," *The American Political Science Review*, LVIII (1964); 361–82; H. McClosky and J. H. Schaar, "Psychological Dimensions of Anomy," *American Sociological Review*, 30 (1965), 14–40; L. W. Milbrath, *Political Participation* (Chicago: Rand McNally, 1965); P. Mussen and A. Wyszyinski, "Political Personality and Political Participation," *Human Relations*, 5 (1952), 65–82; D. Riesman and N. Glazer, "Criteria for Political Apathy" in A. W. Gouldner (ed.), *Studies in Leadership* (New York: Harper, 1950), esp. 540–47; M. Rosenberg, "The Meaning of Politics in Mass Society," *Public Opinion Quarterly*, 15 (1951), 5–15; "Some Determinants of Political Apathy," *Public Opinion Quarterly*, 18 (1954), 349–66; "Misanthropy and Political Ideology," *American Sociological Review*, 21 (1956), 690–95.

⁵ *Op. cit.*, p. 187.

[6] *Ibid.*, pp. 187–88. "Disagree" responses to items 1, 3, 4, and 5, and an "agree" response to item 2 were coded as "efficacious." The authors combined these items, exclusive of item 2, which was thought ambiguous, by means of Guttman scale analysis in order to produce scale types. Item 2 happens to be the only item running in a positive direction. Thus the resulting scale may be subject to acquiescence response set.

[7] Cf. L. W. Pye and S. Verba (eds.), *Political Culture and Political Development* (Princeton: Princeton University Press, 1965), p. 522.

[8] The eight items were scattered through our eight cities' "Citizenship Attitudes #9" questionnaire which was administered to 12,052 purposively selected white, public school children, both middle class and working class in origin, in eight large metropolitan areas (two of each of the four major regions of the U.S.). The questionnaire was administered to the children in their regular classrooms in late 1961 and early 1962. These items were located as follows: 1. p. 16 #72, 2. p. 16 #74, 3. p. 17 #18, 4. p. 19 #29, 5. p. 19 #31, 6. p. 22 #43, 7. p. 22 #45, 8. p. 30 #27. Question 8 was part of a series: p. (#22–29).

[9] The computations were performed at the University of Chicago on an IBM 7094 using a variable N tetrachoric correlation routine.

[10] In error, we included two of our independent variables, reading achievement and I.Q., among the items used for this series of factor analyses. It turns out that these two measures of intellectual ability "load" on this component at grades 5, 6, and 8 (but not at grades 3, 4, and 7). The loadings of these two variables were as follows: reading achievement, .50, .50 and .37 at grades 5, 6, and 8 respectively; I.Q., .37, .41, and .32 at grades 5, 6, and 8 respectively. These have been omitted from Table 1.

[11] See our earlier report, "The Child's Image of Government," in R. Sigel (ed.), "Political Socialization: Its Role in the Political Process," *The Annals of the American Academy of Political and Social Science*, 361 (1965), pp. 40–57.

[12] We are brought to such a cautious and somewhat intricate interpretation because here we are examining a set of attitudes and cognitions still in process of formation rather than in the full-fledged state usually encountered and tested among adults. With children we need to revise our conception of survey research and expect to handle materials much less tractable, in part because they are less well-defined and certainly less stable. Political orientations in process of formation are less easily investigated with instruments designed to detect and measure developed ones. But an exciting aspect of our data is that in spite of this we have been able to discover in children a structure of attitudes toward efficacy that shows a persistent identity as they move from third through eighth grade.

[13] Our procedure in scoring was to cluster-score the five highest-loading items, weighting each item equally and giving the child a score from 1 to 16. The precise scoring procedure was to add up the scores on each of the items, which could range from 1 to 4 (eliminating the middle or "don't know" option). For children who answered three of the five questions other than "don't know" we multiplied his three-item score by 5/3. A similar procedure was used for children answering four questions other than "don't know" (i.e., multiplying by 5/4). Children who failed to answer at least three of the five items were not scored. Scores ranged from 5 to 20. Final scores, after subtracting 4, ranged from 1 to 16.

[14] Our findings that this norm appears relatively early in childhood and that there is a fairly rapid growth of positive feeling in relation to it suggest that what several other observers have speculatively proposed, with less direct evidence, is true. Lane, for example, noted in *Political Life* (p. 151) that the S.R.C. data in *The Voter Decides* show a steady distribution of political efficacy over the (adult) age span to the middle fifties. From this he conjectured that "it appears that the standard of influence, then, is established relatively early—and is not the product of occupational experience so much as of the family and strata where one is reared, plus the personality support which such an attitude implies." The authors of *The Voter Decides* (p. 187) themselves refer to political efficacy as a "broader and more enduring" political value and attitude. In *The American Voter* the authors went even further when they argued that "variables of this sort, in contrast to measures of involvement in the current election, may be conceived as lying at a

relatively 'deep' level in any hierarchy of dispositions. That is, they represent highly generalized orientations toward the world of politics and could be expected to remain rather stable over a period of time. In this sense they are approaching 'personality' status'' (p. 516). This statement suggests that the disposition is likely to begin to form in childhood, when personality development is at its peak, a suspicion that is now reinforced for the first time by data.

[15] Cf. *The American Voter*, p. 516.

[16] Cf. *The American Voter*, p. 515n.; E. Douvan and A. M. Walker, *op. cit.*

[17] We used as an indicator of socio-economic status the occupation of the respondent's father or guardian obtained either from the child in the classroom questionnaire administration or from the school files. In cases where neither was available, an estimate was used based on the average rank of the occupations of the fathers of the child's classmates in the child's own grade and school system.

[18] The first-order partial correlations of I.Q. with efficacy, holding SES constant are as follows (where $1 = $ Eff., $2 = $ I.Q., $3 = $ SES):

Grade	3	4	5	6	7	8
$r_{12.3}$	.10	.24	.30	.31	.31	.28

The first-order partial correlations of SES with efficacy holding I.Q. constant are:

Grade	3	4	5	6	7	8
$r_{13.2}$	.13	.15	.15	.10	.10	.13

[19] Cf. *The Voter Decides; The American Voter;* L. Milbrath, *op. cit.*; R. Lane, *Political Life;* H. Eulau, *op. cit.*; R. Dahl, *op. cit.*; J. E. Horton and W. Thompson, "Powerlessness and Political Negativism"; A. Kornhauser, *et al., op. cit.*

[20] *Op. cit.* p. 191.

[21] Cf. O. G. Brim, Jr. and S. Wheeler, *Socialization After Childhood* (New York: Wiley, 1966), pp. 8, 21 and 35ff

[22] *Op. cit.*, p. 19.

PART FOUR

Relationships
between Leaders and Citizens

In most casual discussions of democracy, one of the important topics is that of the relationship between leaders and followers. In scholarly terms, what seems to be at issue in these discussions is whether the policy preferences of citizens have any bearing upon the policy enactments of leaders. Recent research tends to question the extent to which this causal relationship exists. The readings in this section contain information which can be applied to the controversy concerning how much impact the citizenry really has on political leaders.

Rokkan raises the possibility that political parties—especially their ideological position and the social makeup of their membership—have major roles in maximizing this relationship. His discussion (Chapter 15) centers on the political participation of individual citizens in the Western democracies. Rokkan terms research on this topic "microanalysis" because our measurements are based upon individuals, the smallest unit of political analysis. However, while much of our prior research has been at the micro-level, Rokkan argues for combinations of measurements of individual behavior with measurements on larger units. Thus, we could examine the impact of social organizations or, at the highest level, political systems on individual behavior.

In explicitly evaluating the importance of such "macro-level" variables for understanding individual behavior, Rokkan provides a perspective for theorizing about the relationship between leaders and followers. Comparisons at the highest level—among different political systems—leads us to the following observations.

The Western political systems upon which most of our research is based vary over time in how democratic their political processes are. For example, the full equalization of suffrage is of comparatively recent accomplishment and seems to be an almost irresistible development which occurs when any degree of citizen participation is allowed. The source of this development is the competition for power among political parties. As suffrage approaches full equality, we would expect to find social and economic differences increasingly reflected in politics, i.e., the policy bias against lower status groups would decrease.

Yet even among systems that are equally democratic as far as formal criteria are concerned, there still exist different relationships between status and participation, especially at the higher participation levels. Differences in this respect between the United States and Norway seem to be due to the greater ideological cleavage among the Norwegian political parties. Therefore, it is possible that citizen demands depend not only upon the nature of social cleavages in the society, but also upon the extent that those cleavages are made politically relevant. This latter variable, in turn, seems to be in part dependent upon the kind of political debate which characterizes partisan competition in the political system. As a result, even in a democratic system we might expect little relationship between citizen preferences and leadership policy stands if the extent of party divergence is truncated, because fewer policy demands would then be made by the citizenry.

However, citizen demand for policy enactments is only one possible condition that would maximize the relationship between leaders and citizens. Another possible source is one in which a third party makes demands which benefit a group or groups in the acquiescent citizenry. For example, in this formulation interest groups may make demands directly upon government. Because of the complexity of organizational life, interest-group demands may serve as functional equivalents for those from most of the citizens at large, i.e., most major interests may be served.

Such thinking is quite common in political science; but little research upon this precise question has been done. Lewis A. Froman's analysis (Chapter 16) does treat a portion of this problem. First he finds that interest-group strength in the American states has an impact on government outcomes. If interest groups had no measurable effect on government, we could not very well argue that they served in the place of citizen demands on leadership. Instead, the findings indicate an effect on the nature of the constitutional system in the state. In general, stronger interest groups provide constitutional structures with greater access, e.g., greater emphasis on electing officials rather than appointing them, and easier amendment procedures. Thus not only do interest groups affect government, they also maximize the constitutional conditions for their future impact on government.

While these constitutional changes may be termed democratic, they may or may not provide for a greater correspondence between general preferences of citizen and leader. However, greater access at least provides the opportunity for influence by someone other than the formal office holders. Therefore, where political parties are not of the nature which increases citizen influence, interest groups may provide a second-best approximation.

The foregoing discussion may lead us to predict a relationship between the preferences of leaders and citizens. This prediction would be based upon the patterns which we in turn predict would maximize such relationships in democracies. But our predictions must be tested. Warren E. Miller and Donald E. Stokes (Chapter 17) test this relationship between Congressmen and their constituencies in the United States. They find that constituency attitudes are related to Congressional roll call votes to varying degrees depending upon the political issue considered. The strongest relationship occurs in the area of civil rights. In the area of foreign policy, little relationship at all seems to exist, while the strength of the relationship in the area of social-welfare legislation falls between those of the other two issue areas.

From the point of view of providing answers to our problem, this chapter indicates that in the United States citizen attitudes have their greatest impact on the issue of civil rights. As far as the other two issues are concerned, Congressmen appear to be relatively free to make up their minds without paying much attention to the preferences of the citizens in their districts. Thus it is quite possible that, except for a few aberrant Congressmen and except for super-charged issues like civil rights, Congressmen pay attention only to the highly active minority of citizens and to the special interest groups that may be affected by particular issues at hand.

If this is the case, why doesn't the American political system (and any others similar to it) disintegrate? One answer lies in several readings in the previous section: many citizens, especially the more active ones, have positive attitudes about the processes of the political system. They therefore provide support for the stability of these processes over time, even though the processes may not result in leadership enactment of these citizens' preferences.

Another answer which is similar to that above, but which is more closely related to relationships between citizens and leaders, is that citizens value not only the processes of the system, but also the institutions and the officials who happen to occupy roles in the institutions at some point in time. Fred I. Greenstein's selection (Chapter 18) shows the generally positive feeling of citizens for Eisenhower and the Presidency in the 1950's. Moreover, his analysis indicates that the feeling of official benevolence is highest among children in the early grades in school and tends to decline somewhat with increasing grade level. These results lead to the conclusion that positive attitudes are a result of early socialization (or perhaps early psychic needs) and tend to remain as residuals even among adults. Therefore, representation of citizen preferences by leaders may be quite poor at any one point in time in a democracy and yet stability may continue to be the order of the day if the citizens have been socialized to thinking in positive terms about these dramatic objects in the system.

CHAPTER 15

The Comparative Study of Political Participation: Notes Toward a Perspective on Current Research*

Stein Rokkan

THE EMERGENCE OF MICROPOLITICS

However academic, the discipline of politics has not escaped the impact of changes in the conditions and contexts of governmental decision-making. New tasks for inquiry and interpretation have come to the fore as new developments have brought about new inflows of data.

In the first phases of the growth of nation-states the emphasis was on the analysis of data produced at the upper levels of each hierarchy and at the centers of decision-making: the outputs of commands, regulations, and laws from monarchs, cabinets, courts, administrative agencies, parliaments, and councils, and the records of deliberations and bargains within and between such bodies as well as within parties, clubs, and associations of notables and other prominent power holders.

With the gradual extension of the suffrage and the growth of mass parties in the Western polities during the nineteenth and twentieth centuries the conditions for scholarly work on politics underwent change; the entry into politics of the underprivileged strata of the national communities and the organization of standardized "one citizen, one vote" elections not only set new tasks for research but also called for new approaches and new techniques of study. The expansion of the representative bases of each regime and the mobilization of all accountable citizens into direct confrontation with the issues of politics brought about an extraordinary increase and diversification in the data for research: not just statistics on turnout and party support but also information on the memberships of the parties, the attendance at their meetings and demonstrations, the circulation of their newspapers and their campaign literature, the growth of support from

Reprinted from Austin Ranney, ed., *Essays on the Behavioral Study of Politics* (Urbana: University of Illinois Press, 1962), pp. 47–90, by permission of the University of Illinois.

voluntary associations, and the results of canvasses and polls. These data did not easily lend themselves to treatment by the traditional methods of historiography nor could it be dealt with through the established procedures of institutional description; it could only be systematically exploited through the use of techniques of statistical analysis, and it could only be meaningfully interpreted within the broader framework of the concepts and models of the generalizing sciences of society.

It took some time before the potentialities of these new bodies of data were fully realized by Western students of politics, but from the 'thirties onward there was unmistakable evidence of academic recognition of statistical studies of parties, popular movements, and mass reactions to politics. The spectacular expansion of empirical research in the social sciences stimulated the development of new techniques and new approaches to the study of what came to be called "micropolitics"—the analysis of the individual citizens' reactions to the political events and alternatives in their communities.

Three fundamental technical and methodological developments accelerated the growth of this branch of politics: first, the development of statistical machinery for the handling of the often overwhelming masses of individual or aggregated data; second, the development of probabilistic procedures for sampling in the handling of existing data as well as in the collection of new data; and third, the establishment in one country after another of organizations for the conduct of interview surveys of mass reactions to politics.

THE CHALLENGE OF COMPARATIVE MICROANALYSIS

Vast bodies of data on micropolitical behaviors have been accumulated in the democracies of the West over recent decades, and increasing numbers of studies have been undertaken to establish distributions, to trace trends, and to account for differences in such data. The bulk of these studies have limited themselves to one national setting. They may have compared data for different local communities, constituencies, and regions, but they have stayed within the over-all structure of the national political system. Very few studies have ventured beyond the one national setting and sought to account for constituencies and differences across several systems.

The early comparative studies of turnout and party vote hardly went beyond the collation of parallel series of aggregate figures. Herbert Tingsten was the first to see the potentialities of comparative microanalysis in the exploration of general propositions about factors in political behavior. He was particularly concerned with the reactions of the newest entrants into the national mass electorates, the workers and the women, and he assembled statistics for a variety of elections and referenda in the countries of the West to test hypotheses about conditions likely to affect their actions in this new institutional setting.[1]

With the growth of organized interview research in the countries of the West after World War II came a scattering of attempts at comparisons of data on voters and the background and motivation of their decisions, but only a handful of these studies went beyond the collation of independently produced tabulations toward a detailed consideration of the system contexts of the reactions reported on in the interviews.[2] There is much to be mined from the rapidly growing archives of the private, academic, and governmental survey organizations in the different countries.[3] Much the same questions about socio-economic origins and current status have been asked in extensive series of election surveys for each country, and some of these surveys have gone far beyond the obvious questions about turnout and party choice and inquired into motivations for the vote, party images, exposure to party campaign efforts, interest and level of information, participation in politics and community life. The collation of comparative tables from independently designed and organized surveys will invariably prove tricky and the interpretation of findings from such "secondary analysis" will often be fraught with hazards, but this is clearly an essential step in the development of systematic research on the dynamics of mass reactions to politics in systems of differing structure.[4] So far, we have records of only half a dozen attempts to go further in the direction of designing and carrying out cross-nationally co-ordinated survey operations in a series of countries to ensure a basis for systematic comparisons; the most extensive program of this kind is probably the one currently under way at Princeton and Yale universities under the direction of Gabriel Almond.[5] Such programs of co-ordinated cross-national research are costly and confront social scientists with complex but challenging problems of design and organization. Not only does it become possible to ensure better coverage of items and variables across the countries to be compared, but it also becomes possible to standardize field procedures, question sequences, and response classifications; to evaluate with greater precision the comparability of the data; and, what is crucial in this line of analysis, to explore, in much more detail than through secondary analysis of independently conducted surveys, the structural contexts of the individual reaction to politics.

In analyses of one-nation records of elections and other consultations of the general citizenry, the structural contexts of such microbehaviors are regularly overlooked or deliberately disregarded. The electoral codes are assumed to be uniformly enforced throughout the system, the alternatives facing the citizen are taken to be roughly equivalent in all communities, and the instituted procedures for registering and aggregating the citizen's decisions are assumed to make the data comparable across the entire nation-state. Such analysis, consequently, will focus on the variations in the individual reactions to these uniform sets of stimuli, not on the possible effects of variations in the local settings of the electoral decisions. Such assumptions will generally prove justifiable in analyses of citizen reactions in referenda and plebiscites within unitary nation-states, but will rarely hold for analyses of sequences of elections between parties. Even in highly centralized systems, there will be marked local differences in the range and character of the alternatives presented to the citizens on polling day, not just because of the variations in the group appeals of the party candidates but even more because of the variations in the extent of local resistance to partisan conflict. Even highly disciplined national party organizations are not able to present the same alternatives to the citizens in all constituencies, let alone at elections at all levels of government. Such variations in the range and character of the alternatives facing the citizen, whether from one national election to another or from one level of government to another, are bound to affect in various ways not only his behaviors on successive polling days but also his basic sense of identification with one contesting party rather than another. In our ecological analysis of commune data for turnout in Norway, we have found telling evidence of the importance of variations between national and local elections: if *fewer* parties present themselves at local than at national elections in the given commune, turnout will be *low* also at the national elections, but if the *same* range of party alternatives is presented at local as at national elections, turnout will be *average or high*. This raises intriguing problems of "macro-micro" analysis of the sequences of steps in the electoral decision-making process. The national party organizations set alternatives for the actual or potential leaders in each constituency, the constituency parties set alternatives for the actual or potential party officials in each unit of local administration, and only the local party organizations are in a position to ensure that the same broad alternatives of choice are put before the general citizenry in every election.[6] The behavior of the citizen at the polls represents his decisions between institutionally set alternatives and reflects in one way or another his experiences flowing from decisions among alternatives in earlier elections. Even in a system of completely "nationalized" politics, therefore, any analysis of electoral behavior will be incomplete as long as it has not traced the effects of differences between communities and changes over time in the ranges and characteristics of the alternatives presented to the electorate.

This goes *a fortiori* for analyses within federations of states differing not only in their party systems but in their electoral provisions and procedures. Within the United States, V. O. Key, Jr., has urged the importance of comparative community studies for an understanding of the "macro contexts" of individual political decisions; such studies "might shed light on the questions of the relation between the extent and nature of citizen participation and the character of political systems in the large."[7] So far, however, the vast majority of political behavior studies in the United States has either concentrated on single communities or dealt with samples of the entire national electorate. There are indications, however, of a trend toward increasing investments in comparative data gathering across communities differing in the formal and institutional settings of their politics as well as in their party traditions and their leadership. The controversy over methodology and theory in the study of "community power elites" has stimulated a great deal of interest in the comparison of local political systems,[8] but the comparative studies so far undertaken have concentrated on top decision-makers and influential people rather than on the general citizenry and its reactions.[9] The most promising designs for detailed quantitative analysis of the impact of macroforces on micro-behaviors, the Rossi–Cutright[10] and Eldersveld–Katz[11] studies of precinct and ward variations in the efficacy of party organizations, have so far been developed within metropolitan and other large urban areas. Similar explorations of the effects of structural contexts on citizen decisions at the polls have been attempted at the county and the state levels. The regional panel surveys organized by the Bureau of Applied Social Research at Columbia University were motivated by such concerns.[12] The Survey Research Center at the University of Michigan has endeavored to strengthen the tie-in between studies of national cross-sections and studies of local communities and has shown, in the analysis of the nationwide sample data for the 1956 election, that it is possible to find meaningful ways of analyzing within this research design the effects of differences in the "macro" contexts of the electoral act. Angus Campbell and his co-workers have shown how the state-to-state differences in suffrage requirements affect the lifetime frequency of turnout at elections both in the North and the South and have documented the importance of the formal rules of registration as well as of the form of the ballot for the actual voting of citizens differing in the strength of their partisanship and their concern with politics.[13] Warren Miller has gone further to an exploration of the effects of county-to-county differences in the character of the party system[14] on individual political orientations and decisions and has taken an important step toward bridging the "micro-macro" gap through the design of a nationwide study of the interrelations between party candidates for Congress and the citizens in their constituencies.

These developments in the design and organization of cross-community and cross-constituency studies within national systems cannot fail to influence the continuing efforts to advance comparative microanalyses across different nations; they force us to differentiate our comparisons by levels in each system, they alert us to new sources of variations, and they add further perspective in our interpretations of similarities and differences.

With the accumulation of attempts to assemble parallel micro-tabulations across differing political systems has come an increasing concern with the underlying logic of such comparisons and with the "grammar" of cross-national research. So far, no single scholar has ventured a frontal attack on these problems; what we find in the literature are varieties of hints and suggestions but hardly a single attempt at a systematic treatment. This is true for comparisons in most fields of the social sciences[15] and is eminently true of comparative politics.[16] This is a challenge to all scholars concerned to advance the codification of the procedures of observation, analysis, and inference in the study of politics. What I can do toward this end in this paper is very little; I shall suggest some distinctions I have found important in my current work on electoral and other forms of political behavior, I shall present a chart for the location of major variables in the comparative study of such microdata, and I shall try to formulate and discuss in historical and comparative terms three central problems in the study of citizen participation in public affairs.

PARADIGMS AND MODELS FOR COMPARISONS OF MICRODATA

Comparisons of micropolitical data lead to analyses in two distinct directions: (1) the direction of the structurally set restraints on the decisions recorded—the rules of procedure and the enforcement practices, the number of alternatives and the difference between them, the methods used in aggregating the choices and determining the outcomes, and the probabilities of "pay-off" for choices of each of the given alternatives; and (2) the direction of the personal background of the choice between the given alternatives, the experiences and expectations, the group pressures and the individual motivations prompting the choice for one alternative rather than another.

In the language of David Easton's model of the political process,[17] the restraints on the microdecisions constitute outputs from the system; they regulate and set conditions for the feedback flow of inputs into the system from the general territorial population. In any such system changes in the outputs will occur whenever the variations in the inputs exceed critical limits. With the rapid changes in the socio-economic bases of politics in the Western systems during the nineteenth and the early twentieth century went a series of crucial changes in the outputs of restraints on micro-decisions: political citizenship rights were extended to vast numbers of hitherto unrecognized members of the national community, the formal equality of all citizens was recognized through the institution of "one citizen, one vote" rules, and procedures were introduced to ensure the compulsory anonymity of each vote. Since the end of World War I these basic restraints have been maintained without much change in the majority of Western systems despite marked variations in the outcomes of elections and other consultations. The rules for the aggregation of votes into mandates have proved much less stable and have been modified again and again under the impact of changing constellations of microdecisions. The restraints on the number and the range of alternatives facing the individual citizen will, within flexible limits, vary with the results of successive consultations of the given constituency; this holds true for the "pay-off" probabilities for each of the choices open to him. A party may lose so many votes at time t_1 that will prove unable to present itself as an alternative at time t_2. Two parties may compete so hard to reach the majority point that they may become indistinguishable in their appeals and their policy commitments and provoke the development of splinter movements presenting new alternatives to the citizens.[18] Changes in the alignments of socio-economic groupings behind the parties in a system may bring about greater dissensus or increasing consensus across party lines and as a result make for changes in the ranges of alternatives open to the citizenry at election time.[19]

These "macro-micro" interdependencies have been recognized again and again in analyses of electoral and other political behavior data, but the implications have nowhere been spelled out in any detail in a comparative framework.

The studies we find in the literature may roughly be grouped in four classes according to the direction of the analysis: (1) "micro-micro" studies focusing on relationships between individual background characteristics, roles, cognitions, and motivations on the one hand and political dispositions and decisions on the other; (2) "macro-micro" studies exploring the effects of variations and changes in structural contexts on the rates of given political decisions and on the strength and direction of "micro-micro" relationships; (3) "micro-macro" studies concerned with the effects of the attitudes and decisions of the general citizenry on the policies, strategies, and tactics of the parties and on the operation of the established systems of structural restraints on decision-making; and finally, (4) "macro-macro" studies concerned with the functions of given structural restraints in the maintenance, legitimation, and stabilization of the over-all political system.

A conscientious classification of all the categories of variables taken into account in studies of each of these types would require a great deal of space. It is enough here to point to a series of distinctions of possible "orders of comparison" in the exploration of "micro-micro" and "macro-micro" propositions; this is done in Table 1.

This typology starts out from direct comparisons of the aggregated rates

Table 1. A Typology of "Orders" of Comparisons: Microcomparisons of Lower Complexity

Order	Alternatives set for Citizen		Collectivities significant for Citizen (C)	Citizen's		Examples of propositions derived and/or derivable from the given order of comparison
	National Level (N)	Local Level (L)		Regular Roles (R)	Political Behavior (B)	
First:					micro	(1) Turnout rates (B) for national electorates higher in western Europe than in the U.S.
Second: N	macro				micro	(2) Turnout rates (B) higher in systems with official registration and short ballots (N) than in systems with voluntary registration and complex ballots.
L		macro			micro	(3) Turnout rates (B) for localities increase with the proportions of votes cast for dominant party (L).
C			macro		micro	(4) Turnout rates (B) for localities increase with increasing socio-economic or cultural homogeneity (C).
R				micro	micro	(5) Turnout rates (B) higher for men and married citizens than for women and single citizens (R).
Third: NL	macro	macro			micro	(6) Turnout rates (B) for localities increase with one party dominance (L) in PR systems (N), not in plurality systems.

Type				Proposition
NC	macro	*macro*	micro	(7) Turnout rates (B) for localities more likely to increase with increasing socio-economic homogeneity (C) within markedly status-polarized party systems (N).
NR	macro	*macro*	*micro*	(8) Educational differential in political participation (R-B) smaller the more marked the status polarization of the national party system (N).
LC	macro	*macro*	micro	(9) Turnout rates (B) not so likely to increase with increasing socio-economic homogeneity (C) in non-partisan local elections (L).
LR	*macro*	macro	*micro*	(10) Educational differential in political participation (R-B) will be more marked the less partisan the politics of the locality (L).
CR	macro	*macro*	*micro*	(11) Status differential in turnout (R-B) decreases with increasing residential segregation of workers *vs.* others (C).

Sources:

(1) H. Gosnell, *Why Europe Votes* (Chicago: University of Chicago Press, 1930), Chap. 8; cf. S. Rokkan and A. Campbell, "Citizen Participation in Political Life: Norway and the United States of America," *International Social Science Journal*, Vol. 12 (1960), pp. 71–72.

(2) Gosnell, *op. cit.*, pp. 185–87.

(3) E. Allardt, *Social struktur och politisk aktivitet* (Helsinki: Söderström, 1956), pp. 30–33. The alternative proposition, that turnout will be highest in closely contested districts was documented by Gosnell, *op cit.*, Tables II, V, VII and pp. 199–201. Tabulations for Britain indicate that the highest turnouts will be found either in closely contested constituencies or in heavily labor-dominated ones, cf. H. G. Nicholas, *The British General Election of 1950* (London: Macmillan and Co., 1951), p. 318.

(4) Allardt, *op cit.*, pp. 56–59.

(5) Tingsten, *op. cit.*, M. Dogan and J. Narbonne, *Les françaises face à la politique* (Paris: Armand Colin, 1955), Chap. 6; Allardt, *op. cit.*, pp. 124–30.

(6) Rokkan and Valen, *op. cit.*, pp. 36–37.

(7) Implications of finding in Rokkan and Campbell, *op. cit.*, not documented.

(8) Rokkan and Campbell, *op. cit.*, pp. 84–89 and 93–96.

(9) Not documented.

(10) Not documented; derivable from P. H. Rossi, *op. cit.*, pp. 37–42.

(11) This is Tingsten's "law of the social center of gravity," *op. cit.*, pp 170–72; cf. E. Allardt and K. Brunn, "Characteristics of the Finnish Non-Voter," *Transactions of the Westermarck Society*, Vol. 3 (1956), pp. 55–76; Lipset, *op. cit.*, pp. 205–07.

of given political behaviors within territorial units—comparisons of such familiar statistics as those for relative turnout and party strength or those of less accessible data such as the proportions of dues-paying party members, of attendants at party meetings, of subscribers to party journals, of listeners to party broadcasts, and of active "opinion leaders." These are all examples of "dependent" variables. It is the task of comparative analysis to account for variations in such rates through breakdowns at successive levels of the political system. In the schematic typology presented here only four such levels have been distinguished: (1) the level of the roles and statuses of the individual actor in the collectivities and the organizations of which he is part; (2) the level of the macrocharacteristics of such collectivities or organizations, whether aggregated across their members or determined by their structure, their leadership, or their position in the established conflict alignments in the political system; (3) the structural restraints on microdecisions at the local level, the level of the most immediate unit of elective government in the actor's regular environment; and (4) the structural restraints on micro-decisions at the national level, the level of the total territorial system within which the actor is a political subject.

Several further levels could no doubt be distinguished, but these are the ones most likely to prove useful in comparisons across unitary nation-states; federations add further complexity to any scheme of comparison.

Only three orders of comparison are identified and exemplified in the chart; only very few comparisons so far attempted go any further, although this is logically perfectly possible.

The "second order" comparisons most frequently found in the research literature are of the "micro-micro" variety; such comparisons are essentially replications of the same analytical breakdowns within a variety of localities and national systems to test the generality of differences in political behavior between individuals in different roles. Most of Tingsten's analyses were of this order; he studied differences in turnout and "left-right" voting by sex, age, marital status, education, and occupation. His most important analyses, however, went beyond this stage; in these he concerned himself with the broader social settings most likely to bring about such "micro-micro" relationships. He showed for several localities that the socio-economic homogeneity of the residential area affected the differences in turnout between workers and middle class citizens and, what was sociologically of even greater interest, that this curve for "residence-sensitivity" was marked-ly steeper for women than for men.[20]

The following were clearly "third order" comparisons: localities and areas were ranked on given unit characteristics to determine the effects of the residential environment on the political behaviors of citizens differing in their role positions within the community. This type of comparison has become a major analytical device in political sociology; the much-discussed theories about the stabilizing impact of increasing cross-class communication and the radicalizing effects of working-class isolation clearly prompt continued application of such third order comparisons.[21] In these comparisons, the structural restraints set by the electoral procedures and the party systems are deliberately disregarded, at least in the first rounds of analysis; the comparisons aim at the establishment across a variety of political systems of generalizations about political reactions in residential environments differing in their socio-cultural homogeneity. The rationale for cross-national studies of this kind is two-fold: by going beyond the one nation, the *number of cases* that can be tested is vastly increased, and the *range of variability* in the cases is extended. The between-community variability within the given nation may be very small and produce only minor variations in the dependent behaviors; to get data on cases farther apart on the given collectivity variable it is essential to go to a number of different national settings. This, of course, goes for any group or collectivity of potential political relevance for the citizen who is part of it   families, work organizations, unions, churches, sects, voluntary associations, or parties. I have myself suggested as a possible task for comparative political research the collection of data on the degree of "status distinctiveness" of the major parties of the West and the testing of hypotheses about the effects of within-party homogeneity vs. heterogeneity on the recruitment of active participants.[22] What is important here is perhaps not so much the establishment of invariant relationships as the identification and analysis of deviant cases; this may give us new cues to the historical study of particular developments and alert us to sources of variations at higher levels within each system. Third order comparisons of the recruitment channels within different parties could in this way lead on to "fourth order" comparisons of the local settings of these processes and to "fifth order" comparisons of the over-all national decision-making structures and the limits they set for the parties and their active participants.

Our tentative typology of comparisons implies a "model" of the complex processes leading to individual political decisions. The typology singles out as crucially important in the flow of influences on the given political act the roles the individual has in his life environments, the collectivities he identifies with, the choices open to him within his immediate local community, and the choices open to him as a subject of a national political system. These have been the basic categories of variables in research on electoral statistics since the early pioneers, and they are still the ones that account for the greatest number of tabulations in the literature. The development of survey research has made it possible to go much further in the differentiation of variables within each of these categories and, what is even more important to enrich the analysis through the addition of information on other phases in the process—on the exposure to influences from the mass media and the immediate role environment; on reactions to conditions within these environments; on identifications with politically relevant collectivities; on images of ideologies, parties, and alternatives for action; on the interest manifested in political affairs; and on the manifold forms of private or public participation in conflicts over policies and between parties. This extraordinary wealth and diversity of data cannot easily be fitted into a coherent theory of the processes at work in such differing structural contexts. In planning our program of electoral studies in Norway we did not attempt to construct anything like a "conceptual model" for such research, but we did find it helpful to work out in some detail a "location chart" for the principal variables to be taken into account either in the design of the actual data-gathering instruments or in the analyses and interpretations of the information assembled. In comparing our Norwegian data with evidence from studies in other countries we have found this a useful framework for the discussion of similarities and differences; it is therefore reproduced here, after some revision, as Table 2.

This chart represents essentially an attempt at a codification, within the limits of a two-dimensional schema, of the designs of data gathering and analysis now in use in research on elections and other forms of mass participation in politics. The "locations of politically relevant variability" are ordered along two axes: a "macro-micro" axis running from the conditions in the total political system down through the influences on the citizen in his everyday roles to his actual decisions during the campaign and on polling day, and a time axis running from the situation in the citizen's family of origin through the changes in his environment during the formative years of early adulthood to his current situation.

In its basic structure this two-dimensional schema will be seen to be closely akin to the notion of a "funnel of causality" so suggestively set out by Angus Campbell and his co-workers in their discussion of strategies of research in their volume on the 1956 presidential election.[23] The focus is on the terminal acts of choice at the election under study, in our chart these are located in the lower right corner; in the funnel model they are at the end of the narrowing stem. In both models time is a central ordering dimension; the final political act is traced back to conditions and events in the life history of the citizens and the system that he is part of. In the Michigan model the conditions at each cross-section in time are ordered from a central core of politically relevant and personally experienced events toward a periphery of politically irrelevant events beyond the actor's ken. In the chart we used in designing our Norwegian studies, we focused on what we considered to be the analytically relevant conditions at each cross-section in time and ordered these by levels in the political system: at the first level, nearest to the terminal acts under study, the citizen's behaviors in other political contexts, his privately expressed concerns with public issues, and his public participation in policy-influencing organizations or in political parties; at the second level, his images and judgments of the political alternatives open to him; at the third, his orientation and attitudes to critical issues in his regular environments and his identifications with collectivities engaged on one side or the other in given conflicts; at the fourth, his roles and activities in his regular environments, the collectivities he spends the bulk of his time in; at the fifth, his exposure to political influences in these environments, through majority pressure, through active opinion leaders, and through the mass media; at the sixth, and this is the first "macro" level, the messages, the information, the arguments, and the appeals sent to him from the organizations and the corporate units active in the contests for support within the system; at the seventh, the actual alternatives set by the system for the ordinary citizen, locally as well as nationally; and finally, the eighth level, the given state of the system, the external pressures on it, the cleavages within it, and the alignments of forces among the full-time decision-makers, whether political, administrative, economic, or cultural.

A chart such as this is not a substitute for a rigorous design; it simply serves as a guide to remind us of sources of variation to be taken into account whether data on the sources can be assembled or not. What is important here is that it underscores the need to take contexts into account in comparing data on political behavior, whether within one national system or across several systems.

CONTRASTING CONTEXTS OF CITIZEN PARTICIPATION IN DECISION-MAKING: THE ELECTORAL VS. THE TRADITIONAL AND THE ORGANIZATIONAL

The lines of influence set out in our chart converge on the terminal acts of choice on election day: the choice between turning out and staying home, the choice between the n lists or the n candidates.

These acts constitute inputs into the process of decision-making for the territorial community, but they make up only one of the great variety of categories of such inputs. Individual acts of disobedience or resistance, spontaneous demonstrations, public articulations of opinion, mass media campaigns, demands, appeals, and threats from organized movements and interest groups, offers and counteroffers in bargains between corporate units, and reactions and suggestions flowing back from administrative agencies are examples of inputs to be taken into account in any analysis of the processes of decision-making in the nation-state. How do the electoral inputs fit into this broader framework of articulations of demands and

Table 2. Location Chart for Variables in Election Research

SYSTEM DIMENSION

Citizen's Life Cycle				
State of System	External circumstances; central decision-making; cleavage bases; conflict alignments	→ Changes		→ Current state
Alternatives for Citizen	Suffrage requirements; electoral procedures, barriers; party organizations, differences on policy. *Nationally:* Range of party choice, chances to gain mandates, power. *Locally:* Nonpartisan traditions	→ Changes		→ Current alternatives
Message Flows — Sources	Governmental, official; parties, movements, organizations; publicists, ideologues	→ Changes in volume content, lines of argumentation		→ Current campaign ←MACRO| MACRO →
Message Flows — Channels	*Mass:* mass media, party literature, rallies. *Role:* local party workers, opinion leaders	→ Changes in channels		→ Current campaign
Message Flows — Exposure	*Mass:* accessibility, nearness to urban centers. *Role:* nearness to activists; political divisions within / between role environments	→ Changes in accessibility		→ Current campaign ←MICRO| MICRO →
Roles in Regular Environments	*Parents' roles/activities* Community; kin, friendship circles; household; work milieu; associations; church, sect	*Own entrance* Socialization; → formal education; apprenticeship	*Mobility* Residential; social; marital; → occupational; economic; religious	→ *Current roles/activities* Community; kin, friends; household; work milieu; associations; church, sect

SYSTEM DIMENSION

→ MICRO

	Past (Parents'/early)	Entering	Own current
Orientations Identifications	*Parents' orientations to/identifications with* Own community, kin, ethnicity; paternal authority; economic conditions, prospects; workmates, unions; church, sect; parties	*Own on entering adulthood* Conformity—revolt ↑	Own current orientations/ identifications ↑
Perceived Alternatives	*Parents' perceptions/images* Local political alternatives, difference in policies, leaders, support, chances to gain mandates, majority — National political alternatives	*Own early perceptions/images* Changes in local context ↑ — Changes nationally ↑	Own current perceptions/images ↑
Political Behavior — Private	*Parents' behaviors* Interest in, knowledge of politics; information seeking; articulateness on issues; commitments on issues; party preference	*Own on entering electorate* "Socialization" to political activity/inactivity ↑	Own current level of private participation ↑
Political Behavior — Public	*Parents' behaviors* Open advocacy of policies activity in policy-influencing organizations; party membership, subscriptions	*Own on entering electorate* Recruitment to active participation ↑	Own current public/organizational activity ↑
	Elections { Active campaign work / Turnout / Party vote }	First votes ↑	Own current turnout; current party vote ↑

TIME DIMENSION →

aggregations of pressure?[24] This is a problem of central importance in the integration of approaches to the study of political processes: important in the analysis of the functional unity of systems and important in the study of the motivations and manifestations of individual participation in the affairs of the community and the nation.

This problem has a crucial historical dimension. The processes of centralization and democratization during the nineteenth and the early twentieth century brought about a more and more marked contrast between the electoral and the other channels of participation in decision-making; the seemingly irresistible trend toward the formal standardization of procedures and enforcement practices gradually sets the electoral mode of aggregation distinctly apart from other modes, both from the traditional influences of locally dominant families and from the emerging influences of functionally differentiated national organizations.

In full-fledged political democracies, electoral acts of participation will differ from other acts on three crucial counts: (1) the universality of access—all accountable adults without severe criminal records are given the vote, however peripheral their concern for politics and public affairs and however dependent and subordinate their roles in their community or their organizations; (2) the equality of influence—each vote cast counts as one anonymous unit of influence and is completely divorced from the person and the roles of the participating citizen; and (3) the privacy and the "irresponsibility" of the participant's act—the vote is given the status of a "privileged communication" to the territorial authorities, there is no feedback to the citizen's other roles in his community, and it is consequently up to each voter to decide whether or not to reveal his act and take responsibility for it in his day-to-day environment.

The history of the movement toward formal democracy in the West could appropriately be written as an analysis of the sequences of decisions that led to the adoption and enforcement of these three institutional solutions to the problem of the legitimacy of representation. What was central in this development was the growing acceptance of the concept of the *unit citizen* of the nation-state acting in abstraction from his particular roles in the organizational and institutional structure of society. It is tempting to see the development of these channels for mass participation in politics as one element in the complex series of processes that led to the growth and integration of territorially defined nation-states. The extension of political citizenship rights to all accountable adults and the equalization of all votes within a standardized system of electoral decision-making were two of the several important facets of an over-all process of political mobilization within the national territory — a process bringing about a steady increase in the proportion of the territorial population standing in direct, unmediated communication with the central authorities.[25] It is not difficult to trace this process in the history of the consolidation and integration of the nation-states in the West in the nineteenth century, and there are important parallels in the current developments in the new states in Africa and Asia.[26] Essentially what we find is a process of institutional innovation leading to the imposition of formally equal obligations and to the granting of formally equal rights to all accountable adults independent of differences in their established influence through roles in the kinship system, the local community, or other corporate bodies. Direct taxation, military conscription, and compulsory education would be major examples of formally universalized obligations to the nation-state, while equality before the courts, social security provisions, and universal suffrage would be the principal examples of national citizen rights.[27] We rarely find any straight progression toward the universalization of all these obligations and all these rights; what we find is a series of temporary compromises in a complex bargaining process between major power groups in each polity.

What needs to be emphasized in this context is that this process of nation-building brought with it almost as a matter of necessity the enfranchisement of vast masses of politically inarticulate citizens and at the same time made it formally possible for them to cut off traditional allegiances to the local communities and their hierarchies of influence. Edmund Burke was probably the first to see the growth of formal equality in this perspective; he denounced the French Revolution for instituting an abstract equality of citizenship in order to insure greater centralization under the national government. Alexis de Tocqueville went further in this analysis of the parallel movements toward national integration and universal suffrage. He saw in the growth of *démocratie* a part-process in the total mobilization of all adult subjects into direct, unmediated relationships to the nation-state. *Démocratie* implied more than an extension of political citizenship rights to the bourgeoisie and the lower classes; it stood for a trend toward the disintegration of all intermediate authorities between the government and the mass of legally equal citizens. In fact, for Tocqueville the leveling of all differences in legal and political status among the subjects of the regime was at the heart of the over-all trend toward a centralization of territorial authority in the nation-states; the demands of the subjects for greater equality strengthened the claims of the centralized state, and the central power holders reinforced these same demands in order to undercut all interference from intermediary powers, whether feudal, local, or associational. Tocqueville prophesied that this dialectical process would be accelerated through the growth of manufacturing industries and the decline of local power based on agriculture—industrialization not only would bring with it changes in the social structure and intensify the demands for equality of status but would also create conflicts that would increase the need for regulations of local affairs by the central government.

How did these projections into the future fit the actual facts of the political developments in the Western nation-states during the hundred years that followed? Tocqueville proved remarkably prophetic at one level —the level of the development of formal political institutions and regulations. The continued growth of the manufacturing industries *did* bring about increased centralization of the national decision-making systems and *did* lead to the equalization of citizenship rights and obligations; by the end of World War I practically all nations of the West had introduced universal manhood suffrage, and a majority of them also extended these rights to women. What Tocqueville was less ready to see was that this development toward formal equalization could proceed *pari passu* with the steady growth of a pluralist network of associations and corporate bodies; the systems of "one citizen, one vote" decision-making were gradually balanced off, so to speak, against systems of bargaining, consultation, and representation among growing numbers of interest organizations, voluntary associations, and public bodies. Tocqueville saw this coming in his description of the political and civil associations in the United States, but somehow these insights did little to change his central vision of the growth of mass democracy. He did not see that the institutionalization of formal equality would not only allow, but sometimes even encourage, the persistence of traditional loyalties to local notables and trusted spokesmen in guilds and associations and, what was to become even more important, set the stage for the growth of new organizations.

THREE CENTRAL PROBLEMS FOR COMPARATIVE RESEARCH ON CITIZEN PARTICIPATION

Gabriel Almond has argued persuasively for the development of "dualistic models" in the comparison of political systems at different stages of growth; a system may be "modern" "universalistic", and "achievement-oriented" at one level and in one of its channels of decision-making and still remain "traditional", "particularistic," and "ascriptive" at other levels and in other channels of decision-making (Almond and Coleman, *op. cit.*, pp. 20–25). National political systems are "multistructural"; the growing complexity of the economy may bring about a variety of differentiated rational-legal systems of decision-making, but the traditional local structures will invariably persist in one form or another and decisively affect the actual functioning of the new institutions.

Almond urges the importance of this perspective in functional comparisons of total systems. The perspective is of equal importance in the study of the structural contexts of individual participation in decision-making. Almond's primary example highlights the contrast between the opportunities for formal participation opened up by the extension of the suffrage and the persistence of earlier structures of dependence on local spokesmen; the contrast between the assumptions of equality, anonymity, and individual choice underlying the institutions of mass democracy and the discovery in *The People's Choice*[28] and a long series of other empirical studies of the importance of face-to-face communication with opinion leaders in the immediate environments of the enfranchised citizen.

Students of political behavior have again and again been struck by this contrast between the "one citizen, one vote" provisions of political democracy and the persistent inequalities in the actual processes of decision-making. Study after study has underscored the contrast between the high proportions of voters and the very low proportions of politically concerned and alert citizens within the mass electorate; on the one hand a large majority of *only-voters*, of citizens who turn up at their polling stations but show very little articulate concern about the issue of politics, only rudimentary knowledge of the alternatives, and no willingness to take an active part in the conflict between the parties, and on the other hand a small minority of active participants in the political system, of articulate and informed citizens motivated to act and to take a stand.

These inequalities have persisted in all mass democracies; they invariably become even more marked with the extension of the suffrage to women. The improvement of educational standards, the spread of the mass media of communication, and the organizational work of the mass parties may have helped to raise the "political literacy" levels in most systems, but the basic inequalities in participation have remained. The persistence of the inequalities raises a series of questions about the implications of the introduction of universal suffrage for the functioning of modern political systems So far, such questions of functional relationships have mainly been raised in discussions of evidence from single countries.[29] To gain a comparative perspective on such "macro-macro" consequences we shall clearly have to do much more to collate data from countries differing in their characteristic sequences of development toward full-fledged democracy and differing in the political alignments of the masses of citizens enfranchised through these developments. We need *historical* comparisons of the processes of decision-making which led to the expansion of the electorate and the standardization of registration and voting procedures; we need *statistical* comparisons of trends in political reactions of the masses of lower class citizens and of women after their entry into the electorate; and we need *institutional and structural* comparisons of the different ways in which the pressures of the mass electorate, the parties, and the elective bodies are dovetailed into a broader system of decision-making among interest organizations and private and public corporate units.

These are the three sets of problems I consider crucial in any systematic study of the structural contexts of political participation: (1) the series of decisions which *set the formal conditions* for the political mobilization of the masses of inarticulate subjects within each territory, (2) the actual *rates of mobilization* to political activity and the conditions making for higher or lower rates, (3) the conditions for given types of tie-ins between party-political activities and participation in *other policy-influencing groups, collectivities and organizations.*

This is not the place for detailed discussion of the current status of research on each of these problems. I shall limit myself to a few suggestions of promising lines of analysis.

The Institutional Settings and the Structural Restraints

Discussing the progress of democracy in the United States, Alexis de Tocqueville pointed to an "invariable rule in the history of society"—once the first step had been taken to reduce the qualifications for the vote, it would be impossible to halt the movement at any point short of universal suffrage.[30] It is extraordinary to see how Tocqueville's projections turned out to fit the actual developments toward full-fledged formal democracy in nation-state after nation-state. The decisions to extend the vote were not uniformly a response to pressures from below; they were as often the results of contests for influence at the top and of deliberate moves to broaden the bases for an integrated national power structure. The French Revolution had sown its plebiscitarian seeds, and the success of Napoleon III had a distinct impact on political minds in western Europe.[31] By a much-debated historical coincidence, the two great Conservative leaders, Disraeli and Bismarck, proceeded in 1867 within months of each other to extend the suffrage further than their Liberal antagonists had wanted.[32] In both cases these "leaps in the dark" were motivated by a profound belief that the entry of the working classes into the electorate would strengthen the unity and stability of the nation-state. Disraeli expressed great faith in the working class and saw a major source of strength for the Conservative party in these new entrants into the electorate. In the words of a *Times* obituary sixteen years later, Disraeli discerned the Conservative working man "in the inarticulate mass of the English populace" just as "the sculptor perceived the angel in a block of marble."[33] Bismark also saw a major ally against the Liberals in the working class and was clearly very much influenced in his decision by his secret conversations with Ferdinand Lassalle—the Junker and the Socialist found a common ground in their belief in the integrating and centralizing impact of the introduction of universal manhood suffrage.[34] The motive for extending the suffrage to the workers was patently not to create a channel for the articulation of the interests of the economically dependent strata; the objective was to strengthen the policies of centralization by enlisting the support of the least articulate classes in German society. Bismarck even toyed with the possibility of introducing a system for ensuring numerical support through the tacit acquiescence of the inarticulate masses; the votes of those who did not turn out were to be counted in favor of the governmental candidates.[35] Lassalle developed the idea (he called it his *Zauberrezepte*)[36] of ensuring results in the same direction by a system of obligatory voting. This idea was not taken up in the debate over the constitution of the North German Federation but was later to become a standard strategy in efforts to ensure an equilibrium of power in mass suffrage systems.[37]

At the heart of the bitter debates over the extension of the suffrage were conflicting expectations concerning the repercussions of the entry of the "politically illiterate" into the arena: conflicting views of the allegiances and probable reactions of these masses once they were enfranchised and conflicting evaluations of the possibilities of controlling and channeling these new forces. Liberals tended to express fear of an irresponsible and disruptive radicalization of politics; Conservative and Christian party leaders were more likely to see in the enfranchisement of the lower classes and of all women a major strategic move in the stabilization of the national system against the attacks from the Socialist Left. An extraordinary variety of institutional compromises were tried out in response to these conflicting pressures. The history of these innovations is not of merely antiquarian interest; these developments set the stage for the organization of mass politics in each country and the particular solutions reached at each stage helped to determine the conditions for the integration of the lower classes into the national community.

In a systematic comparison of the sequences of decisions that led to the introduction of full-fledged formal democracy a great number of dimensions of institutional change would have to be considered. For the present purposes a simplified schematic chart has been prepared (Table 3) to set in relief some of the salient differences between western European countries in the developments that led to the enfranchisement of the politically least articulate strata of each population.[38] This chart takes into account only three dimensions of variation: the steps in the extension of the suffrage, the decisions on the weighting of the votes, and the steps toward the privatization of electoral preferences.

A comparison of these sequences of decisions reveals some marked contrasts both in the number of years and the number of steps it took to

Table 3. Comparative Chronology of Suffrage Extensions: Some Contrasts in Western Europe

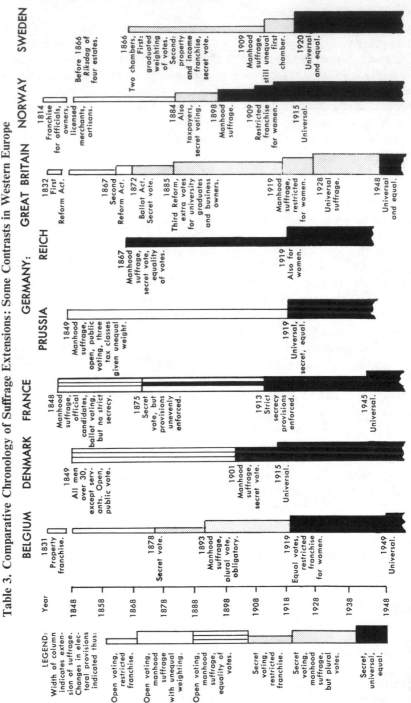

LEGEND:
Width of column indicates extension of suffrage. Changes in electoral provisions indicated thus:

Open voting, restricted franchise.

Open voting, manhood suffrage with unequal weighting.

Open voting, manhood suffrage, equality of votes.

Secret voting, restricted franchise.

Secret voting, manhood suffrage, but plural votes.

Secret, universal, equal.

BELGIUM
1831 Property franchise.
1878 Secret vote.
1893 Manhood suffrage, plural vote, obligatory.
1919 Equal votes, restricted franchise for women.
1949 Universal.

DENMARK
1849 All men over 30, except servants. Open, public vote.
1901 Manhood suffrage, secret vote.
1915 Universal.

FRANCE
1848 Manhood suffrage, official candidates, ballot voting, but no strict secrecy.
1875 Secret vote, but provisions unevenly enforced.
1913 Strict secrecy provisions enforced.
1945 Universal.

GERMANY: PRUSSIA
1849 Manhood suffrage, open, public voting, three tax classes given unequal weight.
1919 Universal, secret, equal.

GERMANY: REICH
1867 Manhood suffrage, secret vote, equality of votes.
1919 Also for women.

GREAT BRITAIN
1832 First Reform Act.
1867 Second Reform Act.
1872 Ballot Act. Secret vote.
1885 Third Reform, extra votes for university graduates and business owners.
1919 Manhood suffrage, restricted for women.
1928 Universal suffrage.
1948 Universal and equal.

NORWAY
1814 Franchise for officials, owners, licensed merchants, artisans.
1884 Also taxpayers, secret voting.
1898 Manhood suffrage.
1909 Restricted franchise for women.
1915 Universal.

SWEDEN
Before 1866 Riksdag of four estates.
1866 Two chambers, First: graduated weighting of votes. Second: property and income franchise, secret vote.
1909 Manhood suffrage, still unequal first chamber.
1920 Universal and equal.

Year
1848
1858
1868
1878
1888
1898
1908
1918
1928
1938
1948

reach universal suffrage and in the decisions taken at the point of entry into politics of the hitherto unrecognized strata of the population.

It would be difficult to devise an electoral measure more calculated to alienate the lower classes from the national political system than the one promulgated in Prussia in 1849: all adult men were given the vote, but the workers and the lower middle class were given only a token chance to influence the elections because of the three-class division of the electorate. What is even more remarkable about the Prussian case is that it was possible to maintain for more than two generations a system of universal manhood suffrage with oral voting at public sessions. Of other countries only Denmark kept up provisions for public voting for any length of time after the introduction of near-universal manhood suffrage. In France the provisions for secrecy were largely nominal far into the era of the Third Republic; mayors and other officials had little difficulty in controlling the votes of the less articulate. In most other countries of western Europe provisions for the secrecy of the vote either preceded or were developed *pari passu* with the extension of the suffrage.

The extraordinary contrast between the electoral systems of Prussia and the Reich from 1870 to 1918 has given rise to a great deal of discussion among historians and political theorists. In Prussia there was a system of extremely unequal, open, and indirect elections; in the Reich, a system of equal, secret, and direct voting, which was for a Diet without decisive influence in the affairs of the nation. There is a wealth of evidence to show that this constellation of institutions was highly dysfunctional; the extension of the suffrage appeared to encourage the participation of the lower classes, but the contrast between the two systems of elections made for widespread resentment and helped to isolate the workers in permanent opposition to the regime.

Ernst Fraenkel has recently suggested that the introduction of secret voting in the Reich contributed decisively to the isolation of the urban working class in *eine soziale Ghettopartei.*[39] What he has in mind is that the deep resentments caused by the Prussian system of unequal and open voting could find secret and safe expression in votes for the Reichstag without any pressure on the ordinary voter to articulate his feelings openly in his community. In the deeply divided German society, the introduction of secret voting in fact tended to keep the newly enfranchised citizens in isolation outside the national political system and clearly did not contribute to the integration of the polity.

Interestingly enough, the evidence for the developments in other countries, particularly in Britain, suggest the opposite. The Ballot Act was passed five years after the decisive extension of the suffrage in 1867 and coincided with the great efforts of the Conservative party to organize clubs of workingmen for political action. The Ballot Act drastically reduced the opportunities for local influence on the worker vote through bribery and chicanery but at the same time made it possible for the "deferent working man" to vote with his superiors without making this an issue in his day-to-day life with his fellow workers. The decisive difference between the developments in Britain and in Germany after the extension of the suffrage in 1867 was no doubt due to the action of the parties; in Britain both the Conservatives and the Liberals developed mass organizations aimed at the new entrants into the electorate; in Germany the parties on the right remained *Nonoratiorenparteien* and left it to the Social Democrats to develop a network of political, social, and cultural organizations for the workers which kept them clearly apart from the rest of the body politic. The introduction of secret voting in both countries accentuated these differences in development.

This contrast raises a series of intriguing questions about the functions for political systems of the introduction of institutions for the safeguarding of the privacy of the voting act. It is remarkable how little attention has been given in the literature to the effects of these profound changes in electoral procedures.[40] What can be said at this stage will of necessity be based on speculation and only scattered and unsystematic evidence.

Tocqueville would clearly have seen in the provisions for secrecy a further extension of the tendency for the centralizing nation-state to enter into direct communication with each individual subject and to undermine all intermediary powers. The essential effect of the secrecy institution is to accentuate the equality of each voter by isolating him from the hierarchical influences in the local community. Through the secrecy provisions the power of the local aristocracy, the notables, and the clergy is further reduced and, to follow the Toqueville model, the tendencies toward centralization correspondingly strengthened.

In sociological terms we might say that in the situation of secret voting the individual adult is cut off from all his roles in the subordinate systems of the household, the neighborhood, the work organization, the church, and the civil association and set to act exclusively in the abstract role as a citizen of the over-all political system; there will be no feedback from what he does in this anonymous role to what he does in the other roles and therefore no need for him to take responsibility for the act of voting in his everyday interaction in his regular environment.

The obvious manifest reasons for introducing the secrecy provisions were the numerous public scandals over attempts at intimidation and bribery. The primary motive for the introduction of the ballot system was to make it possible to escape sanctions from superiors; this was the essence of the Chartists' early demands and has also been a basic concern of working-class movements.

What has been less emphasized in histories of electoral institutions is that the provisions for secrecy could cut the voter off from his peers as well as his superiors. It is often overlooked that there are two distinct elements in the secrecy provisions: the first is to make it *possible* for the voter to keep his decision private and avoid sanctions from those he *does not* want to know; the second is to make it *impossible* for the voter to prove how he voted to those he *does* want to know. The very rigorous rules set up in country after country for the invalidation of all irregularly marked ballots was directed to the second point; they were devised to ensure that the citizen could no longer treat his vote as a commodity for sale. He might well be bribed, but the price per vote would clearly decrease as soon as it proved impossible to check whether it was actually delivered.[41] The salient point here is that by ensuring the complete anonymity of the ballots it became possible not only to reduce bribery of the economically dependent by their superiors but also to reduce the pressures toward conformity and solidarity within the working class.

The secrecy provisions clearly constituted an important mechanism of escape for the politically inarticulate entrants to the electorate. The actual political effects of making the vote private varied enormously, however, with the organizational environments of these citizens.[42] In Germany the Social Democratic party was able, at least in the major cities, to create a highly homogeneous working-class environment through the development of a wide variety of secondary organizations; it became what Sigmund Neumann has called *eine integral Partei*, a party that could claim the allegiance of its voters in all their social roles and therefore could isolate them from disturbing cross-pressures. In this case the introduction of secret voting for the Reichstag contributed further to the isolation of this subsystem since it reduced to a minimum the need for community interaction about political differences. In Britain the mass-directed efforts of the Conservative and the Liberal parties subjected the new entrants into the electorate to conflicting pressures; in this situation the institution of secrecy became an important device for the stabilization of the system since it allowed legitimate withdrawal from open political strife, not just by abstaining from the vote, but also by keeping preferences private and without consequence in everyday life. With increasing social mobility and the cross-cutting influences brought about by expanding associations in the community and the nation, more and more workers must have come under conflicting political pressures and must have felt the need for such provisions for the privatization of the act of voting.

What is crucial here is that this need for privatization tends to be much more marked among the politically inarticulate than among those who for one reason or another have become motivated to concern themselves with public issues. Under regulations for secret voting there is an important *asymmetry* in the system–voter relationship; the system is pledged to the safeguarding of the secrecy of the vote, but the worker is under no legal obligations to keep his preferences private, however little he can do to provide direct proof of his actual behavior at the poll. The institution of secret voting in this way places every citizen before another set of alternative decisions: should he keep his vote completely to himself, as is his right, or should he make his preferences known to others within his primary groups only, to those within the organizations and associations he is part of, or to the general public?

This, in fact, brings about a stratification of the electorate on a "privacy-publicity" dimension: from those who never reveal their vote to anyone to those who publicly take their stand on the alternatives set and openly proclaim how they will or have voted. The active and militant in the political parties clearly cannot make much use of the secrecy provisions which may be important for them in the choice of particular candidates. However, it is part of their community role to commit themselves publicly between the major alternatives.

The Political Mobilization of the Inarticulate Strata

The effects of the secrecy provisions on the behavior of the masses of workers and later of women enfranchised through the final universalization of the suffrage have never been systematically studied. The marked contrasts in the turnout proportions between parallel elections in Prussia and in the Reich have frequently been documented, but no detailed ecological comparisons of results in open elections and results in secret elections have, as far as I have been able to ascertain, ever been attempted. Erik Högh has under way a fascinating analysis of the electoral registers for a sample of Danish constituencies from the period of open elections: here it will be of the greatest interest to analyze the extent of participation and the political preferences of the various categories of manual workers.

Comparative research on the processes of entry into politics is indeed still in its infancy. Tingsten was probably the first to give serious attention to the study of the electoral records for the last to be enfranchised, the workers and the women.[43] His actual analyses, however, did not go beyond the first step in this process, the use of the vote. Statistics on the turnout of the latest entrants into the electorate were available for some countries. Statistics on their further advances into the political arena have generally proved much more difficult to assemble and, what is crucial here, much more difficult to break down by categories of the electorate.

Maurice Duverger assembled an important body of comparative information on party memberships and established trends in the member–

voter ratios for mass parties in western Europe.[44] These, however, were all derived from aggregate figures for entire parties, without any breakdowns by the occupation or the sex of the member. Historical statistics on the recruitment of party members from the ranks of the latest entrants into the electorate may still be assembled for the better-documented parties, but the data are often fragmentary and hard to evaluate. The outlook for historical comparisons is markedly better for the ultimate steps in participation in each system, the competitive participation in candidacies and the actual participation in decision-making in formally established elective offices. For such studies there will generally prove to be an abundance of documentary materials available for coding and counting, but so far hardly anything has been done in any country to assemble such statistics for the lower rungs of political systems. There is a growing body of literature on the recruitment of participants in central, national decision-making,[45] but to reach fuller understanding of the "entry-into-politics" process, we shall clearly have to collect data on candidates and officers in samples of local administrative districts.[46]

Data on the socio-economic backgrounds of party members, candidates, and elected officials can to a large extent be assembled from regularly maintained "bookkeeping" records. Sources of this kind will only rarely, however, offer detailed data for analyses of the paths of recruitment and the over-all patterns of participation in community life, in policy-influencing organization, and in the flow of public and private communication about the polity and its affairs. To ensure a basis for such analyses we will normally have to proceed to direct data gathering, either through local enquiries and the use of informants or through personal interviews. Two distinct strategies of data gathering have been developed in such studies: the one starts out from rosters of organizationally visible participants (for example, party members,[47] party officials,[48] candidates, and elected officials); the other is to select cross-sectional samples from the electorate-at-large and to rely on breakdowns by levels of activity within the samples. Each procedure has its drawbacks as well as its advantages; the ideal solution is a design that combines the two.[49] Studies focusing exclusively on the visible participants will only allow very few comparisons with the rest of the electorate. Cross-sectional studies will allow a wide range of direct comparisons but in most cases will have to be prohibitively large to permit analyses of upper-echelon participants.[50] The basic difficulty, however, lies in the time dimension; in most Western countries it took years after the final extension of the suffrage before adequate survey data started to get accumulated. Any time series that can be established for the recruitment of active participants among the lower strata and among women will be very short indeed. Something can be done through breakdowns by age within the samples, even more through systematic use of recall questions about the activity levels in the family or origin, and through analyses of social and political mobility, but serious gaps in our knowledge of the time sequences in the "entry-into-politics" processes will remain whatever we do in this direction.

However limited the possibilities of historical comparisons, cross-national analyses of survey data are clearly essential in any attempt to reach some understanding of the implications of mass suffrage for the functioning of Western-type political systems. Comparisons of the extent and scope of participation within the lower socio-economic strata can help us to gain insight into the functional importance of the right to vote: What does the suffrage mean for citizens in these strata? Is voting a peripheral activity of little consequence, or does it fit in with a wider range of participant activities in the community, in associations, in politics? Sample surveys can give us data on these wider contexts of participation, and comparisons of such data across communities and across national systems can give us clues to an under-standing of the importance of the structural settings and the alternatives in the system for the recruitment of active participants from the lower strata within each society.

Our recent attempt at comparing data on participation from two systems differing as much from each other as Norway and the United States[51] points to a possible line of research in this direction. Our principal concern here was with the extent of political participation within the lower strata of two electorates: the workers as contrasted with the salaried em-ployees, the professional people and the businessmen; the primary-educated as contrasted with the secondary-educated and the college-educated. We found for both countries the usual differences in turnout between the strata, and we found consistent differences in the same direction for the extent of attention to the mass media during the campaign. We dealt with replications of "micro-micro" breakdowns. What changed the character of the analysis was the finding that there were no such uniform differences between the strata for organizational activity in politics. Using a simple index of participation based on party membership, attendance at meetings, and electoral work, we found no consistent differences between strata in the Norwegian sample but a marked and consistent one in the United States. We interpreted this to reflect the contrast between the two regimes in the alternatives set for the citizens, both as voters and potential recruits to party activity: in Norway a markedly class-distinct, "status-polarized" party system, in the United States much less correspondence between the lines of socio-economic cleavage and the lines of political conflict.[52] To explore this further we proceeded to a third-order "macro-micro-micro" compari-son (CR-B in the typology suggested in Table 1). We placed the parties in the two systems in order of rank according to the proportions of manual workers among their voters, and we found that the class character of the parties made a decisive difference in the recruitment of active participants in political work. In the Norwegian Labour party we found manual workers more likely to be active than middle class voters. In the more heterogeneous Democratic party in the United States we found a tendency in the opposite direction: the level of participation was slightly lower for workers than for middle class voters. The most marked status differentials in participation were found within the parties with the lowest proportions of working-class voters—the opposition parties in Norway and the Republican parties in the United States. This, of course, cannot be taken to be conclusive evidence; the differences were found within nation-wide cross-sections and will need to be tested by categories of communities. However, the findings do suggest important hypotheses for continued comparative research: they accentuate the importance of assembling data on the character of the political choices confronting the worker, on the opportunities open to him for experience and training in organizational skills, and on the channels of recruitment from class-distinct associations such as unions to membership and activity in political parties.

Perhaps the most important set of factors to be taken into account in any cooperative study of participation bears on the organizational bases for the recruitment of active supporters in party-political work: How open, direct, and stable are the channels of recruitment from the given economic cultural, or religious organization to the given party? What are the alternative "policy pay-offs" of other affiliations, other modes of influence, or for the given organization? What are the alternative prospects of achievement and advancement for the active participants in the given organization?

Questions along these lines may be raised for any association or organization and for any party. They are of particular importance in comparative studies of the socio-economic bases for party conflict. In pushing further our tentative comparisons between Norway and the United States, these are exactly the questions we shall want to explore in detail: the character of the tie-ins between the different labor unions and the parties, the distinctiveness of the union votes, the extent of recruitment from union activity to political activity, and the relationships between union activity and participation in other organizations and associations in the community and the nation.[53]

Party-Political Activity, Community Influence, and Organizational Power

With these questions we are already at the heart of another important area for comparative research: the study of factors which cause differences between systems and changes within systems in connection with the importance of party politics and elections in the over-all process of decision-making for the territorial population.

In an attempt to clarify issues in the current debate over method and theory in the study of community power structures, Peter Rossi recently suggested a typology and a set of hypotheses of general importance in comparative research on participation.[54]

Rossi's basic concern is with community conditions making for separation between the political elite and the economic elite. In terms of our discussion the focus of his analysis is on conditions for the development of two distinct channels of decision-making, one based on mass suffrage and party organization, the other based on professional status, managerial position, and the control of wealth.

Rossi specifies three sets of conditions for the development of such separate channels: (1) the *size* of the community—this determines the extent to which local government offices will be full-time roles segregated from any other roles of the incumbents; (2) the strength of *partisan traditions* in local government, the stability and competitive .character of the local party system; and (3) the extent of *"political crystallization*,[55] the extent to which the social structure of the community is reflected in the divisions of the electorate at the polls.

Rossi sees a "natural strain" in community life toward overlap and congruence between the economic and political dominance. This is the normal situation in small communities in the United States, whether run by the Democrats in the South or the Republicans in the North. There is a tendency in the same direction in larger communities with strong traditions of nonpartisan "managerial" governments; such traditions generally tend to strengthen the position of the local economic elite and to prevent the growth of "countervailing powers" deriving their strength from the mass suffrage.

A marked separation between political and economic elites will generally be found in northern cities governed by Democratic politicians deriving their power from socio-economically and ethnically distinct electorates. In such communities the level of status polarization will regularly be found to be as high as in countries with clearly class-divided party systems throughout their territory.[56] If we compared just these United States cities with cities in a country with a major labor party such as Norway we should *not* find differences of the magnitude we reported for nation-wide samples. It is important to note that in the United States a high level of status polarization in the division of local votes does not appear to increase appreciably the recruitment of working class citizens to public positions. Comparative evidence from communities differing in the level of status polarization should not be very difficult to assemble, but the scattered local studies at hand are not always easy to compare for rates of recruitment. Reviewing such evidence as is at hand, Rossi finds that the cleavage between the political and the occupational elites will largely tend to be a cleavage within the world of business and the professions; the leaders in the "public" sectors of such communities are most likely to be recruited from the ranks of small businessmen and lawyers at the hearts of extensive networks of local face-to-face acquaintances while the leaders in the "private" economic and professional sectors are more likely to derive their power from positions in large-scale, territory-wide organizations cutting across a variety of localities.[57]

Here we touch on an important theme on the analysis of the implications of mass suffrage for the functioning of pluralist political systems: What changes will occur in the over-all processes of decision-making with the mobilization of the less articulate electorates for political action and with the consequent growth of independent centers of electoral power?

Rossi hypothesizes that the three basic strategies used by economic elites in countering the effects of this growth of electoral power will be these: (1) the promotion of nonpartisan electoral systems and of technically neutral administrative agencies; (2) the intensified proliferation of privately controlled community institutions and voluntary civic associations serving as instruments of influence and pressure in conflicts over local policies; and (3) the development of state-wide or nationwide interest organizations to influence policies beyond the control of the local political elite.

Hypotheses of this kind may be tested either diachronically or synchronically. Several attempts have been made to establish trends toward a withdrawal of the economic elites from local politics in the United States over the last decades,[58] but the factors accounting for such trends are complex and certainly cannot be attributed solely to the growth of independent electoral power centers. Synchronic comparisons of the extent of private policy-influencing activity through community institutions and voluntary associations have, to my knowledge, never been attempted in the United States. Rossi's hypothesis is that such activities would be more extensive when the separation of the economic from the political elite in the community is more marked. The basic task here would be to find some meaningful measure of the "importance" of the private institutions and the voluntary associations in each community; mere statistics on size of memberships and the economic roles of the active participants would not be likely to take us very far in this direction.

Whatever the technical difficulties of testing the hypotheses suggested by Rossi, the underlying reasoning about the processes of decision-making in mass-suffrage systems will clearly prove important in future attempts at cross-national comparisons.

The most straightforward of the tasks to be taken up in comparative research on these wider contexts of participation is the collation of national statistics on the recruitment of members and officers in different categories of voluntary associations. Studies of the linkages between association memberships and political activity have been undertaken in several countries over the last years,[59] and evidence on the character of such linkages can now be assembled for a wide range of structurally different systems. The studies so far undertaken have focused on social activities in the community and in wider organizations as sets of conditioning variables in explaining levels of political partisanship and participation. The simplest way of establishing the linkages have been by direct counts of the total number of nonpolitical memberships and offices held by each respondent and by analyses of the correlations with indices of political activity. In moving toward comparative analyses of channels of influence on community policy-making it will clearly be essential to go beyond such crude correlations; voluntary associations and private organizations will have to be differentiated not only according to their substantive goals and their membership criteria[60] but also in terms of the socio-economic background and political partisanship of their clientele and their leaders and, what is of particular importance here, in terms of the "pay-off" probabilities of action through parties vs. action directly on policy makers and administrative agencies. Detailed studies along these lines would require the co-ordination of institutional analyses and surveys of samples of community leaders as well as of the rank-and-file electorate. Attempts in this direction have been made in some countries,[61] but research in this area is still at a very early stage of development.

Comparative research along these lines may help us to gain further insight into the implications of the processes of political change in systems undergoing economic growth. With the early phases of industrialization went a variety of tendencies toward both greater integration of the national decision-making machinery and a widening of the representative bases of each regime. The introduction of mass suffrage made it possible to mobilize the lower strata of economically dependent citizens into distinct political parties and set the stage for the development of new channels of influence on the processes of decision at local and national levels. At the same time, and partly in reaction to these developments, most systems of the West witnessed an extraordinary growth in the scope and activity of voluntary associations and interest organizations. With the continued growth and diversification of each national economy, these networks of organizations tended to cut across the earlier party-political divisions and to create cross pressures making for a lowering of the polarization in the system.[62] If Rossi is right in his conjectures, we are faced here with an intriguing process of historical dialectics; the extension of the suffrage increased the chances for a status polarization of national politics, but this very polarization brought about a proliferation of sectional and functional organizations which in turn tended to soften the over-all strains in the system and reduce the level of polarization.[63] What we tend to find is an accumulation of forces making for a narrowing of the alternatives for national politics, a fragmentation of the networks of policy-influencing organizations, and a consequent decline in the importance of the decisions of the electorate-at-large. This may tend to lower the level of general political participation and to alienate from politics sizable sections of the once enfranchised citizenry, leaving the basic decisions to a bargaining process between interest organizations, parties, and agencies and departments of the national bureaucracy. We see tendencies in these directions in many countries of the West; the developments toward *Entideologisierung* and "all party governments" are cases in point.[64] We know far too little about the dynamics of these developments, and we need to do much more to facilitate cooperation and coordination in the study of these problems in different countries.

NOTES

* This paper is a product of work I undertook during 1959–60 as a Fellow of the Center for Advanced Study in the Behavioral Sciences at Stanford, California. I am greatly indebted to the director and staff of the center for all aid and assistance in my work. I also wish to acknowledge my intellectual debts for ideas gleaned in stimulating discussions with Reinhard Bendix, Angus Campbell, James Coleman, Samuel Eldersveld, Heinz Eulau, Daniel Katz, Herbert Kaufman, V. O. Key, Jr., Seymour Martin Lipset, Robert McKenzie, Robert Merton, Talcott Parsons, Peter Rossi, and Carl Schorske.

[1] H. Tingsten, *Political Behavior* (London: P. S. King, 1937).

[2] Large numbers of tables for the social and religious backgrounds of voting in western Europe have been assembled in J. J. deJong, *Overheid en onderdaan* (Wageningen, Netherlands: Zomer & Keunings, 1956) and in M. P. Fogarty, *Christian Democracy in Western Europe* (Notre Dame, Ind.: University of Notre Dame Press, 1957), Chap. 22. Matti Dogan has compared western European survey data on the electoral behavior of women in "Le comportement politique des femmes dans les pays de l'Europe occidentale." *La Condition Sociale de la Femme* (Brussels: Institut de Sociologie Solvay, 1956), pp. 147–86, and on the party allegiances of workers in "Le vote ouvrier en Europe occidentale," *Revue Française de Sociologie*, Vol. 1 (1960), pp. 25–54. S. M. Lipset has assembled an extensive file of tabulations and IBM cards from a wide variety of surveys of a number of Western countries and has reported some of his findings in *Political Man* (Garden City, N.Y.: Doubleday and Co., 1960) especially Chaps. 6 and 7.

[3] On the possibility of developing an international archive of raw data from interview surveys, see a report to the Ford Foundation by York Lucci and Stein Rokkan, *A Library Center of Survey Research Data* (New York: Columbia University School of Library Service, 1957). The Roper Public Opinion Center at Williams College has now built up a substantial archive of IBM cards and other records of surveys not only from the United States, but also from a number of other countries. The files of the center have been open to qualified scholars, but the center itself does not undertake comparative evaluations or analyses of the data assembled.

[4] On the problem of "levels" in comparative studies see H. C. J. Duijker and S. Rokkan, "Organizational Aspects of Cross-National Social Research," *Journal of Social Issues*, Vol. 10 (1954), pp. 8–24; and S. Rokkan, "Current Sociological Research: A Note on Trends toward International Comparability," *Transactions of the Third World Congress of Sociology*, Vol. 7 (1956), pp. 51–60.

[5] Earlier attempts include: the nine-nation UNESCO survey of national stereotypes, only peripherally concerned with political behavior, W. Buchanan and H. Cantril, *How Nations See Each Other* (Urbana: University of Illinois Press, 1953); the surveys carried out by the Organization for Comparative Social Research of teachers' politics in seven countries of western Europe, S. Rokkan, "Party Preferences and Opinion Patterns in Western Europe: A Comparative Analysis," *International Social Science Bulletin*, Vol. 7 (1955), pp. 575–96; the Columbia University surveys of opinions in six Middle Eastern countries, D. Lerner, *The Passing of Traditional Society* (Glencoe, Ill.: The Free Press, 1958); the comparative "élite" interviews conducted in Britain, France and West Germany under the direction of Daniel Lerner and currently under analysis at the Center for International Studies at M.I.T.; the studies conducted in a number of countries by the Institute for International Social Research on "protest voting," H. Cantril, *The Politics of Despair* (New York: Basic Books, 1958), and on the foreign policy views of legislators, L. A. Free, *Six Allies and a Neutral* (Glencoe, Ill.: The Free Press, 1959).

[6] For details of the Norwegian program, see S. Rokkan and H. Valen, "Parties, Elections, and Political Behaviour in the Northern Countries: A Review of Recent Research," O. Stammer, ed., *Politische Forschung* (Köln-Opladen, Germany: Westdeutscher Verlag, 1960), pp. 120–25, with bibliography at pp. 237-49. An analysis of the effects of differences in the degree of "politicization" of local elections is given in S. Rokkan and H. Valen, "The Mobilization of the Periphery," *Acta Sociologica*, Vol. 6 (1962).

[7] V. O. Key, Jr., *Politics, Parties and Pressure Groups*, 4th ed. (New York: Thomas Y. Crowell Company, 1958), p. 638.

[8] The simple technique of "élite sociometry" used in F. Hunter, *Community Power Structure* (Chapel Hill: University of North Carolina Press, 1953), was taken up in a wide variety of local studies but has lately come under vigorous attack from Robert A. Dahl and his co-workers at Yale University: see Dahl's article "A Critique of the Ruling Élite Model," *American Political Science Review*, Vol. 52 (1958), pp. 463–69; and the detailed discussion of studies of this type in N. W. Polsby, *Community Power and Political Theory* (unpublished Ph.D. dissertation, Yale University, 1960).

[9] Peter H. Rossi has suggested a typology of local political systems and a set of hypotheses about the socio-cultural bases of community politics which can only be put to a test through such "macro-micro" studies: see "Power and Community Structure," *Midwest Journal of Political Science*, Vol. 4 (1960), pp. 390–401, and "Theory and Method in the Study of Power in the Local Community," a paper delivered at the Conference on Metropolitan Leadership, Northwestern University, April 1960.

[10] P. Cutright and P. H. Rossi, "Grass Roots Politicians and the Vote," *American Sociological Review*, Vol. 23 (1958), pp. 171–79; cf. Rossi and Cutright, "The Impact of Party Organization in an Industrial Setting," in M. Janowitz, ed., *Community Power Systems* (Glencoe, Ill.: The Free Press, 1961), pp. 81–116.

[11] D. Katz and S. J. Eldersveld, "The Impact of Local Party Activity upon the Electorate," *Public Opinion Quarterly*, Vol. 25 (1961), pp. 1–27.

[12] W. McPhee and W. Glazer, *Congressional Voting* (to be published soon by the Free Press of Glencoe, Ill.).

[13] A. Campbell and W. Miller, "The Motivational Basis of Straight and Split Ticket Voting," *American Political Science Review*, Vol. 51 (1957), pp. 273–312. See also A. Campbell, P. E. Converse, W. E. Miller, and D. E. Stokes, *The American Voter* (New York: John Wiley & Sons. Inc., 1960), Chap. 11.

[14] W. Miller, "One-Party Politics and the Voter," *American Political Science Review*, Vol. 50 (1956), pp. 707–25.

[15] Social anthropologists have, for obvious reasons, paid more attention to these problems than other social scientists: cf. J. W. Whiting, "The Cross-cultural Method," in

G. Lindzey, ed., *Handbook of Social Psychology* (Cambridge, Mass.: Addison-Wesley, 1954), Vol. 1, pp. 523–31; and O. Lewis, "Comparisons in Social Anthropology," in W. L. Thomas, Jr., ed., *Current Anthropology* (Chicago: University of Chicago Press, 1956), pp. 259–92.

[16] None of the discussions of the methodology of comparative politics published over the last decade deal in any detail with microcomparisons. G. Heckscher's account of the IPSA symposium, *The Study of Comparative Government and Politics* (London: Allen & Unwin, 1957) has hardly more than one page about cross-national analyses of electoral statistics. The most important contribution to theory development and model construction in comparative politics is Gabriel Almond's introduction to G. Almond and J. S. Coleman, eds., *The Politics of Developing Areas* (Princeton, N.J.: Princeton University Press, 1960), pp. 3–64. This, however, is only indirectly concerned with microcomparisons.

[17] D. Easton, "An Approach to the Analysis of Political Systems," *World Politics*, Vol. 9 (1957), pp. 383–400. Compare the further development of this model in Almond and Coleman, *op. cit.*, pp. 12–25.

[18] For formalizations of such "micro-macro" interdependencies, see particularly A. Downs, *An Economic Theory of Democracy* (New York: Harper and Brothers, 1957), Chap. 8.

[19] The possibility that the realignment of voters brought about by continued economic growth will push further toward between-party consensus is discussed in S. Rokkan, "National Consensus and Political Participation" (Stanford: Center for Advanced Study in the Behavioral Sciences, 1960, mimeo.).

[20] Tingsten, *op. cit.*, pp. 126–27, 170–72. Cf. R. E. Lane, *Political Life* (Glencoe, Ill.: The Free Press, 1959), pp. 262–64.

[21] S. M. Lipset and J. Linz, *The Social Bases of Political Diversity* (Stanford: Center for Advanced Study in the Behavioral Sciences, 1956), Chap. 7; A. Kornhauser, *The Politics of Mass Society* (Glencoe, Ill.: The Free Press, 1959), Chap. 12.

[22] S. Rokkan, "Citizen Participation in Political Life: Introduction," *International Social Science Journal*, Vol. 12 (1960), pp. 13–14.

[23] Campbell, *et al.*, *op. cit.*, pp. 24–32.

[24] The concepts of "interest articulation" and "interest aggregation" are discussed in detail in Almond and Coleman, *op. cit.*, pp. 33–45.

[25] For an attempt to develop this concept in detail, see K. Deutsch, *Nationalism and Social Communication* (New York: John Wiley & Sons, Inc., 1953), pp. 100–101. For a fascinating analysis of the role of the mass media in such processes of political mobilization, see Lerner, *op. cit.*

[26] The term "political mobilization" is discussed by D. A. Rustow, *Politics and Westernization in the Near East* (Princeton, N.J.: Center for International Studies, 1956), pp. 16–18. Comparative studies of the impact of mass suffrage in underdeveloped countries are essential for an understanding of factors making for integration or dissensus: cf. W. J. M. Mackenzie and K. Robinson, eds., *Five Elections in Africa* (Oxford: at the Clarendon Press, 1960); and T. E. Smith, *Elections in Developing Countries* (London: Macmillan and Co., Ltd., 1960). A fascinating account of the effects of the introduction of a system of mass elections in a traditional, highly stratified society is J. J. Maquet and M. d'Hertefelt, *Élections en Société féodale: une étude sur l'introduction du vote populaire au Ruanda-Urundi* (Brussels: Académie royale des Sciences coloniales, 1959).

[27] The most remarkable single-nation study of such processes of change is T. H. Marshall, *Citizenship and Social Class* (London: Cambridge University Press, 1950).

[28] P. F. Lazarsfeld *et al.*, *The People's Choice* (New York: Duell, Sloan and Pearce, Inc., 1944). Similar findings are reported for Sweden by B. Anderson and C. O. Melen, "Lazarsfeld's Two-Step Hypothesis: Data from Swedish Surveys," *Acta Sociologica*, Vol. 4 (1959), pp. 20–23. Cf. also L. Himmelstand, *Social Pressures Attitudes and Democratic Processes* (Stockholm: Almquist & Wiksell, 1960). sect. 2.5.5.

[29] See particularly B. Berelson, "Democratic Theory and Public Opinion," *Public Opinion Quarterly*, Vol. 16 (1952), pp. 313–30; B. Berelson, P. F. Lazarsfeld, and W. N. McPhee, *Voting* (Chicago: University of Chicago Press, 1954), pp. 314–17; R. S. Milne

and H. C. Mackenzie, *Marginal Seat* (London: The Hansard Society, 1958), Chap. 13; Lane, *op. cit.*, pp. 340–48; Campbell *et al.*, *op. cit.*, Chap. 20.

[30] A. de Tocqueville, *De la Démocratie en Amérique* (Paris: Gosselin, 1835), Vol. 1, Chap. 4.

[31] Cf. particularly H. Gollwitzer, "Der Cäsarismus Napoleons III im Widerhall der öffentlichen Meinung Deutschlands," *Historische Zeitschrift*, Vol. 173 (1952), pp. 23–76.

[32] For the developments leading to the Second Reform Act, see particularly C. Seymour, *Electoral Reform in England and Wales* (New Haven, Conn.: Yale University Press, 1916). For the decision of the North German Federation, see H. Oncken, *Historisch-politische Aufsätze u. Reden* (Munich: Oldenbourg, 1914), Vol. 2. pp. 157–92; and W. Gagel, *Die Wahlrechtsfrage in der Geschichte der deutschen liberalen Parteien* (Düsseldorf: Droste, 1959).

[33] The London *Times*, April 18, 1883, quoted in R. T. McKenzie, *British Political Parties* (London: Macmillan and Co., 1955), p. 147. The most recent discussion of the Conservative belief of "one man, one vote, one value" is in Sir Ivor Jennings, *Party Politics, I: Appeal to the People* (Cambridge: Cambridge University Press, 1960), pp. 18–28.

[34] E. R. Augst, *Bismarcks Stellung zum parlamentarischen Wahlrecht* (Diss. Leipzig, 1916); and G. Mayer, *Bismarck u. Lassalle* (Berlin: Dietz, 1929).

[35] Mayer, *op. cit.*, p. 36; E. Eyck, *Bismarck* (Erlenbach-Zürich: Rentsch, 1945), Vol. 1, p. 601.

[36] Letter to Bismarck, January 13, 1864, in Mayer, *op. cit.*, p. 81.

[37] For a general review of these developments, see K. Braunias, *Das parlamentarische Wahlrecht* (Berlin: de Gruyter, 1932), Vol. 2, pp. 35–45.

[38] For secondary sources see: C. Seymour and D. P. Frary, *How the World Votes* (Springfield, Mass.: Nichols, 1918), 2 vols.: and Braunias, *op. cit.*, Vol. 1.

[39] E. Fraenkel, "Parlament und öffentliche Meinung," in *Zur Geschichte und Problematik der Demokratie: Festgabe für H. Herzfeld* (Berlin: Duncker & Humblot, 1958), p. 178.

[40] The formal history of the Anglo-Saxon systems is well covered in J. H. Wigmore, *The Australian Ballot System* (Boston: Boston Book Co., 1889); and E. D. Evans, *A History of the Australian Ballot System in the United States* (Chicago: University of Chicago Press, 1917). On other systems, see G. Mayer *Das parlamentarische Wahlrecht* (Berlin: Haering, 1901), pp. 528–65. Also, see Braunias, *op. cit.*, Vol. 2, pp. 168–74.

[41] See Seymour, *op. cit.*, pp. 434–35. For details on the effect on the "vote market," see H. J. Hanham, *Elections and Party Management: Politics in the Time of Disraeli and Gladstone* (London: Longmans, Green and Co., 1959), Chap. 13.

[42] This, of course, is the theme of Ostrogorski's volumes. For a detailed account of developments in England, Scotland, Wales, and Ireland, see Hanham, *op. cit.* For developments in Germany see particularly G. A. Ritter, *Die Arbeiterbewegung im wilhelminischen Reich* (Berlin: Dahlem, Colloquium, 1959); and T. A. Nipperdey, *Die Organisation der deutschen Parteien vor 1918* (Düsseldorf: Droste, 1961).

[43] Tingsten's work on the behavior of recently enfranchised groups needs to be completed and systematized on a variety of points. Quite particularly, it would be of great theoretical interest to undertake comparative analyses of the rate of "politicization" in the peripheral areas of each nation-state, the remote, less "modernized" areas of the national territory. This is a central concern in our current studies of electoral participation in Norway, to be reported on in the volume *Valg i Norge*, now in preparation. We find clear evidence that women are least prone to vote in the less accessible, least politicized areas along the coast. It is of interest to note that similar differences in the votes for women appeared in German statistics just after the introduction of female suffrage: cf. Gabriele Bremme, *Die politische Rolle der Frau in Deutschland* (Göttingen, Germany: Vandenhoeck & Ruprecht, 1956), p. 45, but have tended to disappear in postwar elections. This has been interpreted in terms of a process of "mobilization" by E. Paul in E. Paul, ed., *Wahlen und Wähler in Westdeutschland* (Villingen, Germany: Ring-Verlag, 1960), pp. 156–63.

[44] M. Duverger, *Political Parties* (London: Methuen, 1954), Chap. 2.

[45] Cf. H. D. Lasswell *et al.*, *The Comparative Study of Elites* (Stanford: Stanford University Press, 1952); D. Marvick, ed., *Political Decision-Makers: Recruitment and Performance* (Glencoe, Ill.: The Free Press, 1961).

[46] Our Norwegian program of research on parties, elections, and political behavior includes a study of the recruitment to local elective offices, but so far only for elections after World War II: cf. Rokkan and Campbell, *op. cit.*, pp. 81–84.

[47] Two examples are: O. Rantala's work on the membership of the Conservative party in Finland, *Konservatiivinen puolueyhteiso* (Helsinki: Tammi, 1956); and Renate Mayntz's study of the CDU members in a district of Berlin, *Partieengruppen in der Grossstadt* (Cologne: Westdeutscher Verlag, 1959).

[48] An example is H. Valen and D. Katz, "An Electoral Contest in a Norwegian Community," in M. Janowitz, *op. cit.*, pp. 207–36.

[49] Two attempts in this direction are: Katz and Eldersveld, *op. cit.;* and Valen and Katz, *op cit.*

[50] This, of course, will vary with the administrative structure and the population density of the country. Figures for Finland and Norway indicate that up to 2 per cent of any nationwide sample will be candidates for offices in local elections: see the articles on "Finland" and "Norway and the United States of America" in S. Rokkan, ed., "Citizen Participation in Political Life," *International Social Science Journal*, Vol. 12 (1960), esp. pp. 31–32 and 81–84.

[51] Rokkan and Campbell, *op. cit.*,

[52] For general discussion of "status-polarization," see Campbell *et al.*, *op. cit.*, Chap. 13.

[53] A report of a comparison of union-party tie-ins is in progress.

[54] Rossi, "Theory and Method in the Study of Power in the Local Community."

[55] This is the term introduced by G. E. Lenski, *American Sociological Review*, Vol. 19 (1954), pp. 405–13; in this context it is synonymous with the term "status polarization" used elsewhere in this paper.

[56] Correlations by precinct between economic/ethnic indices and the Democratic vote have been found to be very high in such cities: see Rossi and Cutright, *op. cit.;* and Katz and Eldersveld, *op. cit.*

[57] This contrast is discussed in some detail by Rossi in a thought-provoking paper recently prepared for the Fund for the Advancement of Education," 'Public' and 'Private' Leadership in America" (May, 1960, mimeo.).

[58] R. O. Schulze, "The Role of Economic Dominants in Community Power Structure," *American Sociological Review*, Vol. 23 (1958), pp. 3–9; also: "The Bifurcation of Power in a Satellite City" in M. Janowitz, *op. cit.*, pp. 19–80.

[59] For the United States, see the secondary analyses of NORC data by C. R. Wright and H. H. Hyman, "Voluntary Association Memberships of American Adults." *American Sociological Review*, Vol. 23 (1958), pp. 284–94. For Finland, see: Erik Allardt *et al.*, "On the Cumulative Nature of Leisure-Time Activities," *Acta Sociologica*, Vol. 3 (1958), pp. 165–72. For Germany, see: E. Reigzrotzski, *Soziale Verflechtungen in der Bundersrepublik* (Tübingen, Germany: Mohr, 1956). For Norway see: S. Rokkan, "Electoral Activity, Party Membership and Organizational Influence," *Acta Sociologica*, Vol. 4 (1959), pp. 25–37. For Sweden, see: H. Zetterberg, "Voluntary Associations and Organized Power," *Industria International* (in press).

[60] Cf. A. M. Rose, *Theory and Method in the Social Sciences* (Minneapolis: University of Minnesota Press, 1954), Chap. 3.

[61] Reports are in preparation on the efforts made toward this end within the Norwegian program of research on parties, elections, and political behavior.

[62] This point of view has been developed in further detail for Sweden by H. Zetterberg, *op cit.*

[63] N. W. Polsby, *op. cit.*, Chap. 7, has suggested such a cyclical pattern for developments in United States cities since the peak inflows of ethnically distinct lower class citizens.

[64] Cf. especially O. Kirchheimer, "The Waning of Opposition in Parliamentary Regimes," *Social Research*, Vol. 24 (1957), pp. 127–56; and A. Vulpius, *Die Allparteienregierung* (Frankfurt a/M: Metzner, 1957).

CHAPTER 16

Some Effects of Interest Group
Strength in State Politics*

Lewis A. Froman, Jr.

The literature on interest groups is, by and large, either heavily abstract and theoretical or highly concrete and descriptive. There are, on the one hand, several attempts to provide a theoretical framework for the study of interest groups, the major foci being either "the group basis of politics"[1] or "mass society."[2] On the other hand are numerous case-studies which describe in some detail, either for a particular policy[3] or for a particular interest group,[4] relevant political activities which lead to inferred conclusions about the impact that such groups have on the issue or issues. What we lack, and what is needed to raise the study of interest groups to the level of empirically-based generalization, are studies which collect data and generalize about interest groups using multiple units of analysis.

This observation is not meant to depreciate or undervalue the important theoretical and descriptive contributions which have been made in the examination of the role of interest groups in governmental systems. It is simply to state a fact about the literature and to plead for more systematic data collection and empirically-based generalization from which verified propositions about interest groups may emerge.

I think there are two major reasons why the literature on interest groups lacks a comparative base. First, many of the concepts which are employed in theories about interest groups are difficult to operationalize for data collection. Such concepts as "cohesion," "access," "resources," etc., represent complex phenomena and would involve a good deal of effort to apply rigorously and empirically. Take, for example, the interesting proposition that *ceteris paribus*, "interest groups with high cohesion are more effective than interest groups with low cohesion." Clearly this is an important assertion which attempts to explain why some interest groups may have more influence than others. How such a proposition might be tested is, unfortunately, also clear. Simply take a sample of

Reprinted from *American Political Science Review*, Vol. 60, No. 4 (December, 1966), pp. 952–62, by permission of the American Political Science Association.

interest groups, devise measures of group cohesion and political effectiveness, collect the data on both measures, and see whether the proposition is confirmed or invalidated.

Second, it is usually very difficult and expensive to collect data on a wide variety of groups which might then be used for purposes of generalization. Such data is not generally available, and what is available is often incomplete, inaccurate, or both. Even to collect such relatively simple data as group size often presents serious problems in compiling membership lists, deciding who is a member and who isn't, perhaps identifying those who feel some allegiance to the group but who may participate in the activities of the group only minimally, and other equally knotty problems. To attempt to determine, across groups, what difference a particular independent variable (such as cohesion, group size, leadership ability, etc.) may have in the distribution of political outcomes raises formidable data problems indeed.

This paper will suggest how a comparative base for generalization about the activity of interest groups may be developed. I will attempt to answer the question: Do political systems that vary in the strength of their interest groups also vary in a systematic way with regard to certain structural and output variables within their respective political systems? That is, can we explain certain differences in political systems by knowing something about the strength of interest groups within the system? The data to be employed will be for forty-eight state governments within the United States.[5] It is by now a truism to assert that states may provide a convenient laboratory to test certain propositions about politics. The number of states, the fact that they are all part of a larger political system (and hence share many things in common) while at the same time providing a certain amount of diversity make the states a useful data source in which to generalize and test political hypotheses.

THE FIRST SET OF DEPENDENT VARIABLES

Political scientists have long been interested in questions regarding constitutions and constitution-making. By and large the focus of attention has been on national constitutions and more particularly the Constitution of the United States. It is very difficult, however, to make generalizations about constitutions if the unit of analysis is a single document.

What will concern us here is how state constitutions differ in certain respects from one another, and how these differences might be explained. There are, of course, a large number of possible differences in state constitutions. State constitutions may vary, for example, in the kinds of governments they establish (unicameral vs. bicameral legislatures, a large number of elected executive officials vs. a large number of appointed officials, elected vs. appointed judiciaries, etc.). State constitutions may also vary in the detail in which they cover various aspects of government, and in the discretion which they give to public officials to carry out certain functions. They may also vary in the specific content which they give to questions of public policy (labor practices, regulation of utilities, transportation problems, etc.).

The differences among state constitutions which are of most interest to us here have to do with how specific and comprehensive they are, how easy or difficult they are to amend, how often proposals are made to amend the constitution, and how often the respective constitutions are in fact changed. More specifically, there are four dependent variables in which we will be primarily interested.[6]

1. *Length of Constitution.* State constitutions vary greatly in their length. We are not, however, interested in length of constitutions in and of itself but rather assume that the longer the constitution the greater the range of activity it attempts to cover and the more specific and detailed it is in its provisions. Length of constitution, then, will be used as an indirect measure of extent of coverage and specificity.

2. *Number of Amendments Proposed.* What we are interested in here is the number of official proposals which have been made to amend the respective state constitutions. The measure to be employed will control for age of constitution by taking the number of proposed changes for each state and dividing by the number of years the constitution has been operative.

3. *Number of Amendments Adopted.* This measure is similar to the previous one except that amendments actually adopted rather than simply proposed is the unit employed. Age of constitution is again appropriately controlled.

4. *Percentage of Amendments Adopted.* This is the ratio of amendments adopted to amendments proposed for each state and is expressed in a simple percentage.

Table 1 gives some indication of how the states vary on these four measures.

As can be seen from Table 1, there is a wide diversity among states with respect to these four variables. Now, assuming that constitutions are one of the mechanisms through which advantages and disadvantages are distributed in a political system, we would expect that differences in length of constitutions and the frequency with which they are amended would help us to understand, in some measure, how responsive states are to demands made by groups within the political system.

Table 1. Median and Range for States on the Four Dependent Variables

	Median	Range
Length of Constitution (No. of words)	15,000	4,840–227,000
Number of Amendments Proposed Per Year	1.35	.31–12.63
Number of Amendments Adopted Per Year	.65	.10–9.98
Percentage of Amendments Adopted	58%	23%–94%

Source: *The Book of the States, 1964–1965* (Chicago: The Council of State Governments, 1964), p. 12.

THE INDEPENDENT VARIABLE

The role of interest groups in political systems is an extremely important, and hotly contested, open question. At one level we can talk of the functions which most interest groups, or interest groups collectively, perform in political systems. David Truman, Robert Dahl, William Kornhauser, and V. O. Key, Jr., for example, suggest that, among other functions, interest groups:[7]

1. Channel communications to decision-makers,
2. help structure alternative policy choices,
3. act as buffers between the government and the people,
4. help check demands made by others,
5. provide for functional representation,
6. compartmentalize access to decision-makers,
7. lead to a system of minorities rule,
8. provide people with an emotional outlet.

This kind of analysis helps us to understand how interest groups in general fit in with other aspects of a society and polity. What we are interested in here, however, is a somewhat different question. It would be useful to know whether variations in interest group strength make a difference with respect to structural and output variables of political systems. More specifically, do interest groups vary in strength from state to state, and if so, might this variation help to explain why certain other variables also vary?

The major question of this section, then, is how may states be classified according to strength of interest groups? The answer, "obviously," is that some measure of "strength" must be developed by which the states may be ranked. This task would, equally obviously, be an exceedingly difficult, expensive, and time-consuming enterprise.

It is possible, however, to employ a probably less valid and less reliable technique to measure interest group strength. The Committee on American

Legislatures of the American Political Science Association sent question-naires to political scientists located in the various states asking them to judge whether interest groups in their respective states were strong, moder-ately strong, or weak.[8] On the basis of the responses to this questionnaire the Committee then classified state interest groups into the three categories.

Judgmental measures are not unique with this study. Several psycho-logical measures, for example, rely on this technique (rating scales of various kinds).[9] Seymour Martin Lipset's seminal piece on social requisites of democracy also relies heavily on a judgmental measure of whether countries are democratic and stable.[10] A recent comparative study of polyarchy also employs ratings on several variables.[11]

It is not that, if the authors mentioned above had their "druthers," they would choose this technique rather than another. It is simply that it has advantages in reducing crucial costs of research. The use of this type of measure certainly invites some criticisms, and where it is used it should be viewed as providing only tentative answers to the questions which it attempts to answer. It does, however, provide a useful first step until better resources become available.

On the basis of this classification of state interest group systems into strong, moderate, and weak, Harmon Zeigler, in a very useful study, relates this classification to other variables which help to show why states are likely to vary in strength of interest groups, and how such variation is related to political party structure and legislative cohesion. Zeigler finds that states with stronger interest groups are also more likely to be (1) one-party states, (2) states which have legislative parties with weak cohesion, (3) less urban, (4) less wealthy, and (5) less industrial. Table 2 presents these findings from Zeigler's study.

What we will do now is to employ the Committee's classification of state interest group systems and see whether this classification helps us to explain variations among the states in the four dependent variables pre-viously described.[12]

THEORY, HYPOTHESES, AND FINDINGS

Why would one expect strength of interest groups and certain aspects of state constitutions to be related to one another, and what would be the expected relationships?

The answer to the first part of the question, the theory underlying the expected associations, is that where interest groups are stronger one manifestation of this greater strength as compared with weaker interest group systems would be a larger number of requests for, and the actual giving of special privileges and advantages. This distribution of special

Table 2. The Strength of Pressure Groups in Varying Political and Economic Situations

Social Conditions	Types of Pressure System[a]		
	Strong[b]	Moderate[c]	Weak[d]
	(24 states)	(14 states)	(7 states)
Party Competition			
One-party	33.3%	0%	0%
Modified One-Party	37.5%	42.8%	0%
Two-Party	29.1%	57.1%	100.0%
Cohesion of Parties in Legislature			
Weak Cohesion	75.0%	14.2%	0%
Moderate Cohesion	12.5%	35.7%	14.2%
Strong Cohesion	12.5%	50.0%	85.7%
Socio-Economic Variables			
Urban	58.6%	65.1%	73.3%
Per Capita Income	$1,900	$2,335	$2,450
Industrialization Index	88.8	92.8	94.0

[a] Alaska, Hawaii, Idaho, New Hampshire, and North Dakota are not classified or included.

[b] Alabama, Arizona, Arkansas, California, Florida, Georgia, Iowa, Kentucky, Louisiana, Maine, Michigan, Minnesota, Mississippi, Montana, Nebraska, New Mexico, North Carolina, Oklahoma, Oregon, South Carolina, Tennessee, Texas, Washington, Wisconsin.

[c] Delaware, Illinois, Kansas, Maryland, Massachusetts, Nevada, New York, Ohio, Pennsylvania, South Dakota, Utah, Vermont, Virginia, West Virginia.

[d] Colorado, Connecticut, Indiana, Missouri, New Jersey, Rhode Island, Wyoming.

Source: Harmon Zeigler, "Interest Groups in the States," in Herbert Jacob and Kenneth N. Vines (eds.), Politics in the American States (Boston: Little, Brown, 1965), p. 114.

advantages would be predicted to show up in a political system in a number of ways. For example, we might hypothesize that in states with stronger interest groups the latter would have relatively greater success with state legislatures in receiving legal protection and encouragement for their activities. It would also not be unreasonable to suppose that states with stronger interest groups would differ with respect to the ways in which laws are administered and adjudicated. It would be interesting for example, to observe if such states also differ in the manner in which administrative personnel are recruited and appointed and, consequently, in the decisions which are reached concerning various regulations and distributions within the political system. An investigation of part of this hypothesis will appear near the end of this paper.

We would also, however, expect there to be a relationship between strength of interest groups and state constitutions. If we assume that constitutions essentially lay out important ground rules by which the game of politics will be played, and that they may place certain restrictions or give certain dispensations to the players involved in the game, then we would expect variations in state constitutions to be intimately related to variations in other aspects of political systems. Generally, we would expect state constitutions in states which have stronger interest groups to reflect, in certain systematic ways, a greater amount of interest group activity than do the constitutions in states with weaker interest groups. More specifically, we would hypothesize the following relationships:

1. The stronger the interest groups, the greater the length of state constitutions.

This hypothesis follows in that states with stronger interest groups would be predicted to make greater efforts to achieve special advantage through constitutional provisions which refer to their activities. These efforts would result in longer and more detailed constitutions than in states with weaker interest groups. Table 3 presents data which tests this hypothesis.

As can be seen from Table 3, the twenty-four states which are classified as strong-interest-group states have constitutions which average 33,233 words in length; the fourteen states which are classified as moderate in interest group strength have constitutions which average 17,985 in length; and the seven states which are classified as weak in interest group strength have constitutions which average 14,828 in length.

2. The stronger the interest groups, the greater the number of proposed amendments.

Table 3. Relationships Between Strength of Interest Groups and Three Dependent Variables

Strength of Interest Groups	Average Length of Constitution	N^1	Average No. of Proposed Amendments Per Year	N^2	Average No. of Adopted Amendments Per Year	N^3
Strong	33,233	24	2.97	19	1.58	22
Moderate	17,985	14	1.14	12	.76	14
Weak	14,828	7	.68	5	.41	7

[1] Alaska and Hawaii are excluded from this and the following tables. In addition, Idaho, New Hampshire, and North Dakota were not classified by strength of interest groups.

[2] Arkansas, Colorado, Connecticut, Delaware, Iowa, Michigan, North Carolina, Utah, and Washington are excluded for lack of data.

[3] Michigan and North Carolina are excluded for lack of data.

Sources: The Book of the States, 1964–1965 (Chicago: The Council of State Governments, 1964), pp. 12–15, and Harmon Zeigler, "Interest Groups in the States," in Herbert Jacob and Kenneth N. Vines, eds., Politics in the American States (Boston: Little, Brown, 1965), p. 114.

If the theory we have suggested is correct, then we would expect states with strong interest groups to have more proposals for constitutional changes than states with moderately strong interest groups which, in turn, would have more proposals for changes than would states with weak interest groups. This hypothesis would reflect a greater number of attempts to gain some special constitutional status.

The data from Table 3 confirm this hypothesis. The average number of proposed amendments per year in states with strong interest groups is 2.97, in states with moderate interest groups 1.14, and in states with weak interest groups .68.

3. The stronger the interest groups, the greater the number of amendments which are adopted.

As with proposed amendments, we would expect stronger interest group states to have a larger number of changes in the constitution than in states with less strong interest groups.

From Table 3 we can see that the data confirm the hypothesis. Strong-interest-group states have an average of 1.58 amendments adopted per year, moderate states an average of .76, weak-interest-group states an average of .41.

Additional support for this hypothesis, and for the theory being proposed here, is the following. We would also expect states with longer constitutions to have a greater number of changes in their constitutions. This follows if we assume, as we have been doing, that longer constitutions indicate a larger range of activities provided for in the constitution, and a greater specificity and detail. The greater constitutional comprehensiveness in states with longer constitutions would also suggest a greater need to revise the constitution as economic, social, and political changes occur. Hence, we would predict that the longer the constitution, the greater the number of amendments. Table 4 provides data on this point.

As Table 4 indicates, the average number of amendments adopted per year increases as the average length of the constitution increases.

Since states with stronger interest groups tend to have longer constitutions (Table 3), and since states with longer constitutions tend to have a greater number of amendments (Table 4), hypothesis three, the stronger the interest group, the greater the number of amendments which are adopted, is directly derivable from these other hypotheses. The fact that this three-step chain of hypotheses is true at all three steps lends additional validity to the general theory being proposed here. It is also interesting to note that both strength of interest groups and length of constitution have an independent effect on the number of amendments adopted. When each is held constant the relationship with the other and number of amendments adopted is attenuated, but still present.

Table 4. Relationship Between Length of
Constitution and Number of Constitutional
Amendments Adopted

Length of Constitution	Average No. of Adopted Amendments per year	N[1]
Less than 10,000 words	.27	7
10,000–19,999	.67	18
20,000–29,999	.78	12
30,000 and over	3.04	9

[1] Michigan and North Carolina are excluded for lack of data.
Source: The Book of the States, 1964–1965 (Chicago: The Council of State Governments, 1964), pp. 12–15.

4. States with moderately strong interest groups will have the highest percentage of amendments adopted.

This hypothesis, although not immediately obvious, follows from the following argument. To this point our data indicate a positive relationship between strength of interest groups and both number of amendments proposed and number of amendments adopted. It is clear, however, that it is easier to propose an amendment than to get an amendment adopted. States with strong interest groups, then, would be expected to have a larger number of amendments proposed and a larger number of amendments adopted, but since it is easier to propose amendments than to have them ratified, their rate of success would not be expected to be the largest among the states.

Similarly, states with weak interest groups have the fewest number of amendments proposed and the fewest number of amendments adopted. But, again, since it is easier to propose than to adopt, weak interest group states would not have the highest rate of success. This reasoning would predict that states with moderately strong interest groups would have the highest ratio of amendments adopted to amendments proposed. Table 5 provides data on this hypothesis.

As Table 5 indicates, it is the states with moderately strong interest groups that have the highest percentage of amendments which are proposed adopted. States with strong interest groups have a ratio of adopted amendments to proposed amendments of 54.8 per cent, states with moderate interest groups 62.8 per cent, and states with weak interest groups 52.6 per cent. Those states with the weakest interest groups have the lowest rate of success, but those states with the strongest interest groups do not have the highest rate of success. Indeed, their rate of success is much closer to weak interest group states than to moderately strong ones.

**Table 5. Relationship Between Strength of
Interest Groups and Percentage of
Proposed Amendments Adopted**

Strength of Interest Groups	Average % of Amendments Adopted	N^1
Strong	54.8%	19
Moderate	62.8%	12
Weak	52.6%	5

[1] See footnote 3, Table 3.
Source: See Table 3.

A POSSIBLE ALTERNATIVE EXPLANATION

Before accepting the above theory and hypotheses relating strength of interest groups to variations in state constitutions, it might be useful to explore a possible alternative explanation.

States also differ considerably in the extent to which it is easy or difficult to amend their constitutions. Some states, for example, require a two-thirds, or three-fifths majority of the legislature and/or passage by two successive legislatures to propose and ratify constitutional amendments. All states but one also require a popular referendum after legislative action, but require differing majorities in the referendum. In addition, states also differ on whether they allow constitutional amendments to be proposed by initiative, and have different ways of calling together and proposing amendments in constitutional conventions.[13]

Given these widely varying practices in states, an index of difficulty of proposing and ratifying constitutional amendments was constructed. This index is derived from the three major ways in which the constitution may be amended and therefore reflects: (1) legislative difficulty, (2) presence or absence of the initiative, and (3) constitutional convention difficulty in proposing and ratifying constitutional amendments. One point was given to each state if a majority greater than a simple majority is required in the legislature, one point if approval by two sessions is needed, and one point if ratification by a majority vote in the election rather than a majority vote on the amendment is required. Additionally, one point is given if there are no initiative procedures in the state. With regard to constitutional conventions, one point is given if greater than a majority in the legislature is required to call a constitutional convention, one point if approval is needed by two sessions of the legislature, one point if a referendum on whether there should be a constitutional convention is necessary, one point if a majority in the election rather than a majority on the proposition is required, one point if after the constitutional convention ratification of the amendment is required (one-half point is given if no provision is in the constitution for a referendum ratifying the amendment but the legislature may determine if a referendum is necessary), and one point if ratification requires a majority in the election rather than a majority on the amendment.

This index of difficulty of amending the constitution, then, can vary from 0 to 10. The median score was 4, the range from 1 to 9. Fifteen states had scores of 3.5 or less, sixteen had scores from 4 to 5, and fifteen had scores from 5.5 to 9.

Given this wide range in difficulty in amending state constitutions, we would expect that such variation might have an impact on the number of amendments which are adopted by the states. More specifically, we would hypothesize that the greater the difficulty in amending the constitution, the fewer the number of amendments which will be adopted. Table 6 provides the data to test this hypothesis.

Table 6. Relationship Between Difficulty in Amending the Constitution and Average Number of Amendments Adopted Per Year

Score on Difficulty of Amending Constitution	Average No. of Adopted Amendments Per Year	N[1]
Less than 3.5	1.29	15
4–5	1.32	16
5.5–9	.66	15

[1] Michigan and North Carolina are excluded for lack of data.
Source: See Table 4.

Table 6 only partially confirms the hypothesis. Those states with the most difficult procedures to amend the constitution do have fewer amendments adopted, but the states with the easiest procedures do not have the greatest number of amendments adopted.

This partial explanation of why states vary in the number of changes in their constitutions may be further explained, however, by variation in states in strength of interest groups. Consistent with our theory, it may be proposed that states would be expected to vary in ease or difficulty in amending their constitutions by strength of interest groups. That is, we would expect the following hypothesis to be true: the stronger the interest groups, the less the difficulty in amending the constitution. Table 7 presents data on this hypothesis.

The data from Table 7 confirm the relationship between strength of interest groups and difficulty of amending the constitution. States with

Table 7. Relationship Between Strength of Interest Groups and Difficulty of Amending the Constitution

Strength of Interest Groups	Average Difficulty of Amending the Constitution	N
Strong	4.21	24
Moderate	5.00	14
Weak	5.65	7

Sources: See footnote 3, Table 3.

strong interest groups have a difficulty score of 4.21, states with moderately strong interest groups have a score of 5.00, and states with weak interest groups have a difficulty score of 5.65. Hence we may say that even though the number of changes in the constitution is related to difficulty of amending the constitution as well as strength of interest groups, the reason why this additional explanation is at least partially true is because strength of interest groups is also related to difficulty of amending the constitution.

One further piece of data will also help to confirm the theory being proposed here. Since states with strong interest groups have longer constitutions (Table 3), and since strong interest group states also have constitutions which are easier to amend (Table 3), we would also expect there to be a relationship between length of constitution and ease of amendment. More specifically we would hypothesize the greater the length of the constitution, the less the difficulty in amending the constitution. Table 8 provides data on this hypothesis.

Table 8. Relationship Between Length of Constitution and Difficulty of Amending State Constitution

Length of Constitution	Average Difficulty of Amending the Constitution	N[1]
Less than 10,000 words	6.29	7
10,000–19,999	4.58	18
20,000–29,999	4.71	12
30,000 and over	4.11	9

[1] Michigan and North Carolina are excluded for lack of data.

Source: See Table 4.

As can be seen from the Table, this hypothesis is for the most part confirmed. The states with the shortest constitutions have the most difficult amending procedures, and the states with the longest constitutions have the easiest amending procedures, although the two sets of states in the middle do not fall in the predicted order.

Summing up this section, then, there is a partial relationship between the difficulty of amending the constitution and the number of changes made in the constitution. However, this relationship can be accounted for by the fact that there is also a relationship between strength of interest groups and ease of amending the constitution. The alternative explanation, then, may be rejected and the original explanation retained. Strength of interest group seems to be a major factor in explaining why states vary with regard to certain constitutional practices.

THE SECOND SET OF DEPENDENT VARIABLES

In the previous sections our concern was with the effect of strength of interest groups on some general features of state constitutions. In this section the focus will shift slightly to a combined constitutional-legislative variable, the method of selection of state officials. States differ widely in the number of office-holders who are appointed as opposed to elected to office. We will be concerned, in the following, with an explanation of this variation.

A priori one might predict that states with stronger interest groups would be *either* more likely or less likely to have a larger number of elected as opposed to appointed officials. The major political variable in either prediction is the ability of interest groups to influence the selection of personnel. Those who would predict that interest groups will have more influence if governmental officials are appointed rather than elected would suggest that interest groups would prefer the politics of dealing with the governor and, in some instances, the legislature, to the uncertainties of electoral politics. If this hypothesis is combined with the already-established hypothesis that strength of interest groups is related to political outcomes then this group would predict that states with stronger interest groups would have a greater number of appointed rather than elected officials.

On the other hand one could, with equal logic, agree that interest groups do want to maintain influence over the selection of governmental personnel but that such influence can better be established if personnel are elected rather than appointed. A governor is likely to be responsive to a wide variety of state interests. In some cases he may be a member of a political party which is less responsive to the concerns of certain interest groups. Gubernatorial appointment combined with legislative confirmation would provide some check on the governor, but interest groups, on balance, might be better able to influence the selection of personnel if such persons were elected in what, for minor positions, would be relatively low turnout elections rather than take a chance with governors. Proponents of this view would deduce an opposite conclusion from that previously advanced: stronger interest group states would have a larger number of elected rather than appointed officials.

How does one choose between these competing theories? Since the logic of each produces contradictory conclusions we might test those conclusions. Although this does not produce a direct test of the competing theories it does provide an indirect test, since the conclusions drawn from each are clearly contrary to each other. Evidence on these derivative hypotheses may support one theory as opposed to the other.

The relationship between interest group strength and selection of governmental officials will be tested in four different ways. First, what is the relationship between interest group strength and the total number of state officials who are elected? Second, what is the relationship of interest group strength and the number of state agencies with elected officials? This relationship will give us some idea of the range of offices which are subject to election.

Each of these variables gives an indication of the overall elective-appointive system within and among states. But what about specific instances? Third, then, what is the relationship between strength of interest groups and the selection of state public utility commissions? Fourth, what is the relationship of strength of interest groups with the selection of judges on state courts of last resort? Table 9 provides data to test these four relationships.

From Table 9 it is clear, in each instance, that states with strong interest groups rely more heavily on election of state officials than do states with weaker interest groups. The stronger the interest groups the greater the number of elected officials, the greater the number of state agencies with elected officials, the greater the likelihood that public utility commissions will be elected, and the greater the probability that judges on state courts of last resort will be elected.

The data, then, lend support to the second of the alternative theories. States with stronger interest groups are better able to isolate governmental agencies and officials from executive or legislative influence than are states with weaker interest groups, and are more likely to have agencies of government which are independent from the governor and legislature.

One further bit of evidence lends additional support to this conclusion. Given the evidence that elections rather than appointments are related to strong interest groups, it may also be inferred that those states with strong

Table 9. Relationship Between Strength of Interest Groups and Four Dependent Variables

Strength of Interest Groups	Average No. of State Elected Officials	Average No. of State Agencies With Elected Officials	% of Elected State Public Utility Commissions	% of Elected State Courts of Last Resort	N
Strong	19.54	9.17	50	79	24
Moderate	14.64	7.14	7	57	14
Weak	7.71	5.86	0	43	7

Source: The Book of the States, 1964–1965 (Chicago: The Council of State Governments, 1964).

interest groups would have shorter terms of office than those states with weaker interest groups. This would provide additional control by interest groups by making governmental officials run for office more frequently and hence be less independent from outside influence. Table 10 provides data on terms of office of judges of state courts of last resort.

The data in Table 10 confirm this hypothesis. Length of term for judges on state courts of last resort decreases as strength of interest groups increases.

SUMMARY AND CONCLUSIONS

We began our discussion by suggesting that the literature on interest groups, generally speaking, lacks studies which attempt to test generalizations about interest group activity. The emphasis on theory and/or case studies we attributed to two factors: (1) difficulty in operationalizing theoretical concepts, and (2) difficulty and expense in collecting data for many interest groups or on many policies.

This study attempts to test several propositions about the relationship between strength of interest groups and variations among states with regard to structural and output variables centering on the constitution and the election of state officials. A theory was developed which explained why state governments would have such wide variations in their constitutions and the political processes surrounding them. More specifically the following hypotheses about strength of interest groups were tested and confirmed:

1. The stronger the interest groups, the greater the length of the state constitutions.

2. The stronger the interest groups, the greater the number of proposed amendments.

3. The stronger the interest groups, the greater the number of amendments which are adopted.

4. States with moderately strong interest groups will have the highest percentage of amendments adopted.

5. The stronger the interest groups, the less the difficulty in amending the constitution.

6. The stronger the interest groups, the greater the number of state elected officials.

7. The stronger the interest groups, the greater the number of state agencies with elected officials.

8. The stronger the interest groups, the greater the likelihood that state public utility commissions will be elected.

9. The stronger the interest groups, the greater the probability that judges on state courts of last resort will be elected.

10. The stronger the interest groups, the shorter will be the terms of office of judges on state courts of last resort.

**Table 10. Relationship Between Strength of Interest Groups
and Average Length of Term of Judges on
State Courts of Last Resort**

Strength of Interest Groups	Average Length of Term	N
Strong	7.58	24
Moderate	11.21	14
Weak	13.43	7

Source: The Book of the States, 1964–1965 (Chicago: The Council of State Governments, 1964).

In addition, the following subsidiary hypotheses were also tested:

11. The longer the constitution, the greater the number of amendments which are adopted.

12. The longer the constitution, the less the difficulty in amending the constitution.

13. The greater the difficulty in amending the constitution, the fewer the number of amendments which will be adopted (partially confirmed).

All of these hypotheses confirm the theory which has been proposed here. Variation in strength of interest groups does have an impact on political systems. It was expected that states with stronger interest groups would be characterized by attempts by those groups to gain special advantages. Since constitutions are one of the vehicles through which advantages and disadvantages are distributed in political systems, these attempts would have an effect on the length of the constitution, the amending procedures within states, and the number of changes which are made. Since the selection of governmental personnel is also of primary concern to interest groups, it would be expected that differences in selection procedures would also vary by interest group strength. The data presented in this paper lend credence to these suppositions.

STATISTICAL APPENDIX

A political scientist must, with some data projects, give attention to the possible conflict between data analysis sophistication and general readability. In the text I have attempted to present the findings in the simplest way possible consistent with accuracy and at least minimum precision. However, there are techniques of data analysis which provide more powerful data manipulation. One of these techniques, appropriate for this analysis, is multiple regression analysis. This statistical appendix will present the findings in terms of correlation coefficients, holding some variables constant where appropriate.

Two points, however, should be made immediately. First, the results of the multiple regression analysis are entirely consistent with the findings already reported. The interpretation of the data also remains the same. Second, the entire analysis was performed in two steps, one with all of the states (in most cases this is forty-five states), and the second with the eleven former Confederate states dropped from the analysis. It has been found consistently that in many respects southern states differ from northern states. However, the propositions reported here are true whether one includes or excludes the southern states.

The correlation coefficients for the propositions listed in the summary, in the same numerical order, are as follows (correlations in parentheses exclude the southern states):
1. .36 (.34), 2. .40 (.33), 3. .30 (.25), 4. curvilinear, 5. $-.30$ $(-.31)$, 6. .26 (.27), 7. .52 (.45), 8. .41 (.45), 9. .32 (.31), 10. $-.43$ $(-.42)$, 11. .53 (.53), 12. $-.24$ $(-.24)$, 13. $-.12$ $(-.17)$ (partial relationship reported).

In addition, the relationship between interest group strength and number of constitutional amendments adopted, with length of constitution held constant is .19. Similarly, the relationship between interest group strength and number of constitutional amendments adopted, with difficulty of amending the constitution held constant is .24.

The relationship between strength of interest groups and number of state elected officials is not affected by population size.

NOTES

* I wish to thank Sheen T. Kassouf, Deane E. Neubauer, Jack W. Peltason, and Howard Rosenthal for their comments on an earlier draft of this paper.

[1] See, for example, David B. Truman, *The Governmental Process* (New York: Knopf, 1951), Chaps 2 and 3; Earl Latham, *The Group Basis of Politics* (Ithaca: Cornell University Press, 1952), Chap. 1; E. E. Schattschneider, *The Semisovereign People* (New York: Holt, Rinehart & Winston, 1960); and Harmon Zeigler, *Interest Groups in American Society* (Englewood Cliffs, N.J.: Prentice-Hall, 1964), Chaps 1–3. There is also a voluminous journal literature discussing the pros and cons of "the group approach." See, for example, Stanley Rothman, "Systematic Political Theory: Observations on the Group Approach," *American Political Science Review*, 54 (March, 1960), pp. 15–33.

[2] See William Kornhauser, *The Politics of Mass Society* (New York: Free Press, 1959).

[3] See Raymond A. Bauer, Ithiel de Sola Pool, and Lewis Anthony Dexter, *American Business and Public Policy* (New York: Atherton, 1963) for a policy case study which also develops very useful and interesting theory.

[4] See Joseph R. Monson, Jr., and Mark W. Cannon, *The Makers of Public Policy* (New York: McGraw-Hill, 1965), for a number of discussions of particular interest groups and their activities.

[5] Alaska and Hawaii are excluded.

[6] Data from *The Book of the States, 1964–1965* (Chicago: The Council of State Governments, 1964), pp. 12–15.

[7] David B. Truman, *op. cit.*; Robert A. Dahl, *A Preface to Democratic Theory* (Chicago: University of Chicago Press, 1956); William Kornhauser, *op. cit.*; and V. O. Key, Jr., *Politics, Parties, and Pressure Groups* (New York: Crowell, 1964), 5th ed.

[8] Belle Zeller (ed.), *American State Legislatures* (New York: Crowell, 1964), Chap. 12, especially Table 9, pp. 190–91.

[9] See, for examples, Claire Selltiz, Marie Jahoda, Morton Deutsch, and Stuart W. Cook, *Research Methods in Social Relations* (New York: Holt, Rinehart, & Winston, 1961).

[10] Seymour Martin Lipset, "Some Social Requisites of Democracy," *American Political Science Review*, 53 (March, 1959), pp. 69–105.

[11] Deane E. Neubauer, *On the Theory of Polyarchy: An Empirical Study of Democracy in Ten Countries* (Ph.D. thesis, Yale University, 1966).

[12] A note of caution, however, should undoubtedly be entered here. The measurement of "strength" of interest groups being employed may probably best be construed to mean strength of interest groups vis-à-vis the state legislature. At least this is the sense in which it appears that the Committee defined strength. It is certainly the case that interest groups could vary in strength in a number of different ways. For example, size of membership, or number of groups may, under certain conditions, be appropriate measures of strength. As strength of interest groups is being used here it will be defined primarily in terms of legislative activity.

In addition, the results of this study must be interpreted cautiously since the time periods in which the independent and several of the dependent variables were measured are not coterminous. Strength of interest groups was measured by the Zeller Committee in 1954. Length of constitution and difficulty of amending the constitution (a variable to be introduced later in this paper) correspond to this time period, but the three variables having to do with amendments (number proposed, number adopted, and percentage of amendments adopted) are measured to the date when each state's current constitution was adopted. In several cases this reflects many years. It is therefore necessary, in three of the propositions, to make the assumption that strength of interest groups in states is a relatively stable phenomenon. Although there is not much evidence to support or deny the validity of this assumption, it does not appear unduly unrealistic to make it. Changes in governments, barring revolutions, are likely to take place slowly. If this is the case it does offer a certain plausibility to the assumption.

[13] For descriptions of the differing state systems, see *The Book of the States, op. cit.*, pp. 13–15.

CHAPTER 17

Constituency Influence in Congress*

Warren E. Miller
Donald E. Stokes

Substantial constituency influence over the lower house of Congress is commonly thought to be both a normative principle and a factual truth of American government. From their draft constitution we may assume the Founding Fathers expected it, and many political scientists feel, regretfully, that the Framers' wish has come all too true.[1] Nevertheless, much of the evidence of constituency control rests on inference. The fact that our House of Representatives, especially by comparison with the House of Commons, has irregular party voting, does not of itself indicate that Congressmen deviate from party in response to local pressure. And even more, the fact that many Congressmen *feel* pressure from home does not of itself establish that the local constituency is performing any of the acts that a reasonable definition of control would imply.

I. CONSTITUENCY CONTROL IN THE NORMATIVE THEORY OF REPRESENTATION

Control by the local constituency is at one pole of *both* the great normative controversies about representation that have arisen in modern times. It is generally recognized that constituency control is opposite to the conception of representation associated with Edmund Burke. Burke wanted the representative to serve the constituency's *interest* but not its *will*, and the extent to which the representative should be compelled by electoral sanctions to follow the "mandate" of his constituents has been at the heart of the ensuing controversy as it has continued for a century and a half.[2]

Constituency control also is opposite to the conception of government by responsible national parties. This is widely seen, yet the point is rarely connected with normative discussions of representation. Indeed, it is remarkable how little attention has been given to the model of representation implicit in the doctrine of a "responsible two-party system."

Reprinted from *American Political Science Review*, Vol. 57, No. 1 (March 1963), pp. 45–56, by permission of the American Political Science Association.

When the subject of representation is broached among political scientists, the classical argument between Burke and his opponents is likely to come at once to mind. So great is Burke's influence that the antithesis he proposed still provides the categories of thought used in contemporary treatments of representation despite the fact that many students of politics today would advocate a relationship between representative and constituency that fits *neither* position of the mandate-independence controversy.

The conception of representation implicit in the doctrine of responsible parties shares the idea of popular control with the instructed-delegate model. Both are versions of popular sovereignty. But "the people" of the responsible two-party system are conceived in terms of a national rather than a local constituency. Candidates for legislative office appeal to the electorate in terms of a *national* party program and leadership, to which, if elected, they will be committed. Expressions of policy preference by the local district are reduced to endorsements of one or another of these programs, and the local district retains only the arithmetical significance that whichever party can rally to its program the greater number of supporters in the district will control its legislative seat.

No one tradition of representation has entirely dominated American practice. Elements of the Burkean, instructed-delegate, and responsible party models can all be found in our political life. Yet if the American system has elements of all three, a good deal depends on how they are combined. Especially critical is the question whether different models of representation apply to different public issues. Is the saliency of legislative to the public so different in quality and degree on different issues that the legislator is subject to very different constraints from his constituency? Does the legislator have a single generalized mode of response to his constituency that is rooted in a normative belief about the representative's role or does the same legislator respond to his constituency differently on different issues? More evidence is needed on matters so fundamental to our system.

II. AN EMPIRICAL STUDY OF REPRESENTATION

To extend what we know of representation in the American Congress the Survey Research Center of The University of Michigan interviewed the incumbent Congressman, his non-incumbent opponent (if any), and a sample of constituents in each of 116 congressional districts, which were themselves a probability sample of all districts.[3] These interviews, conducted immediately after the congressional election of 1958, explored a wide range of attitudes and perceptions held by the individuals who play the reciprocal roles of the representative relation in national government.

The distinguishing feature of this research is, of course, that it sought direct information from both constituent and legislator (actual and aspiring). To this fund of comparative interview data has been added information about the roll call votes of our sample of Congressmen and the political and social characteristics of the districts they represent.

Many students of politics, with excellent reason, have been sensitive to possible ties between representative and constituent that have little to do with issues of public policy. For example, ethnic identifications may cement a legislator in the affections of his district, whatever (within limits) his stands on issues. And many Congressmen keep their tenure of office secure by skillful provision of district benefits ranging from free literature to major federal projects. In the full study of which this analysis is part, we have explored several bases of constituency support that have little to do with policy issues. Nevertheless, the question how the representative should make up his mind on legislative issues is what the classical arguments over representation are all about, and we have given a central place to a comparison of the policy preferences of constituents and Representatives and to a causal analysis of the relation between the two. In view of the electorate's scanty information about government it was not at all clear in advance that such a comparison could be made. Some of the more buoyant advocates of popular sovereignty have regarded the citizen as a kind of kibitzer who looks over the shoulder of his representative at the legislative game. Kibitzer and player may disagree as to which card should be played, but they were at least thought to share a common understanding of what the alternatives are.

No one familiar with the findings of research on mass electorates could accept this view of the citizen. Far from looking over the shoulder of their Congressmen at the legislative game, most Americans are almost totally uninformed about legislative issues in Washington. At best the average citizen may be said to have some general ideas about how the country should be run, which he is able to use in responding to particular questions about what the government ought to do. For example, survey studies have shown that most people have a general (though differing) conception of how far government should go to achieve social and economic welfare objectives and that these convictions fix their response to various particular questions about actions government might take.[4]

What makes it possible to compare the policy preferences of constituents and Representatives despite the public's low awareness of legislative affairs is the fact that Congressmen themselves respond to many issues in terms of fairly broad evaluative dimensions. Undoubtedly policy alternatives are judged in the executive agencies and the specialized committees of the Congress by criteria that are relatively complex and specific to the policies at issue. But a good deal of evidence goes to show that when proposals come before the House as a whole they are judged on the basis of more general evaluative dimensions.[5] For example, most Congressmen, too, seem to have a general conception of how far government should go in the area of domestic social and economic welfare, and these general positions apparently orient their roll call votes on a number of particular social welfare issues.

It follows that such a broad evaluative dimension can be used to compare the policy preferences of constituents and Representatives despite the low state of the public's information about politics. In this study three such dimensions have been drawn from our voter interviews and from congressional interviews and roll call records. As suggested above, one of these has to do with approval of government action in the social welfare field, the primary domestic issue of the New Deal-Fair Deal (and New Frontier) eras. A second dimension has to do with support for American involvement in foreign affairs, a latter-day version of the isolationist-internationalist continuum. A third dimension has to do with approval of federal action to protect the civil rights of Negroes.[6]

Because our research focused on these three dimensions, our analysis of constituency influence is limited to these areas of policy. No point has been more energetically or usefully made by those who have sought to clarify the concepts of power and influence than the necessity of specifying the acts *with respect to which* one actor has power or influence or control over another.[7] Therefore, the scope or range of influence for our analysis is the collection of legislative issues falling within our three policy domains. We are not able to say how much control the local constituency may or may not have over *all* actions of its Representative, and there may well be pork-barrel issues or other matters of peculiar relevance to the district on which the relation of Congressman to constituency is quite distinctive. However, few observers of contemporary politics would regard the issues of government provision of social and economic welfare, of American involvement in world affairs, and of federal action on behalf of the Negro as constituting a trivial range of action. Indeed, these domains together include most of the great issues that have come before Congress in recent years.

In each policy domain we have used the procedures of cumulative scaling, as developed by Louis Guttman and others, to order our samples of Congressmen, of opposing candidates, and of voters. In each domain Congressmen were ranked once according to their roll call votes in the House and again according to the attitudes they revealed in our confidential interviews. These two orderings are by no means identical, nor are the discrepancies due simply to uncertainties of measurement.[8] Opposing candidates also were ranked in each policy domain according to the attitudes they revealed in our interviews. The nationwide sample of constituents was ordered in each domain, and by averaging the attitude scores of all constituents living in the same districts, whole constituencies were ranked on each dimension so that the views of Congressmen could be compared with those of their constituencies.[9] Finally, by considering only the constituents in each district who share some characteristic (voting for the incumbent, say), we were able to order these fractions of districts so that the opinions of Congressmen could be compared with those, for example, of the dominant electoral elements of their districts.

In each policy domain, crossing the rankings of Congressmen and their constituencies gives an empirical measure of the extent of policy agreement between legislator and district.[10] In the period of our research this procedure reveals very different degrees of policy congruence across the three issue domains. On questions of social and economic welfare there is considerable agreement between Representative and district, expressed by correlation of approximately 0.3. This coefficient is, of course, very much less than the limiting value of 1.0, indicating that a number of Congressmen are, relatively speaking, more or less "liberal" than their districts. However, on the question of foreign involvement there is no discernible agreement between legislator and district whatever. Indeed, as if to emphasize the point, the coefficient expressing this relation is slightly negative (-0.09), although not significantly so in a statistical sense. It is in the domain of civil rights that the rankings of Congressmen and constituencies most nearly agree. When we took our measurements in the late 1950's the correlation of congressional roll call behavior with constituency opinion on questions affecting the Negro was nearly 0.6.

The description of policy agreement that these three simple correlations give can be a starting-point for a wide range of analyses. For example, the significance of party competition in the district for policy representation can be explored by comparing the agreement between district and Congressman with the agreement between the district and the Congressman's non-incumbent opponent. Alternatively, the significance of choosing Representatives from single-member districts by popular majority can be explored by comparing the agreement between the Congressman and his own supporters with the agreement between the Congressman and the supporters of his opponent. Taking *both* party competition and majority rule into account magnifies rather spectacularly some of the coefficients reported here. This is most true in the domain of social welfare, where attitudes both of candidates and of voters are most polarized along party lines. Whereas the correlation between the constituency majority and congressional roll call votes is nearly $+0.4$ on social welfare policy, the correlation of the district majority with the non-incumbent candidate is -0.4. This difference, amounting to almost 0.8, between these two coefficients is an indicator of what the dominant electoral element of the constituency gets on the average by choosing the Congressman it has and excluding his opponent from office.[11]

These three coefficients are also the starting-point for a causal analysis of the relation of constituency to representative, the main problem of this paper. At least on social welfare and Negro rights a measurable degree of congruence is found between district and legislator. Is this agreement due to constituency influence in Congress, or is it to be attributed to other causes? If this question is to have a satisfactory answer the conditions that are necessary and sufficient to assure constituency control must be stated and compared with the available empirical evidence.

III. THE CONDITIONS OF CONSTITUENCY INFLUENCE

Broadly speaking, the constituency can control the policy actions of the Representative in two alternative ways. The first of these is for the district to choose a Representative who so shares its views that in following his own convictions he does his constituents' will. In this case district opinion and the Congressman's actions are connected through the Representative's own policy attitudes. The second means of constituency control is for the Congressman to follow his (at least tolerably accurate) perceptions of district attitude in order to win re-election. In this case constituency opinion and the Congressman's actions are connected through his perception of what the district wants.[12]

These two paths of constituency control are presented schematically in Figure 1. As the figure suggests, each path has two steps, one connecting the constituency's attitude with an "intervening" attitude or perception, the

Figure 1. Connections Between a Constituency's Attitude and Its Representative's Roll Call Behavior

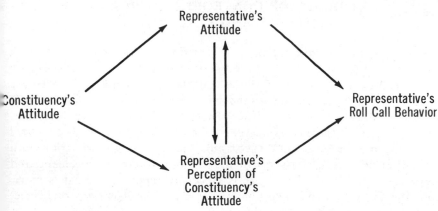

other connecting this attitude or perception with the Representative's roll call behavior. Out of respect for the processes by which the human actor achieves cognitive congruence, we have also drawn arrows between the two intervening factors, since the Congressman probably tends to see his district as having the same opinion as his own and also tends, over time, to bring his own opinion into line with the district's. The inclusion of these arrows calls attention to two other possible influence paths, each consisting of *three* steps, although these additional paths will turn out to be of relatively slight importance empirically.

Neither of the main influence paths of Figure 1 will connect the final roll call vote to the constituency's views if either of its steps is blocked. From this, two necessary conditions of constituency influence can be stated: *first*, the Representative's votes in the House must agree substantially with his own policy views, or his perceptions of the district's views, and not be determined entirely by other influences to which the Congressman is exposed; and *second*, the attitudes or perceptions governing the Representative's acts must correspond, at least imperfectly, to the district's actual opinions. It would be difficult to describe the relation of constituency to Representative as one of control unless these conditions are met.[13]

Yet these two requirements are not sufficient to assure control. A *third* condition must also be satisfied: the constituency must in some measure take the policy views of candidates into account in choosing a Representative. If it does not, agreement between district and Congressman may arise for reasons that cannot rationally be brought within the idea of control. For example, such agreement may simply reflect the fact that a Representative drawn from a given area is likely, by pure statistical probability, to share its dominant values, without his acceptance or rejection of these ever having been a matter of consequence to his electors.

IV. EVIDENCE OF CONTROL: CONGRESSIONAL ATTITUDES AND PERCEPTIONS

How well are these conditions met in the relation of American Congressmen to their constituents? There is little question that the first is substantially satisfied; the evidence of our research indicates that members of the House do in fact vote both their own policy views and their perceptions of their constituents' views, at least on issues of social welfare, foreign involvement, and civil rights. If these two intervening factors are used to predict roll call votes, the prediction is quite successful. Their multiple correlation with roll call position is 0.7 for social welfare, 0.6 for foreign involvement, and 0.9 for civil rights; the last figure is especially persuasive. What is more, both the Congressman's own convictions and his perceptions of district opinion make a distinct contribution to his roll call behavior. In each of the three domains the prediction of roll call votes is surer if it is made from both factors rather than from either alone.

Lest the strong influence that the Congressman's views and his perception of district views have on roll call behavior appear somehow foreordained—and, consequently, this finding seem a trivial one—it is worth taking a sidewise glance at the potency of possible other forces on the Representative's vote. In the area of foreign policy, for example, a number of Congressmen are disposed to follow the administration's advice, whatever they or their districts think. For those who are, the multiple correlation of roll call behavior with the Representative's own foreign policy views and his perception of district views is a mere 0.2. Other findings could be cited to support the point that the influence of the Congressman's own preferences and those he attributes to the district is extremely variable. Yet in the House as a whole over the three policy domains the influence of these forces is quite strong.

The connections of congressional attitudes and perceptions with actual constituency opinion are weaker. If policy agreement between district and Representative is moderate and variable across the policy domains, as it is this is to be explained much more in terms of the second condition of constituency control than the first. The Representative's attitudes and perceptions most nearly match true opinion in his district on the issues of Negro rights. Reflecting the charged and polarized nature of this area, the correlation of actual district opinion with perceived opinion is greater than 0.6, and the correlation of district attitude with the Representative's own attitude is nearly 0.4, as shown by Table 1. But the comparable correlations for foreign involvement are much smaller—indeed almost negligible. And

Table 1. Correlations of Constituency Attitudes

| | Correlation of Constituency Attitude with | |
| | Representative's Perception of Constituency | Representative's Own |
Policy Domain	Attitude	Attitude
Social welfare	.17	.21
Foreign involvement	.19	.06
Civil rights	.63	.39

the coefficients for social welfare are also smaller, although a detailed presentation of findings in this area would show that the Representative's perceptions and attitudes are more strongly associated with the attitude of his electoral *majority* than they are with the attitudes of the constituency as a whole.

Knowing this much about the various paths that may lead, directly or indirectly, from constituency attitude to roll call vote, we can assess their relative importance. Since the alternative influence chains have links of unequal strength, the full chains will not in general be equally strong, and these differences are of great importance in the relation of Representative to constituency. For the domain of civil rights Figure 2 assembles all the intercorrelations of the variables of our system. As the figure shows, the

Figure 2. Intercorrelations of Variables Pertaining to Civil Rights

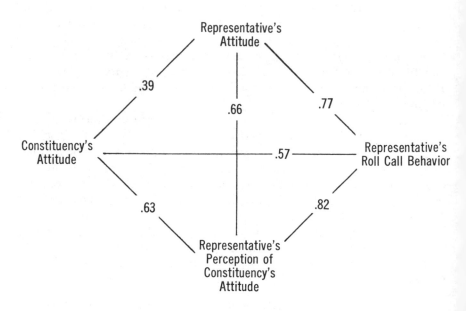

root correlation of constituency attitude with roll call behavior in this domain is 0.57. How much of this policy congruence can be accounted for by the influence path involving the Representative's attitude? And how much by the path involving his perception of constituency opinion? When the intercorrelations of the system are interpreted in the light of what we assume its causal structure to be, it is influence passing through the Congressman's perception of the district's views that is found to be preeminently important.[14] Under the least favorable assumption as to its importance, this path is found to account for more than twice as much of variance of roll call behavior as the paths involving the Representative's own attitude.[15] However, when this same procedure is applied to our social welfare data, the results suggest that the direct connection of constituency and roll call through the Congressman's own attitude is the most important of the alternative paths.[16] The reversal of the relative importance of the two paths as we move from civil rights to social welfare is one of the most striking findings of this analysis.

V. EVIDENCE OF CONTROL: ELECTORAL BEHAVIOR

Of the three conditions of constituency influence, the requirement that the electorate take account of the policy positions of the candidates is the hardest to match with empirical evidence. Indeed, given the limited information the average voter carries to the polls, the public might be thought incompetent to perform any task of appraisal. Of constituents living in congressional districts where there was a contest between a Republican and a Democrat in 1958, less than one in five said they had read or heard something about both candidates, and well over half conceded they had read or heard nothing about either. And these proportions are not much better when they are based only on the part of the sample, not much more than half, that reported voting for Congress in 1958. The extent of awareness of the candidates among voters is indicated in Table 2. As the table shows,

Table 2. Awareness of Congressional Candidates among Voters, 1958

		Read or Heard Something about Incumbent[a]		
		Yes	No	
Read or Heard Something about Non-Incumbent	Yes	24	5	29
	No	25	46	71
		49	51	100%

[a] In order to include all districts where the House seat was contested in 1958, this table retains ten constituencies in which the incumbent Congressman did not seek re-election. Candidates of the retiring incumbent's party in these districts are treated here as if they were incumbents. Were these figures to be calculated only for constituencies in which an incumbent sought re-election, no entry in this four-fold table would differ from that given by more than two per cent.

even of the portion of the public that was sufficiently interested to vote, almost half had read or heard nothing about either candidate.

Just how low a hurdle our respondents had to clear in saying they had read or heard something about a candidate is indicated by detailed qualitative analysis of the information constituents *were* able to associate with congressional candidates. Except in rare cases, what the voters "knew" was confined to diffuse evaluative judgments about the candidate: "he's a good man," "he understands the problems," and so forth. Of detailed information about policy stands not more than a chemical trace was found. Among the comments about the candidates given in response to an extended series of free-answer questions, less than two per cent had to do with stands in our three policy domains; indeed, only about three comments in every hundred had to do with legislative issues of *any* description.[17]

This evidence that the behavior of the electorate is largely unaffected by knowledge of the policy positions of the candidates is complemented by evidence about the forces that *do* shape the voters' choices among congressional candidates. The primary basis of voting in American congressional elections is identification with party. In 1958 only one vote in twenty was cast by persons without any sort of party loyalty. And among those who did have a party identification, only one in ten voted against his party. As a result, something like 84 per cent of the vote that year was cast by party identifiers voting their usual party line. What is more, traditional party voting is seldom connected with current legislative issues. As the party loyalists in a nationwide sample of voters told us what they liked and disliked about the parties in 1958, only a small fraction of the comments (about 15 per cent) dealt with current issues of public policy.[18]

Yet the idea of reward or punishment at the polls for legislative stands is familiar to members of Congress, who feel that they and their records are quite visible to their constituents. Of our sample of Congressmen who were opposed for re-election in 1958, more than four-fifths said the outcome in their districts had been strongly influenced by the electorate's response to their records and personal standing. Indeed, this belief is clear enough to present a notable contradiction: Congressmen feel that their individual legislative actions may have considerable impact on the electorate, yet some simple facts about the Representative's salience to his constituents imply that this could hardly be true.

In some measure this contradiction is to be explained by the tendency of Congressmen to overestimate their visibility to the local public, a tendency that reflects the difficulties of the Representative in forming a correct judgment of constituent opinion. The communication most Congressmen have with their districts inevitably puts them in touch with organized groups and with individuals who are relatively well informed about politics. The Representative knows his constituents mostly from dealing with people who *do* write letters, who *will* attend meetings, who *have* an interest in his legislative stands. As a result, his sample of contacts with a constituency of several hundred thousand people is heavily biased; even the contacts he apparently makes at random are likely to be with people who grossly overrepresent the degree of political information and interest in the constituency as a whole.

But the contradiction is also to be explained by several aspects of the

Representative's electoral situation that are of great importance to the question of constituency influence. The first of these is implicit in what has already been said. Because of the pervasive effects of party loyalties, no candidate for Congress starts from scratch in putting together an electoral majority. The Congressman is a dealer in increments and margins. He starts with a stratum of hardened party voters, and if the stratum is broad enough he can have a measurable influence on his chance of survival simply by attracting a small additional element of the electorate—or by not losing a larger one. Therefore, his record may have a very real bearing on his electoral success or failure without most of his constituents ever knowing what that record is.

Second, the relation of Congressman to voter is not a simple bilateral one but is complicated by the presence of all manner of intermediaries: the local party, economic interests, the news media, racial and nationality organizations, and so forth. Such is the lore of American politics, as it is known to any political scientist. Very often the Representative reaches the mass public through these mediating agencies, and the information about himself and his record may be considerably transformed as it diffuses out to the electorate in two or more stages. As a result, the public—or parts of it— may get simple positive or negative cues about the Congressman which were provoked by his legislative actions but which no longer have a recognizable issue content.

Third, for most Congressmen most of the time the electorate's sanctions are potential rather than actual. Particularly the Representative from a safe district may feel his proper legislative strategy is to avoid giving opponents in his own party or outside of it material they can use against him. As the Congressman pursues this strategy he may write a legislative record that never becomes very well known to his constituents; if it doesn't win votes, neither will it lose any. This is clearly the situation of most southern Congressmen in dealing with the issue of Negro rights. By voting correctly on this issue they are unlikely to increase their visibility to constituents. Nevertheless, the fact of constituency influence, backed by potential sanctions at the polls, is real enough.

That these potential sanctions are all too real is best illustrated in the election of 1958 by the reprisal against Representative Brooks Hays of Arkansas' Fifth District.[19] Although the perception of Congressman Hays as too moderate on civil rights resulted more from his service as intermediary between the White House and Governor Faubus in the Little Rock school crisis than from his record in the House, the victory of Dale Alford as a write-in candidate was a striking reminder of what can happen to a Congressman who gives his foes a powerful issue to use against him. The extraordinary involvement of the public in this race can be seen by comparing how well the candidates were known in this constituency with the awareness of the candidates shown by Table 2 above for the country as a whole. As Table 3 indicates, not a single voter in our sample of Arkansas' Fifth District was unaware of either candidate.[20] What is more, these

Table 3. Awareness of Congressional Candidates among Voters in Arkansas' Fifth District, 1958

		Read or Heard Something about Hays		
		Yes	No	
Read or Heard Something about Alford	Yes	100	0	100
	No	0	0	0
		100	0	100%

interviews show that Hays was regarded both by his supporters and his opponents as more moderate than Alford on civil rights and that this perception brought his defeat. In some measure, what happened in Little Rock in 1958 can happen anywhere, and our Congressmen ought not to be entirely disbelieved in what they say about their impact at the polls. Indeed, they may be under genuine pressure from the voters even while they are the forgotten men of national elections.[21]

V. CONCLUSION

Therefore, although the conditions of constituency influence are not equally satisfied, they are met well enough to give the local constituency a measure of control over the actions of its Representatives. Best satisfied is the requirement about motivational influences on the Congressman: our evidence shows that the Representative's roll call behavior is strongly influenced by his own policy preferences and by his perception of preferences held by the constituency. However, the conditions of influence that presuppose effective communication between Congressman and district are much less well met. The Representative has very imperfect information about the issue preferences of his constituency, and the constituency's awareness of the policy stands of the Representative ordinarily is slight.

The findings of this analysis heavily underscore the fact that no single tradition of representation fully accords with the realities of American legislative politics. The American system *is* a mixture, to which the Burkean, instructed-delegate, and responsible-party models all can be said to have contributed elements. Moreover, variations in the representative relation are most likely to occur as we move from one policy domain to another. No single, generalized configuration of attitudes and perceptions links Representative with constituency but rather several distinct patterns, and which of them is invoked depends very much on the issue involved.

The issue domain in which the relation of Congressman to constituency most nearly conforms to the instructed-delegate model is that of civil rights. This conclusion is supported by the importance of the influence-path passing through the Representative's perception of district opinion, although even in this domain the sense in which the constituency may be said to take the position of the candidate into account in reaching its electoral judgment should be carefully qualified.

The representative relation conforms most closely to the responsible-party model in the domain of social welfare. In this issue area, the arena of partisan conflict for a generation, the party symbol helps both constituency and Representative in the difficult process of communication between them. On the one hand, because Republican and Democratic voters tend to differ in what they would have government do, the Representative has some guide to district opinion simply by looking at the partisan division of the vote. On the other hand, because the two parties tend to recruit candidates who differ on the social welfare role of government, the constituency can infer the candidates' positions with more than random accuracy from their party affiliation, even though what the constituency has learned directly about these stands is almost nothing. How faithful the representation of social welfare views is to the responsible-party model should not be exaggerated. Even in this policy domain, American practice departs widely from an ideal conception of party government.[22] But in this domain, more than any other, political conflict has become a conflict of national parties in which constituency and Representative are known to each other primarily by their party association.

It would be too pat to say that the domain of foreign involvement conforms to the third model of representation, the conception promoted by Edmund Burke. Clearly, it does in the sense that the Congressman looks elsewhere than to his district in making up his mind on foreign issues. However, the reliance he puts on the President and the Administration suggests that the calculation of where the public interest lies is often passed to the Executive on matters of foreign policy. Ironically, legislative initiative in foreign affairs has fallen victim to the very difficulties of gathering and appraising information that led Burke to argue that Parliament rather than the public ought to hold the power of decision. The background information and predictive skills that Burke thought the people lacked are held primarily by the modern Executive. As a result, the present role of the legislature in foreign affairs bears some resemblance to the role that Burke had in mind for the elitist, highly restricted *electorate* of his own day.

NOTES

* The research reported here was made possible through grants of the Rockefeller Foundation and the Social Science Research Council, whose support is gratefully acknowledged. The authors are indebted also to Ralph Bisco and Gudmund R. Iverson for invaluable assistance.

[1] To be sure, the work of the Federal Convention has been supplemented in two critical respects. The first of these is the practice, virtually universal since the mid-19th century, of choosing Representatives from single-member districts of limited geographic area. The second is the practice, which has also become virtually universal in our own century, of selecting party nominees for the House by direct primary election.

[2] In the language of Eulau, Wahlke, et al., we speak here of the "style," not the "focus," of representation. See their, "The Role of the Representative: Some Empirical Observations on the Theory of Edmund Burke," American Political Science Review, Vol. 53 (September, 1959), pp. 742–56. An excellent review of the mandate-independence controversy is given by Hanna Fenichel Pitkin, "The Theory of Representation" (unpublished doctoral dissertation, University of California, Berkeley, 1961). For other contemporary discussions of representation, see Alfred de Grazia, Public and Republic (New York, 1951), and John A. Fairlie, "The Nature of Political Representation," American Political Science Review, Vol. 34 (April–June, 1940), pp. 236–48, 456–66.

[3] The sampling aspects of this research were complicated by the fact that the study of representation was a rider midway on a four-year panel study of the electorate whose primary sampling units were not congressional districts (although there is no technical reason why they could not have been if the needs of the representation analysis had been foreseen when the design of the sample was fixed two years before). As a result, the districts in our sample had unequal probabilities of selection and unequal weights in the analysis, making the sample somewhat less efficient than an equal-probability sample of equivalent size.

It will be apparent in the discussion that follows that we have estimated characteristics of whole constituencies from our samples of constituents living in particular districts. In view of the fact that a sample of less than two thousand constituents has been divided among 116 districts, the reader may wonder about the reliability of these estimates. After considerable investigation we have concluded that their sampling error is not so severe a problem for the analysis as we had thought it would be. Several comments may indicate why it is not.

To begin with, the weighting of our sample of districts has increased the reliability of the constituency estimates. The correct theoretical weight to be assigned each district in the analysis is the inverse of the probability of the district's selection, and it can be shown that this weight is approximately proportional to the number of interviews taken in the district. The result of this is that the greatest weight is assigned the districts with the largest number of interviews and, hence, the most reliable constituency estimates. Indeed, these weights increase by half again the (weighted) mean number of interviews taken per district. To put the matter another way: the introduction of differential weights trades some of our sample of congressional districts for more reliable constituency estimates.

How much of a problem the unreliability of these estimates is depends very much on the analytic uses to which the estimates are put. If our goal were case analyses of particular districts, the constituency samples would have to be much larger. Indeed, for most case analyses we would want several hundred interviews per district (at a cost, over 116 districts, of several small nuclear reactors). However, most of the findings reported here are based not on single districts but on many or all of the districts in our sample. For analyses of this sort the number of interviews per district can be much smaller.

Our investigation of the effect of the sampling variance of the constituency estimates is quite reassuring. When statistics computed from our constituency samples are compared with corresponding parameter values for the constituencies, the agreement of the two sets of figures is quite close. For example, when the proportions voting Democratic in the 116 constituencies in 1958, as computed from our sample data, are compared with the actual proportions voting Democratic, as recorded in official election statistics, a product moment correlation of 0.93 is obtained, and this figure is the more impressive since this test throws away non-voters, almost one-half of our total sample. We interpret the Pearsonian correlation as an appropriate measure of agreement in this case, since the associated regression equations are almost exactly the identity function. The alternative intraclass correlation coefficient has almost as high a value.

Although we believe that this analysis provides a textbook illustration of how misleading intuitive ideas (including our own) about the effects of sampling error can be, these figures ought not to be too beguiling. It is clear that how close such a correlation is to 1.0 for any given variable will depend on the ratio of the between-district variance to the total variance. When this ratio is as high as it is for Republican and Democratic voting, the effect of the unreliability of our constituency estimates is fairly trivial. Although the content of the study is quite different, this sampling problem has much in common with the problem of attenuation of correlation as it has been treated in psychological testing. See, for example, J. P. Guilford, *Fundamental Statistics in Psychology and Education* (New York, 1956), pp. 475–78.

[4] See Angus Campbell, Philip E. Converse, Warren E. Miller, and Donald E. Stokes, *The American Voter* (New York, 1960), pp. 194–209.

[5] This conclusion, fully supported by our own work for later Congresses, is one of the main findings to be drawn from the work of Duncan MacRae on roll call voting in the House of Representatives. See his *Dimensions of Congressional Voting: A Statistical Study in the House of Representatives in the Eighty-First Congress* (Berkeley and Los Angeles; University of California Press, 1958). For additional evidence of the existence of scale dimensions in legislative behavior, see N. L. Gage and Ben Shimberg, "Measuring Senatorial Progressivism," *Journal of Abnormal and Social Psychology*, Vol. 44 (January, 1949), pp. 112–17; George M. Belknap, "A Study of Senatorial Voting by Scale Analysis" (unpublished doctoral dissertation, University of Chicago, 1951), and "A Method for Analyzing Legislative Behavior," *Midwest Journal of Political Science*, Vol. 2 (1958), pp. 377–402; two other articles by MacRae, "The Role of the State Legislator in Massachusetts," *American Sociological Review*, Vol. 19 (April, 1954), pp. 185–94, and "Roll Call Votes and Leadership," *Public Opinion Quarterly*, Vol. 20 (1956), pp. 543–58; Charles D. Farris, "A Method of Determining Ideological Groups in Congress," *Journal of Politics*, Vol. 20 (1958), pp. 308–38; and Leroy N. Rieselbach, "Quantitative Techniques for Studying Voting Behavior in the U.N. General Assembly," *International Organization*, Vol. 14 (1960), pp. 291–306.

[6] The content of the three issue domains may be suggested by some of the roll call and interview items used. In the area of social welfare these included the issues of public housing, public power, aid to education, and government's role in maintaining full employment. In the area of foreign involvement the items included the issues of foreign economic aid, military aid, sending troops abroad, and aid to neutrals. In the area of civil rights the items included the issues of school desegregation, fair employment, and the protection of Negro voting rights.

[7] Because this point has been so widely discussed it has inevitably attracted a variety of terms. Dahl denotes the acts of *a* whose performance *A* is able to influence as the *scope* of *A*'s power. See Robert A. Dahl, "The Concept of Power," *Behavioral Science*, Vol. 2 (July, 1957), pp. 201–15. This usage is similar to that of Harold D. Lasswell and Abraham Kaplan, *Power and Society* (New Haven: Yale University Press, 1950), pp. 71–73. Dorwin Cartwright, however, denotes the behavioral or psychological changes in *P* which *O* is able to induce as the *range* of *O*'s power: "A Field Theoretical Conception of Power," *Studies in Social Power* (Ann Arbor: Research Center for Group Dynamics, Institute for Social Research, The University of Michigan, 1959), pp. 183–220.

[8] That the Representative's roll call votes can diverge from his true opinion is borne out by a number of findings of the study (some of which are reported here) as to the conditions under which agreement between the Congressman's roll call position and his private attitude will be high or low. However, a direct confirmation that these two sets of measurements are not simply getting at the same thing is given by differences in attitude-roll call agreement according to the Congressman's sense of how well his roll call votes have expressed his real views. In the domain of foreign involvement, for example, the correlation of our attitudinal and roll call measurements was .75 among Representatives who said that their roll call votes had expressed their real views fairly well. But this correlation was only .04 among those who said that their roll call votes had expressed their views poorly. In the other policy domains, too, attitude-roll call agreement is higher among Congressmen who are well satisfied with their roll call votes than it is among Congressmen who are not.

[9] During the analysis we have formed constituency scores out of the scores of constituents living in the same district by several devices other than calculating average constituent scores. In particular, in view of the ordinal character of our scales we have frequently used the *median* constituent score as a central value for constituency as a whole. However, the ordering of constituencies differs very little according to which of several reasonable alternatives for obtaining constituency scores is chosen. As a result, we have preferred mean scores for the greater number of ranks they give.

[10] The meaning of this procedure can be suggested by two percentage tables standing for hypothetical extreme cases, the first that of full agreement, the second that of no agreement whatever. For convenience, these illustrative tables categorize both Congressmen and their districts in terms of only three degrees of favor and assume for both a nearly uniform distribution across the three categories. The terms "pro," "neutral," and "con" indicate a relative rather than an absolute opinion. In Case I, full agreement, all districts relatively favorable to social welfare action have Congressmen who are so too, etc.; whereas in Case II, or that of no agreement, the ordering of constituents is independent in a statistical sense of the ranking of Congressmen: knowing the policy orientation of a district gives no clue at all to the orientation of its Congressman. Of course, it is possible for the orders of legislators and districts to be *inversely* related, and this possibility is of some importance, as indicated below, when the policy position of non-incumbent candidates as well as incumbents is taken into account. To summarize the degree of congruence between legislators and voters, a measure of correlation is introduced. Although we have used a variety of measures of association in our analysis, the values reported in this article all refer to product moment correlation coefficients. For our hypothetical Case I a measure of correlation would have the value 1.0; for Case II, the value 0.0. When it is applied to actual data this convenient indicator is likely to have a value somewhere in between. The question is where.

Case I: Full Policy Agreement

| | Constituencies | | | |
Congressmen	Pro	Neutral	Con	
Pro	33	0	0	33
Neutral	0	34	0	34
Con	0	0	33	33
	33	34	33	100%

Correlation 1.0

Case II: No Policy Agreement

Congressmen	Constituencies			
	Pro	Neutral	Con	
Pro	11	11	11	33
Neutral	11	12	11	34
Con	11	11	11	33
	33	34	33	100%

Correlation 0.0

[11] A word of caution is in order, lest we compare things that are not strictly comparable. For obvious reasons, most non-incumbent candidates have no roll call record, and we have had to measure their policy agreement with the district entirely in terms of the attitudes they have revealed in interviews. However, the difference of coefficients given here is almost as great when the policy agreement between the incumbent Congressman and his district is also measured in terms of the attitudes conveyed in confidential interviews.

[12] A third type of connection, excluded here, might obtain between district and Congressman if the Representative accedes to what he thinks the district wants because he believes that to be what a representative *ought* to do, whether or not it is necessary for re-election. We leave this type of connection out of our account here because we conceive an influence relation as one in which control is not voluntarily accepted or rejected by someone subject to it. Of course, this possible connection between district and Representative is not any the less interesting because it falls outside our definition of influence or control, and we have given a good deal of attention to it in the broader study of which this analysis is part.

[13] It scarcely needs to be said that demonstrating *some* constituency influence would not imply that the Representative's behavior is *wholly* determined by constituency pressures. The legislator acts in a complex institutional setting in which he is subject to a wide variety of influences. The constituency can exercise a genuine measure of control without driving all other influences from the Representative's life space.

[14] We have done this by a variance-component technique similar to several others proposed for dealing with problems of this type. See especially, Herbert A. Simon, "Spurious Correlation: A Causal Interpretation," *Journal of the American Statistical Association*, Vol. 49 (1954), pp. 467–79; Hubert M. Blalock, Jr., "The Relative Importance of Variables," *American Sociological Review*, Vol. 26 (1961), pp. 866–74 ; and the almost forgotten work of Sewall Wright, "Correlation and Causation," *Journal of Agricultural Research*, Vol. 20 (1920), pp. 557–85. Under this technique a "path coefficient" (to use Wright's terminology, although not his theory) is assigned to each of the causal arrows by solving a set of equations involving the correlations of the variables of the model. The weight assigned to a full path is then the product of its several path coefficients, and this product may be interpreted as the proportion of the variance of the dependent variable (roll call behavior, here) that is explained by a given path.

A special problem arises because influence may flow in either direction between the Congressman's attitude and his perception of district attitude (as noted above, the Representative may tend both to perceive his constituency's view selectively, as consistent with his own, and to change his own view to be consistent with the perceived constituency view). Hence, we have not a single causal model, but a whole family of models, varying according to the relative importance of influence from attitude to perception and from perception to attitude. Our solution to this problem has been to calculate influence coefficients for the two extreme models in order to see how much our results could vary according to which model is chosen from our family of models. Since the systems of equations in this analysis are linear it can be shown that the coefficients we seek have their maximum and minimum values under one or the other of the limiting models. Therefore, computing any given coefficient for each of these limiting cases defines an interval in which the true value of the coefficient must lie. In fact these intervals turn out to be fairly small; our findings as to the relative importance of alternative influence paths would change little according to which model is selected.

The two limiting models with their associated systems of equations and the formulas for computing the relative importance of the three possible influence paths under each model are given in Figure A.

Figure A

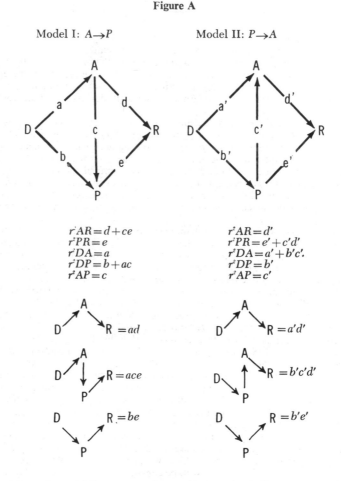

Model I: $A{\rightarrow}P$ Model II: $P{\rightarrow}A$

$r_{AR}=d+ce$
$r_{PR}^{2}=e$
$r_{DA}^{2}=a$
$r_{DP}^{2}=b+ac$
$r_{AP}^{2}=c$

$r_{AR}^{2}=d'$
$r_{PR}^{2}=e'+c'd'$
$r_{DA}^{2}=a'+b'c'$.
$r_{DP}^{2}=b'$
$r_{AP}^{2}=c'$

$D \nearrow^{A} \searrow R = ad$

$D \nearrow^{A} \searrow R = a'd'$

$D \nearrow^{A}_{\downarrow} {}_{P}\nearrow R = ace$

$D \searrow {}_{P}\uparrow^{A} \searrow R = b'c'd'$

$D \searrow_{P}\nearrow R = be$

$D \searrow_{P}\nearrow R = b'e'$

[15] By "least favorable" we mean the assumption that influence goes only from the Congressman's attitude to his perception of district attitude (Model I) and not the other way round. Under this assumption, the proportions of the variance of roll call behavior accounted for by the three alternative paths, expressed as proportions of the part of the variance of roll call votes that is explained by district attitude, are these:

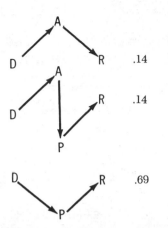

Inverting the assumed direction of influence between the Congressman's own attitude and district attitude (Model II) eliminates altogether the effect that the Representative's district attitude can have had on his votes, independently of his perception of district attitude.

[16] Under both Models I and II the proportion of the variance of roll call voting explained by the influence path involving the Representative's own attitude is twice as great as the proportion explained by influence passing through his perception of district attitude.

[17] What is more, the electorate's awareness of Congress as a whole appears quite limited. A majority of the public was unable to say in 1958 which of the two parties had controlled the Congress during the preceding two years. Some people were confused by the coexistence of a Republican President and Democratic Congress. But for most people this was simply an elementary fact about congressional affairs to which they were not privy.

[18] For a more extended analysis of forces on the congressional vote, see Donald E. Stokes and Warren E. Miller, "Party Government and the Saliency of Congress," *Public Opinion Quarterly*, Vol. 26 (Winter, 1962), pp. 531–46.

[19] For an account of this episode see Corinne Silverman, "The Little Rock Story," Inter-University Case Program series, reprinted in Edwin A. Bock and Alan K. Campbell, eds., *Case Studies in American Government* (Englewood Cliffs, 1962), pp. 1–46.

[20] The sample of this constituency was limited to twenty-three persons of whom thirteen voted. However, despite the small number of cases the probability that the difference in awareness between this constituency and the country generally as the result only of sampling variations is much less than one in a thousand.

[21] In view of the potential nature of the constituency's sanctions, it is relevant to characterize its influence over the Representative in terms of several distinctions drawn by recent theorists of power, especially the difference between actual and potential power, between influence and coercive power, and between influence and purposive control. Observing these distinctions, we might say that the constituency's influence is *actual* and not merely *potential* since it is the sanction behavior rather than the conforming behavior that is infrequent (Dahl). That is, the Congressman is influenced by his calculus of potential sanctions, following the "rule of anticipated reactions" (Friedrich), however oblivious of his behavior the constituency ordinarily may be. We might also say that the constituency has *power* since its influence depends partly on sanctions (Lasswell and Kaplan), although it rarely exercises *control* since its influence is rarely conscious or intended (Cartwright). In the discussion above we have of course used the terms "influence" and "control" interchangeably.

[22] The factors in American electoral behavior that encourage such a departure are discussed in Stokes and Miller, *loc. cit.*

CHAPTER 18

The Benevolent Leader:
Children's Images of Political Authority

Fred I. Greenstein

Society's training of the young, including formal and informal citizenship instruction, character training, and the processes which lead to the development of different personality types, has been seen as an important determinant of adult political behavior by theorists since Plato. In addition, much of our traditional folklore, not to mention much 20th century literature on personality development, national character, authoritarianism, and electoral preference, points to the utility of examining the individual's early years as one means of illuminating his mature actions.[1]

The present paper considers one aspect of the child's political development—the genesis of his attitudes toward political leaders and the possible ways that this developmental process may affect his adult responses to the formal wielders of power. Citizens' orientations to political authority have a complex and imperfectly understood, but obviously important, bearing on the equilibrium of a body politic.

Two classes of data will be considered: survey literature giving some indication of how adults respond to political leaders, and results of a study of 659 New Haven public and private school children of widely varying socio-economic status, ranging from fourth- through eighth-graders (about nine to thirteen years of age). Paper-and-pencil questionnaires were administered to this sample between January and March of 1958. Findings from these sources are supplemented by a smaller collection of prolonged interviews with individual children and many informal encounters with groups of school children and teachers over a period of about two years.[2]

I. ADULT ORIENTATIONS TO POLITICAL LEADERS:
AMBIVALENCE

Adult orientations to political leaders display a curious inconsistency,

Reprinted from *American Political Science Review*, Vol. 54, No. 4 (December 1960), pp. 934–943, by permission of the American Political Science Association.

which must be noted to give meaning to my New Haven pre-adult findings. To begin with, political roles, such as Senator, Mayor, Governor, and Judge, are in general highly esteemed by adults in the United States. Over the years, the many studies of occupational prestige have shown that people rank these roles well above all but an occasional civilian role (such as physician) in terms of importance and status.[3] On the other hand, responses are much more variable when people are asked to rate individual public officials. The best barometer of this variation is probably the American Institute of Public Opinion's monthly estimates of presidential popularity. For over two decades, national cross-sections have been asked questions such as the following:

Do you approve or disapprove of the way President X has been handling his job? During his first term in office, favorable responses to President Truman ranged from 87 per cent to 32 per cent. Roosevelt and Eisenhower also fluctuated in popularity, although not as sharply.[4]

Perhaps as a function of this blend of respect for high political roles and more qualified opinions toward the men who fill these positions, the mere fact of incumbency seems to have a positive effect on a leader's popularity. Thus it has been found that shortly after a president is elected people who were hitherto opposed to him upgrade their evaluations. This probably is a specific case of what has more generally been called the *fait accompli* effect. For example, support for a law increases after it has been passed and, conversely, people are less likely to back policy proposals if they are told that it will be necessary to change a law, or amend the constitution, to achieve this goal.[5]

But this is not the whole story. As is well known, distinctly anti-"politician" and anti-"politics" views are widespread in the population. The survey literature abounds with evidence that substantial groups of people agree that "It is almost impossible for a man to stay honest if he goes into politics," that it is at best dubious for a young man to make politics his career, and so forth.[6] Unsympathetic images of politics and the politician also are revealed by a great many adults in responses to various questions about the individual's political efficacy, as measured for example by willingness to agree with the statement "I don't think public officials care much what people like me think."[7]

The seeming inconsistency between this set of attitudes and responses to individual political leaders and roles has led one recent commentator to write of "the ambivalent social status of the American politician."[8]

II. CHILDREN'S ORIENTATIONS TO POLITICAL LEADERS: UNQUALIFIED SYMPATHY

Possibly the most striking outcome of the New Haven study was the finding that the prevailing adult skepticism and distrust of politics and the politician simply did not seem to be present in the grade school sample. In spite of a variety of attempts to evoke such responses during my preliminary inter-viewing and pretesting, there was no evidence even of a frame of reference which would make it possible to use questionnaire items tapping the dimension of political cynicism. Moreover, although the final New Haven questionnaires contained a number of items which might have evoked spontaneous references to the malignancy of politicians, only one or two of the 659 children made statements which could be construed in this way.[9]

Let us now note some more specific findings.

(1) Children are like adults in their ranking of high political roles. Members of the New Haven sample were asked to tell which of a number of adult roles are "most important." Choices offered included the President and Mayor, authority figures of the immediate environment such as school principals and teachers, as well as physicians, clergymen, police chiefs, and judges. At every age level, there were more references to the President and Mayor than to any of the other roles.

Table 1, which reports the responses of the youngest group in this sample, shows that even by the age of nine this orientation has become firmly entrenched. Both political executives were mentioned by over ten

Table 1. Judgements of Which Adult Roles Are "Most Important" by Fourth Grade Children*

Roles	% Choosing Each Role
President	80
Mayor	79
Doctor	57
Police Chief	51
Judge	48
School Teacher	35
Religious Leader	32
School Principal	22
Number of Cases	111

* Children were permitted four choices, so the percentages exceed 100. The mayor's prestige may be a function of the great per-sonal popularity of New Haven's incumbent city executive. See the note to Table 2.

per cent more fourth graders than even the prestigeful physician. Evidently the importance of political roles is learned early; just how early cannot be determined from this sample. However, the following passage from an interview with a seven-year-old (beginning second grade) is illuminating

Interviewer: Have you ever heard of the President of the United States?
Robert: Yes.
I: What is his name?
R: Eisenhower.
I: What does he do?
R: Well, sometimes he . . . well you know . . . a lot of times when people go away
   he'll say goodbye and he's on programs and they do work.
I: What kind of work does he do? Do you know any more about it?
R: (after thought) Studying.
I: What sorts of things does he study?
R: Like things they gotta do . . . like important . . . what's happening and the
   weather and all that.
I: Now tell me this. Who is more important, the President of the United States or
   a doctor?
R: (Pause) The President.
I: Who do you think is more important, the President of the United States or a
   school teacher?
R: (Emphatically) President!
I: Why is the President more important?
R: They do much more work and they're much importanter. School teacher isn't.
I: (After being told in response to further questions that the President also is
   more important than a store keeper and than a general in the Army): Who do
   you think is more important than the President?
R: (Long pause) Lemme see . . . I don't know.

Robert's answers provide some insight into how political learning takes place. Not only does he have a firmly entrenched assessment of the President's importance, but he has also—as his attempt to explain the President's duties in terms of a work-a-day seven-year-old frame of reference shows—acquired this assessment in the virtual absence of cognitive information. Evaluations and "affective knowledge" about political leaders seem to precede the factual information on which they might be "based."

The younger New Haven children were almost devoid of political knowledge. All but a handful of them knew the names of the President and Mayor, but few knew much more than this. Within the brief age span of this sample, the level of political information increases considerably, as can be seen in Table 2. But the structure of cognitive information is erected on a foundation of feelings, assessments, and opinions; and the development of critical faculties waits on a later stage. Estimates of the importance of political leaders, incidentally, follow the same developmental course as another adult orientation—party identification. New Haven children described themselves as Republicans or Democrats long before they were able to make any meaningful statements about the parties, or even to link the party labels with the names of conspicuous leaders such as the President and Mayor.[10]

Table 2. "Reasonably Accurate" Responses to Selected Political
Information Items, by School Year*

Information Asked	School Grade				
	4th	5th	6th	7th	8th
President's name	96%	97%	90%	99%	100%
Mayor's name	90	97	89	99	97
President's duties	23	33	44	65	66
Mayor's duties	35	42	50	66	67
Governor's duties	8	12	23	36	43
Role of State Legislature	5	5	9	24	37
Number of Cases	111	118	115	135	180

* A correct response to the items "President's name" and "Mayor's name" involved writing the names of the appropriate official on the questionnaire. Children in the lower grades were given assistance in spelling when necessary. Rather "generous" criteria were used for classifying descriptions of political executives and legislatures as "reasonably accurate." Coding and administration techniques are described in detail in Greenstein, *op. cit.* The high degree of familiarity with the Mayor's name and duties probably is due to the unusual popularity of that individual at the time, rather than to a general conspicuousness of city executives. Pre-tests in a nearby town showed that only 40 per cent of the fifth graders knew the First Selectman's name and fewer could describe his role.

(2) Another point at which the New Haven children's orientations can be compared, at least tentatively, with adult responses, is in their ratings of individual political leaders. Following the various information items which called, for example, for descriptions of the duties of the Mayor, Governor, and President (reported in Table 2), the children were asked to evaluate these leaders on a four-point scale ranging from "very good" to "bad."

Here children's responses did not merely reflect what might be expected from comparable adult samples. Their modal assessment of each of the three incumbents was in the highest possible category—"very good."[11] Judging from the way national cross-sections of adults responded to the opportunity to rate President Eisenhower during the (shortly post-sputnik) months of this survey, children's views of political leaders are substantially more favorable than those of their elders. Table 3 contrasts the New Haven responses with the American Institute of Public Opinion's February 1958 report of the President's popularity. Needless to say, this juxtaposition of New Haven findings with national survey data must be treated as suggestive, rather than conclusive. However, differences between these groups in evaluation of the President are considerable. Adults seemed to be about five times more willing to criticize the chief executive.[12]

New Haven responses to items dealing with political efficacy also suggests that children are far more positive in their political orientations than adults. Less than two per cent of the children said that they would not vote when

Table 3. Children's Evaluations of Three Political Executives Contrasted with Adult Evaluations of President Eisenhower During the Same Time Period

	Children			Adults*
	The Mayor	The Governor	The President	The President
Very Good	62%	40%	71% ⎫	
Fairly Good	27	28	21 ⎬ Approve 58%	
Not Very Good	4	2	4 ⎫	
Bad	1	—†	1 ⎬ Disapprove 27	
Don't Know	6	30	4	No Opinion 15
Number of Cases	651‡	643‡	649‡	

* February 1958 AIPO findings, reported in March 1958 release. These findings are based on a national sample. On their comparability with the New Haven data, see footnote 12.

† Less than 1 per cent.

‡ Number of cases does not equal complete sample due to invalid responses.

they reached twenty-one. And over two-thirds agreed that "it makes much difference who wins an election," in contrast to the markedly smaller proportions of adult samples making such statements.[13]

(3) I have already noted that various items in the New Haven questionnaire might have stimulated spontaneous references to graft, corruption, political immorality, and so forth, if these images were important in children's perception of politics, and that such references were not made. However, a totally different set of orientations did emerge spontaneously in response to several of the open-ended items.

These were the six items asking for descriptions of the duties of local, state, and federal executives and legislative bodies (Table 2). The items were quite unstructured, simply asking, "What sorts of things does the Mayor (etc.) do?" As might be expected, most of the children who were able to respond made rather straightforward factual assertions—"The Mayor runs the city"; "Congress makes laws"; etc. What was surprising, however, was that a conspicuous minority of the children volunteered affective or affectively-toned responses—especially in descriptions of the Mayor and President. As noted above, only one or two of these statements were unsympathetic. Several classes of response are worth examining in more detail.

A. Services to Children. About ten per cent of the respondents eschewed reference to more widely recognized duties of the mayor and mentioned child-related portions of his role. For example:

[The Mayor] makes parks and swings. (Fifth grade girl)

[The Mayor] repairs the parks, roads, schools, and takes the snow off the roads when it snows. (Fifth grade boy)

It is a reasonable assumption that when a child's first image of a political leader is in terms of pork-barrel indulgences to the child, his image is a favorable one.

B. General Benevolence. More generally, children tended to describe political leaders as "helping," "taking care of," and "protecting" people. Benevolent perceptions of this sort were especially evident in descriptions of the President and Mayor, but also occasionally were apparent in descriptions of the Governor and of legislative bodies. For example:

[The President] deals with foreign countries and takes care of the U.S. (Eighth grade boy)

[The Mayor] helps people to live in safety. . . . The President is doing a very good job of making people be safe. (Fourth grade girl)

[The President] gives us freedom. (Eighth grade girl)

[The Board of Aldermen] gives us needs so we could live well. (Fourth grade girl)

In a few cases children went so far as to perceive political authority as a direct source of economic support:

[The Mayor] pays working people like banks. (Fifth grade boy)

[The Mayor] sees that schools have what they need and stores and other places too. (Fifth grade girl)

[The Mayor] helps everyone to have nice homes and jobs. (Fourth grade boy)

C. Normative Role. In addition, some children characterized political leaders in positive normative terms—either as people who "do good things," or as people who are specialists in making moral judgments:

[The President does] good work. (Sixth grade boy)

[The Mayor] sends men to build parks for us and make our city be a good one. (Fourth grade girl)

[The President] makes peace with every country but bad. (Fifth grade boy)

[The Mayor] talks business to all the people and says what's wrong or bad. (Fourth grade girl)

I think that he [the President] has the right to stop bad things before they start. (Fifth grade girl)

The frequency of "child-related" references to the Mayor, and of generally "benevolent" and "normative" references to the Mayor and President is shown in Table 4. Here we see that statements of this sort were made by some children at every age level, but that benevolent imagery declines with age. Although the total of these classes of images rarely exceeds 15 per cent in any cell of Table 4, what is remarkable is that any images of this sort are expressed in answer to such bland, unstructured stimulus questions. Moreover, there were additional descriptions of political

Table 4. Children's Images of the Mayor and President, by School Year*

	School Year				
	4th	*5th*	*6th*	*7th*	*8th*
The Mayor					
Child related duties: "makes parks and swings"	15%	14%	1%	11%	15%
Benevolence: "helps us" "gives us freedom"	20	16	9	3	4
Normative role: "does good things" "tells what is right or wrong"	7	12	13	8	12
Number of Cases	55	82	98	115	151
The President					
Benevolence	26%	11%	5%	5%	4%
Normative	5	9	11	3	7
Number of Cases	62	80	95	112	160

* Percentages are based on those children who were able to produce a description of the executive role, whether or not the description was "reasonably accurate" (excluding grossly inaccurate or vague statements). The coding is described in Greenstein, *op. cit.*

leaders with favorable connotations which do not fit as readily into a few simple categories. For example, some children placed emphasis on the wisdom, capability, and solicitousness of public officials:

[The President] is in charge of the United States and has many wise men to tell him what is best. (Sixth grade boy)

[The President] worries about all the problems of all the 48 states. Takes care of threatening wars by holding peace conferences. (Seventh grade boy)

[The Mayor] has to keep track of everything that happens in New Haven. (Sixth grade boy)

The spontaneous appearance of these images suggests that appropriately structured questions would show the imagery of benevolence to be considerably more common among grade school children than Table 4 indicates.[14]

The New Haven findings may be summarized as follows: children are at least as likely as adults to perceive high political roles as being important; they seem to be more sympathetic to individual political leaders (and, in general, to politics) than are adults; in at least some cases their actual images of political leaders are qualitatively different from the images one would expect adults to hold, especially in the emphasis on benignancy; and, most important, the widespread adult political cynicism and distrust does not seem to have developed by eighth grade (age 13). Each of these observations rests on a limited sample of respondents, and several are based on fortuitous findings, or comparisons which can only be made tentatively.

They are internally consistent and seem to be convincing, but further verification (using more varied and refined techniques) clearly is necessary. However, in this discussion which follows I shall for the moment assume their validity and consider their potential significance.

III. THE CHILD'S VIEW OF POLITICAL AUTHORITY: ITS SIGNIFICANCE

Two questions are raised by the foregoing data: (1) Why is the child's early view of political authority so strikingly favorable? (2) What, if any, effect does this aspect of an individual's development have on his adult political behavior?

Fully convincing answers to these questions, particularly the second, are not available. This is so not only because the New Haven data are limited, but also because the existing body of generalizations linking childhood experience to adult behavior is quite rudimentary.[15] Speculative answers, however, are a necessary first step to designing research which will extend our understanding of the dynamics of citizens' orientations toward political leaders.

(1) Although many lasting political orientations are acquired before adolescence—for instance, attitudes about the importance of major governmental roles and identifications with parties—early political learning seems to be quite casual. Young children, including the nine- and ten-year-olds who make up the youngest groups in this sample, have few interests beyond the environment of their immediate circle. And in New Haven there seemed to be little formal adult effort to shape the political information and attitudes of grade school children. Social studies curriculum guides, for example, do not suggest teaching until the sixth grade the subject matter which once was known as civics. Only in eighth grade is there mandatory provision for such training.

Nevertheless, political learning progresses during the preadolescent years (Table 2). This learning has many sources. The most important of them—at least as a determinant of attitudes—undoubtedly is the family.[16] Here (though I have no data based on direct observation) much of the learning probably is inadvertent and incidental to normal family activities. Similarly, inadvertent learning surely takes place in the schools, even in the absence of formal requirements for civic instruction, if only through politically related experiences such as patriotic observances. Among other sources of political learning, the mass media seem to be extremely important, especially during election campaigns.[17]

One antecedent of the highly idealized childhood political images may be whatever political communications are intentionally transmitted to children by their agents of socialization. Even parents and teachers who are personally vehement in their castigation of "politicians" may soften or sugar-coat the political explanations they pass on to children. However, it is likely that the socializing agents pass on something considerably more important than specific political attitudes—namely, general orientations toward the adult world. The child, through the entirety of his experiences with adults, acquires a frame of reference within which to place an especially important class of adult—the political leaders.[18] This seems to be the best way to explain the remarkable lack of political cynicism among children. Children certainly cannot be completely insulated from adult attitudes of distrust toward politics. Rather, it may be hypothesized, that, having learned to see adults as many times life size, children simply misperceive and otherwise screen out the discordant negative elements in the adult political environment.

Psychoanalytic theory suggests an integral connection between the feelings one develops toward figures in the primary environment (such as parents) and one's later responses to individuals in the secondary environment (such as politicians). The latter relationships become invested with deep personal feelings, sometimes in the form of direct reflections of primary group relationships, sometimes in the form of compensating reactions to them.[19] This notion is now quite familiar and in fact has been thoroughly vulgarized in the form of popular journalistic references to political "father figures." Vulgarizations notwithstanding, it may have considerable empirical substance. At any rate, a degree of clinical evidence supporting the hypothesis has accumulated.[20] That young children's descriptions of political leaders reflect imagery of benevolence, protectiveness, exceptional sagacity, etc., also is consistent with this hypothesis, although this is scarcely "proof" that an unconscious linking of primary and secondary figures has taken place.[21]

As we have seen the child's glowing political imagery shows signs of attrition (mainly in the use of "benevolent" language), during the five-year span of this sample. But the greatest change away from political euphoria probably is during adolescence. Disillusionment, following increased realistic political understanding, might produce such changes. Another, likely cause would be the adolescent's need to assume adult mannerisms including in some cases an inside dopester's appraisal of politics. Adolescence is, at any rate, a time for felling idols and perceiving the commanding figures of one's adult environment in a more fallible light.

(2) How does knowledge that the political learning sequence is from childhood idealism to adult realism and cynicism add to our understanding of citizens' responses to political authority? To answer this some further remarks on adult orientations to political leaders are necessary.

The cynical imagery of Americans seems to be less functionally relevant to their political behavior than the positive side of their responses—their respect for high political leaders and their frequent willingness to hold individual leaders in great esteem. This is evident not merely from such relatively narrow mechanisms as the *fait accompli* effect and the general willingness to accept the verdict of elections. The oft-proclaimed stability of the American political system—in spite of a remarkably heterogeneous population—suggests more broadly that powerful psychological mechanisms encouraging political obedience are present in the citizenry. These mechanisms may be as important as many of the more familiar historical, political, economic, and social factors which are drawn on to explain the complex phenomenon of political stability.

Psychologists of various schools, ranging from psychoanalysis to learning theory, have argued that "learning which takes place early in life should have especially great influence on lasting personality characteristics."[22] It also may be that political and social orientations which are acquired early will be particularly influential in adult behavior. As we have seen, the more negative attitudes toward political leaders are chronologically late arrivals, whereas the firm impression that leaders are important people emerges early and almost unconsciously—years before the child has more than a smattering of factual political information. Thus when the adult is in conflict between his two inconsistent assessments of political leaders, the longest held of these would be most likely to influence his response. In this respect it is worth noting that party identification, which also is acquired before the age of political reasoning, is a more important determinant of adult electoral choice than other motivating variables.[23]

The uniquely positive conceptions and misconceptions of leaders displayed by New Haven respondents, statements such as "The Mayor pays working people like banks," certainly are not important in the conscious political imagery of adults. But even here the fact that they once existed may be of some importance in understanding adult political behavior. If the psychoanalytic hypotheses linking political imagery to the primary group relationships which are vital in molding the personality are valid, it could follow that some early political images exercise an unconscious effect on adult choices. To the degree that responses to political authority are deeply rooted in the personality additional predictions might be made. For example, clinical experience suggests that in times of personal or community crisis individuals might tend to resume their earlier ways of viewing authority.

IV. RESEARCH PROSPECTS

So far I have attempted to relate two aspects of the way orientations towards political leaders develop, to the likelihood that these orientations will be influential in adult life. I have suggested that if the orientation is learned early, or if it becomes tied to intimate primary group experiences, it should have an especially strong effect on later behavior. To this a single more specific hypothesis about the possibility of regression has been added. Further theorizing and research is necessary to generate more in the way of specific, testable hypotheses. At present the general theories of development which have been spun out by Freud, Piaget, Sullivan, and Erikson, for example, have received only limited empirical verification and are poorly correlated with the empirical norms of development reported by child psychologists and the little which is known about the genesis of political and social orientations.

Theory building and hypothesis elaboration might best proceed in the context of concrete research, since little is known in detail at present about how political behavior develops.[24] The following are some of the *desiderata* of such research:

A. We need to know more about children's political images. The data presented in this paper are no more than a first approximation of how children perceive political authority. Do they differentiate between a wider range of political roles than those presented in the New Haven questionnaire? How do their responses vary over time and space? How prevalent are responses of the sort which arose spontaneously in the present study— imagery of benevolence, for example? New instruments will have to be developed to explore these responses in further detail.[25]

B. We need information on the types of independent variables which are related to differences in childhood political response. Do images of political leaders vary with the child's personality type? Do they vary with his family structure? In view of the continuing interest of social scientists in a number of disciplines in relationships between personality, culture, and social organization, there should be increasing possibilities for interdisciplinary collaboration.

Broader sampling of demographic groups will furnish insight into additional independent variables. Here the speculations about the political stability of nations earlier in this paper suggest that cross-cultural investigation may be promising. Recent studies of children's responses to (nonpolitical) authority figures by Gladys and Harold Anderson show substantial national differences in such perspectives as the expectation of punishment for a misdemeanor.[26]

C. Most important (and most difficult), we need ways of determining in some more precise manner than has been possible here what effects early orientations have on later political behavior. Here progress will be slowest, but by the same token validated propositions will be most rewarding. To a considerable extent advances will be dependent upon accomplishments in basic socialization research. This is an area of investigation in which experiments are not normally possible and knowledge accumulates somewhat uncertainly on the basis of correlational studies. Again, collaboration with ongoing research in other disciplines is both desirable and possible. For example, there have been many longitudinal projects which followed the same samples of children over varying periods of time.[27] Other procedures short of the longitudinal study also exist for studying socialization.[28]

As inevitably slow as the early stages of such research may be, the long run possibilities are exciting. For, as John Dollard has commented, if "the life of the individual is a single connected whole," it will be necessary, in order to enrich our understanding of adult political existence, "to peer down the long avenue of the individual life to see how the present-day event matured."[29]

NOTES

[1] The first thoroughgoing consideration of the problems in studying political socialization, including a summary of much past research which is germane to understanding political development, is Herbert Hyman's *Political Socialization* (Glencoe, 1959). Emphasis on the socialization process as a determinant of adult behavior does not, of course, carry the implication that "only ... childhood events determine adult behavior." Cf. Nathan Leites, "Psycho-Cultural Hypotheses about Political Acts," *World Politics*, Vol. 1 (1948), pp. 102–19.

[2] For a full report of the larger study from which these findings are drawn, along with a more detailed discussion of its methodology, see Fred I. Greenstein, *Children's Political Perspectives: A Study of the Development of Political Awareness and Preferences among Pre-adolescents*, unpublished doctoral dissertation, Yale University Library. The major methodological point which should be noted here is that the respondents consist of the populations of three public and one private school, rather than a probability sample of New Haven children. As a rough means of compensating for this difficulty, socioeconomic status was controlled in the data analysis. However, since SES differences are not relevant to the present discussion, data for all respondents are presented combined.

When data are reported by age, systematic variations between the younger and older age groups are treated as evidence of developmental changes. It is always possible, however, in a cross-sectional study that some other variable is responsible for apparent age differences. Therefore, further validation of statements about development by longitudinal procedures is desirable. For a discussion of the relative merits of cross-sectional and longitudinal research, see the articles by John B. Anderson and Margaret Mead in Leonard Carmichael, *Manual of Child Psychology* (New York, 1954).

I am deeply indebted to Robert E. Lane for his thoughtful criticism at every stage of this project. Earlier drafts of this paper profited from comments by James David Barber, Harold D. Lasswell, Richard D. Schwartz, and Jerome H. Skolnick.

[3] See "Jobs and Occupations: A Popular Evaluation," *Opinion News*, Vol. 9 (September 1, 1949), pp. 3–19; Mapheus Smith, "An Empirical Scale of Prestige Status of Occupations," *American Sociological Review*, Vol. 8 (1943), pp. 185–92; Harvey C.

Lehman and Paul A. Witty, "Further Study of the Social Status of Occupations," *The Journal of Educational Sociology*, Vol. 5 (1931–32); George W. Hartmann, "The Prestige of Occupations," *The Personnel Journal*, Vol. 13 (1934–35), pp. 144–52. For an early attempt at cross-cultural study, see Jerome Davis, "Testing the Social Attitudes of Children in the Government Schools in Russia," *American Journal of Sociology*, Vol. 32 (1926–27), pp. 947–52.

[4] The variations in Truman's first-term popularity are summarized in Bernard Berelson *et al.*, *Voting* (Chicago, 1954), p. 258. Public responses to Roosevelt may be found in Hadley Cantril and Mildred Strunk, *Public Opinion 1935–1946* (Princeton, 1951). For Eisenhower's popularity see the regular news releases of the AIPO.

[5] Hadley Cantril, *Gauging Public Opinion* (Princeton, 1944), pp. 43–44; Paul F. Lazarsfeld *et al.*, *The People's Choice* (New York, 1944), p. 38; Paul F. Lazarsfeld, "Public Opinion and the Classical Tradition," *The Public Opinion Quarterly*, Vol. 21 (1957), p. 47.

[6] Cantril and Strunk, *op. cit.*, p. 584; National Opinion Research Center, *The Public Looks at Politics and Politicians*, Report No. 20, March 1944.

[7] Angus Campbell *et al.*, *The Voter Decides* (Evanston, 1954), pp. 187–94.

[8] William C. Mitchell, in the *Western Political Quarterly*, Vol. 12 (1959), pp. 683–98.

[9] This is not to say that children never develop aversions to *individual* political leaders, although as is shown below, they probably are less likely than adults to do so. One item which did evoke spontaneous negative references to individual politicians asked the child to "Name a famous person you *don't* want to be like." About 15 per cent of the respondents named a political leader of the present or of the recent past. Interestingly, more than half of these references were to foreign leaders such as Nikita Khrushchev. Follow-up interviews suggested that some of the negative references to domestic leaders were rejections of the responsibility of being (say) president, rather than personal criticisms of the leader.

[10] Moreover, they expressed the party identification which was "appropriate" for their demographic group. The children's reports of familial party preferences support the familiar thesis that membership in American political parties is "inherited." How party identification develops and the relationship between this process and the development of other orientations which affect adult electoral choice will be discussed in a subsequent publication.

[11] The report of these findings in Table 3 shows not only that ratings of the three incumbent political executives were exceptionally favorable, but also that few children failed to express an opinion. In fact, two-thirds of the sample evaluated all three leaders, although, as can be seen from Table 2, many fewer were able to describe the duties of each of these individuals. This raises the possibility that responses to the evaluation item may be "invalid," as a result, for example, of perseveration. I do not believe that this is so for the following reasons:

(1) Some variations in ratings of the three leaders emerged, within the context of a general willingness to (a) evaluate and (b) make a highly positive assessment. For example, "don't know" was checked with respect to the lesser known Governor more often than with respect to the Mayor and President.

(2) Seventh and eighth grade children evaluated a non-incumbent political leader, Adlai Stevenson, as well as the three incumbents. Stevenson's ratings were much less favorable than Eisenhower's (with a modal response of "fairly good").

(3) Within the general tendency to produce favorable ratings, differences between subgroups in the sample were evident. Children with Democratic party identifications were significantly more likely to give high ratings to the Democratic Mayor and Governor, and Republicans were significantly more favorable toward Eisenhower.

(4) The possibility of checking "don't know" was emphasized in the administration instructions, and this alternative appeared before the other possibilities in the questionnaire. In addition, each evaluation item was separated from the next by a series of intermediary items. The anonymity of questionnaire responses was stressed.

Rather than being an artifact of the questionnaire, I suspect that the responses reported in Table 3 are further evidence of children's early propensity to make political judgments in the absence of much information. Cf. Nicholas Babchuck and C. Wayne Gordon, "The Child as a Prototype of the Naive Informant in the Interview Situation," *American Sociological Review*, Vol. 23 (1958), pp. 196–98.

[12] At least three points of non-comparability should be noted: the differences in population; the differences in question wording; and the differences in response alternatives. With these major reservations in mind, the following additional AIPO findings on President Eisenhower, for the months surrounding this survey, may be noted. (AIPO releases November 1957, January and March 1958).

	Approve	Disapprove	No Opinion
November 1957	57%	27%	16%
January 1958	60	30	10
March 1958	52	33	15

The November AIPO report, which controls for region, suggests that Southern responses may have inflated the "disapproval" column. In that month, Eastern states were reported as 65 per cent approve, 21 per cent disapprove, and 14 per cent no opinion. This still is considerably more than the 5 per cent of the New Haven children who checked the "bad" and "not very good" alternatives.

[13] For example, in the Survey Research Center's 1952 election study sample, only a fifth of the respondents claimed that "it would make a great deal of difference to the country whether the Democrats or the Republicans win the elections." Angus Campbell *et al.*, *The Voter Decides* (Evanston, 1954), p. 38. The same reservations about comparability of samples, question wording, and response alternatives expressed in note 12, above, are also relevant here.

The Survey Research Center reports that 43 per cent of the respondents replied "some difference, minor differences." Compare a 1946 cross-section of the national population which was asked: "Do you think it makes much difference or only a little difference which party wins the elections for Congress this fall?" About half said it made "much difference," about 30 per cent "little," and the remaining 20 per cent was divided evenly between "no difference" and "no opinion." Cantril and Strunk, *op. cit.*, p. 582.

[14] Another class of political imagery is worth noting. A small percentage of the respondents (but some in each of the four schools which make up the sample) coped with the problem of organizing their fragmentary political information by using hierarchical concepts. They saw politics, even in the case of individuals and institutions which are formally co-ordinate, in terms of a chain of command. For example:

The Mayor gets orders from the President . . . The President gives orders to the Governor. (Fifth grade girl)

[The Mayor] handles the minor problems and if it is too big he goes to the Governor. (Seventh grade boy)

[The Mayor] takes the problems of the town. He [The Governor] takes the hard problems. (Fifth grade boy)

One notably ingenious misconception combined hierarchy with benevolence. The fifth grade boy whose statement that "The Mayor pays working people like banks" was cited above went on to say, "The Governor pays mayors. . . . The President pays the Governor." Again the appropriate instrument might reveal that this way of perceiving politics is reasonably common in childhood and, perhaps, that it is related to certain types of nonpolitical—e.g., primary group—experiences. See footnote 21, below.

[15] For a useful summary of this literature, see Irvin L. Child, "Socialization," in Gardner Lindzey, *Handbook of Social Psychology* (Cambridge, 1954), pp. 655–92. Also Alex Inkeles and Daniel J. Levinson, "National Character: the Study of Modal Personality and Sociocultural Systems," *ibid.*, especially pp. 997–98.

[16] Cf. Hyman, *op. cit.*, Chap. 4.

[17] Cf. Greenstein, *op. cit.*, pp. 55–74.

[18] Contemporary children's literature, which presents a painfully benevolent portrayal of the wider environment, would tend to reinforce such a frame of reference. Books such as *Our Friend the Farmer* and *How the Policeman Helps Us* are couched in language which closely resembles some of the pre-adolescent descriptions of political leaders reported above.

[19] This thesis is advanced in Harold D. Lasswell, *Power and Personality* (New York, 1948), pp. 156–57. Also see C. W. Wahl, "The Relation Between Primary and Secondary Identifications," in Eugene Burdick and Arthur J. Brodbeck, *American Voting Behavior* (Glencoe, 1959), pp. 262–80.

[20] Sebastian DeGrazia, "A Note on the Psychological Position of the Chief Executive," *Psychiatry*, Vol. 8 (1945), pp. 267–72; W. R. D. Fairbairn, *An Object Relations Theory of Personality* (New York, 1954), pp. 223–29; Frans Alexander, "Emotional Factors in Voting Behavior," in Burdick and Brodbeck, *op. cit.*, pp. 300–307; Richard E. Renneker, "Some Psychodynamic Aspects of Voting Behavior," *ibid.*, pp. 399–413.

[21] The hierarchical imagery reported in footnote 14 provides an illustration of the types of linkage which may take place. In each instance the child clearly has meager factual information about the roles he is attempting to describe. His allusion to a chain of command seems to result from an attempt to organize what fragmentary information he has. This may be seen in further detail in a follow-up interview with a sixth grade boy who had responded hierarchically on his questionnaire:

Interviewer: What sorts of things does Mayor Lee do?
Larry: Well, he keeps the city together and tells them what to do.
I: Tells who what to do?
L: Well, let's see. He probably tells some of the most important people and then they tell the ones that are less important and they keep on going.
I: What kinds of people are these? Do you mean any people in the city?
L: No, like the police chief and the head of the schools or something.

. . . .

I: What do you think the Governor does?
L: Well, be probably tells the mayors what to do and he probably tells other people what to do.
I: When you say "probably," does that mean you're sort of guessing about what he does?
L: Yes . . . He has to tell *somebody* what to do.

. . . .

I: President Eisenhower, what does he do?
L: He probably tells the governors what to do.
I: Can you think of any other things that he might do?
L: He probably tells the people that are going to foreign countries to present a thing or something he wants that if they might be interested in. (*sic*)
I: What kind of a thing do you mean?
L: Well, like a peace treaty or something.

That Larry turns "automatically" to hierarchy as an organizing principle, suggests that his prepolitical experiences have taught him to view the world in terms of "telling people what to do." One might hypothesize, for example, that children responding in this way are more likely to come from families in which parental authority follows similar patterns.

[22] Child, *op. cit.*, p. 678.

[23] Angus Campbell and Donald E. Stokes "Partisan Attitudes and the Presidential Vote," Burdick and Brodbeck, *op. cit.*, p. 357.

[24] The sequence of development of certain classes of political response in the New Haven sample is summarized in Greenstein, *op. cit.*, Chap. 11.

[25] Projective devices of the Thematic Apperception variety are promising techniques. For a novel projective procedure, which has received preliminary application, see John L. Kennedy and Harold D. Lasswell, "A Cross-Cultural Test of Self-Image," *Human Organization*, Vol. 17 (1958), pp. 41–43.

[26] A bibliography of portions of this study which have been published is contained in Harold H. Anderson *et al.*, "Image of the Teacher by Adolescent Children in Four Countries: Germany, England, Mexico, United States," *Journal of Social Psychology*, Vol. 50 (1959), pp. 47–55. The Andersons have kindly made available to me unpublished portions of their data.

[27] For a guide to ongoing research, see the regular reports of the Children's Bureau in the bulletin *Research Relating to Children*. A bibliography of longitudinal studies has been assembled by A. A. Stone and Gloria C. Onque, *Longitudinal Studies of Child Personality: Abstracts with Index* (Cambridge, 1959).

[28] A logical first step would be to extend cross-sectional sampling of various age groups beyond the age-range of the present study. For an interesting attempt to use survey data collected over a period of several years to simulate developmental analysis, see William M. Evan, "Cohort Analysis of Survey Data," *The Public Opinion Quarterly*, Vol. 23 (1959), pp. 63–72.

Lasswell has proposed an ingenious procedure for combining the convenience of cross-sectional research with the merits of studies following the same individuals over time. Harold D. Lasswell, "The Method of Interlapping Observations in the Study of Personality and Culture," *Journal of Abnormal and Social Psychology*, Vol. 32 (1937), pp. 240–45. In addition, the systematic examination of adult recollections, especially under clinical conditions (see note 21) has barely begun.

[29] *Criteria for the Life History* (New Haven, 1935), p. 27.

PART FIVE

Democracy and Policy Outcomes

The readings in Part Five bear on the single most important question in constructing a theory of democracy. Simply put, this question is: Why are we interested in something called democracy anyway? Our answer is that in democracies the *results* of government activity are quite different from those in other types of political systems. Speaking more scientifically, we would say that democracy is an important specifying variable in explaining public policy outcomes.

The notion that the policy results under democracy are different is a legacy that comes down to us from normative theory. The pro-democratic argument in that tradition is that democracy should be valued because it gives us valued outcomes. Generally, two broad classes of outcomes are emphasized: liberty and equality. Thus we can prevent governments from violating the people's liberties by making the government accountable to the people. The conclusion is the result of a definition (accountability being somehow included in the definition of democracy) and an assumption (people will be motivated to do, and to make government do, that which is in their interest). It is easy to see that the same definition and assumption lead to statements concerning attempts to utilize government to equalize social and economic differences under conditions of democracy.

In the more immediately appropriate empirical tradition, the strategy has been to treat these outcomes as hypotheses. This strategy is consistent with the overall scientific emphasis to minimize the number of assumptions one makes and to treat as many statements as possible as factual ones subject to test. Therefore, the normative tradition provides us with a fairly rich collection of hypotheses with which to begin the theory-building process.

In most of the empirical work that tests if outcomes are maximized by democracy, analyses which utilize some aspect of liberty as an outcome are almost nonexistent. However, a few studies do treat aspects of socio-economic equality, although the measures vary in how directly or indirectly they are related to the concept. One of the early studies which treats the concept in this way is V. O. Key's *Southern Politics*. Key did not have a direct measure of policy outcome, and he speaks specifically of aspects of party competitiveness rather than of democracy. However, from his theoretical discussion of representativeness, it is apparent that he is dealing with this hypothesis. Thus, as the degree of democratic representativeness (facilitated by two-party competition) increases, we can expect a decrease in the extent of bias against lower-status groups in the content of public policy. While Key does not test this proposition, it provides the theoretical backdrop for his work and for the essays presented in this section.

The selection by Phillips Cutright (Chapter 19) does deal directly with measures of the variables in the above proposition. Cutright investigates whether nations with high scores on an index of political representativeness will in general have high scores on a measure of social-insurance experience. Although there is a correlation between these variables, it is reduced markedly when a control for economic development is introduced. On the other hand, changes in social security coverage follow positive changes in level of representativeness much more closely in the developed than in the non-developed nations. Thus, "nations at very high levels of economic development are able to take advantage of stable government or positive political change, and they are likely to move toward completing the normal pattern of social-insurance programs."

Cutright's first test with the control for economic development indicates that, in large part, economic development and representativeness are not "additively" related to social-insurance outcomes cross-nationally. That is, the policy outcomes in this area are not simply a function of the level of economic development *plus* the level of representativeness in the nations studied. Not only are the latter variables less than independent, but Cutright also finds that they combine in complex ways to result in social-security policy. The impact of representativeness on changes in policy is greatest among the more highly-developed nations.

This finding suggests a non-additive relationship between these variables. Such a result indicates a much more complex impact from democracy than normally assumed in non-empirical works.

The analysis by Thomas R. Dye (Chapter 20) closely parallels that of Cutright. In the American states, Dye finds high correlations between three different types of variables: socioeconomic environment, political process, and policy outcomes. The process variable, malapportionment, tends to reduce the "liberalness" of policies relating to taxation, social welfare, and education in the states. However, the states that are low in socioeconomic development are also less liberal in these respects. The problem for Dye, then, is whether these policies are outcomes of malapportionment or are simply due to economic development. He proceeds to examine the relationships between malapportionment and these policies when the socioeconomic factor is controlled. Once again the control for socioeconomic development reduces markedly the relationship between the political variable and public policy.

This result leads to the inference that these policy outcomes are due to the level of social and economic development in the state, regardless of how badly apportioned the state legislature is. This finding and inference is rather unexpected. Certainly our intuitive notions of what democratic institutions are about would lead us to expect malapportionment to make a difference in policy enactments.

If we remind ourselves that apportionment is only one aspect of how representative political institutions are, we can quite easily imagine that many of the states may be quite representative for other reasons. Moreover, given the limited range of democracy in the world, when we deal only with the American states, for the most part we have isolated our analysis to the democratic end of the continuum. This probably completely overshadows any additional variation in representativeness that we may measure with apportionment, given our poor ability to measure such phenomena at the present time. In this perspective, the high correlation between economic development and public policy in the states is quite consistent with Cutright's cross-national conclusions concerning changes in representativeness and social-security policy among the economically developed nations.

The third selection of Part Five treats another important area concerning policy outcomes—the spending of money. Without funds to enforce or carry out programs, public policies may be merely "on the books" without making substantive differences to society. To have an impact that is more than symbolic, policy outcomes normally have to be more than legislative enactments; they have to be applied by some administrative agency. It is this application phase of policy which requires the expenditure of funds.

Otto A. Davis, M. A. H. Dempster, and Aaron Wildavsky (Chapter 21) find great stability in the budgetary process of the U.S. national government. In large part, the budgetary requests to Congress from the administrative agencies (through the Bureau of the Budget) are some function of what Congress appropriated for the agency in the previous year. Likewise, what Congress appropriates for expenditure by the agencies is some function of the agencies' requests. We, of course, do not have the motivations of the individual administrators and Congressmen available for investigation. However, the budgetary process operates as if reciprocal

expectations of the two types of participants—legislative and executive—
were based upon the past behavior of each. These expectations would then
allow each to second guess the future behavior of the other and to make
compensations for this behavior in budgetary requests on the one hand and
in appropriations on the other.

The possibility that this is the operative process raises the question of
whether elected officials are able to control public policy by controlling
expenditures. The folklore of American politics places much emphasis on
"control of the purse strings." In addition, our notions of democracy
include the necessity of policy control by elected representatives. The
findings, however, present a picture of equilibrium in expenditure which is
achieved by the reciprocal process just described. The control that is
possible in this picture is only an incremental one which makes changes at the
margins but does not substantially alter programs once they have been
instituted. The evidence gives scanty support for the ability of elected
officials to make major changes in expenditure levels in the face of requests
from the permanent bureaucracy.

Yet the evidence does not *entirely* conflict with our earlier assumptions
about democracy. The authors find that one factor responsible for upsetting
the stability of the budgetary process is change in administration, especially
if it is accompanied by the President's party achieving a majority in Congress
at the same time. A new stability is eventually established—a finding
consistent with the overall pattern of reciprocal expectations and behaviors.
However, changes in the magnitude of the constants in the models of the
process do coincide with changes in administration, even though the
variables in the models remain the same across administrations.

In general, these selections do not support some of the most commonplace assumptions about democratic politics; but the research findings in
these three essays should not lead to the inference that democracy has *no*
impact on public policy. Instead, we find the world more complex than the
assumptions anticipated. Instead of direct and additive impacts from
democracy and economic development, the findings of Cutright and Dye
may be read as showing that one of these variables can be considered to
specify the impacts of the other on public policy. Instead of creating
wholesale change in the factors which give rise to appropriation levels for
programs, we find that elected officials modify the emphasis given to these
factors. However, we cannot expect a satisfactory answer to our original
question—"Are the results different under democracy?"—if we require that
answer to be stated in absolute terms. Therefore, the following pages should
be read from the following perspective: To what *extent* are the policy results
under democracy likely to be different from those under non-democratic
conditions?

CHAPTER 19

Political Structure, Economic Development and National Social Security Programs[1]

Phillips Cutright

Comparative sociological studies of political systems in modern nations have, in recent years, experienced impressive theoretical development. Attention has been focused on the "functional prerequisites" for political democracies, the structural conditions generating political stability or instability in "democratic" states, and the value structures necessary for a democratic order.[2] A number of excellent studies of political stability in non-democratic nations exist, but when more than one nation is studied, the comparison is usually limited to somewhat similar underdeveloped nations. When comparisons between democratic and non-democratic nations are made, the number of observations (nations) is severely limited by the absence of scales and indexes relevant to the analytical variables guiding the analysis.[3]

Elsewhere the author has developed and tested a scale of the complexity of national political organization.[4] The development of similar scales that would increase the number of nations in comparative studies and serve to aid in the selection of a few nations to fit the requirements of special studies is clearly a desirable goal. One aspect of this article is the development of a scale that can be applied to nations throughout the world. It measures the development of national programs to provide populations with insurance against severe loss of income under stated conditions, that is, the general level of social security development in the nations of the world. Because such national programs are an output of government activity, the analytical value would seem to go beyond the concrete phenomena directly measured. The scale can be used as a yardstick against which governments with varying characteristics can be compared.[5] It may allow one to measure, for example, one aspect of what democratic governments *do* that may distinguish them from non-democratic governments.[6]

Reprinted from *American Journal of Sociology*, Vol. 70 (March 1965), pp. 537–51, by permission of the University of Chicago Press. Copyright © 1965 by the University of Chicago.

In this paper we develop an index of the general level of social security in different nations that is a direct consequence of one kind of government activity (i.e., legislation or government order). We then analyze the relationship of this index to an index measuring the political representativeness of nations and to other indicators of economic and social development. The general purpose of the analysis is to assess the importance of representativeness in governmental organization to the social security and welfare of national populations. Our working hypothesis is that governments in nations whose political structures tend to allow for greater accessibility to the people of the governing elite will act to provide greater social security for their populations than that provided by governments whose rulers are less accessible to the demands of the population. The theoretical contribution of this analysis is toward an application of the construct of representativeness (or accessibility) to actual government activity.

MEASURING NATIONAL SOCIAL SECURITY

Perhaps one of the more striking developments of the twentieth century has been the effort by national governments to protect that portion of the population that is, for one reason or another, not in the employed labor force. National social-insurance programs, initiated in Europe near the end of the nineteenth century, first dealt with the problem of income loss resulting from industrial work injury, a problem that was greatly intensified by the expansion of industrial activity. As urbanization and industrialization (and their social and political correlates) continued, social-insurance programs covering other types of risks—sickness, old age, unemployment—began to appear.

Though there exists some detailed information on the extent of coverage or the level of benefits provided by various national social-insurance schemes, these data are available for only a few nations. In a study that concentrated on the economic correlates of certain social-insurance programs, Henry Aaron was able to locate adequate detailed data on twenty-two nations—all economically well developed—and subjected these data to an intensive multiple-regression dummy variable analysis.[7] These data on program coverage and benefit levels showed that the most powerful explanatory variables were (1) years of experience with the program (number of decades since its initiation) and (2) various indicators of national economic development. If one knows how long a nation has had certain programs and what its level of economic development is, then one can assess how the nation will rank in coverage and benefit levels relative to the remaining twenty-one nations in the sample. (The homogeneous economic and political character of the nations in Aaron's study should be noted.

Correlations are often low within homogeneous groups; the present instance is an exception to this rule.) Aaron suggests that the relationships among his variables may not be the same in less-developed nations; but the question is not whether the regression is the same but whether Aaron's detailed study can be applied to a slightly different type of analysis that will allow us to get around the problem of lack of detailed program data in many nations. If number of years' experience with a program is highly correlated with the total expenditures, benefit levels, and coverage of a program, then the number of years can be used as an indicator of the level of program development.

However, the lack of detailed and comparable data on social security programs is not the only stumbling block in the way of international comparisons. We have also to establish that what we call social security programs are conceptually related. The fact that custom and administrative usage have grouped different types of programs under a common label (social security) is not proof that these programs are interrelated and form a continuum along which nations may be placed in order from high to low social security development. The first task is to offer some evidence that we can talk about the social security development of nations because a definite pattern of program occurrence or non-occurrence exists among the nations of the world.

PATTERNS OF SOCIAL SECURITY PROGRAM DEVELOPMENT

There are five major types of social security programs.[8] Of the seventy-six nations outside Africa[9] that had achieved independent political status by 1960, seventy-one had begun work-injury programs, fifty-eight had sickness and/or maternity programs, fifty-six had programs grouped under old-age, invalidism, and death, forty had some type of family allowance plan, and twenty-seven had unemployment-insurance programs. This frequency distribution does not, in itself, tell us that a nation with an unemployment program is necessarily more or less advanced toward a social-insurance goal than is a nation with only a work-injury program. There are several ways to approach this question, but perhaps the simplest is with the Guttman scale.[10] If several discrete items, in this case the five types of social-insurance and benefit programs, form a Guttman scale, we can say that the scale is measuring an underlying dimension along which each of the items may be placed in a known order, and that a given combination of items (i.e., social-insurance programs) represents a higher place along a continuum of social-insurance development than some alternative combination.

The five major types of social security programs do form a Guttman scale. A nation can have between zero and five programs, and we have six possible perfect-scale types with varying combinations of programs. Twenty-two nations in our sample are in the first perfect-scale type, having all five programs, while the second type contains thirteen nations lacking only unemployment insurance. It is interesting that seven of these thirteen nations were Soviet Russia and its satellites. A third perfect-scale type contains the twelve nations that had neither unemployment nor family allowances, but did have the three other programs. The five nations in the fourth scale type lack, in addition to unemployment and family-allowances programs, a program to provide for the aged, invalidism, and/or death. They have both work-injury and sickness programs. In the fifth scale type are six nations with work-injury programs only, and the final scale type contains five nations with no programs at all. Thus sixty-three of the seventy-six countries are in perfect-scale types. It is worth noting that, had we included African nations, the sixth scale type would have had many more nations, with a resulting increase in the coefficient of reproducibility (CR) to about .98. However, even without this group the CR is .966, considerably above the usually acceptable level of .90.

Because the items do form a Guttman scale, these scale types may be used to rank order the nations of the world according to the extent to which they have developed a social-insurance program. The scale does not necessarily tell us whether a nation in scale type 1 has a better or more comprehensive old-age program than a nation in scale type 2, but it does indicate that the general social security coverage of the population outside the employed labor force is better in scale type 1 than in scale type 2, 3, and so on.

A CUMULATIVE MEASURE OF THE YEARS OF SOCIAL-INSURANCE PROGRAM EXPERIENCE

Because the programs form a Guttman scale, it is possible to apply a measure that distinguishes more than six levels of social security development. The measure is, simply, the years of experience with social-insurance programs for each of the seventy-six nations for the period 1934–60. This statistic is similar to that used by Aaron for well-developed nations, and from the above analysis it appears applicable to less-developed nations as well.

An index of a nation's social insurance program experience (SIPE) can be computed by totaling the number of years from 1934 through 1960 that the nation had a given type of program in operation. For each of the five programs, a score of from 0 to 27 is possible. A score of 27 on each program would yield a maximum SIPE score of 135.[11]

The following analysis concentrates on the relationship of SIPE scores to various aspects of national political and economic life. The final section focuses on a social-insurance completion index and relates scores on this index to political and economic levels and changes from 1928 to 1960.

SIPE scores are one possible index of the responsiveness of governments to the needs of the governed. A nation that lacks work-injury or old age insurance programs may or may not have the economic base capable of supporting such programs, but the extent to which governments initiate and improve insurance programs may reflect much more than the operation of an automatic and economically triggered mechanism.

Nevertheless, it is also the case that the ability of a government to begin a program is closely related to the nation's level of social and economic development. The SIPE scores of the seventy-six nations have been correlated with 1960 indexes of energy consumption, urbanization, literacy, and political representativeness (PRI),[12] and the full matrix of product-moment correlations is shown in Table 1.

The highest correlation is between energy consumption and SIPE. This correlation of .90 accounts by itself for 81 per cent of the variation around the mean SIPE score. It is much higher than the correlation of energy consumption with PRI, literacy, or urbanization. Further, it is considerably higher than the zero-order relationship between literacy and SIPE. This indicates that the level of economic development has a powerful role in determining the level of social-insurance development, and that we must control for level of economic development as measured by energy consumption as well as for level of political development in any analysis of the amount of change in social-insurance programs from the 1930's through the early 1960's.

Table 1. **Zero-Order Correlation Matrix of Energy Consumption, Urbanization, Literacy, Political Representativeness, and Years of Social-Insurance Program Experience, 1960***

	Urbanization	Literacy	PRI	SIPE
Energy consumption	72	81	61	90
Urbanization	—	64	58	58
Literacy	—	—	76	83
PRI	—	—	—	74

* All variables except SIPE have been T-scored; $N=76$.

Source data for energy consumption, urbanization, and literacy are taken from the U.N. *Demographic Yearbook* and the U.N. *Statistical Yearbook*. The primary source for political data is the *Political Handbook of the World: Parliaments, Parties, and Press* (New York: Harper & Bros. [for the Council on Foreign Relations], annual publication 1928–62).

The high correlations between social security development and energy consumption or political representativeness do not mean, however, that urbanization and the literacy level of the population are not also important correlates of social security development. Quite the opposite is true. In general, nations with high levels of SIPE also have high literacy rates and tend to be highly urbanized. Nations with low levels of urbanization or literacy have less-developed social security programs as well as lower levels of energy consumption and political representativeness.

Although this analysis centers on the relationship of economic development and PRI, it should not be assumed that a change in one or both of these variables alone would be sufficient (although it might be necessary) to produce changes in social security. Changes in the levels of literacy and urbanization of the population usually occur concomitantly with changes in PRI or energy consumption. It would appear that the probability of an increase in the level of social-insurance development is greatest when all four variables are rising. This view is compatible with the proposition that changes in major institutional areas of the society do not proceed far without reacting on each other as well as on lesser aspects of life. Institutions are interdependent. The matrix of correlations is evidence in support of this hypothesis—at the level of national social systems.

In the following section we test the hypothesis that the levels of economic development and PRI will have independent and joint effects on SIPE Economic development was selected because of its high correlation with SIPE and political development because it is central to analysis.

ANALYSIS OF NATIONAL DIFFERENCES IN YEARS OF SOCIAL-INSURANCE PROGRAM EXPERIENCE

Table 2 presents the mean SIPE scores for nations at five levels of economic development—as measured by energy consumption—and four levels of political development in 1930. The mean social-insurance experience of these nations and the number of nations is shown.

In the upper left-hand cell is a single nation with 99 cumulative years of program experience and immediately below it are three nations with a mean of 25 years' experience. (The reader may prefer to collapse cells having only one case with adjacent cells before comparing individual cells with column means.) The mean SIPE scores associated with each level of economic development are in the "row mean" column. The twenty-one nations with the highest level of economic development had an average of 114 years of cumulative social-insurance program experience from 1934 through 1960. Nations in the second highest group had an average of eighty-three years' experience while the ten nations at the lowest level had

Table 2. Mean Years of Social-Insurance Program Experience
by Mean 1930–60 Energy Consumption and 1930 Level of Political
Representativeness[a]

Mean Energy Consumption 1930–60	1930 PRI[b]				
	Dependent Nations	Below Mean	Above Mean	Highest Nations	Row Mean
I	99 (1)	101 (2)	114 (4)	116 (14)	114 (21)
II	25 (3)	93 (4)	100 (5)	102 (3)	83 (15)
III	36 (1)	88 (4)	62 (5)	54 (2)	67 (12)
IV	30 (8)	44 (9)	54 (1)	—	39 (18)
V	18 (5)	7 (4)	63 (1)	—	18 (10)
Column Mean	30 (18)	59 (23)	86 (16)	107 (19)	70

[a] Nations are placed into energy consumption levels according to their T-score. Groups I and II are above the mean of 50; Groups III, IV, and V are below the mean. Groups I and V contain nations that were more than one standard deviation from the mean.
[b] Number in parentheses $= N$.

an average of only eighteen years' experience. The same pattern of decreasing length of program experience is found within each column. We may conclude that the level of economic development is related to SIPE; statistical control for political development does not remove the positive association between the two.

The mean SIPE scores associated with each level of 1930 PRI are in the bottom row of Table 2. The scores show a steady gain with increasing PRI levels. The eighteen nations with dependent political status in 1930 have a mean score of thirty years compared to 107 years for the nineteen nations with the highest PRI scores. This pattern of larger SIPE scores with higher PRI levels holds at the first, second, and fourth levels of economic development. The third level does not fit the general pattern—this "deviant" row may explain why the correlation between PRI and SIPE was "only" .74— and the association in the lowest economic level is also of dubious strength.

Controlling first for one and then for the other variable, then, we see that each is related to the SIPE scores. We should note that the ten nations at the lowest level of economic development have considerably lower SIPE scores than the nations at the next highest level of development. For these nations, it is level of economic development rather than level of political development that determines the level of social-insurance program experience. In terms of causal sequence, it appears that before positive change in political structure can bring about positive change in social-insurance program development, a nation must have experienced some economic growth.

Table 2 supports our working hypothesis. In general, governments in nations with more representative political structures have provided greater social security coverage to their populations. Among self-governing nations there is a nearly uniform increase in government social security activities from one level of representativeness to the next. However, nations with the highest PRI scores—those we would normally call "democratic"—do not really differ qualitatively from those nations of parallel economic development that are in the next lowest PRI group. This finding will be discussed at the conclusion of this paper.

In the next section the idea that changes in political structure are associated with changes in years of social-insurance experience will be tested.

CHANGES IN YEARS OF SOCIAL-INSURANCE PROGRAM EXPERIENCE AND CHANGES IN PRI

Table 3 shows the relationship between changes in political representativeness and changes in SIPE. Since the amount of change in PRI is strongly associated with initial level of PRI (as seen in the disproportionately high gains made by the initially lowest PRI group), it is important to control for 1930 PRI level; level of economic development is not controlled. Nations are ranked in each column according to the size of their gain or loss in political representativeness between 1930 and 1960. Reading down the columns, a near-perfect correlation can be seen between changes in PRI and changes in SIPE. Even within the initially highest PRI group, the twelve nations whose political structure remained perfectly stable throughout the period had an average gain of 121 years of experience; the three that ended at the same level as they began but experienced instability in between (Japan, Uruguay, and Costa Rica) had an average increase of eighty-one; and the two that declined in political representativeness (Canada and Columbia) had a gain of only seventy-six years.

We might note that SIPE gains also are strongly associated with initial PRI level. The largest gains in social insurance are found in nations that began the time period with a maximum political-representativeness score. Reading across the rows in Table 3, within each PRI-change interval there is a positive association (slightly reversed in only one case) between 1930 PRI level and SIPE gains.

A NON-CUMULATIVE MEASURE OF SOCIAL-INSURANCE DEVELOPMENT

An alternative measure of social-insurance development in a nation is, for some purposes, more satisfactory. Instead of using a cumulative measure of years of program experience, we can examine the political situation surrounding major changes in a nation's social-insurance programs (i.e., each time

Table 3. Mean Change in Social-Insurance Program Experience, 1934–60, and Size of Change in Political Representativeness Index, 1930–60

				1930 PRI								
Ranked PRI Change Interval	Dependent (N=18)			Below Mean[b] (N=20)			Above Mean[b] (N=15)			Highest[b] (N=17)		
	PRI Gain	N	SIPE Gain	PRI Gain	N	SIPE Gain	PRI Gain	N	SIPE Gain	PRI Gain	N	SIPE Gain
Largest	23	3	63	13	4	97	7	6	114	0	12	121
Second	16	6	31	5	7	56	3	3	70	0	3[c]	81
Third	11	4	22	3	3	20	−2	3	66	−8	2	76
Fourth	6	5	14	0	6	49	−5	3	65	[d]	[d]	[d]

[a] Controlled for PRI.

[b] Soviet satellites (Albania, Bulgaria, Hungary, Poland, Rumania, and Czechoslovakia) are omitted from this table as our scoring of PRI changes excluded those caused by external domination. They are included in all other tables.

[c] These three nations began and ended the period with the highest PRI scores, but were unstable during the period.

[d] No cases.

a new program is launched). An index can then be developed to measure the extent to which a nation is moving toward social-insurance program completion (SIPC). Completion is used here to mean that a nation has begun to tackle the needs associated with the five basic types of social security programs, and not to refer to the extent of coverage of the population by any or all programs. Some examples of how the SIPC index is constructed follow.

If a nation had three programs in 1928, it can introduce only two additional programs. Assume that such a country experiences a positive political change in 1932 and in 1934 adds one program. Between 1932 and 1934 no political changes occur. A score of 50 (i.e., 50 per cent of the total change possible in social-insurance program coverage) is awarded to that specific 1932 political change. If, however, the nation experiences a positive change in 1932 and a negative change in 1933 and adds a social-insurance program in 1934, the positive 1932 political change receives a score of zero and the negative 1933 change a score of 50. The social-insurance-program completion index is, therefore, a measure of the amount of social-insurance change associated with each change in PRI.[13] The mean SIPC change per nation is calculated in the following manner. For positive and negative PRI changes (computed separately), if a nation has more than one change, the sum of the SIPC index scores associated with these changes is divided by the number of changes. Next, the average SIPC scores for each nation are summed and divided by the number of nations to get the mean SIPC change per nation. For nations with no PRI changes, the mean SIPC change per nation is merely the sum of the nations' SIPC scores divided by the number of nations.

It was suggested earlier that social-insurance programs may represent a measure of the responsiveness of government to the social needs of the population. If so, we would expect not only that social-insurance development would be associated with a *high level* of political representativeness but also that a *positive change* in political representativeness would be *followed* by an increase in social-insurance program coverage. The gain in SIPC index should be larger in association with positive political changes than with negative political changes.

Table 4 presents the results of an analysis of SIPC changes associated with political changes of both types. In the time covered, a total of ninety-eight positive political changes and an average increase in SIPC of twenty-two are found. In the same period, there were seventy negative changes with an increase in SIPC of eleven per negative change; a net gain of eleven points is associated with each positive change.

A slightly different statistic which allows us to consider SIPC changes in nations experiencing *no* political change between 1928 and 1960 is the mean

**Table 4. SIPC Index Gains Associated with Positive,
Negative, and No Changes in PRI**

Direction of PRI Change	Mean SIPC Change* per PRI Change	Mean SIPC Change per Nation
Positive	22 (98)	38 (56)
Negative	11 (70)	20 (41)
No change	Not applicable	87 (16)

* Numbers in parentheses are the number of PRI changes and the number of nations.

SIPC change per nation. Table 4 shows that fifty-six nations experienced a positive political change, forty-one had negative changes, and sixteen experienced no change. A net advantage of nearly twenty points per nation goes to countries with positive rather than negative changes, but a still larger SIPC increase of eighty-seven is found among nations that had no political change at all. These stable nations are nearly all at the highest level of economic and political development, a condition favorable to maximum SIPC changes.

Table 5 controls for the level of economic development and shows the amount of social-insurance program-completion change associated in any economic level with either positive or negative political changes or with stable political systems.

At the highest level of energy consumption there were five nations that experienced positive political changes with an average social-insurance index increase of eighty, while seven nations that experienced negative changes had an increase of only seventeen per nation. The thirteen nations with completely stable political structures had an increase of ninety-two. At the second level of energy consumption there is no difference in the amount of social-insurance program-coverage gains between countries with positive or negative change, but the two nations (Finland and Italy) with stable PRI experience have a gain of seventy-five. The third level of economic development again shows the expected pattern with a score of forty-seven associated with positive political change compared to a score of twenty-three associated with negative change. In like fashion, the fourth energy-consumption level reveals an increase of thirty-nine associated with positive change and only eleven with negative change, while the single nation with stable government (Saudi Arabia) had an increase of forty. At the lowest level of development, the ten nations with positive increases had an average of only seven in social-insurance program completion. There were very few cases of negative change and no cases of stable governments in this category. Part of the reason for the small number of negative changes

Table 5. SIPC Index Gains per Nation Associated with Positive, Negative, and No Changes in PRI[a]

Energy Consumption Level and Type of Political Change	Mean SIPC Index Change per Nation Following Each PRI Change			Number of Nations	Net Number of Nations
Level I:					
Positive	80	—	—	5	8
Negative	—	17	—	7	
No PRI change	—	—	92	13	13
Level II:					
Positive	35	—	—	13	13
Negative	—	35	—	9	
No PRI change	—	—	75	2	2
Level III:[b]					
Positive	47	—	—	10	11
Negative	—	23	—	8	
Level IV:					
Positive	39	—	—	18	18
Negative	—	11	—	17[c]	
No PRI change	—	—	40	1	1
Level V:[b]					
Positive	7	—	—	10	10
Negative	—	—	—	(4)[d]	

[a] Level of energy consumption controlled.
[b] Levels III and IV had no nations without at least one PRI change between 1928 and 1960.
[c] Includes four cases from lowest level.
[d] Combined with negative group in Level IV.

is that nations at this level of economic development have minimal PRI scores to begin with and thus have little room to decrease.

If we look down the columns in Table 5, we see some irregularities in the pattern associated with positive and negative PRI changes—there is not a perfectly steady decline in the size of the score from one energy-consumption level to the next.[14]

Regardless of the method used, the conclusion seems clear enough: Nations at very high levels of economic development are able to take advantage of stable government or positive political change, and they are likely to move toward completing the normal pattern of social-insurance programs. Social security growth is less likely to follow a negative PRI change than a positive change at *any* level of economic development. Again it is seen that nations with the lowest level of economic development are not introducing social insurance programs even when they have a positive PRI change. On the one hand, this reinforces the earlier conclusion that for these nations a rise in the level of the economy must precede the introduction of social-insurance programs. On the other hand, a positive change in political representativeness will tend to induce economically more-developed nations to introduce new social security programs.

DISCUSSION

An index (SIPE) measuring the general level of social security protection legislated or otherwise directed by the national government was developed. The SIPE index was closely related (.90) to the level of economic development, literacy (.83), and to a lesser extent (.58) urbanization. The .74 correlation of the SIPE index with the Political Representativeness Index (PRI) was found, after further analysis, to be related to variation in the SIPE index when the level of economic development was controlled.

The effect of different levels of political representativeness on the development of national social security programs varied with the level of economic development enjoyed by the nation. In nations with very low economic development, the push for social security development has, in most cases, yet to begin, despite the presence in this group of several different levels of political representativeness. This finding was interpreted in terms of the necessity of certain technological and bureaucratic prerequisites for successful introduction of social-insurance schemes. However, nations that have this capability (Levels I through IV) do not always exercise it. Within the mid-range of economic development (III and IV), the level of PRI was not powerfully related to SIPE. Nations in the upper two economic-development strata not only had high SIPE scores but within each stratum SIPE was positively related to PRI. In general, the political condition that was most strongly related to low levels of social security development was colonial or quasicolonial status. With few exceptions (especially that of Iceland) little was done by occupying powers to institute social security programs. The difference between being politically dependent and being politically self-governing appears (Table 2) critical to the early development of social security programs. Once political independence is achieved, the degree to which the national government becomes more and more representative is also related to how rapidly the government acts to introduce national social security programs. This is most clearly demonstrated at the higher levels of economic development. In a separate analysis that controlled for the 1930 PRI level and ranked the 1930–60 PRI change against 1934–60 gains in SIPE, the size of PRI changes was positively related to SIPE gains.

A second index (SIPC) of government activity in the social security field was devised. A score was computed that measured the degree to which any new program instituted by a nation moved that nation closer to complete program coverage. Analysis of these scores revealed that social-insurance completion followed more upon positive political changes than upon negative political changes, whatever the level of economic development. Also, the few nations that enjoyed stable political structures had larger social security completion scores than did unstable nations.

If we are willing to speak of nations with the highest PRI scores as being democratic and of nations with lower scores as something less than democratic, we can engage the question of whether people living in a democracy enjoy levels of social security protection that are not provided to populations in other political systems. The analysis indicated that only a small difference could be found between nations at the very highest PRI level and a second group of nations above the mean on PRI. Further, at the upper levels of economic development even nations below the mean on PRI had SIPE scores close to those of the democratic nations.

The evidence presented in this paper supports the idea that national political, economic, and social systems are interdependent. Changes in the complexity of organization in one sphere are followed by changes in organization in other areas. The specific activities that engage the attention of national governments are not independent of the general level of development. Quite the contrary is true. In spite of very great differences among nations in ideological orientation as well as in type of political organization, we found that actual activities of government in the social security field were strongly related to the complexity of social organization in economic, social, and political institutions. Nations with high levels of economic development but with less than "perfect" (i.e., democratic) political systems had government activities highly similar to those undertaken by democratic governments. Further comparative studies of government activities in other areas of social life will aid in understanding this conclusion. One might see the activities of government as intimately related to the problem of maintaining motivation and order in societies as well as being a response to the democratically organized demands of the population. A government can act without being told what to do. The scholar operating within a democratic context (and especially that of the United States) may tend to view government activities as being dependent upon the demands of secondary groups. A major but tentative conclusion that can be drawn from this study of government activity is that it need not await the petition of secondary groups. The role (or even the existence) of politically relevant secondary groups in guiding government decisions in many of the nations included in this study is modest.

In many nations we would conclude that the introduction of social security measures is a response by government to changes in the economic and social order that is not strongly affected by some degree of departure from ideal democratic organizational forms. Similar levels of social security coverage are found in nations whose governments are thought to act in response to the popular will as occur in nations whose governments are thought to act with less regard to public demands. It appears that the the level of social security in a nation is a response to deeper strains affecting the organization of society. Governments may ignore human needs, but there are rather tight limits on the extent to which they may ignore organizational requirements.

APPENDIX A
YEARS OF SOCIAL-INSURANCE PROGRAM
EXPERIENCE, 1934–60, BY NATION

Nation	Years
Afghanistan	15
Albania	53
Argentina	75
Australia	118
Austria	121
Belgium	135
Bolivia	54
Brazil	101
Bulgaria	100
Burma	34
Cambodia	27
Canada	106
Ceylon	52
Chile	129
China	37
Colombia	46
Costa Rica	62
Cuba	81
Czechoslovakia	97
Denmark	117
Dominican Republic	55
Ecuador	86
Finland	96
France	135
Germany	115
Great Britain	124
Greece	100
Guatemala	30

Nation	Years
Haiti	10
Honduras	9
Hungary	104
Iceland	99
India	49
Indonesia	26
Iran	40
Iraq	40
Ireland	125
Israel	45
Italy	133
Japan	88
Jordan	6
Laos	0
Lebanon	36
Luxembourg	122
Malaya	37
Mexico	65
Mongolia	0
Nepal	0
Netherlands	130
New Zealand	131
Nicaragua	39
Norway	121
Pakistan	27
Panama	67
Paraguay	63
Peru	77
Philippines	41
Poland	95
Portugal	100
Romania	98
Russia	98
Salvador	39
Saudi Arabia	28
South Korea	0
Spain	131
Sweden	122
Switzerland	104
Syria	29
Thailand	5

Turkey	44
United States	95
Uruguay	92
Venezuela	48
Vietnam	31
Yemen	0
Yugoslavia	115

APPENDIX B

The index used to measure differences among national political structures is computed according to a point system. Parliament and the executive branch of government are scored as follows.

A. Parliament scoring

2 points if the largest party has less than 70 per cent of the seats in the lower or only chamber and achieved the seats through elections.

$1\frac{1}{2}$ points if the largest party has 70 per cent or more but the second party has at least 20 per cent.

1 point if the largest party has 70 per cent or more and the second party has less than 20 per cent.

$\frac{1}{2}$ point if the largest grouping in parliament is over 70 per cent with the second less than 20 *and* they do not represent parties selected by election but are appointed to represent trade, commerce, ethnic, or other interests. Includes Fascist and Communist party systems.

No points if there is no parliament, if a former parliament is dissolved during the year by coup or revolt, if it is a "constituent assembly," or if the nation still has colonial status.

B. Executive scoring

$1\frac{1}{2}$ points for each year under a chief executive who was selected by a party or parliament under conditions meeting the 70 and 20 per cent rule.

$1\frac{1}{2}$ points if the chief executive is elected directly by the people in a competitive election held at the usual time, regardless of the 70–20 rule.

1 point when the chief executive is selected by a party that is a sustaining force (has existed for 5 years as a party in parliament), but the party composition (is not a multiparty system) violates the 70–20 rule.

1 point when the executive is selected by a party in a system that fails to observe the usual election time or goes outside the rules for having an election or has a non-competitive election or fails the 70 per cent rule.

$\frac{1}{2}$ point for junta, clique, non-party selection of leaders, or when existing leaders remain in power beyond the regular time.

No points to independent nations with hereditary rulers having chief executive power.

No points to nations with dependent colonial status or occupied by a foreign power.

In order to maintain a distinction between dependent and independent nations, $\frac{1}{2}$ point was added to the over-all raw PRI score of each independent nation, while colonial or dependent nations received a score of zero.

It was possible for a nation to achieve from 0 to 4 points each year. A mean yearly PRI score was computed for each of the following four time periods: 1928–34; 1935–44; 1945–54; 1955–61, and a total of 304 scores (four for each of the seventy-six nations) was amassed and T-scored. The four distributions were T-scored separately as well. (A simple technique for computing the T-score is given in Allen E. Edwards, *Statistical Methods for the Behavioral Sciences* [New York: Holt, Rinehart & Winston, 1954]. For a single variable, T-scoring the raw data will yield a distribution with a mean of 50 and a standard deviation of 10.)

NOTES

[1] My thanks to E. Palmore for criticism and helpful suggestions. The opinions expressed are those of the author and do not reflect the opinion of the Social Security Administration.

[2] William Kornhauser (*The Politics of Mass Society* [Glencoe, Illinois: Free Press, 1959]), in particular, gives a detailed discussion of the concept of "representativeness" and democratic pluralism. Robert R. Alford (*Party and Society: The Anglo-American Democracies* [Chicago: Rand McNally & Co., 1963]) examines longitudinal data bearing on the relations between political parties and the social structure of five democracies. S. M. Lipset ("Democracy and the Social System," in Harry Eckstein [ed.], *Internal War: Problems and Approaches* [New York: Free Press of Glencoe, 1964]) develops a framework for analyzing the value patterns that support democratic government.

[3] See Dick Simpson, "The Congruence of Political, Social and Economic Aspects of Development," *International Development Review*, VI (June, 1964), pp. 21–25.

[4] P. Cutright, "National Political Development: Measurement and Analysis," *American Sociological Review*, XXVIII (April, 1963), pp. 253–64. That study also argues the case for scales rather than crude qualitative categories in international studies. See n. 12 of the present article for a description of the revised political representativeness index used in this study.

[5] An inventory of municipal services in Bristol, England, and Seattle, Washington, revealed remarkable similarities "even in two cities where the governmental power is based on different philosophies. In Bristol the Labor (socialist) party holds political dominance with its leaders in almost all key legislative positions. In Seattle, a conservative local government rules (Republican). Yet each city has almost the same amount of municipal ownership and control" (William H. Form and Delbert C. Miller, *Industry, Labor and Community* [New York: Harper & Bros., 1960], p. 501).

[6] There has been relatively little systematic work on the consequences for national populations of living under more or less representative governments. Studies of this sort often compare only totalitarian and democratic governments, highlighting the impact of government activity on the expression of individual freedoms.

Unfortunately, an inventory of the activities of national governments, or even a conceptual scheme to aid in their classification, is not at hand. Comparative studies of the outputs of national governments are limited by the lack of scales of those activities, and relatively little attention has been given to classification of the activities. Available indicators of government activities are not, however, being fully exploited. Thus, studies using measures of education, health, or demographic conditions do not examine these phenomena as though they were related to government activity. For example, we are more likely to see a certain level of education as a requisite for democratic government than to view government activity as vital for the development of national education levels.

[7] Henry Aaron, "Social Security in an Expanding Economy" (unpublished doctoral dissertation, Harvard University, 1963).

[8] All data pertaining to social security programs are taken from U.S. Department of Health, Education, and Welfare, Social Security Administration, *Social Security Programs throughout the World*, 1961 (Washington, D.C.: Government Printing Office, 1961). Discussion of the characteristics of each type of program can be found in that document.

[9] This part of the analysis is based on research initially focused on the correlates of political development, which for statistical reasons omitted all African nations in order to avoid spuriously high correlations. The seventy-six nations are listed in Appendix A.

[10] S. A. Stouffer, *et al.*, *Measurement and Prediction* (Princeton, N.J.: Princeton University Press, 1950), pp. 60–90. For a more recent explication of Guttman scaling see Allen L. Edwards, *Techniques of Attitude Scale Construction* (New York: Appleton-Century-Crofts, 1957), pp. 172–98.

[11] SIPE scores for each of the seventy-six nations are shown in Appendix A. Data on political structure are available for as early as 1928, and that time is used in analyzing the introduction of new social-insurance programs later in this paper. The base year for computing the years of program experience is 1934 rather than 1928, however. This is the product of error, not design. However, if 1928 had been used, there would be little difference beyond adding five points to the range of the scale; the relationships with other variables would remain the same.

[12] See Appendix B.

[13] One feature of the SIPC index that should be considered in future work is the correlation between economic and political development and the size of the score awarded to a single program change. Since nations at high development levels will also be more likely to have had several programs by 1928, they will also receive "extra" credit when they introduce their next program. Whether it is more difficult for a nation to launch its first than its last program is not the issue here. Comparison of the results using this index as opposed to another is a matter for investigation rather than for debate. Although it might be expected that larger scores would be associated with the economically and

politically more-developed nations, this does not justify assuming that high scores should be associated with positive rather than with negative political changes. Controls for economic-development levels will also be introduced to reduce the spurious association between large scores and high economic-development scores.

[14] An alternative method of computing SIPC change per political change rather than per nation provides a somewhat more consistent table when broken down in the same way as Table 5. At each level of energy consumption the average SIPC index change following each PRI positive change is larger than for negative PRI changes. The pattern of decline in SIPC change associated with decreasing energy consumption is also consistent for both positive and negative PRI change.

CHAPTER 20

Malapportionment and Public Policy
in the States

Thomas R. Dye

Commentators on state policy have often implied that malapportionment seriously affects the policy choices of state legislatures. In the literature on state politics it is frequently argued that there are important policy differences between urban and rural constituencies and that malapportionment, by over-representing rural interests, grants them a real advantage in policy-making.[1] It is also frequently predicted that reapportionment on a population basis will bring about noticeable shifts in many state policies.[2]

Malapportionment of state legislatures has been successfully challenged on the grounds that it denies to the citizens equal protection of the laws.[3] This challenge was essentially a normative one, stemming from deeply held values about political equality.[4] The merits of this type of challenge do not lend themselves to empirical verification. However, statements about the effect of malapportionment on public policy, and predictions about the policy consequences of reapportionment, can be tested empirically. Such tests, of course, in no way reflect upon the moral quality of the proposition "as nearly as practicable one man's vote should be equal to another's."[5] But they can help us to know what to expect in the way of policy changes in the wake of reapportionment. In the past, proponents of reapportionment have been very enthusiastic about its expected consequences. Having attributed a lack of party competition, unfair distributions of state funds conservative tax schemes, unprogressive education policies, and penny-pinching welfare programs to rural over-representation, they naturally expect to see these conditions changed by reapportionment. Court-ordered reapportionment is viewed as a source of strength for state legislatures rather than an infringement of a heretofore exclusive prerogative of these bodies. Reapportionment, it is said, will help states come to grips with important domestic problems in the nation and reassume their rightful place in our federal system.

Reprinted from *Journal of Politics*, Vol. 27, No. 3 (August 1965), pp. 586–601, by permission of the Southern Political Science Association.

In contrast, a few scholars have sounded a note of caution regarding the expected consequences of reapportionment. On the basis of roll call analyses in the Missouri and Illinois legislatures, David Derge concluded that metropolitan and non-metropolitan legislators seldom opposed each other in unified voting blocs.[6] It is difficult to see how reapportioning legislatures to reduce rural over-representation would have much effect on policy making, if we accept Derge's conclusions that only infrequently do rural-urban divisions influence legislative decisions anyway. Duane Lockard also entered a caveat about the consequences of malapportionment. With specific references to conditions in Massachusetts and Connecticut he asked: "Do states with fair apportionment respond to urban appeals more readily? If anyone has made a systematic study of this, I am unaware of it, but limited evidence does not seem to indicate that the states with fair apportionment are any more considerate of urban problems than states with malapportionment."[7] Herbert Jacob was equally skeptical of the consequences of malapportionment. He computed rank-order correlation coefficients for the relationship between malapportionment and party competition, highway fund distributions, and certain welfare expenditures for the fifty states. On the basis of low coefficients, he concluded, "it is improbable that it (reapportionment) will substantially invigorate state governments or dissolve the stalemates which sap public confidence in them."[8]

The purpose of the study reported here was to examine systematically the impact of malapportionment on party competition and public policy in all fifty states. If the policy choices of malapportioned legislatures are noticeably different from the policy choices of well-apportioned legislatures, and these differences in policies can be traced to malapportionment rather than some other condition, then reapportionment can be expected to have a significant impact on state policies. However, if the policy choices of well-apportioned and malapportioned legislatures do not differ significantly, or if differences which do occur are the product of some condition other than malapportionment, then more caution is warranted regarding the policy changes that reapportionment may bring. The same test applies to expectations about the impact of reapportionment on party competition. Only if there is significantly more party competition in well-apportioned legislatures than in malapportioned ones, and this increased competition is attributable to apportionment rather than some other condition, is one safe in predicting that reapportionment will bring about greater party competition.

MEASURING MALAPPORTIONMENT

Several measures of the malapportionment of state legislatures are available. Perhaps the most common measure is the theoretical minimum percentage of a state's population that can elect a majority of each house.[9] The two minimum percentages for each chamber can be added to provide an index of malapportionment for the legislature as a whole. Percentages are additive in this case because the real denominator is the power of each house to influence policy and this is assumed to be real. In 1960 this index ranged from a low of 37 for Nevada with the least representative legislature to a high of 96 for Oregon with the most representative legislature. Hereafter this measure is referred to as the "index of representativeness."

Another index was devised by David and Eisenberg to focus on urban under-representation in state legislatures.[10] Because urban areas are most likely to be the subject of discrimination, the authors felt that urban under-representation should be a specific object of measurement, in addition to theoretical measures of representativeness. In order to determine the degree of descrimination against urban areas, David and Eisenberg computed the "value" of a vote cast in the largest urban counties of each state. First they computed the average population of a single member district in each state. Actual constituencies were then compared to these average constituencies: the "value" of a vote was represented by the ratio of an actual constituency to the average constituency in each state. For example, in a district with twice the population of the state's average district, the value of a vote would be .50. The "value" of a vote in the largest category of county in each state was computed for each house and then the measures for both houses were averaged to provide an "index of urban representation" for each legislature. In 1960 this index ranged from a low of .12 for Georgia, where the largest countries were most discriminated against in apportionment, to a high of 1.05 in Louisiana, where the largest counties were granted the greatest legislative representation.

A third measure of malapportionment is the technically sophisticated "apportionment score" proposed by Glendon Schubert and Charles Press.[11] The apportionment score combines inverted coefficients of variation for each state (divide the population of the average district by the standard deviation of all districts and subtract the quotient from 1.0) with statistical measures of skewness and kurtosis in the distribution of districts by size of population. The result is an index that measures the combination of variance, skewness, and kurtosis in the populations of legislative districts in each state. According to this scale, in 1962 Massachusetts, with the highest apportionment score, was technically the best apportioned legislature in the nation and Indiana, with the lowest score, was the worst.

All three of these measures—the index of representativeness, the index of urban under-representation, and the apportionment score—are used in this study. Each measure depicts a slightly different aspect of malapportionment; each results in a slightly different ranking of states.[12] The first measure focuses on the theoretical minimum proportion of a state's population that can control the legislature, the second measure focuses on urban under-representation, and the third measure focuses on the degree to which a state's apportionment scheme approaches the statistical concept of normality. In the analysis to follow we shall evaluate the political relevance of each of these measures.

MEASURING PUBLIC POLICY

Measuring state policy choices is an even more difficult task than measuring malapportionment. In the 1960–61 legislative biennium, more than 104,000 bills were introduced in the state legislatures throughout the nation. Each bill rejected or enacted represents a separate policy choice. What policies are to be selected in order to assess the impact of malapportionment? It was decided to select 30 measures of state policy in three of the most important subject matters of state politics—education, welfare, and taxation. Education is the largest category of state spending. In fact, with the exception of national defense, education is the nation's largest public undertaking. The responsibility for this undertaking rests with the fifty state governments. Twelve variables reflecting important attributes of state educational systems were selected for analysis:

> Public School Expenditures Per Pupil in Average Daily Attendance, 1960–61
>
> Average Annual Salary Per Member of Instructional Staff, 1961–62
>
> Male School Teachers as a Percent of Total, 1961–62
>
> Pupil-Teacher Ratio: Enrollment Per Member of Instructional Staff 1961–62
>
> Percent of Elementary Teachers with B.A. Degree, 1962
>
> Percent of Secondary Teachers with M.A. Degree, 1962
>
> Drop-out Rate: High School Grads in 1963 as Percent of 9th Graders in 1959
>
> Percent of Selective Service Examinees Disqualified for Failing Mental Test, 1962
>
> Average Size of School District in Pupils, 1961–62
>
> State Participation: School Revenues from State as Percent of Total School Revenue, 1961–62
>
> Federal Participation: School Revenues from Federal Sources as Percent of Total School Revenues, 1961–62
>
> Per Capita State Expenditures for Higher Education, 1961

Welfare expenditures are the second largest category of state expenditures. Although many state welfare efforts are federally assisted, responsibility for welfare programs and benefits rests with the fifty state governments. Ten welfare variables were selected for analysis:

Average Weekly Payment Per Recipient Unemployment Compensation, 1961

Average Monthly Payment, Old Age Assistance, 1961

Average Monthly Payment Per Family, Aid to Dependent Children, 1961

Average Monthly Payment, Aid to Blind, 1961

Average Monthly Assistance, Medical Assistance for Aged (Kerr-Mills), 1961

Per Capita State and Local Expenditures for Welfare, 1960

Per Capita State and Local Expenditures for Health and Hospitals, 1960

State Participation: Percent State Expenditures of Total Expenditures for Welfare, 1960

State Participation: Percent State Expenditures of Total Expenditures for Health and Hospitals, 1960

Federal Participation: Per Capita Federal Grants to the State for Health, Welfare and Related Purposes, 1960

Eight measures of tax burden and revenue structure in the states were also selected:

Total State and Local Tax Revenues Per Capita, 1960

State Revenues Per Capita, 1960

State Revenues as a Percent of Total State and Local Revenues, 1960

Percent of Total State and Local Revenues from Federal Sources, 1960

Income Tax Revenues as a Percent of Total Tax Revenues, 1961

Sales Tax Revenues as a Percent of Total Tax Revenues, 1961

Alcohol and Tobacco Tax Revenues as a Percent of Total Tax Revenues, 1961

Motor Fuel and Vehicle Tax Revenues as a Percent of Total Tax Revenues, 1961

All 30 variables were obtained for each of the fifty states.[13]

MEASURING THE IMPACT OF MALAPPORTIONMENT ON PUBLIC POLICY

The method chosen to assess the impact of malapportionment on party competition as well as state education, welfare, and tax policies was that of linear regression analysis. First, simple correlation coefficients were computed for the relationships between the several measures of malapportionment and the selected measures of state policy. These simple coefficients show the extent to which differences in policies among the fifty states are associated with malapportionment, but they do not deal with the possibility that some other intervening variables and not malapportionment, might account for these differences. For example, if it is shown that, in general, wealthy states are better apportioned than poor states, it might be that differences in the policies of well-apportioned and malapportioned states are really a product of the fact that the former are wealthy while the latter are poor. If this were the case, policy differences between the states might be attributed to wealth rather than malapportionment. Other intervening variables might be urbanization, industrialization, or the educational level of the state's population. Several studies have shown these socio-economic variables, all of them interrelated, to be associated with variations in state policies.[14] In order to isolate the effect of malapportionment on state policies from the possible effects of socio-economic variables, it is necessary to control for these latter variables. This required that partial correlation coefficients be computed which would show the relationship between malapportionment and the several measures of state policies while controlling for the effect of urbanization, undustrialization, income, and education. If relationships between malapportionment and state policies which appear in simple correlation coefficients disappear when socio-economic variables are controlled, then we may conclude that there is no independent relationship between malapportionment and public policy. On the other hand, if the correlation coefficients between malapportionment and state policies remain significant, even after the effects of socio-economic variables are controlled, then we may more readily conclude that malapportionment does have an independent effect on public policy.

In interpreting correlation coefficients in this study, it was decided to dismiss as insignificant those coefficients which might easily have occurred by chance. An analysis of variance test for the significance of r identifies those coefficients which could occur by chance more than 5 out of 100 times in the correlation of any set of random digits.[15] All calculations are made on the basis of observations about all 50 states (except with regard to party competition for which Nebraska and Minnesota are dropped from analysis because of their non-partisan character). Given a constant number of observations in all correlations, it is possible to state that only simple coefficients above .30 and partial coefficients above .35 are significant at the .05 level, and that all other coefficients can be dismissed as likely to be a product of chance.

MALAPPORTIONMENT AND PARTY COMPETITION

Before turning to a discussion of malapportionment and public policy, let us briefly consider the impact of malapportionment on party competition in state legislatures. Party competition in state legislatures is measured here by the percentage of total seats in each house of the legislature between 1954 and 1964 which were held by the majority party. Percentages are then inverted so that the competition scores in the house and senate of Alabama, Arkansas, Louisiana, Mississippi, and South Carolina, where the minority party did not hold a single seat during those years, are set at 0 and all other scores range upward. If it is true that malapportionment adversely affects party competition, then malapportioned legislatures should be less competitive than well-apportioned legislatures, and these differences in competition should be attributable to malapportionment rather than some other social or economic condition.

Table 1. The Relationship Between Malapportionment and Party Competition in State Legislatures, Controlling for the Effect of Four Socio-Economic Variables

Party Competition 1954–1964	Malapportionment					
	Index of Representation		Urban Under Representation		Apportionment Score	
	Simple	Partial	Simple	Partial	Simple	Partial
Lower Houses	.13	.28	.44	.35	.39	.27
Upper Houses	.06	.30	.50	.38	.43	.29

Note: Figures at the left under each heading are simple correlation coefficients for 48 states; figures at the right are fourth-order partial coefficients which control for the effect of urbanization, industrialization, income, and education.

The simple correlation coefficients in Table 1 indicate a significant relationship between the index of urban under-representation and party competition in both upper and lower chambers. Discrimination against urban areas in representation is associated with decreases in party competition. However, this relationship noticeably weakens when the effects of urbanization, industrialization, income, and education are controlled. The apportionment score also appears related to party competition in simple correlations, but this relationship falls well below accepted significance levels once socio-economic variables are controlled.

Coefficients obtained with the index of urban under-representation are higher than those obtained with either the index of representativeness or the apportionment score. Both of these latter two indices measure malapportionment in an abstract sense and not its discrimination against a particular interest. We might conclude that malapportionment itself does not affect party competition except when it operates to discriminate against urban areas. However, none of the coefficients in Table 1 are very high. Urban under-representation at best can explain less than 25 per cent of the variation among the several states in party competition. Factors other than urban under-representation must be looked to in order to account for 75 per cent of the total variation in party competition among the states.

MALAPPORTIONMENT AND PUBLIC POLICY

Table 2 shows the relationship between malapportionment and 30 separate measures of education, welfare, and tax policies in the fifty states. Simple correlation coefficients are shown at the left under each measure of malapportionment, while partial coefficients—controlling for the combined effect of urbanization, industrialization, income, and education in the states —are shown at the right. Perhaps the most striking feature of Table 2 is that none of the coefficients are very high. For the most part, variations in public policy among the states can *not* be explained by malapportionment.

In the field of education, it might be hypothesized that malapportionment results in lower per pupil expenditures, lower teachers' salaries, and higher pupil-teacher ratios, which in turn produce lower teacher qualifications, higher drop-out rates, and more selective service mental failures. The signs of the coefficients in Table 2 tend to bear out these relationships, but few of the coefficients obtain at a level of significance that would merit much confidence in these hypotheses. None of the coefficients under the index of representativeness or the apportionment score are statistically significant. This helps confirm our suspicion that malapportionment in its technical aspects has no policy relevance. Only six of the twelve simple coefficients under the index of urban under-representation are above the level of significance and only four of these hold up well once socio-economic variables are controlled. Urban under-representation is slightly related to higher pupil-teacher ratios, higher drop-out rates, and increased state and federal participation in public school finance. Yet these relationships are not so close to warrant predictions about changes in these policies once urban areas are given better representation. Per-pupil school expenditures decline with increases in malapportionment, yet this relationship is clearly a product of the fact that pupil expenditures are greater in the rural, less wealthy, agricultural states; once socio-economic variables are controlled, the relationship between pupil expenditures and malapportionment disappears. Likewise the relationship between low teachers' salaries and malapportionment also disappears once socio-economic variables are controlled.

Few policy variables in the welfare field appear related to malapportionment. The closest relationship is between urban under-representation and state participation in the provision of health and hospital services. Yet urban under-representation accounts for only 11 per cent of the total variation

Table 2. The Relationship Between Malapportionment and State Education, Welfare and Tax Policies Controlling for the Effect of Four-Economic Variables

| | Malapportionment | | | | | |
| State Policy Measures | Index of Representation | | Urban Under-Representation | | Apportionment Score | |
	Simple	Partial	Simple	Partial	Simple	Partial
Education						
Per Pupil Expenditures	.12	.06	.36	.12	.09	.01
Average Teachers' Salaries	.28	.20	.30	−.17	.01	.27
Teachers With B.A.	.24	.18	.13	.29	.12	.24
Teachers With M.A.	.07	.10	.14	.07	.09	.04
Male Teachers	.22	−.01	.15	.01	.01	−.10
Pupil-Teacher Ratio	−.11	−.23	−.31	−.40	−.15	−.21
Drop-out Rate	.06	.29	.37	.53	.15	.29
Mental Failures	−.09	−.27	−.15	−.26	−.16	−.14
Size of School Districts	−.24	−.31	−.10	−.20	−.14	−.15
State Participation	−.25	−.34	−.32	−.42	−.23	−.28
Federal Participation	−.06	−.13	−.33	−.38	−.07	−.18
Higher Education Expenditures	−.07	−.07	−.15	−.07	−.16	−.20
Welfare						
Unemployment Benefits	.17	.20	.29	.09	.13	.03
Old Age Benefits	−.01	.07	.37	.04	.01	.06
ADC Benefits	.12	.11	.49	.06	.14	.09
Blind Benefits	−.08	.16	.32	.09	.01	.02
Kerr-Mills Benefits	.13	.18	.34	.27	.05	.05
Welfare Expenditures, Per cap.	.04	.05	.09	.01	−.17	.02
Health Expenditures, Per cap.	−.21	.03	−.01	.01	−.08	.05
State Participation, Welfare	−.12	−.17	−.26	−.11	−.08	−.05
State Participation, Health	.10	.06	.34	.31	.17	.18
Federal Participation	.01	−.08	−.31	−.18	−.28	−.29
Taxation						
Total Taxes Per capita	.15	.05	.26	.17	.01	.09
State Revenue Per capita	−.16	−.07	−.18	−.17	−.10	−.09
State Percent of Total Revenue	−.01	−.06	−.30	−.20	−.13	−.10
Federal Percent of Total Revenue	−.03	−.09	−.36	−.23	−.04	−.08
Income Taxes	.12	.07	.14	.01	.02	.05
Sales Taxes	−.14	−.15	−.20	−.20	−.14	−.09
Alcohol & Tobacco Taxes	.14	.04	.13	−.01	.02	.07
Motor Fuel Taxes	.22	.08	.01	.04	−.19	.14

Note: Figures at the left under each heading are simple correlation coefficients for 50 states; figures at the right are fourth-order partial coefficients which control for the effect of urbanization, industrialization, income, and education.

among the states in the extent of their participation in the health field. The level of payments to recipients of unemployment compensation, old age assistance, aid to dependent children, and aid to the medically indigent aged under Kerr–Mills laws, appears to be slightly related to urban under-representation on the basis of simple coefficients. Most of these coefficients disappear, however, once socio-economic variables are controlled. In short, the relationship between urban representation and welfare policies among the fifty states is a product of intervening socio-economic variables. There is no evidence that reapportionment will bring any noticeable liberalization of welfare policies.

Not one of the relationships between malapportionment and the eight selected tax policies are statistically significant. It is doubtful, for example, that reapportionment will bring higher tax levies. Neither total state and local taxes per capita nor total state revenues per capita are significantly related to apportionment. While federal grants constitute a larger share of the revenue of malapportioned states, this is merely a product of the fact that these states tend to be less wealthy; the relationship between federal support and malapportionment disappears when socio-economic variables are controlled. State revenues are a larger share of total revenues in mal-apportioned states, but this relationship also appears as a product of socio-economic variables rather than malapportionment itself. It was hypothesized that well-apportioned states would place greater reliance in their tax structure on progressive income taxation, while malapportioned states would rely more on regressive sales taxation. The signs of the coefficients in Table 2 tend to confirm this hypothesis, but the coefficients are so low the relationships so slight, that they might easily have occurred by chance. Certainly there is no evidence that reapportionment will bring about any substantial changes in state tax structures.

It is interesting to note that the few significant policy correlations derived in this study were obtained with David and Eisenburg's index of urban under-representation. This index measures the degree to which a particular political interest is affected by malapportionment rather than the existence of malapportionment in the technical sense. The failure to obtain any significant policy correlates with the index of representativeness suggests that the theoretical minimum population which *could* control a legislature is not a relevant political variable. Nor does the extent to which the populations of legislative districts approach a normal statistical curve, as measured by the Schubert and Press apportionment score, appear to be a politically relevant variable. Schubert and Press rebuked earlier scholars for their technically unsophisticated measures of malapportionment ("the difference in the costs for the computation of precise and crude indices is ... minimal").[16] Yet it turns out that David and Eisenburg with their less sophisticated measure came closer to identifying the relevant political aspect of malapportionment than Schubert and Press. For malapportionment becomes relevant when it operates to discriminate against specific political interests in a state.

CONCLUSION

On the whole, the policy choices of malapportioned legislatures are not noticeably different from the policy choices of well-apportioned legislatures. Most of the policy differences which do occur turn out to be a product of socio-economic differences among the states rather than a direct product of apportionment practices. Relationships that appear between malapportionment and public policy are so slight that reapportionment is not likely to bring about any significant policy changes. Of course, these conclusions are predicted on results obtained from analyzing 30 selected measures of public policy in three separate fields—education, welfare, and taxation. Conceivably malapportionment could have a more direct effect on some area of policy-making that was not investigated. However, expenditures for welfare and education, the liberality of welfare benefits, teachers' qualifications and salaries, the quality of public education, the tax burden, the revenue structure, and the extent of state participation in education, health, and welfare, are certainly among the most important issues in state politics And apportionment practices seem to have little impact on the outcome of these issues.

At this point it seems appropriate to enter a caveat regarding the conclusions that can be drawn from these operations. All that has been shown is that reapportionment is not likely to have a direct impact on party competition or on certain policy outcomes. This is *not* to say that reapportionment will have no effect on state political systems or processes. Quantification necessitates a simplification of what may be a very complex question. The consequences of reapportionment may be so subtle and diverse that they defy quantitative measurement. Perhaps the consequences in each state will vary so much that direct interstate comparisons are inappropriate. Certainly we need more refined analyses of the impact of apportionment systems on state political processes and policy outcomes; we especially need more "before and after" studies of reapportionment. But these operations do succeed in challenging the easy assumptions and simple generalizations about the effects of malapportionment on public policy, and they caution us not to expect major policy changes in the wake of reapportionment.

How can we account for the bitter political battles fought over reapportionment in many states if malapportionment really has little effect on public policy? Perhaps the explanation lies in the distinction between the potential for power and the exercise of power. Certainly malapportionment overweights rural representation in legislatures. Malapportionment may give rural legislators a potential for power over their urban counterparts, *but* if they do not vote together with a high degree of unity to oppose urban interests on actual questions of public policy, their "power" may be more hypothetical than real. Legislative control can change hands and still leave policies unchanged if there are few policy differences between those placed in power and those dispossessed. Suburban voters, for example, may be just as conservative as the rural voters whose voice they may replace. In addition, divisions other than rural-versus-urban may characterize much of the legislative process: divisions between the parties, between a Governor's supporters and his opponents, between economic interests and organized groups, between liberals and conservatives, between labor and management, between regions of a state, and so forth. Reapportionment could change the distribution of power between rural and urban constituencies and yet have so subtle an effect on these other divisions that few policy changes would result. In short, even rural-urban divisions are affected by reapportionment; these divisions are only one of many types of legislative divisions.

These conclusions need not moderate enthusiasm for reapportionment. The moral case for equality of representation is as compelling as it ever was. The impact of reapportionment on public policy, however, may be somewhat less sweeping than many expect.

NOTES

[1] See Charles Adrian, *State and Local Governments* (New York: McGraw-Hill, 1960), pp. 306–7; Daniel Grant and H.C. Nixon, *State and Local Government in America* (Boston: Allyn and Bacon, 1963), pp. 204–5; Richard Frost, "On Derge's Metropolitan and Outstate Legislative Delegations," *American Political Science Review*, Vol. 53 (September, 1959), pp. 792–95; Commission on Intergovernmental Relations, *A Report to the President for Transmittal to Congress* (Washington: U.S. Government Printing Office, 1955), p. 39; Malcolm Jewell, *The State Legislature* (New York: Random House, 1962), pp. 30–33; V. O. Key, Jr., *American State Politics: An Introduction* (New York: Knopf, 1956), pp. 76–77.

[2] See "After Redistricting Decision—Where States May See Changes in Taxes, Welfare, Highways," *U.S. News and World Report*, July 6, 1964, pp. 34–36; and "A New Charter for State Legislatures," *Time*, June 26, 1964, pp. 22–23.

[3] *Baker* v. *Carr*, 369 U.S. 186 (1962); *Reynolds* v. *Sims*, 84 S.Ct. 1362 (1964).

[4] E.g., "The conception of political equality from the Declaration of Independence to Lincoln's Gettysburg Address, to the Fourteenth, Fifteenth, Seventeenth, and Nineteenth Amendments can mean only one thing—one person, one vote." *Gray* v. *Sanders*, 83 S.Ct. 801 (1963), p. 809.

[5] *Wesberry* v. *Sanders*, 84 S.Ct. 526 (1964), p. 530.

[6] David Derge, "Metropolitan and Outstate Alignments in the Illinois and Missouri Legislative Delegations," *American Political Science Review*, Vol 53 (December, 1958), pp. 1051–65.

[7] Duane Lockard, *The Politics of State and Local Government* (New York: Macmillan, 1963), p. 319.

[8] Herbert Jacob, "The Consequences of Malapportionment: A Note of Caution," *Social Forces*, Vol. 43 (December, 1964), pp. 256–61.

[9] Manning J. Dauer and Robert G. Kelsay, "Unrepresentative States," *National Municipal Review*, Vol. 44 (December, 1955), pp. 571–75.

[10] Paul T. David and Ralph Eisenberg, *Devaluation of the Urban and Suburban Vote*, Bureau of Public Administration, University of Virginia, 1961.

[11] Glendon Schubert and Charles Press, "Measuring Malapportionment," *American Political Science Review*, Vol. 58 (June, 1964), pp. 302–27; and corrections published December, 1964, pp. 966–70.

[12] The simple correlation coefficients between these three measures are as follows: index of representativeness and urban under-representation: .45; index of representativeness and apportionment score: .52; urban under-representation and apportionment score: .65.

[13] Sources of data on education, welfare and tax variables were: U.S. Office of Education, *Statistics of State School Systems 1961–62* (Washington: U.S. Government Printing Office, 1963); National Education Association, *Rankings of the States 1963* (Washington: National Education Association, 1963); U.S. Bureau of Census, *Statistical Abstract 1963* (Washington: U.S. Government Printing Office, 1963).

[14] See, for example, Jerry Minar, *Social and Economic Factors in Spending for Public Education* (Syracuse: Syracuse University Press, 1963); Richard E. Dawson and James A. Robinson, "Inter-party Competition, Economic Variables and Welfare Policies in the American States," *Journal of Politics*, Vol. 25 (May, 1963), pp. 265–89.

[15] The analysis of variance test determines the possibility that any coefficient might have been obtained by correlating sets of 50 random numbers from an imaginary infinite universe of states. It does not matter that the fifty states are a universe rather than a sample. The allusion to sampling in tests of significance is a hypothetical one. It helps us to determine whether the correlations which are obtained might have been obtained by correlating various columns of 50 digits found in a table of random numbers. See Hubert M. Blalock, *Social Statistics* (New York: McGraw-Hill, 1960), pp. 302–5.

[16] Schubert and Press, *op. cit.*, p. 311.

CHAPTER 21

A Theory of the Budgetary Process*

Otto A. Davis
M. A. H. Dempster
Aaron Wildavsky

There are striking regularities in the budgetary process. The evidence from over half the non-defense agencies indicates that the behavior of the budgetary process of the United States government results in aggregate decisions similar to those produced by a set of simple decision rules that are linear and temporally stable. For the agencies considered, certain equations are specified and compared with data composed of agency requests (through the Bureau of the Budget) and Congressional appropriations from 1947 through 1963. The comparison indicates that these equations summarize accurately aggregate outcomes of the budgetary process for each agency.

In the first section of the paper we present an analytic summary of the federal budgetary process, and we explain why basic features of the process lead us to believe that it can be represented by simple models which are stable over periods of time, linear, and stochastic.[1] In the second section we propose and discuss the alternative specifications for the agency-Budget Bureau and Congressional decision equations. The empirical results are presented in section three. In section four we provide evidence on deviant cases, discuss predictions, and future work to explore some of the problems indicated by this kind of analysis. An appendix contains informal definitions and a discussion of the statistical terminology used in the paper.

I. THE BUDGETARY PROCESS

Decisions depend upon calculation of which alternatives to consider and to choose.[2] A major clue toward understanding budgeting is the extraordinary complexity of the calculations involved. There are a huge number of items to be considered, many of which are of considerable technical difficulty.

Reprinted from *American Political Science Review*, Vol. 60, No. 3 (September 1966), pp. 529–47 by permission of the American Political Science Association.

There is, however, little or no theory in most areas of policy which would enable practitioners to predict the consequences of alternative moves and the probability of their occurring. Nor has anyone solved the imposing problem of the inter-personal comparison of utilities. Outside of the political process, there is no agreed upon way of comparing and evaluating the merits of different programs for different people whose preferences vary in kind and in intensity.

Participants in budgeting deal with their overwhelming burdens by adopting aids to calculation. By far the most important aid to calculation is the incremental method. Budgets are almost never actively reviewed as a whole in the sense of considering at once the value of all existing programs as compared to all possible alternatives. Instead, this year's budget is based on last year's budget, with special attention given to a narrow range of increases or decreases.

Incremental calculations proceed from an existing base. (By "base" we refer to commonly held expectations among participants in budgeting that programs will be carried out at close to the going level of expenditures.) The widespread sharing of deeply held expectations concerning the organization's base provides a powerful (although informal) means of securing stability.

The most effective coordinating mechanisms in budgeting undoubtedly stem from the roles adopted by the major participants. Roles (the expectations of behavior attached to institutional positions) are parts of the division of labor. They are calculating mechanisms. In American national government, the administrative agencies act as advocates of increased expenditure, the Bureau of the Budget acts as Presidential servant with a cutting bias, the House Appropriations committee functions as a guardian of the Treasury. and the Senate Appropriations Committee as an appeals court to which agencies carry their disagreements with House action. The roles fit in with one another and set up patterns of mutual expectations which markedly reduce the burden of calculation for the participants. Since the agencies can be depended upon to advance all the programs for which there is prospect of support, the Budget Bureau and the Appropriations Committees respectively can concentrate on fitting them into the President's program or paring them down.

Possessing the greatest expertise and the largest numbers, working in the closest proximity to their policy problems and clientele groups, and desiring to expand their horizons, administrative agencies generate action through advocacy. But if they ask for amounts much larger than the appropriating bodies believe reasonable, the agencies' credibility will suffer a drastic decline. In such circumstances, the reviewing organs are likely to cut deeply, with the result that the agency gets much less than it might have with a more moderate request. So the first guide for decision is: do not come in *too* high. Yet the agencies must also not come in too low, for the reviewing bodies assume that if agency advocates do not ask for funds they do not need them. Thus, the agency decision rule might read: come in a little too high (padding), but not too high (loss of confidence).

Agencies engage in strategic planning to secure these budgetary goals. Strategies are the links between the goals of the agencies and their perceptions of the kinds of actions which will be effective in their political environment. Budget officers in American national government uniformly believe that being a good politician—cultivation of an active clientele, development of confidence by other officials (particularly the appropriations subcommittees), and skill in following strategies which exploit opportunities—is more important in obtaining funds than demonstration of agency efficiency.

In deciding how much money to recommend for specific purposes, the House Appropriations Committee breaks down into largely autonomous subcommittees in which the norm of reciprocity is carefully followed. Specialization is carried further as subcommittee members develop limited areas of competence and jurisdiction. Budgeting is both incremental and fragmented as the subcommittees deal with adjustments to the historical base of each agency. Fragmentation and specialization are increased through the appeals functions of the Senate Appropriations Committee, which deals with what has become (through House action) a fragment of a fragment. With so many participants continually engaged in taking others into account, a great many adjustments are made in the light of what others are likely to do.

This qualitative account of the budgetary process contains clear indications of the kind of quantitative models we wish to develop. It is evident, for example, that decision-makers in the budgetary process think in terms of percentages. Agencies talk of expanding their base by a certain percentage. The Bureau of the Budget is concerned about the growth rates for certain agencies and programs. The House Appropriations Committee deals with percentage cuts, and the Senate Appropriations Committee with the question of whether or not to restore percentage cuts. These considerations suggest that the quantitative relationships among the decisions of the participants in the budget process are linear in form.

The attitudes and calculations of participants in budgeting seem stable over time. The prominence of the agency's "base" is a sign of stability. The roles of the major participants are powerful, persistent, and strongly grounded in the expectations of others as well as in the internal requirements of the positions. Stability is also suggested by the specialization that occurs among the participants, the long service of committee members, the adoption of incremental practices such as comparisons with the previous year, the fragmentation of appropriations by program and item, the treatments of appropriations as continuously variable sums of money rather than as perpetual reconsiderations of the worth of programs, and the practice of allowing past decisions to stand while coordinating decision-making only if difficulties arise. Since the budgetary process appears to be stable over periods of time, it is reasonable to estimate the relationships in budgeting on the basis of time series data.

Special events that upset the apparent stability of the budgetary process can and do occur. Occasionally, world events take an unexpected turn, a new President occupies the White House, some agencies act with exceptional zeal, others suffer drastic losses of confidence on the part of the appropriations subcommittees, and so on. It seems plausible to represent such transient events as random shocks to an otherwise deterministic system. Therefore, our model is stochastic rather than deterministic.

The Politics of the Budgetary Process contains a description of strategies which various participants in budgeting use to further their aims. Some of these strategies are quite complicated. However, a large part of the process can be explained by some of the simpler strategies which are based on the relationship between agency requests for funds (through the Budget Bureau) and Congressional appropriations. Because these figures are made public and are known to all participants, because they are directly perceived and communicated without fear of information loss or bias, and because the participants react to these figures, they are ideal for feedback purposes. It is true that there are other indicators—special events, crises, technological developments, actions of clientele groups—which are attended to by participants in the budgetary process. But if these indicators have impact, they must quickly be reflected in the formal feedback mechanisms—the actions of departments, the Bureau of the Budget, and Congress—to which they are directed. Some of these indicators (see section IV) are represented by the stochastic disturbances. Furthermore, the formal indicators are more precise, more simple, more available, more easily interpreted than the others. They are, therefore, likely to be used by participants in the budgetary process year in and year out. Present decisions are based largely on past experience, and this lore is encapsulated in the amounts which the agencies receive as they go through the steps in the budgetary cycle.

For all the reasons discussed in this section, our models of the budgetary process are linear, stable over periods of time, stochastic, and strategic in character. They are "as if" models: an excellent fit for a given model means only that the actual behavior of the participants has an effect equivalent to the equations of the model. The models, taken as a whole, represent a set of decision rules for Congress and the agencies.

II. THE MODELS

In our models we aggregate elements of the decision-making structure. The Budget Bureau submissions for the agency are used instead of separate figures for the two kinds of organizations. Similarly, at this stage in our analysis, we use final Congressional appropriations instead of separating out committee action, floor action, conference committee recommendations, and so on. We wish to emphasize that although there may be some aggregation bias in the estimation of the postulated structure of decision, this does not affect the linearity of the aggregate relationships. If the decisions of an agency and the Bureau of the Budget with regard to that agency depend linearly upon the same variable (as we hypothesize), then the aggregated decision rule of the two, treated as a single entity, will depend linearly upon that variable. By a similar argument, the various Congressional participants can be grouped together so that Congress can be regarded as a single decision-making entity. While the aggregating procedure may result in grouping positive and negative influences together, this manifestly does not affect the legitimacy of the procedure; linearity is maintained.[3]

Our models concern only the requests presented in the President's budget for an individual agency and the behavior of Congress as a whole with regard to the agency's appropriation. The models do not attempt to estimate the complete decision-making structure for each agency from bureau requests to departments to submission through the Budget Bureau to possible final action in the Senate and House. There are several reasons for remaining content with the aggregated figures we use. First, the number of possible decision rules which must be considered grows rapidly as each new participant is added. We would soon be overwhelmed by the sheer number of rules invoked. Second, there are genuine restrictions placed on the number of structural parameters we can estimate because (a) some data such as bureau requests to departments, are unavailable, and (b) only short time series are meaningful for most agencies. It would make no sense, for example, to go back in time beyond the end of World War II when most domestic activity was disrupted.[4]

Since the agencies use various strategies and Congress may respond to them in various ways, we propose several alternative systems of equations. These equations represent alternative decision rules which may be followed by Congressional and agency-Budget Bureau participants in the budgetary process. One important piece of data for agency-Budget Bureau personnel who are formulating appropriations requests is the most recent Congressional appropriation. Thus, we make considerable use of the concept "base", operationally defined as the previous Congressional appropriation for an agency, in formulating our decision rules. Since the immediate past exercises such a heavy influence on budgetary outcomes, Markov (simultaneous, difference) equations are particularly useful. In these Markov processes, the value of certain variables at one point in time is dependent on their value at one or more immediately previous periods as well as on the particular circumstances of the time.

We postulate several decision rules for both the agency-Budget Bureau requests and for Congressional action on these requests. For each series of requests or appropriations, we select from the postulated decision rules that rule which most closely represents the behavior of the aggregated entities. We use the variables

y_t the appropriation passed by Congress for any given agency in the year t. Supplemental appropriations are not included in the y_t.

x_t the appropriation requested by the Bureau of the Budget for any given agency for the year t. The x_t constitutes the President's budget request for an agency.

We will also introduce certain symbols representing random disturbances of each of the postulated relationships. These symbols are explained as they are introduced.

A. Equations for Agency-Budget Bureau Decision Rules. The possibility that different agencies use different strategies makes it necessary to construct alternative equations representing these various strategies. Then, for each agency in our sample, we use time series data to select that equation which seems to describe best the budgetary decisions of that agency. In this section we present three simple models of agency requests. The first states agency requests as a function of the previous year's appropriation. The second states requests as a function of the previous appropriation as well as a function of the differences between the agency request and appropriation in the previous year. The third states requests as a function of the previous year's request. In all three linear models provision is made for a random variable to take into account the special circumstances of the time.

An agency, while convinced of the worth of its programs, tends to be aware that extraordinarily large or small requests are likely to be viewed with suspicion by Congress; an agency does not consider it desirable to make extraordinary requests, which, might precipitate unfavorable Congressional reaction. Therefore the agency usually requests a percentage (generally greater than one hundred per cent) of its previous year's appropriation. This percentage is not fixed: in the event of favorable circumstances, the request is a larger percentage of the previous year's appropriation than would otherwise be the case; similarly, the percentage might be reduced in the event of unfavorable circumstances.

Decisions made in the manner described above may be represented by a simple equation. If we take the average of the percentages that are

implicitly or explicitly used by budget officers, then any request can be represented by the sum of this average percentage of the previous year's appropriation plus the increment or decrement due to the favorable or unfavorable
circumstances. Thus

$$(1) \qquad\qquad x_t = \beta_0 y_{t-1} + \xi_t$$

> The agency request (through the Budget Bureau) for a certain
> year is a fixed mean percentage of the Congressional appropriation
> for that agency in the previous year plus a random variable
> (normally distributed with mean zero and unknown but finite
> variance) for that year.

is an equation representing this type of behavior. The average or mean
percentage is represented by β_0. The increment or decrement due to circumstances is represented by ξ_t, a variable which requires some special explanation. It is difficult to predict what circumstances will occur at what time to
put an agency in a favorable or unfavorable position. Numerous events
could influence Congress's (and the public's) perception of an agency and
its programs—the occurrence of a destructive hurricane in the case of the
Weather Bureau, the death by cancer of a friend of an influential congressman, in the case of the National Institutes of Health, the hiring (or losing)
of an especially effective lobbyist by some interest group, the President's
becoming especially interested in a program of some agency as Kennedy
was in mental health, and so on. (Of course, some of them may be more or
less "predictable" at certain times to an experienced observer, but this fact
causes no difficulty here). Following common statistical practice we may
represent the sum of the effects of all such events by a random variable that
is an increment or decrement to the usual percentage of the previous year's
appropriation. In equation (1), then, ξ_t represents the value which this random variable assumes in year t.

We have chosen to view the special events of each year for each agency
as random phenomena that are capable of being described by a probability
density or distribution. We assume here that the random variable is normally
distributed with mean zero and an unknown but finite variance. Given this
specification of the random variable, the agency makes its budgeting decisions as if it were operating by the postulated decision rule given in equation
(1).

An agency, although operating somewhat like the organizations
described by equation (1), may wish to take into account an additional
strategic consideration: while this agency makes a request which is roughly
a fixed percentage of the previous year's appropriation, it also desires to
smooth out its stream of appropriations by taking into account the difference

between its request and appropriation for the previous year. If there were an unusually large cut in the previous year's request, the agency submits a "padded" estimate to make up for the loss in expected funds; an unusual increase is followed by a reduced estimate to avoid unspent appropriations. This behavior may be represented by equation or decision rule where

(2) $$x_t = \beta_1 y_{t-1} + \beta_2(y_{t-1} - x_{t-1}) + \chi_t$$

> The agency request (through the Budget Bureau) for a certain year is a fixed mean percentage of the Congressional appropriation for that agency in the previous year plus a fixed mean percentage of the difference between the Congressional appropriation and the agency request for the previous year plus a stochastic disturbance.

χ_t is a stochastic disturbance, which plays the role described for the random variable in equation (1), the β's are variables reflecting the aspects of the previous year's request and appropriation that an agency takes into account: β_1 represents the mean percentage of the previous year's request which is taken into account, and β_2 represents the mean percentage of the difference between the previous year's appropriation and request $(y_{t-1} - x_{t-1})$ which is taken into account. Note that $\beta_2 < 0$ is anticipated so that a large cut will (in the absence of the events represented by the stochastic disturbance) be followed by a padded estimate and visa-versa.[5]

Finally, an agency (or the President through the Bureau of the Budget), convinced of the worth of its programs, may decide to make requests without regard to previous Congressional action. This strategy appeals especially when Congress has so much confidence in the agency that it tends to give an appropriation which is almost identical to the request. Aside from special circumstances represented by stochastic disturbances, the agency's request in any given year tends to be approximately a fixed percentage of its request for the previous year. This behavior may be represented by

(3) $$x_t = \beta_3 x_{t-1} + \rho_t$$

> The agency request (through the Budget Bureau) for a certain year is a fixed mean percentage of the agency's request for the previous year plus a random variable (stochastic disturbance).

where ρ_t is a stochastic disturbance and β_3 is the average percentage. Note that if the agency believes its programs to be worthy, $\beta_3 > 1$ is expected.[6]

These three equations are not the only ones which may be capable of representing the actual behavior of the combined budgeting decisions of the agencies and the Bureau of the Budget. However, they represent the agency-Budget Bureau budgeting behavior better than all other decision rules we tried.[7]

B. Equations for Congressional Decision Rules. In considering Congressional behavior, we again postulate three decision equations from which a selection must be made that best represents the behavior of Congress in regard to an agency's appropriations. Since Congress may use various strategies in determining appropriations for different agencies, different Congressional decision equations may be selected as best representing Congressional appropriations for each agency in our sample. Our first model states Congressional appropriations as a function of the agency's request (through the Budget Bureau) to Congress. The second states appropriations as a function of the agency's request as well as a function of the deviation from the usual relationship between Congress and the agency in the previous year. The third model states appropriations as a function of that segment of the agency's request that is not part of its appropriation or request for the previous year. Random variables are included to take account of special circumstances.

If Congress believes that an agency's request, after passing through the hands of the Budget Bureau, is a relatively stable index of the funds needed by the agency to carry out its programs, Congress responds by appropriating a relatively fixed percentage of the agency's request. The term "relatively fixed" is used because Congress is likely to alter this precentage somewhat from year to year because of special events and circumstances relevant to particular years. As in the case of agency requests, these special circumstances may be viewed as random phenomena. One can view this behavior as if it were the result of Congress' appropriating a fixed mean percentage of the agency requests; adding to the amount so derived a sum representing by a random variable. One may represent this behavior as if Congress were following the decision rule

$$(4) \qquad\qquad y_t = a_0 x_t + \eta_t$$

The Congressional appropriation for an agency in a certain year is a fixed mean percentage of the agency's request in that year plus a stochastic disturbance.

where a_0 represents the fixed average percentage and η_t represents the stochastic disturbance.

Although Congress usually grants an agency a fixed percentage of its request, this request sometimes represents an extention of the agency's programs above (or below) the size desired by Congress. This can occur when the agency and the Bureau of the Budget follow Presidential aims differing from those of Congress, or when Congress suspects that the agency is padding the current year's request. In such a situation Congress usually appropriates a sum different from the usual percentage. If a_1 represents the mean of the usual percentages, this behavior can be represented by equation or decision rule

$$(5) \qquad\qquad y_t = a_1 x_t + v_t$$

where v_t is a stochastic disturbance representing that part of the appropriations attributable to the special circumstances that cause Congress to deviate from a relatively fixed percentage. Therefore, when agency aims and Congressional desires markedly differ from usual (so that Congress may be said to depart from its usual rule) the stochastic disturbance takes on an unusually large positive or negative value. In order to distinguish this case from the previous one, more must be specified about the stochastic disturbance v_t. In a year following one in which agency aims and Congressional desires markedly differed, the agency makes a request closer to Congressional desires, and/or Congress shifts its desires closer to those of the agency (or the President). In the year after a deviation, then, assume that Congress will tend to make allowances to normalize the situation. Such behavior can be represented by having the stochastic disturbance v_t generated in accordance with a first order Markov scheme. The stochastic component in v_t is itself determined by a relation

$$(6) \qquad\qquad v_t = a_2 v_{t-1} + \epsilon_t$$

where ϵ_t is a random variable. The symbol v_t therefore stands for the stochastic disturbance in the previous year (v_{t-1}) as well as the new stochastic disturbance for the year involved (ϵ_t). Substituting (6) into (5) gives

$$(7) \qquad\qquad y_t = a_1 x_t + a_2 v_{t-1} + \epsilon_t$$

The Congressional appropriation for an agency is a fixed mean percentage of the agency's request for that year plus a stochastic disturbance representing a deviation from the usual relationship between Congress and the agency in the previous year plus a random variable for the current year.

as a complete description of a second Congressional decision rule. If Congress never makes complete allowance for an initial "deviation," then $-1 < a_2 < 1$ is to be expected.

To complete the description of this second Congressional decision rule, we will suppose $0 < a_2 < 1$. Then, granted a deviation from its usual percentage, Congress tends to decrease subsequent deviations by moving steadily back toward its usual percentage (except for the unforseeable events or special circumstances whose effects are represented by the random variable ϵ_t). For example, if in a particular year $v_{t-1} > 0$ and if in the following year there are no special circumstances so that $\xi_t = 0$, then $v_t = a_2 v_{t-1} < v_{t-1}$. The deviation in year t is smaller than the deviation in year $t - 1$. However, if $-1 < a_2 < 0$, after an initial deviation, Congress tends to move back to its usual rule (apart from the disturbances represented by the random variable ϵ_t) by making successively smaller deviations which differ in sign. For example, if $v_{t-1} > 0$, then apart from the disturbance ϵ_t it is clear that $v_t = a_2 v_{t-1} < 0$, since $a_2 < 0$. Finally, if $a_2 = 0$, decision rule (7) is the same as the previous rule (4).

The specialization inherent in the appropriations process allows some members of Congress to have an intimate knowledge of the budgetary processes of the agencies and the Budget Bureau. Thus, Congress might consider that part of the agency's request (x_t) which is not based on the previous year's appropriation or request. This occurs when Congress believes that this positive or negative remainder represents padding or when it desires to smooth out the agency's rate of growth. If Congress knows the decision rule that an agency uses to formulate its budgetary request, we can let λ_t represent a dummy variable defined as $\lambda_t = \xi_t$ if the agency uses decision rule (1); $\lambda_t = \beta_2(y_{t-1} - x_{t-1}) + \chi_t$ if the agency uses decision rule (2); and, $\lambda_t = \rho_t$ if the agency uses decision rule (3). Suppose that Congress appropriates, on the average, an amount which is a relatively fixed percentage of the agency's request plus a percentage of this (positive or negative) remainder λ_t. This behavior can be represented by the "as if" decision rule

$$(8) \qquad\qquad y_4 = a_3 x_t + a_4 \lambda_t + v_t$$

The Congressional appropriation for an agency is a fixed mean percentage of the agency's request for a certain year plus a fixed mean percentage of a dummy variable which represents that part of the agency's request for the year at issue which is not part of the appropriation or request of the previous year plus a random variable representing the part of the appropriation attributable to the special circumstances of the year.

where v_t is a stochastic disturbance whose value in any particular year represents the part of the appropriation attributable to the agency's special circumstances of the year. One might expect that Congress takes only "partial" account of the remainder represented by λ_t so $0 < a_4 < 1$.

III. EMPIRICAL RESULTS

Times series data for the period 1947–63 were studied for fifty-six non-defense agencies in the United States Government. The requests (x'_t) of these agencies were taken to be the amounts presented to Congress in the President's budget. For eight sub-agencies from the National Institutes of Health, data for a shorter period of time were considered, and the requests (x_t) of these eight sub-agencies were taken to be their proposals to the Bureau of the Budget.[8] In all instances the Congressional decision variable (y_t) was taken to be the final appropriation before any supplemental additions. The total appropriations (without supplements) of the agencies studied amounted to approximately twenty-seven per cent of the non-defense budget in 1963. Over one-half of all non-defense agencies were investigated; the major omissions being the Post Office and many independent agencies. A minimum of three agencies were examined from each of the Treasury, Justice, Interior, Agriculture, Commerce, Labor, and Health, Education and Welfare Departments.[9]

If the agency-Budget Bureau disturbance is independent of Congressional disturbance,[10] the use of ordinary least squares (OLS) to estimate most of the possible combinations of the proposed decision equations is justified. OLS is identical to the simultaneous full information maximum likelihood (FIML) technique for most of the present systems. This is not so, however, for some systems of equations because of the presence of an auto-correlated disturbance in one equation of the two and the consequent non-linearity of the estimating equations. In equation (6) the stochastic disturbance for year t is a function of the value of the disturbance in the previous year. In a system of equations in which auto-correlation occurs in the first equation, an appropriate procedure is to use OLS to estimate the alternative proposals for the other equation, decide by the selection criteria which best specifies the data, use the knowledge of this structure to estimate the first equation, and then decide through use of appropriate criteria, which version of the first equation best specifies the data.

The principal selection criterion we used is that of maximum (adjusted) correlation coefficient (R). For a given dependent variable this criterion leads one to select from alternative specifications of the explanatory variables, that specification which leads to the highest sample correlation coefficient. The estimations of the alternative specifications must, of course, be made from the same data.[11] The second criterion involves the use of the d-statistic test for serial correlation of the estimated residuals of a single equation.[12] This statistic tests the null hypothesis of residual independence against the alternative of serial correlation. We used the significance points for the d-statistic of Theil and Nagar.[13] When the d-statistic was found to be significant in fitting the Congressional decision equation (4) to an agency's data, it was always found that equation (7) best specified Congressional behavior with respect to the appropriations of that agency in the sense of yielding the maximum correlation coefficient. A third criterion is based on a test of the significance of the sample correlation between the residuals of (4) and the estimated λ_t of the equation selected previously for a given agency. David's significance points for this statistic were used to make a two-tailed test at the five per cent level of the null hypothesis that the residuals are uncorrelated.[14] When significant correlation occurred, it was always found that Congressional decision equation (8), in which a function of the deviation from the usual relationship between request and the previous year's appropriation enters explicitly, best specified appropriation behavior with respect to the agency in question.

The statistical procedures were programmed for the Carnegie Institute of Technology's Control Data G-21 electronic computer in the 20-Gate algebraic compiling language. The selection among alternate specifications according to the criteria established was not done automatically; otherwise all computations were performed by machine. Since the results for each agency are described in detail elsewhere,[15] and a full rendition would double the length of the paper, we must restrict ourselves to summary statements.

The empirical results support the hypothesis that, up to a random error of reasonable magnitude, the budgetary process of the United States government is equivalent to a set of temporally stable linear decision rules. Estimated correlation coefficients for the best specifications of each agency are generally high. Although the calculated values of the multiple correlation coefficients (R's) tend to run higher in time series than in cross-sectional analysis, the results are good. We leave little of the variance statistically unexplained. Moreover the estimated standard deviations of the coefficients are usually much smaller than one-half of the size of the estimated coefficients, a related indication of good results. Table 1 presents the frequencies of the correlation coefficients.

Table 1. Best Specifications for Each Agency Are High

	Frequencies of Correlation Coefficients										
	1 – .995	*– .99*	*– .98*	*–.97*	*– .96*	*– .95*	*– .94*	*– .93*	*– .90*	*– .85*	*– 0*
Congressional	21	8	15	4	5	2	2	1	5	2	2
Agency-Bureau	9	2	2	8	5	2	4	3	5	11	10

The fits between the decision rules and the time series data for the Congressional decision equations are, in general, better than those for the agency-Bureau of the Budget equations. Of the 64 agencies and sub-agencies studied, there are only 14 instances in which the correlation coefficient for the agency (or sub-agency) equation was higher than the one for the corresponding Congressional equation. We speculate that the estimated variances of the disturbances of the agency-Budget Bureau decision rules are usually larger because the agencies are closer than Congress to the actual sources that seek to add new programs or expand old ones.

Table 2 presents a summary of the combinations of the agency-Bureau of the Budget and Congressional decision equations. For those agencies studied, the most popular combinations of behavior are the simple ones represented by equations (4) and (1) respectively. When Congress uses a sophisticated "gaming" strategy such as (7) or (8), the corresponding agency-Bureau of the Budget decision equation is the relatively simple (1). And, when Congress grants exactly or almost exactly the amount requested by an agency, the agency tends to use decision equation (3).

Table 2. Budgetary Behavior Is Simple

Summary of Decision Equations

Agency-Budget Bureau		1	2	3
	4	44*	1	8
Congress	7	1	0	0
	8	12	0	0

*Including eight sub-agencies from the National Institutes of Health.

Our discussion thus far has assumed fixed values for the coefficients (parameters) of the equations we are using to explain the behavior underlying the budgetary process. In the light of the many important events occurring in the period from 1946 to 1963, however, it seems reasonable to suppose that the appropriations structure of many government agencies was altered. If this is correct, the coefficients of the equations—literally, in this context, the values represented by the on-the-average percentages requested by the agencies and granted by Congress—should change from one period of time to the next. The equations would then be temporally stable for a period, but not forever. The year when the coefficient of an equation changes from one value to another is termed the "shift point." The time series we are using are so short that it is possible to find only one meaningful shift point in each of the two equations that describe the budget request and appropriation best fitting an agency. We, therefore, broke each time series into two parts and used Chow's F-statistic[16] to determine temporal stability by testing the null hypothesis that the underlying coefficients did not shift (against all alternatives) for the individual equations. We used four categories for the coefficients of a decision equation defined as follows:

Temporally very stable: The F-statistic is small and the coefficients estimated from the first and last parts of the series are virtually the same.

Temporally stable: The F-statistic is small, but the coefficients estimated from the first and last parts of the series appear to be different.

Not temporally stable: The F-statistic is large but not significant at the ten per cent level and the coefficients estimated from the first and last parts of series appear to be different.

Temporally unstable: The F-statistic is significant at the ten per cent level.

Of the Congressional decision equations, six were temporally very stable, 12 were temporally stable, 12 were not temporally stable, and 28 were temporally unstable. Of the agency-Bureau of the Budget decision equations, four were temporally very stable, 18 were temporally stable, 18 were not temporally stable, and 18 were temporally unstable.[17] Since a substantial majority of cases fall into the not temporally stable and temporally unstable categories it is evident that while the process is temporally stable for short periods, it may not be stable for the whole period.

Table 3 presents a summary of the combinations of the agency-Bureau of the Budget and Congressional decision equations when each series is broken into two parts. These specifications are referred to as "first period" and "second period" for all agencies even though the years at which the time series were broken vary. While the most frequent combinations of

**Table 3. Congressional Behavior Tends
to Become More Sophisticated**

First Period Decision Equations			
	1	2	3
4	45	0	10
7	1	0	0
8	2	0	0
Second Period Decision Equations			
	1	2	3
4	35	1	9
7	1	0	0
8	12	0	0

behavior are the simple ones represented by equations (4) and (1) respectively, there is a marked tendency for Congressional behavior to become more sophisticated: the incidence of the gaming behavior represented by equation (8) increases over time.[18]

The budgetary process seems to become more linear over time in the sense that the importance of the "special circumstances" appears to diminish. Table 4 presents frequencies of the correlation coefficients for the first and second periods. Although there is a different number of correlation coefficients in each period (111 in the first period and 114 in the second)[19] Table 4 shows clearly that fits are better for the second period, which is sufficient evidence of increasing linear tendencies. To us it seems reasonable to expect an increasing use of simplifying rules of thumb as the budget grows in size and the pressure of time on key decision makers increases. Yet this is only one of a number of possible explanations. For example, the data are not deflated for changes in the price level during the early years. Since there were larger increases in the price level during the early years, this might help explain why the fits are better during the second period.

Table 4. The Budgetary Process Is Becoming More Linear

Frequencies of Correlation Coefficients											
$1 - .995 - .99 - .98 - .97 - .96 - .94 - .92 - .90 - .80 - .60 - 0$											
First Period	9	5	8	5	3	6	8	4	18	24	21
Second Period	27	5	13	8	8	15	7	5	12	8	6

When only one shift point is presumed, most shifts are discovered during the first two budgets of the Eisenhower Administration (1954–1955). Table 5 presents, for both Congressional and Agency-Budget Bureau decision equations, frequencies of the shift points for (a) those equations whose coefficients are in the not temporally stable or temporally un-stable categories and (b) those agencies for which the decision rules of the participants appeared to change. While it is certainly possible that shift points do not occur as dramatically and as sharply as shown here, and that it may take

**Table 5. Likely Shift Points Are Concentrated in the First Years
of the Eisenhower Administration**

Year	*Frequencies of Shift Points*															
	'48	'49	'50	'51	'52	'53	'54	'55	'56	'57	'58	'59	'60	'61	'62	T
Congressional	0	2	3	1	0	1	17	16	1	1	3	0	0	1	0	46 (40)
Agency-Bureau	0	2	4	0	2	3	15	13	3	0	2	1	0	2	1	37 (36)

several years for actual behavior to change noticeably, Table 5 nevertheless makes it clear that likely shifts are concentrated in the first period of the Eisenhower administration.

We said, in Section II, that we expected β_0, β_1 and β_3, to be greater than one, and β_2 to be negative. In 56 instances this expectation is satisfied, but eight exceptions were noted. In the two cases where the estimated $\beta_3 < 1$, explanations are immediately available. First, the fit for the Bureau of Employment Security is not good. Second, the Office of Territories evidences most un-Parkinsonian behavior: its activities decline with a decrease in the number of territories. In the six other exceptions, the estimated coefficient is $\beta_0 < 1$. For three of these, Congress tends to appropriate an amount greater than the request, and two of the three represent an interesting phenomenon. When those parts of requests and appropriations directly related to loans are omitted from the data for both the Rural Electrification Administration and the Federal Housing Administration, the estimated coefficients are of the magnitudes expected with $\beta_0 > 1$ and $a_0 < 1$. However, when the data relating to loans are included, then $\beta_0 < 1$ and $a_0 > 1$. Apparently, Congress favors the loan programs more than do the agencies or the Budget Bureau.

As a rule, the d-statistics resulting from fitting the best specifications were not significant. It would thus appear that all major underlying trended variables (with the possible exception of variables with the same trend) have been accounted for by these specifications. When an exception to this rule did exist, the authors made a careful examination of the residuals in an effort to determine the reason for such a situation. It appeared that in most of these instances the cause was either (a) that the coefficients shifted slowly over several years and not abruptly at one point in time, or (b) that restricting the search to only one shift point left undetected an additional shift either very early or very late in the series.

In an attempt to unmask the trended variable most likely (in our opinion) to have been ignored, and to cast some light upon the notion of "fair share", final appropriations y_t for each agency were regressed on total non-defense appropriations z_t. This time series was taken from the *Statistical Abstract of the United States*. The results were poor. Indeed, the sample correlations between y_t and z_t are usually worse than those between y_t and x_t. Moreover, the d-statistics are usually highly significant and the residual patterns for the regression show the agency's proportion of the non-defense budget to be either increasing or decreasing over time. However, it should be noted that even those exceptional cases where the agency trend is close to that of the total non-defense appropriation do not invalidate the explicit decision structure fitted here. A similar study, with similar results, was conducted at departmental level by regressing y_t for the eight National Institutes of Health on y_t for the Public Health Service, the agency of which they are a part. Finally, the y_t for selected pairs of agencies with "similar" interests were regressed on each other with uniformly poor results.

Although empirical evidence indicates that our models describe the budgetary process of the United States government, we are well aware of certain deficiencies in our work. One deficiency, omission of certain agencies from the study, is not serious because over one-half of all non-defense agencies were investigated. Nevertheless, the omission of certain agencies may have left undiscovered examples of additional decision rules. We will shortly study all agencies whose organizational structure can be traced. We will also include supplemental appropriations.

A more serious deficiency may lie in the fact that the sample sizes, of necessity, are small. The selection criterion of maximum sample correlation, therefore, lacks proper justification, and is only acceptable because of the lack of a better criterion. Further, full-information maximum likelihood estimators, and especially biased ones, even when they are known to be consistent, are not fully satisfactory in such a situation, although they may be the best available. However, the remedy for these deficiencies must await the results of future theoretical research on explosive or evolutionary processes.

IV. THE DEVIANT CASES AND PREDICTION: INTERPRETATION OF THE STOCHASTIC DISTURBANCES

The intent of this section is to clarify further the interpretation of the stochastic disturbances as special or unusual circumstances represented by random variables. While those influences present at a constant level during the period serve only to affect the magnitude of the coefficients, the special circumstances have an important, if subsidiary, place in these models. We have indicated that although outside observers can view the effects of special circumstances as a random variable, anyone familiar with all the facts available to the decision-makers at the time would be able to explain the special circumstances. It seems reasonable therefore to examine instances where, in estimating the coefficients, we find that the estimated values of the stochastic disturbances assume a large positive or negative value. Such instances appear as deviant cases in the sense that Congress or the agency-Budget Bureau actors affected by special circumstances (large positive or negative values of the random variable) do not appear to be closely following their usual decision rule at that time but base their decisions mostly on these circumstances. The use of case studies for the analyses of deviant phenomena, of course, presupposes our ability to explain most budgeting decisions by our original formulations. Deviant cases, then, are those instances in which particular decisions do not follow our equations. It is possible to determine these deviant instances simply by examining the residuals of the fitted equations: one observes a plot of the residuals, selects those which appear as extreme positive or negative values, determines the year to which these extreme residuals refer, and then examines evidence in the form of testimony at the Appropriations Committees, newspaper accounts and other sources. In this way it is possible to determine at least some of the circumstances of a budgetary decision and to investigate whether or not the use of the random variables is appropriate.[20]

Finally, it should be pointed out that in our model the occurrence of extreme disturbances represents deviant cases, or the temporary setting aside of their usual decision rules by the decision-makers in the process, while coefficient shifts represent a change (not necessarily in form) of these rules.

From the residuals of one-half of the estimated Congressional decision equations, a selection of 55 instances (approximately 14 per cent of the 395 Congressional decisions under consideration) were identified as deviant.[21] Table 6 shows the yearly frequency of the occurrence of deviant cases. It is apparent that deviancy grows in years of political change: in 1948 the Republican 80th Congress made a determined effort to reduce appropriations

Table 6. Deviant Cases Cluster in Years of Political Change

Year	'48	'49	'50	'51	'52	'53	'54	'55	'56	'57	'58	'59	'60	'61	'62	'63
Number of Cases	8	2	1	1	1	4	6	4	1	1	2	3	4	2	8	7

submitted by the Democratic President; the years 1953 through 1955 mark the beginning of Eisenhower's Presidency; the large number of deviant cases in 1962 and 1963 are related to the accession to office of Kennedy and Johnson. The latter category of deviant cases, we will explain later, may be mis-classifications in the sense that the passage of time and the corresponding accumulation of additional evidence may reveal shift points, i.e., changes in the "average percentages" of the decision processes, rather than "exceptional circumstances." Nevertheless, this fact causes no particular problem in light of our purposes here, and the cases may be viewed as if they are appropriately classified.

Table 7 categorizes the cases according to estimates of why deviance occurred. It should be noted that the largest category, significant policy change, involves the lack of a budgetary base for the agency in question. In

Table 7. Deviant Cases May Be Viewed As Random Events

Categories of Deviance	Number of Cases
Significant policy change	20
Fiscal policy change	8
Felt need of Congressional supervision	6
Amended estimate due to a time factor	6
Single event	5
Large new legislative program	4
Reorganization of agency	1
Non-identifiable	5
TOTAL N =	55

order to highlight the meaning we give to random phenomena, an illustration of each category follows. This analysis explains why, although the deviant cases are understandable to an experienced observer or participant, an outsider would have to regard them as essentially random disturbances to an otherwise deterministic system. Indeed, no two events in the categories of Table 7 are likely, *a priori*, either to be the same or to occur in any particular year.

Significant Policy Change
The Southwestern Power Administration is typical of agencies whose appropriations fluctuate unduly because basic policy is being negotiated. Deviance was evident in 1948, 1949, 1954 and 1955. The SPA continually requested funds for the building of transmission lines, and Congress repeatedly eliminated the request from their appropriations, insisting that private enterprise would supply the necessary facilities. In 1948 the Bureau of the Budget recommended $7,600,000 of which only $125,000 was appropriated, with stringent and explicit instructions that printing and mailing of materials calculated to increase clientele among rural and municipal electrical cooperatives cease.

The Korean War increased demands for electric Power. Deviance occurred in 1955 not because of appropriations cuts but because of House floor amendments and Senate Appropriations Committee increases. Public policy then became stabilized as Congress established a budgetary base. The following years fit our equations.

Fiscal Policy Changes
The Foreign Agricultural Service's 1963 appropriation is deviant in appropriation figures, but because $3,117,000 was provided by transferring funds from Sec. 32, the total budget for FAS is close to the Budget Bureau's initial request.

Felt Need of Congressional Supervision
The House Committee reports on Office of Territories for 1953 show a lack of confidence in the agency. The tenor can be judged by House Report 1622: "The Department was advised last year that the Committee did not intend to provide appropriations for an endless chain of capital investment in the Alaska Railroads. Army testimony was conflicting as to the need for a road and railways. There is need for a coordinated plan before the Committee can act intelligently with regard to the railroad."

Amended Estimate Due to Time Factor
Typical of this type of deviance is the Commodity Stabilization Service's appropriation for 1958. On the basis of figures from County Agricultural Agents, Secretary Ezra Taft Benson scaled down his request from $465 million to $298 million. A more accurate estimate was made possible because of added time.

Large New Legislative Program
This is especially apt to affect an agency if it is required to implement several new programs simultaneously. The Commissioner of Education said in reference to the student loan program, "We have no way of knowing because we never had such a program, and many of the institutions never had them." The NDEA Act alone had ten new entitlements.

Reorganization of an Agency
The only sample is the Agricultural Marketing Service's appropriation for 1962. Funds were reduced because of a consolidation of diverse activities by the Secretary of Agriculture and not through reorganization as a result of Congressional demands.

Non-identifiable
This applies, for example, to the Public Health Service where a combination of lesser factors converge to make the agency extremely deviant for 1959, 1960, 1961, and 1962. Among the apparent causes of deviance are publicity factors, the roles of committee chairmen in both House and Senate, a high percentage of professionals in the agency, and the excellent press coverage of health research programs. No one factor appears primarily responsible for the deviance.

Our models are not predictive but explanatory. The alternate decision equations can be tried and the most appropriate one used when data on requests and appropriations are available. The appropriate equation explains the data in that, given a good fit, the process behaves "as if" the data were generated according to the equation. Thus, our explanatory models are backward looking: given a history of requests and appropriations the data appears as if they were produced by the proposed and appropriately selected scheme.

The models are not predictive because the budget process is only temporally stable for short periods. We have found cases in which the co-efficients of the equations change, i.e., cases in which there are alterations in the realized behavior of the processes. We have no *a priori* theory to predict the occurrence of these changes, but merely our *ad hoc* observation that most occurred during Eisenhower's first term. Predictions are necess-arily based upon the estimated values of the coefficients and on the statistical properties of the stochastic disturbance (sometimes called the error term). Without a scientific method of predicting the shift points in our model, we cannot scientifically say that a request or an appropriation for some future year will fall within a prescribed range with a given level of confidence. We can predict only when the process remains stable in time. If the decision rules of the participants have changed, our predictions may be worthless: in our models, either the coefficients have shifted or, more seriously, the scheme has changed. Moreover, it is extremely difficult to determine whether or not the observation latest in time represents a shift point. A sudden change may be the result either of a change in the underlying process or a temporary setting aside of the usual decision rules in light of special circumstances. The data for several subsequent years are necessary to determine with any accuracy whether a change in decision rules indeed occurred.

It is possible, of course, to make conditional predictions by taking the estimated coefficients from the last shift point and assuming that no shift will occur. Limited predictions as to the next year's requests and appropri-ations could be made and might turn out to be reasonably accurate. However, scholarly efforts would be better directed toward knowledge of why, where and when changes in the process occur so that accurate pre-dictions might be made.

The usual interpretation of stochastic (in lieu of deterministic) models may, of course, be made for the models of this paper, i.e., not all factors influencing the budgetary process have been included in the equations. Indeed, many factors often deemed most important such as pressure from interest groups, are ignored. Part of the reason for this lies in the nature of the models: they describe the decision process in skeleton form. Further, since the estimations are made, of necessity, on the basis of time series data, it is apparent that any influences that were present at a constant level during the period are not susceptible to discovery by these methods. However, these influences do affect the budgetary process by determining the size of the estimated coefficients. Thus, this paper, in making a comparative study of the estimated coefficients for the various agencies, suggests a new way of approaching constant influences.

No theory can take every possible unexpected circumstance into account, but our theory can be enlarged to include several classes of events. The concentration of shift points in the first years of the Eisenhower administration implies that an empirical theory should take account of changes in the political party controlling the White House and Congress.

We also intend to determine indices of clientele and confidence so that their effects, when stable over time, can be gauged.[22] Presidents sometimes attempt to gear their budgetary request to fit their desired notion of the rate of expenditures appropriate for the economic level they wish the country to achieve. By checking the Budget Message, contemporary accounts, and memoirs, we hope to include a term (as a dummy variable) which would enable us to predict high and low appropriations rates depending on the President's intentions.

V. SIGNIFICANCE OF THE FINDINGS

We wish to consider the significance of (a) the fact that it is possible to find equations which explain major facets of the federal budgetary process and (b) the particular equations fitted to the time series. We will take up each point in order.

A. It is Possible to Find Equations for the Budgetary Process. There has been controversy for some time over whether it is possible to find laws, even of a probabilistic character, which explain important aspects of the political process. The greatest skepticism is reserved for laws which would explain how policy is made or account for the outcomes of the political process. Without engaging in further abstract speculation, it is apparent that the best kind of proof would be a demonstration of the existence of some such laws. This, we believe, we have done.

Everyone agrees that the federal budget is terribly complex. Yet, as we have shown, the budgetary process can be described by very simple decision rules. Work done by Simon, Newell, Reitman, Clarkson, Cyert and March, and others, on simulating the solution of complex problems, has demonstrated that in complicated situations human beings are likely to use heuristic rules or rules of thumb to enable them to find satisfactory solutions.[23] Braybrooke and Lindblom have provided convincing arguments on this score for the political process.[24] Wildavsky's interviews with budget officers indicate that they, too, rely extensively on aids to calculation.[25] It is not surprising, therefore, as our work clearly shows, that a set of simple decision rules can explain or represent the behavior of participants in the federal budgetary process in their efforts to reach decisions in complex situations. The most striking fact about the equations is their simplicity. This is perhaps partly because of the possibility that more complicated decision procedures are reserved for special circumstances represented by extreme values of the random variable. However, the fact that the decision rules generally fit the data very well is an indication that these simple equations have considerable explanatory power. Little of the variance is left unexplained.

What is the significance of the fact that the budgetary process follows rather simple laws for the general study of public policy? Perhaps the significance is limited; perhaps other policy processes are far more complex and cannot be reduced to simple laws. However, there is no reason to believe that this is the case. On the contrary, when one considers the central importance of budgeting in the political process—few activities can be carried on without funds—and the extraordinary problems of calculation which budgeting presents, a case might better be made for its comparative complexity than for its simplicity. At present it is undoubtedly easier to demonstrate that laws, whether simple or complex, do underlie the budgetary process than to account for other classes of policy outcomes, because budgeting provides units of analysis (appropriations requests and grants) that are amenable to formulating and testing propositions statistically. The dollar figures are uniform, precise, numerous, comparable with others, and, most important, represent an important class of policy outcomes. Outside of matters involving voting or attitudes, however, it is difficult to think of general statements about public policy that can be said to have been verified. The problem is not that political science lacks propositions which might be tested. Works of genuine distinction like Herring's *The Politics of Democracy*, Truman's *The Governmental Process*, Hyneman's *Bureaucracy in a Democracy*, Neustadt's *Presidential Power*, Buchanan and Tullock's *The Calculus of Consent*, contain implicit or explicit propositions which appear to be at least as interesting as (and potentially more interesting than) the ones tested in this paper. The real difficulty is that political scientists have been unable to develop a unit of analysis (there is little agreement on what constitutes a decision) that would permit them to test the many propositions they have at their command. By taking one step toward demonstrating what can be done when a useful unit of analysis has been developed, we hope to highlight the tremendous importance that the development of units of analysis would have for the study of public policy.

B. The Significance of the Particular Equations. Let us examine the concepts that have been built into the particular equations. First, the importance of the previous year's appropriation is an indication that the notion of the base is a very significant explanatory concept for the behavior of the agencies and the Budget Bureau. Similarly, the agency-Budget Bureau request are important variables in the decisions of Congress. Second, some of the equations, notably (7) and (8) for Congress, and (2) for the agency-Budget Bureau, incorporate strategic concepts. On some occasions, then, budgeting on the federal level does involve an element of gaming. Neither the Congress nor the agencies can be depended upon to "take it lying down." Both attempt to achieve their own aims and goals. Finally, the budgetary process is only temporally stable. The occurrence of most changes of decision rules at a change in administration indicates that alterations in political party and personnel occupying high offices can exert some (but not total) influence upon the budgetary process.

Our decision rules may serve to cast some light on the problem of "power" in political analysis. The political scientist's dilemma is that it is hardly possible to think about politics without some concept of power, but that it is extremely difficult to create and then to use an operational definition in empirical work. Hence, James March makes the pessimistic conclusion that "The Power of Power" as a political variable may be rather low.[26] The problem is particularly acute when dealing with processes in which there is a high degree of mutual dependence among the participants. In budgeting, for example, the agency-Budget Bureau and Congressional relationships hardly permit a strict differentiation of the relative influence of the participants. Indeed, our equations are built on the observation of mutual dependence; and the empirical results show that how the agency-Budget Bureau participants behave depends on what Congress does (or has done) and that how Congress behaves depends on what the agency-Budget Bureau side is doing (or has done). Yet the concept of power does enter the analysis in calculations of the importance that each participant has for the other; it appears in the relative magnitude of the estimated coefficients. "Power" is saved because it is not required to carry too great a burden. It may be that theories which take power into account as part of the participants' calculations will prove of more use to social science research than attempts to measure the direct exercise of influence. At least we can say that theories of calculation, which animate the analysis of *The Politics of the Budgetary Process* and of this paper, do permit us to state and test propositions about the outcomes of a political process. Theories of power do not yet appear to have gone this far.

In the field of economics, work has long been done on organizational units called industrial firms. In political science, however, despite the flurry of excitement over organization theory, there has been no empirical demonstration of the value of dealing with various public organizations as comparable entities. By viewing governmental bodies not as distinctly different agencies but as having certain common properties (here, in budgetary calculations and strategies), we hope to have shown the utility to empirical theory of treating organizations *qua* organizations. Despite the differences among the organizations studied—some follow different decision rules and are affected by different random disturbances—it is analytically significant to explain their behavior by virtue of features they share as organizations.

It should be clear that we are dealing with general models of organizations and not with individual policies. One cannot say anything directly about water, land, health, or other transportation policies, from inspection of our models of a given agency. But this limit is not inherent in our approach. It is possible, for example, to calculate from our data present and future estimated rates of growth for virtually all domestic agencies since World War II. Agencies with similar growth rates may be segregated and examined for common features. The growth rates of agencies in similar areas of policy such as public health and natural resources, may be compared, and the fortunes of policies in those areas deduced. Individual agencies may be broken down into sub-units or the courses of certain policy programs charted to explain the differential treatment they receive. While pursuing this type of analysis, we hope to have one advantage. We shall be working from a general model of the budgetary process. It will, therefore, be possible for us to locate our efforts within this larger scheme. To know whether one is dealing with a normal or deviant case, to know one's position in this larger universe, is to be able to give more general meaning to the individual and particular circumstances with which one must be involved in handling small parts of the total process.

The general mode of analysis we have developed here may be pursued in many different contexts. Similar studies could be undertaken in state and local governments as well as foreign countries.[27] Private firms and public agencies may be conceptualized in parallel terms through their budgetary mechanisms.[28] By comparing the processes underlying budgeting in a variety of political and economic systems, it may be possible to state more elegantly and precisely the conditions under which different forms of behavior would prevail.

APPENDIX

On the Definition of Terms

Certain of the technical terms required in the paper are here given informal definitions.

Coefficient. A coefficient of an equation is a parameter or number that is said to have some given but usually unknown value. The α's and β's used in the models are the coefficients of the equations in which they appear.

Since the values of the coefficients are usually unknown, they must be estimated statistically from available data. In this paper, the coefficients (α's and β's) are average representations of the real percentages of requests made by agencies and appropriations granted by Congress.

Linear. An equation is linear if it has no square or higher order terms. Thus $y = \alpha x$ is linear whereas $y = \alpha x^2$ is not linear. (Remember that for two variables linear means "in a straight line.")

Stochastic. A variable is stochastic, a term meaning random, if the particular value that it assumes is a matter of chance and the set of values that it can assume is capable of being described by a probability distribution or density. The distribution gives the probability of the random variable assuming the various allowable values.

Variance. The variance is defined as $E(x - \mu)^2$ where x is a random variable, μ is its mean, and E stands for "the expected value of." One can think of variance as a measure of the dispersion or spread of the probability distribution governing the random variable.

Linear Regression Equation. A linear regression equation is a particular model of the relationship between two or more variables. The model has the form

$$y_i = \beta_0 + \beta_1 x_{1i} + \beta_2 x_{2i} + \ldots + \beta_k x_{ki} + \epsilon_i$$

where β_0 is the unknown constant term, the other β's are unknown coefficients, and ϵ_i is a random variable. In this notation, y_i represents the value of the dependent variable on the ith observation and $x_{1i}, x_{2i}, \ldots, x_{ki}$ represents in a similar manner the values of the independent variables for the same observation. From a set of n observations, each of which consists of particular values for the dependent and independent variables, the regression operation estimates values for the unknown coefficients and the constant term; the regression operation also estimates n values of the random variable, which are called residuals. When the sets of observations on the dependent and independent variables refer to successive periods, the observations are called time series and we say that the values of y_i are generated by a stochastic process.

Stochastic Disturbance. This is a name for the random variable in a regression equation. It is also called the error term. Thus, in the equation $y_t = \alpha x_t + \epsilon_i$, the term ϵ_i represents a stochastic disturbance (or random variable), which is usually assumed to be normally distributed with mean zero and finite but unknown variance.

Difference Equation. An equation which describes the value of a variable in one period in terms of the value of either that variable or another variable in some previous period is a difference equation, For example, $x_t = \beta y_{t-1}$ is a difference equation. If a random variable is present, the equation is called a stochastic difference equation. Thus, if ϵ is a random variable, $x_t = \beta y_{t-1} + \epsilon_i$ is a stochastic difference equation and the successive values of x may be thought of as a stochastic process.

Unstable, Evolutionary or Explosive Process. A process is said to be unstable, evolutionary or explosive if the expected values of the successive values taken by the process are increasing. For example, the stochastic difference equation $y_t = \gamma y_{t-1} + \epsilon_i$, where $\gamma > 1$, generates an evolutionary process.

Serially Independent. If successive realizations of a random variable are serially independent, the value it assumes in one period is independent of the value it assumed in a previous period. This can be described mathematically as $E(x_t | x_{t-1}) = E(x_t)$, meaning that the expected value of random variable x at period t does not depend upon the value that the random variable x assumed at period $t - 1$. It follows that the expected simple correlation between x_t and x_{t-1} will be zero, if the random variable x is serially independent. For example, in our models, the assumption of serial independence of the disturbances reflects the belief that special circumstances in one year either do not affect special circumstances in succeeding years or that their influence enters explicitly into our model (as in equation (8) and the equations of footnote 4).

The Meaning of a Markov Process

For our purposes, a Markov process generating some random variable x, is a process for which the value of x at time t depends upon the values assumed by that random variable at one or more earlier periods plus the value assumed by some stochastic disturbance at time t. A Markov process is "first order" if the variable x_t takes on a value that depends only upon the value of the variable x_{t-1} in the previous period plus the value of a stochastic disturbance at time t. Thus

$$x_t = \alpha x_{t-1} + \epsilon_t$$

is a first order Markov process where ϵ_t is a random variable with a given distribution and α is a non-zero constant. A second order Markov process can be described by

$$x_t = \alpha_1 x_{t-1} + \alpha_2 x_{t-2} + \epsilon_t$$

where both α_1 and α_2 are non-zero constants. The value of the variable x_t now depends upon its values in two previous periods.

On the Meaning of Goodness of Fit

An intuitive notion of good fit for a linear regression equation is that in a scatter diagram the observations should cluster about the fitted line.

Probably the most popular measure of good fit is the square of the multiple correlation coefficient (R^2), which may often be interpreted as the percentage of the variance of the dependent variable that is explained by the postulated linear relationship (regression). For our models, however, this interpretation is not valid, although the adjusted R gives a rough measure of the goodness of fit. The closer to 1 that the adjusted R is, the better the fit.

On Standard Deviations of Coefficient Estimates

Speaking roughly, these standard deviations measure the reliability of the estimates of the coefficients. The smaller the estimated standard deviation, the more accurate the estimated coefficient is likely to be. If we had another series of data generated from the same process, the smaller the standard deviation of the coefficient (estimated from the first data) in relation to the size of this coefficient, the more likely it is that a new estimate made on the basis of the hypothetical new series of data would be close to the estimate made from the original data. Generally, one hopes the estimated standard deviation of the coefficient is at least as small as one-half the size of the estimated coefficient.

On Biased and Unbiased Estimators

Think of the problem of trying to determine the average IQ of students at a large university. Suppose the administration would not allow access to records and one did not wish to give IQ tests to all students. One might select a certain number of students at random (a sample) and give them the tests. The test scores of these students are sample observations. One might compute the average of these test scores and claim that he has an estimate of the mean IQ of all students at the University. The estimator is the formula for the average of the sample observations. If he repeated the process, taking a new sample, it is possible that the estimator would produce a slightly different estimate of the mean. However, the estimator would still have a certain expected value. If the expected value of the estimator can be proven to equal the population parameter (the mean IQ of all the students) then the estimator is said to be unbiased. Otherwise, it is said to be biased.

On Consistent Estimators

An estimator is consistent if it approaches nearer and nearer to the true value of a parameter (in our case, a coefficient) as the size of the sample is increased. A consistent estimator may be biased (it may approach closer to but never actually equal the parameter), but if the sample from which it is estimated is large enough this bias will be small.

On Least-Squares Estimators and the Meaning of Temporally Stable Processes

This discussion specifically refers to process (4) although it is equally applicable to all processes. Consider

$$y_t = \alpha_0 x_t + \eta_t$$

where α represents the coefficient of the equation or the "on the average" percentage of the request that is granted by Congress and η_t is a stochastic disturbance (random variable) that represents the variation in the request over time that may be assigned to special circumstances. We assume that η_t is normally distributed with mean zero and finite but unknown variance. The coefficient is unknown and must be estimated on the basis of available data. The data are the requests x_t and the corresponding appropriations y_t. We do not know the values assumed by the stochastic disturbance. Our estimates of the values assumed by the stochastic disturbance are the residuals of the fitted regression equation. If, for a given agency, we observe the requests and appropriations over a specified period of time, we could plot the data in a scatter diagram (Fig.1). The line drawn in Figure 1 would be our estimated line (the line resulting from our estimate of α).

Figure 1.

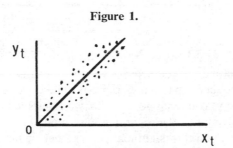

The vertical positive and negative distances of the points from the fitted line are the values of the residuals, our estimates of the values assumed by the stochastic disturbance. The least-squares estimates of the coefficients are those values of the coefficients which make the sum of the squares of these distances a minimum. In Figure 1, there is no discernible pattern of departure of the points from the line.

Thus, we can say that the process is temporally stable (i.e., fixed over time) and presume that the true value of the coefficient (we know only its estimated value) remained constant during the period under consideration. A temporally stable process is one in which the value of the true coefficient does not change during the period under consideration. This should not be confused with a stable or non-evolutionary process, i.e., one whose values do not tend to grow, but fluctuate about some level.

If we again plotted the requests and appropriations data for an agency and found the results to be as in Figure 2, the longest line would represent our first fitted equation (or the equation resulting from our first estimate of the value of the coefficient). The points (alternately the residuals) form a pattern of departure from the fitted line. In the early years (a) they fall mostly above the line and in the later years (b) they fall mostly below the line. The process must have been temporally unstable for the period as a whole, i.e., the coefficient had one true value during the first years of the period and a different true value during the last years.

Figure 2.

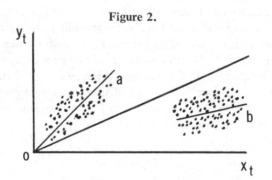

A temporally unstable process is one in which the true coefficient assumes two or more values during the period under consideration. Since we only know the estimated coefficient, we must examine the residuals to determine whether such a pattern is present. Then, we select what appears to be the probable year of change, and fit two lines such as those drawn in above. We then compute the F-Statistic to make our statistical test to determine, at a given level of significance, whether or not the true value of the coefficient shifted. If it was found to shift, the process was temporally stable for some period of time but not necessarily for the entire series of time periods examined.

The Meaning of a Shift Point and a Break Point

The two second lines fitted to Figure 2 represent the true process. The year during which the coefficient changes (the year when the pattern shifts from clustering about line (a) to clustering about line (b) is referred to as a shift point. If what appears at first to be a shift in the true value of the coefficient is actually an alteration in behavior so that one equation fits the first sub-period and another equation must be used for the second sub-period, we still refer to the year of the change in realized behavior as a shift point. Break point is the term used to describe a suspected shift point but for which the F-test indicates that the true coefficient value did not shift.

NOTES

* The research was sponsored by Resources for the Future. We received valuable criticism from Rufus Browning, Sam Cohn, W. W. Cooper, Richard Cyert, Nelson Polsby, Herbert Simon, and Oliver Williamson, research assistance from Rose Kelly, and editorial assistance from Jean Zorn. Mrs E. Belton undertook the laborious task of compiling the raw data. We are grateful to Resources for the Future and to our colleagues, but the sole responsibility for what is said here is our own.

¹ See the Appendix for explanations of terms and concepts.

² The description which follows is taken from Aaron Wildavsky, *The Politics of the Budgetary Process* (Boston, 1954). Portions of the comments on the House Appropriations Committee are from Richard Fenno, "The House Appropriations Committee as a Political System: The Problem of Integration," *American Political Science Review*, 56 (1962), 310–24.

³ See H. Thiel, *Linear Aggregation of Economic Relations* (Amsterdam, 1954).

⁴ Our subsequent discussion of "shift" or "break" points should also make clear that it is not realistic to expect meaningful time series of great length to be accumulated for most agencies in the United States government.

⁵ Since some readers may not be familiar with the notation we are using, a brief explanation may be in order. As a coefficient of the equation, β_2 is an unknown number that must be estimated from the data, and this coefficient multiplies another number $(y_{t-1} - x_{t-1})$ that may be computed by subtracting last year's request from last year's appropriation. We want the equation to say that the agency will try to counteract large changes in their appropriations by changing their normal requests in the next year. If the agency asks for much more than it thinks it will get and its request is cut, for example, the expression $(y_{t-1} - x_{t-1})$ will be a negative number written in symbolic form as $(y_{t-1} - x_{t-1}) < 0$. A rule of multiplication says that a negative number multiplied by another negative number gives a positive number. If an agency pads its request, however, it presumably follows a cut with a new request which incorporates an additional amount to make allowance for future cuts. In order to represent this behavior, that is to come out with a positive result incorporating the concept of padding, the unknown coefficient β_2 must be negative ($\beta_2 < 0$).

⁶ The agency that favors its own programs should increase its requests over time. In the absence of the stochastic disturbance (when the random variable is 0), the request in a given year should be larger than the request in the previous year so that $x_t > x_{t-1}$. Therefore, the unknown coefficient β_3 must be larger than one ($\beta_3 > 1$) since it multiplies last year's request.

⁷ Other gaming strategies are easily proposed. Suppose, for example, that a given agency believes that it knows the decision rule that Congress uses in dealing with it, and that this decision rule can be represented by one of (4), (7), or (8), above. Presume, for reasons analogous to those outlined for (8), that this agency desires to take into account that positive or negative portion of the previous year's appropriation y_{t-1} that was not based on the previous year's request x_{t-1}. This consideration suggests

$$x_t = \beta_4 y_{t-1} + \beta_5 \Delta_{t-1} + \delta_t$$

as an agency decision rule where Δ_{t-1} is a dummy variable representing in year $t-1$ the term not involving x_{t-1} in one of (4), (7) or (8) above. If one believes that agency and Bureau of the Budget personnel are sufficiently well acquainted with the senators and congressmen to be able to predict the value of the current stochastic disturbance, then it becomes reasonable to examine a decision rule of the form

$$x_t = \beta_6 y_{t-1} + \beta_7 \Delta_t + \sigma_t$$

where Δ_t is defined as above. No evidence of either form of behavior was found, however, among the agencies that were investigated. We also estimated the parameters of the third order auto-regressive scheme for the requests of an individual agency

$$x_t = \beta_8 x_{t-1} + \beta_9 x_{t-2} + \beta_{10} x_{t-3} + \tau_t$$

in an attempt to discover if naive models would fit as well as those above. In no case did this occur and generally the fits for this model were very poor. A similar scheme was estimated for the appropriations y_t of an individual agency with similar results with respect to equations (4), (7) and (8) above. Since the "d" statistic suggests that no higher order Markov process would be successful, no other rules for agency behavior were tried.

[8] Agency proposals to the Bureau of the Budget are not reported to the public and could be obtained only for these eight sub-agencies.

[9] Three interrelated difficulties arise in the analysis of the time series data x_t, y_t, for an agency. The first problem is the choice of a technique for estimating the parameters of the alternate schemes in some optimal fashion. Given these estimates and their associated statistics, the second problem is the choice of criteria for selecting the model best specifying the system underlying the data. Finally, one is faced with the problem of examining the variability of the underlying parameters of the best specification. We believe that our solution to these problems, while far from optimal, is satisfactory given the present state of econometric knowledge. See our presentation in "On the Process of Budgeting: An Empirical Study of Congressional Appropriations," by Otto Davis, M. A. H. Dempster, and Aaron Wildavsky, to appear in Gordon Tullock (ed.), *Papers on Non-Market Decision Making*, Thomas Jefferson Center, University of Virginia. See especially section 4 and the appendix by Dempster, which contains discussions and derivations of estimation procedures, selection criteria and test statistics for the processes in Section II of this paper.

[10] We make the assumption that these two disturbances are independent throughout the paper. Notice, however, that dependence between the disturbances explicitly enters decision equation (8) of section II and those of footnote 7. For these equations, the assumption refers to the disturbance of the current year. That is, we allow the possibility that special circumstances may affect a single participant (Bureau of the Budget or Congress) as well as both. When the latter case occurred, our selection criteria resulted in the choice of equation (8) as best specifying Congressional behavior.

[11] We are estimating the unknown values of the coefficients (or parameters) of regression equations for each agency. All of our estimators are biased. We use biased estimators for the simple reason that no unbiased estimators are known. The property of consistency is at least a small comfort. All of our estimators are consistent. It might be noted that all unbiased estimators are consistent, but not all consistent estimators are unbiased.

[12] This statistic is known as the Durbin-Watson ratio. A description of the test may be found in J. Johnston, *Econometric Methods* (New York, 1963), p. 92.

[13] H. Theil and A. L. Nagar, "Testing the Independence of Regressional Disturbances," *Journal of the American Statistical Association*, 56 (1961), 793–806. These significance points were used to construct further significance points when necessary. See Davis, Dempster and Wildavsky, *op. cit.*

[14] The test is described in T. W. Anderson, *An Introduction to Multivariate Analysis* (New York, 1958), pp. 69–71. See Dempster's appendix to Davis, Dempster, and Wildavsky, *op. cit.*, for some justification of the use of the test.

[15] See Davis, Dempster, and Wildavsky, *op. cit.*

[16] G. C. Chow, "Tests of Equality between Sets of Coefficients in Two Linear Regressions," *Econometrica*, 28 (1960), 591–605, and the appendix to Davis, Dempster, and Wildavsky, *op. cit.*

[17] In a few instances an inspection of the residuals indicated that a shift point occurred so early or so late in the series that it was not possible to compute a meaningful stationarily F-Statistic. In these few cases the deviant observations were dropped and the usual analysis performed on the shortened time series. Thus we "forced" a break in every case in order to perform subsequent operations.

[18] The apparent discrepancy between the latter part of Table 3 and Table 1 is caused by the fact that for two agencies, the Bureau of the Census and the Office of Education, although the agency-Bureau of the Budget decision equations are temporally stable and best specified as (1), when a shift point is forced, the criteria indicate (3) for the latter period.

[19] Some of the shift points appeared to occur so early in the series that it was not possible to calculate a correlation coefficient.

[20] The importance of analyzing deviant cases is suggested in: Milton M. Gordon, "Sociological Law and the Deviant Case," *Sociometry*, 10 (1947); Patricia Kendall and Katharine Wolf, "The Two Purposes of Deviant Case Analysis," in Paul F. Lazarsfeld and Morris Rosenberg (eds.), *The Language of Social Research* (Glencoe, 1962), pp. 103–37; Paul Horst, *The Prediction of Personal Adjustment: A Survey of the Logical Problems and Research Techniques* (New York, 1941); and Seymour Lipset, Martin Trow, and James Coleman, *Union Democracy* (New York, 1960).

[21] We are indebted to Rose M. Kelly, a graduate student in the Department of Political Science, University of California, Berkeley, who did the research on the deviant cases and provided the data for Tables 6 and 7.

[22] See Wildavsky, *op. cit.*, pp. 64–68, for a discussion of clientele and confidence. In his forthcoming book, *The Power of the Purse* (Boston, 1966), Richard Fenno provides further evidence of the usefulness of these categories.

[23] Geoffrey P. E. Clarkson, *Portfolio Selection: A Simulation of Trust Investment* (Englewood Cliffs, N.J., 1962); G. P. E. Clarkson and H. A. Simon, "Simulation of Individual and Group Behavior," *American Economic Review*, 50 (1960), 920–32; Richard Cyert and James March (eds.), *A Behavioral Theory of the Firm* (Englewood Cliffs, N.J., 1963); Allen Newell, "The Chess Machine: An Example of Dealing with a Complex Task by Adaptation," *Proceedings of the Western Joint Computer Conference* (1955), pp. 101–8; Allen Newell, J. C. Shaw, and H. A. Simon, "Elements of a Theory of Human Problem Solving," *Psychological Review*, 65 (1958), 151–66; Allen Newell and H. A. Simon, "The Logic Theory Machine: A Complex Information Processing System," *Transactions on Information Theory* (1956), pp. 61–79; W. R. Reitman, "Programming Intelligent Problem Solvers," *Transactions on Human Factors in Electronics*, HFE-2 (1961), pp. 26–33; H. A. Simon, "A Behavioral Model of Rational Choice," *Quarterly Journal of Economics*, 60 (1955), pp. 99–118; and H. A. Simon, "Theories of Decision Making in Economics and Behavioral Science," *American Economic Review*, 49 (1959), 253–83.

[24] David Braybrooke and Charles Lindblom, *A Strategy of Decision* (New York, 1964).

[25] Wildavsky, *op. cit.*, pp. 8–63.

[26] James March, "The Power of Power," in David Easton, editor, *Varieties of Political Theory* (Englewood Cliffs, N.J., 1966), pp. 39–70.

[27] See the forthcoming studies by John P. Crecine on budgeting in Pittsburgh, Detroit and Cleveland, and by Donald Gerwin on the Pittsburgh School District. Aaron Wildavsky will attempt to apply variations of the models in this paper to Oakland, California.

[28] Aaron Wildavsky, "Private Markets and Public Arenas," *The American Behavioral Scientist*, Vol. 9 No. 7 (September 1965), pp. 33–39.

PART SIX

Methodology and Future Research

"Where do we go from here?" In this final group of readings, we attempt to present our answer to such a question. Hopefully, our answers will aid theory-building in this area. Therefore, the final essay of this volume sums up, integrates, and extrapolates some new areas for testing and research. Our answers will take the form of a recommendation of a methodology to be added to our store of theory-building techniques and an integration of some of the existing findings as one jumping-off point for further theoretical developments.

The selection by Charles F. Cnudde and Donald J. McCrone (Chapter 22) is an application of a causal modeling technique to important political data. The technique allows us to make inferences about causal relationships from empirical associations, if we view the associations from the perspective of a set of assumptions. Statements concerning causal relationships are probably the most frequent type of social science findings. Often, however, researchers use cautious synonyms for the word "cause," such as X "leads to" Y, or Y "is dependent upon" X, and so on. Used properly, causal modeling makes explicit the fact that we wish to deal with causal relationships, that to do so we must make assumptions, and that therefore we are dealing in the realm of inference.

Since many of our hypotheses concerning democratic processes are at heart causal, the method seems particularly appropriate to theory-building about democracy. An interesting example is that concerning the linkage between public opinion and behavior of elected representatives. This linkage is an association between what the public wants and what leaders do, which in a democracy often is thought to be overriding. Note that a causal direction is built into this thinking: first the public wants leaders to do something and then the leaders do it.

Cnudde and McCrone attempt to trace out the mechanisms which bring about linkage on civil rights policy, the one area of national policy where linkage seems to take place. (Miller and Stokes in Chapter 17 find associations in social welfare and foreign policies to be so weak that it is difficult to say that much linkage takes place in these areas.) With Congressional roll call votes as the dependent variable and constituency attitudes as the independent variable, Cnudde and McCrone infer that the association which occurs is due more to the ability of Congressmen to perceive public desires than to the ability of the public to choose Congressmen on the basis of policy commitment.

In the final essay (Chapter 23), we attempt to draw together several threads. In doing so we treat propositions from the literature as causal statements, as if the causal modeling technique had been applied. While this allows us to string together numerous causal relationships, the relationships themselves are probabilistic. As a result, the integrative statement we present must be treated as hypotheses.

In general, the integration follows the S-O-R metaphor with which we began. We have divided the discussion into categories emphasizing environmental factors, factors and processes internal to democracies, and policy responses. The same environmental factors in the presence of one type of internal process will provide the stimulus for one type of response and in the presence of another process, a quite different response. Thus, the approach gives us a basis for making statements concerning causal links, and it also provides us with a theoretical expectation of interaction effects between these variables.

CHAPTER 22

The Linkage Between Constituency Attitudes and Congressional Voting Behavior: A Causal Model*

Charles F. Cnudde
Donald J. McCrone

Warren E. Miller and Donald E. Stokes' publication in 1963 of a preliminary report on the Survey Research Center's representation study is an important landmark in the development of empirical political theory.[1] That report addressed itself to the crucial theoretical question of the linkage between mass political opinions and governmental policy-making.[2] More specifically, the report found considerable policy agreement between Congressional roll call votes and the attitudes of the individual Congressman's constituency.[3] This policy agreement was then interpreted through several causal paths and the Congressman's perception of his constituency's attitudes was found to be the main path by which the local district ultimately influenced Congressional outputs.

The main body of the report dealt with the broad civil rights issue dimension, and, by specifying the perceptual path by which constituency influence is brought to bear, documented the effect of political issues despite the generally low level of political information held at the mass level. Thus, the Congressmen, through their broad cognitive evaluations were aware of how far they could proceed in determining their civil rights roll call votes on the basis of their own attitudes before risking the displeasure of their constituents.

Beyond such major substantive contributions the representation study introduced to political science a variance-apportioning technique similar to that developed by Sewall Wright, in 1921.[4] Through this variance-apportioning technique, the importance of the perceptual link was isolated and evaluated. This study, then, symbolizes the growing recognition in political

Reprinted from *American Political Science Review*, Vol. 60, No. 1 (March 1966), pp. 66–72, by permission of the American Political Science Association.

science of the importance of more sophisticated methodological tools in the process of theory building.

I

This essay seeks to continue this trend toward empirical theory building in political science. A technique for making causal inferences is utilized to resolve two theoretically important problems left unresolved in the original constituency influence study.

In the representation study the authors report the following paradigm showing intercorrelations between constituency's attitude, representative's perception of constituency's attitude, representative's attitude, and representative's roll call behavior on the civil rights dimension. Each of these variables, which we shall call D, P, A, and R, respectively, was linked to every other variable through causal arrows. The inclusion of all possible causal arrows follows the authors' statement of the hypothetical conditions of constituency influence.

Broadly speaking, the constituency can control the policy actions of the Representative in two alternative ways. The first of these is for the district to choose a Representative who so shares its views that in following his own convictions he does his constituents' will . . . The second means of constituency control is for the Congressman to follow his (at least tolerably accurate) perceptions of district attitude in order to win re-election. . . . Out of respect for the processes by which the human actor achieves cognitive congruence we have also drawn arrows between the two intervening factors, since the Congressman probably tends to see his district as having the same opinion as his own and also tends, over time, to bring his own opinion into line with the district's.[5]

Figure 1, then, represents the model of constituency influence which the authors derive conceptually. This conceptual causal model is then evaluated empirically to determine how well it interprets constituency influence. Each conceptually possible path from D to R is assumed to be operative and the authors move directly to a test of how effective each is. Thus, each conceptually possible direct path is evaluated as an interpretation of the indirect relationship between constituency attitude and representative's roll call behavior through the computation of influence coefficients. The perceptual path, running from D to P to R, is found to be the major link accounting for the relationship between D and R. Nevertheless, the path from D to A to R is found to be of some consequence in interpreting the relationship, indicating that recruitment as such has a direct effect.[6]

The use of the variance-apportioning technique also means that the authors must leave the question of the direction of causation between the two intervening variables A and P unanswered, i.e., whether the Congress-

Figure 1. Intercorrelations of Variables Pertaining to Civil Rights—Whole District*

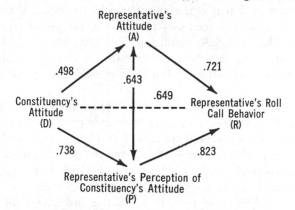

* The correlations used in this essay are not taken from Warren E. Miller and Donald E. Stokes, "Constituency Influence in Congress," *American Political Science Review*, 57 (1963), p. 52. The original coefficients have been corrected to remove the attenuation of correlation due to the sampling of constituents. The basis of this correction is explained in Warren E. Miller and Donald E. Stokes, *Representation in the American Congress* (Englewood Cliffs, N.J.: Prentice-Hall, Inc., in press).

man's attitudes distort his perceptions, or his perception of district attitudes influences his own attitudes. The reported influence coefficients are computed with causation going from *A* to *P*. This is consistent with general psychological theory which holds that attitudes are firmer and longer-lasting than perceptions. This model is also the "least favorable" as far as the total contribution of the Congressman's perceptions to the original relationship is concerned.[7] However, the original study declared that either causal direction is possible.

The present analysis will apply two similar theory building techniques to the civil rights model. First, the Simon-Blalock causal model analysis is used to resolve the two questions: are all the possible causal paths operative? what is the direction of causation between the representative's perception and his attitude? The Simon-Blalock technique enables us

to make causal *inferences* concerning the adequacy of causal models, at least in the sense that we can proceed by eliminating inadequate models that make predictions that are not consistent with the data.[8]

The logic of the Simon-Blalock technique, then, requires the consideration of various alternative causal models. The causal models are tested for adequacy by utilizing the empirically established intercorrelations. If the prediction equations for any given causal model do not conform to the actual relationships among the variables in the model, then it is rejected.[9]

After testing each causal model, if only one fits the data, then we can infer from its adequacy that it is the causal model to adopt. If more than one model fits the data, it is necessary to resort to the use of regression coefficients to infer the most likely candidate.[10] Briefly, Blalock's additions to the Simon technique provide a basis for inferring causal relationships, not only through spurious correlations,[11] but also by establishing indirect and direct effects.

Second, Miller and Stokes' variance-apportioning technique is used to evaluate the effectiveness of various intervening variables in interpreting a relationship between independent and dependent variables.[12] This evaluation will proceed only after we have inferred the correct causal model by use of the Simon-Blalock method. The Simon-Blalock technique can also be used to evaluate intervening variables, but the value of the variance-apportioning technique is that it gives the proportion of the original relationship that the intervening paths explain.[13]

This analysis makes most of the causal assumptions made in the original study. On the theoretical level, the most important of these is that constituency attitude is the independent variable and the representative's roll call behavior is the dependent variable.

This paper also accepts the other assumptions necessary for the use of product-moment correlations in the original study: that departures from multivariate normality and normally distributed errors are not great, that relationships are additive and linear. It also assumes that the other causes of each variable are not correlated with the other variables in the system of relationships and causation is uni-directional.

II

Alternative Causal Models

The first test to be made of the constituency influence model involves whether, in fact, the direct link between A and P exists at all. If A and P are correlated only because they are both related to D, then there would not be a direct relationship between A and P and the question of causal direction would be superfluous. Model I shows graphically this possibility.

Restricting our attention to the first half of the model (the relationship between D, A, and P), we note that Model I predicts that D is an independent variable producing variation directly in the variables A and P. Neither A nor P in that case would be producing variation in each other. If Model I is correct there would be no developmental sequence in either the direction of D to A to P or in the direction of D to P to A. The first equation in Table 1 shows the Simon-Blalock test of this model.

Model I

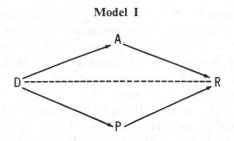

No direct link between P and A.

The very poor degree of fit between the actual correlation between *A* and *P* and the predicted correlation if there were no direct relationship between *A* and *P* indicates that Model I is incorrect empirically. The large difference between .643 and .368 indicates that at least to some degree there is a

Table 1. Prediction Equations and Degrees of Fit for Models of Constituency Influence—First Half

	Predictions		*Degrees of Fit*	
Models	*Predicted*		*Actual*	*Difference*
I. $rDA\ rDP = rAP$	(.498) (.738) = .368		.643	.275
II. $rDA\ rAP = rDP$	(.498) (.643) = .320		.738	.418
III. $rDP\ rPA = rDA$	(.738) (.643) = .475		.498	.023

developmental sequence between *D*, *A*, and *P*. Once a direct relationship between *A* and *P* is found, the next step is to determine whether this relationship is entirely due to a developmental sequence. Model II predicts that the relationship between *A* and *P* is entirely a part of a developmental relationship from *D* to *A* to *P*.

If Model II is correct, then the causal direction of the relationship between *A* and *P* would go from *A* to *P*. This hypothesis is a necessary part of the

Model II

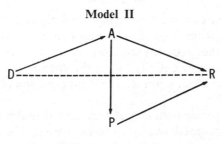

Development Sequence from
D to A to P.

developmental sequence which is predicted. This, incidentally, is also the causal direction included in the "least favorable" model of the Miller and Stokes study. Were this developmental sequence to fit the data, the inference would be that no direct relationship between D and P existed. Instead, the correlation between D and P would be accounted for by the relationship from $D \rightarrow A \rightarrow P$. The second equation of Table 1 shows the test of Model II.

The poor degree of fit between .738 and .320 indicates that P is not without some independent and direct effect from D and that therefore Model II is incorrect. If there is a developmental sequence from D to A to P it does not entirely account for the correlation between D and P. To some degree, then, D also has a direct effect upon P.

Thus far, this analysis indicates two findings:

1. To some extent there is a developmental sequence involving D, A, and P.
2. To some extent D has a direct effect upon P.

The direction of causation between A and P is still unknown, but these two findings lead logically to the next test. Thus, assuming D to be a truly independent variable in this system, the fact that D has a direct effect upon P and that there is some kind of developmental sequence in the system leads to the hypothesis that the sequence goes from D to P to A. Model III shows graphically this prediction.

Model III

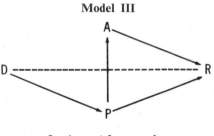

Development Sequence from
D to P to A.

In Model III the causal direction of the relationship between A and P is hypothesized to go from P to A. This sub-hypothesis is necessary to the total hypothesis of the predicted sequence. Also, if the correlation between D and A were found to be entirely due to the D to P to A sequence, then D would have no direct effect upon A. The third equation of Table 1 tests this model.

Unlike the two previous models, this model has an almost perfect fit to the data. The close correspondence between the actual .498 and the predicted .475 correlations provides a basis for inferring that the developmental sequence does indeed go from D to P to A. This test also enables us to infer that the direction of causation which was unresolved in the original study, goes from P to A. Moreover, the accuracy of the fit indicates that the developmental sequence accounts for the entire relationship between D and A. The lack of a direct relationship between D and A is, therefore, a modification of the model presented in the original study. Two points which have implications for empirical political theory can be derived from this new model.

Model III, by showing that constituency attitude and representative's attitude are not directly related on the civil rights dimension, has important consequences for the problem of linkage between mass attitudes and governmental policy-making in democratic societies. This analysis indicates that constituencies do not influence civil rights roll calls in the House of Representatives by selecting Congressmen whose attitudes mirror their own. Instead, Congressmen vote their constituencies' attitudes (as they perceive them) with a mind to the next election. Constituency influence is not provided by candidate recruitment but by elite cognitions.

Such cognitions, in this specialized population of political elites, do not operate as psychological theory would normally indicate. Rather than finding perceptions to be influenced by attitudes, this study shows that the reverse is true. In the area of civil rights especially, Congressmen are in a political situation in which significant rewards accrue to those who perceive their constituency's attitude correctly and vote on that basis. The deprivations are so severe that little room can be allowed for the Congressman's own attitudes to distort this perception. In fact, representatives are motivated to bring their own attitudes (or, at least, their public attitudes) into line with their perceptions of constituency attitude. In the case of Congressmen voting on civil rights the dynamics of the political situation strongly influence psychological processes.

The import of these theoretical statements is dramatized by the fact that both the Congressman's perceptions and his attitudes have direct effects on his roll call votes. Table 2, testing the second half of the constituency influence model (involving the interrelationships between A, P, and R) indicates that the causal arrows between A and R and P and R cannot be

Table 2. Prediction Equations and Degrees of Fit for Constituency Influence Model—Second Half

Models	Predicted	Actual	Difference
	Predictions		*Degrees of Fit*
1. $rPA\ rAR=rPR$	$(.643)(.721)=.464$	.823	.359
2. $rPA\ rPR=rAR$	$(.643)(.823)=.529$	.721	.192

removed. In order for the constituency attitude to be translated into Congressional behavior, the Congressman must perceive his constituency's attitude and vote accordingly, or he must change his attitudes to meet his perception of his constituency's attitude and then vote according to his new attitude. Model III, then, is the new constituency influence model developed through an empirical test of the conceptually possible models presented in the Miller and Stokes study.

In the original analysis, the authors of the representation study concentrated upon both the Congressman's attitude and his perception of his constituency's attitude as interpretations of the link between his constituency's attitude and his roll call votes. The new paradigm presented in this analysis points out that only his perceptions can be thought of as providing this link, while his own attitudes are related to his constituency's attitudes through his perceptions. One question remains to be dealt with by this analysis: how well do the Congressman's perceptions interpret the link between constituency attitude and roll calls on civil rights?

The Congressman's perceptions were found to provide the major link between constituency and roll call in the original analysis. The present analysis clearly confirms this point. Miller and Stokes found that the three possible paths interpreting the root relationship explained nearly all of that relationship. Of these paths, that going from constituency attitude to perception to roll call by itself explained about two thirds of the relationship between constituency attitude and roll call.[14] Since the present analysis removes the weakest path, the two perceptual paths have to be reexamined as the sole possible interpreters of the constituency's influence on Congressional behavior. Table 3 shows the influence coefficients for these paths.

Table 3. Equations for Influence Coefficients for Two Perceptual Paths as Interpreters of the Linkage Between Mass Attitudes and Policy

1. $b = r^2 DP = .5446$	
2. $c = r^2 PA = .4134$	$be/r^2 DR = .5978$
3. $d = r^2 AR = .5198$	$bcd/r^2 DR = .2778$
4. $e = r^2 PR - cd = .4624$	
5. $r^2 DR = .4212$	Total $= .8756$

The influence coefficients for b, c, and d can be derived directly from the correlation coefficients involved, as illustrated in equations 1, 2, and 3. The influence coefficient for e can be derived from its correlation and from equations 2 and 3. Finally, the proportion of the root path ($r^2 DR$) that each path explains can be calculated and added to give the proportion that they explain together.

Table 3 indicates that the paths from constituency attitude to representative's perception to roll call and from constituency to perception to representative's attitude to roll call account for an impressive 88 per cent of the link between constituency attitude and roll call. The two paths go to this extent in solving the problem of linkage between mass attitudes and civil rights roll calls in Congress. The largest proportion of this linkage is provided by the path from constituency to perceptions to roll call. Nearly 60 per cent of the relationship between constituency and roll call is explained

Figure 2. Intercorrelations of Variables Pertaining to Civil Rights—District Majority*

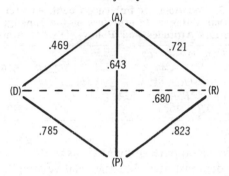

* Data provided by Warren E. Miller and Donald E. Stokes to the authors.

by this path alone, while about 28 per cent is explained by the path which contains the representative's attitudes. These proportions differ from the Miller-Stokes model because the direct link between constituency attitude and representative's attitude has been eliminated. Thus, these are the new weights assigned to the paths linking constituency and roll call after the model of constituency influence has been inferred by utilizing the Simon-Blalock technique.

III

Thus far, we have evaluated the alternative causal models derived from the constituency influence paradigm based on the attitudes of the whole district. In order to strengthen our confidence in the selected causal model, let us briefly evaluate the alternative causal models based on the attitudes, not of the whole district, but only of the majority within the district.

The three alternative causal models for the direction of causation between D, P, and A are evaluated in Table 4 in the same manner as before.[15] The very poor fit between the actual and predicted correlations for Models I and II indicate that they can still be rejected as the correct causal models. Once again, the fit between the data and the predictions from Model III provides a basis for inferring that this is indeed the correct causal model.

Table 4. Prediction Equations and Degrees of Fit for Models of Constituency Influence—District Majority

Models	Predicted	Actual	Difference
	Predictions	Degrees of Fit	
I. $rDA\ rDP = rAP$	$(.469)\ (.785) = .368$	.643	.275
II. $rDA\ rAP = rDP$	$(.469)\ (.643) = .301$	.785	.484
III. $rDP\ rPA = rDA$	$(.785)\ (.642) = .505$	.469	.036

Table 5. Equations for Influence Coefficients for Two Perceptual Paths as Interpreters of the Linkage Between Mass Attitudes and Policy—District Majority

1. $b = r^2 DP = .6162$
2. $c = r^2 PA = .4134$ $be/r^2 DR = .6161$
3. $d = r^2 AR = .5198$ $bcd/r^2 DR = .2863$
4. $e = r^2 PR - cd = .4624$ ———
5. $r^2 DR = .4624$ Total $= .9024$

In Table 5 variance-apportioning analysis of the two intervening paths from D to R also demonstrates that the relative weight between the two paths remains the same. The path from D to P to R still accounts for about twice as much of the variation as does D to P to A to R. One other encouraging aspect of the influence coefficients is the slight rise in the explanatory power of the two intervening paths.

IV

Substantively, on the civil rights dimension, several important findings emerge:

1. The lack of a direct link between Congressmen's attitudes and district attitudes indicates that elite recruitment is not the basis for constituency control.

2. Unlike the private citizen, the Congressman does not distort his perceptions to coincide with his own attitudes. Because the costs of misperceiving are so high for an elected official, his perceptions are likely to cause him to modify his attitudes to fit his reasonably accurate perceptions.

3. The overwhelmingly important impact of Congressmen's perceptions in linking mass attitudes to policy-making, as indicated by Miller and Stokes, is reconfirmed.

4. The relative importance of the indirect impact of perception through congressional attitudes was underestimated in the original study.

5. Finally, the change in the independent variable from whole district

to district majority attitudes reconfirms the inferred causal model and results in only a very slight increment in the explanatory power of the model.[16]

Methodologically, this study reconfirms the implications of the Miller and Stokes article that the use of sophisticated methodological tools is essential in the process of empirical theory building. In particular, it demonstrates the utility of the Simon-Blalock method of causal inference with nonexperimental data. It also highlights the rewards to be attained by the combination of techniques for causal inference and variance-apportioning in one study.

Finally, in regard to the subject of theory building in political science, the cumulative nature of empirical model building needs to be stressed. By explicit articulation of the model of constituency influence and emphasis on establishing empirical relationships, the Miller-Stokes study provides a basis for further development. The application of new techniques and the possible inclusion of new variables is thereby facilitated. This study has focused on the cumulative nature of this model by the adoption of the Simon-Blalock method to provide answers to undeveloped or unresolved questions stemming from the original model. The resolution of these questions also results in a more parsimonious causal model of constituency influence in Congress.

NOTES

* The authors wish to express their gratitude to Warren E. Miller and Donald E. Stokes for providing the data upon which this analysis is based. We gratefully acknowledge the invaluable assistance of Hubert M. Blalock, Jr. and James W. Prothro. The authors, of course, are solely responsible for the analysis.

[1] Warren E. Miller and Donald E. Stokes, "Constituency Influence in Congress," (*American Political Science Review*, 57 (1963), pp. 45–56.

[2] For other material on the linkage problem, see especially V. O. Key, Jr., *Public Opinion and American Democracy* (New York: Alfred A. Knopf, 1961), pp. 441–531.

[3] Briefly, the representation study interrelates three types of data collected in 1958. First, a mass survey was conducted according to probability sampling methods. From this survey central tendencies on attitudinal dimensions were computed for 116 congressional districts. Second, interviews were conducted with incumbent and nonincumbent candidates running for the House of Representatives from these constituencies. The third set of data consisted of Guttman scales of roll call votes taken in Congress on civil rights, social welfare and foreign policy. For a fuller description of the study, see Warren E. Miller and Donald E. Stokes, *Representation in the American Congress* (Englewood Cliffs, N.J.: Prentice-Hall, in press).

[4] Sewall Wright, "Correlation and Causation," *Journal of Agricultural Research*, 20 (1921), pp. 557–85.

[5] Miller and Stokes, "Constituency Influence in Congress," *op. cit.*, pp. 50–51.

[6] *Ibid.*, p. 53.

[7] *Loc. cit.*

[8] Hubert M. Blalock, Jr., *Causal Inferences in Nonexperimental Research* (Chapel Hill: The University of North Carolina Press, 1964), p. 62. Also see Herbert A. Simon, "Spurious Correlations: A Causal Interpretation," *Journal of the American Statistical Association*, 49 (1954), pp. 467–79.

[9] In the three-variable model, for example, if we predict that the relationship between B and C is spurious because they are both dependent variables of A, the Simon-Blalock method predicts that the product of the correlations between A and C, and A and B will equal the correlation between C and B. Thus: $rCB = rACrAB$.

[10] At the very least, then, this method allows us to eliminate logically possible alternative models from our store of explanations. For the utility of regression coefficients, see Blalock, *op. cit.*, pp. 85–87.

[11] For a recent application of the Simon technique, see Thad L. Beyle, "Contested Elections and Voter Turnout in A Local Community: A Problem in Spurious Correlation," *American Political Science Review*, 59 (March, 1965), pp. 111–17.

[12] Miller and Stokes, "Constituency Influence in Congress," *op. cit.*, pp. 52–53.

[13] If B is an intervening variable between A and C, then the product of the amount of variation A explains in B, and B explains in C, gives the proportion of the relationship between A and C that is accounted for by the path from A to B to C. Thus: the proportion of A to C explained by A to B to $C = (r^2AB \times r^2BC)/r^2AC$.

[14] Miller and Stokes, "Constituency Influence in Congress," *op. cit*, p. 53.

[15] It is not necessary to make prediction equations for the relationships between A, P, and R in the latter half of the model for their intercorrelations remain the same. Only the correlations between D and other variables are affected.

[16] The degree to which these substantive findings (and many others) apply to other issue dimensions is the subject of Miller and Stokes' forthcoming book on representation, *Representation in the American Congress, op. cit.*

CHAPTER 23

New Trends in Democratic Theory

Charles F. Cnudde
Deane E. Neubauer

At the present time, the research on democracy is beset with a circular problem. Without a theory of democracy, the research is difficult to integrate. However, without some degree of integration, it is difficult to imagine how a theory will be achieved. As a result, the studies in the area are examinations of specific problems which only now and then show cumulative characteristics. Of the possible strategies for breaking into this set of circular difficulties, two present themselves as having the most potential. The first is greater effort at definitional clarity; and the second is to by-pass the definitional problem and attempt to integrate this material as it stands.

This chapter will attempt to cover the highlights of this material and to bring about a partial integration of it. In doing so, we will also relate to problems for future research by examining these two integration strategies in detail. Since most of this volume and the main body of this paper concern the second of these strategies, some introductory remarks dealing with it are needed. We will postpone until later a discussion of *why* we chose this strategy and *how* we go about it. However, in the integration of the material as it stands, we came upon a theory or a partial theory which explains or subsumes many of the findings.

In short, this theory says that mildly autocratic-democratic patterns are inherently unstable. Such systems would move closer to either the democratic or autocratic position. It seems difficult to suppress the political liberties of one or a few sectors of society for long periods and still maintain liberty for the rest. It is likely that, over time, cleavage over some issue will divide the dominant sectors. Then the incentives of appealing to the oppressed for support become very strong for one or both parties to the cleavage. Under these conditions suppression will be relaxed—the previously suppressed will become the balance of power; or alternatively suppression will increase—those who appeal to the suppressed must also be suppressed. In some cases, then, a decision on a new issue increases the level of democracy as new participants are brought into the system in order to reach the decision.

In other cases, such decisions decrease the level of democracy as new elements are suppressed in order to maintain the suppression of the old. Eventually, events would increasingly move a political system occupying a middle position more and more in one direction or the other. Which direction the movement takes may depend upon the immediate issue, the nature of the cleavages in the society, the history of the system, or other such factors to be isolated in further research.

In any event, we are hypothesizing a theory of a kind of "reverse regression" toward the extremes in which freedom or suppression are achieved. We must also recognize that perfect democracy and perfect non-democracy are ideal states; thus, the regression is simply toward, but never reaching, the extremes.

Thus, the integration of the findings in the area led to a new formulation at a somewhat more abstract level. The rest of this chapter concerns this process. Most of what follows is our attempt at an integration. The conclusions of the chapter draw the integrated material out and reformulate much of it as the regression hypothesis. But before we get to such topics, we must address ourselves to problems in the most difficult strategy of all —that of working at definitional clarity.

DEFINITIONS OF DEMOCRACY

One of the first problems that must be tackled by future efforts in the area of empirical democratic theory is the definitional one. As the readings in this volume indicate, an entire discipline whose only concern is the study of politics has not been able to come up with an agreed upon, yet rigorous, conception of what democracy means. In these selections, this concept has been defined as: the existence of popular sovereignty, political equality, popular consultation, and majority rule (Ranney and Kendall—Chapter 2); and as the opposite of autocracy, a system of personal power irrevocably held (Sartori—Chapter 1). It has been defined as polyarchy or minorities rule by Dahl. In addition, operational definitions have been presented for the resolution of social conflict by: letting the largest possible part of society influence decisions by choosing from alternative candidates for leadership (Lipset—Chapter 7); and preserving the existence of majority rule and minority rights (Prothro and Grigg—Chapter 11).

Perhaps the reason for the lack of precision in our conceptualizations of democracy is that we are looking at the term through the eyes of contemporary behavioral scientists, while historically its usage has been explicitly normative. Because democracy was coined to serve normative functions, it was given different meanings depending upon the normative interests at hand. Under such conditions, consistency in usage is less valuable than flexibility and adaptability. Yet when we attempt to build an empirical theory using a term derived from that tradition, flexibility and adaptability come with the term. The result is the several meanings listed above. This state of affairs may seem tolerable to many students, but it should cause some degree of anguish among those who are aware of the nature of scientific discourse.

Kuehn points out that research is a social enterprise.[1] Disciplines are communities of scholars working out problems together in particular subject-matter fields. Basic to the idea of community are two factors: the communication of research results among the participants and a consensus on the meaning of that research. Consensus may be achieved if scholars agree upon standards of validity and upon ways of interpreting the portions of reality they choose as the field of study. The former area of agreement is an important criterion in testing relationships among operational definitions, while the latter is more directly concerned with purely conceptual definitions. If we assume that the most reasonable state of affairs is one in which conceptual activity precedes operational activity, then scientific disciplines may have grave difficulties if they cannot agree upon *operational* definitions; but without *conceptual* agreement, they are hardly communities at all. In Kuehn's terms, we then have pre- and post-paradigmatic revolutions in which the discipline is grouping for its identity. Only when agreement is reached can research activity settle down into the more normal enterprises of testing hypotheses which have been derived from theories.

Since democracy is one of the most important concepts in political science, the lack of agreement upon its meaning is an indication of how far removed from a paradigmatic stage political science is. Moreover, the lack of agreement upon such a basic term hampers efforts at constructing more general agreement. Aside from these discipline-wide problems, the many uses of the term democracy makes it extremely difficult for scholars to communicate with each other. Due to this communication problem, we have an absence of efforts to integrate the thinking and research on the subject. Yet theory-building presupposes such integration at some stage.

A rigorous definition of democracy upon which the discipline can agree would allow us to integrate much of our research and perhaps to suggest theoretical schemes which are presently only inplicit in our thinking. However, we are asking for a conceptualization of democracy which serves functions for empirical work and yet upon which scholars can agree. This is a tall order, for there appears to be a conflict between the form and content of such a definition.

The form most efficient for empirical purposes is that of a *continuous variable*. Although we rarely find operational measures which have this form in the social sciences, our best work proceeds with concepts which at least theoretically can be viewed as varying by degrees. We then have very explicit notions of relativity, and we can most efficiently construct hypotheses of causes and effects.[2] However, in order to achieve consensus on the definition, the concept would have to at least be consistent with earlier uses of the term, and at best subsume those usages. This means that the new concept must include the content of previous definitions. That content often requires several conditions to be fulfilled before democracy can be said to exist. For example, Prothro and Grigg's definition says that democracy exists when both majority rule and minority rights exist. Even if we view these latter terms as continuous variables, democracy is defined as their intersection. All systems at the intersection and above are democratic; all below the intersection are undemocratic. Thus, the contents of many previous definitions specify a particular form for the concept—a categorical either/or nominal scale. Ranney and Kendall's definition, which increases the necessary conditions to four, compounds the difficulty.

If Ranney and Kendall and Prothro and Grigg represent one common school of research, Sartori represents another. He denies the usefulness of continuous variables in defining democracy. The grounds for this position are that we may have overlapping and somewhat ambiguous assignment of systems to levels of democracy around the midpoint of the continuum. Sartori argues, instead, for an explicit categorical approach in which we place systems in either democratic or autocratic boxes.

Sartori's concern with measurement error may be premature. It is true that at the operational level the unique placement of political systems on a continuum of democracy would become more difficult as we move away from either extreme. However, the regression theory hypothesizes that a distribution of systems on a continuous measure of democracy would be bi-modal. At least there would be few systems at or near the midpoint. This would mean that Sartori's assignment errors would be minimal because few systems would occupy the middle ranges for very long periods of time. His reasons for objecting to a continuous variable may vanish when empirical systems are measured.

Nevertheless, although Ranney and Kendall and Sartori begin with quite different intentions, they arrive at variables having the same form. The former authors wish to speak of a continuous variable, but the content of their definition means that at best they would achieve a partially ordered scale, and at worst, categories. Sartori, by defining autocracy and then defining democracy as its opposite, also achieves a categorical level of measurement. In both cases, the content of these conceptualizations forces upon us a lower level of measurement than we would desire for efficient theory construction.

This fact is not sufficient ground for rejecting the content of the definitions. Indeed, the examples under discussion are perhaps our best statements of what we have meant by democracy. However, the conflict over form and substance underlies the difficulty in achieving consensus on the term. This difficulty may prove to be so great that scholars may eventually take the nominalist way out. They may refuse to deal with the concept at all, but rather they may create new concepts which are more suited to empirical research and which relate only to differing aspects of what previous generations have meant by democracy. Hopefully, such decisions will not be made lightly, and more effort will be expended in conceptualizing democracy before the term is scrapped.

Although the task seems great, the importance of conceptual clarification in future work in the area cannot be clearer. The burden of the present discussion has been to aid future research by demonstrating this importance and outlining the difficulties that must be surmounted. In the absence of conceptual agreement, the present volume tries to integrate the research in this area as it stands. If this integration can successfully break into the circular difficulty in the field, then a summarization and drawing together of the threads of the major research findings should provide theoretical directions for future research. Before turning our efforts in that direction, some comments on the rationale for the attempt are in order.

Even though there is a lack of consistency in the meaning of democracy in the selections we have offered, we will nevertheless attempt to integrate them. That is, the selections will be treated as if they were consistent in their usage. Courage for this procedure is derived from the expectation that when an agreed upon conception of democracy is found, that conception will be consistent with most of the existing usages. As a result, few of the thoughts or findings in these selections would be upset. At the present time, then, the rewards of integration seem to outweigh the slight risk due to these inconsistencies.

On the other hand, the risk due to the quality of the data may be greater. For the most part, the authors of these essays recognize that future research may upset their findings when more precise operational indicators are developed. However, we are placing additional burdens upon these data in that we are trying to interrelate the findings. Although some of the data may not support these burdens (the cross-national data seem especially weak), we have decided to get on with the theory-building job.

The procedure employed in integrating the research will be to trace out what research has found to be the pattern of effects of one variable upon another. If a selection indicates that X has an impact on Z, and another essay infers that Z has an impact on Y, we will integrate this material by stating simply that X affects Z affects Y: by illustration, $X \rightarrow Z \rightarrow Y$. Unless findings or compelling arguments indicate that X has an additional direct effect on Y, we will, for the sake of simplicity, discuss only the sequences as illustrated, while recognizing that such developmental sequences are only hypothetical until tested. In other words, we will draw together the highlights of much of this research in order to construct new and more extensive systems of variables as higher-order hypotheses for further research.

THE SOCIAL AND HISTORICAL ENVIRONMENT

A well-developed system of mass communications which permeates large portions of the society seems to be an important immediate factor bringing about democratic practices. The reasons for this seem to be the necessity of the spread of information for the maintenance of democracy. Although nothing like equality of information exists in even the most democratic systems, democracies require a greater information base at the citizen level than most other types of systems. At a minimum, a functioning democracy requires that most citizens know when elections are to take place, while in non-democratic systems leadership changes are probably most successful in the face of citizen ignorance. Mass communication systems also serve socialization functions, stimulating and increasing political-system effect, thereby maintaining democracy. Finally, mass communications may be only very efficient measures of other environmental factors which affect the nature of political regimes.

Some of these other factors are education and literacy, urbanization, and industrialization. Education and literacy affect the spread of mass communications because these factors provide the audience and in part the producers of the media. Urbanization affects the levels of education and literacy because urbanization is one of the first requirements of modernization, a process which stimulates interest in, and desire for, mass education. Industrialization and urbanization may affect each other: the growth of cities provides the labor force and market society necessary for industrial production; on the other hand, the existence of industrial jobs may draw individuals out of their rural environments to new lives in cities.

In general, democracy is most successful in what we have come to call modernized societies. In these societies, the major social and economic conflicts have been solved or papered-over by the ameliorative effects of economic growth. Democracy seems to be too fragile to survive the conflicts of poorer, less developed social environments.

Historical events also impinge on democratic practices. Lipset notes that societies may go through crises of legitimacy in which pressures well up for change in the nature of the political system. This pattern is related to the factors in the social environment in that a transition to new social structure brings about this crisis if the transition occurs within a historical context in which all major groups have not had access to the political system. It appears, then, that past patterns of events can be specifying conditions for the effects of social and economic factors. The same social factors may have one impact within the context of a set of historical circumstances and a completely different impact within the context of another.

In addition, we may hypothesize that historical factors may have an even more direct effect on economic development. Certain cultural norms are more conducive to industrialization than are others. For example, patterns of value for hard work and deferred gratifications support economic development while the values of the fiesta-siesta syndrome do not. Likewise the market economies of the developed societies are dependent upon feelings of trust and the sense of community in those societies. The development of these cultural values over long periods of time in some societies allowed then to achieve what has been termed modern social and economic organization. At least this has been the common pattern in the West.

We may summarize the processes by which environmental factors affect the development and maintenance of democratic processes by linking each of these variables. Figure 1 presents this summary graphically. The integration of the effects of environmental factors as we see it allows for the possibility of reciprocal relationships between historic events and industrialization and between industrialization and urbanization. Theories exist specifying feedback relationships between several of the other variables

Figure 1. The Impact of Environmental Factors on Democracy

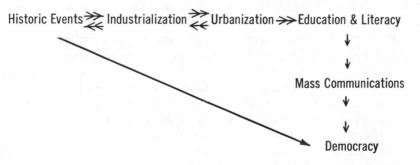

as well. However, the impact of mass communications on education and education on urbanization seem relatively minor compared to opposite effects. Therefore, we are sacrificing relatively little rigor for the sake of greater parsimony in theory construction by treating these relationships as one-way effects.

However, once industrialization has begun, it would seem to have important consequences for later historic events. Social scientists generally hold that the change from rural or craft-based economies to industrialization is such a dramatic shift that changes or modifications in existing social organization follows. For example, changes in the division of labor brought about by industrialization tend to create new systems of social stratification in which achievement rather than ascription provides status criterion. As a result, the growth of industry provides new roles and status criteria which in turn provide opportunities for upward mobility for large proportions of the society. While new economic status dimensions develop, older political and social status dimensions may exist concurrently. Because of a temporary imbalance in status dimensions, short-run dislocations often lead to historic events such as the rise of radical political movements and industrial and political violence. These events are primarily conflicts between representatives of the traditional and modern orders.

With changes in status and roles, new patterns of value also tend to develop. These values support and rationalize the change in the ways of doing things. Just as the new ideology tends to seize upon historic events which arise out of temporary dislocations, dramatizing the events and raising then to the level of myths, it will also reinterpret older historic events, emphasizing aspects of those events which are in harmony with the new order.

These arguments lead us to expect that history not only shapes the rate of industrialization in societies, but that industrialization also shapes the nature or at least our view of the nature of historic events. Therefore, we hypothesize a reciprocal relationship between these environmental factors over time.

In general, this set of hypotheses concerning the impact of environmental factors states that political practices cannot be completely separated from historical circumstances, from the level of economic development, and from the nature of social organization. Instead, these latter terms are important categories of independent variables which affect each other and the development of regime types. Therefore, we have begun our explanation of democracy by sorting out the findings on the sequences of the links between these variables and democracy. The generalization implicit and explicit in the analysis is that democracy is the result of a developmental sequence from historic events to industrialization to urbanization to education and literacy to mass communications to democracy. In addition, there are possibilities of a direct effect from historic events to democracy and effects from industrialization to historic events and from urbanization to industrialization.

However, Neubauer's analysis indicates than many of these independent variables do not have the same effect when undemocratic countries are excluded. This suggests that environmental factors may result in a certain minimum level of democracy, but that variation in the degree of democracy among systems that meet the minimum level is due to additional variables. Thus, when only democratic systems are analyzed, we are dealing primarily with the highly industrialized and modernized systems. Since, in general, these environmental factors produce democracy, we have, in effect, controlled for those factors by removing the undemocratic systems from the analysis. Yet by reducing environmental factors to essentially constants, we can observe the impact of additional variables on the still theoretically meaningful variation among the democracies.

In a very real sense, we are now no longer dealing with a range of variation in regimes which runs from the very undemocratic to the very democratic, but instead with one which runs from the somewhat democratic to the very democratic. Therefore, the two pieces of evidence do not conflict so much as they deal with different degrees of variation in operational definitions. The importance of Neubauer's findings is that of setting the stage for a proper interpretation of the effect of environmental factors. These factors seem to bring about the conditions necessary for the operation of political variables, which in a somewhat democratic context tend to produce even greater degrees of democracy. What some of those political variables are which operate once the democratic threshold has been reached is the topic of the next section of this chapter.

POLITICAL VARIABLES AND DEMOCRATIC STABILITY

By viewing these research reports from the perspective of the amount of variation on democracy measured, we are able to integrate the findings from large-scale cross-national studies such as Cutright's with those from observations of patterns within one or a few democratic systems. That is, the findings from one political system do not need to stand alone as descriptive of that system. Instead, knowledge of its levels of economic development and democracy allow us to place the patterns extant within a comparative context. In this way, we may estimate what other types of variables are important once environmental factors have had their effect.

In the literature, political systems at the highly democratic end of the empirical range of variation of democracy are usually termed as having a high level of *democratic stability*. That is, such systems are not only highly democratic; it also seems to work out empirically that those systems are very likely to have been democratic for long periods of time. We can imagine a four-celled typology constructed of these categories: very democratic, somewhat democratic, democratic for a long time, and democratic for a short time; however, the cells opposite the main diagonal are hardly populated at all. It may be theoretically rewarding to analyze the deviant cases that fall in these cells. However, research on empirical democratic theory is just beginning to track down the general cases. For the time being, then, researchers seem to do little violence to the over-all pattern when they use the phrases "high degree of democratic stability" and "high degree of democracy" interchangeably.

One of the political factors that relates to the system stability, in addition to environmental factors, is the intensity of policy preferences in the society. Few would argue that extremist views exist at the margins of most, even very democratic, societies. However, when intense preferences become the norm, democracies become unstable; that is, the system under such conditions tends to become less democratic.

The reason for this relationship is that intense preferences are difficult to satisfy. According to the essay by Edelman (Chaper 4), rather moderate preferences may be easily satisfied with symbolic rewards. It is also likely that demands made by groups with extreme preferences will tend to be primarily at the symbolic level. Since symbolic demands may be increased indefinitely, little in the way of policy outcome at either symbolic or substantive levels would satisfy these preferences. Political leaders in the face of citizen demands that are difficult to satisfy, either because these demands are substantive ones opposed by the rest or society or because they are symbolic, have only a few alternatives. They may attempt to minimize these demands by changing the rules of the game, thus creating limitations on citizen influence on policy making. On the other hand, political leaders may become immobilized or even actively attempt to maintain the status quo. As a result of this, unsatisfied demands lead large numbers of the population to become politically frustrated or alienated. If such a situation continues, new demands to change the rules of the game will find support among these citizens. Changes then are likely to move the system in undemocratic directions, especially if the primary motivation for change is frustration.

Perhaps there are additional alternatives available to innovative elites. However, the route most emphasized in the literature on democracy is the second—maintaining the status quo. The first—changing the rules—is found most frequently in the literature on the developing and post-colonial nations. The main point, however, is that with either alternative the most frequent outcome is a threat to democratic procedures in the systems involved.

An intervening variable in this relationship is the level of political participation by the citizens. Generally speaking, the literature holds that intensity of policy preferences is related to level of participation. Although many factors affect participation, most of which may be subsumed under what we have called environmental influences, individuals with the most intense preferences are said to participate at higher rates than others. It is this high rate of participation by large numbers of citizens with intense preferences that threatens democratic stability. These relationships often, at least implicitly, underlie the thinking of political scientists when they conclude that low levels of participation can be functional.

However, it is interesting to note that another factor which *increases* democratic stability—citizen allegiance to democratic rules of the game—is also positively related to political participation. Although the allegiant are motivated by sense of citizen duty to participate, there is evidence that the relationship also works in the other direction. That is, merely becoming involved in the workings of a political system tends to increase one's commitment to the nature of those workings. Additional research is needed into the processes involved here. The preliminary conclusions available tend to confirm in the area of politics what organizational theorists find to be the effect of participation in decision-making generally: participation leads to allegiance.

Since citizen allegiance tends to increase system stability, we would expect that increases in participation would eventually increase stability by increasing allegiance. Likewise, increases in the intensity of policy preferences would increase stability by increasing levels of participation and therefore allegiance. Yet we stated earlier that one conclusion of research in this area was that intensity of policy preferences tended to decrease stability. It would appear that the findings are in conflict. Perhaps we can sort out our thinking here by simplifying the relationships with an illustration of the direct effects which are in conflict.

In Figure 2 plus and minus signs are utilized to indicate whether the relationships are positive or negative. If a chain of activity begins at the

Figure 2. Interrelationships Between Political Variables

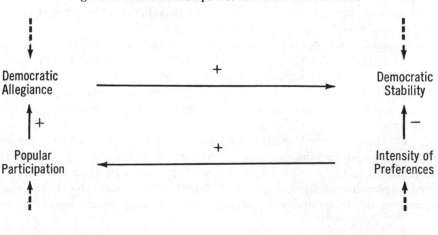

variable of preference intensity, some increase in the level of that characteristic among large sections of a society will probably lead to some degree
of instability rather quickly. However, in general we would then expect
greater participation on the part of those who experience the rise in intensity.
Greater participation should lead to increased allegiance to the rules of the
game if these hypotheses are true. The outcome of greater allegiance is
increased stability.

Since it appears that the initial increase in intensity ends in conflicting
effects, one might hypothesize that after temporary fluctuations, the net
impact on democracy of an increase in intensity would be negligible. To be
sure, it is quite possible that the positive and negative effects would cancel
out. Such a possibility would depend upon the relative weights of these
impacts and of the competing effects of outside variables (represented in
Figure 2 by the broken arrows). The fact that we can imagine this possibility,
however, indicates that increases in intensity may not necessarily threaten
democratic practices, as many writers in the area of democratic theory have
suggested. Instead, it is an empirical matter, as yet not thoroughly investigated, as to whether the result will be reduced democracy or no long term
reduction after short term instability.

The configuration of relationships illustrated in Figure 2 also has
implications for another aspect of the functional apathy argument. A major
reason why apathy may be functional is that the apathetic are also those
citizens who tend to have the lowest level of allegiance to the existing rules
of the game. If they participated, they might support demagogic appeals to
reduce the level of democratic practice. Thus the system is more likely to
survive without change when those not committed to the system fail to make
demands upon it.

However, we have seen that it is quite possible that mere participation
increases one's level of allegiance. If this is the case, then we would expect
that even though an increase in intensity may bring about short-run instability, it would also bring long-run stability. The reason for this is that
the existence of a body of unallegiant apathetics presents the threat of
future instability. A crisis, for example, could stir such a group to participate. The sudden participation of large numbers of these individuals may
be more than the system can withstand without change. Thus, the possibility
of a crisis at some future time, means that low levels of participation are
functional only in the short run.

On the other hand, gradual increases in the level of participation may
lead to long-run stability. Such participation leads to increased commitment,
an increase in the proportion of the citizenry which participates may increase the extent of democratic commitment in the society. In other words,
increased participation helps to guard against the problem posed by the

existence of nonallegiant apathetics by reducing the relative size of this group.

Thus far, the discussion has treated the relationship between preferences and governmental outcomes rather loosely, For example, a relationship between these factors is implicit in the expectation that the participation of nonallegiant apathetics may result in threats to democracy. Although the literature indicates that some such relationship exists, especially in policy areas that come closest to being threats to democracy, the processes that underlie the relationship are complex indeed. By examining the place of policy outcomes in this system of variables, we hope to sort out the effect of these processes on system stability and the effect of stability on them.

POLICY OUTCOMES

There are some indications in the literature that the stability of democratic rules of the game is not just a product of socialization to democratic norms. Instead, it is possible that, in addition to the effect of socialization, political leadership may limit even short-run instability by minimizing the development of intense preferences through their own responses to policy. How this comes about depends, first of all, on the nature of policy-making in democratic contexts.

Research on the factors that are related to policy outcomes tends to emphasize fairly simple models of interrelationships. The most common model utilizing the three classes of variables that we have been concerned with is shown in Figure 3.

Figure 3

Environmental Factors ⟶⟶ Democratic Practices ⟶⟶ Policy Outcomes

In this system of variables, the hypothesis anticipates a developmental sequence in which the democratic practice factors intervene between environmental factors and policy outcomes. A somewhat more complicated theoretical structure that may be hypothesized is seen in Figure 4.

Figure 4

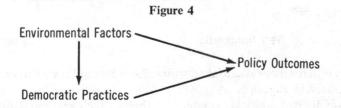

Here environmental factors are not restricted to a single, indirect effect, but in addition have an impact on policy outcomes over and above that which

is transmitted through democratic practices. Mathematically speaking, we are working within the framework of additive relationships when constructing these two models.

There are, of course, other possibilities within the additive framework. Yet comparatively unresearched are alternatives within a non-additive set of assumptions. Indeed, there are non-additive possible relationships which are consistent with much of the traditional thinking about democracy. For example, it is part of the common lore of discipline to think that democratic practices maximize the transmission of general social cleavages into policy outcomes. That is, democracy, however defined, includes the sharing of power or influence by wider sections of society than non-democratic alternatives. Demands may be made for outcomes by more widespread sets of preferences under democratic systems. Mechanisms for the translation of demands into policy are somewhat more open and routinized in such systems. Therefore, by widening the degree of representation, democracy in practice results in a greater tendency for the enactment of preferences of the lower social strata. Since policy is less skewed in favor of the higher status groupings in democracies, we expect a greater association between environmental factors like socioeconomic development and policy outcomes. In other words, we would hypothesize a decline of some sort in the relationship between the two factors as systems become less democratic. Such a decline is presented in Figure 5.

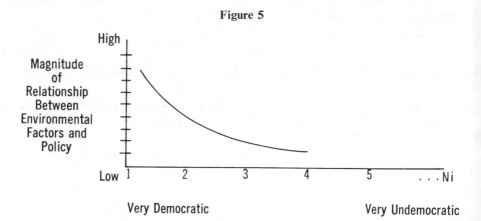

Figure 5

In terms of hypothetical causal relationships we would state this expectation as illustrated in Figure 6.

If we divided political systems into those which are highly democratic and those which are highly undemocratic by establishing some cutting point, we would expect a higher relationship in the democratic than in the un-

Figure 6

Democratic Systems   Undemocratic Systems

Environmental   Public   Environmental   Public
Factors   ──────▶   Policy   Factors   Policy

democratic. Moreover, in the ideal case we would expect a very strong relationship in the former and none in the latter.

Placing Dye's findings (Chapter 20) within this context makes clear that they are consistent with the expectations of democratic theory. While the American states exhibit much variation in political structure and form, for the most part they would fall among the democratic cases in any rating of existing political systems. For that reason, we would expect moderate-to-strong relationships between environmental factors like socioeconomic development and social welfare policy outcomes in the states.[3] Additional support for this hypothesis can be drawn from Cutright's article (Chapter 8). Not only does he find that the simple additive relationship can be rejected, but that cross-nationally where the variation on democracy is greater than among the states, the data support the non-additive relationship.

If we can conclude, then, that preliminary confirmation can be found in the literature on the hypothesis of a closer translation of socioeconomic features into policy as we move from very democratic to very non-democratic systems, what information do we have on the mechanisms that underlie the translation. When processes within the same system are examined, we have controlled for most of the variation level of democracy in the system. Yet if such examinations are made over time, they may yield information on whether change in policy outcome follows change in environment.

The appropriation of expenditures within the American national government is an output area that has been rather systematically analyzed with time-series data. The findings thus far appear to be rather mixed, as far as supporting our hypothesis is concerned. These outputs seem to be a function of agency variables, such as previous allocations or requests. This may mean that expenditure of money is really determined by some sort of law of inevitability. Once a decision is made to establish and to fund a new agency, bureaucratic forces take over to preserve the agency and to maintain its level of funding, or more likely, to progressively increase this level. If this is the case, then once established, substantive programs become functions of internal bureaucratic forces and become isolated from later changes in the environment. As a result, even if external factors change status cleavages, distribution of policy preferences, or even political leadership, they may not have the effect of changing or ending existing programs. Such changes may come to be bureaucratically impossible.

Certainly the findings indicate that expenditures are not as responsive to the elected leadership as the ideal model of democracy specifies. An awareness that that model is an ideal means that we would be surprised indeed if the reality of the situation were as responsive. The findings, however, do not indicate that expenditures are completely unresponsive to changes in leadership. To be sure, expenditures are a function of past expenditures, but *how much* they are a function of past behavior varies with administrations. The following idealized equations made clear what is involved in the distinction between these concepts:

Condition A	Condition B
$Y = 1.5\ X$	$Y = 0.5\ X$

Under both conditions, Y is a function of X, i.e., X is the single best predictor of Y. However, under Condition A it takes one and one-half X to give us one Y, while under Condition B we get one Y for only one-half X. Thus, how much Y is a function of X varies with the condition (measured by A and B). If these equations measured future (Y) and past (X) expenditures, under Condition B expenditures would be reduced by 50 per cent from what they were previously and under Condition A they would be increased by 50 per cent. Research on the magnitude of the constants is therefore as important as that on finding the most predictive independent variable when we want to make inferences about control over expenditure. The fact that the greatest variation in the value of the constants occurs when the changing conditions are from Democratic to Republican administrations means that leadership alternation is not an unimportant factor in the budgetary process.

This evidence that the elected leadership has an impact on an important, perhaps controlling, system output dimension leads us to expect that leadership plays an important role in the process underlying the relationship between environment and policy outcomes. Of course, classical democratic theory also leads us to expect this. In democracies, citizens select their leaders, therefore leaders do what the citizens want. In part, what the citizens want obviously depends upon the changing socioeconomic environment in which they exist. Thus, we might hypothesize an underlying sequence from environmental change to citizen control of leadership to leadership alternation to policy change. However, while we find some support for the broad relationship between environment and policy and the underlying impact of leadership on policy, the full chain of effects is broken. The weak link is citizen control of leadership, a link which findings suggest is marginal at best.

The findings instead suggest a revision of the traditional theory, substituting leadership perception of citizen preferences for citizen control.

That is, to the extent that there is a relationship between citizen preferences and policy, it occurs primarily because leaders somewhat accurately perceive those preferences. The findings also indicate a rank order among broad policy areas in the strength of the citizen preference-policy output relationship. The strongest relationship is in the civil rights area; social welfare is next, and foreign policy last. At the level of the general citizenry, it seems likely that opinions about identifiable out-groups, such as Negroes, are likely to be very intensely felt and that opinions about issue areas far removed from immediate experience, such as foreign policy, are likely to be extremely low in intensity. We hypothesize that the accuracy of leadership perception depends upon intensity of citizen preference.

A fairly plausible argument can be constructed which would provide a theoretical underpinning for this hypothesis. For a variety of reasons, many leaders may want to know the preferences of the citizenry, and they may want to enact policies which are consistent with those preferences. However, when preferences are not very intense, few manifestations of preferences occur. Thus, the leader has very little to go on in deciding upon what the citizens want. More likely than not, his perceptions then will be distorted by his own preferences on the policy. In that case, if his perceptions coincide with citizen preferences at all, the relationship may be spurious or due to chance.

However, where preferences are intense, perceptions are likely to be more accurate. If we place this hypothesis in the chain of hypotheses and findings already considered, we have a sequence from environment to intensity of preferences to leadership perceptions to output. Thus, there may be a relationship between citizen preferences and policy even though the citizens may not have the information on leadership action required by the leadership control link in classical theory. However, the environment-policy relationship may exist as, but to a less than perfect degree than, classical theory predicts, and may be due to underlying relationships which differ from those specified by the theory.

It is also possible to place this sequence within the larger pattern of variables which relate to democratic stability. Not only do we usually think that democracy structures the environment-output relationship, scholars also tend to feel that when the environment-output relationship is high, democratic stability is enhanced. In other words, a major theoretical proposition in our thinking on democracy has been the idea that democracy is maintained by the enactment of policies which have support among broad sectors of the society. This proposition raises the possibility that if intense preferences are somewhat accurately perceived by leaders who then structure outputs to satisfy these preferences, the outputs thus adopted will tend to increase system stablility. Thus, leaders may perceive accurately enough to estimate growing intensity of preferences among sectors of the society and to respond to that growth through policy enactment before the intensity develops to the point at which it endangers the stability of the system. At the present time the validity of this theoretical structure is of course tentative. However, our discussion has shown that it develops out of separate and scattered findings and is consistent with the general notions of some of our classical thinking on democracy.

More importantly this kind of thinking explains some political patterns contained in related bodies of findings. If the theoretical structure we hypothesize were at work, one of its results would be a low intensity of policy preferences. Leaders anticipate rising intensity and through policy-making short circuit the potential relationship between intensity and instability. Most of the empirical research on political behavior at the mass level in the United States indicates that low levels of intensity on policy preferences characterize that political system.[4] Our interpretation of this state of affairs is that it is a by-product of the level of system stability.

Another pattern that this structure explains is the low relationship between attitudes on policy and political behavior in the United States. In general, political participation is only weakly linked with current policy issues. Instead, political behavior is primarily a habitual response produced by factors like partisanship and memories of social crises of bygone ages and is secondarily a volatile response to the personal qualities of political leaders and "band-wagon" effects in the immediate social context.[5] The relative unimportance of issues is consistent with our model. In the model, participation may be produced either by preference intensity and/or environmental factors or both. Preferences, however, due to leadership action, remain at low levels of intensity in the United States. Therefore, we would expect that, relatively speaking, participation would be less the result of policy preferences than of environmental factors like social status and community sentiment.[6]

A third pattern that the model predicts is the stability of democratic practices in America in the absence of mass consensus on democratic values. Since the model specifies opposite signs for the effects of intensity and democratic allegiance, the level of democratic practice in the system can remain relatively high and constant when agreement to democratic values is low if preference intensities are also low. Simply put, it is relatively easy for institutions responsive to popular will to survive if few popular demands are made upon them. We would predict, then, that if the level of preference intensities increases the enactment of valued outputs or the level of democratic agreement would have to similarily increase; otherwise system instability would ensue.

The increase in racial violence in northern U.S. cities seems to be an example of such instability. Negroes have increasingly become aware of political processes for solving social problems. They therefore have translated their hope for social and economic equality into political preferences. While minority status makes these preferences increasingly intensely held, system outputs have not made any practical differences in Negro life. Instead, there is some evidence that the gap between Negro and white income level has actually increased in recent years. Assuming that agreement to democratic values is at the same level among Negroes as it is among other Americans, we would expect intense preferences of Negroes in the absence of policy change to result in instability. The model therefore not only explains the existence of stability but also instances of its absence.

CONCLUSIONS

In general, an integration of the research on democracy provides us with some interesting possibilities for the continuing development of theory in the area. Once historical and environmental forces influence political practices in democratic directions, we hypothesize that a regression will take place: practices will become increasingly democratic or a reversion to a less democratic state will occur. Some of the environmental factors which specify which extreme the system will move toward are levels of mass communications and levels of economic, educational, and urbanization development. In addition, we have speculated that the nature of the cleavages in society, as well as the nature of the issues over which groups are divided, are important influences in this process.

However, if the system does move toward the democratic end of the continuum, there are two results: further movement tends to be of only a limited degree and that movement which does occur tends to be in a democratic direction. The first process is that underlying democratic stability and the second is the evolution toward increasingly democratic forms. Both contribute to our notion of a regression toward extremes over time and both find support in the literature.

One of the most important relationships supporting democratic stability involves citizen preferences, leadership awareness of those preferences, and policy outcomes. In this relationship, the leadership enacts policies which the citizenry would demand if they felt intensely enough about policy to make demands. Through such enactments, leaders head off the growth of intense preferences that would otherwise well up in mass support of policies if long periods of contention took place. As a result, intense preferences exist only among very small sectors of the population. Most of the day-to-day politics concerning highly charged controversies are salient only to these more involved participants. One theoretical possibility here is that those with intense preferences would attempt to change the rules in order to change issue outcomes. But since highly active participants adhere to democratic values, conflict over issues does not lead to movements to change the rules of the game.

Therefore, it is quite possible for systems to remain fairly stabilized at a democratic level even though many citizens do not agree to democratic procedures, Thus, leadership regulation of policy outcomes can help to produce low intensities of preferences among those citizens who are least supportive of democratic values. As long as the least supportive citizens also have low intensities of preferences, the system will be relatively free from undemocratic demands originating at the mass level.

Alternatively, when leaders do not or cannot produce outcomes which are valued by citizens, problems develop for which no solutions are being offered. As the problems grow in magnitude, citizen awareness and, eventually, preference intensity increase. With increasing intensities will come greater probabilities for demands from the citizenry for solutions. As a result, the chance that the solutions that are offered are consistent with democratic practices depends upon how much the citizens value democracy.

Many of the deviant cases of the regression theory are consistent with this pattern. Instances of instability, when systems quickly moved from very democratic to very undemocratic positions, occurred during times of economic crises when the existing system could not solve pressing problems. Another possibility is the failure to bring about the integration of widely different cultural or ethnic groups through democratic practices.

The type of citizen control over leadership postulated in traditional democratic theory is not a threat to democracy when we can assume widespread agreement on democratic values among the citizenry. But in rejecting the support for that assumption, at least within the United States, the research on democracy leads us to the conclusion that such citizen control instead represents a tendency toward a breakdown in the level of democratic practices that exist. We conclude, then, that a more complex type of citizen control is operative—one in which leaders avoid direct control by going most of the way toward enacting citizen preferences. Thus, it is possible that citizens may get what they want without direct control. But in avoiding direct control by the citizenry, the leadership tends to avoid mass threats to democratic practices.[7]

Yet if we can understand why systems may not become less democratic in the face of disension over democratic values, why should we expect systems to become more democratic under these conditions? In answering this question, we are dealing with the second factor in the regression hypothesis—the evolution toward increasingly democratic forms. We argued that it is difficult for repression to take place without a movement toward a state in which it is applied to either almost everyone or to almost no one. Yet how can this movement take place in the face of the absence of consensus on democracy at the citizen level? Our expectation is that a shift in a democratic direction can take place if the shift is accompanied by gradual increases in the participation level among the citizenry. Increased participation will tend to result in a more widespread commitment to democratic values. This commitment will, in turn, allow existing political practices to become even more democratic without the challenges from undemocratic elements that otherwise would develop.

Thus, it appears that very rapid expansion of participation may threaten democratic stability by increasing the influence of the normally low participants (among whom we tend to find a lack of democratic commitment). On the other hand, a very gradual increase in the participation level may be a precondition for extending the democratic character of the rules of the game. These statements mean that citizen commitment sets bounds on the impact of changes in the participation level. Within those bounds, increases in participation will make possible further development in democracy. But if the participation level increases beyond those bounds, democratic stability becomes threatened. Indeed, participation growth which takes place within the commitment bounds not only paves the way for higher levels of democracy, but it does so at an exponential rate. That is, such growth also increases the future bounds within which further participation growth can take place and still result in democratic effects.

It is important to note that the exponential rate that is referred to does not imply rapid growth. It is not rate over time directly, but rate relative to growth in participation. Thus, an increase in participation has an exponential effect on increasing the level of democracy. Since participation can increase only very gradually over time without having undemocratic effects, the impression of rapid increase in democracy over time would not be necessitated by the theory. But once a system develops in a democratic direction, it tends to become increasingly democratic and tends not to switch from a very democratic to a very undemocratic level. The regression theory, therefore, makes compatible and subsumes the notions of democratic change and democratic stability which we find in the literature.

More specifically, the regression theory suggests that we may account for the political development of nations in terms of the three developmental types illustrated in Figure 7. The left hand side of the developmental continuum represents the undemocratic extreme, the right hand side of the democratic extreme, and the center that range of mixed democratic and undemocratic practices which we assume to be inherently unstable. The theory asserts that in the course of Western history a variety of factors set in motion a

Figure 7

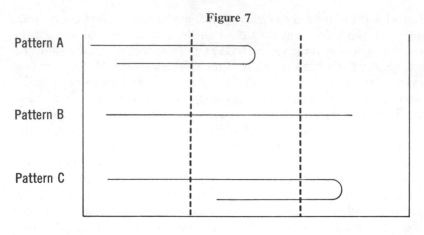

Pattern A

Pattern B

Pattern C

Undemocratic   Democratic

general, but uneven, development toward democratic national government.

It is this initial movement toward democratic forms which is isolated by factors such as social and economic development, the values of the Judeo-Christian tradition, the centralization of nation states following the decline of feudalism and the like. Those systems which achieve high levels on these factors tend to move the greatest distance in the democratic direction. We take this movement as given.

The center of the developmental continuum is represented by what is commonly called the participation crisis: that period immediately preceding and following the demand for entry or the actual entry into the political process of groups previously excluded from participation (e.g., working-class groups or racial groups). The pattern of institutional relationships characteristic of this period is inherently unstable. The demand and satis-faction cycle will either produce satisfaction with the system, or the system will change. Thus, the center of the continuum represents a threshold level in the movement toward increasingly democratic practices. Political pro-cesses involving relationships between leaders, followers, and policy will move some societies to greater levels of democracy, while causing a reversion among others. These movements are represented by Patterns B and A respectively; and the relationships which result in one pattern rather than the other have been at the heart of this chapter. Under the theory, Pattern C would rarely take place. The emphasis given such examples in the litera-ture seems to be due to the drama of extreme change rather than to the prevalence of cases.

If we possessed sophisticated measures of democracy, it would be possible to specify the location at any point in time of any nation. Time sequence analysis would indicate its rate of movement along the continuum, as well as indicate the consistency in direction of the movement. In the absence of such precision, we can only assert that:

1. The broad historical changes we observe follow:
   A. A degree of general movement toward democracy over time,
   B. Upon which is superimposed further movement toward either extreme; and
2. The theory which predicts these movements subsumes and integrates much of the previous research that we have examined.

In this chapter we have interwoven many findings and statements which we think have implications for democratic theory. The main task has been to find out if this interweaving can lead to new formulations and thereby short-circuit some of the difficulties in theory-building in this area. However, we would be remiss if we did not also point out that the separate propositions themselves usually are only preliminary conclusions of the original authors. Therefore, much more research, indeed, is needed to complete the verification of these findings. In addition, further research is needed to verify the more extended statements that result from inter-linking these findings. However, we do feel that this attempt at theory-building has been a success. Therefore, to us the more interesting problems for research are those brought into focus by the regression hypothesis. Of these the most rewarding appear to be:

1. Does such a regression take place?
2. If so, can we specify the conditions for its maximization?
3. And of these conditions, is the balance between citizen commitment and participation an important one?

Most of the literature and, therefore, most of our discussion has been about movement in the democratic direction. Thus, the whole area of change in the undemocratic direction also needs additional research. But despite the large areas that require further research, enough findings concerning *democracy* do exist in the literature for us to be somewhat more systematic about theory-building on this topic. The purpose of the volume has been to apply some interesting theory-building strategies to these findings and to show the relationship of this field to the other areas of political science.

NOTES

[1] Thomas S. Kuehn, "The Structure of Scientific Revolutions," *International Encyclopedia of Unified Science*, II, No. 2 (Chicago: University of Chicago Press, 1962).

[2] In other words, unless our concepts are of this nature, we have difficulty thinking of them as mathematical functions of other variables. See Carl G. Hempel, "Fundamental Concept Formation in Empirical Science," *International Encyclopedia of Unified Science*, II, No. 7 (Chicago: University of Chicago Press, 1952), pp. 4–5.

[3] Whether malapportionment also interacts with environmental factors (exhibits non-additive properties) to produce policy outcomes probably depends upon our ability to measure the intervening variable with precision, given the fact that we are already controlling for "representativeness" to a large degree by confining the analysis to the American states.

[4] Any analysis of voting or public opinion would bear out this contention, but see especially, Angus Campbell, *et al.*, *The American Voter* (New York: John Wiley & Sons, Inc., 1960), and V. O. Key, Jr., *Public Opinion and American Democracy* (New York: Alfred A. Knopf, 1961).

[5] For these effects, see Campbell, *et al.*, *op. cit.*, and Bernard Berelson, *et al.*, *Voting* (Chicago: University of Chicago Press, 1954).

[6] The overwhelming importance of these factors on participation even in the South where most observers would expect greater "politicization" than elsewhere in the U.S. is examined in Donald R. Matthews and James W. Prothro, *Negroes and the New Southern Politics* (New York: Harcourt, Brace & World, Inc., 1966).

[7] We should again emphasize that the findings concerning the effect of participation in democratic politics on adherence to democratic values are important underpinnings of our theory. Since leaders participate at the highest levels, they would tend to be extremely committed to democratic practices.